D0457166

The Long Reach of the Sixties

The Long Reach of the Sixties

*LBJ, Nixon, and the Making
of the Contemporary Supreme Court*

LAURA KALMAN

OXFORD
UNIVERSITY PRESS

OXFORD
UNIVERSITY PRESS

Oxford University Press is a department of the University of Oxford. It furthers
the University's objective of excellence in research, scholarship, and education
by publishing worldwide. Oxford is a registered trade mark of Oxford University
Press in the UK and certain other countries.

Published in the United States of America by Oxford University Press
198 Madison Avenue, New York, NY 10016, United States of America.

© Oxford University Press 2017

All rights reserved. No part of this publication may be reproduced, stored in
a retrieval system, or transmitted, in any form or by any means, without the
prior permission in writing of Oxford University Press, or as expressly permitted
by law, by license, or under terms agreed with the appropriate reproduction
rights organization. Inquiries concerning reproduction outside the scope of the
above should be sent to the Rights Department, Oxford University Press, at the
address above.

You must not circulate this work in any other form
and you must impose this same condition on any acquirer.

Library of Congress Cataloging-in-Publication Data
Names: Kalman, Laura, 1955– author.
Title: The long reach of the Sixties : LBJ, Nixon, and the making of
the contemporary Supreme Court / Laura Kalman.
Description: New York, NY : Oxford University Press, 2017.
Identifiers: LCCN 2016036598 | ISBN 9780199958221 (hardback)
Subjects: LCSH: United States. Supreme Court—Officials and employees—Selection
and appointment—History—20th century. | Judges—Selection
and appointment—United States—History—20th century. | United States—Politics and
government—1963–1969. | United States—Politics and government—1969–1974. |
BISAC: HISTORY / United States / 20th Century. | LAW / Legal History.
Classification: LCC KF8742 .K35 2017 | DDC 347.73/2634—dc23
LC record available at https://lccn.loc.gov/2016036598

1 3 5 7 9 8 6 4 2

Printed by Sheridan Books, Inc., United States of America

In Memory of
Newton Kalman, 1920–2010
Celeste Garr, 1924–2010
John Morton Blum, 1921–2011
Lee Kalman, 1919–2014
Protectors, Promoters, Teachers, Friends

CONTENTS

PREFACE

On February 13, 2016, friends found the body of the Supreme Court's preeminent conservative in his suite at a hunting resort in West Texas. Seventy-nine-year-old Antonin Scalia had unexpectedly died of natural causes just as the nation moved into an unusually fraught presidential primary season. With the court frequently divided on big issues four to four between "liberals" and "conservatives," and another seventy-nine-year-old justice, Anthony Kennedy, casting the swing vote, "Scalia's Death Offers Best Chance in a Generation to Reshape Supreme Court," the *New York Times* declared. Since President Obama had almost a year left in office and promised to fulfill his constitutional duty by naming a new justice, his fellow Democrats expected him to do so, though many doubted that the Republican Senate would confirm the nominee. After all, less than two hours before the public learned of Scalia's death, Senate Majority Leader Mitch McConnell of Kentucky had incensed Democrats by declaring that "it only makes sense that we defer to the American people who will elect a new president to select the next Supreme Court justice."[1]

Five weeks later, Obama nevertheless nominated Merrick Garland, a white Harvard College and Law School alumnus. Like almost all justices since the mid-1970s, Garland was a federal judge with sterling credentials. He had been articles editor of the *Harvard Law Review* and had clerked for two legendary judges, Henry Friendly and William Brennan. He had also served as a partner in one of the capital's preeminent law firms, federal prosecutor in the Bush I administration, and deputy assistant attorney general in the Clinton administration before Clinton successfully named him to the DC Circuit Court of Appeals. By some standards Garland was centrist; by others, he was a centrist liberal slightly to the right of the court's liberals. While he was the best the Republicans could hope for, a Justice Garland seemed likely to move the court leftward. Senate Republicans simply refused to hold hearings.[2]

Obviously, the Supreme Court nomination would play a critical role in the political season. By this time, Americans had grown accustomed to the eruption of periodic battles royal over Supreme Court vacancies, particularly when the president's party did not control the Senate. Some traced the origins of this state of affairs to Ronald Reagan's unsuccessful nomination of Robert Bork in 1987. In fact, it began over twenty years earlier, when Lyndon Johnson and Richard Nixon created a new kind of presidential politics around nominations to the Supreme Court.[3]

The Long Reach of the Sixties shows how, between 1965 and 1971, Supreme Court nominees and their confirmations became critical to presidential politics. As Lyndon Johnson and Richard Nixon, the Senate, prospective justices, members of the court, interest groups, and the public mobilized, they created and politicized the modern nomination and confirmation process. The period saw two successful Supreme Court nominations and two failed ones by Johnson, and four successful Supreme Court nominations and two failed ones by Nixon. The quest to enlist the court in consolidating presidential power provoked clashes that had lasting consequences for the court's political significance and the selection and confirmation of Supreme Court justices that still resonate today.

Scholars have long focused on the turning point that Roosevelt's 1937 court-packing plan posed for president, court, and country. After the resolution of that crisis, however, the court and its membership consumed space in presidents' partisan calculations only sporadically. FDR wasted little time worrying about the Senate's reaction to his prospective Supreme Court nominees or what they would do as justices—which may be one reason they fought with each other so much. That pattern continued under Truman, Eisenhower, and Kennedy.[4]

Then, when LBJ and Nixon in rapid succession tried to enlist the court in service of their presidencies, the Senate asserted itself and nominations became controversial. Just as we evaluate the impact of presidential nominees on the court, we need to examine prospective justices in the context of the presidency. As Johnson and Nixon saw it, they needed a clearer idea of what potential candidates for court vacancies would do because the Supreme Court under Earl Warren was making waves by transforming the meaning of the Constitution for civil rights, criminal procedure, internal security, reapportionment, religion, and speech. With their expansive vision of the political chessboard and potential chess pieces, LBJ and Nixon modeled for their successors how the president should and should not factor the court into the politics of the presidency.

With his first nomination, Johnson sought to install a spy at the Supreme Court, to maintain the tradition of the "Jewish seat," and to continue keeping tabs on the Justice Department. With his second, Johnson created the "black seat" by naming the first African American to sit on the court at a time when he worried that the civil rights consensus underlying Cold War liberalism was teetering. With his two failed nominations in 1968, LBJ hoped to reward devoted friends and to sustain the ideological momentum of the Warren Court, though he had some reservations about it. Like Chief Justice Warren, LBJ considered the court part and parcel of his Great Society. For that and other reasons, Republicans and Southern Democrats derailed the nominations in a brawl centered around Johnson's attempt to name "cronies" to the court; the Warren Court's civil rights, criminal law, and obscenity decisions; and charges of financial impropriety.[5]

The Warren Court became Richard Nixon's quarry. He used it to win election in 1968 and to unify, shape, and broaden the modern Republican Party. As president, he tried to create vacancies by getting rid of two of the court's most liberal members. He also nominated six individuals to the Supreme Court whom he touted as "strict constructionists" or "constitutionalists" who would roll back the work of the Warren Court. Now, liberal Democrats, often aided by moderate or progressive Republicans, mounted a counterattack.

The Long Reach of the Sixties turns the spotlight on Johnson's and Nixon's attempts to populate the court between 1965 and 1971. Using recordings of presidential telephone conversations, along with archival sources, it grounds the efforts by LBJ and Nixon to shape the court in the political history of their presidencies. It places the ideological contest over the court within the context of the struggle between the executive, judicial, and legislative branches of government, as well as interest group mobilization. The fights that followed fixed the image of the Warren Court as "activist" and "liberal" in one of the arenas where that image matters most, the contemporary Supreme Court appointments process.

The book also investigates the ways in which "the sixties," a period that lasted into the early seventies, have haunted and scarred that process. Of course, Supreme Court nominees had faced attack before the late Warren era. But even by the standards of the nineteenth century, when confirmation struggles over Supreme Court justices routinely occurred, the fights about nominees from 1967 to 1971 proved exceptionally contentious. If how we react to a Supreme Court nominee depends on whose ox is gored, what makes this period special is that Warren Court partisans and antagonists alike had plenty of oxen at risk for slaughter.

We improve our understanding of the combination of political and constitutional developments that have made so many nominations since the mid-twentieth century so significant if we root the modern Supreme Court appointments process in the sixties. But we should recognize that just as contingency pervades history, it plays a large role in this story. Like other presidents, LBJ and Nixon named people to the Supreme Court according to Holmes's proverbial "felt necessities of the time," and, as ever, all history "teaches" us is that history turns on a dime. If political science is too neat to instruct Americans on how to govern, history is too messy.

Nevertheless, in a real and often unfortunate way, Johnson's and Nixon's tussles over nominations have shaped how the Warren Court is remembered and how justices have been chosen and confirmed ever since. The struggles also led Republicans and Democrats to portray the Warren Court as "too activist" and "too liberal" in the contemporary appointments process. As a consequence, even when members of their own party controlled the Senate, two gun-shy presidents in the late twentieth and twenty-first centuries appointed moderate progressives to the court who rejected judicial "liberalism" and "activism." That pattern, I argue, reflects Democrats' acceptance of the inaccurate portrayal of the Warren Court that its opponents promoted during the sixties.

Like stereotypes, adages exist for a reason. Trite as it is to point to Faulkner's observation, "The past is never dead. It's not even past," I have the historian's fondness for doing so. This book had its origin in a prior one, a file and a policy. More than thirty years ago, I began work on a biography of Abe Fortas. In the Library of Congress, I discovered the notes of *New York Times* reporter Fred Graham on his conversations with Supreme Court members after Nixon had forced Fortas's resignation. Justice Potter Stewart had stressed that he and his colleagues "work hard, don't go out on nights when there are arguments," and that most had stopped lecturing for fees or serving on foundation boards. Justice William Rehnquist had informed Graham that "the justices are cut off to some extent by others' awe of them" and that "they have been cut off further by the [F]ortas scandal; thinks this is not a good thing." These documents started me wondering about a larger issue. How had the last days of the Warren Court affected the Supreme Court as an institution and shaped its impact on the presidency?[6]

At the time, I put these questions aside to concentrate on learning about Fortas in the archives that housed his traces. As much as I loved my stints at the Johnson Library, one of its policies stymied scholars. Anyone who studied LBJ knew how important the telephone was to him. And ironically, the president who loathed wiretaps had secretly recorded more than 640 hours of his most important conversations, which he used instead of a stenographer's notes to ensure that promises made were kept. At Johnson's direction, the library had closed the tapes until 2023, fifty years after his death, at which time LBJ had instructed the archivist of the United States or the director of the library to listen to them for the purpose of deciding whether the recordings should be "promptly resealed or examined by the appropriate security officials of the government for possible clearance."[7]

Although Johnson's Daily Diary revealed that the president recorded many conversations with Fortas, I reluctantly concluded that I could not wait for their release to finish my biography. If I lived until 2023, I would be sixty-eight. If the brittle tapes had not crumbled by then, and if officials decided against "promptly" resealing the recordings, government clearance would take years. I vowed to listen to the recordings if ever they became available and enjoyed comforting visions of spending my retirement in my favorite presidential library reading room hunched over recording equipment.

My biography of Fortas appeared in 1990. The following year, Oliver Stone's "JFK" excoriated the official, governmental explanation in the Warren Commission's report that Lee Harvey Oswald acted alone in assassinating President Kennedy. Far more likely, Stone suggested, that Kennedy planned to withdraw the United States from Vietnam after he won a second term in 1964 and that Vice President Lyndon Johnson and the military–industrial complex consequently staged a coup d'état that included the president's assassination. The ludicrousness of its premise caused me to walk out of the theater in disgust three times when I first viewed "JFK," but the film proved good for something. In 1992, Congress reacted to the interest it stimulated by enacting legislation requiring the release of all data in government archives related to the president's murder. Among other things, the "JFK Series" conversations in the Johnson Library lay bare LBJ's antagonism toward Robert Kennedy. Perhaps in part because so many showed the president at his worst, LBJ Library Director Harry Middleton, after consultation with Lady Bird Johnson and the archivist of the United States, promised to open all the tape recordings, not just those involving the assassination. Disregarding LBJ's wishes, archivists began the arduous process of reviewing the recordings, which they made available in batches over the next sixteen years.[8]

When lightning struck the library on the first day of the release, some may have wondered whether Johnson was angry. He need not have been. He had tried so hard to appear presidential in public that he sometimes seemed dull, but the tapes allowed us to see him in his element: earthily persuasive, mercurial, sometimes manic, often paranoid. Unlike letters and memoranda, which he rarely drafted himself, the tapes provided a portrait of him at work. To be sure, it was incomplete, since LBJ did not record all his conversations. And, Bruce Schulman stresses, we must beware the delusion that by transforming "scholars into eavesdroppers," audio creates "a direct, unmediated experience of history—sans bias, sans censorship, sans interpretation." But given the frequent outrageousness of LBJ's behavior on the tapes and the many instances on which he spoke of keeping them away from researchers, there seemed little possibility that the president crafted the performances to impress those who would write about him later.* Of course, one can never be certain of anything with Johnson. He always considered his historical reputation, and the recordings often made him sympathetic (to me, anyway) by testifying to his anguish over the Vietnam War and his dedication to steering his civil rights and poverty programs through Congress. At Lady Bird Johnson's funeral, the chairman of the LBJ Foundation imagined the words with which her husband welcomed his wife to the hereafter: "Even though you and Harry Middleton opened those sealed White House tapes about 40 years earlier than I had directed, it was another wise decision by you. It actually seemed to have helped my reputation."[9]

At the same time that the Johnson tapes became available, the notorious Nixon recordings did too. Miraculously, the University of Virginia's Miller Center of Public Affairs made both sets of presidential recordings available online, and Luke Nichter featured the Nixon recordings at Nixontapes.org. I listened to them in my study, office, classroom, car, and hotel rooms and on planes, and I once played them for guests at Thanksgiving dinner. Because of Johnson's mistrust of the Department of Justice, under the leadership of, first, Robert Kennedy, and then, Kennedy's chosen successor, Nicholas Katzenbach, as well as LBJ's interest in courts and nominations, the Johnson recordings provided a particularly rich portrait of legal and judicial affairs. Like the Nixon tapes, they told a fascinating story about presidents, Congress, and the court.

But this tale was more than technological. The vast quantity of documents related to the Supreme Court at the presidential libraries of Johnson and his successors, as compared to the Eisenhower and Kennedy Libraries, also suggested that as the court became more politicized in the mid-1960s, presidents became more conscious of its significance in American life and to their own survival. In this respect, too, the archives testified to the long shadow cast by the 1960s and the Warren Court over the contemporary Supreme Court, history, and memory.

As chapter 1 shows, when LBJ became president in 1963, he had to contend with Kennedy holdovers. Frustrated in particular by Attorneys General Robert

---

* Rumors of the tapes' existence circulated in Washington during the Johnson Presidency. JFK's personal secretary, Evelyn Lincoln, who worked briefly in the Johnson White House, told the historian and Kennedy adviser, Arthur Schlesinger, Jr., about them over lunch in March 1964. "They are immediately transcribed by the girls in her old office and then given to the President the first thing in the morning, so he can see what he said," Schlesinger noted in his journal. (If only that had been the case! By no means all tapes were transcribed). "What a treasure trove for the historian! and what a threat to the rational and uninhibited conduct of government." Arthur Schlesinger, Jr., *Journals 1952-2000*, ed. Andrew Schlesinger and Stephen Schlesinger 225 (New York: Penguin, 2007). It thus seems likely that some of those with whom LBJ spoke suspected or knew they were being taped, and they may have behaved accordingly. Abe Fortas, for example, spoke quietly, but he often spoke unusually softly on the tapes. Perhaps he wanted to make it difficult for historians to learn what he said.

Kennedy and Nicholas Katzenbach, the new president turned to his confidant—in Washington parlance, his "crony"—superlawyer Abe Fortas, to do the attorney general's sensitive work satisfactorily, and Johnson made Thurgood Marshall the nation's first African American solicitor general. Chapter 2 investigates the president's sense that he needed an ear at the court, his installation of Fortas there, his continued reliance on Fortas to circumvent the attorney general, and the impact of inner-city rebellions and other issues on his political calculations for the Justice Department and the court. Chapter 3 roots LBJ's nomination of Marshall to the court and his creation of "the black seat" in the president's problems at the Justice Department and other political travails, and demonstrates how the Warren Court became a bogeyman for the Supreme Court appointments process. As chapter 4 shows, the fight over the court grew bipartisan and more furious when the president unsuccessfully tried to make Fortas chief justice and name Homer Thornberry as associate justice during an election year. Chapter 5 delves into the last days of the Warren Court, Fortas's resignation under fire, and how those events affected Nixon's selection of Judge Warren Burger as Chief Justice of the United States. Chapter 6 studies the president's "Southern Strategy" for the Republican Party and his failed attempts to apply it in 1969 and 1970 by nominating first Judge Clement Haynsworth of South Carolina and then Judge G. Harrold Carswell of Florida to the court before Nixon was forced to settle on Judge Harry Blackmun, a midwesterner. Chapter 7 tells the strange story of the president's efforts to nominate successors to Justices Hugo Black and John Harlan in 1971 that resulted in the court appointments of Lewis Powell and William Rehnquist. The epilogue explores the shadow these struggles of the Johnson and Nixon years cast over the contemporary nomination and confirmation process and the court itself.

Yet this story does not start at the court. Instead, we turn to the executive branch in chapter 1. There LBJ's certainty that the lawyers he inherited from his predecessor did not represent his best interests led to a classic inside-the-beltway struggle between him and his Justice Department.

The Long Reach of the Sixties

1

A New President Seeks Power, 1963–65

After John Kennedy's assassination in Dallas, "I was catapulted without preparation into the most difficult job any mortal man can hold," Lyndon Johnson remembered (figure 1). He proved himself masterfully. But the continuity he craved and called for as he tried to take control came at a price. Fatefully, the new president felt compelled to shackle himself to Kennedy's survivors—and especially to Attorney General Robert Kennedy.[1]

That meant the significance of Kennedy's Justice Department for LBJ's infant presidency became apparent just as Johnson was reminded how controversial Chief Justice Earl Warren was, shoved Warren further into the spotlight, and came to recognize the importance to his own success of two topics that loomed large on the Warren Court's agenda, civil rights and liberalism. LBJ also realized his own susceptibility to a scandal that he feared the Justice Department would prosecute. The difficulty of managing Justice and controlling its presentation of legal matters to the Supreme Court and Congress as long as Kennedy or his desired heir, Nicholas Katzenbach, remained in charge became clear too. Because of the presence of Kennedy and Katzenbach, LBJ could not control his most crucial department even after he became president in his own right. He had to satisfy himself with end runs around the attorneys general to whom history had yoked him by tapping Abe Fortas and Thurgood Marshall for help. Later, he would "reward" both with jobs on the court and use them to rid himself of a meddlesome attorney general.

Assuming Command

On Sunday, November 24, 1963, as Chief Justice Earl Warren put the finishing touches on the eulogy for JFK that Mrs. Kennedy had asked him to deliver, his daughter summoned him to watch a television broadcast about Jack

Figure 1 Waiting for the oath of office to be administered to LBJ on November 22, 1963. Homer Thornberry, LBJ's friend and congressman whom he would nominate to the Supreme Court in 1968, is standing behind him. Like other photographs of the swearing-in, this one featured a disproportionate number of Johnson loyalists. Though Jacqueline Kennedy would ultimately be at the new president's side, and her aides, Pamela Turnure and Mary Gallagher, would stand behind her, few Kennedy men wanted to watch LBJ take the oath. From left to right: Mac Kilduff (lower left corner), Judge Sarah T. Hughes, Gen. Clifton, Jack Valenti, Jesse Curry, Lady Bird Johnson, President Lyndon B. Johnson, Mary Gallagher (behind Thornberry), Cong. Homer Thornberry, Lem Johns, Cong. Jack Brooks, Pamela Turnure. LBJ Library. Photo by Cecil Stoughton.

Ruby's shocking murder of the president's alleged assassin, Lee Harvey Oswald. Minutes later, Warren spoke in the Capitol rotunda (figure 2). He seemed sure where the blame for the death of "this great and good President" lay. "What moved some misguided wretch to do this horrible deed may never be known to us, but we do know that such acts are commonly stimulated by forces of hatred and malevolence, such as today are eating their way into the bloodstream of American life," he lamented. Warren pleaded with Americans to swear off "the hatred that consumes people, the false accusations that divide us, and the bitterness that begets violence. Is it too much to hope that the martyrdom of our beloved President might even soften the hearts of those who would themselves recoil from assassination, but who do not shrink from spreading the venom which kindles thoughts of it in others?"[2]

For the chief justice, the villains were the very right-wing extremists who had long also had him in their sights. And some agreed. When Yale Law School Dean Eugene Rostow spoke with White House aide Bill Moyers later that afternoon,

Figure 2   Chief Justice Earl Warren eulogizing JFK in the Capitol, November 24, 1963, to mourners led by Attorney General Robert Kennedy, Mrs. Kennedy, and Caroline Kennedy. Standing from left to right: Senate Majority Leader Michael Mansfield; Stephen Smith, Kennedy brother-in-law; the new president (behind RFK); Kennedy brother-in-law Peter Lawford, comforting seven-year-old daughter Sydney; Kennedy sister Patricia Lawford, next to Mrs. Kennedy and Caroline Kennedy. PhotoQuest/Archive Photos.

Moyers mentioned that the experiences of the past few days had been "symptomatic" of "the breakdown of respect for law and order" reflected in signs urging members of Congress to "Impeach the Supreme Court." The court had become a political lightning rod in some parts of the country when Earl Warren took its helm and, with his colleagues, ordered the desegregation of public schools in 1954, then nibbled at the Cold War consensus by protecting the rights of dissenters. Its decisions then and later increased the powerful antipathy toward Warren and his court that, according to its enemies on the Far Right, was empowering underdogs instead of following the Constitution. In fact, the signs posted by the right-wing John Birch Society were more pointed than Moyers acknowledged. They read "Impeach Earl Warren."[3]

Rostow was telephoning the White House to urge the appointment of a special presidential commission to study the assassination of Kennedy now that Oswald would never stand trial for it. To Johnson's irritation, Deputy Attorney General Nicholas Katzenbach embraced the idea. The president realized that he had "to assure the country that everything possible was being done to uncover the truth" about events in Dallas. With Ruby's murder of Oswald, LBJ discovered, national outrage at Kennedy's death "turned to skepticism and doubt. The atmosphere was poisonous and had to be cleared," lest conspiracy theorists rush to the judgment that the assassination represented the work of Russia, Cuba, the state of Texas, or even Johnson himself. But because the murders of Kennedy and Oswald were state, not federal, crimes, LBJ had initially resolved to leave them to Texas authorities, who planned to convene a court of inquiry, pursuant to state law, and the FBI, which had already begun to investigate them. Johnson told columnist Joe Alsop that he had spent several hours "going over this thing from A to Z" with the "ablest" and "truest civil liberties lawyer in this town in my judgment." The attorney (obviously Abe Fortas) had stressed that "the White House *must* not—the President *must* not—inject himself into, uh, local, uh, killings." Fortas told presidential commission proponents that Americans would read too much into Johnson's selection of its members and "the country is upset enough and if the President supersedes the ordinary procedures, it would further shake people's trust and confidence." Few agreed. Alsop warned LBJ that non-Texans did not believe in Texas justice and that the Left mistrusted the FBI.[4]

As the new president and his adviser beheld the negative reaction to the Texas court of inquiry, they became convinced that it would proceed "on the assumption that Kennedy's assassination was a communist plot." And they began to worry about the congressional investigations that the court of inquiry would not forestall. Changing course, LBJ and Fortas now seized on the establishment of a blue-ribbon presidential commission to head off a circus in Texas and in Congress.[5]

The president believed that only the chief justice could chair it. Given Warren's unpopularity with the Far Right and his rush to blame it for JFK's death, LBJ might have made a wiser choice. Yet Warren, after all, was a Republican and, as head of the federal court system, the symbol of judiciousness and fairness. His appointment would sound a reassuring note of bipartisanship.[6]

Consequently, LBJ gave Fortas the job of recruiting the chief justice. But when Johnson wanted an update, Fortas could say only that in an effort "to handle this with the greatest tact," he had tasked Deputy Attorney General Katzenbach and Solicitor General Archibald Cox with obtaining Warren's consent, instead of approaching the chief justice himself. "Well, we need it right quick," LBJ stressed, because members of Congress were already trumpeting news of the commission "all over the damned place. When you talk to the leaders, it's just like talking into a big microphone." Fortas, who was Jewish, permitted himself a rare "Oy" when the president added that Representative Hale Boggs was already discussing the commission on the floor of the House. "I'll call Nick immediately and see if he's got a report," Fortas assured Johnson. "He should've gone over there right away. I really gave him the hotfoot this morning."[7]

The deputy attorney general, however, soon relayed bad news. Warren had informed Katzenbach and Cox that he had no time for the job and that it violated the principle of separation of powers for a Supreme Court justice to sit on a presidential commission. If he participated and the commission's findings resulted in litigation, the chief justice would have to disqualify himself. Warren also gave Katzenbach and Cox a history lesson about the impact of extrajudicial activities on the court. "I told them," Warren wrote later, that "the acceptance of diplomatic posts by Chief Justice Jay and Ellsworth had not contributed to the welfare of the Court, that the service of five Justices on the Hayes-Tilden Commission had demeaned it, that the appointment of Justice Roberts as chairman to investigate the Pearl Harbor disaster had served no good purpose, and that the action of Justice Robert Jackson in leaving Court for a year to become chief prosecutor at Nuremberg after World War II had resulted in divisiveness and bitterness on the Court." Katzenbach realized that he and Cox had not proven "very persuasive." The reason was simple. At bottom, both of them agreed with Warren.[8]

Here was LBJ's first clear signal after Dallas that the Justice Department represented a potential problem. First, Katzenbach promoted a presidential commission when Johnson did not want it. Then, when LBJ agreed to one, Katzenbach could not enlist the president's choice to chair it.

Only a session with Johnson himself in which the president convinced Warren that the very future of the republic and avoidance of nuclear war lay on the line turned around the chief justice. The president told the story later that day to his mentor, Senator Richard Russell, a conservative Georgia Democrat. After Warren twice refused him, LBJ related, the president replied, " 'I think you'd put on your uniform [from] World War I'—fat as you are—'and do anything you could to save one American life. Now I'm surprised that you, the Chief Justice of the United States, would turn me down.' And he started crying, and he said, 'Well, I won't turn you down. I'll just do whatever you say.' But he turned the Attorney General down." As ever, LBJ relished his own persuasiveness, mocked those who succumbed to it, and exuberantly embellished. Johnson would have known that Russell routinely expressed "my indignation and contempt" for "Warren and his leftist group" to constituents. Thus, the president portrayed the chief justice as weak and built himself up by suggesting that Warren first rejected Attorney General Robert Kennedy, rather than Kennedy's deputy attorney general and solicitor general.[9]

Having secured Warren's assent, LBJ had to sell the Warren Commission to others, Russell chief among them. "I couldn't serve there with Chief Justice Warren," Russell disconsolately—and vainly—protested when Johnson telephoned him to read the announcement of the commission's formation and its members, including Russell, that he had already released to the press. "I don't like that man, and . . . I don't have any confidence in him, though

I realize," Russell added caustically, "he's a much greater man in the United States nearly—today than almost anyone." Unmoved, Johnson reminded Russell, "I served under you—and I don't give a damn if you have to serve with a *Republican*, if you have to serve with a *Communist*, if you have to serve with a *Negro*, if you have to serve with a *thug*"—before assuring his friend that only his mother had meant more to him than the senator. House Republican Minority Leader Charles Halleck of Illinois also considered Warren a bad choice. "I was a little disappointed in . . . the speech the Chief Justice made [about the assassination], and I'm talking real plainly," Halleck told Johnson. "He's jumped the gun, and of course, I don't know whether the right wing was in this or not." Senate Judiciary Committee Chairman James Eastland of Mississippi counseled Johnson to select the Warren Court's leading dissenter, Justice Harlan, instead of the chief justice.[10]

Here was the combination of Southern Democratic and Republican opposition that had stalled liberal legislation since 1938 and that would sabotage Warren and LBJ's attempt to retain control of the court in 1968. Even before LBJ had announced the establishment of a commission, the conservative *Chicago Tribune* reported that the American Communist Party had demanded that Warren head it. Almost hopefully, the *Tribune* predicted that LBJ's insistence on the chief justice might cause his first clash with Congress. It did not. His problems in creating the Warren Commission, however, underscored for Johnson the importance of taking charge of the Justice Department.[11]

As the establishment of the Warren Commission suggested, in death, JFK became larger than life. Kennedy's advisers and admirers extolled his style. To many who saw JFK as the personification of sixties coolness, the new president fell woefully short. Writer Susan Douglas was thirteen at the time of Kennedy's murder. "I didn't know then that behind the images of John-John and Caroline frolicking in the Oval Office, behind the nationally televised speeches asserting that segregation was immoral and would not be tolerated, behind the glittering White House parties for artists and intellectuals, it was old-style politics as usual," she remembered. "So when I saw that vulgar turkey neck, Lyndon Johnson being sworn into office, I felt that youth had been robbed and betrayed" and that the "the forces of reaction and cynicism had triumphed over idealism." So did many others. Consequently, in the 1960s, when admiration of JFK peaked, LBJ was compared constantly and unfavorably to his predecessor.[12]

Johnson knew all too well that he came out poorly. Born in 1908, he was just nine years older than Kennedy, who had proclaimed in 1961 that "the torch has been passed to a new generation of Americans—born in this century, tempered by war, disciplined by a hard and bitter peace, proud of our ancient heritage— and unwilling to witness or permit the slow undoing of those human rights to which this Nation has always been committed." LBJ too was a child of the twentieth century. But he seemed much more elderly than his predecessor.[13]

Unlike JFK, who had grown up in luxury in the Northeast, Johnson hailed from the Texas Hill Country. He had not gone to Harvard, but to Southwest Texas State Teachers College. He lacked inherited wealth, he had massive ears, and he had faded into complete obscurity during his thousand days as vice president. After a honeymoon with the press that showcased his persuasive power during his first days in office, President Johnson could not control the media as effectively as President Kennedy had done or as Johnson himself had done as Senate majority leader, and press leaks drove LBJ wild. Reporters did not always find him credible. As an aide reported later, and recordings of the presidential telephone conversations amply bore out, the "problem was exacerbated because LBJ became the most gullible victim of his own revisionist claims. He would quickly come to believe what he was saying even if it was clearly not true," as when Johnson irately denied to his staff that he was ever irate. One of his press secretaries put it succinctly: "The first victim of the Johnson whopper is always Lyndon Baines Johnson."[14]

Where JFK proved a compassionate boss who welcomed dissent, President Johnson sometimes struck those who worked for him as sadistic, though he proved magnanimous, even loving, on occasion. He demanded absolute fealty even when he did not deserve it. Johnson railed at "the Kennedy cult" who portrayed him as "a cornpone," but he did seem unpolished and paternalistic next to his predecessor. He outraged dog owners when he publicly picked up his beagle, Him, by the ears. Privately, the president compared Him's loyalty to that of Texas Mexican Americans. "My Mexicans, most of them can't read and write," but "they're just like my beagle," LBJ laughed to labor leader Walter Reuther. "My beagle runs up and he smells my ankles, and he knows that this is the *man*, right here!"[15]

Although LBJ had hitched his wagon to the New Deal star of Franklin Roosevelt, liberals began to doubt Johnson's sincerity as they watched him move rightward with Texas and national politics in the 1940s and when he became Senate majority leader in the 1950s. They knew that Johnson's words changed depending on his audience. Had Calvin Trillin, who prided himself on gauging "a white Southerner's racial views by the way he pronounced the word 'Negro,'" followed LBJ around during the 1960s, the reporter would have found Johnson using every pronunciation imaginable. Trillin probably would have had that experience with many other white Southerners. In LBJ's case, though, the speech variations seemed especially significant. Predictably, JFK's selection of Johnson as his running mate provoked liberal dismay.[16]

Just as LBJ prided himself on his adaptability, however, so the new president understood that both powerful Americans and the prevailing mood might favor the liberalism for which he personally felt considerable sympathy. In the aftermath of the assassination, Americans sought unity and leadership. Johnson knew, of course, that the conservative coalition in Congress retained rock-solid control of key committees. Yet like the JFK–LBJ agenda that the Warren Court worked to advance, liberalism—"an understanding that the federal government had the responsibility, power, and ability to reduce inequality, protect historically oppressed minorities, champion American interests and values around the world, and balance the private sector's singular focus on making money with a broad concern for the nation's long-term good"—might well prove the wave of the future in November 1963. And Johnson himself was a creature of consensus; his favorite biblical verse, Isaiah 1:18: "Come now, and let us reason together." He understood that civil rights activists had maximized their power and changed the political climate in their televised struggles with Southern racists. He also believed that blacks *and* whites from his region would prosper only if the South made itself more attractive to outside investors by swearing off segregation and discrimination and joining the rest of the nation. (Like so many others at the time, LBJ possessed an idealized view of racial progress in the North and the West.) Consequently, he realized that he must use his extraordinary curiosity about, and understanding of, people to promote liberalism and win over those who suspected him of closet conservatism.[17]

That included Kennedy staffers like Richard Goodwin, who was called in to LBJ's bathroom for a consultation. "I had never before seen a president taking a shit," Goodwin recalled. (He had, however, sometimes been summoned while JFK was taking a bath.) While Goodwin stood—"the President had the only seat in the room"—Johnson studied his reaction. As Goodwin came to realize, LBJ had intentionally selected the setting. "His display of intimacy was not gross insensitivity, or an act of self-humiliation, but an attempt to uncover, heighten, the vulnerability of other men—the better to know them, to subject them to his will." Apparently satisfied by the aide's lack of squeamishness, the president said he needed Goodwin more than Kennedy had and could accomplish more too: "I loved Jack Kennedy, just like you, but he never really understood the Congress. I do." Johnson pledged to use that knowledge to enact the civil rights and other liberal legislation that Southern Democrats and Republicans had bottled up during Kennedy's presidency. "It's a once-in-a-lifetime opportunity, for you, for me, for the country."[18]

LBJ was not just being vain and grandiose. The same qualities that threatened to destroy him—ambition, paranoia, insecurity—also made him capable of greatness. He had been in Congress longer than JFK, he cared about it more, and in fact he did understand it better. Awed politicos marveled that Johnson knew which senator had "been screwing a Negro woman for years," her telephone number, and when to enlist her to persuade her reluctant man to vote for civil rights. As a Southerner, LBJ could speak the language of those from his region who opposed the civil rights agenda and sometimes tamp down their virulence. And when Johnson exclaimed to Richard Russell, "Good God, I'd rather hear your voice than Jesus," he testified to the bonds of a long relationship that made members of Congress more eager to help him than Kennedy, who had shown little interest in them. Further, as journalists Rowland Evans and Robert Novak famously wrote, LBJ's "overwhelming personality" enabled him to subject those in Congress to "The Treatment," whose tone might be one of "supplication, accusation, cajolery, exuberance, scorn, tears, complaint, the hint of threat," even all of them, somehow, at once. Of course, he was no magician, though he often was portrayed as one by wistful liberals later and by many of his contemporaries in 1963–64 when Johnson was successfully steering JFK's program through Congress (with the notable exception of those in the Kennedy circle like Arthur Schlesinger, Jr. who fumed privately that the new President was "living intellectually off the Kennedy program" and off the "Kennedy people" and derogated his "ability to transmute boldness into banality."). Without a doubt, however, LBJ was a savvy tactician who possessed advantages that JFK had lacked.[19]

Kennedy's death placed LBJ in charge and gave him the chance to maneuver his predecessor's stalled program past congressional conservatives and to present it as a memorial to the martyr. If Johnson could accomplish that, he knew that all things would prove possible. Understanding that Kennedy's men provided continuity, and believing that he could not clean house as Truman did when he succeeded Roosevelt, Johnson skillfully convinced all Kennedy loyalists, not just Goodwin, to remain in his service. He and they knew that they were making an uncertain gamble. "We have supposed that Johnson so badly needed the Kennedy people for the [1964] election that we would retain a measure of power for eleven months," Arthur Schlesinger Jr. was soon confiding to Attorney General Robert Kennedy. "But he has shown, I believe, that we are weaker— a good deal weaker—than we had supposed. He has understood that the only sanctions we have are resignation and/or revolt—and that both sanctions are meaningless, and will seem sour grapes, unless they are provoked by a readily understandable issue—and this LBJ will do his best to deny us." So the president would keep on "the Kennedy people," but as he did in establishing the Warren Commission, the new president would frequently also try to circumvent them.[20]

In the case of the Justice Department, which could make or break his infant presidency, LBJ's adjustment proved especially delicate. While FDR concentrated political power in the postmaster general's office, the Justice Department became the nerve center of the presidency after World War II. As Washington columnist Drew Pearson said, the power had moved to Justice, "which can decide to prosecute or not to prosecute for income tax evasion; whether to pardon or not to pardon; and whom to appoint as judges, U.S. attorneys, U.S. marshals." For that reason, Truman awarded Democratic National Committee Chair Howard McGrath the attorney generalship, Eisenhower appointed former Republican National Committee chair Herbert Brownell to the slot, and JFK acquiesced when his father informed him that his brother, Robert, Kennedy's campaign manager but a relatively inexperienced lawyer, would prove ideal for the post. But the influence of the Justice Department extended far beyond patronage. The many duties of the attorney general included attending to how the executive branch, Congress, and the judiciary handled a host of important issues ranging from antitrust to wiretapping, defending the administration's position before the Supreme Court via the solicitor general, and overseeing the FBI and other law enforcement agencies. Consequently, attorneys general were traditionally presidential, as well as party, loyalists. As LBJ put it, "There are two jobs in this man's government that you want only your mother to fill—and even her not on every day: Commissioner of Internal Revenue and Attorney General."[21]

And although Johnson and President Kennedy had a correct, even sometimes warm, relationship, contemporary journalists and historians ever since have demonstrated that LBJ and Robert Kennedy loathed each other. Robert Kennedy blamed Johnson for trying to deny his brother the presidential nomination in 1960 by launching a whispering campaign about JFK's health and worked to withdraw the vice presidential nomination after LBJ had accepted it. Then, when he remained on the ticket, Johnson recalled, RFK "humiliated" him by treating him contemptuously or ignoring him, and creating an atmosphere in which other Kennedy associates felt free to do both. To some extent, similarities between LBJ and RFK accounted for the tensions between them. Both could be rude and ruthless. And just as liberals condemned Johnson for his conservatism in the 1950s, so they castigated Kennedy during that decade for riding roughshod over civil liberties as he crusaded against domestic communism, organized crime, and labor racketeering as chief counsel of the Senate Rackets Committee. Both RFK and LBJ believed that the ends justified the means. All the while, each considered the other an immoral opportunist.[22]

Yet no adult, save the president's widow, was as closely bound to John Kennedy in the public's eyes as Attorney General Robert Kennedy, and Johnson considered him vital now. Given the importance of both RFK and the Justice Department to his administration, LBJ labored mightily to smooth things over with Kennedy. The attorney general obviously had little use for the new president, however. Deputy Attorney General Katzenbach recalled that "[e]verything Bobby said about Johnson was negative and often bitter," and that RFK predicted a rightward turn by Johnson and questioned the sincerity of the new president's commitment to civil rights. The suspicion pervaded the Justice Department.[23]

Moreover, understandably, Kennedy's mind was not on the attorney general's job. Robert Kennedy was grieving for the man he still called "the President" or "President Kennedy" in even "the most intimate circumstances." (He referred to LBJ as the "new fellow" or "Lyndon Johnson.") His office files bulged with evidence that he was evaluating his own future and how best to finish the job his brother had started. So did those of others: Within three weeks of the assassination, Arthur Schlesinger was observing in his journal that "Bobby obviously has no confidence and no taste for Johnson and obviously wants to be President himself." How, then, to proceed? Should RFK try to convince LBJ to name him Secretary of State, or come the 1964 election, vice president? The latter position seemed especially desirable since it would leave him, as Katzenbach said, well positioned to "cut off" another usurper when Johnson finally left office. Newspapers began charting RFK's interest in the vice presidency within a month of the assassination, and intimates began working to win it for him, so much so that Kennedy would later dispatch economist John Kenneth Galbraith in a futile attempt to assure Johnson that "the tactless activities—indeed any activities—on his behalf have been wholly beyond his control." Or should Kennedy run for the Senate from the state of New York, although he had not lived there since he was a child?[24]

RFK was also keeping tabs on his brother's men within the administration to ensure that they did not draw too close to LBJ. He was building his brother's and his own legacies by arranging the "insider" histories and memoirs that would be written by Schlesinger and others about JFK, his administration, and the assassination; planning and raising money for the Kennedy Library; and supervising the development of the Kennedy Center, the JFK gravesite, and other memorials. He was also increasing Johnson's fears of a Kennedy restoration through widely publicized trips to the Far East and Eastern Europe. Under the circumstances, Katzenbach said, LBJ "left the department alone." Nor could the new president count on any help from the White House counsel's office, where a JFK holdover remained in charge.[25]

Predictably, Johnson turned to Abe Fortas to operate as a shadow attorney general and do the sensitive legal work of the new administration. Fortas had grown up in Memphis in modest circumstances, attended Southwestern at Memphis, and won a scholarship to Yale Law School, where he compiled a stunning record and served as editor-in-chief of the *Yale Law Journal*. When Fortas, then twenty-two, finished his third year at Yale in 1933, the faculty invited him to join it. Like his Yale mentors and lifelong friends, Thurman Arnold and William O. Douglas, Fortas also wanted to become part of Franklin Roosevelt's New Deal. For the next few years, he commuted between Washington and New Haven while bouncing between government agencies and the classroom. By 1941, he had become under secretary of interior to Harold Ickes.

Just as Ickes was known both as "Honest" and "Horrible" Harold, so opinion about Fortas was mixed. In a town remarkable for its residents' opportunism, some found his king-sized. Fortas was capable of projecting emotions he did not feel. Depending on what he believed necessary, he might play tyrant, backstabber, sycophant, or devoted friend. He adored his wife, Yale law graduate Carolyn Eugenia Agger, a petite, cigar-smoking feminist. She admitted to owning "at least" 150 pairs of shoes, and she was an exceptionally able attorney, as well as an accomplished and fanatical gardener. But Fortas pursued other women with the same passion that he poured into mistrusting the media. His roots in the South as a lower-middle-class Jew made him an outsider, but he reinvented himself as the quintessential Washington insider. Indeed, Fortas, who was short and who spoke quietly and elegantly with a well-hidden Southern accent, shared many characteristics with the towering and frequently noisy Johnson, who became acquainted with him in the 1930s and cultivated him when Fortas became under secretary. Johnson once admiringly told a reporter that Fortas "could cut a fellow's pecker off, . . . but he'll do it clean and neat and wrap it up nice and tie it with a ribbon and pour perfume all over it."[26]

Fortas and Johnson stayed close when Fortas left government and became one of the proverbial New Dealers who had come to Washington to do good and remained to do well. With Thurman Arnold, who moved from Yale to the Justice Department to the DC Circuit, and former Federal Communications Commission chair and Truman administration insider, Paul Porter, Fortas established the celebrated Washington law firm of Arnold, Fortas & Porter and went to work guiding corporations through the very regulations he had once drafted to stymie them. At the same time, Fortas won praise from liberals and the Left by doing plenty of pro bono work. Among other things, he defended Owen Lattimore and other victims of McCarthyism for little or no money, broadened the legal definition of insanity, and successfully made the case for indigent criminal defendants' right to counsel before the Warren Court in *Gideon v. Wainwright*. In 1948, when the election results catapulting LBJ into the Senate were disputed, Fortas saved the seat for his friend, and he proved his usefulness to Johnson repeatedly afterward.

Life was good until the assassination. Fortas and Agger, a tax expert who became one of his partners, lived in a large Georgetown house. On weekends and in the summer, they escaped to their nineteenth-century farmhouse overlooking the Long Island Sound in upscale, liberal Westport, Connecticut. Fortas, an enthusiastic violinist and violist close to Isaac Stern and Pablo Casals, entertained corporate clients and fellow chamber musicians there and in Georgetown. But after the events in Dallas, President Johnson began to call on Fortas night and day. The attorney's advice tended toward the cautious and legalistic, and some around LBJ questioned Fortas's political judgment. No one, however, doubted his loyalty to Johnson or his skill as a lawyer. Fortas would prove indispensable to the new president as Johnson struggled to accomplish the transition, adapt to and work around the Justice Department, and control the damage caused by a potentially poisonous associate.

School for Scandal

In these first days of his administration, Johnson's ability to get things done appealed even to members of the press who later would revile him. When *Washington Post* publisher Katharine Graham telephoned to ask a favor, he greeted her cheerily: "Hello, my sweetheart, how are you? ... You know, the only one thing I dislike about this job is that I'm married and I can't ever get to see you. I just hear that sweet voice, and it's always on the telephone, and I would like to break out of here and be like one of these young animals down on my ranch, jump a fence." After the laughter subsided, LBJ obligingly agreed to deliver a speech to newspaper publishers, and Graham begged him to ignore the rudeness of Kennedy strategist and speechwriter Ted Sorensen. The Johnson White House had tapped Sorensen to write the president's first speech to Congress calling for continuity after the assassination, then irritated him by bringing in Fortas and others to tamper with the draft. (Sorensen's elegy for Kennedy, whom he considered "the greatest man of our time," would have had LBJ say, "I who cannot fill his shoes must occupy his desk.")

As Johnson stressed to Graham, Sorensen's speech "was a great tribute to a great man, but the Congress expected a little something else." It wanted to know where LBJ stood and what legislation he would propose. So, while the prima donnas griped that "Abe Fortas put this paragraph in and took my paragraph out," Fortas wrote the section urging Congress to honor Kennedy's memory by immediately enacting his stalled civil rights bill.

LBJ then instructed the publisher on the difficulty of forcing Congress to move. All its members had been on vacation when he needed to talk with them about the Warren Commission, the president groused to Graham. "Charlie Halleck was out hunting turkey," while others had gone home or to the beach. "And they are not passing anything. And they are not going to," although "justice and equality" demanded it. So instead of producing stories about Bobby Baker and whether he had procured prostitutes for US senators, the president continued, *Washington Post* reporters should be "asking these fellows, 'Where did you spend your Thanksgiving holidays? Tell me about it. Was it warm and nice?' "[27]

Bobby Baker had become a concern of Johnson's during his final days as vice president and was one reason the new president worried so about the Justice Department, now, and the Supreme Court, later. Like his one-time mentor, Secretary of the Senate Baker, or "Little Lyndon," as senators referred to the man charged with supervising their chamber's daily operations, was a natural con artist. Baker bragged that as a boy, he had routinely escaped school by persuading his teachers that a developmentally disabled classmate needed him to escort her home. When Johnson left the Senate to become vice president, his fix-it man acquired even more power. By Baker's account, the new Senate majority leader, Montana's Mike Mansfield, encouraged him to run the show. But after Baker became a millionaire, the *Washington Post* ran a series of articles accusing him of influence peddling.[28]

When the Senate Rules Committee and Robert Kennedy's Justice Department launched an investigation of Baker early in the fall of 1963, what Evans and Novak called "the most bizarre Washington scandal of the 1960s" erupted. Naturally, it was accompanied by speculation about whether Lyndon Johnson, a wealthy man despite—or, many suspected, because of—decades of government service, had illegally or inappropriately enriched himself as a senator. That talk propelled journalist William Lambert and others at *Life* Magazine to explore how Johnson had become rich.[29]

Since *Life* had loosened a swarm of reporters around his home in Texas, the vice president surely knew that the magazine was digging into the story of how he had amassed his own fortune. LBJ also surmised that the Kennedys were fretting about some rumors linking him to the recently arrested Texas con man, Billie Sol Estes, and others suggesting that Johnson had benefited from the Pentagon's strange decision to award the TFX fighter aircraft contract to a financially shaky Fort Worth company. Indeed, before the assassination, LBJ feared that the Kennedys planned to use the Baker scandal to remove him from the ticket in 1964. So Johnson was relieved when Fortas agreed to represent Baker. He knew his friend would look after his interests, as well as the client's. Foolishly, Fortas prevailed on the vice president to get out the message that Baker had never been his "protégé" and that the two men had worked together simply because the Senate Democrats had elected Baker secretary of the Senate when Johnson became Senate majority leader. Although technically true, that was clearly a stretch, since the Democrats had just ratified Johnson's choice. Here was Fortas at his most legalistic and one reason that some close to LBJ said he lacked political sense.[30]

Fortas more adroitly distanced President Johnson from Baker after the assassination. The attorney cited his own new duties at the White House as the excuse for turning over representation of Baker to Washington superlawyer Edward Bennett Williams. But Fortas's removal reduced Johnson's control over the Baker matter. As he moved into the Oval Office, LBJ became frantic about the danger posed to his presidency by revelations related to Baker, whose indictment Justice Department officials had asked a federal grand jury to consider.[31]

And no wonder. *Life* halted its investigation after Kennedy's assassination. "I thought we ought to give the guy a chance," Lambert said of Johnson, although perhaps the magazine just considered it dangerous to take on a president. But the very day that Kennedy died, Senate Rules Committee staff members were interviewing Baker's associate, Don Reynolds, about Senator Lyndon Johnson's past demands for, Reynolds would allege then or later, kickbacks, campaign contributions, and a $100,000 payoff for arranging a lucrative contract. After all the investigations and headlines, the worst proven in the hearings about Johnson— with respect to Reynolds, anyway—was that after LBJ bought a life insurance policy from him, Reynolds was evidently apprised, presumably at LBJ's instigation, that he should purchase $1,208 (about $9,400 in 2016 dollars) in advertising time from the Johnsons' radio and television station and present the Johnson family with a nice hi-fi that cost him about half as much, both of which Reynolds obligingly did.[32]

But penny-ante corruption had endangered the Truman and Eisenhower administrations, and the " 'Bobby Baker case' . . . has stirred up more gossip and speculation over influence peddling than anything in years," the *New York Times* reported. Further, even though Democrats controlled the Senate and could helpfully circumscribe the Baker inquiry in Congress, one historian has suggested that President Johnson worried that it "might expand from business improprieties, where the evidence against him was weak and indirect, to campaign finance, an issue on which he had flouted the law throughout his career." The disclosures might prove embarrassing, regardless of whether LBJ "flouted" the law or "skirt[ed]" it, as an aide maintained. (As president, Johnson once reprimanded a fundraiser who had illegally taken a contribution on federal property by reminding him that the Hay-Adams Hotel had been built "so that people like you could have a place to go to accept political contributions.")[33]

LBJ understood that he needed power over the Justice Department to resolve the Baker matter. He knew he would lack that as long as RFK remained. Though he wanted Kennedy to go, he needed Kennedy to stay. In fact, by December 1963, LBJ was worrying that Robert Kennedy soon would resign and dispatched Clark Clifford to see the attorney general.

Like Fortas, Clifford had come to Washington to join the government, but where Fortas had served Roosevelt, Clifford's master had been Truman. Like Fortas too, Clifford then established his own successful law firm and remained a political insider. Clifford was taller and more handsome than Fortas. His voice was honeyed, and he was famous for the way he steepled his hands as he portentously spoke. Since the 1950s, Johnson had often called on Clifford and Fortas to argue two sides of an issue for him when he needed to reach an important decision. But where those in the know considered Fortas a well-connected "lawyer's lawyer," many wrote Clifford off as just well connected. Clifford had shrewder political instincts than his friend, however, and where Fortas's loyalty was to LBJ, Clifford had also ingratiated himself with the Kennedys. Clifford had played a vital role in the Eisenhower–Kennedy transition, and though he refused all posts in JFK's administration, he served on the president's Foreign Intelligence Advisory Board and burnished his standing as power broker by doing other odd jobs for Kennedy.

After a two-hour meeting with Robert Kennedy in December 1963, Clifford reported to the president that "we really had it out," and "I'm just authorized to say now that he's going to stay." That was good news because it avoided an outright split between Kennedy and Johnson forces. "I know how hard the past six weeks have been for you," LBJ soon wired his attorney general. "Under the most trying circumstances your first thoughts have been for your country. Your brother would have been very proud of the strength you have shown," and Johnson reiterated that as he himself worked to be worthy of JFK's trust, he sought RFK's "counsel and support." But soothing words did nothing to make Baker and other distractions disappear. LBJ also understood that he required the whip hand over the Justice Department not just because of Baker but because the success of his presidency depended on realization of his civil rights agenda, which he and Justice would oversee together.[34]

For all the variations in the way he articulated that agenda, LBJ genuinely yearned for racial and economic equality and knew that they were intertwined. He also understood that he would win acclaim if he succeeded where Kennedy had failed by persuading Congress to enact legislation aimed at eradicating both. After pledging his commitment to fiscal austerity to Walker Stone in early 1964, Johnson warned the conservative journalist, in terms designed to sell him on it, "You won't like my poverty [program]. I'm going to try to teach these nigras that don't know anything how to work for themselves, instead of just breeding." Johnson made the point only slightly less offensively when he informed Reverend Dr. Martin Luther King Jr. how easy it was to figure out "what $8 billion in education, what $1 billion in health, and what a billion and a half in poverty will do if it goes to people who earn less than two thousand dollars a year" (about $15,000 in 2016 dollars). "You know who earns less than two thousand, don't you?" the president chuckled, in a transparent reference to African Americans.[35]

Johnson's remarks reflected both his fear that civil rights activists and liberals would say that he did not embrace their goals and his anxiety that Congress did not share them. At the time, presidents often had to slip African American judicial nominees past Southern segregationist Democrats who controlled the Judiciary Committee by appointing them while the Senate was not in session. In January 1964, the president grumbled to a civil rights leader who urged him to carry out Kennedy's plan to award recess appointments to two African Americans, Spottswood Robinson and Leon Higginbotham, that the black media was unfairly portraying him as bigoted. Just over an hour later, the president told African American leader Roy Wilkins that he wanted credit for the Robinson and Higginbotham appointments that he was announcing that day and spoke of the civil rights legislation. "If we lose this fight, Roy, we're going back ten years," LBJ stressed. Like the Bobby Baker issue, his desire to have his greatness as a leader recognized, his desire to integrate the South with the rest of the nation, and his own commitment to equality required him to become the master of the Justice Department.[36]

The president chafed while Baker continued to preoccupy the media, and RFK honored his commitment to remain at the Justice Department. For all Johnson's attempts to reassure Robert Kennedy that "they're never going to separate us as far as I'm concerned" and to recognize him by presenting him one of the pens with which he signed the landmark 1964 Civil Rights Act that ended segregation in public accommodations, LBJ did not trust the attorney general—though not nearly as much as he was to mistrust Kennedy later. Occasionally, the two were in sync. The first inner-city riot or rebellion that summer occurred in New York in July, two and a half weeks after LBJ had signed the Civil Rights Act. Eight more would follow by Labor Day, typically sparked by complaints about police mistreatment and/or miserable rat-infested housing, and making 1964 the first of "the long hot summers" that scarred the 1960s. Combined with continuing problems in the South that made civil rights a millstone around the Democrats' neck in the upcoming presidential campaign, LBJ and RFK agreed. But more often, at least as Johnson perceived it, Kennedy proved nonresponsive, indifferent, or contemptuous. "When this fellow looks at me, he looks at me like he's going to look a hole through me like I'm a spy or something," Johnson confided to a friend that month.[37]

Frustrated because RFK wanted to be offered the vice presidency and strangely fearful that his rival might somehow seize it, Johnson summoned Kennedy to the White House in late July of 1964. LBJ then gave a blow-by-blow account of the meeting to Clifford, who had provided the president with his talking points. He was not asking Kennedy to join the ticket, the president informed RFK, but wanted his participation in the campaign and "thought that he had a bright future in the party [and] would be willing to do what I could to contribute to it." After Kennedy agreed to help, Johnson asked if he wanted to remain at the Justice Department.

Kennedy said he did not and asked LBJ to name Deputy Attorney General Katzenbach as his successor. As Johnson recounted the conversation, RFK also warned him about Bobby Baker: "There's something that showed up where it might be interpreted that he violated the law. They'll want to know why we haven't done something, and if we do do something, it will prove embarrassing." As Kennedy got up to leave, according to the president, he said, with a smile, "'Well, you didn't ask me. But I think I could have done a hell of a job for us.'" Johnson responded, "'Well, I think you *will* do a hell of a job for us.' I looked at him very straight, proud, and said, 'And for yourself too.'"[38]

Had he been able to see the future, perhaps LBJ would have realized that he erred in leaking his own version of the showdown with RFK to select reporters, and possibly also in refusing to offer Kennedy the vice presidency. Had the president offered the job and RFK accepted it, LBJ would not have had the satisfaction of winning a presidential election on his own. He would have given Robert Kennedy's hopes of succeeding him a big boost too. Yet Johnson could more easily have kept a close watch on the Democratic rival who worried him even more than Republican ones. And as LBJ told Hubert Humphrey, the person he ultimately did select for the slot, the only vice president Johnson had ever known who possessed "any influence" was FDR's running mate, John Nance Garner, and Garner lost his in Roosevelt's second term. "I had none because Kennedy wouldn't *give* me any," he complained. Because a vice president exercised only as much power as a healthy president awarded him, President Johnson would have had the added pleasure of humiliating Vice President Robert Kennedy by giving him nothing to do beyond dispatching him to funerals. Moreover, Johnson had little use for Humphrey, whom he found garrulous (or, as LBJ would have put it, had "hydrophobia" and foamed at the mouth). No one ever called Kennedy loquacious.[39]

Here was an important moment in our story. Kennedy, who was dropping hints that he would like to become secretary of state the day after LBJ publicly ruled him out as running mate, joking to reporters and politicians about his vice presidential nonselection a week later, and announcing that he would run for a Senate seat as New York's Democratic nominee in another three weeks, had saddled LBJ with Katzenbach in exchange for avoiding an open break. By forcing Katzenbach on the president, Kennedy set in motion the improbable chain of events that would lead LBJ to pick Thurgood Marshall as solicitor general and Supreme Court justice and prompt the president to move Katzenbach to the State Department. But of course, nothing was inevitable, and there would be many twists and turns along the way.[40]

From the president's perspective, at least, Katzenbach represented an improvement over Kennedy. A graduate of Exeter, Princeton, and Yale Law School, and a Rhodes Scholar, Katzenbach possessed the usual Kennedy administration credentials. The forty-two-year-old was disarmingly self-effacing. When Katzenbach talked about the two years he had spent as a German prisoner of war after he left college in his junior year and his plane was shot down, it sounded as if he viewed the experience as a chance to catch up on his reading. (He managed to do so much of it that Princeton awarded him a degree six weeks after Katzenbach's return to college.) He had taught at Yale and University of Chicago Law Schools before joining the Justice Department when Kennedy became president. Katzenbach had excelled as Robert Kennedy's deputy attorney general since 1962, and LBJ named him acting attorney general at summer's end in 1964.[41]

Like Johnson, the new acting attorney general preferred to do business by telephone and in the shadows, but he proved able in the spotlight, as he showed in 1963 in Tuscaloosa. There Katzenbach confronted Governor George Wallace, who had settled on the publicity stunt of protesting desegregation by blocking the door to the University of Alabama when two African American students tried to register for its classes. "We could have treated the students as registered without going through all that," Katzenbach remembered later. Attorney General Kennedy, however, thought Wallace might turn nasty and provoke violence if he were not allowed "his moment in the sun or in the shade as it really was." It was Katzenbach who Wallace maneuvered into the sweltering heat. Though photos of the incident showed the big and bald Katzenbach mopping his forehead, he was famous for keeping cool, and the *New York Times* hailed his "unflappability." The Kennedys admired his calm head in a crisis.[42]

But Katzenbach's limited usefulness to Johnson in one became clear just before the 1964 presidential election. While LBJ was campaigning for himself and Robert Kennedy in New York, Fortas and Clifford alerted the president that reporters had learned of the recent arrest of Johnson's de facto chief of staff, Walter Jenkins, in a Washington YMCA men's restroom on a morals charge. Fortas and Clifford, rather than the Justice Department, ran damage control. They hospitalized Jenkins for hypertension and exhaustion and tried to keep the arrest out of the papers by stressing the damage of publication to Jenkins's wife and six children. They proved only partially successful. But at LBJ's direction, Fortas managed to clear campaign finance materials and other potentially harmful documents out of the disgraced aide's office safe before the beginning of the FBI investigation that LBJ was now forced to order.[43]

The news of Jenkins's arrest confounded the president. It wasn't that extramarital sex shocked LBJ, who had plenty of it, but that Jenkins had been caught having sex with a man. "It just shocks me as much as it does if my daughter committed treason," Johnson exclaimed as he obsessed over the impact of the scandal on his campaign. One key Democratic political operative had already identified Bobby Baker and questions about how LBJ made his money as the Republicans' best issues. "What's the political effect of it on top of Baker?" Johnson kept asking those close to him about Jenkins's arrest. The wave of scandals, he worried, might cause him to lose the election to Republican candidate Barry Goldwater or ruin his tenure if he won. Just as administration corruption had tainted President Warren Harding during the 1920s, so it might undo him. "We've got to protect the office of the Presidency," LBJ told Acting Attorney General Katzenbach when they finally spoke on the second day of the Jenkins scandal. "We're going to have to be a little careful on the Baker thing." Like FDR before him and Nixon afterward, LBJ wanted to unleash the IRS on those in his way—in this case, Baker associate Don Reynolds. Katzenbach resisted. As Johnson complained, Goldwater was making an issue out of "Bobby Baker, Walter Jenkins, and Billie Sol Estes" on the campaign trail, and the president wrongly anticipated a "Billie Sol Estes bombshell" before the election for which he wanted the Justice Department prepared. "[W]e can't be a Harding."[44]

Nothing could stop the LBJ bandwagon in 1964. His Republican opponent, Senator Barry Goldwater, had won conservatives' hearts when he refused to renounce the John Birch Society, fantasized about bombing the Kremlin's restroom, condemned civil rights legislation as federal coercion, derogated the war on poverty on a trip to Appalachia, confided his dream of ending Social Security to the aged, informed farmers that he disliked subsidizing them, and proclaimed the breakdown of morality and order. The moderates who still dominated the GOP, however, cringed whenever Goldwater opened his mouth, and LBJ embodied the optimistic "can do" spirit of the early mid-1960s. Johnson won a record 61% of the popular vote, forty-four states and the District of Columbia, and the election transformed Congress by filling it with liberals. LBJ knew, however, that he might not always prove so lucky in his opponents. Even before, and especially after, he won the presidency in his own right, he developed what his best political adviser, Lady Bird Johnson, referred to as "a Harding complex."[45]

Robert Kennedy's move to the Senate only exacerbated it (figure 3). LBJ had campaigned for Kennedy, he griped the day after the election, and won hundreds of thousands more votes than him in New York, yet he barely received any thanks when the senator-elect claimed victory. First, Johnson angrily anticipated, the *New York Times* "is going to try to make a Warren Harding out of us on account of Baker and Jenkins." Next, liberal Republicans, Kennedy Democrats, and columnists would allege that the nation had voted against the conservative Goldwater, instead of giving Johnson a mandate.[46]

Even as LBJ spoke, however, the *Times* was acclaiming "the Johnson landslide" as a triumph for liberalism and hinting that the Republican Party might be

Figure 3 LBJ campaigning with RFK in New York, 1964. LBJ Library. Photo by Cecil Stoughton.

headed for extinction. Under Johnson's guidance too, the 89th Congress would exceed even his own most extravagant hopes. There, LBJ and the liberals now possessed "the huge majorities they needed to prevent conservative committee chairmen from thwarting their domestic policy aims," Julian Zelizer has written. The possibilities for legislation appeared "limitless," not just because liberal Democrats now possessed "the votes necessary to pass bills and kill filibusters," but also because scarred moderate Republicans "were running as fast as they could from all positions that might allow Democrats to brand them as right-wing extremists in the wake of ultraconservative senator Barry Goldwater's landslide loss." So, as it turned out, the president worried needlessly. Yet his mistaken predictions did reveal his fear of scandal.[47]

The Search for an Attorney General

Given his anxiety, Johnson stressed repeatedly, he needed a loyal attorney general to defend him from persecutors and dispense the plums. "There have been about 78 people rumored as the next Attorney General," the Justice Department's deputy press secretary told a friend soon after Johnson's landslide. "The fact is that we have no idea what is going to happen. I think Nick is still in the ball game, but I have no idea what inning it is." Others thought he was out of it altogether: Evans and Novak reported that "no one in Washington" would "bet a plugged nickel" on Election Day that the president would select Katzenbach.[48]

Doubtless eager to deflect the president's attention, Fortas predicted the day afterwards that Clifford would accept the job. Johnson seemed dubious. "I think he's wonderful, and I think you're wonderful," he replied. But the president's enemies in Congress might try to worm LBJ's secrets out of Fortas. And when President Kennedy appointed Clifford to the Intelligence Board, Johnson continued, the press had said, "They just got . . . one of Truman's cronies. Just a Washington fixer that . . . was no great legal shakes." The press would want an attorney general like Tom Walsh, who had painstakingly investigated the Harding scandals, LBJ believed. Clifford's Missouri roots might mean that the South would accept his appointment at the Justice Department, however, and Johnson foresaw that civil rights issues would continue to preoccupy the administration. "I just wonder if the Bar thinks he's more than an aide to Truman."

Fortas kept pressing. "I don't know that he has been in court much . . . but you don't need it for that post," he said to the president of Clifford. "We've just got to have our own man in there," and it was worth "taking a little heat" on the nomination from Congress, "rather than run a risk of getting somebody who isn't entirely our man." If Kennedy had lost his race, Fortas continued, "I might feel differently about it. I'm scared because the young man that was elected in New York is certainly going to try to keep his clutches" on the Justice Department. Clifford had assured him that Kennedy's potential was "vastly overestimated" and that RFK would self-destruct, Fortas added. But Fortas himself feared that Kennedy "may try to appear as the knight in shining armor." He might even carve out a position for himself as a Democratic version of "Senator [John] Williams," the Delaware Republican who lived to uncover corruption in the Truman and Eisenhower administrations and sparked the congressional investigation of Bobby Baker. Johnson remained anxious about Kennedy too: "I thought he had a lot of trouble ever getting around to mentioning me last night. Didn't you?" Kennedy could not bring himself to do so, Fortas answered. "That's the terrible thing," the attorney continued. "Of course, he wouldn't have had a Chinaman's chance if it hadn't been for the tremendous votes you rolled up there." And the two old friends were off, stoking the president's insecurity.[49]

FBI Director J. Edgar Hoover, who also despised Robert Kennedy, fed LBJ's anxiety too. "Your former boss" was sending messengers to Fortas to say that Johnson must remove the "Acting" from Katzenbach's title, the president warned Hoover. RFK was also engaged in "inside blackmail" by spreading the word that Johnson was hesitating because Katzenbach too strongly favored civil rights. Just as bad, Hoover told the president, Katzenbach was bringing back to the Justice Department the same ruthless people whom Kennedy had borrowed to work on his Senate campaign. (Hoover, whose own enthusiasm for civil liberties was erratic, piously added that while he had shared Kennedy's desire to imprison labor leader Jimmy Hoffa, he had wanted to do so "legally and constitutionally.")

The news that Johnson was considering Fortas and Clifford should have reassured Hoover. Yet while he said nothing against Fortas, Hoover did tell the president that Clifford was too intimate with the Kennedys. "No, he's for me," Johnson said, and Clifford would take the job, "but I don't know how close you'd all be." Fortas was obviously Johnson's first choice. "I think he belonged to some liberal organizations [during the 1930s] that would give us some trouble [in the Senate] and I don't want to get into that," he mentioned to Hoover. But Johnson would get into it, the president made clear, if his friend would accept the post. Fortas, however, told LBJ that Congress would make him "a whipping boy" at confirmation hearings because he kept Johnson's confidences and he refused any appointment. No one else seemed right for the job.[50]

In the coming days, Johnson would continue to focus wistfully on Fortas and Clifford. In January 1965, he offered Katzenbach the directorship of the CIA. Though the acting attorney general made it clear he lacked experience in intelligence and did not want the job, he expressed a desire to serve "you and my country" wherever Johnson needed him. Katzenbach, who soon would infuriate Johnson (as Fortas duly reported to the acting attorney general) by informing LBJ that "I could no longer serve in an 'acting' capacity" and that the president must appoint a permanent attorney general for the sake of the Justice Department and the administration, left the White House believing that LBJ would not keep him where he was.[51]

Johnson did intend to install someone else at the Justice Department and give Katzenbach a consolation prize. Katzenbach had done an "A+ job," the president told Richard Russell soon afterward. Nevertheless, he was "Bobby's closest friend and Bobby's closest man," an assessment that doubtless would have surprised RFK and Katzenbach. "The person that I want to be my Attorney General—the person I respect most from the legal standpoint and from the compassionate standpoint and from the integrity standpoint—is Abe Fortas," whom LBJ had known since "we were both young Southerners up here running around, trying to find our way and supporting Roosevelt and the New Deal." When Bobby Baker had gotten into trouble, he retained Fortas because "he knew that I thought that Fortas was the ablest lawyer in the country." Though Clifford remained another possibility, Johnson informed Russell, "he's not quite as patient with me as you are" and is "a little cooler customer and a little more of a Fancy Dan. More country club." Fortas understood people from Johnson City, Texas, better than Clifford did, the president mentioned. There was the problem of the "liberal outfits" to which Fortas had belonged as a New Dealer, but he had become a famous corporate lawyer.

Was the Fortas nomination worth any problems it might cause him? LBJ asked Russell. Yes, Russell said emphatically. "He says he does not want to come," Johnson replied, and that "they" would say "I'm putting Baker's lawyer in as Attorney General" if he did. After Russell reassured him that no "great commotion" would ensue, Johnson consulted Senate Judiciary Committee Chair James Eastland, another conservative Southern Democrat. Eastland stressed that LBJ needed what he currently lacked, an attorney general whose first loyalty was to the president. "That's right," Johnson mused. "I've got to have a man kind of like my priest—that I confess to and I say, 'Here are the problems. Now you tell me what the law is and tell me how to fix it.'" Eastland promised to cooperate if Fortas appeared before him at confirmation hearings, though he warned that he had heard "these Jewish organizations don't want a Jew Attorney General" and doubted "you can get him."[52]

Fortas did remain resolute. Quite apart from his fear that he would become a "whipping boy" for Johnson, he had his own reasons to decline the offer. As attorney general, he would lose any independence from the president. He also loved his law practice, which enabled him to epitomize the corporate liberalism that LBJ personified by representing both the powerful and the disfranchised. Moreover, Fortas feared the impact of the departure on his firm, which he managed. Further, the job would pay a small fraction of the $173,274 he had reported as his income from practicing law in 1964 ($1.3 million in 2016 dollars), although Carol Agger earned a substantial income of her own. Most important, Agger did not want him to take the position for all those reasons and recalled arguing with Johnson for well over an hour about whether he should do so. "It's work to say to LBJ you can't have him," she said years later.[53]

Clifford too turned Johnson down the following week, despite efforts by LBJ and Fortas to strong-arm him into taking the job. Later, Clifford would stress that he believed that Katzenbach "deserved" to become attorney general and that Johnson had "unjustified" suspicions about Katzenbach's loyalty. Perhaps. Like Fortas, however, Clifford simply did not want to become attorney general. He too had his own lucrative law practice, foreign policy engaged him more than domestic matters, and he also feared that he would lose the ability to speak candidly by joining the president's official family. "It was not easy to say no to Lyndon Johnson without getting him mad, but I managed it," Clifford recalled afterward.[54]

The refusals of Fortas and Clifford to head the Justice Department probably frustrated LBJ. As he would have recognized, they knew him extremely well. It may even have occurred to him that those most loyal to him remained wariest of him.

Surely Johnson realized, though, that the unwillingness of Fortas and Clifford to join his cabinet left him with few options. While JFK's foreign policy appointees were staying on, Kennedy's political and domestic advisers, many of whom had signed lucrative publishing deals to write tell-alls about their boss and his successor, were leaving. Johnson did not regret their departure, but he did worry about the books and the "little cult" of former Kennedy advisers and the media "that runs around out there in Georgetown together." As a result, honoring Robert Kennedy's wishes that Katzenbach succeed him seemed prudent.[55]

Capitulating, the president invited the Katzenbachs to the White House one evening in late January, where they found LBJ "at his most charming." The president said he was naming Katzenbach attorney general, and Mrs. Johnson graciously welcomed Katzenbach and his wife, Lydia, "into the family." She was putting on a game face. Katzenbach "was a Bobby Kennedy man from the beginning, and that will be a hard blow to some of the closest Johnson people," Mrs. Johnson confided to her diary in an unusually pessimistic entry. "I do not feel close to either one of them. We are poles apart."[56]

Attorney General Katzenbach

The first disagreements were about policy. Soon after Attorney General Katzenbach had finally transferred his belongings into the cavernous office where Robert Kennedy had once tossed footballs, civil rights activists gathered for a march in Selma, Alabama. They planned to dramatize the refusal of many white Southerners to allow African Americans to vote and to pressure Johnson into sending voting rights legislation to Congress. They hoped to provoke a confrontation with Sheriff Jim Clark, a made-for-the-media racist, and they succeeded beyond their wildest expectations as Clark and his forces unleashed dogs on the marchers and violently attacked and beat them before television cameras.

Katzenbach monitored the crisis and fended off for as long as he could a stream of suggestions from the president to send federal troops to Alabama. "Have we got any legal right to go in with troops to stop a deputy sheriff from hitting a citizen over the head?" LBJ asked the day after segregationists had fatally beaten a marcher, Reverend James Reeb. "No, Mr. President," Katzenbach answered—not unless "a lot more people got hit" and the Justice Department could argue that local law enforcement officials were conspiring to defy the law. Like the Kennedys, the attorney general had a robust conception of federalism. As Katzenbach said, "LBJ was far less hesitant than President Kennedy or Bobby to call in the army, which I attributed, rightly or wrongly, to the fact that he was from south Texas and did not carry the political freight of a northern liberal among southerners." Katzenbach now told the president that sending in troops would prove "disastrous." Many disagreed. Crowds picketed the White House and occupied the Justice Department to urge the dispatch of federal troops and the enactment of voting rights legislation.[57]

Five days before the president finally federalized the National Guard, Johnson joined the civil rights community in demanding a Voting Rights Act in a brilliant speech before Congress. "What happened in Selma is part of a far larger movement which reaches into every section and state of America," he observed, "the efforts of American Negroes to secure for themselves the full blessings of American life. Their cause must be our cause too." Not just African Americans, but all Americans, "must overcome the crippling legacy of bigotry and injustice." Making the mantra of the civil rights movement his own, LBJ concluded, after pausing dramatically, "And we shall overcome." Katzenbach, who had marched into the Capitol with other cabinet members, thought the speech "pure Johnson in its passion and simple eloquence. In common, I suspect, with many others, I almost fell out of my chair." The attorney general still fretted that the Republicans whose support the president needed to compensate for Southern Democratic defections would dilute the bill.[58]

Yet as the legislation made its way through Congress, liberal Democrats who wanted to strengthen it proved more embarrassing. The recently ratified Twenty-Fourth Amendment to the Constitution outlawed the poll tax that the South had used to prevent impoverished African Americans from voting in federal elections and which the Supreme Court had declared constitutional in the 1937 case of *Breedlove v. Suttles*. The Voting Rights Bill proposed banning the literacy tests that Southerners had long used to disfranchise African Americans, but not poll taxes, in nonfederal elections. Senator Ted Kennedy of Massachusetts, with his brother's support, moved to achieve a long-standing ambition of civil rights activists and introduced an amendment to the Voting Rights Bill that would ban the poll tax in all nonfederal elections.[59]

LBJ too wanted to eliminate the poll tax, but Katzenbach told him that the Kennedy brothers' provision was unconstitutional. If all states used the poll tax to discriminate against people of color, Congress might prohibit it by statute, the attorney general reasoned. But since some, such as Vermont, employed the poll tax for other reasons, it would take another constitutional amendment to outlaw the poll tax in all elections. As with his reluctance to send in troops, Katzenbach may have been overly cautious. In fact, he acknowledged later, he and many lawyers believed that because the poll tax had so frequently been used to keep African Americans from voting, the court might well declare it unconstitutional. Katzenbach was also playing a dangerous game vis-à-vis LBJ. When Robert Kennedy asked the attorney general "whether Teddy's amendment was a problem for me," Katzenbach recalled, "I told him I was pretty confident we had the votes to defeat Teddy, so if it was doing Teddy any good politically, there was no reason for him to lay off." The administration did have the votes to beat the Kennedys and to offset Southern defections in the Senate—barely—thanks in large part to Everett Dirksen, who yoked his Republicans to liberal Northern Democrats, just as he had done with the Civil Rights Act of 1964. But as Katzenbach admitted afterward, the fight in the Senate spurred liberals and civil rights leader Martin Luther King Jr. to take up the cause in the House, which included a poll tax ban in the bill.[60]

Only after lots of public squabbling did Katzenbach break the resultant impasse by negotiating a compromise that included language in Section 10 of the Voting Rights Act that poll taxes imposed a burden on the poor, generally, and "in some areas" had "the purpose or effect of denying persons the right to vote because of race or color. Upon the basis of these findings, Congress declares that the constitutional right of citizens to vote is denied or abridged in some areas by the requirement of the payment of a poll tax as a precondition to voting." The act then explicitly directed the attorney general to challenge the constitutionality of the poll tax in the Southern states that still used it to make sure that the courts agreed. Though Congress then overwhelmingly approved the blockbuster Voting Rights Act, or "superstatute," many liberals cried "betrayal." And when Justice Douglas, writing for a majority of the court in 1966, did overrule *Breedlove* and declare all poll taxes in state elections unconstitutional on the grounds that voting was a "fundamental" right, he made no reference whatsoever to the recent abolition of poll taxes in federal elections by the Twenty-Fourth Amendment or to Section 10 and the fact that "Congress had just affirmed the very same constitutional views he was expressing." From LBJ's perspective, then, Katzenbach had embroiled him in an unnecessary battle with congressional liberals.[61]

And an embarrassing one. It is unlikely that Katzenbach told Johnson of his conversation with Robert Kennedy. But naturally, the Kennedys' criticism of his Voting Rights Bill as insufficient rankled the president, just as it would gall him when RFK began to break with administration policy on Vietnam and the Dominican Republic that Johnson had inherited from JFK and had charged Kennedy holdovers with developing. Of course, LBJ also reminded everyone urging approval of the Kennedys' poll tax provision that they bore the blame for the advice that he was receiving from Katzenbach. "I picked him because I thought you guys wanted him," LBJ said to NAACP lobbyist Clarence Mitchell, who diplomatically responded that the civil rights community's disagreement with the attorney general was "intellectual, not emotional" and that it had been "delighted" by the appointment. But Mitchell continued to cite constitutional experts who considered it possible to outlaw the poll tax by statute. "Every President's entitled to his lawyer," LBJ more pointedly remarked to Senator Birch Bayh (D-Ind.). "Katzenbach is the champion of you *all*. He's not [a] Johnson man." There was "no reason why the Kennedys can't get along with

Nick Katzenbach," LBJ added sarcastically. "He lo-v-ves them, and he's loyal to them, and he's devoted to them." The Kennedys "asked me to keep him and I have kept him, and I'm following what he says." If the liberals did not back down, the public would conclude "that we were a bunch of kids fighting among ourselves." Liberals would split the Democratic Party.[62]

"There's not one president in twenty who'd appoint the Kennedy man as Attorney General," Johnson grumbled again after the administration had defeated the Kennedy amendment in the Senate. "But I did it. I thought it was big." And what had he received for it? Martin Luther King had labeled the rejection of the Kennedys' poll tax provision at Katzenbach's insistence "an insult and blasphemy." When the bill looked as if it would succeed in the Senate, the press said it had "been drafted by the Kennedy boys' Attorney General," Dirksen and Mansfield. "But when the son of a bitch gets in trouble, it becomes the *Johnson* bill!"[63]

Even when Congress enacted "the son of a bitch," LBJ remained a chronic complainer, and Katzenbach the proverbial lawyer about whom clients griped. All too often, the attorney general told the president what he could not do. LBJ remembered the 1930s. "I want to assure you," one key New Dealer had then reportedly told his aides, "that we are not afraid of exploring anything within the law and we have a lawyer who will declare anything you want to do legal." That was the kind of lawyer Fortas was and that Johnson wanted. To be sure, as the president may have known, the sloppy lawyering evident in early New Deal legislation helped explain why the Supreme Court had declared so much of it invalid. But unlike FDR, LBJ did not face an obstructionist court, and he knew that Congress might not share his interest in social reform for long. Consequently, a more daring attorney general might have better enabled him to develop policy.[64]

Still, Johnson and Katzenbach worked together harmoniously at first. Appointments especially interested the president because they enabled him to brand his administration and to create obligations. There were plenty of new Justice Department jobs. During the five months that Katzenbach had languished in limbo as acting attorney general, most other division heads had languished right along with him, except at Civil Rights, where LBJ had wisely made internal candidate John Doar assistant attorney general.

The president liked Katzenbach's selections for some key posts. From within his department, Katzenbach recommended moving Ramsey Clark—a Texan, University of Chicago Law School graduate, and son of LBJ's long-time friend, Supreme Court Justice Tom Clark—from the Lands Division to the position of deputy attorney general, where he would oversee patronage and personnel. Katzenbach lit on Clark for the job principally because he knew that Johnson wanted him there. One Johnson loyalist thought that "Nick always felt, well here's Ramsey; he's a Texan. And he may be over here to kind of look over my shoulder." But the two men got along well, and Katzenbach had other reasons to choose Clark. So many Kennedy appointees were leaving the Justice Department that the attorney general's choices proved limited. Clark strongly supported civil rights. And although Katzenbach, whom Johnson sometimes considered rigid, found Clark occasionally inflexible, Clark was always principled. "There were better lawyers available, but none more idealistic in his view of what law should accomplish," the attorney general recalled, and he believed that he and Clark would make a good team. Katzenbach also pleased Johnson by installing Barefoot Sanders, another Texan, at the helm of the Civil Division; Fred Vinson Jr., son of Earl Warren's predecessor as chief justice, at the Crime Division; and Edwin Weisl Jr., son of LBJ's great friend, New York lawyer and politico Ed Weisl, at the Lands Division.[65]

At worst, Johnson showed only moderate distaste for the attorney general's other early personnel recommendations. Even then, his tone with Katzenbach was usually teasing, generally a good sign. "Think about it over the weekend," LBJ instructed on one occasion. "Talk to your wife. Maybe she's got an old boyfriend. Looks like to me she has pretty good judgment of men the way she picked you!"[66]

The president wanted the attorney general to receive credit for the appointments because he knew the applause would redound to the administration. "I've got more Phi Beta Kappas than anybody in the country," LBJ complained to Katzenbach, but a "wheeler-dealer" image. "Show that you've brought young, practical lawyers that can try lawsuits, who at the same time are up at the top of their class." Informed that Katzenbach was considering Professor Donald Turner from Harvard, "probably the outstanding younger man in the country," as assistant attorney general in charge of antitrust, however, Johnson balked. "Can't you get me somebody in the Midwest or South or West, besides all these Harvard men?" the president inquired before hyperbolically claiming that nine of the ten men he named to government positions had Harvard degrees. "Now I know it's a hell of a good school, and I'm for it, and I don't mind them having 30 percent." There were "two states that get everything—Wisconsin and this goddamned Harvard." Only LBJ could transform Harvard into a state. But his tone with Katzenbach remained good-natured, even affectionate, very different from the one he would use later in speaking about Turner, who got the job.[67]

Johnson still had high hopes for presenting the Justice Department as a place where liberalism shone bright and as the place where, as the meritocratic-minded president put it, "excellence" was "written over every brow." Justice Department press officers "should start leaking right quick that this Katzenbach is a modest, shy guy, but he won his spurs with Johnson himself," the president instructed his attorney general. They should let the media know that "there's never been a

President and Attorney General more close unless it was the Kennedy brothers," and that LBJ supported Katzenbach "in any damn thing he wants to do."[68]

Still, the president remained watchful. "I'm getting a little uncomfortable about some of the people around us," he told Fortas in mid-1965. Though Johnson valued his and Kennedy's secretary of state, Dean Rusk, far more than JFK ever did, the people in Rusk's department "just screw me to death." There was a "little bit" of a problem in the Justice Department too.[69]

Solicitor General Archibald Cox, who had taken a leave from the Harvard Law faculty to serve in the Kennedy administration, wanted to keep on doing his job, but only if LBJ specifically asked him to remain. Katzenbach pressed Johnson to do so, and the president got angry when Justice Department officials "slipped over a letter for me to sign, asking Archibald Cox to stay on Solicitor, saying he's the best one they ever had." He had never found Cox "too damn effective," Johnson told Fortas, and "I see no reason why we got to keep the top . . . law job in the country for one of Kennedy's professors." To Ramsey Clark, who shared Katzenbach's reverence for the solicitor general, LBJ dismissed Cox as "a burr-head" with "a pompadour" who "clerked for the Kennedys."[70]

Solicitor General Marshall

The president had his own candidate for the solicitor general's job, Second Circuit Judge Thurgood Marshall. As head of the NAACP Legal Defense and Educational Fund for more than twenty years, the great-grandson of a slave had one of the most significant legal careers of the twentieth century. From the 1930s through the 1950s, Marshall had braved threats of violence from racists as he used his shoestring budget to take his traveling civil rights law office through the South. To millions, he embodied the struggle for racial equality and color-blind justice. The greatest civil rights lawyer of his age, Marshall had won twenty-nine of the thirty-two cases he argued before the Supreme Court. "He brought us the Constitution as a document like Moses brought the people the Ten Commandments," said one NAACP official. At Marshall's urging, the Supreme Court struck down segregation in voting, housing, buses, railroads, public schools, and state universities. Of his most famous victory, *Brown v. Board of Education*, which established that "separate but equal" public elementary and secondary schools were inherently unequal, Marshall said, "We hit the jackpot." In the words of his friend and biographer, Carl Rowan, Marshall was "driven, sometimes compassionate, but often ornery; hard-working, hard-cussing and sometimes hard-drinking; hard-to-get-along with under pressure, self effacing and graceful in triumph."[71]

As always, Johnson had several reasons for focusing on Marshall now. First, civil rights activists were pressing him to name an African American to a high government position. Early on, Martin Luther King had let the president know that he and other leaders "have a strong feeling that it would mean so much to improve the health of our whole democracy . . . to have a Negro in the Cabinet."[72]

Yet the leading candidate was Robert Weaver, who had administered the Housing and Home Finance Agency for the last five years. JFK had said publicly that if Congress approved a Department of Housing and Urban Development, as it seemed likely to do, he would make Weaver secretary. Although Johnson acknowledged "a moral obligation" to Weaver, the president saw him as a "Kennedy man." More important, LBJ did not have much faith in Weaver's abilities, and neither did others in the cabinet or Congress. As Weaver's biographer observed, their assessments reflected white liberal hypocrisy and arrogance, as well as the fact that he "was not a dynamic leader in the Johnson administration." He was "a scholarly technocrat" with a PhD from LBJ's least favorite university "and a loner." *And* he irritated the president by campaigning openly for the job and behaving as if he deserved it. "I find that Weaver is pretty much of a martyr," LBJ told Roy Wilkins. Though civil rights leaders publicly expressed their support for Weaver, some did not sound that enthusiastic privately. As it turned out, Johnson made Weaver the first African American cabinet member in January 1966, when the president belatedly installed him at the Department of Housing and Urban Development after humiliating him by leaving him dangling for months, as he had done with Katzenbach. But during 1965, the president had not yet definitely decided on Weaver. Perhaps he hoped that by naming Marshall solicitor general he could stop a groundswell from developing for Weaver.[73]

LBJ was also losing his administration's most high-profile African American. As the president had reminded King, he had already placed an African American "in charge of every bit of the information that went to all of the 120 nations" when in January 1964, he named journalist Carl Rowan director of the US Information Agency (USIA). LBJ had consulted extensively with congressional Southerners beforehand to ensure that they would not punish the USIA for the appointment by reducing its appropriations and sending Rowan "home one day without his peter." Ever eager for credit, the president had also stressed to civil rights leaders that since the USIA director sat with the National Security Council and "has to tell the Secretary of State what we say abroad," Rowan would be "real powerful." But given Rowan's demands for meetings, presidential telephone calls, and luxury cars, Johnson quickly came to regard his new USIA director as a self-important and needy liability. By 1965, Rowan wanted to resign, and the president had no objections—as long as there was another African American to take his place. "I want people to say that I'm losing one Negro but getting another," LBJ explained to Katzenbach.[74]

Marshall appealed to the president in a way that neither Weaver nor Rowan did. Unlike Weaver, Marshall was not close to the Kennedys, who had only bowed to pressure to send him to the Second Circuit after Marshall refused a district court judgeship. Marshall had gone to Howard, not Harvard. Like LBJ, Marshall was a splendid raconteur, and like the president, he possessed a sense of humor that intermingled "irony and triumph." He was a brilliant advocate, and Johnson appreciated the potential of federal courts to advance the cause of civil rights. Just as much as he understood the dramatic possibility of appointing an African American to argue the government's cases before the court, LBJ early became captivated by the idea of naming the right African American to the Supreme Court after preparing him and the nation for the move.[75]

So despite Katzenbach's recommendation of Cox, LBJ telephoned Marshall on July 7, 1965, and asked him to become solicitor general. It meant a pay cut and the loss of life tenure, the president said. But "I want the top lawyer in the United States representing me before the Supreme Court . . . to be a negro" and to be "a damn good lawyer that's done it before." Then came the appeal to patriotism and the reminder that the Cold War required American progress on civil rights. The appointment, Johnson stressed, would help the American "image, abroad at home." And finally, a hint that the president might harbor still larger plans for Marshall in the future: "I want you to have the experience and be in the picture. I'm not discussing anything else . . . and I don't want to make any other commitments" or "bribe or mislead you." Johnson meant for Marshall "to have the training and experience of being there day after day." LBJ hoped "to do this job that Lincoln started and I want to do it the right way," and he intended "to be the first president that really goes all the way. . . . But I don't want anybody to be able to clip me from behind. I want to do it on merit." By the time the president finished the pitch, Marshall had accepted. "The answer's 'yes,'" he said—though as Marshall told the story later, he asked for time to consult his wife.[76]

With that conversation, Johnson had now staffed the Justice Department as best as he was able. The Kennedy shadow continued to loom large over it in the person of Katzenbach, but LBJ still needed to conciliate the Kennedys. Now the president turned his attention to the court.

2

Musical Chairs, 1965–66

Once he had done his best to tame the Justice Department, Lyndon Johnson started worrying about the Supreme Court. Secrecy shrouded its operations, and the president knew the court could both promote and endanger his agenda. He protected himself by taking extraordinary steps to change its personnel and to create two new vacancies there. First, LBJ convinced Justice Arthur Goldberg to go to the United Nations so that he could install Abe Fortas in Goldberg's place. Then, moved by both political expediency and his vision of liberalism, Johnson used Justice Fortas to influence the court, while still counting on him to run interference in the Justice Department. Then, still stymied by Attorney General Katzenbach's loyalty to the ever more troublesome Robert Kennedy and straining to prove his own commitment to civil rights, the president began looking for a chance to substitute a loyalist for Katzenbach at the Justice Department and to create a second vacancy on the court for Thurgood Marshall in the process.

No president had so meddled with the court since Roosevelt tried to increase its size and pack it with liberal justices in 1937. Yet neither members of Congress nor the public knew of the full extent of Johnson's machinations. And during the first two-thirds of the twentieth century, most legislators assumed that the Senate must approve presidents' Supreme Court selections. So LBJ shuffled personnel, his power unchecked.

LBJ's Court

Like Warren Harding, the 1930s cast a long shadow over Lyndon Johnson. Because LBJ had boldly backed FDR's controversial effort to pack the Supreme Court with additional justices in 1937, he always understood a president's need to dominate not just the executive branch, but the legislature and judiciary as well. Just as he feared that the public would compare withdrawal from Vietnam with appeasement of Hitler, so he recalled Roosevelt's struggle with a court that repeatedly struck down New Deal legislation. When Congress rejected FDR's proposal to increase the court's size in 1937 and pack it with liberal justices, the president sustained his first big domestic policy loss. That emboldened conservative Southern Democrats, who had reluctantly followed Roosevelt when he was popular, to jump ship. They joined Republicans in constructing a formidable coalition that blocked all civil rights and social reform legislation for the next quarter century until LBJ became president. So it was not surprising that when Johnson was fretting that the House might reject his 1964 poverty bill, he would tell one person after another, as he successfully lobbied for its passage, that he had not been "beat yet" and that if he suffered defeat now, he would become as impotent as FDR after the Senate shelved court packing: "They're gonna say the King's dead." The crisis that moved Roosevelt to battle the court also reminded LBJ of the importance of having a court that would uphold Great Society legislation.[1]

The court that LBJ faced made favorable decisions likely. Chief Justice Earl Warren presided over it genially, forcefully, and effectively. Psychoanalysts might speculate that Warren's commitment to society's marginalized grew out of his early commitment to Progressivism and/or his regret over having urged the internment of Japanese Americans as a California politician during World War II. Whatever the cause, the concern was real.

That did not endear the chief justice to those on the right. Some evidently concluded that politicians lacked respect for precedent and made bad judges. By the late 1950s, conservative Southern senators were fruitlessly introducing bill after bill in Congress that would have required Supreme Court nominees to have logged at least five years of service on a federal or high state court before Supreme Court appointment.[2]

Nor was Warren popular with sticklers among legal scholars. Liberals then dominated the legal academy. Virtually all law professors worshipped at the shrine of *Brown v. Board of Education* and sympathized with other Warren Court decisions. But at Harvard, some legal process scholars preached that the court that they had condemned for undemocratically functioning as a "superlegislature" when conservatives controlled it in the 1930s had become a "superlegislature" for liberals a quarter century later. They also charged that Warren Court opinions too often proved unsupported by legal principle or precedent and featured "sweeping dogmatic statements" and "the formulation of results accompanied by little or no effort to support them in reason." At Harvard, one alumnus remembered, "it was common to mock Warren for often asking from the bench whether a particular legal position was 'just.' Sophisticated legal scholars did not speak that way." The leader of this pack of sophisticates was the court's only Jewish justice, Felix Frankfurter, who managed the bloc opposing Warren. The former Harvard professor and New Dealer became the patron saint of judicial restraint and deference to the executive and legislative branches after FDR sent him to the court. Frankfurter dazzled his many friends and potential converts and ridiculed those with whom he disagreed. He referred to the chief justice as "that dumb Swede."[3]

Other old New Dealers at the court sympathized with Warren's pragmatic egalitarianism. After his fellow senators confirmed FDR's nomination of Hugo Black of Alabama to the court in 1937, revelations that he once belonged to the Ku Klux Klan raised an uproar. But Black weathered the storm and so firmly aligned himself with civil rights and civil liberties causes until the mid-1960s that wags said where "he used go around in white robes, scaring black people," he now "goes around in black robes, scaring white people." Black's absolutist approach to the First Amendment and his dedication to protecting all speech appalled those like Frankfurter who urged the balancing of individual liberties against the state or federal interest in their regulation. So, too, Black's stand for civil rights embittered many of his former supporters. "In my judgment you have betrayed your friends and the white people of Alabama who, having sent you to the Senate with their ballots are directly responsible for your present position on the Supreme Court bench," one wrote him after *Brown*. As a result, Black could hardly set foot in Alabama to see his relatives and few remaining friends there for the 1950s and the first half of the 1960s. Nevertheless, there were compensations. "As the senior member of this Court," his clerk, John Frank, observed, "he has had the rare triumph of beginning as a [member of a] small minority and seeing many of his views on government and liberty become the law of the land." Black carried the Constitution in his pocket and consulted it as religiously as he played tennis on the court behind his eighteenth-century Alexandria house. The Constitution often led him to where the chief justice wanted to go. Many considered Black the real driving force behind the bloc to which Warren belonged, though Black's power was waning by 1965.[4]

When Louis Brandeis resigned from the court, FDR chose Securities and Exchange Commission Chairman William O. Douglas for the vacancy. Douglas shared Black's First Amendment absolutism and was devoted to civil rights. Douglas overcame polio and poverty to attend Whitman College, then rode the rails to Columbia Law, where he graduated near the top of his class. Before joining the rush of New Dealers to the capital, where he developed a lifelong alliance with the Kennedys and Lyndon Johnson, Douglas taught at Yale during the heyday of legal realism, a jurisprudence aimed at carving out a niche for Yale as the anti-Harvard. The realists, who became champions of *Brown v. Board of Education*, saw law as an instrument of social policy and social science and preached that the fact pattern giving birth to the case might prove more important to its resolution than legal doctrine. In contrast to the legal process scholars, they extolled the instrumentalist style of Warren Court majority opinions, which Douglas himself largely adopted, though he never hesitated to strike out on his own.

Douglas became the court's first celebrity justice. FDR considered him for the vice presidency in 1944, and the justice flirted with a presidential run in 1948. He produced a stream of bestselling books reporting on his travels to Outer Mongolia and other far-flung locales and extolling the environment. By the time LBJ became president, the sixty-five-year-old had also become controversial because of his three marriages, the most recent to a woman of twenty-four. (The fourth would occur in 1966.) Douglas's ribald humor endeared him to friends, but he often treated others contemptuously and his clerks cruelly. Admirers insisted that his genius enabled Douglas to produce opinions with prodigious speed and to accomplish so much off the court. Antagonists contended that the justice, like Warren, cared more about result than reason. The latter group included Frankfurter, with whom Douglas clashed endlessly.[5]

Tom Clark, the father of Johnson's deputy attorney general, Ramsey, was a convivial Texan with a penchant for bow ties. Clark angered civil libertarians by his pursuit of internal security risks as Truman's attorney general and Supreme Court justice. But Clark supported civil rights. He also drafted the majority opinion in the 1961 decision of *Mapp v. Ohio* that threw the Warren Court's criminal procedure revolution into high gear: It held evidence obtained through a search in violation of the Fourth Amendment inadmissible in state, as well as federal, criminal prosecutions. Two years later, after the court had created an uproar by holding in *Engel v. Vitale* that the voluntary interdenominational prayer with which New York public school students started their day violated the establishment clause, Clark produced the majority opinion for eight justices in *School District of Abington Township v. Schempp*. There he wrote that when public schools sponsored recitations of the Lord's Prayer or Bible passages to open school, they violated the establishment clause too. Clark thus sometimes gave Warren a vote, but the chief justice could not count on him.[6]

How his contemporaries viewed Clark's opinions and those of the other justices, of course, was not necessarily how scholars would evaluate them later. Anders Walker has recently shown that by protecting private space through insisting that police acquire warrants before they enter homes, "*Mapp* actually worsened interactions between police and minorities on the street, in part by encouraging police to develop means of stopping suspects," including replacing a "search" of their persons with a violent "frisk" in the hope that evidence would drop to the ground. So, too, even as Corinna Lain exposed how Clark crafted *Schempp* to reassure the public that the court valued the pivotal role of religion in public life, she and Sarah Barringer Gordon emphasized that many schools defiantly continued to open the day with a prayer or Bible reading. And like other Cold Warriors, the liberals on the Warren Court sometimes showed greater interest in securing the façade of democracy than its substance in cases like *Brown v. Board of Education*, Mary Dudziak has maintained, and the court moved too slowly to require meaningful school desegregation. Indeed, by the late 1970s, as the Left developed a more vocal presence in the legal academy, scholars began charging that the rights that the Warren Court so enthusiastically declared just duped the subordinated classes who received them into believing the legal system was fair. And come the millennium, we will see, even liberals were readily admitting that "the Warren Court was neither as progressive nor as successful as its fans have assumed."[7]

During the 1960s, however, "sixties liberals" saw the court and themselves as both courageous *and* mainstream. They *believed* that *Mapp* protected the poor and minorities and that *Schempp* preserved religious liberty. Moreover, they seemed sure that the civil rights decisions, whatever their imperfections, promoted racial equality.

But liberals were not proud of Clark and never considered him one of their own. When they attacked his Supreme Court nomination in 1949, Senator Lyndon Johnson defended Clark, "one of my closest friends," and deplored "some of the testimony, some of the sly references, and some of the smear, dirt, and mud thrown into the hearings in an attempt to reflect on Tom Clark and his lovely family." Accusations that Clark was a presidential intimate and intellectually undistinguished tarnished the justice, as they did two of Truman's other appointees, Chief Justice Fred Vinson and Justice Sherman Minton, both of whom left the court in the 1950s. (Though Harold Burton, the one Republican Truman sent to the court, possessed better credentials than Clark, Vinson, and Minton, he was a presidential pal too.) This pattern of "cronyism" Eisenhower resolved to reverse. "I am determined to do my part to restore the Court to the position of prestige it formerly held in the eyes of the American people," Ike routinely wrote those complaining about the court.[8]

What period "formerly" referred to he did not say, though he probably meant to include both the Roosevelt and Truman eras in his indictment. Some thought Eisenhower had a funny way of doing his part. After he became president-elect, he promised the next court vacancy to Governor Warren, who had accepted the death blow to his own presidential hopes when Senator Richard Nixon delivered the California delegation to Ike at the 1952 Republican Convention and won the Vice Presidency and Warren's everlasting enmity in the process. Originally, the two agreed that Warren would train for the court appointment by becoming solicitor general. But then Vinson died unexpectedly, and Warren signaled that he wanted to become chief justice. Ike decided against promoting any associate justices, and he named Warren chief.[9]

"Almost four years ago," Eisenhower wrote in his diary in 1957, he and Attorney General Herbert Brownell also agreed that "except for the position of

Chief Justice, we would confine our selections for the Supreme Court to people who had served on either minor Federal benches or on the Supreme Courts of various states." The president maintained that "such experience would demonstrate whether the person actually had judicial temperament, judicial craftsmanship, and the willingness to sacrifice income for public service." Further, since only Burton and Warren belonged to the GOP, he and Brownell would seek "a balance on the Court between Democrats and Republicans."[10]

Eisenhower awarded his first associate justice nomination to John Marshall Harlan, the grandson of the justice who protested when all his colleagues voted to uphold segregation on railroads. "Our constitution is color-blind, and neither knows nor tolerates classes among citizens," the first Harlan famously wrote in dissent. First, Brownell convinced the second Harlan, a Republican who had studied law at Oxford and New York Law School before becoming a lion of the Wall Street bar, to join the Second Circuit. Then, just one year later, Brownell sold Harlan to Eisenhower as the only candidate for the court. Many were delighted. Learned Hand, one of the greatest judges of his era, promised Eisenhower that Harlan's appointment "would give general satisfaction to all those competent to judge, and . . . he would at once begin to add to the reputation and moral authority of the Court." Most justices revered Harlan as much as Brownell and Hand. He was as erudite as his ally, Frankfurter; as committed to judicial restraint and craft; and more gracious to intellectual adversaries. Harlan faithfully turned out elegant and well-reasoned opinions even after his eyesight began to fail by 1961 and his secretary had to read them and his mail aloud to him.[11]

Ike's subsequent elevation of William Brennan Jr., a Democrat on the New Jersey State Supreme Court, was designed to please state supreme court justices by adding one of theirs to the mix. It was also meant to appeal to Catholics restive that there was no one of their religion on the court at the moment and whose votes the president wanted in the 1956 election, as well as "to show that we mean our declaration that the Court should be nonpartisan." Some attributed Brennan's effectiveness in winning votes for the Warren–Black bloc to his gregariousness. And Eisenhower, who adopted the practice of inviting the Standing Committee on the Federal Judiciary of the American Bar Association (ABA) to rate Supreme Court nominees' professional qualifications and of interviewing nominees he did not already know, declared himself taken by Brennan's "warm personality." But Brennan also proved as gifted at manipulating legal doctrine as the less progressive Frankfurter and Harlan.[12]

Since the court now frequently divided between those Frankfurter darkly called "the Four"—Warren, Black, Brennan, and Douglas—and Frankfurter, Harlan, Burton, Clark, and Stanley Reed, the next appointment would prove crucial. When Reed retired in 1957, Ike tried to please the Midwest by awarding his spot to Eighth Circuit Judge Charles Whittaker of Kansas, a Republican with a powerful backer who the president thought had "verifiably moderate-to-conservative views." That was a mistake because Whittaker proved the most indecisive justice of the twentieth century. After wavering, he settled in with the Frankfurter–Harlan wing until the pressure of judging drove him to a physical and nervous breakdown.[13]

After Burton's retirement in 1958, the president considered appointing Brownell, who had returned to Wall Street, but he had never been a judge, and Eisenhower feared that "Southern extremists" would stress Brownell's service as attorney general at the time of *Brown* and when Ike sent federal troops to Little Rock in 1957 to desegregate Central High. An alternative candidate was Brownell's assistant attorney general, Warren Burger of Virginia, whom Ike had recently appointed to the DC Circuit, a person "whose record seems to be without blemish" and whose "reputation as a citizen is exemplary." Yet another was Elbert Tuttle of the Fifth Circuit, headquartered in New Orleans, since the president thought it might "be a good idea to have two Southerners on the Court." By now, though, Eisenhower was stressing that Justice Department officials should study candidates' opinions to ensure that they "definitely reflect a middle-of-the-road political and governmental philosophy," and Tuttle became a civil rights crusader.[14]

Instead, the president decided to replace Burton with another Ohio Republican, forty-three-year-old Judge Potter Stewart of the Sixth Circuit, a "blue blood" by virtue of the prosperous Protestantism that enabled Stewart to vacation at the Bohemian Grove and in Bermuda, and his devotion to Yale, whose college and law school he had attended. Stewart was his own urbane person. As a former chairman of the *Yale Daily News*, he enjoyed talking with journalists more than most of his media-shy colleagues. As he saw it, Stewart explained to one later, the court possessed Frankfurter and Black wings when he arrived, both courted him, and "I didn't go whole hog for . . . either of their rather extreme positions." Like Whittaker, though, Stewart would often side with Frankfurter, Harlan, and Clark.[15]

Eisenhower enjoyed an unusual number of court vacancies—the most in the twentieth century, save for FDR and Taft. Significantly, Ike added the prior judicial experience requirement for associate justices and bureaucratized the selection process. Otherwise, he played a traditional demographic game. Like his immediate predecessors, he focused on geography, religion, and, for the most part, those in his own party. Like them, insofar as he thought about the matter, he apparently naively assumed that nominees who shared his political sympathies would write opinions he liked.

Whether or not Eisenhower actually said that he had made two mistakes as president, Warren and Brennan, and they were "both sitting on the Supreme Court," the selection process surely did not work out as he intended. In the parlance of the day, it yielded two liberals, Warren and Brennan, with whom Eisenhower soon became unhappy; one brilliant conservative, Harlan; one conservative nonentity, Whittaker; and one independent, Stewart. Whatever Ike felt about *Brown v. Board of Education*—and the justices thought he did not like it or support them—the president seemed sure that the Warren Court's sympathy for racial and political minorities made it an albatross. "I get more confused every time the Court delivers another opinion," he plaintively complained to his attorney general in 1958. "Who determines whether the Court is legislating or whether it is merely making a decision and issuing necessary orders therewith?"[16]

Yet criticism of the court barely affected the nomination and confirmation process. Within two weeks of announcing Warren's recess appointment as chief justice, Eisenhower had received 116 letters, 85 of them unfavorable. Correspondents complained that Warren "lacked prior judicial experience" and also that "the appointment was dictated by politics," a staffer reported. Denunciations of Warren poured into the Senate Judiciary Committee, many apparently written by conservatives and/or delusionals.[17]

The Senate Judiciary Committee counsel boiled them down to thirty-three charges. Among the accusations that he thought went to the issue of "fitness," which the committee could properly explore, one stretched back to Warren's years as district attorney, when he allegedly was "many times . . . so drunk . . . that his assistants had to help him stand up in court." Most, however, related to his tenure as California's attorney general or governor, when correspondents contended that Warren had been dominated and controlled by "a notorious liquor lobbyist," with whom he had improper connections; "permitted organized crime to establish its national headquarters in California"; promoted corruption in his administration and penalized whistle-blowers; refused to prosecute bookmaking violations; "owned and operated" an "escrow racket"; unfairly favored "the AFL labor monopoly"; had a "100 percent perfect record of following the . . . Marxist . . . revolutionary line"; and "knowingly" made "dishonest" people judges "and thereafter elevated them." Then, too, there was Warren's lack of judicial experience. Among the accusations that the counsel thought did not go to the issue of fitness and were outside the committee's investigatory purview were charges that Warren discriminated against Dust Bowl migrants; supervised the State Unemployment Trust Fund poorly; appointed an unfit person to the state's Audit Authority; unwisely used his power of executive clemency; signed into law an Administrative Procedure Act that was "unconstitutional and un-American"; was "left of center," a socialist, a Democrat, or not "a good Republican"; behaved like "a Roosevelt-Truman New Deal vote-getter"; failed to win the election when he became the Republican candidate for vice president in 1948; did not help Richard Nixon in his 1950 Senate campaign; "toadied" to Truman during the

1952 campaign; was a "One Worlder" who sided with Republican internationalists; befriended an attorney who represented a communist; opposed a loyalty oath for University of California professors and state schoolteachers; promoted "socialized medicine" and a State Fair Employment Practices Act; opposed segregation; vetoed a bill protecting the American flag; and possessed "political philosophies" that would prevent him from judging soundly.[18]

Warren's friend, columnist Drew Pearson, accurately characterized Senate Judiciary Committee Chairman William Langer as "one of the most independent, unpredictable, colorful and cantankerous members of the United States Senate." Langer knew the accusations against Warren were baseless. Nevertheless, after using them to stall consideration of the nomination, he directed that almost all the charges the committee's counsel had identified as worthy of investigation, with the exception of the one about Warren's alleged drunkenness, be read aloud in a hearing attended by the press and public, and they were broadcast throughout the nation. (At the time, many speculated that Langer behaved as he did because the Eisenhower administration had not followed his recommendations on patronage, a hypothesis that the senator and the Justice Department denied.)[19]

But Warren remained safe. Like other chief justices, he did not even attend his own confirmation hearing at which the hearsay against him was rehashed, though some Senate Judiciary Committee members clearly wanted him to do so. Three voted against recommending his nomination to the Senate. Professing to admire Warren, while obviously worried that he would support civil rights, two Democrats, Senators James Eastland of Mississippi and Olin Johnston of South Carolina, called for a nominee with judicial experience and sought a more extended FBI investigation. Another, Senator Harley Kilgore of West Virginia, characterized his vote against Warren as a protest against "the press pressure" on the committee to discharge the nomination. Nevertheless, the Senate Judiciary Committee favorably reported it by twelve to three. And like most successful Supreme Court nominees between 1789 and 1965, Warren was confirmed in the Senate by voice vote.[20]

Once the Senate Judiciary Committee began holding public confirmation hearings as a matter of course in 1938, associate justice nominees appeared at them intermittently, and only routinely beginning with Harlan. And from Harlan's hearing through Brennan's, they easily dodged senators' questions by claiming that controversial issues might come before the court and standing on the principle of separation of powers. No recent phenomenon, evasiveness came especially easily to nominees like Brennan and Stewart, who, like Warren, were named when the Senate was in recess and took their places on the court and began producing and issuing opinions before their confirmation hearings occurred.[21]

All easily survived the confirmation process. Although Southern anger at *Brown v. Board of Education* and Harlan's "scalawag" grandfather did delay consideration of his nomination, the Senate confirmed him by a vote of seventy-one to eleven after a two-day hearing more memorable for the parade of witnesses insisting or denying that Harlan was a "One Worlder" who rejected national sovereignty than for the smaller role played by questions about school desegregation. (Without a doubt, though, the latter issue explained why the nine Southern Democrats among those eleven voted against him). And when Senator Joe McCarthy, who did not belong to the Judiciary Committee and who had passed the peak of his power, insisted that Brennan define communism and explain his attitude toward congressional investigations of it at a brief hearing, colleagues swatted him down, and the Senate confirmed Brennan by voice vote. Only McCarthy voted nay. The Senate followed a similar pattern with Whittaker, whose confirmation hearing proved even more of a charade than Brennan's. (Perhaps it helped Whittaker that his only opposing witness, a civil liberties lawyer who admitted to sympathizing with international communism, attacked the nominee for writing an opinion that upheld the right of a university to fire a professor who refused to answer questions about his communist sympathies.)[22]

Stewart proved less fortunate. His confirmation hearing was the first to occur after a two-month period in which the court handed down a shocking set of opinions that seemed to repudiate its own recent decisions and challenge "democratic bodies." The 1957 decisions provided communists with access to their FBI files, made prosecution of Communist Party leaders a thing of the past, reined in federal and state legislative committees investigating communists and other dissidents, affirmed the importance of academic freedom, and prevented bar associations from excluding communists. "Not since the Nine Old Men shot down Franklin Roosevelt's Blue Eagle in 1935 has the Supreme Court been the center of such general commotion in newspapers and the bar," *Time* said of the "Court's swerve in a new, liberal direction in dealing with cases bearing on the individuals v. government." It took every ounce of Majority Leader Lyndon Johnson's skill to force the Senate to table the Jenner–Butler bill that would have stripped the court of jurisdiction over internal security cases.[23]

Senate Judiciary Committee members vented their anger at the court on Stewart. Notably, their definition of "fitness" had broadened by the time of his hearings. Where the nominee's views on segregation and internal security had been off the table during the Warren confirmation, *Brown v. Board of Education* now took center stage, as Senator John McClellan of Arkansas and his fellow segregationists badgered Stewart about it and, to a lesser extent, the court's internal security decisions. Scot Powe rightly labeled the Stewart hearing a turning point in judicial confirmations in terms of difficult questions asked of the candidate—not that Stewart told senators much of anything other than to say, after repeated questions about *Brown*, "I would not like you to vote for me ... because I am for overturning that decision, because I am not. I have no pre-judgment against that decision." Senators and Stewart also sparred about whether he believed that "the Supreme Court has the power to amend the Constitution of the United States," whether the words of the Constitution had the same meaning they did when the Constitution and amendments were adopted, and whether he considered himself a "creative judge" or one bound by precedent. Senator Sam Ervin of North Carolina provided a lengthy critique of the Warren Court and its recent decisions that had "astounded" him.[24]

Senators Eastland and Johnston no longer pretended to admire Warren either. Their minority report opposing Stewart's confirmation contended that "with a Supreme Court which has invaded the reserved power of the States, which has usurped legislative power, which has invalidated the internal security laws of the Nation, at both the State and Federal levels, which has crippled the investigatory powers of the Congress, and which has handed down a series of decisions that in sum have vastly aided the Communist conspiracy, it is of the highest importance that the Senate shall exercise most carefully its power to confirm or reject a nominee." Eastland and Johnston inveighed against recess appointments and insisted that the hearings had shown that "Stewart thinks the Supreme Court has the power to legislate and to amend the Constitution of the United States," even though Stewart had emphatically denied it did.[25]

They had company on the floor of the Senate, where Senators Richard Russell and Herman Talmadge of Georgia and Strom Thurmond of South Carolina joined them in launching a full-throated protest. Stewart's opponents damned him with faint praise. They conceded that he was "an honorable and capable man," even "an improvement over what we now have on the supreme bench." But they excoriated *Brown* and the internal security decisions and extolled the legal process critique of the Warren Court's craftsmanship. Nevertheless, most senators refused to agree that fitness encompassed ideology, and they voted to confirm Stewart by seventy to seventeen, with only a portion of the Southerners in opposition.[26]

It is unlikely that the nominations of Harlan and Stewart were ever in jeopardy. The Senate rejected nearly one in four Supreme Court nominations during the nineteenth century, particularly during the Tyler, Grant, and Cleveland presidencies. During the first two-thirds of the twentieth century, the confirmation process's era of good feelings, however, it typically approved them by voice vote or overwhelming majority. (That pattern generally held true in lower court appointments as well. But lawmakers' tendency to treat lower court appointments as their personal property made for occasional tense moments between presidents and senators with respect to district court and circuit court nominations. Further, the Republican-controlled Senate Judiciary Committee blocked or delayed confirmation of a large number of Truman's nominees between 1946 and 1948. And segregationists vigorously but vainly attacked Eisenhower's nomination of Solicitor General Simon Sobeloff to the Fourth Circuit in 1956. Since he had represented the government before the court in *Brown*, they saw him as desegregation's champion.)[27]

Even if the nominations of Harlan and Stewart were endangered, that would bring the number of instances during this sixty-year period in which an individual's allegedly "radical" or "reactionary" ideology posed any real threat to his confirmation to just ten. Of the forty Supreme Court nominations made by presidents from Theodore Roosevelt through Dwight Eisenhower, senators held up the 1912 nomination of Mahlon Pitney for nearly a month on the grounds that he opposed labor and social reform before voting approval for it by fifty to twenty-six. After a brutal four-month fight pervaded by anti-Semitism but ostensibly centered on whether Woodrow Wilson's nominee, Louis Brandeis, was radical, unethical, and unprofessional, senators confirmed him in 1916 by forty-seven to twenty-two and made him the first Jewish justice. In 1925, they cleared Harlan Fiske Stone by seventy-one to six after nasty allegations surfaced about his behavior as attorney general and Stone became the first nominee ever to appear before the Senate Judiciary Committee to refute them. In 1930, senators voted for Charles Evans Hughes as chief justice by a two-to-one majority, despite criticism that he toadied to big business and did not support states' rights.[28]

While the Senate handed FDR a defeat on his proposal to increase the number of justices on the court, it accepted his and his successors' control over filling vacancies there. The Senate remained tolerant during the Roosevelt and Truman administrations. Although his fellow senators surely knew that Hugo Black had been a Klansman years earlier, they confirmed him by sixty-three to sixteen in 1937. The Senate Judiciary Committee did not even bother to hold hearings on the Supreme Court nominations of two other senators during this period, James Byrnes and Harold Burton. Felix Frankfurter, the first immigrant in the twentieth century named to the court and the second nominee to appear before the Judiciary Committee, was reviled as a communist and Jew in what Lori Ringhand has called "our first truly modern confirmation, and the first modern confirmation involving . . . [an] outsider." Nevertheless, senators approved Frankfurter by voice vote in 1939, even though anti-Semitism was at its prewar peak and a Jew, Brandeis, was already sitting on the court. (FDR's nomination of another outsider to the court the following year, his Irish Catholic attorney general, Frank Murphy, was never in jeopardy, since the Senate confirmed him by voice vote within two weeks. Where Frankfurter had answered questions largely focused on his past political activities, Murphy, whom some reviled for refusing to use force against sit-down strikers as Michigan's governor, underwent even more of a contemporary-style hearing. He confronted questions about whether he favored property rights, judicial review, recusal, and "administrative absolutism.") And as William Wiecek wrote, "partisan Republican senators . . . determined to settle old scores" from Sherman Minton's days in the Senate and to "take cheap shots at the New Deal" dominated his 1949 hearing, but senators voted to award him a Supreme Court seat by a three-to-one margin.[29]

Only once during the first half of the twentieth century did they prove noncompliant with respect to a Supreme Court nomination. Interest groups had delayed the confirmations of Stanley Matthews in 1881 and Brandeis in 1916 for reasons more ideological than the partisan considerations that caused senators to reject nominees beforehand. Civil rights and labor groups utterly derailed Herbert Hoover's "Southern strategy" to turn white Southerners Republican when the president nominated Fourth Circuit Judge John Parker of North Carolina to the court in 1930. "The methods employed were something new in the history of the United States," Parker stressed afterward. "What was done was to agitate the labor unions and Negro organizations from Washington and New York by means of false propaganda, and to have them bring influence to bear on their Senators. It is almost impossible for a nominee for the Supreme Court to meet this kind of propaganda; for if he descends into a publicity fight of this sort, he is straightway condemned for engaging in tactics unbecoming to a nominee to the highest Bench." For Parker, these attacks on his beliefs and defections from Southern Democrats who wanted to embarrass Hoover for partisan reasons explained why he fell just one vote shy.[30]

Yet after the Parker fight, senators once again functioned as presidential lapdogs with respect to Supreme Court confirmations. The Senate confirmed Hoover's next choice, Owen Roberts of Pennsylvania, an "economic reactionary" whom the civil rights community wanted to believe was "liberal" on race, by voice vote. To be sure, as Joe Crespino and James Heath have stressed, during the 1950s, Senator Strom Thurmond of South Carolina and the seventeen other senators who signed the Southern Manifesto advocating school segregation and assailing *Brown* as "a clear abuse of judicial power" launched their own long "war on the Warren Court" for its "softness" on communism, crime, and, above all, civil rights. And by the end of the Eisenhower era, some used Senate Judiciary Committee hearings to grouse publicly about the court's direction. But all still behaved as if the president had the right to put whomever he wanted on it. "Given the fact that the Senate as a whole has seen fit to reject but one Supreme Court nominee since 1893, it is difficult to support the proposition that the function of the Senate Judiciary Committee is to objectively investigate the qualifications of Supreme Court nominees and decide to recommend confirmation accordingly," one scholar observed in 1965.[31]

Even congressional grumbling subsided under Kennedy, as the same senators who worked so hard to block his domestic legislative program hailed his
Supreme Court nominations. First, Justice Whittaker retired in 1962. "You
ought to be appointed to that vacancy, but . . . we need you too much in the
Administration," Secretary of Labor Arthur Goldberg remembered JFK saying.
Then Robert Kennedy, who saw the civil rights and Cold War agendas as intertwined, became interested in the Supreme Court appointment of Circuit Court
of Appeals Judge William Hastie, the first black editor of the *Harvard Law Review*
and the first African American federal judge. The Kennedys, however, treated the
chief justice more deferentially than the Eisenhower administration. When RFK
spoke with Warren about Hastie, he found the chief justice "violently opposed"
because Frankfurter might beguile Hastie. In Warren's view, Hastie was "not a
liberal" and "would be completely unsatisfactory," Kennedy recalled.[32]

Within the administration, an influential group lobbied for Harvard's Paul
Freund, a Frankfurter disciple and a Jew, but JFK bypassed him too and named
forty-four-year-old Deputy Attorney General Byron White. Raised in modest
circumstances amid sugar beet fields, White was a Phi Beta Kappa graduate
of the University of Colorado. There, he proved a star football player and was
shackled with the name "Whizzer," which he loathed. In short order, he won
a Rhodes scholarship, became the best-paid player in the National Football
League and its rushing leader, and was decorated for Navy service. Graduating
first in his class at Yale Law, he was the first person nominated to the court who
had himself clerked there: White worked for Chief Justice Vinson before settling
in Denver. Then JFK tapped White, whom he had known since the 1930s and
who had written the World War II report that exonerated Lieutenant Kennedy
from wrongdoing when the Japanese rammed his PT boat, to head Citizens for
Kennedy in 1960. After the election, Kennedy tasked White with organizing the
Justice Department. Though White was often ungracious and taciturn, especially with those seeking to recall his gridiron glories, his past made him attractive to JFK, who saw him as "the ideal New Frontier judge." The Senate Judiciary
Committee, which had been relatively flooded with communications from the
public protesting the Clark and Warren Supreme Court nominations, received
just eighteen communications opposing White's nomination, two-thirds of
which focused on his lack of judicial experience. Senator Sam Ervin (D-NC),
a former state Supreme Court justice, grumbled that the president might have
chosen someone from the bench, but Ervin and his colleagues liked the nominee too. White's 1962 hearing, which lasted all of ninety minutes, was a coro-
nation. The Senate confirmed him by voice vote less than two weeks later after
just two pro forma complaints by Southerners applauding White but attacking
the court's "tendency to make sociological rulings on legal matters." As a justice,
White proved as "non-ideological and non-doctrinaire" as JFK himself.[33]

Later that year, Frankfurter resigned after a stroke that he and others believed the Warren bloc's entrance into the "political thicket" of reapportionment had caused. Once again, JFK considered Paul Freund, until Robert Kennedy reminded him that "Freund had refused the position of Solicitor General." The Kennedys then discussed "the necessity of replacing Frankfurter" with a person of his religion, with the president stressing that "the various Jewish organizations would be upset if this appointment did not go to a person of the Jewish faith." If JFK wanted a Jew, RFK contended, the president should select Goldberg.[34]

His was a Jewish Horatio Alger story. The child of Russian immigrants, Goldberg was one of eight children raised in Chicago slums. After his father, a peddler, died, the family's finances became even more precarious. Arthur sold shoes and took other jobs, then graduated first in his class from Northwestern and summa cum laude from its law school. He was just twenty years old. During World War II, he served in the CIA's precursor, the Office of Strategic Services. Then he became general counsel of the United Steelworkers of America; the Congress of Industrial Organizations; and, after he ended the rupture between the American Federation of Labor and Congress of Industrial Organizations, the AFL-CIO. Goldberg, who dreamed of joining the court, had wanted to go to the Justice Department, but JFK appointed him secretary of labor instead. Although he was garrulous, vain, and self-important, he was also endearingly bubbly, confident, and exceedingly energetic and effective in resolving disputes.[35]

So, after enlisting Goldberg to ensure that labor leaders approved of his successor, JFK told his secretary of labor he was announcing his appointment to the court later that day. When Goldberg protested that the administration had not yet consulted the members of the American Bar Association's Standing Committee on the Federal Judiciary, Kennedy said, "Oh Hell, Bobby's doing it over the phone and I'm going ahead anyhow. They can't object to your appointment." There was then no "roll-out" of the nominee and no appearance with him at the announcement. No president even went to court to watch his nominee take the oath until Truman, the first to appear there while in office, attended Burton's investiture. Nor did nominees routinely call on senators before confirmation hearings, undergo "murder boards" to prepare for them, or make opening statements.[36]

Goldberg did at least have the benefit of a fifteen-page position paper. Its undisclosed authors, probably at the Labor or Justice Department, had examined every confirmation hearing since Warren's. They advised Goldberg to read Stewart's and informed him of probable questions "unless your hearing is a pro forma one—like Justice White's." If past proved prologue, the "chief questioners" would be two Warren Court detractors, Ervin of North Carolina and Senate Judiciary Committee Chair James Eastland of Mississippi. There was no reason for fear. As the authors said, "For the most part these questions are ritualistic and pavlovian answers are expected. Like a witness in a law suit, the nominees have fared best when they gave short, forthright answers and did not volunteer too much information or qualify their answers too much." Among other things, the memorandum included possible questions about *Brown* and the role of the Supreme Court. It also predicted that the committee might ask about issues such as civil rights activists' civil disobedience, school prayer, contempt of Congress, reapportionment, obscenity, and right to counsel. "The temptation to do so at this time is particularly strong because of the large number of important cases that were put over from last Term to this and because many people feel that the new Justices will have the deciding votes on these cases. The Committee has generally been willing to accept the nominee's claim that it would be improper of him to discuss issues then before, or likely to come before the Court."[37]

Committee members threw Goldberg more softballs than even the authors anticipated. He received no questions about *Brown*, and Eastland kept quiet or absented himself. Predictably, Ervin griped about Goldberg's lack of judicial experience and asked him whether he was "aware of the fact that many informed, intellectual, and honest and sincere persons, who respect the Supreme Court as an institution of the Government" had lately concluded that "the Supreme Court has usurped and exercised the power of Congress and the States to amend the Constitution, while professing to interpret it." But Ervin's inquiries, like those of his colleagues, did seem formulaic; the senators, satisfied by Goldberg's "pavlovian" responses stressing his commitment to capitalism, his condemnation of communism, his insistence on administering justice with an even hand, and his respect for the rights of Congress and the states. Senators confirmed Goldberg by voice vote, with only Strom Thurmond of South Carolina voting against him. In those halcyon days, conservative Senator Barry Goldwater wired JFK that Goldberg was an "excellent" choice. The Senate Judiciary Committee received fewer than two dozen protests against the nomination from anticommunists, anti-Semites, and conservatives.[38]

Where Eisenhower said he named judges to end cronyism, Kennedy's appointments of both White and Goldberg reinstated it—or, to put it less baldly, rewarded loyal executive branch officials with distinguished academic and professional credentials. Johnson would follow JFK's pattern, though unlike Kennedy, he would appoint two liberals to the court, not one. The Warren Court's glory days, beginning in 1962, also awakened Kennedy's successors to the court's political importance.[39]

Unlike them, JFK considered the court, like all judicial appointments, a sideshow. "I don't know why they all want to go into retirement up there, but they do," he complained. In the case of the Goldberg appointment, the president intended not just to bestow a reward but also to please voters by maintaining the court's "Jewish seat." (His brother, Ted, was then waging his first

Senate campaign, and just before he nominated Goldberg, JFK made Anthony Celebrezze secretary of health, education, and welfare. Ted Kennedy "ran like wildfire through the Jewish and Italian wards of Boston," Tom Wicker reported, and aides "produced this painful but instructive bit of doggerel: Goldberg didn't hurt/And Celebrezze/Made it easy.")[40]

Goldberg's arrival at the court changed everything by giving the bloc composed of Warren, Brennan, Douglas, and Black the crucial fifth vote (figure 4). The Warren Court had been "more of a Frankfurter Court than a Warren Court," except in the realm of civil rights, Goldberg recalled. "With my appointment, the Warren Court became more than a name," he said proudly. "It became an actuality. For the first time since the appointment of Earl Warren as Chief Justice there was a majority for a constitutional approach, which gave full meaning to the great rights safeguarded by the Bill of Rights in the Constitution." Beyond limiting school prayer, the court in 1963 struck down legislation designed to put the NAACP out of the business of litigating segregation and discrimination cases. It proclaimed indigents' right to counsel in state felony cases in *Gideon v. Wainwright*, gave teeth to the prohibition against

Figure 4 Justices of the US Supreme Court, 1962, left to right, sitting: Tom Clark, Hugo Black, Earl Warren, William O. Douglas, John Harlan; left to right, standing: Byron White, William Brennan, Potter Stewart, Arthur Goldberg. Supreme Court of the United States.

unreasonable search and seizure, declared the right of those convicted in state courts to habeas corpus, and broadcast the principle of "one person, one vote" for legislative districting.[41]

With Warren, Black, Douglas, Brennan, and Goldberg there then, LBJ could count on a majority at the court should it scrutinize Great Society legislation. Yet, as he knew, the court had its foes. In the summer of 1963, Brennan publicly mourned the strength of its critics: "There is sectional opposition because of the desegregation cases; state opposition because of recent decisions involving state powers as they relate to aspects of criminal law; rural opposition because of the reapportionment cases, and church opposition because of the prayer case." The situation was not as dire as Brennan suggested. Of course, the South continued to vilify the desegregation decisions. But Kennedy and religious leaders defended the court on school prayer, and Clark's soothing words in *Schempp* about the preeminent place of religion in American society muted some of the outcry over *Engel*. Further, many Americans welcomed the reapportionment and criminal procedure cases as they did become aware of them. Constitutional scholar Barry Friedman stressed that the public "loved" the court's reapportionment decisions and celebrated *Gideon*—which some then thought just changed the situation on the ground in a few Southern states anyway.[42]

Still, like the Warren Court's other decisions, the reapportionment and criminal procedure decisions stood out for politicians, some of whom detested the Warren Court's determination to nationalize the Bill of Rights. In 1963, the Council of State Governments adopted a resolution proposing (1) amendment of the Constitution's Article V to permit proposals adopted by two-thirds of state legislatures to become constitutional amendments without congressional deliberation or a national convention, (2) amendment of the Constitution to end federal judicial authority over state legislative apportionment, and (3) amendment of the Constitution to establish a fifty-justice Court of the Union staffed by the state chief justices to review the Supreme Court's federalism decisions. "I was astounded by the number of States which have seriously considered the proposals of the Council of State Governments," Warren confided to his friend, Arthur Freund, a distinguished Saint Louis lawyer and civil rights activist, and the chief justice found it "shameful" that "the legal fraternity . . . ignored proposals to change our institutions so radically." The American Bar Association reported that the council's proposals were "dead issues" by 1964, thanks in large part to the energy Freund and Warren poured into fighting them. But by then, twelve state legislatures had adopted the first proposal; thirteen, the second; and five, the third.[43]

Barry Goldwater, LBJ's Republican opponent in the 1964 presidential election, was no longer celebrating Goldberg's appointment either. He attacked the court's decisions on criminal procedure, reapportionment, and school prayer. Of the three branches of government, "today's Supreme Court is least faithful to the constitutional tradition of limited government and to the principle of legitimacy in the exercise of power," Goldwater contended to the American Political Science Association. At the Mormon Tabernacle in Salt Lake City, he urged adoption of a constitutional amendment to permit school prayer, and in the South, he promised to appoint federal judges who would "redress constitutional interpretations in favor of the public."[44]

The polarizing rhetoric did nothing to help the Republican candidate. A bipartisan coalition of the nation's leading lawyers, including five past American Bar Association presidents, issued a widely publicized statement rebuking Goldwater for relying on "catch phrases and slogans" in attacking "the ultimate guardian of American liberty." The chair of the House Judiciary Committee denounced his "violent demagoguery" and compared him to Hitler and Mussolini, while columnist Drew Pearson reported that the candidate planned "to pack the Supreme Court with pro-segregationist judges." Although Goldwater fatefully moved law and order to the center of political discourse, Richard Nixon played a far greater role in making it important when he blamed the Supreme Court for its breakdown and made criticism of the court respectable four years later.[45]

Still, Goldwater's attack stung, especially since it came as the court prepared to start a new term. "Not since the Nine Old Men of unhallowed memory struck down the first New Deal almost 30 years ago—perhaps not since John Marshall's Court put the separate states in their places in order to strengthen an adolescent nation—has any Supreme Court used its politico-legal power so broadly and boldly as did Earl Warren's in the term that ended last June," Yale's Fred Rodell announced in the *New York Times*. In *Reynolds* v. *Sims*, for example, the Court invalidated unequally populated state legislative districts because they violated the principle of "one person, one vote." After scoring the majority for cutting "deeply into the fabric of our federalism" with its "profoundly ill-advised and constitutionally impermissible" actions, Justice Harlan concluded his powerful dissent by accusing his brethren of politicizing the judicial process in words that appealed to legal process scholars and political conservatives alike:

[T]hese decisions give support to a current mistaken view of the Constitution and the constitutional function of this Court. This view, in a nutshell, is that every major social ill in this country can find its cure in some constitutional 'principle,' and that this Court should 'take the lead' in promoting reform when other branches of government fail to act. The Constitution is not a panacea for every blot upon the public welfare, nor should this Court, ordained as a judicial body, be thought of as a general haven for reform movements. The Constitution is an instrument of government, fundamental to which is the premise that in a diffusion of governmental authority lies the greatest promise that this Nation will realize liberty for all its citizens. This Court, limited in function in accordance with that premise, does not serve its high purpose when it exceeds its authority, even to satisfy justified impatience with the slow workings of the political process. For when, in the name of constitutional interpretation, the Court adds something to the Constitution that was deliberately excluded from it, the Court, in reality, substitutes its views of what should be so for the amending process.[46]

Reynolds was just one of many controversial decisions handed down during the 1963-64 term. The court had held that counties could not dodge integration by closing their public schools. It had supported civil rights activists who mounted marches and sit-ins. It had begun to attack state antimiscgenation laws. It had declared that the values of free speech and press required the protection of all statements about public figures and officials, except those made with knowledge that they were false or with "reckless disregard" for the truth. It had expanded protection for obscenity. It had voided legislation that denied passports to US citizens with communist connections. It had announced that the privilege against self-incrimination was applicable in state, as well as federal, court proceedings. And it had concluded that self-incriminating statements made in the absence of counsel after suspects' indictment were inadmissible because they violated the right to fair trial.[47]

Even one of the court's "liberal" members worried about its expansive record. Justice Black was now telling his clerks that "nigras had to come in the back door of my Pappy's store" and that there was a private constitutional right to discriminate. That position he reiterated in dissent when he insisted that "the Fourteenth Amendment of itself does not compel either a black man or a white man to trade with anyone against his will." Was the elderly justice promoting property rights over civil rights because he wanted "to be buried in Alabama," as Warren joked? Alternatively, or perhaps additionally, by refusing to consider civil rights activists accused of sitting in and/or trespassing as candidates for constitutional protection, was Black insisting on a distinction between speech and conduct? Was he also revealing an antipathy—which some older members of the civil rights movement and Justices White and Harlan shared—toward a younger generation of activists who had embraced civil disobedience? After all, Christopher Schmidt stressed, "In his opinions, Justice Black returned again and again to his belief that liberties ultimately suffer when protesters take to the streets rather than rely on courts to protect their rights."[48]

As a Yale law professor and legal realist, Fred Rodell revered the Warren Court. But as he acknowledged in his laudatory *Times* article, "its display of judicial force and authority, coming as the culmination of a decade of constitutional change that began with the school-desegregation decision of 1954," was not beloved everywhere. Its work "caused many to conclude that, and others to wonder whether, the Court had gone too far."[49]

Lyndon Johnson was not then among the wonderers. "I doubt if there ever has been or will be again a judicial bench better than . . . the Warren Court," the president told a reporter. "There has never been less friction between the executive, legislative, and judicial branches." The family quarrel between liberals in the academy did not interest him. So what if liberal Harvard law professors who liked the results in the court's decisions attacked their underlying reasoning? What concerned LBJ was what decisions did and how Congress and the public reacted to them.[50]

More than most presidents, he also saw the court as integral to his own past, present, and future. Where the Kennedys viewed judges and justices as "passive spectators," Johnson saw them as partners in treating law as a tool of social policy. The court had made his career possible. When he ran for Senate in 1948, Johnson called on Abe Fortas to defend him against allegations of voter fraud. As the court was not in session, Fortas took the case directly to Justice Black, its representative to the Fifth Circuit. Black listened to the argument that no federal judge should intervene in a state election and set aside the temporary restraining order that would have kept Johnson's name off the ballot. With Fortas, Black saved Johnson's political life. As LBJ saw it, now that he was president, that life depended on a sympathetic court again.[51]

The First Supreme Court Vacancy

What Johnson apparently decided he needed in 1965, Robert Dallek said, was "a mole" at the court to stave off decisions against Great Society legislation, protect his interests, and inform him about its relevant deliberations. In a sense, the president worried needlessly, since the Warren Court would handily uphold all Great Society legislation while he was in office. But his own cautiousness never concerned LBJ, and given his fear of becoming a Warren Harding consumed by scandal, perhaps he reasoned that other issues involving his administration might come before the court for which inside knowledge of its members' thoughts would prove useful.[52]

A number of the justices had long been active in Washington politics and policymaking, and LBJ had close ties to them. The Johnsons and the Clarks had been friends for decades, and when the president had bladder surgery, the telephone rang. "I wanted to tell you we love you," Tom Clark said. Black made it possible for Johnson to become a senator and continued to call him "Lyndon" even after he became president. William O. Douglas described LBJ as "a dear friend." At Christmas 1963, the Goldbergs received a basket of holly, homemade bread, and peach preserves. A card "in Lady Bird's own writing to 'Mr. Justice and Dorothy . . .' [included] sweetly expressed sentiments [and was signed] 'Lyndon and Lady Bird' though I would never dream to call him Lyndon anymore," Dorothy Goldberg remarked. While the chief justice would never warm to LBJ as he had to JFK, Johnson successfully "flattered Warren in the way he did so many other men," one Warren biographer wrote.[53]

By tradition, dating back to the first chief justice, John Jay, it was appropriate for justices to advise presidents on political and policy matters. During the early nineteenth century, G. Edward White has observed, "one could find Supreme Court Justices openly drafting congressional legislation, advising presidents, sitting on cases in which, according to modern standards, they had apparent conflicts of interest, and regularly holding ex parte conversations and communications with lawyers." In those days, justices acted as the guardians of their own moral virtue. Article III, Section I of the Constitution provided that Supreme Court justices, like federal judges, held "their Offices during good Behaviour," and the House of Representatives had only just impeached one Supreme Court justice, Samuel Chase, whom the Senate had acquitted. The American Bar Association did not even exist until 1878 or adopt its Canon of Judicial Ethics vaguely exhorting judges to maintain "official conduct . . . free from impropriety and the appearance of impropriety" until 1924.[54]

While presidents naturally continued calling on helpful justices, then, by the 1960s, they tried to be discreet about it. It was one thing for a chief executive to persuade a justice to accept an extrajudicial assignment, as LBJ did when he pressed Warren to chair the commission investigating JFK's assassination in 1963. Yet when Johnson sought Goldberg's advice about a strike the following year, he wanted the call placed in an aide's name. Presidents or their emissaries also sometimes consulted justices about court appointments, as Robert Kennedy did when JFK was thinking of nominating Hastie. Quasi-political jobs abounded for amenable justices.[55]

But if the president wanted to know about the court's work by the 1960s, he was supposed to read its opinions or, at least, newspaper accounts of them. Then, as now, no one thought that justices should keep presidents or, indeed, anyone in the executive branch or Congress apprised of the court's deliberations as it took and resolved cases. That President-Elect James Buchanan had helped shape the contours of *Dred Scott* by privately lobbying his friends on the court and had known what it would hold before its public announcement was now considered almost as shameful as the opinion itself. Though one obituary for Fred Vinson had reported that "the President and the Chief Justice had telephones by their beds, and regularly held long talks late at night, in which the President received Mr. Vinson's advice and counsel on many problems," no one alleged that Vinson had breached the confidentiality of the court by advising Truman he could constitutionally seize the steel mills for nearly thirty years. "Imagine the outcry if a Supreme Court Justice were caught feeding inside information from the Court to the Justice Department in an explosive case, something like abortion," the *New York Times* editorialized in 1987 after historian Norman Silber and a former Justice Department lawyer revealed that Justice Felix Frankfurter had done just that to help the solicitor general's office frame the government's brief in *Brown v. Board of Education.* "There'd be instant demands for resignation and threats of impeachment for impropriety. Loftiness of purpose or concern for national interest would be no defense." No president, much less one who feared scandal as much as Johnson did, should have consulted a justice about the court's internal deliberations.[56]

Issues of propriety, of course, rarely bothered LBJ. He had seen from his interactions with Katzenbach just how many issues that concerned him and his administration could potentially reach the Supreme Court. Just as the president valued Fortas as a lawyer and saw him as a pragmatic liberal in his own image, he understood that Clark, Black, Warren, Douglas, and Goldberg would not do for the job he envisioned. Though a loyal friend, Clark had never been Johnson's lawyer. Black was a stickler about separation of powers, Johnson did not know Warren that well, and Douglas's and Goldberg's ties to the Kennedys prevented their inclusion in his inner circle. Fortas was the obvious candidate to keep an eye on the court, since issues of propriety did not concern him when they involved LBJ. All the president had to do was to convince Fortas to become a justice. In May 1965, after LBJ dispatched Fortas to negotiate a coalition government in the Dominican Republic, Attorney General Katzenbach informed the president that Justice Harlan was ailing and might resign at term's end. How did the court stack up? the president asked. "If the average fellow was lining them up, he would line five clearly on the liberal side of the Court. That would be the Chief Justice and Black and Douglas and Brennan and Goldberg," Katzenbach answered. "And he would line up on the conservative side—this is crude— . . . Stewart, Clark, White, Harlan." But Katzenbach's prediction proved premature: Harlan remained in his chambers until 1971.[57]

His retirement would not have done LBJ much good anyway. If Johnson replaced any justice but Goldberg with Fortas, two Jews would occupy the bench. The president realized that the public expected a "representative" Supreme Court. Though the concern with a justice's geographical roots had diminished, it still existed. (That was one reason that Nixon thought he could make so much political hay out of the Senate's failure to confirm Southerners, later.) Consequently, like his predecessors, LBJ worried about geography and religion. He should have recalled that during the 1930s, the court had included two Jews: First, Brandeis and Cardozo; then, Brandeis and Frankfurter. Since the end of the 1930s, however, there had been at most one seat for Catholics and one for Jews. Johnson, who always worried about "overdoing" minority appointments, would not have wanted to see Fortas and Goldberg on the court together. He would have reasoned that Goldberg must leave the court to become a prominent Jewish appointee elsewhere in government so Fortas could join it.[58]

Administration needs and Goldberg's background made Health, Education, and Welfare (HEW) one possible place for him. LBJ denied leaks about his unhappiness with HEW Secretary Celebrezze. The president knew Celebrezze yearned to become a judge, though, and would happily name him one if LBJ could find someone for HEW.[59]

Then, on July 14, 1965, the day after LBJ announced his nomination of Thurgood Marshall as solicitor general, United Nations Ambassador Adlai Stevenson suddenly dropped dead on a street in London. He possessed "a marvelous, speaking voice, great charm, elegance, kindness, and a delicious wit," one of the many women in love with him remembered. As governor of Illinois, Stevenson famously vetoed a bill to protect birds by penalizing owners who allowed cats to leave their premises unrestrained with the words, "It is in the nature of cats to do a certain amount of unescorted roaming." As the two-time Democratic nominee for the presidency, he captured the hearts of liberals and intellectuals: Just as Republicans wore "I Like Ike" buttons, so Democrats carried "We Love Adlai Madly" signs. While Stevenson hoped to become secretary of state after Kennedy's election, JFK instead pressed him to accept the Ambassadorship to the United Nations, a position that came with a palatial Waldorf apartment, but, as Stevenson soon discovered, no power.[60]

President Johnson had promised Stevenson a larger role in formulating foreign policy. ("You know things are ten times better for me than they were before," Stevenson tactlessly informed Arthur Schlesinger several weeks after the assassination.) Then LBJ ignored his UN Ambassador too. As Stevenson began to doubt the American course in foreign policy he told the president he was considering a run in 1964 from New York for the US Senate. He had support; the *New York Times* greatly preferred him to Robert Kennedy. But Lady Bird Johnson said her husband told Stevenson he was "made for this role you're in." Although the answer obviously surprised him, she recorded, when LBJ "pitilessly" insisted that he must remain at the United Nations, Stevenson stayed at the "job in which he was, in theater terms, perfectly cast."[61]

Now Stevenson was gone, and at a moment when Johnson faced momentous decisions about whether to send hundreds of thousands of Americans to fight in Vietnam. The president hated the war but felt compelled to wage it. If the communists won control in Southeast Asia, he worried, Americans would brand him "soft" on communism and render him impotent to win the domestic reform legislation that mattered so much to him. Consequently, LBJ wanted to replace Stevenson with someone who, in his more cynical moments, the president would have called one of the "peace lovers." The new ambassador must ask questions about the wisdom of escalation and symbolize Johnson's commitment to ending the conflict through a negotiated settlement. He must showcase the president's appreciation for opposing points of view.[62]

One obvious candidate was Stevenson's long-time friend, Under Secretary of State George Ball, who had filed a sixty-seven-page memorandum warning that "once on the tiger's back, we cannot be sure of picking the place to dismount." The day after Stevenson's death, the president told Secretary of State Dean Rusk, "I rather like his [Ball's] willingness to be a little independent." Even after Rusk warned "we could come to a point later in the fall" where Ball stopped supporting the administration's policy, LBJ continued to speak in terms of moving him over to the United Nations "for whatever time that he would give us." But Johnson decided to leave Ball where he was because "he knows so damn much" and, possibly, because he heard Rusk's warning.[63]

The president's eyes may have lit on Harvard economist John Kenneth Galbraith, JFK's ambassador to India, although LBJ never mentioned Galbraith in his many recorded conversations about the position. At Stevenson's memorial service in the Washington Episcopal National Cathedral on July 16, Galbraith received unsettling news as he sat with Arthur Schlesinger Jr. and Ted Kennedy. "During the first hymn, in a scene direct from Evelyn Waugh, Schlesinger or Kennedy, perhaps both, began to pass me information: Oh God, our help in ages past/Our hope for years to come/You are the first on Lyndon's list/In our eternal home."* Since Galbraith had no interest in the job, he realized that he needed a candidate if Johnson mentioned the United Nations ambassadorship. He remembered that his friend, Arthur Goldberg, had told him "that after his intensely active years as a labor lawyer, politician and Secretary of Labor, the Court involved a severe case of decompression. Its much more deliberative pace was a great and by no means wholly welcome change." Of course, by now, Goldberg

---

* In Waugh's *Decline and Fall* (New York: Back Bay, 2012), 254, Paul Pennyfeather and Philbrick dodge rules barring communication between prisoners in chapel by relying on the musical version of Psalm 90, "Oh God Our Help in Ages Past," to discuss Mr. Prendergast's murder:

> "'O God our help in ages past.' sang Paul.
> 'Where's Prendergast to-day?'
> 'What ain't you heard? 'e's been done in.'
> 'And our Eternal home.'"

had served on the court for three years, and even if he adjusted to it with difficulty, he loved the institution.[64]

Galbraith, however, was desperate. To his relief, the president did not offer
him the post when he and his wife stopped by the White House later that day,
though LBJ did speak of the difficulty of replacing Stevenson. "But I was intent
on avoiding all risk; I told him of my meeting with Goldberg and that Goldberg
was a little bored on the Court." Galbraith later acknowledged that he had "no
justification for using the word bored" and that Goldberg was "justifiably angry
when he heard about it." Galbraith's admission came in 1971, when former president Johnson reported the conversation in his memoir and also wrote that he
had personally confirmed that Goldberg was "restless" at the court (figure 5).
Goldberg, who spent the rest of his life denying his boredom on the bench,
responded by publicly calling LBJ a liar.[65]

But all that discord lay in the future when the president summoned Justice
Goldberg to the White House on Saturday, July 17. There, aide Jack Valenti
alluded to an appointment to HEW. "I said, 'I'm walking out, I'm not interested
in HEW,'" Goldberg remembered. At that point, he said, Valenti disappeared,
and when the justice's turn came to confer with Johnson, LBJ said he wanted
to discuss "the U.S. ambassadorship and a key role in the Vietnam situation."
Leaving the White House, Goldberg summoned his friend, Daniel Moynihan,
and reported that LBJ had asked him to become United Nations ambassador.

Figure 5 President Johnson and Justice Arthur Goldberg on Air Force One en route to
Adlai Stevenson's funeral. LBJ Library. Photo by Yoichi Okamoto.

"The Justice was in the turmoil one might expect," Moynihan stressed later. "He had not the least desire to leave the Court. I am as certain of this as one man can be of another's feeling." Only LBJ's "urgent and pressing appeal" might possibly sway him.[66]

The following day, LBJ advised his Federal Bureau of Investigation liaison, Deputy Associate Director Cartha "Deke" DeLoach, that he would appoint Fortas to an important position and asked for an update of his FBI file. According to the president, "Fortas had belonged to a number of communist front organizations" during the 1930s. (They had not been that when Fortas and other New Dealers joined them. It was not until the Cold War began that people like Tom Clark and Senator Joe McCarthy caused some New Dealers to erase their own leftist pasts by branding the civil rights, anti-Nazi, and other progressive organizations that had often interested them in the 1930s "communist fronts.") But according to LBJ, the attorney "had matured and was now a well trusted, loyal individual. The President stated he trusted Fortas as much as he did Lady Bird and even more so with respect to advice regarding business and international matters." LBJ planned to announce the appointment "within the next day or so," and he "wanted to find out first exactly what opposition he would encounter after he named Fortas." He instructed DeLoach to interview eleven ideologically diverse senators. When LBJ included Robert and Ted Kennedy, DeLoach reported, "I interrupted . . . and asked him if he was serious," and the president said that he wanted them to "go on record" so that they could not issue "adverse press statements" later. DeLoach guessed that LBJ intended to make Fortas Stevenson's successor.[67]

By the next day, July 19, the Monday of Stevenson's burial in Illinois, LBJ was sounding out congressional members about the United Nations post. He had settled on Goldberg for the United Nations, he explained to Richard Russell, because his efficiency and excellence as an extemporaneous speaker would make him good with the Russians. "Also, he's a bulldog, and he is pretty abrasive." Oddly, LBJ thought it good that the justice resembled a "bloated banker." Goldberg "looks like he is power," he said approvingly. Although Johnson worried about the Arab reaction, he relished the symbolism of the appointment. It would show that the United States did not discriminate and boost his standing with liberals: "I think this Jew thing would take the *New York Times* and all this crowd that gives us hell all the time" by storm while putting "a Johnson man" in the United Nations. "I guess the lawyers would cuss me for taking him off the Court," the president continued, and Senator Russell agreed that Goldberg's "a man that I'd hate to get taken off the Court." Who would replace him? "I'm going to put Abe Fortas on . . . if I could," LBJ answered.

Russell asked the obvious question. Why not leave Goldberg at the court and send Fortas to the United Nations? "Well, in the first place I don't think he'd go, second I don't think he is as good a speaker as Goldberg," LBJ answered. "I think Abe Fortas is one of the greatest lawyers of this country and one of my greatest friends but he is a technician, craftsman" and "teacher," while Goldberg was a salesman. "He's like I am, he has shined some shoes in his day, . . . he has sold plenty of newspapers and he has had to slug it out and he's like a Georgian, Dick." Having strained credulity by comparing Goldberg to a Georgian, LBJ added, "Goldberg has so much a bigger name in the country." Typically, by the time the president was recounting his conversation with Russell to Goldberg and others, the senator had become Goldberg's biggest supporter.[68]

Everyone else with whom he had spoken, Johnson informed Goldberg, was aboard too. LBJ was at his most persuasive, although Joe Califano, his top domestic adviser, recalled that the president did not have to do as much arm-twisting as he and Goldberg insisted. As Goldberg would subsequently admit, the United Nations position proved enticing because he feared that "we were going to get enmeshed in Vietnam," and he had the "egotistical feeling . . . that I could influence the President to not get overly involved." He had the president's promise that the ambassadorship would assume greater importance. And, at LBJ's direction, Goldberg would ask the Security Council to collaborate with the United States in developing a Vietnam peace formula soon after he moved to the United Nations. Goldberg reasonably imagined that he would become a top foreign policy adviser and would negotiate an end to the war. Goldberg, who would campaign unsuccessfully for the governorship of New York in 1970, harbored political ambitions too, and Johnson may have held out the possibility that he might replace Humphrey as vice president if he performed well at the United Nations. Alternatively, Goldberg figured that the president "had picked him for the UN job to resolve a few specific crises," according to his biographer, and that once he did so, a "logical next step, on Johnson's part would have been to reappoint him to the Court," perhaps even as chief justice, since Goldberg knew Earl Warren planned to retire before the next presidential election. At the most, he might become vice president or chief justice; at the least, an associate justice again, since "in Goldberg's mind, Johnson's request carried with it an implied promise of a return to the Court once his UN mission had been accomplished." As the child of immigrants, Goldberg felt an enormous debt to the United States, and the symbolism of becoming the United Nations' first American Jewish ambassador also pleased him. When he stressed to Johnson that he was "a proud Jew," LBJ reassured him. "I don't want to be a President that says you can't be my top Ambassador . . . any more than I want to say a Negro cannot sit on the Supreme Court."[69]

LBJ was so sure that Goldberg would take the ambassador's job that he offered his seat on the court to Fortas before Goldberg accepted. "I can't help it that they think you're smart and they think you're patriotic and they think you're able," the president told Goldberg, "and so we've gone too far now. Except Abe Fortas says he won't take the job of the Supreme Court justice." He read Goldberg Fortas's July 19 letter declining the position:

> Again, my dear friend, I am obligated and honored by your confidence and generosity—to an extent which is beyond my power adequately to acknowledge.
>
> But after painful searching, I've decided to decline—with a heart full of gratitude. Carol thinks I should accept this greatest honor that a lawyer could receive—this highest appointive post in the nation. But I want a few more years of activity. I want a few more years to try to be of service to you and the Johnson family. And I want and feel that in justice I should take a few more years to stabilize this law firm in the interests of the young men who have enlisted here.
>
> This has been a hard decision—but not nearly as hard as another [the attorney generalship] which had the virtue of continuing association with your trials and tribulations and greatness.
>
> I shall always be grateful.

"I did not keep a copy—I did not write it for the record," Fortas maintained. Unlikely. The letter deleted and denied his most important reason for turning down LBJ. Certainly, Fortas felt ambivalent about joining the court in 1965, and he led the lawyers at his firm to believe that the prospect did not interest him. Most likely, he would have preferred to swell the family coffers for a few years, wait for Earl Warren to retire, and then join the court as chief justice. (As it turned out, that latter course would have greatly enhanced his chances for confirmation as chief justice.) Without a doubt, however, the idea of joining the court sooner or later appealed to him. One of his wife's closest friends recalled that he was "delighted" at the prospect of becoming a justice and was "greatly touched and honored" by LBJ's offer. Carol Agger, however, no more wanted Fortas to become a justice than attorney general. She thought Fortas, then fifty-five, too young for the position, and she did not think him ready to reenter government. More important, even though she would earn a Washington law partner's salary if he joined the court, he would not. A justice earned less than a quarter of Fortas's income, and she and Fortas had just bought a Georgetown mansion requiring substantial work that they planned to staff with a housekeeper, cook, two maids, and a laundress. Ever protective of his wife, Fortas simply tried to insulate Agger from the rumors circulating like wildfire through Washington that her greed prevented him from accepting the job. He was not hiding behind her. Though they had no children and two large incomes, and money mattered to both of them, it obsessed her. His stance did not daunt Johnson. "We'll just have to start working on him tomorrow," LBJ informed Goldberg.[70]

The president did not quite mean that literally. The next day belonged to Goldberg. Johnson announced his UN nomination in the Rose Garden as Dorothy Goldberg, who shared her husband's reluctance to leave the court, looked on, her expression "unmitigated Stone Age." ("There *is* nothing higher that I know of than to be on the Supreme Court and commissioned to [do] 'justice, justice wilt thou pursue,'" she said privately, although by 1972, particularly given the way Goldberg helped Israel from the United Nations, she was also criticizing those who "increasingly shake their heads and say if only he had stayed on the Court.") LBJ stunned everyone, including Goldberg's adoring Supreme Court colleagues. Some Arab diplomats privately criticized the appointment, but many Americans cheered, and the Senate unanimously confirmed him. As Johnson hoped, the *New York Times* rejoiced. "Once the initial shock . . . wore off, many an American must have wondered himself why he hadn't thought of Justice Goldberg too—because the more one ponders this selection the more logical, even the more brilliant it appears," it editorialized. "His tact, persuasiveness and ingenuity, his ability to arrange a compromise without sacrifice of principle, his activism, enthusiasm and pragmatism—these are qualities as applicable at the United Nations as in the world of labor, the law and government."[71]

Minutes after he told the press that Goldberg was going to the United Nations, an obviously elated Johnson telephoned Galbraith and revealed part of his grand plan. "Well, you got your man named," the president said boisterously. "My God," Galbraith replied. "How does Arthur feel about it?" The economist sounded conscience stricken. "He was very pleased," LBJ said. "And while he likes the Court, . . . he loves peace more and he thinks he has a better chance to do something about it here." Johnson continued that once Goldberg's name surfaced, "we couldn't say we turned him down because he was a Jew." Obviously dazed, Galbraith agreed. "And I'm going to appoint Thurgood Marshall to the Court," LBJ added. "I haven't told anybody that, and I don't want you to. Not to succeed him [Goldberg]," but after Marshall served as solicitor general for a while and argued a number of cases. "And at the end of a year or two no one can say that he's not one of the best-qualified men that has ever [been] appointed. And then I'm going to appoint him." Seizing the chance to burnish relations with Kennedy men, LBJ read Galbraith some news statements lauding the ambassador-designate and promised that "I'd just kiss you almost" for relaying other ideas. The president also tasked Galbraith with touting Goldberg: "I don't want this man that's going to speak for us with 120 nations to get smeared because of his race."[72]

Reaching out to Robert Kennedy and other liberals by assuring them that he wanted peace in Vietnam and progress on civil rights required preserving the balance on the Warren Court too. The following day, Johnson went to work on

Fortas. "I got your letter and I'm mighty sorry," the president said. "[I]t was a sweet, gracious, lovely letter that only you could write. And I regretted it. But we'll debate it a little later." He wanted Fortas to come up with names for the court that would ensure "we have the best appointee anybody could ever conceive of. And I want to get away from Harvard." He sought a lawyer who was "a little left of the center. About what I think I am"—and what everyone thought Fortas was—and someone of Warren's "stature, temperament, disposition, and philosophy." A Republican would be excellent. "Incidentally," LBJ added, he had just received a "perfect" FBI report on Fortas. Clearly, the president had not given up.[73]

He never seriously considered anyone else. "I could make him take it," Johnson told Deputy Attorney General Clark two days later, although "they'd raise hell" about Fortas's connection to Bobby Baker. When Clark reminded Johnson that he had other friends, the president read aloud Fortas's letter. "That's loyalty, isn't it?" LBJ asked. Mrs. Johnson had given Fortas the "third degree," he then volunteered, and the attorney had insisted that he would prove more useful to the president off the court. That was wrong, Clark observed, since justices had long advised presidents. Sharing LBJ's belief that there was but one Jewish seat, Clark warned Johnson that if he appointed a Jew now, he could not appoint Fortas later if another vacancy materialized. "Think we'd get much hell on Abe Fortas?" the president asked. No, Clark responded. "My gosh, ever since I started law school, I['ve] heard he's . . . a lawyer's lawyer." Fortas's role in the Baker case amounted to "practically nothing," and if anything directly involving Johnson came before the court, he could recuse himself. "It would be a truly distinguished appointment. History will show you appointed a truly great justice."[74]

The attorney general, who had taken a course from Fortas at Yale and "used to think if I ever got into serious, serious trouble, I would want Abe to represent me," gave the president the same advice. "If you did not know him he would be my first recommendation—and still is," Katzenbach wrote. "The appointee should reflect you on political philosophy and, therefore, be identified as an open-minded, judicious liberal. This is particularly true because this appointment could change the Court on some issues were the appointee to be clearly conservative." LBJ also needed "an outstanding prestige appointment." Fortas fit the bill. When the president fretted that reporters would criticize him for putting a "crony" on the court, the attorney general answered, "They're going to say you're lucky to have known him, not that he's a crony." Like Clark, Katzenbach also stressed that justices had always counseled presidents and that Justice Fortas could remain a Johnson adviser.[75]

So LBJ kept pushing. "I think he was overweening in this instance," Lady Bird Johnson remarked. Yet she also emphasized that her husband believed that Fortas must want the job and considered him the most qualified candidate. On

July 27, after announcing Celebrezze's nomination to the Sixth Circuit and that of Carnegie Corporation president John Gardner as HEW secretary, Johnson spent two hours with Fortas. The next day, the president telephoned the lawyer at 11:48 A.M. LBJ was announcing that he would send an additional fifty thousand troops to Vietnam at 12:30 P.M., and he wanted some good news. "Are you going to watch my press conference today?" he asked. "Absolutely," Fortas replied. "How's your blood pressure?" Johnson asked. "A little worried of what you may do," Fortas said with an anxious chuckle. LBJ laughed too. "Well, anything I do will be all right, won't it?" Without giving his friend time to reply, the president asked if he wanted to watch the conference with Mrs. Johnson. "Oh, could I?" Fortas asked eagerly. "I don't know what will happen or what questions or anything I'll get," LBJ continued. "But don't be surprised."[76]

"Abe, I'm sending fifty thousand boys to Vietnam today and I'm sending you to the Supreme Court," Joe Califano remembered LBJ saying when Fortas arrived at the White House. "Johnson spoke firmly, not lightly, and the tone of his voice as well as the expression on his face made it clear that he would nominate Fortas, whatever his wishes," just as he put Arthur Goldberg at the United Nations. Fortas surrendered quickly, probably in part because he really wanted to become a justice and knew that history could only be managed up to a point, and in part because he, like so many others, could not repel a determined Johnson. The president made the announcement at his televised press conference minutes later, in a small rollout that featured the nominee at his side. After a luncheon with Johnson, Fortas and Califano proceeded to the nominee's new house in Georgetown, where Fortas pointed to a hole reserved for a central air conditioning system that had just become too expensive.[77]

Once again, Johnson got his man by twisting an almost willing arm (figure 6). He had continued Kennedy's pattern of turning to a well-regarded colleague as justice. Although Fortas had never formally joined the executive branch after Johnson became president, he had operated as the functional equivalent of one of its members. As Kennedy had done with Goldberg, LBJ had also won liberal applause. Just as Goldberg, who rightly viewed Fortas as a "jurisprudential clone," confided to LBJ that he now felt "a whole lot better" about leaving the court, so the appointment reconciled the Warren–Black wing to Goldberg's departure. Douglas had already urged Fortas upon Johnson for the next vacancy, and Black told Warren that he had let the nominee know "that both of us hoped he would agree to come to the Court. He seemed much gratified, and I was glad we gave him the message."[78]

Yet there were signs of restiveness on the right that could have coalesced. On hearing of her husband's elevation, Carol Agger had locked herself in her office to cry. She remained furious at the president and her husband for some time afterward. The appointment had created "a very serious crisis" for the couple,

Figure 6 LBJ and Abe Fortas the day after the president announced his devoted adviser's nomination to the court. LBJ Library. Photo by Yoichi Okamoto.

Douglas confided to Black. "She said her life had been ruined," Johnson protested to Senate Majority Leader Mansfield, just as Roberta Vinson had when Truman named her husband chief justice. "These women! Their lives get ruined mighty easy." Fortas hoped to placate Agger by postponing his confirmation hearing until they had gone away together. Although the mainstream media recognized Fortas's liberalism and still lauded the appointment, LBJ feared that the delay would give conservatives time to score points. They could allege, he worried, that Fortas had inappropriately used his government influence on behalf of clients, wrongly pleaded with newspapers to delay releasing news of Walter Jenkins's arrest, represented Bobby Baker, and cared too much about civil rights and civil liberties.[79]

Katzenbach told the president that Judiciary Committee member Roman Hruska, the second-ranking Republican, had shown him some forty telegrams urging him to block Fortas because he was a "liberal" and "Communist." Hruska, a Nebraska Republican, dismissed their senders as John Birchers. Indeed, when the Senate Judiciary Committee files finally became available to researchers fifty years after the nomination, it appeared that the telegrams' authors had all read the same attack on Fortas as a "knee-jerk left-winger" and LBJ's long-time "personal Mr. Fix-It" in the conservative publication *Human Events*. LBJ had received telegrams too, he told the attorney general, along with "a good many" saying the "certain races," presumably Jews and possibly African Americans, had taken over the government. The president designated Katzenbach Fortas's "principal lobbyist," kept Fortas in town, and insisted on a hasty Supreme Court confirmation hearing.[80]

It was the last pro forma one for quite a while. In retrospect, LBJ's elevation of Fortas in 1965 marked the end of the era of good feelings in Supreme Court nominations. Consider, for example, the Senate Judiciary's reaction to the first witnesses against Fortas. Both were redbaiters who accused the nominee of associating with known communists in the 1930s and of passing off commu-nist witnesses as ex-communists in the 1950s. The committee—which, Mary McGrory observed, included "several fierce Redhunters"—was "bored" and "visibly irritated" by both and treated them as crackpots.[81]

As Fortas made no opening statement, it was on to the main event, the ques-tioning of Johnson's nominee. With other Southern senators and Republicans, Senator McClellan worried that the court had become too protective of crimi-nals. But he seemed satisfied that the nominee agreed with him, particularly after Fortas stressed that lawmen must possess an "adequate opportunity" to question suspects. No one even mentioned *Griswold v. Connecticut*, where seven justices had recently discovered a constitutional right to privacy, though *Griswold* would become the focus of many future confirmation hearings after the Supreme Court relied on it to declare a right to abortion. When one senator tried to pin down Fortas's views on reapportionment, the others criticized him. "We have always felt that it would be unfair to ask any nominee for any judicial office to give a legal opinion on the basis of a hypothetical question," one reassured Fortas. Senators asked the nominee about Walter Jenkins, but not Bobby Baker. Hruska wanted to know whether Fortas's friendship with the president would affect his ability to function as a judge. "Let me take this opportunity to say to you that there are two things that have been vastly exaggerated with respect to me," the nominee puckishly replied. "One is the extent to which I am a Presidential adviser, and the other is the extent to which I am a proficient violinist." (Fortas had probably anticipated the question: He was rarely that funny, spontaneously.) No relation-ship he had "with the President would in any way bear upon the discharge of my functions in the Court," Fortas continued. "It could not be." And after Senator Ervin made a chummy comparison between the Senate and mules that didn't kick according to the rules, the committee adjourned less than three hours after it had come to order.[82]

Conservative Southern Democrats and Republicans dominated the pro-ceeding chaired by segregationist James Eastland of Mississippi. Yet all com-mittee members apparently welcomed the nomination. By contrast, when later that year, LBJ tried to do a favor for the Kennedys by giving their longtime ally, Francis Morrissey, a district judgeship, senators quickly derailed it on the grounds that Morrissey possessed a "quickie" law diploma from a fly-by-night operation, had failed the bar exam, and lacked trial experience. But Fortas's judicial philosophy, or ideology, remained the elephant in the room that none of them seemed eager to address.[83]

In part, that reflected the sense, then current, that a president appropriately appointed anyone he wished to the court, as long as the person possessed good credentials and character. Why else would a conservative Southerner like Russell, who had no use for the Warren Court majority, characterize Goldberg as someone he hated to see leave the court, unless, perhaps, he was being sarcastic? (When Russell was caustic, however, he usually sounded that way.) In part, the reluctance to focus on Fortas's jurisprudence showed LBJ's good sense in appointing a lawyer with a shorter paper trail than that of a judge or academic- -though whether the president had thought of that was unclear, and had the senators analyzed Fortas's, they would have found that it demonstrated commitment aplenty to expanding civil rights and protecting civil liberties. In part, the unwillingness to probe reflected respect for Fortas's record and his performance. "Abe was letter-perfect as a witness, about as good a witness as he is a lawyer," Katzenbach told LBJ. He handled McClellan expertly, and the senator would "not want to be against him" anyway. As that remark suggested, above all, senators feared challenging the liberal consensus and the president who then embodied it. So, too, Marshall's twenty-minute confirmation hearing as solicitor general proved, the *New York Times* said, "surprisingly placid." The Judiciary Committee approved Marshall by 8-2, with Eastland and McClellan voting against him. It unanimously endorsed Fortas.[84]

Confirmation now became preordained. Characteristically, LBJ still worried. After instructing Katzenbach to prepare speeches for Fortas's congressional supporters, the president mischievously suggested that "it would make for better relations" if Kennedy delivered one. (He did not). As it had done so often before and for the last time ever, the Senate approved the Supreme Court nominee by voice vote after a little grumbling about how Fortas had handled the Walter Jenkins affair and despite a warning from Strom Thurmond that the nominee was "utterly lacking in judicial temperament." The same day, it confirmed Marshall as solicitor general in the same way.[85]

"Convict That Damn Carmichael"

Johnson had every reason to rejoice on Wednesday, August 11, Joe Califano remembered. The previous Friday, the president had signed the Voting Rights

Act into law. On Wednesday, the Senate voted on Fortas and Marshall. "He'd capped the day with a successful meeting, where he was at his persuasive, needling, good-humored best, getting wrangling governors and mayors to act together to battle the worst drought in the history of the Northeast." LBJ looked forward to a long weekend in Texas.[86]

That night, however, Los Angeles exploded when African Americans living in its inner city rose up against alleged police misconduct. For much of the five-day Watts conflagration that left thirty-four dead, a wounded LBJ remained secluded at his ranch. He understood that Watts represented more of a cohesive revolt against oppression than a spontaneous, undisciplined riot. "We are on a powder keg," the president said privately. He made no mention of the inflated rents and prices that inner-city residents paid, the drug trafficking and police corruption that they sometimes encountered, or their charges of police brutality. Yet Johnson maintained that "[t]hey have absolutely nothing to live for, 40% of them are unemployed, these youngsters live with rats, and have no place to sleep, and they all start from broken homes and illegitimate families." Martin Luther King urged him to launch the poverty program in Los Angeles. The president readily agreed to do so. Though he focused on aiding families, lest he seem to reward violent protesters, he had already fused poverty, crime, and civil unrest for the public by presenting the war on poverty as a war against crime and civil unrest. Califano now witnessed "how acutely Johnson feared that the reforms to which he had dedicated his presidency were in mortal danger, not only from those who opposed [them], but from those he was trying to help."[87]

Yet, like NAACP Director Roy Wilkins and the others whom LBJ consulted about Watts, King represented "the older Negro Establishment," staffer Harry McPherson told the president. The White House had few contacts among the young who had taken to "the streets." And militants might not listen "to advice from middle-aged and elderly men in their vested suits and regimental stripes."[88]

Although Thurgood Marshall was one of those middle-aged men in vested suits, the president trusted and needed him. Ten months later, LBJ convened the first national civil rights conference held at the White House. The "bomb throwers" at the Student Nonviolent Coordinating Committee boycotted the June 1966 event, which they denounced as "rigged," and the administration sidelined King because of his growing opposition to the Vietnam War. But LBJ sounded upbeat as he presented Marshall to the audience. "I have a very unusual pleasure and pride to introduce to you a great soldier," he proclaimed. "I might say that the President of the United States does not often have the opportunity to introduce another speaker." LBJ happily did so because Marshall had "established in the field of civil rights a beachhead from which we shall never retreat." Johnson's speech, McPherson remembered, proved "an unexpected and flawless triumph," while Marshall's helpfully accentuated the law's role in achieving transformative social change for African Americans.[89]

But the president remained nervous. Earlier in his administration, civil rights and the war on poverty had provided justifications for changes in the criminal justice system by leading much of the public to equate the Harlem cop on the beat "with the 'red-necked sheriff'" who brutalized protesters at Selma and to mistrust police treatment of the poor and minorities. When the White House held its conference, *Time* still reassuringly reported that academics ridiculed the FBI's insistence that violent crime was rising and its crime statistics as "not worth the paper they're written on." Deputy Attorney General Ramsey Clark said the same thing. That the FBI's statistics were untrustworthy, however, did not mean the nation lacked a crime problem. Moreover, by 1966, the media and the Right were racializing crime by trumpeting the need for "law and order," a phrase one Southern senator agreed with Clark had become a euphemism for white concern about black-on-white crime. LBJ felt the ground shifting underneath his feet. As he saw it, the liberal interracialism of the earlier 1960s could crumble under a wave of unrest in inner cities throughout the country and concern about "crime in the streets"—which *Time* explained was "an omnibus label encompassing all the wellsprings of urban unrest from ghetto riots to muggings in middle-class neighborhoods." And indeed, *Time* would soon characterize crime in the United States as "a national disgrace" that threatened "the very foundation of the Great Society" and decry "the Negro riots that keep tearing at American cities" as the "greatest single source" of the fear that "violence is in the ascendant over cooperation, disruption over order, and anger over reason."[90]

The "rioter" who most bothered LBJ was Stokely Carmichael, the new Student Nonviolent Coordinating Committee (SNCC) chairman elected after a leadership struggle that forced out the more moderate activist, John L. Lewis. Carmichael regarded Roy Wilkins and other administration stalwarts as reactionaries. He charged that white liberals had abandoned the entire civil rights movement when it revealed that racism was not unique to the South. Soon he would persuade the SNCC to expel whites. And Carmichael galvanized civil rights workers marching from Memphis to Jackson with his cry of rage just three weeks after the summer 1966 White House conference at which Marshall spoke: "This is the twenty-seventh time that I've been arrested. I ain't going to jail no more." African Americans had to "take over" and preach "Black Power." To make matters worse, he linked black power to draft resistance, and he possessed a wicked sense of humor and a genius for sloganeering. "The war in Vietnam is Lyndon Johnson's war," he told college students at Halloween. "If Lyndon wants to go, then take Lady Bird and Luci and all the rest. But am I going? Hell, no!" It was he who made "Hell, No, We Won't Go!" the shout of the antiwar movement. His biographer understood that "Carmichael now took his place alongside

Martin Luther King as one of America's two most important black political leaders" and that the White House and FBI "took Carmichael as seriously as they did King, at times more so, since they feared that he might personally start a national race war."[91]

As the cry of "Black Power" spread from the Southern marches and sit-ins to inner cities elsewhere in the country, Wilkins defiantly countered that "black Power" was "the father of hatred and the mother of violence." LBJ claimed he cared about neither "black power" nor "white power," but "American democratic power," and that the government was "doing everything we can, as quickly as we can . . . to improve these terrible conditions that exist in the ghettos." Progress came slowly. "But we have done more in the last 24 months than has been done in any similar 24-year period to face up to these conditions of health, education, poverty, and discrimination."[92]

Without a doubt, though, it was becoming harder to convince white Americans to join the president on the quest. David Carter observed that when Mississippi officials beat peaceful civil rights marchers that summer, whites paid little attention. They seemed more taken by "the fault lines" in the civil rights movement, which stood out in bold relief as activists "chanted 'Freedom Now' and 'Black Power' in a competitive black antiphony." Imprisoned by his own insistence on consensus, LBJ blamed Carmichael for the defeat of the year's civil rights bill, which would have provided for open housing. Small wonder he worried that along with the inner cities, his own power in Congress was going up in flames.[93]

Because Johnson believed that challenges to liberalism from the Left just increased the power of the Right, he saw the court as part of the problem and solution. In addition to declaring the right to vote fundamental in 1966, the justices helpfully upheld the constitutionality of the Voting Rights Act and struck down the use of literacy tests to disfranchise minority voters. As Carmichael began shouting "Black Power" in the South, the court also upheld activists' First Amendment rights to protest by staging sit-ins at segregated libraries. The majority opinion in that sit-in case, *Brown v. Louisiana*, was one of Fortas's first, and he carefully nodded toward anxiety about civil unrest by emphasizing that the court might judge less peaceable action differently. The newest justice's opinion sparked an indignant dissent contending that no constitutional provision "forbids any one of the 50 states of the Union, including Louisiana," to make "sit-ins" or "stand-ups" in their public libraries illegal. "Trembling with rage and shaking his finger at the courtroom audience, Black blistered the majority with a thirty-minute assault that made his strongly phrased written dissent seem pale by comparison," the *Washington Post* reported. While Justice Black spoke, Douglas sent Fortas a note: "You can now see what I meant last summer when I said the majority of the Court was moving toward the anti-Negro side."[94]

Perhaps the liberal consensus on the court was at risk for reasons both political and personal. Each year, Brennan and his clerks prepared a private history
of the term. In 1966, they suggested that some of the remarks in Black's "high-
pitched dissent on 'law and order' " in *Brown v. Louisiana*, "such as those accusing the majority of being distrustful of the ways of the Deep South, apparently
distressed Justice Fortas, and they did not soothe an already strained personal
relationship between Justices Black and Fortas." Obviously, Black's enthusiasm
for Fortas's appointment had cooled. Fortas tried periodically to win him over
with blandishment, but Black, who lived by the aphorism "Never too much,"
was not buying. According to John Frank, Black "regards Abe as too much of a
zealot" for liberal causes, like civil rights, juvenile justice, and privacy, and "he
simply doesn't like Fortas very well."[95]

Another 1966 decision would have as ominous implications as *Brown
v. Louisiana*, given the racialization of crime. In June, the court handed down
Miranda v. Arizona. A bare majority led by Warren and including Black, Douglas,
Fortas, and Brennan ruled that the police must advise all criminal suspects in
custody of their rights to remain silent and to an attorney. Justice Tom Clark
complained that the decision went "too far too fast." Future Supreme Court
Justice Lewis Powell, a member of the National Crime Commission chaired by
Katzenbach that LBJ had recently appointed, was distressed too. He claimed
"general agreement" among commission members "that *Miranda* was an unfortunate decision, freezing into constitutionally guaranteed rights an elaborate
set of rules which could far better have been left in a more flexible posture, and
resulted in added handicaps to the process of detecting and prosecuting criminal
conduct."[96]

In fact, however, Corinna Lain showed nearly forty years later, based on the
line of cases leading up to *Miranda*, law enforcement officials "had anticipated
a much stronger ruling from the Court," possibly one forbidding police interrogation in the absence of counsel, and surely "breathed a sigh of relief when
Miranda was decided." The justices had declined to make the ruling retroactive.
Moreover, the state still possessed sufficient evidence to justify a guilty verdict
for Miranda and many others when it retried them without the tainted confessions. And enough law enforcement officials, including the FBI, already used the
warnings to know that suspects would frequently waive their rights, the National
Crime Commission's executive director rightly assured the press. Perhaps the
decision was more problematic because it reinforced the status quo. Because the
commission ultimately "dodged the debate surrounding *Miranda*," however, it
missed the chance to make an argument that the decision would not make much
difference to conviction rates and gave conservatives the chance to charge that
its report "deliberately" omitted discussion of the impact of the Warren Court's
decisions on crime.[97]

The media and pollsters fueled the impression that the crime rate was increasing not alongside those decisions, but because of them. *New York Times* legal affairs correspondent Fred Graham was writing at the time of the decision that the general toleration of *Miranda* indicated that the country largely accepted the Warren Court's handiwork. By 1970, however, he had released a book about the Warren Court's criminal procedure decisions tellingly entitled *The Self-Inflicted Wound* in which *Miranda* took center stage. And as Lain pointed out, the 1966 Harris Poll misstated *Miranda* as holding "that the police could not question a criminal unless he had a lawyer with him," then reported that 65% of its sample opposed it. A National Opinion Research Center Poll that described the decision differently and showed that 65% supported it received relatively little attention. Meanwhile, LBJ conflated race, crime, and civil unrest.[98]

"Now are you all going to do anything on law and order this session and tell these fellows that they got to quit turning over cars and stuff?" the president asked Fortas after the court launched its fall 1966 term. He had been "groaning for us to take some of these cases," the justice answered. The court affirmed dozens of state court convictions by order annually, and he and the chief justice voted "to take some of them up so we can have a big hearing and then affirm with some publicity." But "old Hugo" led the justices who contended that "it's just a waste of time," Fortas volunteered. "The state courts convicted those charged, and why do we have to say, 'Us, too?'" Fortas should "tell them why," LBJ answered. "Just tell them because, by God, we've got riots in all the major cities and it's knocked our polls down 15 percent." Despite the president's last-minute plea to the public that those who preyed "on what is called the 'white backlash'" endangered not just "the interests of Negro Americans, but . . . all who stand to gain from humane and far-sighted government," and that voters should not "repudiate good men—Democrats and Republicans alike—who have given us Medicare, a great education program, a higher minimum wage, new parks and playgrounds, protection for the consumer, the hope for cleaning out our slums and rivers and the air we breathe," the midterm elections of 1966 proved the worst for liberalism since 1950. The conservative coalition of Republicans and Democrats that had frustrated reform for the quarter century between 1938 and 1964 blossomed anew. Liberal Democrats elected on LBJ's coattails in the House in 1964 took a special beating. The GOP won three seats in the Senate and forty-seven seats in the House in 1966, though the Democrats remained in control of Congress, and the Senate Republican victors were liberal and moderate. Law and order hurt the president more than inflation, a growing concern; Vietnam; and everything else "put together," Johnson told Fortas. "Every white man just says, by God, he don't want his car turned over and he don't want some nigger throwing a brick at him. . . . And we've got to do something to shake them up like convict that damn Carmichael."[99]

Actually, the court was about to begin sending more of the message to pro-testers that the president wanted them to hear. Just after the midterm elections, Black won the majority he had sought in *Brown v. Louisiana.* This time, in *Adderly v. Florida,* five justices voted to affirm the conviction of students who demon-strated on jailhouse grounds against the arrest of classmates who tried to integrate movie theaters. The protesters had behaved peacefully and had neither thrown bricks nor overturned cars. Even so, Black maintained in *Adderly* that the protest-ers had engaged in conduct unprotected by the First Amendment and had been lawfully convicted of trespass with malicious intent. Douglas's dissent blasted the majority opinion as tragically "out of step" with the court's previous decisions. He blamed the majority for allowing local authorities to use the law of trespass "to bludgeon those who peacefully exercise a First Amendment right to protest against one of the most grievous of all modern oppressions which some of our States are inflicting on our citizens." To long-time court observers, the divisions between the two former allies now reflected "personal pique," perhaps not just over jurisprudential differences but also, possibly, over Black's discomfort over Douglas's recent fourth marriage to a college senior forty-five years his junior.[100]

And in *Walker v. Birmingham,* which the court handed down at term's end, a majority of the court continued to move in the direction that LBJ liked, and the civil rights community received more bad news. Stewart's majority opinion affirmed a contempt conviction against Martin Luther King and other promi-nent African American ministers for defying an order enjoining a Good Friday march in Alabama. The state judge who issued the injunction there relied on a Birmingham city ordinance prohibiting parades without a permit that the court would unanimously hold unconstitutional in another Stewart opinion two years later. But to the majority, the ordinance and injunction were severable. "This Court cannot hold that the petitioners were constitutionally free to ignore all the procedures of the law and carry their battle to the streets," Stewart insisted in *Walker.* "One may sympathize with the petitioners' impatient commitment to their cause. But respect for judicial process is a small price to pay for the civilizing hand of law, which alone can give abiding meaning to constitutional freedom." Brennan's dissent condemned the majority's pieties about patience. "We cannot permit fears of 'riots' and 'civil disobedience' generated by slogans like 'Black Power' to divert our attention from what is here at stake," he contended—"not violence or the right of the State to control its streets and sidewalks, but the insulation from attack of ex parte orders and legislation upon which they are based even when patently impermissible prior restraints on the exercise of First Amendment rights, thus arming the state courts with the power to punish as a 'contempt' what they otherwise could not punish at all."[101]

If Fortas ever told the president that, along with Warren and Brennan, he joined Douglas's vigorous dissent in *Adderly*, there is no record of it. Nor, probably, did he inform his friend that he privately described Brennan's *Walker* dissent, which he also signed, as "magnificent." Though LBJ probably would have preferred Fortas to side with the majority in *Adderly* and *Walker*, his friend kept faith with his own vision of liberalism even as he kept an eye on the court for the president. And perhaps LBJ reasoned that dissents fed the impression that the court was usefully changing course. After all, in part because of the "blistering" tone of Brennan's dissent in *Walker*, news reports helpfully stressed that the court was changing its tune and taking a hard line toward demonstrators.[102]

It is easy to understand why LBJ thought the court's opinions reflected on him in 1966, though it is less clear why he thought that its justices should care about his standing in the polls. At bottom, he identified everything with himself. With some justification, he perceived the Warren Court and the Great Society as two halves of the same whole that would flourish or falter together. That was why he urged Fortas to tell the justices they had to do "something about law and order." At the same time, the president still yearned for the civil rights community's acclaim and still pinned much of his hope for winning it on his plan to put Marshall on the court. He was also becoming increasingly dissatisfied with the situation in the Justice Department.

"Bugging, American Style"

If the court seemed to be moving in LBJ's direction, the Justice Department was not. The year 1966 was difficult for Nicholas Katzenbach. Johnson obviously thought that Fortas had even more time for him as a justice than as an attorney. "I wish you would talk to Nick every day or so," the president had instructed. "See what he is doing." As ever, LBJ anguished about the Justice Department's plans with respect to Bobby Baker, as the president showed when he interrupted Fortas's delayed vacation with his wife to ask whether he should nominate David Bress as DC's US attorney. Bress's clients included a company in which Bobby Baker had been a major shareholder, and "I'm thinking it might raise a lot of stories," Johnson fretted. Fortas reassured him that it would not because the distinguished attorney had represented the corporation, not individuals. But the Senate held up the nomination while members made speeches against Baker.[103]

By now, Baker's indictment on charges of theft, conspiracy, and tax evasion seemed inevitable. When it happened, the president and Fortas faulted Katzenbach for not forcing Robert Kennedy's friend, William Bittman, and other Criminal Division lawyers in the Justice Department who took the case to the federal grand jury to eliminate some of the counts. And when they let

Katzenbach know how they felt, the attorney general whined—or as LBJ would have put it, "cried"—that he had lost sleep over his decision to side with his lawyers. In the president's eyes, a double standard existed. When Katzenbach suspected the White House counsel, a JFK legacy, of questionable financial conduct, the attorney general had allowed him to resign, LBJ complained, but the Justice Department was "so conscientious" about Baker.[104]

Too conscientious, it turned out. First, when the "most sensational political trial in recent history" began, the *Washington Post* trumpeted Baker's testimony that he had turned "to the best friend I ever had around the Capitol, the then Vice President" when financial ruin threatened and that LBJ had arranged for Senator Robert Kerr of Oklahoma, an oil magnate and mutual friend, to give Baker $50,000. (One issue of the trial involved whether the senator, now dead, had made a gift of the money, as Baker claimed, or Baker had stolen it.) Then a jury found Baker guilty on all counts: He would spend fifteen months in prison. "Aw, hell," Johnson grieved. "He's guilty of a lot of things—all of us are—but not this." The Justice Department "had destroyed 'Little Lyndon'" Baker, and "murdered the daddy," the president bitterly remarked. He remained convinced that Robert Kennedy launched the Baker inquiry. "I believe this boy's got a commitment to his former boss to see these things through," LBJ commented of Katzenbach. That was unfair, though his attorney general did not possess the depth of Fortas's allegiance toward the president. (Few did.) "I think we bought a bad one there," LBJ now said.[105]

The president complained about the other divisions in the Justice Department too, especially Antitrust, headed by Harvard's Donald Turner. LBJ found it too eager to block mergers he favored. Naturally, Johnson also remained despondent about leaks. "They just gut me every day, Nick's people," the president groused in one conversation with Fortas.[106]

As Johnson, seconded by Fortas, became more doubtful of Katzenbach's loyalty, the two men became increasingly skeptical of Robert Kennedy's—if that were possible. Increasingly, by 1966, the Vietnam War consumed liberals in official Washington, and the very individuals who had been promoting the growth of executive power since the Progressive era had begun trying to seize some of it back for Congress in the hope of changing the course of foreign policy. ("It is evident now that this delight in a strong Presidency was based on the fact that, up to now, all strong Presidents in American history have pursued policies of which one has approved," Arthur Schlesinger wryly observed.) Johnson blamed Kennedy for leading liberal senators' rebellion over Vietnam, he told the attorney general, and he was now certain that his rival sought the presidency. "I have no objections to Bobby becoming President of this country," he implausibly insisted to Katzenbach. "I, just by God, want to be a President myself and I think it ill-behooves the Kennedys after all I have done for the Kennedys to not reciprocate the treatment that I have given them. Everything they have ever asked . . . , I have done except put Bobby on the ticket for Vice President." Johnson repeated the litany: He had named Katzenbach attorney general, campaigned for RFK, and approved Morrissey's nomination. Katzenbach should tell Kennedy that the disharmony and divisiveness he sowed would make the nomination worthless. "I do not say anything against him," the president lied. "You never did do much on that project, did you?" LBJ asked the next month. "I tried, Mr. President," Katzenbach said. "He listens, but I do not seem to get any reaction judging from the newspapers."[107]

Katzenbach and Kennedy soon gave Johnson fresh occasion for mistrust in a complicated and convoluted tale of divided loyalties that involved the court, RFK, and the FBI. Wiretapping and bugging now moved to the forefront of the president's list of worries and, LBJ believed, even threatened his political survival, while over at the FBI, J. Edgar Hoover was certain that they jeopardized his. While Fortas and Johnson protected the "presidency" (really, LBJ), Hoover guarded the bureau's self-interest. As events unfolded, Johnson, Fortas, and Hoover displayed an eager readiness to compromise the court's independence to wound Kennedy, and all became convinced that Katzenbach had to go (figure 7).

Figure 7 Uneasy allies: LBJ, Attorney General Katzenbach, and FBI Director J. Edgar Hoover. President Lyndon B. Johnson flanked by J. Edgar Hoover on left and Nicholas Katzenbach on right. LBJ Library. Photo by Yoichi Okamoto.

Johnson did not share the Kennedys' enthusiasm for electronic surveillance. The Kennedys "used it for national affairs, which was a cute way" of creating the impression that their surveillance targeted those who leaked "atomic secrets," he griped to Fortas, "and national affairs was Bobby Baker and anyone that opposed them." When he heard that Joe Alsop was spreading rumors around Washington in the spring of 1965 that the president had ordered Alsop's phones tapped, LBJ first told Katzenbach that male menopause had rendered the columnist crazy. "I'm a red-hot-one-million-two percent civil liberties man, and I'm just *against* them," the president continued emphatically. Though he did not stop taping his own telephone conversations, LBJ signed an order that summer prohibiting wiretapping and bugging, except in the capacious category of national security and with the attorney general's preapproval.[108]

But what about the earlier wiretapping and bugging that the Justice Department had used to battle organized crime? Ably represented by Edward Bennett Williams, Bobby Baker had vainly alleged prior to his conviction that extensive Justice Department wiretapping "tainted" the evidence that the government planned to use against him at trial. In May 1966, the Supreme Court declined to review the tax evasion conviction of Baker's business associate, Fred Black, a lobbyist with ties to the Las Vegas gambling world. Black, a former neighbor of Vice President Johnson's, maintained that publicity about Baker prejudiced his case. Even before Black filed a petition for rehearing, Solicitor General Marshall, with Katzenbach's support and over the protest of J. Edgar Hoover, made a startling disclosure to the court: During a 1963 criminal investigation, FBI agents bugged Black's hotel suite and recorded conversations between him and his attorney. Though Marshall swore that the Justice Department had not used the information in Black's prosecution, Fred Black again asked for dismissal of his conviction.[109]

The court responded by doing something equally surprising. It ordered the Justice Department to file a memorandum indicating who approved, and by what legal authority, the FBI's bugging of Black. "I've watched the Supreme Court for a long time, [and] I never saw anything like it," Ramsey Clark told LBJ. He feared that Marshall would emerge from the episode looking "awful," and that would reflect poorly on his promoters too. "We've got a big investment in him. We've got a lot riding on him."[110]

The court's directive set off a cycle of finger-pointing about who had sanctioned the bugging that would last through 1966. Senator Robert Kennedy lost no time intimating to the press that FBI Director Hoover had ordered the illegal bug installed in Black's suite without the permission of Attorney General Robert Kennedy. Moreover, Johnson told the Speaker of the House, RFK sent word that unless the president stopped Hoover, Kennedy would "declare war." Because no one could control the director, who did what he wanted and justified it by leaking, LBJ was stuck. "I've had war declared for three months," he complained. "It's just one column after another everyday." Johnson could hope to improve his position only by seizing the opportunity to paint RFK as hostile to civil liberties *and* by siding with Hoover, whom the president held in an uneasy embrace. Neither LBJ nor Deputy Attorney General Clark believed that Kennedy had clean hands, and, in one of his more hopeful moments, the president told his powerful personal secretary, Mildred Stegall, that the controversy actually gladdened him: "This puts the finger on Bobby Kennedy where it belongs. Edgar certainly has the goods on Bobby."[111]

Unsurprisingly, Attorney General Katzenbach did find Kennedy truthful. That created problems for Hoover, who by this point lacked any faith in Katzenbach and who considered the Black case "the greatest crisis" in the FBI's history, one that might even lead to exposure of the bureau's merciless surveillance of Martin Luther King. Hoover decided that he had to protect the FBI and himself by pressing for language in the Justice Department's memorandum indicating that Attorney General Kennedy had information about Fred Black that he could only have inferred would have come from a bug. That would make it clear that Kennedy, as Hoover's nominal boss, had known and implicitly approved of the bug. But Katzenbach balked at Hoover's demand. Understandably, the attorney general retained some loyalty to RFK, who hammered him to include assurances in the supplemental memorandum that Kennedy had not known of the Black or any other bugging. After LBJ's personal secretary confided to DeLoach that the president feared that "the Attorney General appears to be 'fronting' for others, namely Bobby Kennedy," DeLoach decided to speak with a member of the court.[112]

Fortas was the obvious contact. At LBJ's direction, DeLoach and the justice were already ineffectively conspiring to sabotage the romance of the president's daughter, Lynda Byrd, with actor George Hamilton. The justice also served as the FBI's agent in convincing Brennan to withdraw his offer of a clerkship to activist Michael Tigar: Fortas warned his colleague that if he hired such a radical, Congress might conduct an inquiry into the court that would embarrass Tigar, Brennan, and the court. These kinds of tasks LBJ expected of Fortas, and the justice willingly performed them. So DeLoach telephoned Justice Fortas to say "that I wanted to see him about a matter which he might consider bordered on a violation of judicial ethics," he related in the first of a series of informal memoranda about the case for Hoover's second-in-command, Clyde Tolson. Fortas laughed, said that DeLoach could talk with him about anything, and invited him to breakfast.[113]

Assuming DeLoach's memorandum describing their conversation the following day is accurate, as it may well be,* he and Fortas did talk about anything and everything. The topics included teamster Jimmy Hoffa's appeal of his jury-tampering conviction, from which Fortas had planned to disqualify himself. Now the justice was wondering whether Robert Kennedy, as attorney general, had known of any "irregularities" in the FBI's investigation of Hoffa, and when DeLoach said that RFK had asked the reluctant bureau to bug an attorney against its will, "Justice Fortas replied that he had felt such might be the case and that under the circumstances he would sit with the rest of the Court on the Hoffa case and would make certain that Kennedy was exposed." (Ultimately, Fortas thought better of that. He decided against participating, and the court satisfied the government by returning the case to the lower courts, which ruled the bugging irrelevant to Hoffa's conviction.) The two men also discussed Courtney Evans, a former FBI employee who had become close to Attorney General Kennedy while working as the liaison to the Justice Department, and DeLoach horrified Fortas by letting him know that Evans now worked for Katzenbach. They spoke about Ramsey Clark, whom the justice confided was "a dreamer," and Fortas learned that the FBI saw him as a "Johnson man." Yet another agenda item was the FBI's excellent reputation at the court.

The fight between Hoover and Katzenbach over the language about bugging in the supplemental memorandum, though, occupied them most. DeLoach filled in Fortas on the attorney general's "evasive tactics" in defending RFK. While Hoover would "furnish the Attorney General specific, honest, hard-hitting answers to the Supreme Court's questions, we nevertheless knew that Katzenbach would throw our answers out the window and present his own slanted version to the Supreme Court," DeLoach reported. By his account, Fortas agreed and said "the entire matter boiled down to a continuing fight for the Presidency. He added that of course if facts, as possessed by FBI concerning

---

* Obviously, the memoranda describing DeLoach's conversations about the case could represent an attempt to lay down a paper trail exonerating Hoover of responsibility for the bureau's illegal acts. Informal memoranda were not serialized or indexed in the FBI's central record system and, along with Hoover's memoranda for the personal and confidential files, were intended to be destroyed. That the memoranda survived thus suggests that Hoover could have seen them as a way of implicating Kennedy and protecting himself. Yet the nature of the documents also suggests their authenticity, since the FBI generally reserved informal memoranda for information that could incriminate the bureau. Moreover, Fortas's personal papers at Yale include correspondence between Hoover and LBJ's chief of staff, Marvin Watson, about the standoff between the FBI and Katzenbach over the supplemental memorandum. Finally, the justice had a long past of treating Johnson's enemies as his own. Though I cannot be absolutely certain DeLoach's informal memoranda accurately set out his conversations with Fortas, I am inclined to believe that they did.

Kennedy's approval of wiretapping were made known to the general public that it would serve to completely destroy Kennedy."

That was a welcome prospect, but Fortas hoped to insulate the court from the task. According to DeLoach, the justice volunteered that after Solicitor General Marshall "ineptly and inadequately" presented the bugging issue to the court, all the justices met confidentially, with White, RFK's former deputy attorney general, "trying to defend Bobby Kennedy." They decided that if they sent the case back to the trial court to resolve whether the snooping tainted Black's right to a fair trial, Katzenbach would fix the outcome by choosing "a patsy" as federal judge who would do as the attorney general wished. The justices, some of whom were "belligerent" towards Kennedy and Katzenbach, opposed that, and some seemed especially eager to see the court figure out who had authorized the bugging.[114]

Under the circumstances, Fortas told DeLoach that he himself would prefer to "slip in the back door" to see the president. The justice planned to advise LBJ to appoint a reliable arbitrator to collect the evidence and report to the court who had approved the bugging. That approach, Hoover told DeLoach approvingly, would "protect the President and the FBI and could spell 'back seat' for Katzenbach and Kennedy." Yet after Fortas and LBJ expanded the idea of a friendly arbitrator into a three-person committee and decided on its membership, Johnson decided against it. That was wise: Fortas's plan would have made it publicly evident that the president had lost confidence in his attorney general.[115]

So Katzenbach continued to wrangle with Kennedy and the FBI about the language in the supplemental memorandum. The pressure about who approved the bugging continued until the morning of July 13, 1966, when the attorney general received a hand-delivered handwritten note at 10:30 from Kennedy:

> Dear Nick,
> As you know this is a damn important matter for me. I just don't want to receive a shaft—It's not deserved—and anyway I don't like them deserved or not. I'm getting too old I guess.
> I can't write you as many memos as J. Edgar Hoover. And there is no sense in our talking about it by phone.
> I feel strongly about it and I write you just that as there's not much else to say.
> Best, Bob[116]

Kennedy should have had more faith in Katzenbach. At best, the Justice Department's supplemental memorandum filed late that afternoon fuzzed over responsibility for the bugging, Ramsey Clark told LBJ. That was wishful thinking. Especially as interpreted by the Kennedy loyalist who acted as the Justice Department press spokesman, the memorandum blamed the misbehavior on the FBI. "The gist of the Solicitor General's shocking admission to the Supreme Court . . . can be summarized very simply: J. Edgar Hoover has had, at least until just lately, a standing authorization to violate the law whenever he thought he could serve the public interest by doing so," the *Washington Post* said in an editorial entitled "Bugging, American Style."[117]

With Fortas and White recusing themselves from the Black case, the court divided. Initially joined by Justice Black, who later switched sides, Harlan and Stewart hoped to send the case back to the lower court to resolve whether the bugging had violated Fred Black's right to a fair trial and a new trial was required. That was what Katzenbach and Marshall wanted. Warren, Brennan, Clark, and Douglas preferred doing as Fred Black asked, vacating his conviction, and ordering a new trial. Most likely, some sought to get the squabble about who authorized what out of the headlines. The *Washington Post* reported that Hoover and Kennedy were now "all but" calling "each other liars," with Hoover reporting to friendly members of Congress and journalists that Kennedy "not only knew of FBI eavesdropping in criminal cases but stepped it up while he was Attorney General," and the senator heatedly denying it. ("J. Edgar: Oh, Yes You Did; Bobby: Oh No I Didn't," the *New York Daily News* headline read.) Other justices, like Douglas, may have hoped to alert the bureau that the court disapproved of bugging. The FBI did not want to hear that message either.[118]

The bureau took solace in a report from a "reliable source," perhaps Fortas, that Fortas and Clark were pressing for the unusual step of scheduling additional oral arguments on the Black case at the court. There they would put Solicitor General Marshall "on the griddle," rebuke him for his evasiveness and failure "to put some individuals on the spot," and force into the open "Bobby Kennedy's actions and the encouragement of the usage of microphones and other electronic devices." The source added "that all Justices, with the exception of [Kennedy friends] Douglas and White, are quite angry" over Katzenbach's handling of the brief.[119]

The FBI may have tried to promote its preferred outcome by forcing Douglas to recuse himself. If he did so, the court would be evenly split, since Justice Black had not yet changed sides, and it might move in the bureau's ideal direction. Douglas's ties to a charitable foundation established by Las Vegas casino owner Albert Parvin were leaked. Douglas, who was now certain that the court conference room was bugged, refused to withdraw, however, and drafted a separate opinion decrying the "powerful and studied effort to drive me out of this case" and the "vicious articles . . . carrying libelous innuendoes" that unjustifiably and untruthfully linked him with Fred Black, "with the underworld, and with others associated with him." It was not the first time that "powerful forces" had damaged the court by trying "to drive a Justice out of a particular case," Douglas charged. "And in light of the power and influence of the group behind the present effort,

I know that this will not be the last effort." Fortas and Brennan talked their friend out of filing the separate opinion, with Fortas warning Douglas that it might "force the FBI to hop on Parvin with all its resources."[120]

In the end, the court's resolution of the Fred Black case embarrassed, but did not bloody, the FBI. The dispassionate per curiam opinion, written largely by Justice Clark, which Warren, Brennan, Black, and Douglas joined, sided with Fred Black and sent the case back for a new trial—where he was acquitted. It was, Alex Charns concluded, the "the strongest warning to date" the court had given Hoover that it would not tolerate bureau bugging misbehavior. But, possibly thanks in part to Fortas and Clark—for Fortas continued to attend conferences where the case was discussed—the opinion was "a slap on the FBI's wrist." (The following year, the bureau dodged another bullet. The conservative *Wall Street Journal* reported gleefully that after seeming to condemn all bugging in June, the justices who cared so much more about "the rights of poor, black suspects" than they did about police bugging, wiretapping, and use of government informants vis-à-vis organized crime executed a "flip-flop" in December. Although they prohibited warrantless electronic surveillance in cases where "national security" was not at stake, their seven-to-one "pro law-enforcement decision surprised everyone by giving the Court's blessing to judicially authorized electronic eavesdropping.")[121]

It was Katzenbach who received the black eye in the Fred Black case. As he himself acknowledged later, the department's "mealy-mouthed explanation" in the Black case infuriated Hoover, Kennedy, and even Solicitor General Marshall. Like his former boss, Robert Kennedy, Katzenbach had not won any points with Johnson or Fortas either.[122]

By now, LBJ had convinced himself that Kennedy employed a staff of forty in New York to dig up presidential dirt and had agents rifling through Justice Department files for it. There is no way to know whether he was right, as the financial reports of Kennedy's New York office remain closed; the duties of his staffers, unclear. Perhaps Johnson's convictions about Kennedy just showed that he indeed suffered from the clinical paranoia that at least one staffer believed afflicted him. Plenty of people around him shared LBJ's obsession with the senator, though, and proved only too willing to stoke it by passing along rumors about Kennedy's disdain for Johnson, his presidential ambitions, and his supporters. Without a doubt, the tension between the LBJ and RFK forces had become toxic, and Katzenbach had become caught in the crossfire.[123]

The impending serialization of William Manchester's book, *The Death of a President*, written about the assassination with the Kennedys' authorization, exacerbated the ill feeling toward Katzenbach at the White House and panicked Johnson administration members during the second half of 1966. As they knew,

Manchester's book's inclusion of intimate details sent the Kennedys into a frenzy too. The family was weighing a lawsuit to block publication, which Jacqueline Kennedy ultimately brought, then settled. But it was Manchester's portrayal of Johnson as a cretin and the "abrasive relationship between Kennedy and Johnson partisans during the hours aboard Air Force One"—as *Look* Magazine put it on its cover—that agitated LBJ. By Manchester's account, Johnson had treated Mrs. Kennedy thoughtlessly and moved with unseemly haste to become president. The Johnson tape recordings suggest that early versions of the manuscript intimated that LBJ had taken the oath of office with his hand atop JFK's beloved Bible, then pocketed it for historic reasons. The published versions placed Johnson's hand atop the Bible—though in reality, the book was not a Bible, but a Catholic missal, and since it was wrapped in cellophane, "[i]t's not one that had ever been opened," the president privately stressed. Manchester now had an "anonymous cozener" at the foot of Air Force One taking from Judge Hughes JFK's "most cherished personal possession," and one that Kennedy's family "would give a lot to have. . .back." (Doubtless Manchester would have had a field day had he known that the stranger was apparently a security agent, and the Johnsons had the missal, which is today on display in the LBJ Library).[124]

Naturally, such stories increased the president's edginess about "spies." JFK's sister, Eunice, actually telephoned LBJ to assure him that her husband, who oversaw the administration's poverty program, and her mother remained "almost painfully loyal" to Johnson, despite brotherly pressure. "Thank you, Eunice," a bemused-sounding president said before handing her off to Lady Bird Johnson. "I would hope all of 'em would be."[125]

Because Katzenbach had been consulted about the oath, the advance reports about the book increased LBJ's doubts about his devotion. Fortas himself believed that the Kennedys relished the damage the book inflicted on LBJ and were trying to avoid charges of smearing him by going through the motions of trying to halt publication of the story they had originally invited him to write through a lawsuit, which they ultimately settled. "The first battle is to charge us with stealing the Bible [missal], the next battle will be [to charge us with] imposing on Mrs. [Jacqueline] Kennedy, the next battle will be [to charge us with] imposing on Bobby and on his mother," LBJ angrily predicted, and "he will wind up as the great hero and we will wind up as the great thug."[126]

Though polls showed that LBJ was wrong and that the Manchester controversy hurt the images of both Robert and Jacqueline Kennedy, it did damage the attorney general. Thanks to his appointment of Fortas, Johnson now had a friendly ear at the court, but he still lacked control over the Justice Department. For his part, Katzenbach felt wrung out, and he knew Hoover remained furious about the Black case. But LBJ could not allow Katzenbach to leave the administration. He remained a link to the Kennedys and helped protect the president from charges that he practiced government by crony. And while he did not trust Katzenbach where the Kennedys were concerned, the president respected him. The task was to move him to a less sensitive position, where he might do good—and to win a second Supreme Court vacancy for Thurgood Marshall in the process.[127]

3

Bogeyman, 1966–68

In the summer of 1967, when LBJ got that second Supreme Court vacancy and a new attorney general, a few Southern conservatives on the Senate Judiciary Committee placed ideology at the center of the Supreme Court confirmation process for the first time in recent history. They used Thurgood Marshall's nomination to politicize the confirmation process and to turn the Warren Court into a bogeyman. After segregationists spent five days interrogating Marshall about his suitability to become a justice, *New York Times* legal correspondent Fred Graham condemned them. "The situation exposed an anomaly that has developed in the Senate's role in the selection of judges—the chances of Senate disapproval have declined almost to zero, while pressures have increased for the nominees to submit themselves for what is often aimless grilling before the Judiciary Committee," the reporter lamented. According to Graham, because confirmation was preordained, as it had been throughout the twentieth century, this sad state of affairs had convinced many of the importance of "new ground rules" to produce less punishing treatment of nominees. Perhaps those new rules might have emerged had Johnson's power held steady, but placing Marshall on the court became one of his last hurrahs. The Marshall interrogation signaled the start of the transformation of the Supreme Court appointments process, and in a way that lessened presidential power.[1]

The Second Supreme Court Vacancy

LBJ saw his opportunity to move Katzenbach out of the Justice Department while keeping him close in the fall of 1966. Exhausted by his fight against the escalation of the Vietnam War, Under Secretary of State George Ball announced he was leaving government. Though LBJ pretended remorse, he rejoiced. His high opinion of Ball at Stevenson's death had evaporated, particularly after Hoover fingered the under secretary as the source of leaks about Vietnam to the liberal "Georgetown set." In Texas, "we poison eggs once in a while to get these sheep-killing dogs," LBJ laughed to Fortas. The president need only provide Ball some confidential misinformation before he swallowed that egg and delivered it right to Drew Pearson.[2]

LBJ, "backed by Fortas," initially offered Ball's job to Clark Clifford. "I pointed out that it would seriously undercut the Secretary of State if a person known to be a close personal friend and adviser of the President became Under Secretary of State," Clifford wrote later. A contemporary exchange between LBJ and Fortas, however, suggested Clifford said that he would accept the post if the president would soon make him secretary of state. But Johnson remained loyal to Secretary of State Dean Rusk.[3]

Katzenbach felt "flattered and pleased" when LBJ telephoned him to discuss possibilities as under secretary of state. But the attorney general considered Johnson's candidates too "hawkish." Consequently, Katzenbach recalled, to his own surprise, he told the president that the State Department had long interested him and volunteered. As Katzenbach remembered it, LBJ originally demurred and said he was needed at Justice. Nevertheless, within days, the president had offered him the job.[4]

LBJ leapt at the chance to get rid of Katzenbach, just as he had jumped at liberating himself from Ball. He knew the move, which entailed a $5,000 pay cut, looked odd. After startling the capital by tucking news of Katzenbach's transfer to the State Department into a September press conference, the president dodged questions about whether it represented a demotion and whether Tom Clark's position at the court precluded Ramsey's elevation to attorney general. The next day, Johnson peppered Katzenbach with directions, since Katzenbach, the president said slyly, generally received good press and was the "better image-maker" of the two of them. The Justice Department press officer, whom LBJ violently mistrusted, should tell *The New Republic*, *The Nation*, and editorial writers that Rusk had wanted Katzenbach at the State Department from the beginning, and Katzenbach had hoped to go, but the Kennedys had installed him at the Justice Department. That part of the story was true, as was the fact that Katzenbach had told Johnson he would serve wherever needed. The media should learn that his selflessness had "stunned" LBJ and that Katzenbach already had the president's ear on economics and foreign policy, as well as law. "I want some of that to go out . . . for your good and for my good," Johnson stressed. "And a lot of them wonder if I didn't make a secret deal with you to make you Secretary of State." Despite problems at the State Department, Rusk was "going to keep his head high as long as he works for me and you are too." Another interpretation was surfacing that the president also wanted to fight: "Johnson was unhappy with you" at the Justice Department. His voice rising as he convinced himself that he was not, LBJ insisted that dispatching Katzenbach to the State Department was "pure and clean and noble," and he wanted to make sure everyone knew it.[5]

LBJ proceeded circuitously in finding a new attorney general. "This man is going to be mine if I ever name him," he stressed to Fortas, who, equally predictably, declared himself "just 1,000 percent for that." Fortas had talked with Clifford about taking the job, but that was a long shot. The *Washington Post* reported that all indicators pointed to Ramsey Clark.[6]

Johnson had known the thirty-nine-year-old Clark, who had gone to college at the University of Texas and law school at Chicago, since before he wore long pants. The president would sometimes question Clark's common sense, but never his loyalty. As a Texan, however, he might be branded a crony, and his father sat on the Supreme Court.[7]

Yet there was no reason that Justice Tom Clark had to resign from the court if LBJ made his son attorney general or acting attorney general, Katzenbach told the president—before LBJ made it absolutely clear that he was pursuing "a throw daddy from the bench" strategy and would only promote Ramsey Clark if he received another vacancy at the court as a bonus. When Senate Minority Leader Everett Dirksen of Illinois reported that Republicans considered Clark, then very popular on the Hill, "a good, able boy," Johnson asked, "What about the problem with the Daddy on the Court?" "Huh?" Dirksen said, before adding, "Oh, well, of course the Attorney General don't appear before the Court." The solicitor general did. All Dirksen's colleagues agreed that Justice Clark need not leave the court. So what if Charles Evans Hughes Jr. had resigned as solicitor general when Herbert Hoover nominated his father as chief justice?[8]

But LBJ was greedy. He was willing to leave Tom Clark on the court if Ramsey became acting attorney general. As he saw it, a permanent attorney generalship, however, required a family sacrifice. Congress had become a more uncertain ally on civil rights. That made a Supreme Court seat that the president could use to demonstrate his commitment to equality more valuable than ever. Johnson devoutly wished to make Marshall the first African American justice.

So Fortas talked with Tom Clark, obviously at the president's instigation, about Ramsey's future. When Fortas said that "I was interested in his son," and that Justice Clark "ought to be now getting down to the short strokes of what he wants to do," the Texan volunteered that he cared most about Ramsey's success. In that case, Fortas advised, he should consult his brethren on the court about whether he should remain if Ramsey became attorney general. Fortas was certain, based on his own soundings of his colleagues, that they would tell him that Justice Clark must resign in that case. "It will work out if . . . that's what you want," Fortas promised LBJ.[9]

Would the country react favorably to the appointment of Thurgood Marshall as Supreme Court justice? the president asked. Civil rights supporters would, Fortas responded. "There's a lot of feeling on it the other way now, though," LBJ answered, including in the Senate. "Yeah there is and of course it will alter the balance of the Court," Fortas remarked. That got the president's attention. "Now wait a minute," LBJ responded. "How's the Court divided now, five to four?" On many matters, yes, Fortas answered. "And y'all have the four?" No. "Well, that would be six to three then," the veteran vote counter observed. "That'd give us a solid majority, yeah," Fortas replied. "I shouldn't have said 'alter the balance of the Court' . . . because I think that Marshall will vote right—will vote with us." Fortas's first answer may have more accurately reflected his thoughts. It seemed to him, Warren, Brennan, and Douglas that Black had become a less reliable ally on civil rights and the First Amendment, and during the 1966–67 term, his "drift toward the right" in criminal procedure cases would become apparent too. Fortas may have hoped that Marshall's arrival would turn the tide and further liberalize the court, as indeed it did.[10]

Vote predicting aside, Fortas promised to coach Marshall about talking tough on crime for the Senate and reiterated that everyone, except those opposed to the president's efforts to resolve "the Negro problem," would welcome the appointment. "And it might be a good thing for the Court because we're going to pull the reins in a little bit," Fortas continued. Perhaps referring to *Walker v. Birmingham*'s punitive approach toward King and protesters who violated court orders, he assured the president that the court was going to "tell people they have to obey the law. . . . So it might be a good thing to have a Negro there."

LBJ returned to Justice Tom Clark. Did Tom think Ramsey would be offered the position? the president wondered. No, Fortas said, but "he knows that I'm for Ramsey, and he's very, very hopeful." Would Justice Clark's resignation create much discussion? "None," Fortas answered. Though Clark was well liked, he was not "a great jurist." That criticism of the president's old friend stung, and LBJ pointed to Clark's diligence. Ever mindful of pleasing his president, Fortas backtracked and began singing his colleague's praises.[11]

But Johnson interrupted Fortas: "You just know the thing to do is for you not to come to [be] the Attorney General?" People would say the president plotted to put Fortas on the court while the Baker case was hot, then moved him to the Justice Department when it cooled down, his friend warned. (LBJ did not persist, but on another occasion he teased Fortas that the difference between a bull and a steer was that the neutered steer had "'lost his social standing in the community where he resides.' And you've just been cut when I put you on that damn Supreme Court. I wish Carol had never talked me into it." Cue to uproarious laughter.)[12]

The two friends moved on to the Fred Black case. "Will Thurgood mess up your wire-tapping thing?" No, and Marshall would have to disqualify himself anyway. Clark's removal might hurt, but the administration would still win, and at least those on the other side would not gain a vote. (As it happened, of course, Clark was still on the court when it resolved the Black case.) Clark was "solid as a rock" on Black, Jimmy Hoffa, and wiretapping, LBJ subsequently stressed. "You damn fellows get disqualified, but somebody's got to get up there and just raise hell [on behalf of the administration], and I don't believe our new friend [Marshall] would do it." An aggrieved Fortas reminded the president, "I worked on this thing [Black] all damn day and I'm disqualified." (At least Fortas *did* disqualify himself. On another occasion, after Ramsey Clark resisted LBJ's urging against filing a brief with the Supreme Court with respect to the enormous Penn-Central Railroad merger, Fortas told the White House what to include in the justice's brief to soft-pedal the department's obvious doubts about the merger. We do not know what he said to Johnson privately because the president ordered the tape recording of their conversation destroyed. "Astonishingly, Justice Fortas participated in the Court's decision," Joe Califano wrote in a memoir, which, unlike most entries in that genre, drew on exhaustive research in the Johnson Library. He also failed to carry the court. Tom Clark issued the majority opinion delaying the merger. "Damn good thing you had your daddy voting with you on that one or you'd have been screwed," LBJ joked to Ramsey Clark. "Talk about conflicts!" Ramsey laughed. Fortas wrote a dissent that, Califano insisted, quoted "the portion of the Solicitor General's brief that made the very point he had suggested the President have the Justice Department put forth: 'The United States . . . does not challenge the merger itself. Indeed, the Solicitor General has represented to the Court that 'the agencies of the Executive Branch that have substantive responsibilities for the formulation of economic and transportation policy believe that the merger is in the public interest and that its consummation should be promptly effected.'" Fortas also wrote the subsequent majority opinion approving the merger.)[13]

After a detour in which Johnson drilled Fortas on how to answer charges that the president was demoting Katzenbach, it was back to Thurgood Marshall. Even though he had not received "two letters" praising him for naming Robert Weaver the first African American cabinet official, LBJ remained hopeful. "I wonder if this Marshall thing wouldn't kind of rock the Negroes in this country and put them in position where they wouldn't be too mean to me," he mused.[14]

Marshall's nomination as Supreme Court justice and Ramsey Clark's as attorney general had become just as intertwined in LBJ's mind as crime and civil rights. When LBJ spoke with Katzenbach, who was still running the Justice Department and who favored both appointments, on September 24, 1966, however, he learned that Ramsey and Tom Clark were both acting "stiff-necked." The father did not want to damage his son's chances to become attorney general; the son, to deprive his father of a beloved job.[15]

But Katzenbach's exchanges with Justice Clark just led to a misunderstanding— or, perhaps, to an attempt by the justice to keep his seat and to see his son be named attorney general. Four days later, LBJ telephoned Katzenbach to read a note from Tom Clark:

> Dear Mr. President,
> Instead of taking time from your busy day for a personal call I'm writing this private note. Underlined "private." I understand that you wish me to stay on the Court. Some leaders of the American Bar have written me confidentially, saying they'd be glad to secure favorable statements from their president, president-elect, and past-president saying no incompatibility would result by my staying there. I'm sure that the former Attorney General [Katzenbach] and the Solicitor General [Marshall] would say the same. However I have asked these [men] to do nothing on this. I have also spoken to my brothers from Black to White, from C.J. [Chief Justice], and also our newest member [Fortas]. I am certain that no repercussions will result from here. . . . I did read where a reporter asked you about it at the time [of LBJ's announcement that Katzenbach would become under secretary]. In view of this, I thought you should have this information. As you know, the Clarks are all for you wherever it leads, and I need not repeat our concern is only in your best interest.
>
>   Faithfully.

"Now I'm wondering," LBJ asked, his consternation evident, "we haven't given him any impression we want him to stay on the Court at all, have we?" No, Katzenbach said, "unless I did it by inadvertence" in emphasizing Johnson's "affection, friendship, and so forth." The attorney general had highlighted "the difficulties" if Clark remained. Once again, however, Katzenbach contended that unlike the public, "sophisticated lawyers" would not question a Clark as attorney general and a Clark as justice. Sophisticated lawyers, such as Warren and Fortas, would, LBJ retorted. "I don't know how to get him [Clark] word," the president lamented. "I cannot in my judgment, as I see it, go this other route [of naming Ramsey Clark attorney general] with him on the Court."[16]

Enter Fortas. Soon after Katzenbach was sworn in as under secretary on October 3, 1966, Fortas relayed the news that Justice Clark "wants you to know" that he would leave the court "if and when" Ramsey became attorney general. Tom Clark's letter to Warren, which would remain private until LBJ decided on Ramsey's future, said media reports indicated that the president was considering promoting his son, and he would retire if Johnson did. The two Clarks had worked out the "exactly right" solution, Fortas rejoiced.[17]

By now, the president was not just dipping into the court's docket but also dreaming about how Justice Marshall, whose appointment he prudently intended to delay until after the midterm elections, could help restore the luster of the civil rights movement. "We've got to shake them [disillusioned whites] up like [by] convict[ing] that damn Carmichael," LBJ reiterated. "I wish you would let our new Justice write the opinion on it," he added, chuckling. "I believe he has got enough courage to stand up with the Wilkinses . . . and others."[18]

Later that day, the president called Ramsey Clark to say, "You're Acting Attorney General, and I want you to run the Department in first class shape for awhile and then I want to sit down and have a talk with you." As he told Fortas, "Doesn't hurt him to act. Nick acted five, six months." The following month, a hospitalized LBJ pulled out all the stops, grabbed Clark Clifford's arm, pleaded with him to become attorney general, and enlisted Mrs. Johnson to beg him too. To no one's surprise, Clifford refused and recommended Ramsey Clark. With that, Marshall's appointment to the court became more likely than ever.[19]

Yet for LBJ, nothing was ever inevitable. Why, when his record as the lawyer for the National Association for the Advancement of Colored People (NAACP) was so good, had Solicitor General Marshall lost five cases and won nine? the president queried Ramsey Clark repeatedly in 1967. Shouldn't a solicitor general possess a better scorecard? "Thurgood's not that kind," Clark laughed. Marshall refused to saddle anyone else in the office with cases the government would lose, despite reminders that "we've got a lot more interest in you than in anybody in that office" and that he had "a tradition and your people and the president" to honor.[20]

The losses hurt, though, as did Marshall's unfamiliarity with business law, and the rumors that he was indolent, left the solicitor general's office at "midafternoon," and drank too much. To no one's surprise, LBJ "never gave you the satisfaction of feeling that you had a sure bet," recalled civil rights leader Louis Martin. "The line has been that Thurgood is no good as a lawyer—that he will be a black mark on the President's record of excellent appointments," Fortas confided to William O. Douglas in the spring of 1967, soon after LBJ had finally named Ramsey Clark attorney general, and Tom Clark had announced his retirement at term's end in a gracious statement stressing his "pride and joy" at his son's nomination[21] (figure 8).

"If it's not Thurgood, it won't be [Harvard Law School's Paul] Freund, I think," Fortas assured Douglas. (Almost every time there was a vacancy, his friend worried the president would nominate that Frankfurter acolyte to the court.) "I think it's more likely to be a Texan." And indeed the *Wall Street Journal* reported that if Johnson did not choose Marshall, he might select his friend, Fifth Circuit Judge Homer Thornberry. "But my *guess* is that Thurgood will get it," Fortas concluded. There were other African Americans, such as William Hastie, who had attended more elite universities, something that never concerned LBJ, and who would carry less political baggage to the Senate Judiciary Committee than did Marshall, who symbolized the struggle for black equality. But Katzenbach told Johnson that Marshall's past provided the very reason that the president must put him on the court.[22]

Figure 8 Swearing in of Ramsey Clark as attorney general by Justice Tom Clark under the approving eyes of family members Georgia Clark and Tom Clark II, President Johnson, Solicitor General Thurgood Marshall, and Vice President Hubert Humphrey, Great Hall, Department of Justice. LBJ Library. Photo by Yoichi Okamoto.

That was what Johnson wanted to hear. As he had done in the case of the Goldberg vacancy, when he zeroed in on Fortas, he never seriously considered anyone other than Marshall to succeed Clark. Aides underscored that Johnson hungered to integrate the Supreme Court and they said that he and Marshall spoke the "same language." As they stressed, "chemistry" was crucial for LBJ. The president would also have wanted to increase the debt felt by Marshall and his friends. Moreover, Johnson may have criticized Marshall largely "to create suspense," which he always craved, about whom he would select.[23]

Certainly, the trope of the shocked Supreme Court nominee made for good political theater. By now, it had become a staple of the modern confirmation process. Just as LBJ was said to have "surprised" Fortas into joining the court, so Felix Frankfurter loved to recount how he was in his undershorts when FDR telephoned him and astonished him with the news of his nomination. In reality, Frankfurter and his friends had been campaigning for it for months. And like FDR, who loved to spring his "bombshells," Johnson relished catching nominees, the media, and the public unaware. Consequently, Marshall recalled warnings from the president not to expect advancement beyond solicitor general "at least two out of every three times" they spoke, even on the night of June 12, 1967, at a party in honor of the retiring Tom Clark.[24]

Just that day, the justices had unanimously declared state laws prohibiting interracial marriage unconstitutional in *Loving v. Virginia*, a decision that deserves remembrance as "the capstone of the Court's blow to the Jim Crow regime," as well as a ringing defense of the right to marry. Mildred Loving, an African American, and her white husband, Richard, had appealed to the Warren Court to vacate a one-year prison sentence that they had received for violating Virginia's antimiscegenation law, which the court now struck down. Like some white liberals, LBJ probably would have hit the roof had either of his daughters married an African American. During the first half of 1968, he would watch "Guess Who's Coming to Dinner," the film about two white liberal parents who must come to grips with their daughter's marriage to an African American doctor, four times. On at least one of them, he quizzed his guests about their reactions to "a negro marrying a white girl." But the president enthusiastically shared the Warren Court's commitment to attacking the last vestiges of racial discrimination, as the nomination of Marshall, an African American married to a Filipina, would powerfully remind the nation.[25]

Still, Ramsey Clark was reassuring LBJ about Marshall right up to the morning after his father's retirement party. Did the solicitor general's staff like Marshall? Johnson asked at 7:59 A.M. on June 13, 1967. "Yes," Clark said. Then "where did all this wave of stuff go around that he was disappointing as Solicitor General" and was "lazy and shiftless and didn't spend much time doing his homework," LBJ wanted to know, conveniently overlooking the fact that he had spread some of the rumors himself. Some wanted someone else appointed to the court, and

Marshall "doesn't fit the mold," Clark answered. "He's not a Yale man. . . . He's a big easy-going, very humane type person." Some of his fellow judges on the Second Circuit had questioned his intellect and industry, "but . . . how'd he do all these things if he's so lazy and incompetent?" Had Marshall been "regarded as the best the Negroes had" when Clark was a young lawyer? Johnson wondered. "He was the only one anyone knew about outside of a few local practitioners," Clark answered. "His name is a part of American history right now." As the NAACP's chief counsel and as solicitor general, Marshall had argued a staggering number of cases before the Supreme Court.

Would there be "any opposition to his confirmation," which the *Baltimore Sun* had predicted just that morning? Clark anticipated some "foot-dragging in the Judiciary Committee" from senators worried about crime, but "anybody who really wanted to oppose would be kind of hard-pressed." He predicted that the two papers Johnson worried about most, the *New York Times* and *Washington Post,* would cover the confirmation positively too. Get hold of the American Bar Association president, LBJ finally ordered, and direct him to ask the Standing Committee on the Federal Judiciary to rate Marshall. "He can have it done within an hour," Clark soothed.[26]

As Clark observed, the Warren Court's desire to harness the power of law to help outsiders accounted for some of Marshall's losses. In *Miranda,* for one example, the solicitor general contended that the court should not always require the recitation of warnings about suspects' right against self-incrimination and to court-appointed counsel. "We can't equalize the whole thing," Marshall said, in an argument that he subsequently predicted to one police chief the justices would not buy. LBJ, who once had worried aloud to Clark that Marshall would not "send a man to the penitentiary, by God, for raping a woman [even] if you had a photograph of [him doing it]," was telling his acting attorney general approvingly by June 13 that Marshall was "a pretty hard kind of man." The other day, the president continued, he himself had told Marshall that "you and Ramsey and Abe Fortas are just gone crazy. All of you too liberal on these [crime] things." LBJ, a gifted mimic, slipped into Marshall's voice as he related the solicitor general's reply. "'Wait. Wait just a minute there. I'm a Tom Clark crime man.' So that would indicate to me that they [Senate Judiciary Committee members] wouldn't be rough on him . . . if that is known. I guess that's not known."[27]

That June 13 morning, Marshall was scheduled to attend a reception for 121 Presidential Scholars, a distinguished group of high school seniors culled from National Merit Scholar finalists, at the White House. But Ramsey Clark told him to go directly to the Oval Office without attracting any attention instead. Marshall could do that any number of ways, including by tunnel from the Old Executive Office Building, but Clark directed him to enter with the awed tourists awaiting a glimpse of the White House interior. A Secret Service agent peeled him off and dispatched him to the cabinet room, where the solicitor general fruitlessly quizzed Chief of Staff Marvin Watson about the reason for his summons. When Marshall walked into the Oval Office at 11:05 A.M., Clark and LBJ were there. Louis Martin and Clifford Alexander, the president's African American deputy special counsel, who had also been called in without explanation, arrived soon afterward. The president "was having fun with us," Martin explained, but when Marshall, Martin, and Alexander saw who was assembled, "we knew the story."[28]

As Marshall told the tale to one audience, however, the surprise was complete. After he and LBJ "chatted for a few minutes," the president suddenly "looked at me and said, 'You know something, Thurgood?' I said 'No, sir, what's that?' 'I'm going to put you on the Supreme Court,' Johnson announced. "I said, 'Oh, yipe!'" By Marshall's account, he also told LBJ that William Hastie deserved the nomination more, and the president instructed him to "'let me mind my own business'" (figure 9). Without a doubt, Marshall, Martin, and Alexander did sit by while LBJ tracked down a delighted Earl Warren in San Francisco to inform him he was sending Marshall's name to the Senate, and telephoned Senate Majority Leader Mansfield and Minority Leader Dirksen. "He lined these guys up and said, 'Now I'm about to do this and I want you to go with me,'" Martin remembered. "The President just had a ball."[29]

Figure 9 Johnson and Thurgood Marshall in Oval Office the day the president nominated his solicitor general to the Supreme Court. LBJ Library. Photo by Frank Wolfe.

At some point, after watching Johnson work the phone, Marshall remembered asking whether he could tell his wife the news. Hadn't he let her know yet? Johnson asked incredulously. "No. How could I? I've been with you all the time." LBJ would have enjoyed that blunt response. The two men telephoned Cissy Marshall, and Marshall recalled telling her to sit down. LBJ then said he was putting Marshall on the court. "I sure am glad I'm sitting down," Marshall said his wife responded. Like Marshall himself, Mrs. Marshall may have been less astonished than her raconteur husband pretended. Another version of the story had Marshall identifying himself without telling his outspoken wife she was on speaker, "Cissy supposedly replied," to Johnson's amusement, "Did we get the Supreme Court appointment?"[30]

At noon that day, the two big men appeared before reporters. Marshall stood beside the president looking somber, almost grim as LBJ reviewed his record as appellate judge and advocate. The solicitor general's office had presented "some 80-odd cases" to the court during Marshall's tenure and had lost just eight. Marshall himself had appeared before the Supreme Court in fifty-two cases during his entire career, and LBJ's "statisticians" (i.e., Ramsey Clark) had informed him that "probably only one or two other living men have argued as many cases before the Court and perhaps less than half a dozen in all the history of the nation" had done so. The president made no explicit mention of *Brown v. Board of Education*, Marshall's years as NAACP litigator, or race. He did carefully emphasize, however, that Marshall had graduated at the top of his class at Howard Law School (which he had chosen because he had no chance of admission at the all-white University of Maryland Law School). Instead, LBJ said, "He has had a distinguished record as private counsel and as Government counsel in the courts of the land. I believe he has already earned his place in history, but I think it will be greatly enhanced by his service on the Court." Marshall deserved the appointment, he stressed again. "He is best qualified by training and by very valuable service to the country. I believe it is the right thing to do, the right time to do it, the right man and the right place." And LBJ trusted that the Senate would "promptly" consider the nomination.[31]

At the news conference that followed, Johnson's first since the Six Day War ended just three days earlier, questions about Marshall alternated with those about diplomacy. Asked whether he had been urged to appoint "someone more conservative" to the court, Johnson answered that he had received "very little pressure of any kind," and volunteered that the American Bar Association had just rated Marshall "highly acceptable." Beyond that, he made sure that Marshall stayed mum. When a reporter wanted to know how Marshall felt about the appointment, LBJ intervened: "I hope the Justice doesn't go into an extended news conference before his confirmation, but I am sure that if you deal purely with health matters he will be glad to respond." Marshall interjected, "You speak for me, Mr. President. We will wait until after the Senate acts."[32]

Just as Woodrow Wilson had awarded the nomination to Brandeis, the icon of a once-marginalized religious minority, so Johnson was now reserving a Supreme Court seat for a champion of a once-vilified racial minority. In doing so, the president implicitly acknowledged that group's struggle and political arrival. At the same time, LBJ had reinforced the meritocratic ideal as he recited his nominee's outstanding credentials.

That evening, the president spoke more openly about his sense of the nomination's significance. Escorting Marshall into the Presidential Scholars' reception, LBJ apologized for the absence of his solicitor general and Supreme Court nominee that morning. Then having touted Marshall as a symbol of the smart and dedicated public servants presidents needed in Washington, LBJ spoke from the heart about the importance of education. "In the United States we have always prided ourselves for our leadership in free education." But for all the progress, there remained much to do. "For every Albert Einstein—how many immigrants worked out their lives in cotton mills, trapped by poverty?" Johnson asked. "For every Thurgood Marshall—how many talented Negro Americans never escaped the prison of the sharecropper? For every Harry Truman—how many promising young men vanished at 16 into the stores, the factories, and the mines?" The president stressed "our" duty to construct "an educational system which will discover and develop these lost Americans." Education, he believed, provided the route to equality.[33]

And for a moment, LBJ could see that his message of hope and determination was heard. A *Chicago Daily Defender* column "commenting on the Thurgood Marshall appointment in the colloquialisms of the urban Negro," as one White House official stiffly put it, so delighted the president that he wanted it sent to "every leading negro" in the United States. "I think thousands and millions of black kids dig this country a little bit more right now," its author wrote. "Cause they got a powerful piece of evidence—right under their nose—that the sun do move." The Congress of Racial Equality's Floyd McKissick, who had won entry to the University of North Carolina Law School thanks to a lawsuit brought by Marshall, rarely applauded the Johnson administration. He did now. "This has stirred pride in the breast of every black American," McKissick said.[34]

To study the reaction to the Marshall nomination, though, is to be reminded anew of the obvious point that reasonable scholars disagree. We are not chroniclers. We interpret the documents from which we often quote without reproducing them. How we read them depends on many things, including our own characters and something as basic as whether we see the cup as half full or empty. Consider the following paragraph from the *New York Times* editorial, "Marshall to the Court. . . ." After noting that the nomination is "rich in symbolism," it continued:

> There are other judges in the state and Federal courts whose judicial work has been far more outstanding than Mr. Marshall's record during his brief service on the Second Circuit. Nor as Solicitor General did he demonstrate the intellectual mastery of Archibald Cox, his prede- cessor. But, apart from the symbolism, Mr. Marshall brings to the Court a wealth of practical experience as a brilliant, forceful advocate.[35]

One Marshall biographer sees this paragraph as evidence of the "genteel bias" and "concerns about Marshall's intellect" that pervaded press reports of the appointment, while I focus on that last sentence saluting Marshall as "a bril- liant, forceful advocate." So, too, the biographer quotes the portion of the *New Republic* editorial claiming that Marshall had "often" proven "less than brilliant" as circuit court judge and solicitor general. But in my view, Thurgood Marshall *was* even more impressive as a courageous and effective civil rights lawyer than he was as judge or solicitor general. Consequently, I light on another part of the same editorial lauding him as an advocate and stressing that in the "person" of Thurgood Marshall, the civil rights lawyer, "millions of Negroes marched into the courtroom and prevailed," and I observe that the *New Republic*'s influential T. R. B. hailed "the fine appointment."[36]

In my reading, aside from conservative journals like *Human Events*; the *National Review*; small-town Southern newspapers, which assailed the nomina- tion; and the *Wall Street Journal*, which took a wait-and-see attitude, most lead- ing newspapers and periodicals applauded it. Many editorials calmly anticipated that Marshall would prove more "liberal" on civil rights and possibly crime than Tom Clark, as he did, and some forecast that the Supreme Court would henceforward possess a "Negro Seat." If editorials provided any indication, the Warren Court remained popular. Some journalists noted that the appointment could prove politically useful in appealing to black voters. Yet most celebrated the appointment more because of Marshall's achievements and what the eleva- tion of an African American to the court might mean about the United States as a nation. The *Washington Post* exulted: "At long last." For Marshall, the nom- ination, which just twenty years earlier would have been "inconceivable," was "the climax of a distinguished career," and it was a positive step for the nation that, the newspaper predicted, would just provoke isolated Southern opposition. "And this should serve as a demonstration of just how rapidly race relations have improved to those Negro leaders who argue that their people can get their rights only through violence," the *Post* stressed[37] (figure 10).

Figure 10 Marshall's confirmation gave many something to celebrate. "Should Be a Good Fit. It Took Us 177 Years to Make." Washington Daily News Cartoon, June 14, 1967, *Washington Post.* Washingtoniana Division, DC Public Library.

Symbolic Politics

That, of course, was also Lyndon Johnson's hope. As always, Marshall remained his proof of America's forward, if uncertain, march toward racial equality at a time when the inner cities had become cauldrons of rage and despair. Where rioting roiled eight cities and killed eight in 1964, it consumed thirty-one cities and left eighty-six dead during the first eight months of 1967 alone. As Marshall's hearing began, Newark exploded, and Detroit was about to go up in flames (figure 11). "Well," Joe Califano remembered hearing LBJ remark disconsolately after he signed the order federalizing the Michigan National Guard, "I guess it's a matter of minutes before federal troops start killing women and children."[38]

Congress responded to the disturbances by defeating the administration's bill to control rats in the slums as demonstrators chanted inside the Capitol, "rats cause riots." Despite warnings of its possible unconstitutionality, Congress also enacted an antiriot bill aimed at penalizing Stokely Carmichael's Student Nonviolent Coordinating Committee (SNCC) successor, H. Rap Brown, with whom LBJ conflated Carmichael, and anyone else who crossed interstate lines with the intent of provoking civil unrest. When Johnson's advisers discussed the desirability of a meeting between the president and "responsible Negro leaders" like Whitney Young and Roy Wilkins that summer, they stressed its disadvantages. "We really don't have an immediate program to put them," and liberal reporters would "point out that these people have not much more

Figure 11 Marshall's confirmation hearing coincided with trouble in Detroit. President Johnson (seated behind desk) at work on the Detroit crisis with, left to right, Joe Califano, Secretary of Defense Robert McNamara, Secretary of the Army Stanley Resor (obscured), Attorney General Ramsey Clark, George Christian, Justice Abe Fortas, Marvin Watson (back to camera). LBJ Library. Photo by Yoichi Okamoto.

contact with, or power of persuasion over the terrorists"—which was how LBJ's staff referred to the "Carmichael crowd"—than the conservative National Association of Manufacturers. Moreover, "the meeting would be sure to dwell on social needs and programs, when "what the country wants to hear about is to bring riots under control." At this point, one historian emphasized, "police measures to hold back supposedly dangerous communities" interested "those Great Society liberals" more than anything else even though the intensity and vastness of urban unrest suggested that a political rebellion that they needed to attend to was under way.[39]

Congress apparently had lost its will to wage the war for racial equality, and some thought that LBJ had too. Especially once it became evident that not all civil rights leaders supported him on the war, Vietnam sapped his energy and enthusiasm for racial equality at the same time that it "aggravated fissures within the civil rights movement along generational and ideological lines." In his 1967 State of the Union address, the president had urged Congress to wage the war in Vietnam, fight the war against poverty, and authorize "special methods and special funds to reach the hundreds of thousands of Americans that are now trapped in the ghettos of our big cities." As the *New Republic* complained, LBJ "devoted exactly 45 words out of several thousand to civil rights." And in the place of the civil rights legislation he had exhorted Congress to enact in 1964, 1965, and even 1966, the president was now touting legislation to attack the rising crime rate.[40]

The Urban League's Whitney Young reminded white leaders that whether the civil rights "moderates" would prevail over the "militants" depended on whether the white community eliminated the conditions that helped cause the riots. "You've got to give us some victories," Young said. The news about Marshall was hardly all that he had in mind, but it counted. Young wired LBJ that the nomination was "perhaps the most significant event in our generation," and like the *Chicago Daily Defender,* the rest of the black press gave it lots of play. If Marshall's nomination did not stop rats from preying on babies in Harlem, it did underline the president's commitment to racial justice through law. It was symbolic politics at a time when, it was becoming increasingly evident, symbols were just about all that LBJ had left.[41]

Southern senators saw the Marshall nomination as great symbolic politics too. In the words of one of his biographers, Thurgood Marshall had become "Public Enemy No. 1 in the South" because he had felled so many laws championing segregation. When JFK made Marshall the second African American ever on the Circuit Court of Appeals by recess appointment in 1961, Senate Judiciary Committee Chair James Eastland of Mississippi, whose father had lynched two African Americans without punishment, traded a promise to the administration not to block the nomination when it came before the committee for a district court judgeship for his arch-segregationist college roommate. But Eastland still made sure Marshall was put through his paces. As was customary then, the Senate Judiciary Committee Chairman, who had himself received scores of appeals against the appointment of what one correspondent termed "that radical, race-baiting, white-man hating, discriminatory rabble rouser, Thurgood Marshall," referred the nomination for evaluation to a subcommittee. To Marshall's misfortune, Eastland made Senator Olin Johnston of South Carolina its head.[42]

Although not one witness appeared to challenge the nomination and other Senate Judiciary Committee members and senators outside the committee loudly objected to the delay, the subcommittee stalled action on the nomination for nearly a year. During that period, it investigated baseless assertions, later repeated by Southerners on the Senate floor, that as the head of the NAACP Legal Defense Fund (LDF), which had its headquarters in Manhattan, Marshall should have taken the New York Bar Association exam. He had supposedly acted unethically by manipulating the history of the Fourteenth Amendment to suggest that its framers intended to outlaw school segregation in his *Brown v. Board of Education* brief. He had allegedly behaved illegally in Texas by soliciting clients and financing their litigation. He reportedly possessed ties to communist organizations and hostility toward whites. In fact, Marshall, a member of the Maryland bar, legitimately practiced law in the federal courts. Lawyers, judges, and Supreme Court justices routinely massaged history to suit their arguments. Marshall had not been personally involved in the Texas litigation and the lawyer whose behavior was at issue there was not an LDF employee. And as a Cold War liberal, he had always vigorously advocated anticommunism and interracial nonviolence. The investigation of William Hastie, the first African American named to the Circuit Court of Appeals, had proven brutal too as senators interrogated Hastie for three days about his connections to alleged communist-front organizations, but at least no one accused Hastie of bad lawyering. Ultimately, the Senate approved Marshall by fifty-four to sixteen, with only Southern Democrats in opposition.[43]

Senator Johnston had died by the time LBJ nominated Marshall to the court in 1967. When a student at work on a paper about the late senator's attitudes toward race reported that Gladys Johnston had told him that "the Senator was very much an admirer of yours and would 'certainly' have voted for your confirmation," Marshall fairly hooted. "As to Mrs. Johnston's statement that Senator Johnston would certainly have voted for my confirmation, she must have meant my last confirmation. In my original appointment to the Court of Appeals for the Second Circuit, Senator Johnston single-handedly held up my nomination for some eleven months and then spoke against it, and voted against it."[44]

Just as Mrs. Johnston was trying to reshape her husband's image by the time LBJ named Marshall to the court, so living Southern senators were conscious of theirs. In the five years that elapsed between Marshall's appointment to the Circuit Court of Appeals and to the Supreme Court, racism had become less respectable. That was one reason that the Senate Judiciary Committee and the full Senate had approved Marshall so readily in 1965. (Possibly, a threat by LBJ to withdraw his full support from a federal judgeship for Governor James Coleman of Mississippi—a moderate by Mississippi standards, but still a segregationist—if the Senate did not confirm Marshall as solicitor general also helped.) Certainly, bigotry had not disappeared in the United States by 1967. "Naming Marshall, Or Any Negro to Supreme Court Is a Dirty Shame," Georgia's *Augusta-Courier* headline read. "Please sir," one white Arkansas family implored Senator McClellan the day after the nomination was announced, "no nigger on the Supreme Court bench—with looting & burning, & riots, all over the country, and Mr. Johnson conscious only of votes, again please don't confirm. So many feel as we do here." Yet just as many white Southerners insisted to their senators that though Johnson might have appointed Marshall because he was a Negro, they did not oppose him for that reason.[45]

Southern segregationists had become history's losers. As Brad Snyder explained, *Brown v. Board of Education* was well on its way toward canonization. Southerners would not even allude to *Brown* when they faced off against Marshall. Although the hearing "was laden with thinly disguised racism," Paul Collins and Lori Ringhand emphasized, "opponents dared not criticize the case directly, even with its primary architect sitting in front of them."[46]

Like Lyndon Johnson, Southern Democrats could feel the terrain shifting underneath their feet. African Americans in the South would wryly observe that the Voting Rights Act of 1965, which effectively gave them the franchise, would ultimately change Southern politicians from segregationist demagogues to celebrants of their "black brothers and sisters." That transformation had not yet occurred, and the legislation also increased pressure on Democratic lawmakers to reassure white constituents that they supported the Southern "way of life." Signs of change, however, appeared everywhere. Significantly, the percentage of African Americans registered to vote in the Deep South nearly doubled within a year of the passage of the Voting Rights Act, rising to 46%. In South Carolina, Senator Ernest "Fritz" Hollings, a Democrat, won 97% of the black vote in 1966. Given the racism of Strom Thurmond Republicans, Hollings said, "the Negro has no place to go but the Democratic Party." By grounding his vote against Marshall on his antipathy to the Warren Court and its alleged overprotection of criminals, Hollings demonstrated his mastery of dog-whistle politics. His coded language sent a message to white voters and enabled him to retain his appeal for black ones.[47]

Irrespective of the changing composition of their region's voters, Southern senators knew that they fought a losing battle in opposing Thurgood Marshall's appointment to the Supreme Court. That LBJ had outfoxed them seemed clear when they initially responded to the nomination with "silence." Southerners felt beleaguered. Any strategy they developed, they acknowledged, had little promise, because, Senator Herman Talmadge of Georgia told a constituent, "the liberal majority" always overwhelmed "the small bloc of Southern Senators" who contended that "we should have Judges on the Supreme Court bench who will interpret the Constitution as it is written, and not in accordance with their own sociological philosophy." Southerners were alone and, reporters believed, would just go through the motions of assailing the nomination simply to win favorable press at home. A Supreme Court nomination was still considered the stuff of presidential prerogative. Though he had less power than he had between 1963 and 1966, LBJ remained a force. Senators expected him to run for reelection in 1968, and they feared him. Finally, liberal Democrats and all Republicans, with the very obvious exception of Senate Judiciary Committee member Strom Thurmond of South Carolina, were backing Marshall.[48]

In this tough political environment, Southerners on the Senate Judiciary Committee played the long game. The group numbered among its members three Democrats. Committee Chairman James Eastland of Mississippi had become notorious for his "black is red" claims that communists controlled the civil rights movement. Eastland had heretofore focused on challenging presidents' nominations to the lower courts and mostly swallowed their choices for the Supreme Court. John McClellan of Arkansas decried both the civil rights movement and the breakdown of law and order with righteous fury. Sam Ervin of North Carolina, segregation's leading constitutional theorist, had declared on the Senate floor that white Anglo-Saxon Protestants were "the people who made America great." The group also included Thurmond, who had astonished politicians in 1964 by switching parties and declaring himself a "Goldwater Republican," and who was at once "one of the last of the Jim Crow demagogues" and "one of the first of the post–World War II Sunbelt conservatives."[49]

An internal evaluation of Marshall's court of appeals record by a Senate staffer for Ervin and McClellan struck a tone of resigned acceptance and intimated that the nominee might have proven worse. It acknowledged that Marshall did not always favor the criminal, but predicted that "he may aline [sic] himself with the more liberal Justices on the Court, liberal in the sense that they do not readily adhere to precedents. . . . To sum up, he is a 'liberal,' but to the right of Douglas, probably somewhere between Black and Brennan. He is not as dumb as Warren, but he is not as smart as most of the rest."[50]

It was that contempt for the Warren Court majority, rather than Marshall's race or background as a civil rights lawyer, that Marshall's Senate Judiciary Committee opponents decided to showcase. Southern segregationists had long celebrated their states' own low crime rates and contended that "the black freedom struggle encouraged lawlessness." Now white supremacy morphed into disdain for the Warren Court and enthusiasm for "law and order," though the transformation preserved the underlying racism. Demagoguery was supposed to be out; constitutionalism, in. "I have gone into his background on previous occasions when he was appointed to a position that required Senate confirmation," Thurmond said privately of Marshall, and the Senate had nonetheless approved him. "This time I am concentrating my efforts on his views on particular issues concerning constitutional interpretation."[51]

While acknowledging "that appointments to the Supreme Court are entirely within the prerogative of the President of the United States," Thurmond had sent LBJ a personal and confidential letter as soon as Tom Clark's retirement was announced making "a friendly suggestion" that the president should name someone with prior judicial experience to the court. Now, as others in the Senate praised Marshall's selection and added newspaper stories lauding the nomination to the *Congressional Record*, Thurmond became the only senator to oppose it publicly before the hearing. He placed into the *Record* an editorial declaring that *Walker v. Birmingham* would have come out differently had Marshall been a justice, instead of Tom Clark. He maintained that if Marshall won confirmation, the court would become "decidedly more liberal." He complained to constituents that "the liberal viewpoint" often prevailed on the court in five-to-four decisions. "The Justice that Marshall is being named to replace is usually found voting with the 4," and Thurmond feared "that the appointment of Marshall will make the future line-up be 6 to 3. This means that it will require two conservative appointments before Court decisions will reflect a true adherence to both the letter and the spirit of the Constitution" and was, according to Thurmond, reason to oppose Senate confirmation. The solution lay in the appointment of justices "who are more aware of the original intent of the Constitution."[52]

Bogeyman

The Marshall nomination thus became the first instance since *Brown,* the midwife of the modern confirmation process, in which opponents justified their unusually close scrutiny of the nominee with allegations that he would change the balance of power on the court. Further, though Senate Judiciary Committee members had sometimes quizzed recent nominees—most notably, Stewart and Goldberg—about whether the Constitution and its amendments still meant what they did at the time of their adoption, "original intention" now became a desideratum of constitutional interpretation for Marshall's opponents.

Goldberg had characterized himself as an "activist" at his court confirmation hearing. Ervin grafted the word "judicial" on to "activist" and "activism" in Marshall's. Those phrases, "judicial activist" and "judicial activism," had been around since the late 1940s, when Arthur Schlesinger Jr. popularized them as descriptive terms, but had proven insignificant in earlier confirmation hearings. They now emerged as epithets for decrying the Warren Court's politicization of justice and describing those who were allegedly destroying constitutional government. Ervin told constituents that he was opposing the Marshall nomination solely "because I felt that at this time in our nation's history, we could ill afford the addition of another activist to the Supreme Court."[53]

His Southern colleagues jumped on that bandwagon. As a result, Supreme Court Senate scrutiny of nominees often became more intense and partisan. Nominees who had been approved by voice vote as recently as 1965 now faced roll-call votes that required senators to stand up and be counted. Nomination hearings became longer, and sometimes more substantive and confrontational, as participants used them to mobilize public opinion. Most recent hearings had ended in a few hours. Marshall's consumed five days. He made no opening statement and his two home-state senators, Robert Kennedy and Jacob Javits, had barely finished proudly introducing him before the hostilities began.[54]

The first to question Marshall at the hearing was John McClellan. When one constituent privately accused the senator of racism, McClellan refuted the charge by saying that he preferred Marshall to "one or two . . . white men" who were sitting justices. "It is my belief that a majority of the Supreme Court has gone so far astray in their interpretation and application of the constitution, in some of their recent decisions, that they have favored the criminal to the injury of society and have contributed to lawlessness in our country." LBJ should have nominated someone "more conservative." That was the point McClellan publicly made repeatedly. His questions did not relate to Marshall's "legal ability or training or character," or race, he insisted. Nor were they meant to trick him. Rather, they went to the nominee's "philosophy. I have made mistakes in the past . . . by not inquiring further and deeper. But the time has come when I can no longer be silent and not inquire into the philosophy of those who are nominated to this high position."[55]

Did Marshall agree with him that the rising level of crime had "reached proportions where it endangers or jeopardizes the internal security of our country"? (figure 12). McClellan wanted to know. Marshall answered that the crime rate "alarmed" him even as he stressed that whatever the government did about it

2/22/67   "HEY! I JUST KILLED 24 PEOPLE—AND YOU GOT THAT CONFESSION
WITHOUT ADVISING ME OF MY RIGHTS!"

Figure 12 Not everyone approved of the Warren Court's rights revolution. Pat Oliphant cartoon, February 22, 1967. Oliphant copyright ©1967. Reprinted with permission of UNIVERSAL UCLICK. All rights reserved.

had to be constitutional. Of course, McClellan responded, "but we have differences of opinion as to what the Constitution says and means," and now that "5-4 decisions" handcuffing the police had become the norm, "one man's decision often determines what the Constitution is." McClellan interrogated the nominee for nearly an hour about his views on confessions and whether he agreed with the majority in *Miranda*. According to the senator, Marshall could properly provide his views on *Miranda*, "a case that is history." The "ruffled" nominee pointed out that in every confirmation hearing "I have ever read about, it has been considered and recognized as improper for a nominee to a judgeship to comment on cases that he will have to pass upon" and repeatedly "respectfully" refused to answer because there were so many cases before the court involving "variations of the so-called *Miranda* rule." Fred Graham reported that the "thrust-and-parry continued for almost an hour, with both men unyielding and unsmiling, but with only one flash of emotion." That came when McClellan finally quit. "I have to wonder from your refusal to answer," he said in his parting shot, if Marshall did agree with the Warren Court majority. "Well, that is up to you, sir," the nominee angrily replied. "But I have never been dishonest in my life."[56]

McClellan had drawn some blood, but he barely injured Marshall. By day's end, five of the ten Senate Judiciary Committee members present had indicated that they would support the nomination. A sixth, Everett Dirksen, had publicly praised it. Reporters were predicting that a "the committee vote will favor him by a comfortable margin."[57]

That it did, but Marshall's antagonists saw the value of winning by losing and of going down in flames on a national stage. On the second and third days of the hearing, Ervin interrogated Marshall about constitutional interpretation, civil rights, and criminal law. Ervin had sought to insulate himself from charges of racism by assuring reporters he would have voted for the confirmation of William Hastie to the court. Now he set out to prove Marshall's jurisprudence dangerous. "Is not the role of the Supreme Court simply to ascertain and give effect to the intent of the framers of the Constitution and the people who ratified the Constitution?" Ervin suggested. "Yes," Marshall replied, "with the understanding that the Constitution was meant to be a living document." That answer irritated Ervin. "I am always intrigued by this statement that the Constitution is a living document and, therefore, must change," he commented acidly. It just meant that "the Constitution is dead and we are ruled by the personal notions of the temporary occupants of the Supreme Court." Ervin, in turn, aggravated Marshall. Repeatedly, the nominee stressed that a judge or justice "should never . . . use his personal feeling in any fashion in deciding or writing an opinion" and that he did not "not agree with your constantly referring to the Judges' personal views."[58]

Ervin also devoted an hour on the second day to trying unsuccessfully to persuade Marshall to answer questions about the court's criminal confession decisions, especially *Miranda*. Marshall continued to say, accurately, that he was simply following the practice of previous nominees before the committee. The senator, however, disingenuously insisted that Stewart and Goldberg had answered "questions fully and freely about their constitutional and judicial philosophy" and complained that Marshall's reluctance to speak made the hearings "absolutely useless." Yet when Marshall's supporters, Senators Ted Kennedy of Massachusetts and Philip Hart of Michigan, suggested that the committee could infer the nominee's judicial philosophy from his opinions as Second Circuit judge and his briefs as solicitor general, Ervin responded that committee members lacked the time to read them and complained that some of the nominee's opinions went on for more than fifteen pages.[59]

The following day, however, while attacking the Warren Court's recent Sixth Amendment decisions that "invented" a right to counsel for suspects in police lineups, Ervin turned to an opinion by Judge Henry Friendly that Judge Marshall had joined during his tenure on the Second Circuit. It held that eyewitness identification of a suspected murderer who had not been informed of his right to have counsel present violated the Sixth Amendment's guarantee of fair trial. Although a majority of the Supreme Court had subsequently limited the impact of the decision by making it nonretroactive, Ervin still did not like the new rule. "Do you know as a matter of fact that from time immemorial, . . . eye-witnesses have been permitted to look at the accused for the purposes of iden-tification in the absence of counsel?" he queried. Marshall conceded that was true. "So that Judge Friendly and you, in effect, wrote into the sixth amendment something that nobody had even suspected was there before," Ervin said. "We did not write anything into the sixth amendment," Marshall rebuked him. "We applied the law of the land, which was at that time that when a man reached the stage of arraignment, he was entitled to a lawyer." Predictably, that answer did not satisfy the senator, who then critiqued the court's decisions upholding the Voting Rights Act. That was "the first time," Fred Graham reported, that "the questioning touched on a racial issue, even though only Southern members of the committee have fired hostile questions at Marshall, who is the first Negro to be named to the Supreme Court."[60]

First time, but not the last. On day four, Senate Judiciary Committee Chairman Eastland wanted to know if Marshall was "prejudiced against white people in the South" and whether "if you are approved, you will give people in that area of the country and the States in that area of the country the same fair and square treatment that you give people in other areas of the country." After Marshall, of course, responded that he was not and he would, Senator Thurmond tried to ex-pose him as an ignoramus.[61]

"Judge Marshall, in view of the fact that your law practice for the many years, before you came with the Federal Government, was concerned with the 13th and 14th amendments, primarily, I would like to ask you some questions in your area of expertise," Thurmond drawled. The senator then addressed some sixty detailed questions to Marshall about the legislative history of the amendments, including what committee had reported out the Fourteenth Amendment and who belonged to it? Why had "the framers of the original version of the first section of the 14th amendment added the necessary and proper clause from article I, section 8, to the privileges and immunities clause of article IV, sec-tion 2"? What was their purpose in alluding to "the incident involving former Representative Samuel Hoar in Charleston, S.C., in December 1844, as show-ing the need for the enactment of the original version of the 14th amendment's first section"? And what was their reason for contending that if the Constitution of 1787 had included a privileges and immunities clause, the Civil War would not have happened? Marshall could not answer most of the queries, and some of his champions on the Senate Judiciary Committee clearly doubted whether Thurmond could either.[62]

One of them sought to undercut Thurmond and his colleagues with a line of reasoning that would become the refuge of presidential supporters of Supreme Court nominees. Ted Kennedy expressed the prevailing view of the "advise and consent" function of the Senate when he claimed it was limited to ascertaining "the qualifications and the training and the experience and the judgment of a nominee, and . . . it is not our responsibility to test out the nominee's particular philosophy, whether we agree or disagree, but his own good judgment." Ervin, however, insisted that in addition to evaluating a nominee's knowledge of law and legal experience, a senator had "to determine whether he is able and willing to exercise that judicial self-restraint which is implicit in the judicial process." Senator Joseph Tydings of Maryland, a Democrat who supported Marshall, now remarked pointedly that the nominee's "performance" before the committee provided "a great testimony to his judicial restraint."[63]

Thus far, no one had mentioned Marshall's position on the Cold War. Eastland got there on the fourth day. He followed Thurmond's constitutional history interrogation with a question about why Judge Marshall had cited historian Herbert Aptheker's *A Documentary History of the Negro People in the United States* in an opinion. "I don't want to leave the impression that you have ever been a Communist or anything like that," Eastland continued, but had Marshall known that Aptheker was "an avowed Communist and was the leading Communist theoretician in the United States"? Marshall responded that he "positively did not" and would not have cited the book if he had. (The nominee's anticommunism was not nearly as remarkable as his apparent ignorance of Aptheker, a distinguished Marxist historian who was almost as well known a Communist intellectual as Eastland suggested.)[64]

Then Eastland called on the general counsel of the right-wing Liberty Lobby, the only person other than Marshall to testify in open session. That attorney resurrected old claims from Marshall's appellate judgeship confirmation hearing that he had behaved unethically at the NAACP. He contended that Marshall's focus on civil rights made his experience too "narrow" for the court. He also alleged that Marshall had associated with "subversive" organizations and possessed "a record of duplicity and arrogance unparalleled by that of any nominee to high judicial office in recent times."[65]

At this point, the Judiciary Committee adjourned for the weekend. Most believed that Southern senators had helped Marshall by hurting him. If Thurmond wanted to make Marshall "look bad you could have done so in a better and less self-incriminating matter," one South Carolinian complained. "You certainly left no one with the opinion that you were conducting an objective inquiry. It does not make you or our state look good" and just provided ammunition to those who considered Thurmond and Southerners bigoted. *Time* predicted that Southerners' "Yahoo-type" tactics just guaranteed Marshall a strong vote in the Senate. Southerners on the committee who taunted him did so only because of his race, the *New York Times* fumed. They had asked Marshall the same kind of "farfetched questions" that county registrars had dredged up to deny African

Americans the vote before the civil rights legislation of the 1960s discouraged such "literacy" tests. "This performance for the benefit of the rednecks back home exposes the vitriol of the Senators, not the knowledge of Mr. Marshall." It would not halt his confirmation and made "a farce of the Judiciary Committee." The *Washington Post* editorialized that "the essential absurdity of Strom Thurmond subjecting Thurgood Marshall to a quiz on constitutional law . . . puts one in mind, somewhat of a Pekingese baiting a lion." Yet the "buffoonery" was no laughing matter because Thurmond's "grossly improper" intention in his "mischievous inquisition," like that of Eastland, McClellan, and Ervin in theirs, was to learn how Justice Marshall would decide cases, and it was inappropriate for the nominee to tell them. "This hazing of a nominee to the country's highest tribunal at the hands of a Southern coterie whose bias is transparent has been allowed to go on for much too long."[66]

But the hazing continued when the hearings resumed on Monday. McClellan wanted to discuss the constitutionality of wiretapping, and Marshall feinted. "Of course the nominee can say that he doesn't know what he will do until the time comes, but I have got to act before that time comes," the senator exploded. At the very moment of "a crime crisis" in the country, the majority of the court was coddling criminals. The "riots everywhere"—most recently, in Detroit, beginning the day before—showed that some Americans believed that they could violate laws that they disliked. When the majority of the court reversed its positions on age-old constitutional issues "at its whim," the man on the street reasonably decided "that, if the Supreme Court has no regard for precedent in law, and change it when it wants to, why can't I do as I please?" Ervin complained that a Supreme Court justice possessed more power than the chief executive. Though Congress and the Supreme Court could chasten the president, there was "no power on earth that can restrain a Supreme Court Justice in an effective manner except his own self-restraint." Thurmond pressed Marshall on whether Congress could limit the court's appellate jurisdiction and impeach a Supreme Court justice who "blatantly violates the Constitution." On that ominous note, the hearings ended.[67]

For Marshall, significantly, they had been a cakewalk, compared to the hearings to put him on the Second Circuit. "Supreme Court wasn't too bad," he remembered. As he saw it, only an unrepentant Thurmond who trumpeted the nominee's "surprising" ignorance "of the area in which he is almost daily depicted as the outstanding scholar" had posed a threat. His other opponents "just made little statements for the record." Senate Minority Leader Dirksen agreed that the hearing just revealed "little biases," not "substantial opposition." Though they marked the moment at which the appointments process began to change, they had barely bruised the nominee.[68]

"Shining Hour"

Southerners on the Senate Judiciary Committee, of course, continued to deny that prejudice motivated them as they considered whether to report out the nomination. Sam Ervin, who wrote the committee's minority report recommending against confirmation that McClellan, Eastland, and Thurmond all joined, insisted that he acted out of "love" for the Constitution, "with all my mind and all my heart." Marshall, Ervin maintained, was a "constitutional iconoclast" who would align himself with the activists on the court "who seek to rewrite the Constitution in their own images" and who had recently "overruled, repudiated, or ignored" so many precedents, particularly in the field of criminal law. He would oppose Marshall's confirmation lest Americans "be ruled by the arbitrary notions of Supreme Court Justices rather than by the precepts of the Constitution."[69]

Eleven members of the Senate Judiciary Committee lionized Marshall in a report recommending his confirmation submitted by the Michigan Democrat, Philip Hart. For the majority, the nominee was no "constitutional iconoclast" but "perfectly prepared" to join the court. He deserved confirmation "because he is an outstanding lawyer, judge and Solicitor General, not because he is a Negro; but we cannot ignore the fact of his race." His success symbolized the nation's progress in its march toward racial equality at the same time that it underscored "how far we have to go." With an enthusiasm that might have bewildered a later generation focused on the original intention of the Constitution's framers, the majority hailed Marshall's vision of the Constitution as "a living document." It saluted his wisdom in refusing to answer questions about issues that might come before the court. His past close identification with the NAACP no more disqualified him for the judiciary than prior corporate connections rendered other nominees unfit, especially since the NAACP had enabled him to prove and hone his gifts as a lawyer. "The Senate will do itself honor, the Court will be graced, and the Nation benefited by our confirmation of this nominee."[70]

That was the view most senators also articulated. As Ervin, Eastland, Thurmond, and McClellan rehashed their complaints about Marshall on the Senate floor during a six-hour debate over his nomination that one reporter deemed "largely lackluster," they attracted few supporters. In the end, the Senate confirmed Marshall just before Labor Day by sixty-nine to eleven in its first roll-call vote on a Supreme Court nomination since Potter Stewart's. All of Marshall's opponents except Senator Robert Byrd of West Virginia hailed from the Deep South. The GOP remained the party of Lincoln: Except for Thurmond, every one of the thirty-two Republican senators present voted for Marshall. Thirty-seven Democrats did too, including some Southerners—J. William Fulbright of

Arkansas, Al Gore of Tennessee, Ralph Yarborough of Texas, and William Spong of Virginia. The record indicated that of the twenty absent senators, an additional eight would have supported confirmation had they been there, while another four Southern Democrats (John McClellan of Arkansas, Richard Russell of Georgia, George Smathers of Florida, and John Stennis of Mississippi) would have voted no. In her history of the confirmation, Linda Greene stressed that "while the official vote was 69-11, according to the record, eighty-one senators favored the confirmation and fifteen opposed the nomination." And where the Senate had held up Marshall's Second Circuit nomination in 1962 for eleven months, it approved his Supreme Court nomination in just seventy-eight days. Marshall had to wait much longer than most recent nominees for confirmation, but progress had occurred. Senate Majority Leader Mike Mansfield, who celebrated the Senate's action as a "shining hour" for Marshall and the country, agreed. "We have come a long, long way toward equal access to the Constitution's promise."[71]

Doubtless, LBJ had something to do with Marshall's lopsided margin of victory. "Well, congratulations," Marshall recalled the president telephoning to say after the Senate's confirmation, "but the hell you caused me, goddamnit, I never went through so much hell." (Johnson later told Marshall that he lost more support because of the nomination than because of the Vietnam War.) Marshall reminded the president that the appointment had been Johnson's idea. Oddly, LBJ did not tape that phone conversation or any others related to Marshall after he announced the nomination. And the documentary record in the Johnson Library is silent about arm-twisting the president did—which, of course, does not mean he did not do it. Nor did he issue a statement praising Marshall's confirmation, though LBJ joined the audience when Justice Hugo Black swore in Marshall at the Supreme Court as its first African American justice[72] (figure 13).

Whether the Senate's support for Marshall indicated backing for the Warren Court also remained unclear. Marshall's antagonists in the Senate debate repeatedly said that a vote for him would strengthen the Warren Court majority. But just two of his advocates even addressed that issue, and neither sounded altogether confident that the Senate approved of that majority. Jacob Javits pointed out that the Court "does something to a man" and predicted that Marshall would startle skeptics. He also observed that time and again, when Congress confronted unpopular decisions by the court and had to decide whether to "reverse the Supreme Court by legislative action we have not done so—or, at least, we have very rarely done so." To Javits, that history suggested congressional respect for the court. Philip Hart, the Democratic floor manager for the Marshall forces, agreed that justices often behaved surprisingly and that Congress valued the court. "It is easy to react pretty violently when we read in the headlines that the Supreme Court has outlawed prayer; but we have seen the dust settle on that issue, and the position taken by the Court is now, I think, generally regarded by

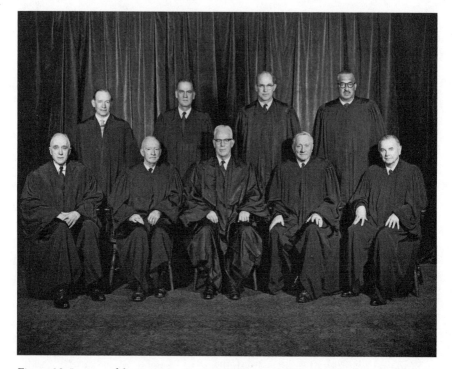

Figure 13 Justices of the Supreme Court, 1967. Seated, left to right: John Harlan, Hugo Black, Earl Warren, William O. Douglas, and William Brennan. Standing, left to right: Abe Fortas, Potter Stewart, Byron White, and Thurgood Marshall. Supreme Court of the United States.

the majority of us as sound, and we are delighted that the Court undertook the heat that it was subjected to in that period."[73]

Journalists who covered the court shared Javits's and Hart's uncertainty about the Senate's attitude toward it. Fred Graham hypothesized in the *New York Times* that "the strong vote for Mr. Marshall seemed to confirm what Court observers had suspected for the past couple of years—that informed public opinion has come to accept the Supreme Court's activism and that many political leaders have concluded that it is a good thing." In contrast to the anger over the court's position on *Brown* and school prayer, "the relatively mild reaction" in 1966 to *Miranda* suggested "that the nation had become markedly inured to thunderbolts from the Supreme Court, and the Marshall vote added weight to that proposition." The Marshall vote could mean that senators and much of the public who picked them really approved of the court's work in crime and civil rights. Other reporters, however, disagreed. "The Supreme Court as an institution was the biggest target in the wordy Senate proceedings that culminated in the confirmation of Thurgood Marshall," John MacKenzie claimed in the *Washington*

Post. Why else had so few stepped up to defend the court in the Senate? It was not hard to find liberals who decried the way racist Southerners talked about the court but who secretly wrung their hands at the justices' eagerness to wade into political thickets. Ron Ostrow of the *Los Angeles Times* agreed that Thurgood Marshall had become the scapegoat for the court and maintained that although those white Southerners who opposed racial equality understood that they had lost the "battle over equal rights for the Negro," they realized they could win a national majority by decrying crime and criminals' rights.[74]

The last claim came closest to the mark. Marshall's race and extraordinary life helped him in the Senate. So did his sparse judicial record which made it impossible for his antagonists to say for certain that he would become the "activist" he did. But some white Southerners obviously realized the political potential of crime and their racialization of it. So, increasingly, did Republicans.

"Things Fall Apart"

If LBJ felt beset when he nominated Thurgood Marshall to the Supreme Court, he felt absolutely beleaguered by the end of 1967. The president who plunged so joyfully into crowds and won election by the largest popular vote in American history in 1964 now dodged hecklers by making his speeches on military bases or in front of small, carefully chosen groups. Reporters and antagonists delighted in exposing Johnson's "credibility gap," or lies. Then there was LBJ's propensity for hammering out backroom deals rather than making his case effectively to the American people. Then there were the issues. The Right made political hay with riots, crime, inflation, the balance-of-payments deficit, and Johnson's attempt to fund both the war on poverty and the Vietnam War. In massive demonstrations, those to Johnson's left shouted that the United States should negotiate a settlement or simply withdraw from Vietnam.[75]

At the same time, the war exposed LBJ's problems in leading and in communicating his vision. At a White House meeting with the press, he was asked why the United States had not stopped bombing North Vietnam. For the next fifteen minutes, *New York Times* reporter Max Frankel recounted, Johnson transformed himself into Saint Francis of Assisi as he poured out "a passionate confession of his yearning for peace and a vivid account of the diligence of his search." The performance lasted until one questioner pointed out the obvious. If LBJ accurately described the situation, perhaps the Right correctly charged that he was not hitting the enemy hard enough. "And suddenly, as if in full regalia, there stood the Commander in Chief ticking off the target lists, the clipped statistics of damage done and the promise of the further pressures planned." Small wonder that LBJ's detractors concluded he just sought to be everything to everyone.

In fact, conservatives outside the Democrats had become disenchanted with "Everyman's President" long ago.[76]

Disillusionment proved even stronger, perhaps, among former sympathizers. Johnson's support for civil rights and Great Society legislation alienated Southern Democrats and working-class whites. The Left, which once had been sure that student protesters could awaken "a sleeping liberal wing of the Democratic Party" and had applauded the Great Society, now denounced "corporate liberalism" and branded the president a war criminal. And because of the war, many liberal Democrats no longer had any use for LBJ either.[77]

In October of 1967, the same month that Johnson saw Marshall sworn in as a justice, some fifty thousand diverse individuals—suburbanites and students, black nationalists and Americans for Democratic Action, lefties and flower children—gathered at the Lincoln Memorial. There they heard the pacifist pediatrician, Benjamin Spock, declare that the enemy "is Lyndon Johnson, whom we elected as a peace candidate in 1964, and who betrayed us within three months, who has stubbornly led us deeper and deeper into a bloody quagmire in which uncounted hundreds of thousands of Vietnamese, men, women and children have died, and 13,000 young Americans too." At least twenty thousand in the crowd then tried to storm the Pentagon and twice breached the lines of twenty-five hundred troops and US marshals surrounding it. Everyone in Washington took notice, including Johnson, who was by now importuning the FBI and CIA to spy on the Left. The president directed his driver to take him around the Memorial and Pentagon on his way home from church so that he could see "what a hippie looked like."[78]

In November, Adlai Stevenson's intellectual heir, Senator Eugene McCarthy of Minnesota, launched his acerbic, witty, and quixotic quest to wrest the Democratic presidential nomination from Johnson. Administration advocates of a negotiated settlement or withdrawal from Vietnam began jumping and being pushed from the ship of state. At Thanksgiving, the White House announced that Secretary of Defense Robert McNamara, who had developed doubts about the war, would leave the Pentagon in early 1968 to become head of the World Bank. "I do not know to this day whether I quit or was fired," McNamara acknowledged decades later, though at the time, he and the White House labored hard and unpersuasively to deny that differences between him and the president accounted for his departure.[79]

Vietnam divided Johnson and Arthur Goldberg too. Moreover, the fellowship between the two had evaporated once Goldberg realized that Johnson was using him as window dressing. He had entered government "full of himself, as always, and full too of a cocksure assurance that he would succeed where Stevenson had failed—that he would not allow himself to be pushed aside and reduced to impotence," Arthur Schlesinger observed. But Goldberg had not succeeded, and the president soon tired of his garrulousness, leaking, and threats to resign. The United Nations ambassadorship that Goldberg held carried cabinet rank, and at a press conference during the first week of December, a reporter asked the president if other changes in the cabinet could be expected. "No," LBJ replied. "I know that 'some kids' have been calling around some of your bureaus predicting that and planning it and these same boys from time to time set up straw men and then knock them down," he added in an obvious jab at Senators Robert and Ted Kennedy.[80]

Two days later, Johnson met with his ambassador. "I want you to do whatever you and Dorothy want to do," LBJ now stressed. "The easiest thing for me to do is accept your resignation and the hardest thing is to read in the press about your wanting to leave." Goldberg claimed that he no longer considered the United Nations job "effective," that the president had supported him "100%" with respect to the United Nations, and that he understood that LBJ had "other advisers for other subjects, such as Vietnam." Johnson pretended not to understand that Goldberg was chastising him: "You're not going to build a case here today about differences on Vietnam because there have not been any differences." The two men agreed that Goldberg probably would leave in the winter. Ultimately, he stayed until April, when, as Johnson put it, he resigned for "the eighteenth time." A chilly public exchange of letters between him and the president heralded his departure.[81]

While Goldberg hesitated, LBJ experienced the most difficult seasons of his presidency yet. On January 23, North Koreans captured the U.S.S. *Pueblo* off their coast. They killed a member of its crew and accused the eighty-two remaining members whom they held for eleven months of violating their territorial waters and spying. Just over a week later, the North Vietnamese and Viet Cong launched the month-long Tet Offensive. Again and again, military leaders and politicians had assured the public that the enemy was in eclipse. Now, recalled Clark Clifford, who had finally succumbed to LBJ's pleas to join the administration and become secretary of defense, the "size and scope" of the Tet Offensive "made a mockery of what the American military told the public about the war and devastated Administration credibility." The shock of seeing the enemy nearly take the American Embassy in Saigon rendered Tet a psychological success and emboldened Robert Kennedy to launch his strongest condemnation yet of the administration's Vietnam policy. Like many, RFK believed that the White House and Pentagon lied when they claimed—accurately, as historians have shown—that Tet represented a military defeat for the North Vietnamese and Viet Cong. "The pressure grew so intense that at times I felt the government itself might come apart at the seams," Clifford remembered. "Leadership was fraying at its very center," and the nation approached "paralysis."[82]

Plenty of people stood ready to fill the leadership vacuum. February brought a declaration by the folksy former governor of Alabama, George Wallace, that he would become a third-party candidate and campaign for the presidency on a law-and-order platform. Wallace castigated Pentagon protesters as "scum of the universe," condemned pacifists as "bearded pseudo intellectuals," and complained that Earl Warren "hasn't enough [knowledge of] law to try a chicken thief." Obviously, he planned to deploy the demagoguery he had once reserved for civil rights activists against new targets. Chicago executives cheered Wallace after he complained that no one could be convicted of a crime any longer and announced, "If you walk out of here and are hit on the head, the criminal is out of jail before you are on your way to the hospital—or while the policeman is telling him his rights, he gets away."[83]

More dangerous for Democrats was Richard Nixon's long-anticipated announcement in March that he sought the Republican nomination and his proclamation that "the real crisis of America today" was "the crisis of the spirit." Nixon touted himself as the only one who could bring a "victorious peace" to Vietnam and unite a nation torn apart by divisions "between the races, between the generations, between the ideologies and between the advocates of lawful change and chaotic violence." The United States, he maintained, could not "afford four more years of Lyndon Johnson in the White House." While New York governor Nelson Rockefeller, Michigan governor George Romney, and California governor Ronald Reagan would also throw their hats into the Republican ring, Nixon became the front-runner.[84]

In March, Eugene McCarthy also upended American politics when he came just 230 votes short of besting the president in the New Hampshire primary. That pollsters showed that the vote was more "anti-Johnson" than antiwar provided the president little comfort. Then, sensing weakness, Robert Kennedy, who shared McCarthy's views about the war but had not endorsed him, validated the president's darkest fears at midmonth and entered the race for the Democratic nomination. He pledged to end LBJ's "disastrous, divisive policies" in Vietnam by "de-escalating" and to fight poverty and racial injustice at home. The Kennedy name and charisma pulled in working-class whites and machine politicians, and RFK electrified audiences on the campaign trail. More than McCarthy, he unified liberals and the Left—black, brown, and white. Intellectuals flocked to Kennedy's support, proving anew to Johnson that like Georgetown journalists, the "Harvards" hated him.[85]

Month's end brought the fateful meeting of the president's internal and external advisers arranged by Clifford, who himself had now turned against the war. Despite briefings that highlighted recent American successes in Vietnam, a majority of the "Wise Men" outnumbered a stunned LBJ and Fortas in urging the president to reject the military's request for more than two hundred thousand additional troops, and to stop the bombing of North Vietnam and negotiate a set-tlement. Then, the afternoon of March 31, Martin Luther King Jr. informed the media that he could not support the president's re-election. He also reaffirmed that thousands of "the tired, the poor, the huddled masses" in his Poor People's Campaign, which Robert Kennedy backed, would camp in Washington until the government had addressed their problems. Did Johnson conclude he could not win if he ran again? Or (and?) did he decide, as he said, that he had no chance of winning peace in Vietnam if he were also campaigning for another term?[86]

When the spent president addressed the nation that evening, he pledged to halt the bombing of the northernmost part of North Vietnam and implored Hanoi to join him in seeking peace. Then he stunned everyone by declaring that he would neither seek nor accept the Democratic nomination. Polls showed his instant popularity. At his first public appearance after the announcement, LBJ seemed puzzled by the audience's ovation. "Poor man," one White House official remarked, "he doesn't remember what a friendly crowd sounds like." Thus began the "happiest" time in his presidency.[87]

It ended abruptly on April 4, when a white extremist assassinated King in Memphis. Riots erupted throughout the country. Ten blocks from the White House, Washington was in flames, and looters rampaged through a department store less than three blocks away. The president ordered federal troops to occupy the capital and met with moderate civil rights leaders, Justice Marshall at his side. Predictably and inaccurately, LBJ blamed the violence on Stokely Carmichael, who had actually tried to keep the peace. (An inaccurate report that Carmichael was mobilizing his forces to burn down Georgetown provided a rare moment of levity. "Goddamn!" LBJ joked. "I've waited thirty-five years for this day!")[88]

In May, just one week after Vice President Hubert Humphrey had announced his own candidacy for the Democratic nomination by ebulliently and oddly embracing "the politics of joy," King's Poor People's Campaign erected Resurrection City, USA, in the shadow of the Lincoln Mall. Its organizers vowed that those who moved there would "plague the Pharaohs of this nation with plague after plague until they agree to give us meaningful jobs and a guaran-teed annual income." Days and days of rain turned the shantytown into a smelly, muddy mess beset by violence and internal strife. Journalists concluded that "King's last dream is turning into a nightmare" that alienated the public without awakening its conscience.[89]

These developments put the court in harm's way. Just before Memorial Day, four hundred residents of Resurrection City invaded the Supreme Court building. They were protesting a decision upholding the right of Washington State to pro-mote conservation by denying the Puyallup tribe special commercial fishing rights. They smashed five windows. After unsuccessfully demanding an interview with Warren or an associate justice, they settled for sending a delegation to decry injustices to the clerk of the court until they were "talked out"—about "broken treaties, lands taken away, deprivation of hunting and fishing rights, desecration of burial places, language restrictions, food supplies and poverty in general."[90]

Some on the Left now shared their discontent with the court. As demonstrators had shut down Columbia University and paralyzed numerous other campuses, most of the justices' tolerance for free expression beyond words was obviously waning. Fortas, for example, who publicly scorned Columbia students' actions as "totally inexcusable from the point of view of even primitive morality," was completing a pamphlet, *Concerning Dissent and Civil Disobedience*. He told one reporter that he had written it because he feared that professors and college students were fearful of being branded "White Uncle Toms" if they spoke out against lawless dissent. His "broadside," with its initial printing of two hundred and fifty thousand copies, insisted that civil disobedience was immoral, impolitic, and illegal when it involved violation of constitutional, valid laws just to dramatize disagreement and that the principle of selective conscientious objection that led some of the young to say they would take up arms against Hitler but not Ho Chi Minh was no good either.[91]

Centrists praised Fortas's pamphlet as "a signal contribution to our understanding of the crisis we are all involved in and to the possibility of its just and peaceful resolution," but the Left panned it. "Since anyone of dozens, if not hundreds, of law professors or their brighter students or a committee of some bar association might, if requested, have accomplished a comparable summary and simplification, it is a little difficult to understand fully why Justice Fortas undertook a task which involved the hazard of appearing to predict his own position on matters which were likely to come before the Court," jibed one young law professor. He speculated that Fortas had written this "intellectually squalid and morally banal" collection of "platitudes" and "pontifications" because he blamed "the decline of Lyndon Johnson" and public support for the war on student dissenters. Historian and activist Howard Zinn responded for the New Left and antiwar movement in a pamphlet that sold more than seventy thousand copies. "For the crisis of our time, the slow workings of American reform [and] the limitations on protest and disobedience set by liberals like Justice Fortas, are simply not adequate," Zinn maintained.[92]

The war of words occurred against the backdrop of the court's decision in *U.S. v. O'Brien*. In that case, handed down the same day the court issued its decision against Native Americans in *Puyallup*, Warren's opinion overturned a First Circuit decision that a law criminalizing the burning, destruction, or mutilation of draft cards abridged "symbolic speech" and consequently was unconstitutional. (Thurgood Marshall did not participate, and the lone dissenter, William O. Douglas, urged his brethren to decide the constitutionality of drafting the young to fight an undeclared war.) The ruling shocked David O'Brien, the appellant who had dramatized his disagreement with government policies by setting his draft card on fire in front of the South Boston Courthouse. "I think this shows that the Administration and the courts are moving toward an oppressive state which will not tolerate political dissent," he told reporters. Eleven women set thirteen draft cards afire on the steps of the court to protest the decision.[93]

The court also continued to roil the Right and the South. The same day the court handed down *Puyallup* and *O'Brien*, Justice Brennan announced *Green v. County School Board*. There the justices unanimously declared their impatience with the slow pace of desegregation, their unwillingness to permit school districts to camouflage continued segregation with "freedom of choice" plans through which students selected their own schools, and their insistence on stamping out racial discrimination in the schools "root and branch." Brennan's clerks cheered that "the mandate for movement is unmistakable." They rejoiced when they heard that the Justice Department's Civil Rights Division had to rework 125 complaints to prod integration of school districts "because the decision was far more forceful than they had anticipated." For the moment, Nixon left it to George Wallace to denounce integration. (By fall, the Republican candidate had heard an audience roar its approval as Wallace blasted the "completely insane" Supreme Court. The Alabamian was also insisting that as Eisenhower's vice president, Nixon had "agreed in advance" to the *Brown* decision that began "the destruction of the public school system." Now, the *New York Times* disapprovingly editorialized, candidate Nixon began talking out of both sides of his mouth and assuring white parents that *Brown* was correct, but "he was opposed to the Federal Government's doing anything effective to enforce the Supreme Court's school desegregation decision.")[94]

Crime, however, was too tempting a target for a Republican determined to play the statesman to ignore, particularly since a recent Gallup Poll suggested that 63% of Americans found American courts "too soft" on criminals. Nixon embraced the unusual strategy of making it crucial to his campaign. By May, the Senate was debating the Safe Streets Bill, which scholars and journalists alike portrayed as "one of the most dangerous assaults on the integrity of the federal judiciary in the nation's history." The Supreme Court's defenders managed to defeat potentially devastating provisions in the House version that would have stripped the federal courts of jurisdiction to review state court habeas corpus proceedings or any confession or lineup identification upheld by the state courts, where more than 95% of criminal cases originated.[95]

Still, anti–Warren Court sentiment ran high enough for the Senate to wound the court. It approved a section supported by candidate Nixon and Senators McClellan and Ervin that tried to overturn *Miranda* by deeming all voluntary confessions admissible in federal and DC courts. Another section the three endorsed, and that the Senate did too, attempted to overturn the court's 1967 decision in *U.S. v. Wade* that the absence of counsel in a criminal lineup after indictment violated the Sixth Amendment guarantee of fair trial. The Senate made all voluntary eyewitness identifications admissible in federal and DC courts. Still another that Nixon, McClellan, and Ervin applauded and that the Senate sanctioned purported to overturn the 1957 decision of *Mallory v. United States*, which had held that no delay should ordinarily occur between arrest and arraignment. It upheld the admissibility of any confession obtained within six hours of arrest in federal and DC courts. The Senate also angered the administration by approving a substantial expansion in the power of law enforcement officials to engage in bugging and wiretapping. The House agreed to the Senate version of the bill, and LBJ signed it. "Although critics of the Supreme Court won a few victories, their defeats were far more significant," the *Los Angeles Times* editorialized approvingly.[96]

Undaunted by a warning from one of his advisers that "any condemnation of the Court will be interpreted as fascist," Nixon gave a widely covered speech on Memorial Day taking aim at *Miranda* and other Warren Court decisions that gave a "green light" to criminals. That set the tone. He promised to appoint people to the court who believed in their mission to *interpret* the law that elected politicians enacted and the Constitution lay out, as well as those who would strengthen "the peace forces, as against the criminal forces."[97]

Like most of his fellow justices, Earl Warren was not immune from the panic over law and order. Like them, the chief received a stream of letters from intimates and strangers blaming the court for increased crime. "It is difficult for me to believe that one like yourself would think that after spending the twenty best years of my life in law enforcement that I would come to this Court for the purpose of destroying law enforcement," he reproved one old friend. On June 10, he may have tried to prove that when he announced the opinion of the court in *Terry v. Ohio*. There, all the justices but Douglas placed the court's seal of approval on the "stop and frisks" that many people of color considered racist as long as the police reasonably feared danger. "*Terry* was at least as significant a victory for the police as *Miranda* had been for the accused and seems a decision out of character for Warren and out of place at the supposed height of the Warren Court," concluded Scot Powe.[98]

But perhaps *Terry* was not so out of character. Perhaps decisions like *Mapp* and *Miranda* were not such victories for the accused. Like other policymakers, Supreme Court justices had to live with the unintended consequences of their actions. Perhaps, as William Stuntz contended in 2011, the Warren Court majority ultimately just increased the importance of defense attorneys, not all of whom were created equal, "by dramatically enlarging" the legal defenses that clever and often expensive lawyers had an incentive to mount for their clients.

It may be that the Warren Court majority's attempts to reduce the gulf between rich and poor defendants actually swelled it. Among other things, those efforts launched an army of overworked public defenders who relegated indigent clients, a disproportionate number of whom were black or brown, to "prison America" by prompting them to accept guilty pleas and concentrated on reducing the time they spent there, rather than obtaining acquittals. In focusing on regulating police behavior and criminal procedure rather than substantive criminal law, the Warren Court made criminal trials "more elaborate." Yet the rush toward plea bargaining ensured that trials became less frequent. Moreover, the court's focus on policing the police moved crime to the center of national politics and prompted legislators who competed for the "tough on crime" moniker to define crimes and sentences more punitively to cause mass incarceration of people of color and/or the poor. Small wonder, Michael Seidman has observed, that today many liberal legal scholars have climbed off the Warren Court's "criminal procedure bandwagon."[99]

Yet at the time, *Terry v. Ohio* looked like an anomalous attempt to keep the Warren Court's "criminal procedure revolution" in step with a white majority concerned about "law and order." By seemingly calling that revolution to a halt, *Terry* drew attention to the extent to which the Warren Court had politicized the judicial process by launching it. For their part, Brennan's clerks considered it a victory that their boss had been able to tone down the rhetoric in an opinion that had originally "read dangerously much like an apology for past decisions which have been charged with having overly restricted the police." Even after Brennan's ministrations, the lone dissenter in *Terry*, Douglas, alleged that the majority was succumbing to "hydraulic pressures . . . to water down constitutional guarantees and give the police the upper hand." The press, too, believed that the court wanted to show its responsiveness to public opinion.[100]

Though Warren might have wavered in *Terry*, he remained proud and protective of his colleagues' record in civil rights and criminal procedure. One week before the court handed down *Terry*, another assassin had murdered Robert Kennedy as he celebrated victory in the California presidential primary. That same night, the last progressive California Republican in the Earl Warren tradition, Senator Tom Kuchel, lost his re-election bid for the Republican Senate nomination. When Warren saw Kuchel, a protégé and friend, at Kennedy's funeral on June 8, the chief justice said, "I just feel so badly about your defeat, I can't talk about it." Like Kuchel's loss, Kennedy's murder filled the seventy-seven-year-old chief justice with foreboding. Warren did not believe his center would hold. He did not think Humphrey could win the election. The Chief Justice despised Nixon, and he wanted the work of the Warren Court continued. Fatefully, he asked Fortas to schedule a meeting for him with the president.[101]

4

"A Man's Reach Should [Not?] Exceed His Grasp"

Summer and Fall, 1968

On June 13, 1968, Warren met with LBJ at the White House for fifteen minutes. "He came down to say that because of age, he felt he should retire from the Court and he said he wanted President Johnson to appoint his successor, someone who felt as Warren did," recorded LBJ's appointments secretary. Johnson, who was preparing to sign the Safe Streets Act into law despite his doubts about its constitutionality and wisdom, shared Warren's sense of jeopardy. LBJ understood, Joe Califano later stressed, "that his Great Society legislation had stepped on many powerful economic and political interests that had the resources to continue to struggle in every available forum" and that "the contest would inevitably play out in the courts long after he left the White House."[1]

When the president optimistically decided that Warren's news might provide him with a way to win victory, he increased the court's significance for the political season. Because of its decisions, the court had become an election year issue before in the presidential campaigns of 1800, 1832, 1860, 1896, 1912, 1924, and 1936, and Nixon had already made it one in 1968. Now, appointments to the court—which were, of course, related to its decisions—would also take center stage in presidential campaigns.[2]

"There Was an Old Woman Who Lived in a Shoe"

Naturally, LBJ asked Warren what he thought about Fortas as his successor. Though the chief justice apparently preferred Brennan or Goldberg, he did not explicitly say so to the president. Like everyone at the court, Warren was well aware of Fortas's private telephone line to the White House and his closeness to

LBJ. The intimacy worried some of the other justices even as they remembered that members of the court had long advised presidents.[3]

Warren had assumed that Fortas would get the nod. "Abe would be a good chief justice," he told the president. According to LBJ, he intimated that he hoped the president would name Arthur Goldberg to take Fortas's place, something that Fortas may have secretly favored. Warren also presented the president with two letters. One declared his "intention to retire as Chief Justice of the United States effective at your pleasure," wording that dated back to 1902, when Justice Horace Gray had told Theodore Roosevelt of his intention to retire. As Warren subsequently explained to an inquiring scholar, he did not know when the president would announce a nomination and he did not want to leave the court without a chief justice if, as occasionally happened, it had to hold a special summer session. A second letter insisted that Warren was retiring "solely because of age."[4]

Though the two men had agreed to keep the news quiet for the moment, it leaked. When Malvina Stephenson, a reporter for Tulsa's KRMG News, attended a wedding at the University Club on June 22, she saw the chief justice in a phone booth there and resolved to ask his plans. "While I waited, all those revealing phrases from Warren began to float across the lobby into my ears," she recounted to her listeners. "He definitely is retiring, no doubt about that, and from all his chuckling he is very relieved to get out. The problem, from what I HEARD, is to get a suitable successor, which is to say, a liberal—not in the image of a Republican choice that might be dictated by a President Nixon and a Senate Republican Leader Dirksen." Her "scoop" showed that Washington was still a small town, but it was also old news. On June 14, the day after LBJ and Warren met, the "Washington Wire" of the *Wall Street Journal* reported that the chief justice had been telling friends he might resign. "Reason: He hopes to have a voice in selection of his successor, doubts Nixon would heed him. Insiders figure Johnson would like to promote Fortas to chief. Fortas is a Warren-type activist, but Warren might prefer Brennan."[5]

Senator Robert Griffin, a forty-four-year-old University of Michigan Law School alumnus, read the *Journal* item while he was flying from his Traverse City home back to Washington. "Casual, friendly, he looks far more like a mild-mannered accountant than the scrappy politician he is," one reporter said of Griffin, and he had long astounded those who underestimated him "by taking on seemingly impossible challenges and emerging victorious." As a Republican congressman, he had engineered the revolt that made Gerald Ford minority leader. Griffin's hero, Governor George Romney, had appointed him to a vacant seat in the Senate in the spring of 1966, and Griffin had won election in his own right later that year. That did not earn him a voice. Relegated to a desk in the chamber's back row, he sat in "Boystown," where new senators were expected to watch, without commenting, on the action. But the *Journal* item and "the sug-gestion that Chief Justice Earl Warren would manipulate his resignation, so that he could have a hand in picking his successor" so worried him, Griffin remem-bered, that he disregarded his staff's advice to keep still. "I do not speak from the standpoint of a critic of the Supreme Court," he stressed to a "nearly empty Senate chamber" on June 21, as rumors of Warren's resignation continued to circulate. "In fact, I agree with most of the Court's decisions." (That was a safe statement to make, since Griffin's constituency included African Americans, labor, Jews, and other powerful supporters of the Warren Court.) But a presi-dential election approached. "If a 'lame duck' President should seek at this stage to appoint the leadership of the Supreme Court for many years in the future, I believe he would be breaking faith with our system."[6]

Although Griffin chose the phrase "lame duck" to get under LBJ's skin, it is unclear that the president even knew of the speech at the time. It would barely have bothered him, anyway. Why should it? Despite his accomplishments in the House, Griffin was a Senate pipsqueak. Moreover, there were plenty of examples of Senate confirmations of Supreme Court nominees and others toward the close of a presidential term. When Griffin did the research *after* delivering his speech, he learned that presidents had successfully appointed eight justices dur-ing their last year in office. And as the freshman himself realized, no one in the Senate seemed terribly interested in what he had to say, beyond one Republican who pledged publicly to back Griffin and a few colleagues who offered a pat on the back and "personal support" without promising him their votes.[7]

Griffin had made a novel argument to which dozens of distinguished law pro-fessors would object on constitutional grounds. Later, its logic would be linked to Johnson's June nomination of Abe Fortas as chief justice and the opposition that derailed it. Named after Senator Strom Thurmond, the so-called Thurmond Rule supposedly would prevent the Senate from voting on judicial candidates beginning in the summer of election years. (What "summer" meant and whether the "rule" covered all judicial candidates, or just controversial ones, depended on the speaker.) But the Senate Judiciary Committee never actually adopted the Thurmond Rule and frequently flouted it. In any event, Griffin deserved credit for it.[8]

The same day that Griffin addressed the Senate, LBJ turned his attention to the Supreme Court. A telephone conversation with Fortas indicated that Johnson did indeed plan to make his friend the first Jewish chief justice. Neither the pres-ident nor the justice found that development worthy of discussion. Fortas was already making frat-boy jokes to William O. Douglas about changes he could make at the court. One intimate recalled that Fortas had known that Johnson had intended to promote him at least since 1966, when Warren, on the eve of his seventy-fifth birthday, smilingly told reporters that he favored compulsory retirement for the judiciary if the executive and legislative branches adopted it too. Realizing that he had a direct line to the president through LBJ's man at the court, Warren also reportedly privately discussed the possibility of retirement with Fortas then. But his colleague was still learning the court and in no hurry to become its chief.[9]

Historians often dodge counterfactuals, but constitutional law experts operate under different norms. According to Geoffrey Stone, "it is highly likely that Fortas would easily have been confirmed as Chief Justice, had Johnson nominated him a year earlier." Certainly, Warren held all the cards, and he and Fortas, two men who prided themselves on their political savvy, may later have looked back ruefully. LBJ possessed greater strength in the Senate in 1966 and even in 1967 and could more easily have won Fortas's nomination. Johnson, too, may have regretted pushing Fortas onto the court in 1965, because, as William O. Douglas said, if the president had allowed Fortas to remain in private practice for three years, then named him as chief justice in 1968, the nomination might well have proven unassailable. Fortas would have possessed no ties to the Warren Court, and no one could have alleged that as a private attorney, he inappropriately advised the president or taught a summer course. Still, like LBJ, Warren and Fortas apparently assumed in 1968 that if LBJ coupled the announcement that he was elevating Fortas to chief with a good nomination as associate justice, the Senate would approve.[10]

Consequently, the real question related to the identity of the next associate justice. If he were still in the White House come January, LBJ confided to Fortas, he would choose John Crooker Jr., whose father had founded the powerful Texas law firm of Fulbright, Crooker and Jaworski. LBJ had known Johnny Crooker, then in his early fifties, since his high school debating days in the 1930s. "He's liberal as hell. He's a red, red-hot Democrat. He's judicious as hell" and could best anyone, even Fortas, in argument. "He's a little boring because he's so damn meticulous and careful." He had excelled at Rice and the University of Texas Law School, and become the resident partner at Fulbright, Crooker and Jaworski's Washington office. "He's rich as hell." But like his "daddy," Johnny Crooker was "still for the people." (That was the highest compliment LBJ could pay.) He had been a stalwart for Johnson at the Democratic National Committee, and the president had recently named him to chair the Civil Aeronautics Board. "He just works day and night for me." But Johnson did not think he could sell the Senate on a Fortas–Crooker team.[11]

That left five candidates—Secretary of Defense Clifford, former deputy secretary of defense Cyrus Vance, Attorney General Ramsey Clark, Secretary of Treasury Joe Fowler, and LBJ's fellow Texan, Judge Homer Thornberry. Ideally, Johnson wanted "someone to last 30, 40 years," and he asked Fortas to look at it from his perspective, "knowing me as you know me and what I want. I want somebody that I'll always be proud of his vote," even if LBJ was not "proud of his opinion" or eloquence. Two on the list obviously were not serious contenders. "Clifford shows his age more than any man I know of at 60, just shows it in his talking," and the president rightly doubted the depth of his interest in liberal social policy. (Although the president did not mention it, his relationship with his secretary of defense had also become strained because of their differences over Vietnam.) Ramsey Clark was "young and liberal," but the Senate might object to him, and "I might not get a Chief Justice."[12]

The patrician Vance was a Wall Street lawyer who had excelled at Yale College and Law School. Johnson had worked with him since the 1950s, when Edwin Weisl, Johnson's great friend and Vance's partner, brought Vance to Washington as counsel for LBJ's Senate Military Preparedness Committee. But a bad back and five children to educate explained Vance's recent departure from the Defense Department for Wall Street. "He can't button his shoes now." Further, with Harlan and Marshall, that would make three New Yorkers on the court. And while LBJ found Vance, whom he still called on to troubleshoot almost every crisis at home or in the world, an able lawyer, the president did not consider him "a liberal at all. That's the one thing I'd have against Vance." Still smarting, probably, from Vance's turnaround on the Vietnam War at the March 1968 "Wise Men" meeting, LBJ told Fortas that Vance was "ultra-conservative." According to the president, Vance was a "pacifist" just "because Bob McNamara sold him on it last month," and he "would be a fascist under proper leadership."[13]

Joe Fowler, Fortas's Yale Law School classmate and fellow New Dealer, was a skilled, loyal secretary of treasury. LBJ valued him as a liberal who had backed the president in his attempts to keep the Great Society alive by arguing that the administration's guns-and-butter agenda required no tax hike. Fowler was a native Virginian with lots of support and close relationships on Capitol Hill. He was personable and, according to his New York Times obituary, "cherubic and courtly." And LBJ admired his methodical and disciplined nature, the fact that he was the kind of person who would stop talking in 9½ minutes if given 10 for a presentation. But, Johnson said, he spoke without "intonation," "inflections," or "goddamits," and "he's awfully boring." Chuckling in agreement, Fortas replied that Fowler might drive Douglas off the court.[14]

Even though he did not possess the credentials of some of the other candidates and was LBJ's age, older than the ideal, Thornberry was obviously the president's first choice. "I've got to have somebody who will carry the moderate[s] and the Republican[s] a little bit, just to have a little appeal to them, just for old times' sake." As a former city councilman, state legislator, and member of Congress, Thornberry would bring a wealth of experience to the court, particularly one, Fortas obligingly added at some point, that so frequently grappled with issues of statutory interpretation. But the "liberal press that will just not give me a fair trial" might not applaud, LBJ fretted. "Hell, I'd be nominated by acclamation on my record for civil liberties and civil rights," he said to Fortas. "But the [New York] *Times* and the [Washington] *Post* are against me because they're just anti-Semitic, by God, and anti-South," the president added incoherently. Johnson believed that "the only damn thing they got against me," since "I've adopted their platform," was that "because I live in Texas, I don't have style." Thornberry, too, would bear the burden of being a Texas politician, albeit one popular with liberals and one who "was never a wheeler-dealer or a manipulator that I'm supposed to be."

Nonetheless, by the conversation's end, he and Fortas had ranked Thornberry first and Fowler second. "Goddamn, I'll tell you this," LBJ summed up his thinking. "If I were an old woman and I lived in a wooden shoe, and my children are starving, the one I would go to first and watch him cry would be Hubert Humphrey," who was not a lawyer. "And then I'd go see Thornberry. Then I'd go see Fowler. And then I would probably go see Vance. And then," the president laughed, "I'd go see Clifford." But Johnson continued to worry that the media and senators would make Thornberry a presidential "crony."[15]

Cronies and Consultations

Of course, they would. As Thornberry's 1995 *New York Times* obituary recognized, Johnson was even closer to Thornberry than he was to Fortas. The child of impoverished deaf and mute parents, Thornberry, an "eminently garrulous man who would as soon chat with a plowman as with a potentate," liked to say that he could not speak until he was three and did not stop talking ever after. His father's death after World War I of influenza when Thornberry was nine made life harder than ever for the boy, who now sold newspapers and worked other jobs. After entering the University of Texas at his mother's urging, Thornberry became Austin and Travis County's youngest deputy sheriff in history, a job he continued to hold when he entered University of Texas Law School. He graduated in the top 15% of his law school class and won a seat in the Texas legislature while he was finishing up at UT. By 1941, he was district attorney in Travis County. During World War II, he served stateside as naval commander. Afterward, he briefly practiced law and became a member of Austin City Council.[16]

He and Johnson had worked as pages in that legislature at the same time when they were teenagers. When Representative Johnson moved up to the Senate in 1948, Thornberry became his congressman. Thornberry and his wife, three children, and devoted and determined mother moved to Washington, where they lived near the Johnsons and saw them frequently.

The families vacationed together, and Thornberry's daughters and son spoke of "Uncle Lyndon" and "Aunt Bird." (As LBJ talked with Fortas in 1968, Thornberry's wife, Eloise, was staying at the White House for a few days.) After LBJ's 1955 heart attack, Thornberry distracted his friend with daily games of dominoes.[17]

Thornberry had helped LBJ win passage of the 1957 Civil Rights Act, which, though feeble, put civil rights on the congressional agenda. The longer Thornberry lived in Washington, the further to the left he moved, though he remained beloved by Congressional Southerners. By the time JFK named him a district judge at Johnson's urging, the *Times* said, "he was such an important liberal voice on the powerful House Rules Committee that he agreed to delay his departures for months to prevent being replaced by a Southern Democrat unsympathetic to the Kennedy program." Thornberry stayed close to LBJ as Johnson awaited word of JFK's death in Dallas and stood behind Johnson as he took the oath of office on Air Force One.[18]

Thornberry served as a federal district judge from late 1963 until 1965. When LBJ wanted to nominate him for an appellate judgeship, Thornberry demurred and told the president he was not "really qualified for it" and another judge could do "a better job." That did not stop Johnson, who chided his friend for his lack of "ambition" and pressed forward. "I don't know of anyone that is missed more from Washington than this wonderful Thornberry family," the president emphasized at his friend's Fifth Circuit swearing-in ceremony on the porch of the LBJ ranch. Of Thornberry himself, the president said, "We hated to see him leave the legislative halls, but we are glad to see him preside in the temples of justice. Because we know that there is no more courageous person, no better and finer human being, and no man with a greater sense of justice and fairness and feeling of equality for all human beings, wherever they live, whatever their color, or whatever their religion, than Homer Thornberry." As LBJ recognized, his friend believed in civil rights. The president was "proud," Thornberry thought, that his fellow Texan wrote the key decision outlawing the poll tax that the Supreme Court upheld and supported racial integration in Fifth Circuit schools, "which, of course, was not easy." By all accounts, Thornberry was not just committed to equal rights, but also extremely decent, fair, and congenial. In evaluating judges, Circuit Court Judge Wade McCree, who would become the second African American Solicitor General under Jimmy Carter, said, he liked to ask himself "whether I could accept an adverse verdict from him with the abiding conviction that I had received a fair hearing in terms of the judge's knowledge of the law, his capacity for patience and his desire to ascertain the truth. Judge Thornberry meets my test." As Thornberry himself apparently understood, he was person of character and a perfectly good, though not exceptionally distinguished, federal judge with a great deal of legislative experience. His name jumped to the top of the list for a Supreme Court appointment in 1968 because of his friendship with the president.[19]

On Saturday morning, June 22, the president continued his "consultations." He had conferred only with Senate Majority Leader Mansfield and Senator Richard Russell, he assured Senate Minority Leader Everett Dirksen. LBJ and Dirksen discussed Eisenhower's disapproval of Warren's performance as chief justice. Since Dirksen, an especially vocal critic of the court's school prayer and reapportionment decisions, shared Ike's displeasure, Johnson knew the news of the chief justice's retirement would please the Senate minority leader. Just as Warren did not fancy enabling Nixon and Dirksen to choose his successor, Dirksen wanted Warren gone. "I want to get the feel" of the Senate, the president then told Dirksen, "because I damn sure don't want any trouble on confirmation." LBJ mistakenly believed that the Senate minority leader could save him strife. Senate Republicans, who were as badly divided over Vietnam as Democrats, increasingly fumed at Dirksen's loyalty to a Democratic president, and the younger Republicans elected in 1966 deferred to him less than their elders had done.

The president's error, though costly, was understandable. Because "the Washington establishment" then considered "strident partisanship" inappropriate, Republicans' dissatisfaction with Dirksen remained muted. Moreover, Dirksen had often provided crucial assistance to the president in the past. The two old politicians were accustomed to viewing each other as powerful, and they also genuinely liked each other. The minority leader's reputation as "The Wizard of Ooze" and his oleaginous or mellifluous voice, depending on who described it, tickled LBJ.[20]

Oddly, the president pretended that he had to promote from within and rationalized that he was making Fortas chief justice because "he's the best lawyer on the Court, and I think all of them [the justices] agree with that." Prudently changing his tone for Dirksen, Johnson also said he wanted "a moderate man on the Court who wouldn't tear up all I have done and who'd be a bit stronger on law and order," someone like Tom Clark. "Marshall told me he'd be that way," and Fortas's recent pamphlet on dissent and civil disobedience demonstrated that he was "going in that direction." In addition to the usual suspects for Fortas's spot, LBJ mentioned Dirksen's friend, the defeated Kuchel, "but I couldn't get him cleared, too liberal." Governor Richard Hughes of New Jersey was another possibility, but, with Brennan there, "that would give me two Catholics from New Jersey." Goldberg would mean "two Jews." The president swatted down Dirksen's suggestion of Judge William Campbell of Illinois, a federal judge since 1940. "I want a man who will be here for awhile," LBJ stressed, and Campbell, like Brennan, was a Catholic. While Mansfield and Russell both thought "very highly of Vance," he told Dirksen, Russell preferred Thornberry. Dirksen ranked

Vance ahead of Thornberry and Thornberry ahead of Fowler but seemed agreeable to any of them.[21]

Clark Clifford pushed back. Later that morning, after the secretary of defense and Fortas attended a meeting on Vietnam, the president asked Clifford and Fortas to accompany him back to his bedroom, where he changed into his pajamas and broached the nominations (figure 14). "The enthusiasm that had long since drained out of him when discussing Vietnam came back in his voice, and his eyes were shining with pleasure at the thought of the wonderful honor he was going to bestow on two of his closest friends, and what they in turn could do for the country," Clifford remembered. The news about Fortas delighted without surprising Clifford. He considered his friend's qualifications outstanding. The prospect of Thornberry, however, alarmed him. "Thornberry was an affable and well-liked politician, but no one ever had considered him Supreme Court material." The secretary of defense had noticed before, and now saw again, that the president "really was not conscious of how much his power had diminished" since he announced that he would not seek reelection.

Clifford cautioned that the Republicans thought they would win in November and while "they would probably accept Abe on his own," they would balk if LBJ tried "to pack the court with your friends at a very late date in the political calendar." The president could guarantee Fortas's confirmation, the secretary of defense advised, by coupling his chief justice nomination with that of a prominent, nonpartisan Republican, preferably one from the Midwest. Clifford even offered a name, the American Bar Association's Standing Committee on the Federal Judiciary chairman, Albert Jenner of Chicago. That was good advice: Robert Griffin later speculated that had LBJ "exercised a bit of restraint" and "sent up the name of only one crony," along with "an unassailable" nominee, confirmation might well have occurred. Johnson, however, balked. "I don't intend to put some damned Republican on the Court," he snapped. Fortas remained quiet while the president and secretary of defense argued. When they asked him who was right, he sided with Johnson and predicted that with the appropriate "handling and preparation," LBJ could sell the package. Fortas's approval clinched the matter for the moment. After they left him to his nap, Fortas told Clifford, "I understand exactly what you were trying to do. I don't know if the President can bring this off, but I couldn't very well sit there and disagree with him when he wants to make me Chief Justice."[22]

Others close to LBJ would also warn him that he contemplated risky business. When Johnson's special counsel, Larry Temple of Texas, worried aloud about the appointment of their mutual friend, Homer Thornberry, Lady Bird Johnson halted Johnson midrebuke: "Lyndon, he may be right about that, and that's what worries me about Homer—although I'd love to see him on the Supreme Court." These skeptics had some impact. On Saturday, the president did mention Jenner

Figure 14 By the summer of 1968, as LBJ considered making Fortas chief justice, the presidency had become agonizing for him. Here he listened to a tape sent by his son-in-law, Captain Charles Robb, from Vietnam. Jack Kightlinger, July 31, 1968. LBJ Library.

and Senator Ed Muskie, a Maine Democrat, as possible candidates, along with Thornberry, Vance, and Fowler. Temple believed, however, that LBJ was just going through the motions and that "almost from the outset he thought of Fortas for the Chief Justiceship and thought of Thornberry for the other position, and then went through the process of eliminating all of the other possibilities."[23]

That was probably the case, and a *New York Times* column that Sunday by the influential Scotty Reston heartened the president. LBJ had "power and history on his side," the journalist stressed. He reminded his readers that John Adams had named John Marshall chief justice as he himself prepared to leave the White House in defeat. Moreover, according to Reston, conservatives lacked the votes in the Senate to block the nomination. Consequently, if, as expected, Johnson decided to name Fortas chief justice, and even if he coupled the nomination with that of the ultra-liberal Ramsey Clark, the Senate would acquiesce.[24]

There was not only no possibility that appointment would go to Ramsey Clark, however, but also even a chance at this point that the president might try to rid himself of the attorney general he had worked so hard to put in office. Later that morning, a White House telephone call to Sunflower County, Mississippi, delayed Senate Judiciary Committee Chair James Eastland, an excellent source of intelligence about the Senate's Republicans and Southern Democrats, from leaving for a wedding. "I could tell because I knew the way Lyndon operated that he was going to appoint Fortas," the senator remembered. As he often did, the president shaded his message for his audience: LBJ touted Fortas's new prudence on civil disobedience and volunteered that Russell considered the justice's attitude "on the nose," along with the Reston column. Russell was relevant because he led the Southerners and might ward off a filibuster of Fortas if he got what he wanted. As the president explained to Eastland, Russell very much hoped to see his friend, Alexander Lawrence, become a federal district judge in Georgia. So LBJ and Fortas were urging Ramsey Clark to overlook segregationist speeches that Lawrence had made as a young man and approve the appointment. Moreover, Johnson wanted the civil rights activists still living in the Resurrection City of King's Poor People's Campaign to leave town, and Clark insisted on getting "them out without throwing them out." Although he never entirely lost his fondness or admiration for the attorney general, the president was impatient about Resurrection City and downright angry about Ramsey Clark's refusal to prosecute Stokely Carmichael for instigating riots. Now there was this new disagreement about Lawrence. He might "have to override" his attorney general, LBJ worried aloud to Eastland. Would the stubborn Clark resign over Lawrence's judgeship?[25]

Johnson believed Dirksen, Russell, and most Democrats would support Fortas, he told Eastland. "The question is, where do I go from there?" If LBJ had Dirksen and Russell, the senator responded, he did not need to worry. "Well,

I haven't got them," the president admitted. He just thought he could coax them on his team. "Or I could just refuse to accept Warren's resignation" and wait for the election. If Humphrey won, LBJ could name Fortas then, and if the Republicans did, Warren would stay in place until Nixon accepted his resignation. "I don't think I'd like to do that, but I could do it." The president sounded relieved when Eastland remarked, "you ought to do it yourself."

Johnson dangled various possible combinations before Eastland, including Fortas–Goldberg, probably to scare him. "No, no, no," the senator responded. Eastland said nothing against Fortas and declared that he liked Thornberry. "If I had my druthers and I didn't have to bother with you and Dirksen and Mansfield—and all the lead bulls, and the newspapers, and the *New York Times*, and all of them—I'd name Homer Thornberry because I know goddamn well what he would do for the next 25 years," LBJ said, although Eastland agreed with him that opponents would "holler cronyism."

The senator, who remained angry about the selection of Thurgood Marshall, proved more enthusiastic when LBJ proposed bringing back Tom Clark instead of Thornberry. "Tom's 69," LBJ volunteered. "But hell, he'd still have ten years to be as old as Warren. I guess the country might say that's tricky putting a Texan back." Eastland said Tom Clark would not have to be confirmed again; Johnson disagreed. "They say a Chief Justice doesn't have to be confirmed, but Fortas said he wouldn't have it if he wasn't confirmed." Eastland saw no reason that Tom Clark could not return to the court while Ramsey Clark remained attorney general. "They" would not "allow that," LBJ answered, forgetting that "they" had consisted only of himself in 1967. "Neither one of them would do it anyway on that basis." Eastland thought Tom Clark "our best idea," then, but doubted "that would be treating Ramsey right." He warned the president that it would just provide fodder for reporters who were already saying "that you are dissatisfied with him." Johnson circled back to Fortas and Thornberry and finally released Eastland after telling the senator to nose around to determine whether the president could confirm them.[26]

Meanwhile, that weekend, Robert Griffin had taken his heretofore lonely crusade against "lame duck" Supreme Court nominations to a meeting with Michigan newspaper editors. Asked how he would react if LBJ named Arthur Goldberg to fill a court vacancy, the surprised senator pledged to support the former justice. "In a sense he has been on leave from the Supreme Court" while he served as United Nations ambassador. "The people more or less expect that he will be returned to the Court." That was an expectation that Johnson was well aware that Goldberg shared, and his champion, Drew Pearson, stopped by the Oval Office for a lengthy visit on June 22. "He would love to be back up there," the president told Mansfield the next day, but LBJ—again, overlooking the fact that two Jewish justices had served together on the court in the 1930s—stuck to the rationalization that he could not nominate two Jews. When Goldberg heard of that response, he angrily branded it camouflage and told his wife that the president was punishing him because of their differences over Vietnam.[27]

Doubtless, Johnson was. But he later volunteered to the press that he had considered naming Goldberg as chief justice before he nominated Fortas. He may have flirted with the idea on Monday, June 24, the same day that more than a thousand DC police descended on Resurrection City to arrest the last protesters there and to clear it out. After many date changes, that was when the president honored outgoing United Nations Ambassador Goldberg and swore in George Ball as his successor. There was no seat for the Goldbergs' son, Dorothy Goldberg said, and "it was strange to invite our friends to his [Ball's] swearing-in, but that is part of today's climate." (Despite his mistrust of Ball, LBJ still believed he needed a "peace lover" or "dove" at the United Nations, and he had worked hard to persuade Ball to take the position. Ball lasted just three months before he quit abruptly.)[28]

That day, Eastland reported to Deputy Attorney General Warren Christopher "that a fight was building up over the Chief Justiceship." At 6:50 P.M., Johnson tried to head it off by inviting Dirksen over for a drink and a deal. Obviously, he clung to the delusion, which the Senate minority leader fostered, that Dirksen could deliver lots of Republicans. Now the minority leader reminded the president that he needed a favor. The Subversive Activities Control Board, which regulated the "subversives" whom Dirksen believed conservatives needed to see him fighting, would expire on June 30 unless Attorney General Clark overcame his civil libertarian scruples and referred cases to it. In a display of presidential power designed to impress Dirksen, LBJ commanded Clark to do so. (When Drew Pearson and Jack Anderson subsequently linked the board's resurrection to Dirksen's support for Fortas, LBJ and Dirksen quickly got their stories straight. "You've never discussed it with anybody in the White House in connection with the Fortas nominations at all" and "no trade" had occurred, the president instructed Dirksen. "That's absolutely true," the senator obligingly and accurately replied. He had first brought up the board "long before we even had any idea Warren might retire"!)[29]

Still, even with Dirksen almost buttoned up, Johnson remained anxious enough afterward to track down his and Russell's friend, Ed Weisl. Sound out Russell about the possibility of making Vance chief justice, LBJ directed. Happily, Weisl reported back the next morning that Russell thought that Thornberry had a better chance of confirmation because of his friendships on Capitol Hill.[30]

Did Johnson seriously consider making Vance, Thornberry, or even Goldberg chief justice instead of Fortas? Larry Temple thought that the idea of a Thornberry chief justiceship might have briefly crossed LBJ's mind. But the president had more confidence in Fortas's legal ability than he did in Thornberry's. Given LBJ's insistence to senators that Thornberry was no "dumbbell" and his certainty that elites looked down on Texans, it is hard to imagine how he would have justified Chief Justice Thornberry.[31]

Perhaps Vance–Thornberry or Goldberg–Thornberry might have had more potential than Fortas–Thornberry. Griffin had painted himself into a corner with his remarks about Goldberg, and Russell admired Vance. Whatever Johnson believed, Vance was no pushover: He resigned as Jimmy Carter's secretary of state a decade later when he disagreed with the president's decision to send a military rescue mission to free American hostages held captive in Tehran. Though Vance did have a bad back, he outlived Fortas. Further, unlike Fortas, but like Thornberry, Vance did not carry the baggage of past identification with the Warren Court. Neither Vance nor Goldberg was a crony. If anything, given the tension between LBJ and Goldberg over Vietnam, Goldberg had become an anti-crony who would also have provided the old Warren Court majority with another vote in Warren's absence, just as Thornberry probably would have sustained its civil rights record. But LBJ was apparently unsure what kind of justice Vance would become, and why should he help Goldberg? As ever, he also wanted to honor loyalty and friendship.

"Improving the Damn Court"

In Fortas and Thornberry, as he saw it, he was not overreaching, but playing a shrewd game. Fortas was "the most experienced, compassionate, articulate, and intelligent lawyer I knew, and . . . I was certain that he would carry on in the Court's tradition," LBJ explained in his White House memoir. Thornberry, "a close friend of mine for many years, . . . was one of the most competent, fair-minded and progressive jurists in the entire South." Moreover, Johnson reasoned, even John McClellan could not remove Fortas from the court. "The only question we're talking about is whether you've got Thornberry or Warren, and I don't think I'm liberalizing the Court with Thornberry, trading him for Warren. I think I'm improving the damn Court!" He also anticipated that Republicans and Southerners would find Fortas and Thornberry "more acceptable than Warren and Goldberg" because the president believed "they are more moderate." Liberals, he thought, would remember that because the president had appointed Thurgood Marshall of New York to replace Tom Clark of Texas, the next vacancy belonged to a Southerner, and Thornberry's record was "about as good a liberal [record] as you can get from that part of the country." The appointments would enable LBJ, a president who delighted in breaking barriers for Jews and minorities, to name the first Jewish chief justice and to reward devotion. Fortas and Thornberry, he believed, would sustain the Warren Court's mission of fostering equality. At the same time, they might rein in judicial protection of criminals and demonstrators. As he saw it, his package responded to his own misgivings about the Warren Court and enabled him to save the best part of it in an age when law and order had become the rallying cry. It also, he believed, would appeal to the Senate.[32]

Prudently, the president also tried to hedge his bets. His letter saluting Warren's accomplishments at the court and accepting his resignation would read, "With your agreement, I will accept your decision to retire effective at such time as a successor is qualified," language similar to that Theodore Roosevelt had used in acknowledging Horace Gray's decision to leave the court. At 12:40 P.M. the following day, Tuesday, June 25, LBJ directed Ramsey Clark to get the letter and the Fortas–Thornberry nominations ready.[33]

Less than half an hour later, the situation became ominous. Although Johnson had not yet even submitted Fortas's and Thornberry's names to the Senate, a bulletin from Eastland to Ramsey Clark at 1:05 P.M. indicated that "a filibuster was already being organized against Fortas . . . and that if it started against Fortas, it would also include Thornberry." The eight to ten senators with whom Eastland had spoken were "very bitter and outspoken against Fortas." Eastland did not say why because he did not need to do so: White Southern Democrats often opposed the Warren Court's criminal procedure and civil rights decisions. McClellan had said that he looked forward to having "that SOB formally submitted to the Senate" so he could fight the nomination. The debate over the chief justice nomination "would tear this country apart." And according to Eastland, Dirksen actually opposed Fortas, though he pretended otherwise. At 4:15 P.M., more discouraging intelligence arrived. Two more Democrats disliked Fortas. Robert Byrd of West Virginia vowed to do "everything in my power" to fight that "leftist," and Russell Long of Louisiana numbered Fortas among "the dirty five" who sided with the criminals against the victim.[34]

Nevertheless, as LBJ pressed forward, he began to receive good news. At the Republican Policy Committee meeting that day, the Senate minority leader confided when Johnson telephoned at 4:53 P.M., those in attendance had talked about whether the president could and should name the next chief justice. Dirksen had assured those present that LBJ remained president until his last day in office, and "I think it cooled off." There had been no discussion of likely nominees. "Am I supposed to nominate somebody the *St. Louis Post-Dispatch* says is a great man that I don't know?" Johnson inquired rhetorically. "And will you go with me on Fortas and Thornberry?" "Yeah," Dirksen promised. Reassure Senator Russell, LBJ ordered Dirksen, "that you will have a much stronger vote on crime and on court things," whatever they were, "than you've ever had before with Warren. . . . A President can't lobby, but I want you to lobby because I damn sure do things for you and you don't even have to tell me to do them."[35]

Then it was time to shore up Thornberry's support among Texans. Johnson knew he could not count on Republican John Tower to sponsor Thornberry. So he called the state's other senator, Ralph Yarborough, a Democrat with whom his relationship was uneasy, at best. "You be working on your statement" supporting Thornberry, LBJ said, after insisting implausibly, "in the last eight years, I've spent two hours with you where I've spent one with him." Afterward, Johnson contacted the prominent Texas attorney and future Watergate special prosecutor, Leon Jaworski, for whom he generally had little use. Jaworski talked and looked "like a puffed-up powder pigeon," LBJ confided to Fortas, "and I'd just like to stick a hat-pin in him and listen to him ooze." But everyone said that Jaworski was "a helluva good lawyer," and the president needed a favor. "I'm going to recommend that Homer Thornberry be kicked up to the Supreme Court from this Circuit Court," and "I'm going to make Abe the Chief Justice. And I expect we'll have a row in the Senate." Jaworski, who had helped with both of Thornberry's prior confirmations, promised to "go all out to get this done."[36]

LBJ was unstinting. The next step was a meeting with Richard Russell, who confirmed what he had told Weisl. He would vote for Fortas and "enthusiastically" back Thornberry. Surely he also inquired about the Alexander Lawrence judgeship, for which, Russell well knew, Johnson was pressing Ramsey Clark. As LBJ remembered it, Russell predicted that Thornberry "would make an outstanding Associate Justice. When you sit in a duck blind all day with a man, he said, you really get to know him," and he understood and trusted Thornberry. Knowing Russell as he did, Johnson thought he sealed the agreement by inviting his friend to share a nostalgic family dinner with the president's daughter and grandson. Afterward, LBJ and Russell tracked down Thornberry at the home of an Austin colleague and gave their friend the good news. "I had always hoped that someday you and I would both be retired and could spend some time on the Pedernales," Thornberry remembered the president saying, but that was "not going to happen." Why not? asked an astonished Thornberry. He was sending up the judge's nomination to the court the next day, LBJ answered. "I was overcome," Thornberry remembered. Good news continued to come in the next morning, when Ramsey Clark reported that the American Bar Association's Standing Federal Judicial Selection Committee, after meeting by telephone for all of an hour, had unanimously rated both Fortas and Thornberry highly qualified.[37]

"We're going to make it," Clark reassured the president. "I don't know," LBJ answered. "I don't like that Bob Byrd stuff and I don't like that Russell Long stuff." The president remained convinced that he had chosen "the best combination." He fussed that about Dirksen telling the press that although he had "thoughts" about the desirability of an outgoing president naming the next chief justice, he would not yet comment on Warren's resignation. Dirksen had told

Johnson, however, "and I've got a record[ing] of it that he'd support me. I guess he wants to try to wait a bit." The president clearly considered Dirksen more important to the crusade than Mike Mansfield. That could have been because LBJ took the Senate majority leader's support for granted and/or did not believe that Mansfield, with whom he had parted ways on Vietnam, could bring along many votes.[38]

Johnson did, however, telephone Mansfield. He had not spoken with Eastland, LBJ fibbed, but the president had heard the Senate Judiciary Committee chair had "hinted" there might be a filibuster. The president had Dirksen's support. Tipping his hand about whom he believed would win the November election, LBJ added that he would "sure hate to see these two appointments blow over to Nixon." "So would I," Mansfield agreed. "I'll do my best."[39]

There was one last intervention from Eastland, who was ushered in to the Oval Office at 10:37 A.M. When LBJ reported Russell's position, Eastland was unfazed. He warned the president that Russell would not vote for Fortas. He was visibly unimpressed by a note that LBJ smilingly handed him indicating that Robert Byrd regretted his intemperateness and appreciated past presidential support. Though Byrd "probably" would vote against Fortas, it said, he would not organize or participate in a campaign against the nominee. Eastland told the president that he strenuously objected to Fortas and cited the justice's recent speech calling on Jews and African Americans to continue working together, which the senator considered "a conspiratorial call for Jews and Negroes to take over America." The most that Eastland would give the president was a promise not to issue a statement against Fortas and to allow the nomination out of committee "at my own time."[40]

At 11:30 A.M., Johnson surprised reporters by summoning them to a press conference in the Oval Office. There he announced that he was nominating Fortas as chief justice and Thornberry as associate justice, though both were absent. Only now did LBJ confirm that Warren had submitted his resignation on June 13 and release the chief justice's two letters and his own response accepting Warren's retirement when his successor qualified. Asked whether he had consulted senators about his nominees, LBJ confirmed that he had spoken with Democrat and Republican leaders, as well as Senate Judiciary Committee Chair Eastland. Did he "anticipate trouble" with Senate ratification of his choices? The president expected "that they would review their records very carefully," and that when they did, "they will meet with the approval of the Senate."[41]

"Subsiding Tempest"

Wishful thinking. Although the full tale of the deliberate *and* instinctive way LBJ selected Fortas and Thornberry awaited the release of the president's telephone conversations, it was immediately evident that the nominations would experience rough sledding. Nonetheless, and despite LBJ's "lame duck" status and the approach of the presidential election, the nominations did, at first, have a good chance of success.[42]

To be sure, Eastland and other powerful Senate Judiciary Committee members made their disapproval clear to the White House. McClellan, "the second ranking man" on the committee, complained that "everybody else" had been consulted except him. "So why should I rush to make known my views. I wonder if we ought not to have real long hearings." Sam Ervin informed the president's legislative liaison that "considering what the Supreme Court has done to the Constitution, I'll have to read Fortas['s] decisions before I can decide." And given the fact that Warren had conditioned his retirement upon qualification of his successor and would soon publicly pledge to remain at the court while or if the Senate dragged its feet in confirming Fortas, Ervin was quickly asking whether the Senate even had a vacancy it could constitutionally fill. At that point, LBJ did indeed "believe that we can get Warren to stay on" if the Senate turned down Fortas. But the vacancy question, Eastland acknowledged in an oral history for the Johnson Library after LBJ left office, and Justice Department attorneys in subsequent Democratic and Republican Administrations agreed, possessed as little validity as the objection that the president was a lame duck. The vacancy issue, however, might prove useful in stalling the hearings. It was dangerous because delay would aid the nominees' opponents. From the outset, when confirmation seemed likely, Johnson was warning his staffers that they needed an early resolution, ideally before Congress adjourned for the nominating conventions in August. Senate Minority Leader Dirksen was a champion at changing course to suit shifting political winds, and "if it drags out," he would "leave us."[43]

Further, on the day that LBJ announced the nomination, half the Republicans in the Senate released a statement drafted by Griffin and George Murphy of California. The eighteen signatories—a group that included conservatives, moderates, and Dirksen's own son-in-law, Howard Baker, from Fortas's own home state of Tennessee—maintained that the next president should choose the next chief justice and any associate justice that might accompany him "after the people have expressed themselves in the November elections. We will therefore, because of the above principle, and with absolutely no reflection on any individuals involved, vote against confirming any Supreme Court nominations of the incumbent President." That pose, Griffin later admitted, proved "unrealistic and naïve." He abandoned it with a bang the following day when he held a press conference to declare that the nominations of Fortas and Thornberry represented "cronyism at its worst, and everybody knows it." Griffin also provided newspapers with their headlines about an upcoming filibuster. Although he realized that "considerably" fewer Republicans than the ones who had signed his statement would commit to participating in a filibuster, he said, he was "prepared to have a very long and extended discussion" of the nomination.[44]

Yet, as Griffin realized, he faced an uphill struggle. Even the *Wall Street Journal*, which charged LBJ with making the court "a political football" by appointing two cronies, one of them "a relatively unknown fellow-Texan," predicted that Fortas might become an "outstanding" chief justice. It saluted his "level-headedness," code for his tolerance of big business mergers, and his "commendable concern for law and order." Other leading newspaper editorials hailed the nominations, Griffin saw, particularly that of Fortas. So did Mansfield, and so did Dirksen in full-throated fashion, finally. Although the media reported that candidate Nixon had said the next president should name the next chief justice, few thought that would happen. Indeed, the Washington press corps and television networks predicted confirmation of both candidates. Newsman Roger Mudd expected that Griffin's group would wage a losing battle, since Southern Democrats were largely publicly keeping mum and "generally seemed to take the position that they could accept Justice Fortas and welcome Judge Thornberry so long as they'd be rid of Chief Justice Warren." Television news journalist and Fortas friend Eric Sevareid also anticipated congressional approval and announced that Fortas would become a great chief justice. "Do you realize that you are fighting the Supreme Court, the American Bar Association, the Democratic Leadership and the Republican Leadership as well as the President of the United States?" Griffin remembered his wife asking. "Just who do you think you are?"[45]

Of course, LBJ nevertheless feared defeat from the start. He always did. To Ramsey Clark, the president fretted, "they're all getting dug in. That's what's dangerous." On June 28, in a conversation with Fortas in which the president declared that the two of them were not cronies because they did not play poker together and LBJ had gone to "a lot more dinners with Dirksen or Mansfield," Johnson estimated that the Fortas–Thornberry forces had "about 50 votes. If we lose Hollings [D-SC] and Russell . . . then we probably have 48 or 49. We have some potential Republicans that we ought to get." The administration had no "leader" to carry its water and respond to the charges lodged by opponents, LBJ complained at the outset. "Mansfield won't do it and Dirksen can't do it." Perhaps Senate Judiciary Committee member George Smathers, a Florida Democrat, could become that leader. He was not seeking reelection and was an old friend of Nixon's and of Fortas's former partner and personal representative to the White House lobbying team, Paul Porter. "I wish everybody in Florida that you know would talk to him," Johnson informed Fortas, especially anyone whom Smathers might hope to snag as a client once he opened his new law office in Washington. Later that day, though, the president received a head count that would have lifted his spirits. With sixty-seven supporting the nomination, it seemed the administration had enough votes to ensure the two-thirds majority necessary to break a filibuster.[46]

So Marge Griffin was skeptical about her husband's endeavor for good reason. By the end of June, Joe Califano said, Johnson had "assumed personal direction of every detail of the effort to secure confirmation of his friend Fortas." On July 1, Smathers became the first Southern Democrat to applaud the nominations when he delivered a speech on the Senate floor drafted by Porter. Smathers characterized Fortas as "gifted" and asked which senators "who love the law . . . can conscientiously condone the prospect that the appointment of a Chief Justice . . . could become a political pawn in this summer's political conventions, a bargaining tool among candidates for high office, a vote-getting device in the November election?" The next day, Dirksen publicly guaranteed that Fortas and Thornberry would "definitely" win confirmation and that no filibuster would occur. When the president's agents met with the Senate minority leader that afternoon, Dirksen was in full battle mode. "We will win this one," he said repeatedly, and he also insisted that he was weaning away some signatories of the Griffin letter. Another Republican source assured the White House that the "Griffin effort is slowly dying."[47]

True, Griffin had some reason to expect support from Southern Democrats because Russell had decided that the Johnson administration was holding the Lawrence nomination hostage for his Fortas vote. On July 1, the president received an outraged letter from the Georgian decrying "the long delay in the handling and juggling" of the Lawrence nomination. After expressing his resentment at "being treated as a child or a patronage-seeking ward heeler," Russell released himself from the duty to honor "any statements" he had made to LBJ about Fortas and Thornberry and declared his resolve to "deal objectively" with the Supreme Court nominations. And sometime around July 4, Russell and Griffin spoke, with the Georgian asking the Michiganian "whether I was serious in my opposition to the Fortas nomination" and would "carry the fight." As Griffin recalled it, when he answered affirmatively, Russell, "the de facto leader of the southern bloc in the Senate," pledged that "he would be with me. That was a turning point in the whole case, as far as I was concerned," the moment when Griffin decided "there was a pretty good chance we would prevail."[48]

Not so fast. First, even if Griffin could count on the Southern Democrats, he knew he was venturing into dangerous territory. He wanted to mount a bipartisan senators' attack on Fortas from all over the country, not a replay of the sectional campaign against Marshall. But recall that while the Democrats included the strongest and weakest supporters of civil rights, every Republican who voted on Thurgood Marshall's nomination, save Strom Thurmond, had approved it. Nixon might be courting the South in a national election, but did Republicans who answered to constituencies from the North, Midwest, and West really want to ally themselves with the Senate's most reactionary members? "Don't openly get caught in an unholy alliance with Southern Democrats," Griffin's notes to himself stressed. The opposition to Fortas must be bipartisan and national, not Southern.[49]

Second, Russell apparently possessed less confidence in Griffin than the freshman senator believed, particularly once LBJ shifted into high gear. After receiving Russell's letter, the president dressed down Ramsey Clark because "your foot-dragging on this has destroyed one of the great friendships I've had with one of the great men that has ever served this country." LBJ now sent emissaries to assure Russell that he had never envisioned a quid pro quo and that Lawrence would receive his judgeship. On July 9, as Dirksen informed the administration that talk of a filibuster had vanished, Russell told Mansfield's legislative aide that "there wouldn't be one, that 'they will just fall apart across the aisle.'"[50]

Four days later, LBJ summoned Russell to the White House and showed him the documents that the administration was sending forward nominating Lawrence. After almost an hour without incident, "the lid blew off," Russell recalled, when LBJ repeatedly alleged that "somebody had undoubtedly poisoned my mind" and that "I had known all the time he had intended to appoint Lawrence." Even now, Johnson did not neglect Fortas and Thornberry. He told Russell that "he had plenty of votes to confirm them both unless I intervened and took an active part in directing the opposition." Russell, who reported becoming "somewhat confused" as LBJ shifted between "complimentary statements of what I had meant to him in times past" and castigations of the senator's letter, reassured the president. "At no time did I make a statement to him as to what I proposed to do about Fortas, but I did tell him twice that I would be glad to support Thornberry for Chief Justice" and did pledge that "I did not intend to undertake to lead any movement in regard to the nominations." Thus, Russell did not necessarily plan to codirect Griffin's crusade. (Several days later, the president sent the Lawrence nomination to the Senate, which quickly confirmed him, and Judge Lawrence began issuing rulings that, ironically enough, integrated the Savannah and Augusta public schools.)[51]

Moreover, the Lawrence judgeship was just one of several providentially to materialize. The same day that LBJ sent it forward, he named another Georgian to the Fifth Circuit, a candidate of Eastland's to the district court in Mississippi, and another individual to the district court in New Hampshire. These nominations might soften up senators whose votes he sought on Fortas–Thornberry. At the very least, the swift confirmation of all of them that followed could fuel White House charges that the Senate was playing politics by dragging its feet on its Supreme Court nominees.[52]

The president wasn't just handing out judgeships either. The White House summoned up all the power of corporate liberalism on Fortas's behalf. It enlisted friendly corporate chieftains and clients of Fortas's former law firm, Arnold & Porter, to lobby their senators and chat up the press. Henry Ford II promised to "get to work on Griffin." Paul Austin of Coca Cola, a longtime Arnold & Porter client, was sure that he could "deliver" Senators Talmadge and Russell of Georgia, Byrd of Virginia, Hill of Alabama, Long of Louisiana, and Hansen of Wyoming. Another Arnold & Porter client, James Ling, a Texan "who collected companies the way boys collect baseball cards," soon launched "a concentrated campaign on behalf of Fortas" in the Senate. The president of Eastern Airlines reported that Eastland's legislative assistant said the senator "will have some fun in opposition initially but ultimately will go along [with] and vote for confirmation." So in addition to promoting Fortas as the candidate of labor groups like the AFL-CIO and the United Auto Workers, both of which enthusiastically backed his nomination, the Administration could sell him as a friend to big business. Senators who wondered aloud why corporate interests were working so hard for confirmation were told that "business and the free enterprise system are behind Abe Fortas" and that the former corporate lawyer "would be an excellent Chief Justice."[53]

And once Eastland was overheard saying, "After [Thurgood] Marshall, I could not go back to Mississippi if a Jewish chief justice swore in the next president," and the National Socialist White People's Party began inveighing against Fortas as "this despicable Jew with a 'red' record that smells to high heaven," the White House could and did insinuate that anyone who disapproved of the nomination did not like Jews either. The American Jewish Committee kept quiet about anti-Semitism as a factor in explaining the opposition to Fortas "first, because we have never believed that the opposition was initially motivated by any such factor, and second, because we thought that any comments by a Jewish organization could be misunderstood and might exacerbate the situation" until the fall, when it became "clear that anti-Semites and extremists" were indeed "exploiting and aggravating" the resistance to Fortas. Long before that, Johnson aide Harry McPherson had told one reporter that "there *are* reactionary voices being raised over this nomination, and that those who have more acceptable purposes in opposing Fortas might find themselves in bed with anti-Semites." The White House helped mobilize Jewish pressure groups and delighted in reports that prominent Jews were "wound up" about the nomination. Griffin remembered fretting frequently about the "'Jewish problem,' not only because I feared that my own position would be misunderstood by many Jewish friends in Michigan, but also because it meant that support would be more difficult to enlist." He continued to worry even after Senator Jacob Javits, the liberal Jewish New York

Republican who ostensibly supported the nominations, promised to "handle" every charge of anti-Semitism lodged against its foes.[54]

Every time any issue involving American Jewry occurred, LBJ thought of the Fortas nomination. After the Ku Klux Klan bombed a synagogue and the home of a Jewish leader in Mississippi, the president telephoned Ramsey Clark. "I would like . . . for us to be on the record, right on this particular day. . . that the Johnson Administration doesn't like this," LBJ said. Senator Stennis of Mississippi might "be a little sober on our nominations, on this Jewish thing, if he realizes that we've got some problems right there." The president himself used the occasion to lobby the FBI's Deke DeLoach to stop the Klan's "guerila warfare" and to urge DeLoach to ask J. Edgar Hoover to remind senators hostile to the nominations that Thornberry would prove tougher on crime than Warren.[55]

And if the combined pressure exerted by the president, his White House staff, corporate leaders, and the Jewish community proved insufficient, Fortas could count on a fully mobilized Department of Justice. Up until this point during the twentieth century, the department had often played a role in nominations, with the attorney general advising the president on prospective justices. But it had not assumed a large and visible role in managing Supreme Court confirmations. Now, the Justice Department prepared memoranda cherry-picking Fortas's opinions to prove he practiced "judicial restraint." As Senator Ervin complained, the department "started to propagandize" the Senate Judiciary Committee and Congress. Both Attorney General Clark and Deputy Attorney General Warren Christopher would testify on behalf of the nominations at the hearings; Clark, to make the case that a vacancy existed, and Christopher, to defend the "judicial restraint" memorandum. LBJ urged Ramsey Clark to delay filing an antitrust suit against Howard Hughes, apparently to avoid irritating the billionaire, a patron of Senator Alan Bible, a conservative Nevada Democrat who was remaining mum about his vote. The level of seen and unseen Justice Department involvement in the confirmation process was unprecedented.[56]

Moreover, though there was great resistance to Fortas in the Senate, it soon became clear that enormous support for him existed there too. After that leader LBJ had yearned for appeared, the nomination pitted two Michiganians against each other. Republican Robert Griffin faced off against Democrat Philip Hart, "a slight, soft-spoken man with a voice loud enough to lead the battle for an end to bigotry and a reputation large enough to be known as 'the conscience of the Senate'" and as one of its most venerated and hard-working liberals. Hart orchestrated the applause for Fortas in the Senate Judiciary Committee and the floor fight for him in the Senate. His participation suggested how much importance liberals attached to the nomination. He devotedly championed Fortas, whom he considered "the best that any appointing authority will be coming up with for a generation."[57]

So if anything, as of early July, the prospects for the nominations seemed good. By now, White House head counts showed as many as seventy-three votes for Fortas. That estimate probably was unrealistic. Still, on July 4, the *Washington Post* editorialized approvingly that the "tempest" over his nomination was apparently "subsiding." It speculated that meant that senators did not want to upset their plans to adjourn before their political conventions by staging a filibuster and seemed certain it meant that they had found "no firm ground on which to make a fight against a nominee as well qualified for the post as is Mr. Fortas." Dirksen's support for the nominees might well settle the matter. "No talkathon without the support of the opposition leadership is likely to get anywhere, and Senator Smathers's praise for the two nominees will have the effect of softening Democratic opposition in the South." The *Post* hailed these "highly favorable omens," since the "last thing the country needs at present is a protracted row over the retirement of Chief Justice Warren."[58]

Still, the president understood that victory would not come easily. That meant that Fortas would have to testify before the Senate Judiciary Committee. Here was a departure. No chief justice nominee had ever appeared before the Senate Judiciary Committee, and no sitting justice, except for recess appointees Brennan and Stewart, had testified either. On the one hand, the White House could have made a good argument that Fortas should not testify. If the Senate Judiciary Committee asked Fortas about his past decisions, as it inevitably would, he would either breach the constitutional commitment to separation of powers by answering them or irritate committee members so much by refusing to do so as to make his appearance counterproductive. Moreover, and contrary to what LBJ had told Eastland, Fortas sensed danger and did not want to testify. On the other hand, Deputy Attorney General Christopher recalled, Fortas had done "superbly well" before the Senate Judiciary Committee in 1965, and he and the White House feared that he would seem "timid" if he declined the invitation to appear three years later. It was only *after* Fortas testified at the hearings and won himself substantial sympathy in the process that the prospects for nominations spiraled downward.[59]

"I Want That Word to Ring in Your Ears"

The hearings also became the moment when the memory of the Warren Court as too "liberal" and "activist" became set in stone for the confirmation process. That was ironic, given how much support remained for both activism and judicial liberalism. Thanks to its opinions, the Warren Court had indeed attracted powerful antagonists by 1968. But recent scholarship has confirmed what was suggested at the time by all those editorials hailing the Marshall and Fortas nominations in 1967–68, some polls, and a number of court watchers: To an extent that would surprise those who painted the Warren Court then and later as outside the mainstream, its decisions largely reflected majority will. After all, even the infamous *Miranda* did not go as far in limiting the police as many had feared, and the court had sounded retreat by approving stop-and-frisks just days before LBJ announced the Fortas and Thornberry nominations. Further, though some of the same senators who tried to make the Warren Court the issue during the Marshall hostilities worked to do so in 1968, their actions again backfired.[60]

Though senators' tactics seemed scattershot, they were not. The underlying issue raised by Fortas's four days of appearance before the committee related to separation of powers—separation of the executive branch from the judiciary and of the judiciary from the legislature. That became apparent the first day when, in a surprising break with tradition, Eastland allowed Griffin to become the Judiciary Committee's first witness, and Griffin called Fortas a crony. "If the doctrine of separate powers is important, what justification could be offered in the event a member of the judicial branch should actively participate on a regular, undisclosed basis in decisions of the executive branch while serving on the Bench?" Griffin asked. Presidents had long appointed "cronies" to the court, Dirksen answered. Lincoln had put his campaign manager, David Davis, on the court; John Kennedy, his deputy attorney general, Byron White. And when Truman named his secretary of treasury, Fred Vinson, chief justice, "nobody got up on his hind legs and shouted cronyism." The "cronyism" charge, Dirksen erupted, was "a frivolous, diaphanous—you know what that means, don't you—gossamer—you know what that means, don't you—argument that just does not hold water." True. Nevertheless, by the following day, when Fortas appeared and referred to "the constitutional limitations" on him as he discussed the court's work with the committee and invoked the principle of separation of powers, he already looked like a hypocrite.[61]

And, some of his opponents suspected, a perjurer. Asked whether he had ever recommended candidates for judgeships or other jobs, Fortas responded that he had never done so. Over the next four decades, it would become clear that his personal files bulged with his evaluations of candidates for White House and judicial positions. Where he said he had just attended a few meetings on Vietnam and had only restated arguments that others had advanced, the documentary record would reveal that he had gone to many and prodded the president to stand firm. Where he denied drafting LBJ's message sending troops into riot-torn Detroit, it would turn out that he had played a key role in its creation. But that lay in the future. To be sure, Fortas made a serious misstep during the early days of the hearings when he declared his pride in aiding Johnson (figure 15). And, after alluding to Detroit and Vietnam, he also outrageously told Senator McClellan, "I guess I have made a full disclosure now because so far as I can recall those

Fortas 'Proud' of Role As a Johnson Adviser

Senate Told Of Aid on Top Issues

By John P. MacKenzie
Washington Post Staff Writer

Justice Abe Fortas said yesterday that he was "proud" to acknowledge that while sitting on the Supreme Court he had helped President Johnson make "fantastically difficult" decisions about the Vietnam war and urban riots.

"I am proud if I at any time have been of the slightest service to the President of my country," said Mr. Johnson's nominee to succeed Earl Warren as Chief Justice of the United States.

Cool and collected during his precedent-breaking session with the Senate Judiciary Committee, Fortas insisted that his role at White House conferences had been strictly limited, that he helped out only when the situation was "critical and desperate" and that his outside activities did not impair his performance on the Nation's highest court.

By Wally McNamee—The Washington Post
"I am proud if I . . . have been of the slightest service to the President of my country."

Figure 15 At his chief justice nomination hearings, Justice Fortas remained defiant and evasive in the face of Senate condemnation of his role as presidential adviser.
John MacKenzie, "Fortas 'Proud' of Role as a Johnson Adviser: Senate Told of Aid on Top Issues," *Washington Post,* July 17, 1968, A1.

are the only two things." That was foolish, because the contemporary media had reported additional though by no means all of the justice's interactions with or on behalf of the White House, about which hostile senators proceeded to grill Fortas, which usually just led Fortas to lie some more.[62]

"Fortas's testimony was so misleading and deceptive that those of us who were aware of his relationship with Johnson winced with each news report of his appearance before the Senate committee," Joe Califano remembered nearly a quarter of a century later in his book about his years with LBJ. (Recall that it drew not just on his memory but research at the Johnson Library as well.)

"Cronyism was now the least of the charges some of us feared." According to Califano, Fortas had counseled LBJ "on the constitutionality of limits on the President's authority to close military bases and of the 1966 D.C. crime bill"; evaluated "the Supreme Court's likely response should the President unilaterally impose wage and price controls"; immersed himself "in shaping Vietnam and economic policies and in advising the President on a variety of crises, ranging from the Detroit riots to the 1967 railroad strike"; and conferred with Johnson "on the Penn-Central case when it was pending before the Supreme Court and then written the Court's final opinion." Scholars detailed additional traces of the justice's imprint on the presidency. Like Califano, though, senators remained unaware of Fortas's assurances to LBJ that the justice was urging his brethren to do something about those "niggers turning over cars" and his reports to the president about court deliberations in the Fred Black case.[63]

Again, however, the concrete evidence from White House files, the justice's papers, and recorded conversations suggesting that Fortas probably committed perjury before the Senate Judiciary Committee only surfaced later and gradually. The media had uncovered just enough in 1968 to suggest that Fortas had not been fully candid about the depth of his involvement in White House affairs. Yet discretion is expected in presidential advisers. And Fortas sounded persuasive when he explained to the Senate that Johnson had turned to him because of their long lawyer–client relationship, declared that he had responded out of patriotism, and echoed Dirksen's reminder that Supreme Court justices traditionally counseled presidents. Further, with one exception, senators had no way to disprove Fortas's claim that none of his interactions with Johnson affected the court. (The exception related to Vietnam: Based on what little they did know about Fortas's involvement in White House policymaking, Senate Judiciary Committee members might have pressed him about how he could decide cases about the constitutionality of the war in the absence of a formal declaration of it, a possible conflict of interest that concerned William O. Douglas. They might also have asked him how he could rule on the constitutionality of draft-card burning.) So when Fortas lectured Senator Ervin, "I cannot conceive of any President of the United States, and certainly not this President, talking to a Supreme Court justice whether his own nominee or not, about anything that might possibly come before the Court as far as the human mind can see," Ervin had to assume the justice was speaking truthfully. What else could Ervin do when Fortas was telling him that "Presidents of the United States do not do that: Justices of the Supreme Court would not tolerate it. That is our country, Senator. That is our country"? Thus, while Fortas's recklessness before the committee was remarkable, it worked to his benefit.[64]

By the time he said that to Ervin, Fortas had already erred by embarrassing the senator. At first, Ervin concentrated on constitutional interpretation. He questioned the nominee about a statement made in a magazine profile: "In his own words, Abe Fortas is a man of the law, and one who believes that the specific meaning of the words of the Constitution has not been fixed." Naturally, that quotation bothered Ervin. Fortas, who had recently responded to a question from Eastland about whether he believed that the words of the Constitution retained their "original meaning" by contending that certain phrases like "due process of law" were not "simple and clear and unmistakable in their meaning," told Ervin that he had often characterized himself as "a man of the law." He did not, however, remember calling constitutional meanings indeterminate. "Certainly I believe firmly, profoundly, that the words of the Constitution are our guideposts, and our only guideposts in deciding what the Constitution has said," along with what judges have "said about the meaning of those words." Did a Supreme Court that "habitually" overruled prior decisions rob law of its value to society? Ervin asked next. "Senator, we should not overrule prior decisions lightly, except in the clearest kind of case," Fortas answered. Then he got cute by quoting from one of Ervin's opinions as a North Carolina Supreme Court justice saying that courts should not follow precedent when that would perpetuate wrongs. "Senator, I would not go that far myself," Fortas observed. "I never voted to overrule but one case," Ervin objected. "Is that right?" Fortas answered. "Well, forgive me for personalizing this. I guess I got a little carried away." The audience, and especially the press, greeted Fortas's excursion into Ervin's past "with great gusto," Griffin saw, and delighted in the way the nominee had cleverly given his interrogator a taste of "his own medicine." Yet, as Griffin said, Ervin did not forget it, and as the hearings continued, he played "a crucial role in developing the case against the Justice."[65]

That case did not rest just on Fortas's role as presidential adviser or his approach to constitutional interpretation, but also on specific decisions by the Warren Court, which, Griffin acknowledged, was "the only real issue in the Fortas nomination" for "many senators." It was not just Fortas, but the Warren Court that was on trial for disregarding the Constitution, Ervin showed, as he proceeded to lay out his disagreement with more than twenty opinions at length, beginning with *Amalgamated Food Employees Union v. Logan Valley Plaza*. There, Fortas joined a majority of the court in declaring a First Amendment right to picket peacefully in a shopping center parking lot open to the public. Though Ervin prudently kept quiet about *Brown v. Board of Education*, he criticized the court's civil rights, labor law, and especially criminal law cases. The senator devoted eighteen minutes alone to *Miranda*. Fortas tried to score points by calling attention to *Terry v. Ohio* and other Warren Court opinions siding with law enforcement and pointing out that when the court ordered a new trial in *Miranda* and other cases, suspects often were found guilty. Just in the last term, the court had affirmed or allowed to stand at least 92% of the eighteen hundred criminal law cases presented to it, he observed. "The cases that are not hard, that are not on the frontier of the law, we handle by orders. ... It is kind of rough when all that is visible on the Court, Senator, are the hard cases." Otherwise, the justice further irritated Ervin by refusing to answer his questions about cases and enduring the critique in silence. Justice Fortas, Ervin complained later, had written "books about cases [apparently a reference to the nominee's pamphlet on dissent and disobedience], he has discussed public issues, [has been] meeting with students, and it also appears he has conferred with the President on various public matters, and also that he called up a friend to get his friend corrected on ... the cost of the Vietnam War." But ever since Thurgood Marshall, Ervin erroneously contended, nominees had invoked "what you might call the so-called judicial nominee fifth amendment."[66]

The attack on the court and on the nomination process that perpetuated it, however, failed. It was not just that many still admired the Warren Court. It was also that, as liberals had insisted during the Thurgood Marshall confirmation hearings, a good number of senators believed it their duty to evaluate nominees on the basis of fitness only, and shrank from attempts to probe ideology through questions about cases, an area where nominees had long been expected to provide evasive answers, anyway. While some declared their opposition to Fortas's judicial behavior, Senate Judiciary Committee member Hugh Scott of Pennsylvania, a moderate Republican, was lining up behind Fortas, his Georgetown neighbor. And Scott argued that senators should not examine "the philosophy of the nominees ... but whether or not they are qualified to serve on the Court by reason of intellectual competence and respect for the constitutional system as well." Further, Griffin acknowledged, Ervin's exposition was technical, almost dull. And when Ervin and others badgered the witness, they sounded as demagogic about crime as Joe McCarthy had about communism in the 1950s. All the while, Fortas won points for his impressive restraint. As Griffin said, by questioning the record of the Warren Court, Ervin simply increased "sympathy for the Justice" during "what was commonly referred to as his 'ordeal.'" (That was the way Fortas thought of it too. "I am *not* a mild man, and it *was* an ordeal," he wrote Philip Hart.)[67]

Strom Thurmond fared even more poorly than Ervin when he tried to make the Warren Court an issue. On July 18, the third day that Fortas came before the committee, Thurmond berated Fortas about the court for over two hours. Recognizing *Brown v. Board of Education* as a battle lost, Thurmond focused his civil rights fire on the court's decisions upholding the Civil Rights Act of 1964 and the Voting Rights Act of 1965. "You expressed your views to the President when he has called you down there, and over the telephone," he admonished Fortas. "Why shouldn't a Senator have the benefit of your views?" And how was it that Fortas could not discuss his reasoning about activists' right to sit in at libraries in *Brown v. Louisiana*, when, in addition to writing the majority opinion there, he had written a pamphlet about the limits of the right to disobey the law in dissenting and spoken about that topic at colleges and universities? Separation of powers was responsible, Fortas answered. "I do not like this situation as a man," he added.[68]

What apparently galled Thurmond even more than the court's positions on civil rights or speech, however, were the court's criminal procedure decisions, and Fortas's refusal to answer questions about them. Suddenly, Thurmond turned his attention to the 1957 case of *Mallory v. United States*, which the Senate had tried to overrule just recently. After the Supreme Court ensured the release of Andrew Mallory, an African American, from death row in 1957, he was arrested for beating a woman in DC in 1958 and raping a woman in Philadelphia in 1960. (Ultimately, Philadelphia police killed Mallory in a gunfight.) As he described the case, Thurmond—by premeditation or spontaneously—worked himself into a rage:

> Does not that decision, Mallory—I want that word to ring in your ears—Mallory—the man happened to have been from my State, incidentally—shackle law enforcement? Mallory, a man who raped a woman, admitted his guilt, and the Supreme Court turned him loose on a technicality. And who I was told later went to Philadelphia and committed another crime and somewhere else another crime because the courts turned him loose on technicalities. Is not that type of decision calculated to bring the courts and the law and the administration of justice in disrepute? Is not that type of decision calculated to encourage more people to commit rapes and serious crimes? Can you as a Justice of the Supreme Court condone such a decision as that?[69]

By this point, as the *Post* sympathetically observed, Fortas had undergone "two days of hazing, . . . but Ervin's criticism had not approached Thurmond's personal verbal assault." Reporters noted the shocked look on the justice's face. They saw how he turned to James Eastland in anticipation that the Senate Judiciary Committee chair would call for order. But Eastland, who "was slouching and reading from a document," seemed oblivious to the scene before him. Fortas said nothing for several moments, then slowly and dramatically responded, "Senator, because of my respect for you and this body and my respect for the Constitution of the United States and my position as Associate Justice of the Supreme Court of the United States, I will adhere to the limitations I believe the Constitution places upon me and will not reply to your question."[70]

Thurmond continued to bolster the justice's case the next day, his last before the committee. By now, a claque had gathered to fortify the nominee. Thurmond questioned whether Fortas agreed with the Pennsylvania Supreme Court chief justice who had charged "that the recent decisions of a majority of the Supreme Court of the United States which shackle the police and courts and make it terribly difficult to protect society from crime and criminals are among the principal reasons for the turmoil and near-revolutionary conditions which prevail in our country and especially in Washington." Now, according to *Time*, the justice permitted himself to display anger for the first time. "No," he answered, to the applause of his supporters. Thurmond denounced "the demonstration," and Eastland threatened to clear the room. "All that happened," Philip Hart soothed, "was that some people were pleased that the Justice did not agree that, whatever the crime rate is, it is a consequence of Supreme Court decisions." None of them seemed like long-haired crazies. "As I look over the room, everybody looks nice and clean and fine and fresh." There had been "mild scattered applause for a statement that I would have applauded myself."[71]

Outside the committee room, too, there was plenty of applause for Fortas, who was apparently winning the match. Distinguished law professors, attorneys, and officers of the American Bar Association leapt to defend him against the "vicious" and disrespectful attacks. Obviously, the Judiciary Committee would not unanimously support the nomination, but a majority of its members would. Those at the White House still believed they had the votes to prevail against a filibuster on the Senate floor.[72]

As the Fortas controversy disappeared into the mists of time, Thurmond's attempt to make "Fortas the scapegoat for the sins of the Warren Court" was remembered as "an effective strategy." But it did not seem one in 1968. Like Griffin, Thurmond's legislative aide mourned that Fortas's opponents had come across as rigid and overbearing bullies; the nominee himself, heroically self-contained. "Our strategy in the Fortas hearings has been a disastrous mistake," James Lucier admonished his boss. Thurmond should not have asked the justice about his reaction to criticism of the court or questioned him about court decisions. "Obviously, he is not going to agree with attacks upon himself," and none of the answers the justice had given would cause any senator to change his vote. "The result is that the line of questioning did not appear to be a sincere attempt to investigate his views; rather, it appeared to be an irrational attempt to delay and harass." Thurmond had turned Fortas "into a martyr" and strengthened him. "Even though our questions were constructed upon the premise that Fortas and the Court have undermined the Constitution, Fortas managed to turn the tables and make it appear that Senator Thurmond was recklessly disregarding Constitutional principles, while he, Fortas, was patiently trying to uphold them in the face of great provocation."[73]

And Thornberry, who spent two days before the Senate Judiciary Committee, provided more of the same. When Ervin put Thornberry on the spot about his poll tax opinion, he proved as unforthcoming as Fortas. "They cannot tell us anything about the future, and they cannot tell us anything about the past, which means they cannot tell us anything," the senator griped before giving up in evident disgust. To Fred Graham, who described how Thornberry looked at his Senate interrogators "unblinkingly as if no answers were expected," the second nominee seemed "more at ease" than Fortas. But Thornberry's prospects for a vote with Fortas were dimming. Eastland was now saying that some committee members refused to question him because of their doubt about the existence of a vacancy and that he would "probably be called back after Mr. Justice Fortas'[s] matter is determined by the Senate." That might mean there was no time to confirm Thornberry during this congressional session.[74]

Thanks in part to Thurmond's overkill, however, Fortas's chances still looked good. The nominee's opponents were not united. Indeed, Griffin, the Northern Republican, and Thurmond, the Southern Republican, and the Southern Democrats all violently mistrusted one another. Theirs was "a shaky alliance at best," one Griffin staffer said. A "key southern aide" voiced a complaint simmering on both sides of the aisle when he maintained that Griffin "was in this fight for his personal glory." Griffin angered Southern Democrats when he contended that Fortas rightly refused to answer questions about his Supreme Court decisions and insisted that there was no need for a filibuster because a majority would defeat Fortas. For his part, Thurmond darkly informed one of his aides that McClellan, Ervin, and Eastland were cowards who might not oppose the nomination unless they were certain of its defeat. In contrast, LBJ's allegiance to Fortas was rock solid. Clearly, Fortas's opponents required a game changer.[75]

"Strom's Dirty Movies"

They found it when James Clancy testified on July 22. The Irish Catholic had encountered pornography as an assistant city attorney when a sexual assault survivor "reported to the police that the person who had raped her had a girlie magazine in his pocket." Clancy decided that pornography produced violence and poisoned the family. By 1968, he had become the attorney for the Citizens for Decent Literature (CDL), a group founded by Charles Keating (who was to achieve a different kind of notoriety in the 1980s when he defrauded investors and helped create the savings-and-loan crisis). Conscious that previous antismut movements had failed because the public mistrusted their connections to the Catholic Church, support for censorship, and self-righteous "humorless puritan[ism]," the CDL maintained that it did not oppose sex, just pornography that met or should be found to have met the legal definition of "obscenity." It was porn, said CDL's stable of social scientists and experts, that caused sex crimes, juvenile delinquency, and homosexuality.[76]

Accompanied by Keating, Clancy came before the Senate Judiciary Committee to allege that in forty-nine of fifty-two of the court's recent decisions in the realm of obscenity law, Fortas had repeatedly cast "the deciding vote" that the material was not obscene. Clancy carried with him a half-hour slide show with highlights of porn films the court's rulings allowed to remain in circulation. He also brought two peep show films available in "adult" movie arcades, "0-7" and "0-12." Clancy was particularly irritated that in its one-sentence ruling in *Schackman v. California*, the court had overturned rulings that "0-7" was ineligible for First Amendment protection because it was obscene.[77]

So what? The obscenity issue, Fortas's defenders correctly observed, was phony. In reality, it was not clear that Fortas had ever cast the deciding vote in any of these opinions, since most of the court's obscenity decisions were unsigned. His one signed dissent in the area actually should have pleased the Citizens for Decent Literature because it argued that states could constitutionally enact laws protecting children from obscenity. The justice had even persuaded a majority of the court to accept a deal that, Scot Powe said, sent a pornographer "to jail without even a fig leaf of due process" to protect a literary work, John Cleland's *Fanny Hill*. *Schackman* itself included no explanation for the decision. The court had overruled the lower court in *Schackman* because the police who seized the film lacked a valid warrant. And although Clancy and Keating could show that in the 1950s, Fortas had submitted an amicus brief to the Supreme Court in defense of a publisher of pornography, even they seemed uncertain that had any bearing on his judicial behavior.[78]

At a time of concern about the erosion of the family and law and order, however, none of the obvious responses to Clancy's charges mattered. Instead, for Fortas's opponents, Clancy's appearance transformed Fortas into the nation's number one porn peddler. "Stamping Out Smut Means Stopping Abe Fortas," vowed one advertisement. And buried within the lengthy memorandum that Clancy and Keating submitted to the committee was an accurate claim: Justice Fortas was the only member of the court in the 1967 case of *Jacobs v. New York* who would have reversed the obscenity convictions of filmmakers and critics Jonas Mekas and Ken Jacobs for screening "Flaming Creatures," Jack Smith's instant underground classic. "To the tune of scratchy recordings of 'Amapola' and other pseudo-Latin rhythms, fantastically draped beings, male and female (although one is often unsure which is which), commingle in settings of Spanish and Arabian décor . . . , parade their genitalia before the camera, and eventually indulge in a ridiculous orgy that seems to coincide with an earthquake," the *New Yorker* reported of the film. To intellectuals, it seemed more of "a spoof of 'forbidden' eroticism and a parody of pornography, rather than the real thing."

As Fortas knew, the *Village Voice* had advertised the screening, a teacher at the New School had shown "Flaming Creatures" in his class, and media critic Susan Sontag did not consider "Flaming Creatures" pornographic. In fact, her paean to the film used it to introduce the concept of "camp" to the mainstream.[79]

Avant-garde praise meant precious little to Strom Thurmond and James Eastland. "I can still see Eastland, cigar in hand, saying the following to me after Clancy's testimony," Griffin's aide remembered later: "You're with Griffin—aren't you? You know this obscenity thing will be the issue that gets Fortas. Once the public is aroused, it'll be all over." It was the only "substantive" comment Eastland ever made to him over the entire fight. "Thanks to Abe Fortas, 0-7 would go down in history with as much popularity as Ian Fleming's 007," Griffin predicted.[80]

Not quite. A contemporary article for *Harper's* entitled "Strom's Dirty Movies" contradicted Thurmond's claim that "0-7" had "shocked" the jaded Washington journalists whom the senator immediately invited, along with other senators, to watch the film. "Mostly the press corps giggled." One scholar later explained that "0-7" was "obviously pornographic," but was "actually pretty tame," featuring a "silent striptease, with no sexual intercourse." Senator Smathers told LBJ that Philip Hart had attended one of the screenings and "didn't think it was so bad."[81]

Yet, as Smathers recognized, this "marginal" issue of obscenity was "pretty dangerous," and "they're really making a big thing out of it." Until now, he explained to the president, Strom Thurmond had looked like "a real nut" and "hasn't really made much sense," but the dirty movies gave people "looking for some reason" to oppose the nominations a chance to complain "that your mother and your sister and your daughters and everybody [else] could go see this damn thing." As Deputy Attorney General Warren Christopher testified about the Justice Department's memorandum making Fortas an apostle of judicial restraint the day after Clancy appeared before the committee, Thurmond ostentatiously thumbed through "several 'girlie' and 'nudist' magazines to the distraction of the entire audience," Griffin's aide remembered. Then the senator peppered Christopher with questions about obscenity, blamed the surfeit of "filthy, obscene material" that threatened the family on the Supreme Court, and announced that Fortas should return to explain his obscenity votes to the Senate Judiciary Committee. "Thurmond Brandishes Nude Pictures, Wants More Testimony from Fortas," read the front page of the *Arkansas Gazette*.[82]

That headline was bound to get Senator McClellan's attention. So were "0-7" and "0-12," when he watched them with other senators. "John was preaching and ranting and raving about how this kind of thing was ruining the life of his grandchildren and everybody else," Smathers informed LBJ. (McClellan should watch Anne Bancroft seduce a young Dustin Hoffman in "The Graduate," the president joked.) Privately, after the hearings had concluded on July 23, McClellan acknowledged to the White House that Fortas was "probably the most able lawyer he knows." Yet he wondered about the justice's "philosophy as it applies to crime" and wanted every Senate Judiciary Committee member to view the films before they voted on the nominations. Predictably, McClellan won a one-week delay on July 23, so he could study the obscenity issue.[83]

McClellan then viewed "Flaming Creatures" with Eastland, a few other senators, and some reporters in a small basement room of the Capitol (figure 16). For the Arkansan, "Flaming Creatures" was not art, just "crude vulgarity." It included same-sex sex, for which he had no tolerance. (As Marc Stein and Tuan Samahon have shown, not just McClellan, but also LBJ and the "liberal" Warren Court majority members who helped make the heterosexual revolution of "the sixties" possible displayed little appreciation for gay rights.) And as McClellan's legislative aide reminded the senator, Fortas was apparently the lone judicial champion of "Flaming Creatures." Damaging in themselves, "0-7" and "0-12" proved lethal when "Flaming Creatures" was added to them. "Is this the type of individual we want as Chief Justice of the Supreme Court of the United States?" McClellan's aide inquired.[84]

Plenty of others were now asking that question. The Citizens for Decent Literature announced its plans to distribute copies of "0-7," "0-12," and "Flaming Creatures" to women's groups and civic organizations. And when the Senate Judiciary Committee recessed for the nominating conventions on August 3 without reporting out the nominations, the battle moved to the press. After viewing "0-12," syndicated columnist James Kilpatrick wrote, "Let me put it bluntly: If this filthy little peep-show qualifies for protection under the lofty ideals of 'freedom of speech and of the press,' as the First Amendment is interpreted by a majority of the high court, something is fearfully wrong." Such outrage, Griffin reported, meant more constituent mail. "The nomination of Abe Fortas as U.S. Supreme Court Chief Justice has run into unexpected trouble," Thurmond crowed. Fortas's antagonists encouraged undecided senators to see the films and decide for themselves. In the next two months, Griffin remembered, "the films were shown dozens of times" to "more than 30 senators," their staffers, and reporters. (No women were invited to the screenings.) "Even those Senators, such as myself, who started the offensive against Justice Fortas on more lofty grounds attended the screenings and were shocked by what we saw." Now that the hearings had ended and the Senate was in recess, the momentum was shifting toward Fortas's opponents.[85]

Nails in the Coffin

Ironically, Fortas still had plenty of support. True, a June Gallup poll had reported that in answer to the question "When new appointments are made by the

Figure 16 Senator Strom Thurmond used the obscenity issue to sink LBJ's attempt to make Fortas chief justice. A 1968 Herblock Cartoon. Copyright © The Herb Block Foundation.

President to the Supreme Court, would you like to have these people be people who are liberal or conservative in their political views?" 51% of the public opted for "conservatives," 30% for "liberals," and 19% had no opinion. But an August Harris poll showed that the public favored Fortas's confirmation by almost a two-to-one margin, and the administration estimated that two-thirds of Senate Judiciary Committee members supported it. So did the "solid majority of the Senate" that considered the nominee "superbly qualified," Philip Hart stressed. The mainstream media continued to stand behind Fortas too, as did the legal profession. At a well-covered press conference, the president of the American College of Trial Lawyers alleged that Thurmond's behavior at the hearings placed him "almost on the lunatic fringe" and that he and "a small group of senators" endangered an independent judiciary. Yale Law School Dean Louis Pollak repeatedly charged that Fortas and Thornberry's opponents posed "a grave threat to the independence of the judiciary and hence to our basic constitutional structure" too. American Bar Association President William Gossett scrapped publicly over the nominations with Griffin, a personal friend, and accused him of playing politics in a way "unworthy of a United States Senator." (For his part, Griffin scorned the ABA for "rubberstamping" the Fortas and Thornberry nominations.) Liberals swallowed their dissatisfaction with Fortas's hawkishness on Vietnam to work hard for his confirmation because of his civil rights and civil liberties record. Some of the nation's most eminent lawyers and law school deans formed the Lawyers' Committee on Supreme Court Nominations to urge the Senate to consider the nominations promptly and fairly.[86]

Nevertheless, LBJ understood that seemed increasingly unlikely. On July 30, he received a report from an associate who had talked with *Newsweek*'s Sam Shaffer. To end a filibuster, the White House needed two-thirds of the senators present to support a cloture motion to stop it. But Shaffer maintained "there are 43 'hard' votes against cloture and that the anti-Fortas group has gained in strength and that the pornography issue has been 'devastating.'" As so often happened, the constituents who opposed a presidential nominee were proving more vocal than those who supported him. Senators' mail was running against Fortas, "in some cases [by] as much as 25 to 1." Moreover, Shaffer said, some Southerners had "discovered that they can placate the Jewish vote by promising to work for arms for Israel and therefore they are not worried about opposition to Fortas." A week later, when Senator Eastland visited the president at his Texas ranch and again predicted defeat, Johnson came to see that "we probably could not muster the votes to put the Fortas nomination through."[87]

But "probably" was not the same as "definitely." LBJ now was telling Joe Califano and others that the opposition to the nomination represented an attack on him, as it did. His enemies had been unable to "bring down the President," Johnson would say, they couldn't repeal his programs, his civil rights bills, but they could bring down Fortas." They must not succeed, and he would keep Congress in session until Christmas to secure the confirmation. "So Johnson dug in, and we all tried harder." When Dirksen telephoned LBJ to wish him happy birthday on August 27, the president wanted to make sure that the senator was not "pulling in" his horns on Fortas. "I told Fortas and these folks you were going to see he's confirmed, and, by God, I want you to stand up there and slug it out." It was difficult, Dirksen chuckled, when Democrats like Eastland, Ervin, and McClellan all opposed the nomination. "Are you less optimistic about Fortas than you were?" LBJ asked. "Well," the senator said before LBJ interrupted to inquire whether Fortas's opponents wanted "Warren to go back on that bench"? "Oh, Christ, I don't want him to go back," Dirksen answered. "I'm going to stay and I'll do my best." As Dirksen's response made it clear, Fortas's Senate opponents cared more about defeating him than his advocates did about championing him. The White House recognized that "Griffin and the Southerners are knocking us around pretty hard every day now," and "we need a lot more enthusiasm among our supporters."[88]

Fortas was becoming less optimistic too, though he displayed a happy face for the media when he vacationed in Westport after the hearings (figure 17). He publicly blamed the reaction against the nominations on the opposition to the Warren Court and hit the speech trail to defend himself. He had listened to critics on the Senate Judiciary Committee in "outraged silence," he informed the National Postal Forum. Some "professed friends of law and order" jeopardized the independent judiciary at the core of the constitutional order, he told the American College of Trial Lawyers. "To set aside the conviction of a man who has been tried in violation of the standards of our constitution is not to set it aside on a mere technicality," he reminded his very enthusiastic audience. "Constitutionalism is not a technicality. This is the phrase that should ring in the Nation's ear."[89]

That was the song Fortas also sang for Warren. Newspapers "covering the entire political spectrum" had hailed the nominations and run "editorials favorable to our cause," he stressed to the chief justice. The Senate opposition reflected "Nixon-Republican partisanship" and the "bitter, corrosive opposition" of some Democrats and Republicans "to all that has been happening in the Court and the country: the racial progress, and the insistence upon increased regard for human rights and dignity in the field of criminal law. Other elements contribute to the mix, but it's my guess that they are minor."[90]

Fortas did not really consider them so minor. To his Connecticut neighbor and close personal friend on the court, John Harlan, who worried about the propriety of justices advising presidents, Fortas defiantly acknowledged he had hurt his chances by helping at the White House. "I have responded—with uneasiness—because of friendship and sympathy for the President. Indeed,

Figure 17 Fortas and Carol Agger on a break in Westport from Washington and the chief justice controversy, Summer 1968. William Sauro, *New York Times*.

looking back on it, I think I agree with myself, and would take the same position all over again because I believe I did bring him some comfort; because I cannot believe that I injured the Court as an institution; and because I really don't care if my response to the President's requests contributes to the withholding of my confirmation as Chief Justice." To his closest friend at the court, William O. Douglas, who was spending the summer in Washington State, Fortas blamed the nominations' reception on the reaction against the Warren Court, opposition to LBJ, and anti-Semitism:

> I don't know how much you have heard about the events relating to my nomination. It's been pretty bloody. All the accumulated venom about practically everything seems to have come to a focus. The principal mouthpieces of evil are Senators Thurmond and Ervin, but as you know, they merely reflect in an articulate way the feeling of others.
>
> Primarily the bitter response mirrors the opposition to what has happened with respect to the racial question and the general revolution of human dignity, reflected by our decisions in the field of criminal law,

etc. Secondarily are the factors of resentment to the President and a small admixture of bigotry towards me. I think the last is quite a small factor, but it would be pointless to say that it doesn't play some part.

Every decent constitutional decision in the last three years, and for some years prior thereto, has been denounced. Now they have discovered that I was part of the majority which voted to clear a lot of "filthy movies."[91]

Reasonable people could disagree about why the nominations had run into a roadblock, and Fortas shaded his explanation, depending on his audience. It was, however, "highly doubtful that the Administration forces could break the threatened filibuster," he confided to Douglas. The only "slight hope," both Fortas and the *New York Times* agreed, lay in something like a strong statement by candidate Nixon opposing a filibuster, which the Fortas forces thought he might make to attract the Jewish vote. The justice may have known that Javits planned to urge Nixon to oppose the filibuster, as the senator did in late August. "I suppose it really depends on Nixon," Fortas told Douglas. "If he thinks a filibuster will hurt, he'll call it off."[92]

That was a pipe dream. Pat Buchanan had urged Nixon to get out front in fighting the nomination and stoked the candidate's fears by repeating rumors that if the Fortas nomination succeeded, Black and Douglas would resign, and LBJ would replace them with Tom Kuchel and Arthur Goldberg. But Nixon was trying to steer a course between the liberal Humphrey and the racist George Wallace by running as the elder statesman who could "bring us together." So, as Buchanan said later, though Nixon "wanted the Fortas nomination killed," the cautious candidate "did not want our fingerprints on the murder weapon." Consequently, he secretly encouraged Fortas's opponents to block the nomination. Given what is now known about Nixon's attitude toward Jews, it seems certain that the candidate cringed when he contemplated a Jewish chief justice administering him the oath of office.[93]

Even though few then realized the intensity of Nixon's anti-Semitism, it was clear at the time that Strom Thurmond had become a "kingmaker" at the Republican Convention in early August when he held the South for Nixon against a challenge from Ronald Reagan. Nixon displayed his gratitude by, among other things, promising to nominate "strict constructionists" to the court who construed the Constitution narrowly and by giving Thurmond a veto over vice presidential candidates. Why would Nixon run afoul of Thurmond by actively opposing a filibuster? Instead, the Republican candidate appeased Jewish voters and responded to Humphrey's allegations that he was "wiggling and wobbling" about Fortas to pay off Thurmond by belatedly announcing in mid-September that he neither supported the nominee nor opposed him and that he opposed a filibuster, just as he opposed "any filibuster." As Washington reporter Robert Shogan observed, Griffin and other Republicans could easily dismiss that as "a pro forma objection." After all, as the *Chicago Tribune* said, by this time, Nixon had allowed the GOP to adopt a platform that "slaps at the Supreme Court confirmations of President Johnson's cronies, Abe Fortas and Homer Thornberry," by declaring that the achievement of law and order required an independent judiciary. Further, in his speech accepting the Republican nomination, Nixon had taken law and order as his theme and stressed that "some of our courts in their decisions have gone too far in weakening the peace forces as against the criminal forces in this country and we must act to restore the balance." In a dig at Ramsey Clark, he had also pledged to appoint an attorney general who would "open a new front against the filth peddlers . . . who are corrupting the lives of children of this country."[94]

Three weeks after that speech at the Republican convention, some of those "peace forces" brutally attacked antiwar and New Left demonstrators who protested outside the Democratic National Convention in Chicago at which Hubert Humphrey received his party's nomination. Although demonstrators engaged in provocative acts, an official report for the National Commission on the Causes and Prevention of Violence found that "on the part of the police there was enough wild club swinging, enough cries of hatred, enough gratuitous beating to make the conclusion inescapable that individual policemen, and lots of them, committed violent acts far in excess of the requisite force for crowd dispersal or arrest." That was also Attorney General Ramsey Clark's opinion, as well as the conclusion of most of the media. "I think we've got a bunch of thugs here, if I may be permitted to say so," the venerable CBS anchorman, Walter Cronkite, observed of the police on the air. But at the time, many Americans who watched and read about the "numbing" violence on the streets of Chicago and the accompanying chaos inside the convention hall in their living rooms sympathized with the police—even though Mayor Richard Daley repeatedly complained of distorted media coverage that he claimed falsely created the impression of police brutality. In addition to providing further evidence of the breakdown of the social fabric, the convention vividly highlighted Johnson's unpopularity in his own party. The politically depleted president had to skip the convention because leading Democrats warned that antiwar delegates might boo him.[95]

The convention, which left the Democrats as divided as the Republicans were united, thus dealt a blow to the hopes not just of Humphrey, who would nevertheless come close to denying Nixon the presidency in November, but to LBJ's court nominees as well. "The violent clashes in Chicago between club-swinging police and youthful antiwar, anti-Humphrey demonstrators" were bound to affect the Fortas fight by "strengthening the hands of those in Congress who have long deplored the breakdown in law and order," one reporter predicted.

Congressional critics would intensify their criticism of Fortas's "decisions that they view as soft on criminals and demonstrators." Those charges, along with the harmony between Republicans, could doom the nominations.[96]

Despite the clear handwriting on the wall, LBJ refused to read it. On September 5, a day after just Eastland and four other Senate Judiciary Committee members had shown up for a committee meeting that was then cancelled for lack of a quorum, both Mansfield and Dirksen said publicly that the prospects for Fortas's Senate confirmation were, as Dirksen put it, "not roseate." Mansfield, Dirksen, and a majority of the Senate still ostensibly sided with the nominee, and the justice still had his vigorous supporters like Philip Hart, but it seemed unlike the Fortas forces they had the votes they needed to break the threatened filibuster. Hours later, the president's press secretary said that Johnson still hoped for confirmation. The following day, LBJ held another surprise news conference about the Fortas nomination and raised the specter of anti-Semitism by referring to the battle over Brandeis. "We believe that there are more than two to one in the committee would favor reporting it if they were permitted to vote" and the "vote is almost that strong in the Senate," he stressed. He had told Mansfield and Dirksen "that in view of the fact that the friends of Justice Fortas felt that between 60 and 70 percent of the people favored the nomination, we should not allow a little group, a sectional group primarily who disapprove of some opinions Supreme Court justices have rendered, to be able, by parliamentary tricks, to filibuster and prevent the majority from expressing its viewpoint." Mansfield thereupon publicly threatened to keep the Senate in session until after the end of the year to force Fortas's confirmation.[97]

So far so good, but LBJ remained dissatisfied. He complained to Ramsey Clark that Dirksen was not providing sufficient support. "He always starts out one way and winds up the other," the president remarked of the Senate's "Master of the U-Turn." Further, Griffin was constantly holding press conferences to "make 40 allegations, and we just get tried and convicted every day." For example, why didn't Senator Javits play the anti-Semitism card instead of pretending that it did not figure into opposition to the nomination? "God almighty," extremists had called Fortas "a red, communist Jew." The president told Clark a favorite story about the candidate who accused his opponent of sleeping with a hog. The moral: "[M]ake the son of a bitch spend the afternoon" doing the research he needed to deny the charge, instead of providing him time to attack. "Now, we don't keep them busy" by, for example, finding some reason that Griffin had made the Fortas case his cause. Why had the senator opposed the nomination before it was announced? LBJ wanted to know. "He wasn't worried about pornography," the president exclaimed of Griffin. "Anybody'd look at his face and tell . . . that doesn't bother him. Pornography! He was just worried that, by God, he . . . couldn't make a partisan, political deal out of the Chief Justice [nomination]."[98]

Griffin was indeed a master of the slow kill. In a July speech at the National Press Club predicting the nomination's defeat and dismissing the idea that anti-Semitism motivated its opponents as a "phony issue," he had promised to present "a great many more facts" about the nominee to the Senate. During the August recess, he had continued collecting them. By the time that Congress reconvened in September, with the nomination still mired in the Senate Judiciary Committee, Griffin had uncovered more evidence about Fortas's relationship with LBJ. A journalist had disclosed, accurately, that with Clark Clifford, Fortas had helped write Johnson's 1966 State of the Union speech. Summoned by the Senate to testify about Fortas's contribution, the defense secretary pleaded a lack of "precise recollection" and the duties of his busy office. Further, Senator Gordon Allott, a Colorado Republican, had alleged that Fortas had participated in drafting the legislation providing Secret Service protection for presidential candidates that the White House had introduced in the aftermath of Robert Kennedy's assassination. That charge was untrue. But the White House, loath to get in a "swearing match" with Allott by labeling him a liar, infuriated Senator McClellan and others by citing executive privilege and refusing to send any administration aide before the Judiciary Committee to refute it.[99]

For Griffin, these two pieces of evidence proved anew that Fortas had not made full disclosure, and he successfully recommended reopening the hearings. Thurmond welcomed that prospect and arranged for more testimony about pornography by an officer in the Los Angeles Police Department Vice Division. He arrived with several films that the senators had not yet seen, along with "two suitcases filled with pornographic materials of all kinds." (Griffin and others continued "enticing" senators to view the films right up until the battle's end.)[100]

Both Griffin and Thurmond cited the new accusations as reason to ask Fortas to testify again. LBJ believed "that it would be fatal if he did not." Attorney General Clark, however, contended that those committee members who scheduled new hearings on September 13 and 16 simply wanted to "embarrass the Court." The justice refused to reappear.[101]

Griffin himself initially refused to touch the most explosive new charge. His office had received an anonymous tip from an American University employee in July that the law school had paid Fortas $15,000, the equivalent of more than $100,000 in 2016 dollars. The dean had raised the money from businessmen's contributions that permitted him to hire the justice to teach a weekly two-hour seminar on law and social policy over the summer. After Griffin concluded that the evidence was too "slim" to make that allegation public, his aide turned it over to Ervin and Thurmond. They ran with it. When Thurmond telephoned American University Law School Dean B. J. Tennery to "invite" him to testify lest he face a subpoena, the dean refused to say how much he had paid Fortas or where he had gotten the money for the justice's salary. Thurmond responded that the committee knew that Fortas had received $15,000 and that he would expect him to provide the names of the donors.[102]

As a consequence, Tennery publicly acknowledged to the committee at the second round of hearings that Fortas's former partner, Paul Porter, had obtained the money from five corporate executives. Three were former clients of Fortas's, and one's son was appealing a fraud and conspiracy conviction in federal court. Because Supreme Court justices at the time, like senators, often received lecture fees, Porter saw nothing wrong with arranging the course. Like everyone else who knew Fortas well, he realized that as a Supreme Court justice, his friend felt financially strapped. But Porter also rightly sensed a "certain restlessness" in Fortas. He realized that his friend, a former law professor, liked to teach, and he reasoned that the topic of law and social policy had long interested Fortas. Though Porter wrote some of the donors to express Fortas's gratitude, that was blarney. In fact, Porter refused to apprise the justice of the contributors' identities, apparently because he did not want to compromise his friend.[103]

Yet the arrangement still seemed inappropriate. Once LBJ nominated him as chief justice, his backers and antagonists agreed, Fortas should have cancelled the seminar, perhaps by citing the need to prepare for the hearings. Alternatively, he should have gotten out in front of any potential embarrassment it might cause by asking Porter to disclose its sponsors. Dirksen was overheard telling Eastland the obvious, "This is going to look awfully bad in print." Even though Fortas did not know exactly who had funded the course, he should have realized how Porter would gather the money to mount it. And although no one could prove that the justice had known who sponsored the seminar before Tennery's testimony, the salary still seemed suspicious; the fee, excessive, particularly after the dean told Thurmond that the most he had previously paid any teacher for a nine-week seminar was "somewhere in the neighborhood of maybe $2,000." Over and over again, hostile senators would observe that Fortas's former partner had solicited contributions from his former clients. Senator McClellan denounced Fortas for citing separation of powers to justify his refusal to answer the Senate Judiciary Committee's question about cases and then discussing them at a university for "about $1,000 an hour."[104]

The lecture fees became yet another excuse to jump ship. Richard Russell cited them, along with the fact that "at least 99%" of his constituent mail on Fortas was negative, when he wrote the president in September saying that he could not support Johnson's chief justice nomination. One Griffin aide judged that the revelations particularly disturbed nine other senators as well. Griffin, who believed that the fees "above all else, had a dramatic—and perhaps decisive—influence on the outcome of the controversy," announced that they raised "serious questions of judicial ethics." Of course, he urged LBJ to withdraw the nomination. His aide recalled that Tennery's testimony had a "devastating effect" on Fortas's prospects and observed that it gave pause to even the *Washington Post*, the *New York Times*, and other strong supporters.[105]

The news about the fees also blindsided the White House. Had Attorney General Clark ordered a new FBI check on Fortas before LBJ nominated him as chief justice, the White House might have received advance warning. (Had Clark done that, he might also have learned that the bureau maintained a morals file on Fortas and that Deke DeLoach had visited the justice at his house during the 1967 Detroit riots to apprise him that "an active and aggressive homosexual" whom the FBI considered a reliable informant was saying that "he had 'balled' with Abe Fortas on several occasions prior to Mr. Fortas's becoming a Justice of the United States Supreme Court." Fortas responded that "he had never committed a homosexual act in his life." Doubtless fearful of LBJ, the bureau did not leak the file until after Johnson's presidency ended.) Yet Clark did not believe in asking for new FBI reports on sitting judges or justices before promoting them because he assumed that they behaved well and worried that such executive branch investigations jeopardized the principle of separation of powers.[106]

White House and Justice Department support for Fortas remained firm. The evening after Tennery testified, Ramsey Clark delivered a slashing speech decrying the partisan politics and hostility to civil rights that he charged lay behind Senate opposition to Fortas. He dismissed the charge that the justice condoned obscenity as "obscene" and described the Senate Judiciary Committee's delay in considering the nomination as a "constitutional crisis" that jeopardized "our system of government: separation of powers, an independent and uninhibited judiciary." Although even LBJ now conceded the hopelessness of Fortas's situation, he loyally refused to withdraw the nomination. "I won't do that to Abe," he informed Joe Califano. The White House lacked the votes for cloture. But LBJ thought that at least, a majority of senators would vote to end the filibuster. "With a majority on the floor for Abe, he'll be able to stay on the Court with his head up," the president said. "We have to do that for him." Because Fortas agreed with that reasoning, the struggle continued.[107]

Now that Fortas had put the last nail in his own coffin, Eastland readied to release the nomination. Though the Senate Judiciary Committee refused to report the Thornberry nomination until the Senate had resolved Fortas's, on September 16, Dirksen let the White House know that the committee would report Fortas's nomination favorably the next day. He and Mansfield agreed, however, "that the 'dirty movies' issue has taken its toll on Fortas, and that the $15,000 fee, while a secondary issue, has been hurtful, particularly since Paul Porter raised the money." They warned that the "floor debate on pornography will be dirty, that

Thurmond tastes blood now, . . . and that the movies were what the opposition needed to make their positions jell."[108]

The following day, the committee voted eleven to six for Fortas. The members of the majority, which included Dirksen, deemed Fortas "extraordinarily well qualified" to become chief justice. They said a vacancy existed, celebrated his commitment to the principle of equal justice, condemned the focus on obscenity as "misdirected," observed that many justices had advised many presidents, and defended the lecture fees. They urged the Senate to avoid setting a "dangerous precedent" by mounting an "ignoble" filibuster. "In the entire history of the Supreme Court, there has never been a case in which the Senate failed to act on a nomination because of a filibuster," they observed. The four senators writing for the minority condemned Fortas and the Warren Court. Ervin derogated Fortas as "one of the judicial activists now serving on the Supreme Court who toy with the Constitution as if it were their personal plaything instead of the precious inheritance of all Americans." Thurmond contended that the justice's opinions "reflected a view to the Constitution insufficiently rooted to the Constitution as it was written." Eastland accused Fortas of joining "ranks with those judicial activists who have become so overzealous in their obsession with the rights of the lawless that they completely disregard the rights of society." McClellan maintained that the court's majority had "set itself up as a superlegislature."[109]

McClellan and other Southerners planned to take a back seat in the forthcoming congressional debate, lest LBJ's allegations that "a small sectional group" was blocking Fortas's elevation gain credibility. They did not intend to remain altogether silent, and McClellan would stand before the Senate, "his arms waving, his voice rising," to decry the president's "obstinate insistence that the Senate confirm this nominee." The *Washington Post* editorialized that the same Southerners who had "for so long stood four-square for 'law and order' as they choose to define it—and for outright defiance of the United States Constitution" now prepared to participate in "the great Fortas filibuster" that threatened "to destroy the independence and integrity of the Supreme Court." As the *Post* reported on September 20, Republicans would lead the "quietly organized" filibuster, "with Southern Democrats, for the first time in years, expected to play the No. 2 role in the talkathon," and with Griffin, the public face of Fortas's opposition, announcing "flatly Fortas will not be confirmed." When reporters discussed that scenario with the Senate minority leader and pressed him as to whether LBJ should withdraw the nomination, Dirksen answered that doing so "would save a lot of discussion" and "juicy headlines." Had he changed his mind about supporting Fortas? a journalist from the *Post* wondered. "I don't know where you got that idea," Dirksen answered. "Of course I am not changing my mind."[110]

But he did. On Tuesday, September 24, the Senate debated a resolution that would have headed off a filibuster by declaring that because Warren had not really resigned, no vacancy existed. It was "authoritatively stated to have been the product of the ingenious mind of Sen. Dirksen," the *Chicago Tribune* disclosed, but he "refused credit" and the text of the resolution reportedly rendered LBJ "wrathful." Probably White House pressure led Mansfield, a weak reed in the crisis, to head off the resolution with a surprise motion that evening to set aside all other Senate business just to *consider* the Fortas nomination. Griffin's two-hour-and-forty-minute speech against the nomination on Wednesday, September 25, signaled the beginning of the filibuster against the motion. Although Griffin now refused to concede that the five-day debate, consuming twenty-five hours of Senate floor time and involving thirty-one senators (with nine speaking for Fortas and twenty-two opposing), constituted a filibuster, most at the time disagreed with him.* As Eastland explained later, "certainly he [Fortas] would have been confirmed or there wouldn't have been a filibuster." After two days of debate, Dirksen announced that he would not vote for cloture.[111]

Here was more bad news for Fortas. In explaining his change of heart, Dirksen alluded to the lecture fees and "things that don't meet the eye." Informed reporters interpreted that as a reference to *Witherspoon v. Illinois*, a recent case in which a Supreme Court majority that included Fortas held that a statute enacted in Dirksen's home state providing for dismissal of any juror with a "conscientious scruple" against capital punishment was unconstitutional. But as Dirksen's biographer said, *Witherspoon* was just a pretext. Another former Fortas enthusiast, ABA President William Gossett, used Dirksen's announcement to acknowledge that "the American Bar Association's Committee on the Federal Judiciary did not have all the facts before it when it said Justice Fortas was highly qualified

---

* Griffin later wrote: "Some would choose to label our efforts a filibuster, but I do not think it was that. Perhaps the Fortas debate is put into proper perspective when it is realized that in 1967 the Senate discussed the investment tax credit bill for 5 weeks; we considered the Congressional reorganization bill for 6 weeks; and in 1968 spent 3 weeks on the crime bill. Reference to the floor rule and tactics employed here refute the filibuster charge. With the cooperation and understanding of Senator Mansfield there were no around-the-clock sessions, Senators were not limited to two speeches on the subject and the opposition to the Fortas nomination did not have a formalized battle plan. What was done was done mostly on the basis of brief consultation [on] the Senate floor. That this was possible is another indication of the sincerity of our effort." Griffin, *The Senate Stands Taller*, his unpublished memoir of the Fortas Fight. Box 284, Griffin MSS. But Griffin's own papers suggest that there was a strategy. In late August, for example, Republican Senate staffers whose bosses opposed the nomination had met and divvied up subjects for their senators to address during the debate. Peter Holmes to Senator, August 23, 1968, Meeting on Fortas-Thornberry Nominations with Senate Backers, Box 285, File: Strategy Meeting, Griffin Papers. And according to the Congressional Senate Research Service, round-the-clock filibusters became less frequent after LBJ left the Senate and senators have "rarely invoke[d]" the rule limiting each senator to two speeches a legislative day on each issue for debate that the Senate considers. Richard Beth and Valerie Heishusen, "Filibusters and Cloture in the Senate," May 31, 2013, https://www.senate.gov/CRSReports/crs-publish.cfm?pid='0E%2C*PLW%3D%22P%20%20%0A, 3, 8.

to be chief justice," which sparked rumors that the ABA might withdraw its endorsement. Asked if Dirksen's shift, which Griffin thought had a "psychological impact," regardless of how many senators the Senate minority leader might bring along with him, hurt the hope for cloture, Mansfield, who had himself publicly branded Fortas's acceptance of the lecture fees "unfortunate," replied, "It sure as hell does."[112]

The Senate majority leader then filed a cloture petition that would require the Senate to vote on limiting debate on Tuesday, October 1, six days before the court's new term would begin. Few "believed it had a ghost of a chance of receiving Senate approval," the *Chicago Tribune* stressed. Fortas remained in that camp. "I very much doubt that we can come close to winning a cloture vote," he had recently written Douglas, "but the hope that I continue to entertain is that Carol and I will somehow survive this degrading and defiling prospect. One would think I've done nothing in my life except to approve obscene movies, plot with LBJ, accept improper fees for teaching, & turn criminals out of jail! Oh, well!" Still, when he reviewed the prospects with Ramsey Clark on September 30, he told the attorney general that "he fully agreed that we should stick it out and press for a vote."[113]

It was not just the Senate that was declaring independence from the president. September 30 marked Warren's fifteenth anniversary at the court. That day, Fred Graham published an article about the chief justice in the *New York Times*. "I'm here, and I'll still be here, so far as this [Fortas] event is undetermined," he had told Graham. But Warren surprised the White House by making it abundantly clear that he had no intention of withdrawing his retirement if the Senate did not approve Fortas—indicating, perhaps, that to LBJ, a "true" vacancy never existed. "Throughout the 35-minute discussion of his plans, Mr. Warren at no time hinted that they were conditional and that he might change his mind about stepping down," Graham emphasized. "Mr. Warren is looking forward to the day when he can leave the Court. . . . He appeared to be a man who has made up his mind to retire and who would do so as soon as a successor—any successor named by President Johnson or the next President—is confirmed." Meanwhile, Vice President Humphrey irritated LBJ with his vow in Salt Lake City that as president, he would halt the bombing of North Vietnam.[114]

Consequently, by Tuesday morning, LBJ's telephone lines were humming with callers who wanted to know what he made of the Democratic presidential candidate's speech and the last phase of the Senate debate, scheduled for noon. One caller was Dirksen. When the senator telephoned at 10:38 A.M., LBJ dissected Humphrey's speech for him and left no doubt that he did not think much of the Democrat's effort to capture the antiwar vote. "Now, what do you know?" Johnson asked. "I don't know a damn thing," Dirksen answered. The two talked briefly about other Senate matters. "Now, I gather you're not going to get your votes—you're not going to cut off cloture," the president finally said. Dirksen agreed. "All right. Then what are we going to do?" Johnson asked, given the fact that Earl Warren had said publicly that he wanted to retire. Dirksen chuckled. "It's up to Mike," he answered.

Then came one of LBJ's favorite lines: "Now, I don't want you to mention this to another human. Can I talk to you that way?" "Yes, sir," Dirksen replied. "What if we sent Tom Clark up there to act as Chief Justice" and got a new attorney general? Johnson reasoned that Clark would not serve long and that Nixon could not object since the age and health of the court's current members meant that he would have at least three vacancies to fill anyway. "[A] lot of folks feel that the Griffin effort was a pure political effort," LBJ added, and that the senator had wrongly contended that "lame ducks shouldn't appoint anybody." Moreover, Southerners like Eastland and McClellan extolled many of Clark's crime decisions. "But I would not want Clark to get butchered," the president stressed. "He served with great distinction, and I think all the conservatives like him. It'd be pretty hard for a Democrat to be against him because he's really on the Court now; he just stepped aside on account of his son." Then came the closer: "Could you support Clark?" Yes, Dirksen said.[115]

Just after 11 A.M., LBJ spoke excitedly with Ramsey Clark about his newest idea for seizing victory from defeat. What if, after the vote on Fortas, the president stayed quiet for a day or two, then called Mansfield and Dirksen to the White House to say that "obviously" a majority of senators "don't want a liberal justice here at this stage of the game," but that "if we named an out-and-out Republican" people "would say I just had to do it" and was "making the court a political football"? Why not return the justice who stepped off the court so "his boy" could become attorney general to the court instead? Ramsey Clark reminded LBJ of the obvious. "The real problem would be [Clark's roots in] Texas and years with you," he said. He would be another crony. "Let's see how we go this morning."[116]

It was a rout. By noon, the floor of the Senate was packed. Marge Griffin sat waiting in the galleries, which were full. So did Carol Agger—who, it would soon be publicized, had lost more than $22,000 of jewelry in a burglary that had occurred over the summer while the Republicans were attacking her husband for coddling criminals. Yet the last day of debate on October 1 proved strangely anticlimactic because no one doubted the result. Robert Griffin, the ostensible leader of the filibuster, "smugly" beheld the proceedings from his "Boystown" seat, feeling "expectant," "subdued," and "buoyant." At noon, he rose to cheer that "for the second time in the history of the United States, the Senate is about to withhold confirmation of a Presidential nomination for Chief Justice" and to claim that as in its 1795 rejection of John Rutledge, the Senate stood "taller when it exercised its constitutional power of advice and consent with care and diligence." Then forty-six of eighty-nine senators voted to cut off debate, while forty-three did not. Fortas had fallen fourteen votes short. He had received the majority Johnson sought for him, but just barely, and his supporters realized that a second motion for cloture would fail too. For the first time, a filibuster had prevented the Senate from confirming a judicial nomination.[117]

As Mansfield moved on to the defense appropriation bill to give the White House and Fortas time to review their options, LBJ consulted Defense Secretary Clifford, who read him the headline "Fortas Foes Win by Big Margin." According to the president, perhaps "one" senator among the forty-five who supported cloture would vote against a second motion to invoke cloture, while "several" among the forty-three who opposed cloture would change. "There're ten absent that would vote for him. There're two absent that'd vote against him. So, just a rough take and you'd be off one or two, it'd be 55-45." Even in the unlikely event that every senator appeared, "you would still be 12 votes off" the 67 that would then be necessary. And if Mansfield fought on, which he did not want to do, "I can't see at this stage that you would win it. They're just getting barrels full of mail . . . all right-wing." Fortas, LBJ reported, had written multiple drafts of an emotional letter withdrawing his nomination and denouncing the Senate that Attorney General Clark and Paul Porter were toning down. "Ramsey thinks that Abe really doesn't want us to submit another name" and wanted the nomination to "die on the vine."[118]

What should the president do next? LBJ floated Tom Clark anew to Clifford, though the president acknowledged that would seem like "a lot of Texas maneuvering." Another possibility was a senator, since senators were more likely to approve of one of their own. Of the possibilities, John Pastore, an Italian American Democrat from Rhode Island, a "damned able lawyer," former state attorney general and governor, and "a hell of a good speaker," was most appealing. When Clifford returned to his proposal of a "sound, distinguished, liberal Republican lawyer of national standing," LBJ told him that every Southern Democrat, save Yarborough of Texas and Gore of Tennessee, had voted against Fortas. (After supporting Fortas when the nomination came before the Senate Judiciary Committee, George Smathers had absented himself on the day that the full Senate decided on cloture.) None of them would want a Republican, "and they're not going to vote for anybody they think will go along" with the Warren Court majority in *Mallory* and *Miranda*. "You wouldn't ever think so," but 62% of Americans had voted for LBJ in 1964, the president added, laughing ruefully. He turned back to Fortas. Why had the justice left a message asking for LBJ to telephone, "instead of him calling the President"? he asked plaintively. (Fortas was one of the relatively few people who could reach the president by telephone just about anytime he wished.) "Hell," Clifford answered, "with the situation at this time, Mr. President, I think, reaching the stage that it has, I think Abe ought to come over and see you . . . I don't think you can talk just over the phone. All that Abe's been to you through the years, and this is the worst ordeal that I about ever saw anybody go through." He was suffering too, LBJ interjected. "It ain't an easy time!" Clifford chuckled.[119]

Despite Clifford's advice, LBJ telephoned Fortas next. "I'm kind of addled," the president confided. "Our people thought we'd get about 52 votes. We had 55 counted a week ago, but a lot of them just didn't come back," and those who did "are just mad as hell" because reprints of the "dirty movies" were being shown in every county, at the National Press Club, "and every old man in the country" who wanted to see "a naked woman" was watching them. For once, Fortas did not subordinate himself to the president. "From my point of view, the best thing to do would be to forget it, and let it [the nomination] just stay up there [in the Senate]," he maintained. Did he want to paralyze the Senate and to endure more cloture votes? Did he think that the Senate might reconsider, perhaps after the election? If so, Johnson set Fortas straight. "You don't mean that we just say, 'Well, we are going to leave it to Nixon voluntarily'?" the president interjected. "Yeah, in effect," Fortas answered. "I don't think I can do that," LBJ said. "I've got to be President. Hell, I've got other people to name every day" for the next four months. "And I just can't say that I just know one man in America that I would recommend as chief justice." Moreover, "I want to fight them. I think they're a bunch of sons-of-bitches." The only way to do that, Fortas responded as he belatedly jumped aboard LBJ's bandwagon, was to send up "a good name." Sounding exasperated, Johnson answered that he would not forward a "bad one."

Then, more gently, the president added, "I think we've got to be satisfied with less than the best because we've tried the best" and lost. "But I don't think we have to take the worst." At first, he had expected that Warren might rescind his retirement, LBJ volunteered, but the Graham interview had made it clear "that's out. Now that changes the whole ballgame" and "our strategy . . . and that was a turn I didn't expect. I thought he'd stay til hell froze over." In the meantime, Fortas's battle was done. "We ought to put it to an end just as quick as we can, tomorrow, I'd think," and decide together whom to nominate next. "Pastore appeals to me a good deal," he concluded. His nomination would put the Senate in "a helluva spot. And I think that keeps Nixon from getting that vote and getting that leader" and would yield a chief justice who voted "right."[120]

The next day, Tuesday, was Yom Kippur. Though Fortas was not an observant Jew, his secretary had barred him from coming to work on the holiest day of the Jewish calendar ever since he joined the court. Now the justice released his letter asking the president to withdraw his nomination. To continue the fight, Fortas reasoned, would ensure more of "the destructive and extreme assaults upon the Court . . . which have characterized the filibuster—attacks which have been sometimes extreme and entirely unrelated to responsible criticism." Then, the Washington Post reported on its front page, "Fortas, who would have been the first Chief Justice of the Jewish faith, left word that he was at home honoring the Yom Kippur holiday and would say nothing further." LBJ's response reiterated that Fortas "is the best qualified man for this high position" and described "the action of the Senate, a body I revere and to which I devoted a dozen years of my life," as "historically and constitutionally tragic."[121]

Washington now buzzed with rumors about the president's plans. Of course, LBJ could refuse to submit another name, but he had plenty of opportunities to nominate someone else as chief justice. One option was to submit a new name before Congress adjourned for the November elections. A second was to announce a recess appointment, though that seemed less likely since Senator Johnson had opposed President Eisenhower's recess appointments. Still, over at the Senate Judiciary Committee, Fortas's opponents were sufficiently worried about that possibility to tell LBJ that they would consider his nomination of his aide, Barefoot Sanders, to the DC Circuit and Fortas's friend, David Bress, to the US District Court if the president promised not to appoint a chief justice while the Senate was in recess. When LBJ expressed interest, senators changed the terms of the deal and said the president must promise not to send up any judicial appointments until the new Congress convened in January. LBJ and his advisers thought they should not relinquish presidential power to Strom Thurmond. What if three Supreme Court justices died on the same day before Nixon took office? Consequently, the president declined the offer, Sanders and Bress did not receive a Senate vote, and the chief justice recess nomination possibility remained on the table. A third option was to call the Ninetieth Congress into special session after the November election, as Johnson was already contemplating doing for other reasons, and to nominate a chief justice then. A fourth was to wait until the Ninety-First Congress had convened in January and do it then.[122]

Arthur Goldberg soon began sending envoys to the White House to indicate that he would take the nomination at any of those times. On Wednesday, Fortas found himself on the platform at NYU Law School with Goldberg to celebrate the centenary of the Fourteenth Amendment. Goldberg stressed his "profound regret" at the Senate's action in his speech and remarked that his wife had recalled Benjamin Franklin's adage: "Do not in public life expect immediate approbation of one's services. One must persevere through insult and injury." When Fortas, who followed, emotionally promised the audience "I shall persevere," he received a long-standing ovation. When Goldberg was not defending Fortas, he was planning his own future. LBJ met with him for an hour on October 10 so he could make his case. "Goldberg just talks *all* the time," LBJ complained to Mansfield on October 16. "He wants to be Chief Justice of the Supreme Court and says you've got to be for him, and Dirksen's got to be for him, and everybody up there is going to be for him if I just got guts enough to name him."[123]

The following day, Goldberg breakfasted with Fortas. "Arthur's a remarkable fella," Fortas told the president, "a combination of self-assurance and ambition that's seldom been seen." In "a long monologue," Goldberg insisted that he could win confirmation if LBJ sent up his name now, in special session, or during the Senate recess. (While Goldberg conceded that he probably could not win confirmation if LBJ waited to do so until the Ninety-First Congress, he promised to take the nomination then too.) Fortas then spoke with Earl Warren and reported that the chief justice "hopes that this will be done." Warren was "ready to resign tomorrow" and wanted only to ensure the survival of a court that would protect LBJ's program. But Johnson doubted that Goldberg could win confirmation. Griffin might stay quiet, "but the same damned old snakes" would bite Goldberg, the president told Fortas. "I'm just amazed he thinks he can be confirmed," Fortas agreed, though he did stress that Goldberg was "a helluva operational guy" who got results.[124]

So was Richard Nixon. After his November victory, he sent word to LBJ that he would welcome the appointment of sixty-nine-year-old Tom Dewey as chief justice. A moderate Republican, former governor of New York, and two-time presidential candidate, Dewey was a famous lawyer and crime-fighter. LBJ and Dewey maintained a cordial relationship, but the president had no intention of making him chief justice. And Nixon turned thumbs down on Eisenhower's second attorney general, William Rogers, who would become his first secretary of state, LBJ reported to Ramsey Clark. "That's interesting, isn't it? Said he's a no good son of a bitch." Clark joked, "That confirms my good opinion of Bill Rogers."[125]

Faced with such alternatives, Goldberg became more appealing to Johnson. In December, LBJ began seriously to consider nominating him either in a special session or when the new Congress met. At the same time, Warren's son-in-law told William Rogers during a golf game that the chief justice worried that Nixon might leave the court without a leader by accepting the resignation of his old foe just as soon as he became president. Sensing an opportunity for an overture, Nixon telephoned Warren on December 4 to ask that the chief justice swear him in as president on Inauguration Day. He also asked Warren to stay on through the remainder of the term. Caught by surprise, Warren acquiesced to both requests. "I tried to get hold of Abe right away and tell him," the embarrassed chief justice explained to LBJ, but he had gone to Puerto Rico.[126]

Then Nixon tried to bar Goldberg's appointment by publicly announcing that Warren had agreed to stay. As Johnson respectfully explained to Warren, the Republican had acted at least in part to avoid the possibility of Goldberg, whom LBJ was still thinking of naming and about whom Dirksen was still sounding out fellow Republicans. The president had told Goldberg's ambassadors, "A) that I don't think he could get confirmed, and I think it would be tragic for his life but

B) if there were evidence that I was wrong I would certainly want to preserve the Court if I could," and "I would certainly regard him as a good appointment." So would he, Warren exclaimed. The chief justice should explain to Goldberg exactly what took place then, the president said, lest he conclude that Johnson had been "playing" him and had known "the whole time this would happen." Warren should also share the information that "I would be willing to name him" if the Senate would confirm him, "but I haven't got that evidence yet, and I don't want to have a tragedy as we did in the case of Abe."[127]

In the end, however, LBJ's advisers concluded that the Senate Judiciary Committee might well reject the Goldberg nomination and that if it did not, the Senate would. Turning down another Jew, particularly one for whom Griffin had said he would vote, "might prove slightly embarrassing for the Republicans but to be repudiated again by the Senate on a Chief Justice nomination would also be embarrassing to the President." So after all the noise about the "Warren Court," the chief justice would stay on and give "the lie to the always flimsy earlier complaints [and, apparently, LBJ's hope] that Warren had phrased his retirement statement so that he could withdraw it unless a replacement to his liking was installed." And Nixon would win the vacancy he coveted at term's end.[128]

For LBJ to determine whether another nomination would succeed, he had to understand the reason for Fortas's defeat. "The truth is that Abe Fortas was too progressive for the Republicans and the Southern conservatives in the Senate, all of whom were horrified at the thought of the continuation of the philosophy of the Warren Court," he explained in his memoir. That was one explanation: Some Republicans and Southern Democrats who knew how to run down the clock disliked the Warren Court's approach to criminal law and civil rights.[129]

There is something to be said for the argument that ideology lay behind Senate voting patterns. But if LBJ had been thinking only in terms of ideological compatibility, instead of ideological compatibility and friendship, he probably could have chosen a legal liberal who could have survived the heat. Given the good chance of Fortas's confirmation at first, it is difficult to imagine how the Senate could have girded itself to defeat someone like William Brennan or Arthur Goldberg or Philip Hart, who lacked Abe Fortas's baggage. "A more sensitive Johnson selection might have resulted in a nomine every bit as liberal as Mr. Fortas but with a background offering conservative Senators little excuse for opposition," one columnist wrote in the *Wall Street Journal*. And what if Johnson had been a more careful strategist? Had the nomination also failed because he could not leave well enough alone? Yes. There was something pathetic about the president's endgame embrace of Clark and Goldberg, the two individuals he had forced off the court. Because of time and LBJ's status as a "lame duck" who no longer bestrode the Senate like the proverbial colossus? Yes. Because LBJ's growing unpopularity had tainted Fortas, the justice-cum-presidential adviser? Certainly. Because Johnson had overreached by naming not just one, but two, "cronies" and Fortas had been caught obfuscating about his role in White House affairs? Definitely. Because the Warren Court's controversial opinions handed the Right a great political issue and its friends had made the colossal blunder of allowing its foes to frame a narrative contending that the court was more out of step with public opinion than it actually was? Positively. Because of the "dirty movies"? Absolutely. Because of the lecture fees? Without a doubt.[130]

The riddle of the Fortas defeat was that this protean causation stew could signify anything its interpreters wished. Thus, Griffin told the press that inflated lecture fees felled Fortas. Phyllis Schlafly portrayed the battle as a seminal moment that "approaches in importance the winning of a Presidential election," one that, in retrospect, marked the arrival on the scene of a "New Right" that fought for family values. For Pat Buchanan, it marked the beginning of "the culture war." Lady Bird Johnson treated it as evidence of "the rising anger against Lyndon and mostly the rising anger against liberalism." Fortas saw it as confirmation of "the fragmentation of liberalism" and the unpopularity of the Warren Court. Philip Hart, however, blamed the defeat on "the lame duck issue, the President's own decline in popularity, the anti-Supreme Court feeling in the country, and Justice Fortas'[s] extra-judicial conduct." And Arthur Goldberg argued that despite his own identification with the Warren Court and political and legal liberalism, he could win confirmation because he lacked Fortas's negatives. Whatever the reason for the failure, the vicious Fortas fight, coming on the heels of the Marshall confirmation, and followed by more hard-fought battles over the next two-and-a-half years, transformed nomination and confirmation politics. With characteristic prescience, Yale's Alexander Bickel anticipated the 1987 Bork battle when he told a reporter in 1968 that "20 years from now the Fortas controversy 'may seem a precursor of what was in the offing.' "[131]

Like the Marshall struggle, the Fortas fight and those that followed on its heels set the prototype for modern confirmation battles. That is not to say that the current nomination and confirmation process would play out in the same way now. In a similar situation today, for example, a White House handler, one would hope, would send a Jewish nominee to synagogue on Yom Kippur and prevent him from bitterly withdrawing his nomination on a holiday that centers around apologizing for one's sins and forgiving those of others. Yet the *seeds* of the contemporary process lay in this period. The Senate Judiciary Committee confirmation hearings of court nominees were not carried live on radio and TV until Reagan nominated Sandra Day O'Connor in 1981. But in Fortas's case, there was intense media scrutiny of nominees and page-one stories about the struggle day after day. There was anger at nominee elusiveness. There was a focus on nominee ethics, character, and private life because of senators' squeamishness about addressing nominee ideology and evasiveness. There was interest group mobilization. There was anxiety about the "politicization" of the court amid awareness that it had become the arbiter of vital national questions. There was stress on the struggle's significance to presidential politics and on the significance of presidential politics to the struggle.

The story unfolding bore resemblance to a play. In Act I, the Warren Commission, the Baker and Jenkins scandals, civil rights, personnel issues, and the Kennedys caused LBJ to worry about the Justice Department and affected his decisions about staffing it. Johnson then dispatched Justice Arthur Goldberg to the United Nations to open up a seat for Fortas at the court and to increase presidential control over it. LBJ also took charge of the Justice Department by sidelining Katzenbach and acquired someone that the president hoped would function as *his* attorney general, Ramsey Clark. Moreover, he ensured that Ramsey Clark's father, Tom, left the court to create a vacancy there for Thurgood Marshall. In Act II, the action moved to Congress, as it mulled over LBJ's effort to leave his mark on the court by putting Marshall on the court, making Fortas chief justice, and appointing his friend, Homer Thornberry, to Fortas's old seat. Congress gave him Marshall, while withholding the Fortas–Thornberry double-play. Act III would feature more conflict as LBJ's successor tried to replace the Warren with the "Nixon" Court.

5

The Last Days of the Warren
Court, 1969

As president, Richard Nixon carefully toed the line between "demagoguing" the court and disparaging its decisions, just as he had done in 1968. He knew that the liberal consensus had not evaporated. The Republican had won barely half a million more votes than his Democratic rival, and the Democrats still possessed healthy majorities in the House and Senate. Making hay with the Warren Court as symbolic target and selected civil rights and crime decisions might help the GOP woo white ethnics in the Northeast and Midwest and Southern whites away from the Democratic Party. If Republicans proved successful, they might become the majority party and destroy the Democratic coalition that dominated American politics from 1932 to 1968 and would control Congress until 1980.

Nixon's ambition meant the political spotlight shone ever more brightly on the court. Just as the election of 1968 solidified many Republicans' identification with conservatism and many Democrats' with liberalism, so it became the moment when presidential candidates began playing up the importance of their elections for the court's membership. As soon as Nixon became president, the White House used threats of jurisdiction stripping and impeachment, along with Warren's retirement, to promote Nixon's dream of melding together Republicans of all stripes, white Democrats in the South, and working-class ethnics elsewhere. During the first months of his administration, it seemed clear that Nixon wanted to accomplish that goal by remaking the court and breaking decisively with Kennedy's and Johnson's cronyism. It turned out, though, that like Johnson, the new president wanted an ally at the court. He found one in his new chief justice.[1]

"A Deliberate Attempt" at Surreptitious Influence

Nothing came easy for Richard Nixon. What motivated him, he once said, were "the laughs and slights and snubs" he suffered growing up poor in

Whittier, California. He had attended a small local college, and although he graduated third in his class from Duke Law School, he could not find a job in a prestigious firm. Only after he had become a senator, become Eisenhower's vice president, and lost the presidency to Kennedy in 1960 did Nixon finally become a Wall Street lawyer. But the work of an attorney in a small town or in New York bored him to distraction, and politics became his refuge. Because of his intelligence, the depth and strength of his "anger," and "personal gut performance," he reflected, he achieved much while those who had it all lazed "on their fat butts."[2]

Like Nixon's ethos, his Washington was dark and gloomy. Unlike LBJ in 1963, the new president could turn his Justice Department over to someone he trusted. Nixon placed his pragmatic law partner and campaign manager, John Mitchell, at the helm of the Justice Department. Attorney General Mitchell's wife, Martha, a bibulous Southern belle, would become a sensation for her candid, late-night telephone conversations with journalists (figure 18). Beloved by friends for his warmth and loyalty, her husband cultivated a "dour, stern, taciturn, forbidding" demeanor for the public. Mitchell became the president's point man in battling the antiwar movement, the Left, and, depending on the moment, school desegregation advocates and antagonists. Mitchell placed Jerris Leonard, a Wisconsin politician and team player, in charge of the Civil Rights Division. The attorney general selected Richard Kleindienst, a blunt Goldwater conservative from

Figure 18 Attorney General John Mitchell and Martha Mitchell in Washington, DC.
David Hume Kennerly/Contributor. Collection: Hulton Archive.

Arizona, soon nicknamed "Mr. Tough," as deputy attorney general. As the "president's lawyer's lawyer," or assistant attorney general in charge of the Office of Legal Counsel, Mitchell chose Kleindienst's brilliant and equally conservative Phoenix friend, William Rehnquist. Like the president, Rehnquist championed "strict constructionist" judges who did not favor expanding the rights of criminal defendants and civil rights plaintiffs.[3]

In the White House, the president surrounded himself with "gut" fighters and reinforced their instincts. The place, one staffer remembered later, was "peopled by competitive political animals" who devoted much of their energy to "self-defeating, vindictive, political gamesmanship" and "who were rewarded in direct proportion to their expressions of fear, suspicion and paranoia." Chief of Staff H. R. Haldeman, a former advertising executive, controlled access to Nixon and relished his role as the "President's son-of-a bitch." Nixon's first White House Counsel was Haldeman's UCLA roommate, John Ehrlichman. Known for his scowl and bushy eyebrows, Ehrlichman spoke of leaving one Presidential patsy "twisting slowly, slowly in the wind." When Ehrlichman became the president's top domestic policy adviser and the "fireman" who extinguished embarrassments, John Dean took his place. Dean would entitle his White House memoir *Blind Ambition*. White House Special Counsel Charles Colson proudly said that he would walk over his grandmother for Nixon, characterized himself as presidential "hatchet man" and designed "dirty tricks" against political opponents.[4]

Despite his efforts to present himself as a man of the people, Nixon mistrusted the public and preferred secrecy to sunshine. Aspiring toward royalty, he went so far as to outfit White House security as elaborately as Buckingham Palace guards. Like LBJ, he saw the press, eastern elites, and the "Georgetown crowd" as enemies. Like Johnson, too, he proved dogged in his persistence: Nixon was someone who courted his future wife by driving her to dates with other men. But in contrast to his predecessor, the new president was solitary. So uncomfortable did the Republican become at state dinners that he pressed aides to cut them down to fifty-eight minutes. (As part of his effort, he banished the soup course on the theory that "men don't really like soup.") He lacked LBJ's interest in and knowledge of Congress too.[5]

Historians, with our passion for periodization, divide about the significance of Nixon's Presidency. Some maintain that "the sixties" ended with Nixon's election, which marked the beginning of a period of conservatism anticipated by Goldwater's candidacy in 1964. Others equally persuasively contend that the "sixties" continued, and that ironically, Nixon's Presidency constituted a liberal high-water mark. As usual, everything depends on where the scholar looks, of course. For one example, conquering poverty was high on liberals' agenda, and in retrospect, one might call Nixon a poverty warrior. During his first term, federal spending on persons in poverty increased dramatically, and reduced the poverty rate, which had been at 21.9% in 1961, 17.3% in 1965, and 12.8% in 1968 to 11.1% in 1973, its lowest point in recent American history. The President proposed the Family Assistance Plan, which would have provided cash payments to every poor family, argued for national health insurance, and signed SSI into law to give aid to the indigent elderly, the blind, and the disabled. Social Security benefits were increased; the food stamps program, expanded. Some of these changes occurred because in another contrast to LBJ, Nixon's passion lay in foreign, not domestic policy. The first President in 120 years to take office at a time when the opposing party held both Houses of Congress, he acquiesced to liberal initiatives more frequently than he advocated them.[6]

To study Nixon's Presidency, though, is to understand that the Warren Court occupied a special place in his calculations. He had made its shortcomings a campaign centerpiece and had pledged himself to changing its direction. If he did not succeed in disempowering the Warren Court, he would seem not just unprincipled, but politically inept. If he triumphed, he would provide the Republicans a boasting point that might help Nixon realize his dream of making them the majority party.

The new administration's first attempt to influence the Warren Court revealed more continuity than change and showed that JFK and LBJ were not the only ones to worry about government eavesdropping. On March 10, 1969, just over a month after Warren administered the oath of office to the president, the court handed down *Alderman v. U.S.* The majority opinion declared that in all cases, even those involving national security, government must provide a defendant with transcripts of any conversations picked up by illegal wiretap or bug on the defendant's premises or in which the defendant participated. In reporting that the Justice Department was expected to request a rehearing on March 13, Fred Graham wrote that its "stunned" officials had depended on Byron White and Thurgood Marshall, two Justice Department veterans, to inform their colleagues on the court that the government was wiretapping and bugging many embassies in the nation's capital, acts it did not want to admit officially and whose illegality it assumed. One alarmed official told Graham that "all a defendant in a routine tax case—or any other Federal case—has to do now is telephone a few foreign embassies, and we'll have to drop the case against him" or show him the transcripts and embarrass the United States in the process.[7]

Justice Department leaders decided that they needed to do more than leak their distress to reporters. On March 12, Attorney General Mitchell dispatched the Justice Department's director of public information, Jack Landau, to disclose to Justice Brennan, an acquaintance, the same information about the embassies that Graham would report in his front-page story the following day. Landau, who was excitable anyway, arrived in a high state of anxiety that became acute when Brennan took him in to repeat his message to the chief justice. In his memoirs, Warren described the encounter as his only "personal experience of a deliberate attempt to surreptitiously influence" a court action. As the chief justice recounted it, he immediately realized "that this young man was only being used as a mouthpiece for others more sophisticated who would not dare to fulfill a mission of this kind" and sent Landau packing. But before he left, Landau twice affirmed that the attorney general wanted the chief justice to know "that he would do anything in his power to head off any Constitutional Amendment or some legislation to curtail the Court's jurisdiction." At that, Warren smelled blackmail. The chief justice then reported on the encounter to the equally outraged justices.[8]

On March 19, the Justice Department filed a petition for rehearing urging the court to exclude foreign intelligence surveillance from *Alderman*. Then, despite his no-blackmail pledge, Attorney General Mitchell virtually invited Congress to submit court-curbing legislation by warning the Senate that *Alderman* might compromise national security. Five days later, the court refused to rehear the case, and Potter Stewart berated the Justice Department. Solicitor General Erwin Griswold, the legendary former Harvard Law School dean and a Johnson holdover, had "mystifyingly" conceded in his *Alderman* oral argument that government surveillances of foreign embassies were "unconstitutional, although he was repeatedly invited to argue that they were not," Stewart chided. Moreover, any "careful reader" of the *Alderman* opinion should have discerned that the court did not there determine the constitutionality of foreign intelligence surveillance.[9]

That was quite a rebuke. The Republican Stewart obviously viewed Nixon's Justice Department as a nest of clowns who could neither argue a case nor understand an opinion. The chief justice himself debated making news of Landau's visit public before deciding against doing so for the present. Warren feared that trumpeting Landau's warning would seem vindictive since the new administration "had campaigned against the Court on the charge it was soft on crime." The chief justice also charitably assumed that because Mitchell's experience lay in bond law, the new attorney general did not yet understand the importance of an independent judiciary. Consequently, Warren kept quiet, and the incident remained secret until Landau left the Justice Department and sparked talk of his own and Mitchell's disbarment by disclosing it to reporters in 1973.[10]

Pace the chief Justice, it was not the first time on his watch that someone had deliberately attempted to "surreptitiously influence" the court. Fortas had done it as LBJ's agent, though he had capably hidden the administration's footprints. Douglas also got it wrong when he characterized Landau's visit "as the first instance in the memory of anyone connected with the Court in which the executive branch has made actual threats to the Court." He should have recalled FDR's court packing plan, just for starters. He might also have remembered World War II and the Nazi saboteurs' case, where, Douglas complained elsewhere in his autobiography, "the Attorney General, Francis Biddle, told the Court that the claims of the saboteurs were so frivolous, the Army was going to go ahead and execute the men whatever the Court did; that the Executive would simply not tolerate any delay. That was a blatant affront to the Court."[11]

The *Alderman* incident may have helped underline for the new president the need for friends at the court. Like a number of his predecessors, Nixon honored the constitutional principle of separation of powers in the breach. Yet he seized on the chance to distinguish himself from LBJ by showcasing his refusal to name "cronies" as justices.

"The Most Thrilling Social Event"

Soon after he moved into the White House, Nixon shrewdly decided to substitute a party honoring the chief justice for the annual presidential dinner for the Supreme Court. Nixon pulled out all the stops with a black-tie event on April 23 for 112, including Warren's six children, secretary, and closest friends. Guests dined on crabmeat imperial, filet mignon rossini with cocotte potatoes and asparagus hollandaise, Caesar salad, a cheese course, and mousse nesselrode. The toasts proved as luxuriant as the menu. Nixon and Warren appeared to bury the hatchet, with the president saluting the chief justice for having served his country well and his guest declaring that he was leaving public life with "no malice in my heart" toward anyone. Thanking Nixon, the chief justice sounded sincere too—and nostalgic. "To have had every one of our family there for such a gathering in the White House is something none of us can ever forget," Warren wrote. "For me it was the most thrilling social event of my half century of public life."[12]

Several of Nixon's rumored chief justice candidates attended the dinner. They included Eisenhower's attorney general, Herbert Brownell, a Wall Street lawyer and close adviser of Nixon's; Brownell's successor as attorney general and Nixon's secretary of state, William Rogers; Attorney General John Mitchell; former New York governor Tom Dewey; Justice Potter Stewart; and Vice President Spiro Agnew. "I'm not going to get it, but I think I know who it's going to be," Rogers told the press. Agnew joked that he wanted to become chief justice because "I'm interested in longevity," while Dewey declared that "I decided a long time ago that I didn't want to come to Washington." One person who aspired to become an associate justice received an invitation too. DC Circuit Court of Appeals Judge Warren Burger, a protégé of Brownell's, arrived at the White House early and asked for a glimpse at the guest list. To his surprise, it included just one other lower court judge, George MacKinnon, a former prosecutor, member of Congress, and friend of the president's, whom Nixon had just put on the DC Circuit Court at Burger's behest. "I turned to my wife," Burger remembered, "and told her just to be natural if she got the feeling people were looking us over."[13]

Burger had lobbied for the promotion to associate justice since before the election. Amid speculation that Nixon would nominate the distinguished Jewish critic of the Warren Court, Judge Henry Friendly, who was also seeking that spot, Burger had written Brownell during the final days of the Fortas–Thornberry battle that Friendly was "damned good—but is he quite the right guy unless Dick wants to negate the anti-Semitic business?" Burger maintained that in the "past, I have been content to let nature take its course—which in high politics it rarely does, as you know." If Fortas was "dead," Warren might "hang on out of that sheer Scandinavian stubbornness." That course would at least carry the advantages of showing the chief justice "in more nearly his true light" and providing time for "the heat on the Fortas business" to subside. Among other things, and despite Johnson and Warren's "shady" attempt to arrange the next chief justice, "something must be done about the Senate handling of confirmations or nobody will want to take a judicial nomination." Burger envisioned "'a code of procedure' for confirmation hearings" that the American Bar Association and others would promulgate. "I know you have many loyalties and demands on you and I shall never embarrass you with any request of mine," he added to Brownell. "But the Midwest (from Ohio to the Rockies is a Hell of a lot of USA!) is not represented on the Topside and ought to be. Before RN gets too firmly fixed I hope that thought will be put to him." Nixon had written Burger "spontaneously" in 1967 to extol his criticism of the Warren Court for crippling police power to obtain confessions from suspected criminals, he volunteered. "Hence he is not unfriendly. Friendly to Friendly however!"[14]

Fortunately, for Burger, Friendly, whose appointment liberals and conservatives would have cheered, suffered from two negatives in Nixon's eyes. He was Jewish and, at sixty-five, elderly for a Supreme Court appointment. The American Bar Association specified sixty-four as its upper limit, though it might well have made an exception for someone of Friendly's stature and its recommendations did not bind presidents anyway.[15]

As his letter to Brownell suggested, Warren Burger was ambitious, convivial, and partisan. "There is nothing stuffy about him, and he has a sense of humor he often turns on himself," one reporter observed. Then sixty-one-year-old Burger was nearly six feet tall, weighed in at two hundred pounds, and sported a leonine white mane. He and his six siblings had grown up poor in Saint Paul, and he sold insurance to finance his way through the University of Minnesota and night school at Saint Paul College of Law, from which he graduated with high honors. In two years, Burger became a partner at a prominent Saint Paul law firm. Now he threw himself into civic and political life as a supporter of Harold Stassen of Minnesota, the liberal and ever-hopeful Republican presidential candidate at whose campaign headquarters Burger first met Nixon in 1948. Burger came to Eisenhower's and Brownell's attention when he helped deny the nomination to Robert Taft by delivering the Minnesota delegation to Eisenhower at Stassen's urging in 1952. After Eisenhower's election, Burger joined the Justice Department as assistant attorney general, and the president named him to the DC Circuit Court of Appeals four years later.[16]

There he remained a "liberal Minnesota Republican" on civil rights even as he plunged zestfully into combat over criminal procedure and the insanity defense with "mine adversary," liberal Judge David Bazelon. "If I were to stand still for some of the idiocy that is put forth as legal and constitutional profundity I would, I am sure, want to shoot myself in later years," Burger told his great friend since childhood and best man, Eighth Circuit Judge Harry Blackmun, whom he was forever importuning to join him on European getaways. "These guys just *can't* be right. So there is nothing to do but resist," though Burger picked his battles carefully. (Blackmun aptly characterized Burger as "a scrapper" with "many friends, in high places and in low, and some insistent enemies.") Nor did Burger display any private patience for "the Bastards" in the Warren Court majority who "went to absurd length[s] in criminal law," and it especially vexed him "that the Eisenhower appointees are doing most of the damage." Publicly, he became a vocal, though respectful, critic of the Warren Court's criminal procedure decisions. "As a Court of Appeals Judge I am bound to follow the Supreme Court's opinions, but not to praise them," Burger would say.[17]

Just after the inauguration, Nixon asked Burger to swear in part of his economic team. The judge privately informed the president that day that the DC Circuit Court of Appeals was "the worst of all the Courts at this level in the country, in his opinion" and successfully urged the appointment of MacKinnon and another "strong" man to vacancies there. By now, the president was touting Burger to his attorney general as "one of the ablest and most responsible Judges I know." A few days later, Mitchell and his deputy attorney general had "a very fruitful meeting" with the judge. Burger followed up with a forceful memorandum for the president about the troubled federal courts. Though Warren's gubernatorial career had led many to anticipate that he "would become the outstanding administrative Chief Justice in our time," he had not, perhaps because "he had to concentrate on learning the craft and techniques of the appellate judge," Burger maintained. "For the dozen years or more in which the Supreme Court has been revamping criminal procedure and details of police function on a case-by-case basis, without adequate data and without adequate records or argument in many of the critical cases, it has neglected the crucial problems of court administration and management." The new chief justice would face a difficult task. He would "come to office at a time when the Court's prestige is perhaps at the lowest ebb in history, certainly in modern times; moreover the Court's standing with Congress is lower than it is with the public." Left unspoken but clear was the hint that one Warren Burger could mightily aid him.[18]

Burger sometimes pretended not to care about his campaign's chance of success. "I am glad that my mood and indeed my deep conviction on the SC business is rational and solid," he assured Blackmun in March 1969. "I can really take it or leave it and if RN doesn't do a lot better in picking his people there (than dear old Ike did), I would not want to be within shouting distance." What could "one man do to stop the nonsense," especially when he could not always count on Harlan and Stewart to side with him? The president could "only straighten that place out if he gets four appointments"—which given the ages of the justices, Nixon might well receive—"and draws on the State and Federal bench for the replacements," since "few lawyers" would understand the extent of the Warren Court's "subversion of the law." As of Warren's April retirement dinner, Burger could reasonably hope for an associate justiceship down the line. "We both know of the 'signs' of favor from the administration," he later confided to Blackmun, but he had "no inkling of the 'center seat' in anything which had come along. That was, and still is, a real bombshell." The events after Warren's dinner helped move him to "the center seat."[19]

"A Question of Ethics"

"The toasts made me cry," Abe Fortas told reporters as he left the White House dinner. Less than a month later, he wept in sadness. Even as Nixon feted Warren, he and administration officials knew that reporter William Lambert of *Life* magazine, who had dug into Johnson's finances in 1963, was excavating Fortas's.[20]

As Fortas struggled to become chief justice in 1968, a government official tipped off Lambert, who some considered "the modern-day father of investigative journalism," that he should examine the relationship between Fortas and Louis Wolfson, who became perhaps the first modern corporate raider. The justice enjoyed the financier and former client, who shared Fortas's immigrant Jewish roots and his interest in civil rights, juvenile delinquency, and other social welfare issues. More prudent people who knew Wolfson, however, checked how many fingers they had left after they shook his hand, and the government had recently convicted him of illegal stock manipulation and conspiracy. By December, the reporter had learned that Fortas had visited Wolfson at his Florida horse farm in 1966 and that the financier had paid Fortas $20,000 (over $145,000 in 2016 dollars) to become a consultant to his family foundation. Lambert also heard that Fortas had concluded that he had no time for the job and returned the money—but only after the financier had twice been indicted. Moreover, Lambert was told, Wolfson had assured Elkin "Buddy" Gerbert and other associates that Fortas would protect them from the government. The reporter put the project aside until April of 1969, when he noticed that the Supreme Court, with Fortas recusing himself—as he routinely did in any case involving a former client—had refused to hear Wolfson's appeal from a Second Circuit decision affirming his conviction. (Oddly, after his release from prison, Wolfson would name his most famous colt, the winner of the 1978 Triple Crown, "Affirmed.") At that point, Lambert resumed work on the story.[21]

Since both Fortas and Wolfson refused to tell him anything, the reporter turned to Nixon's Justice Department for corroborating evidence. How much concrete, independent knowledge officials there possessed of the Fortas–Wolfson relationship remains murky. But Will Wilson, the head of the Justice Department's criminal division, was an old enemy of Lyndon Johnson and no fan of either Fortas or the Warren Court. "I saw myself as ridding the Supreme Court of a man who never should have been on the Court," he later said, and he confirmed Lambert's story. He also seized on the journalist's visit to let John Mitchell and J. Edgar Hoover know that the criminal division would launch its own investigation of Fortas's activities.[22]

When Hoover and Nixon compared notes about the forthcoming *Life* story, the president declared that Fortas should be "off" the court. Ironically, the president ranked Fortas, along with Hugo Black, as one of the ablest justices. Those two had proven most engaged when Nixon appeared before the nine in 1966 to argue that a publication invading its subject's privacy did not deserve First Amendment protection. "I judge them in terms of their questions, and I said, 'boy, I can tell the men in that Court that really had it,'" he remembered. Nixon did not prevail, and his loss in the only case he ever argued before the Warren Court may have helped explain some of his contempt for it. But he felt none for Fortas, who had written the principal dissent coming down on his side. "I never thought he was radical," Nixon said of Justice Fortas, and he was "a brilliant lawyer."* It was "a crime" that Fortas had to go, the president said later, before adding quickly, "Well, it isn't a crime. He brought it on himself." Since Nixon did not consider Fortas a reliable ally, he now wished to take advantage of the justice's

---

* In fact, as Nixon himself became enmeshed in Watergate, he fantasized about placing Fortas on a commission to investigate presidential improprieties. The first justice forced out of office would retain considerable appeal for the first president to resign because of scandal. Stanley Kutler, *Abuse of Power: The New Nixon Tapes*, September 12, 1972 (New York: Free Press, 1997), 140, 141.

relationship with Wolfson. Even if Fortas was no "radical," he was no sure vote for the administration.[23]

Lambert's article, "Fortas of the Supreme Court: A Question of Ethics," appeared on newsstands on Monday, May 5, 1969. Why would a person of the justice's "legal brilliance and high position do business with . . . Louis Wolfson, a well-known corporate stock manipulator known to be under federal investigation?" the journalist asked. He explained that Fortas had received a check for $20,000 from the Wolfson Family Foundation in January 1966, which he had returned that December. "Ostensibly, Justice Fortas was being paid to advise the foundation on ways to use its funds for charitable, educational and civil rights projects," Lambert noted. "Whatever services he may or may not have rendered in this respect, Justice Fortas'[s] name was being dropped in strategic places by Wolfson and Gerbert in their effort to stay out of prison."

While Fortas was hardly the first federal justice or judge who had padded his pocketbook by moonlighting as consultant to a charitable foundation, Lambert obviously disapproved of what he knew about Fortas's relationship with Wolfson. First, that the justice apparently did not realize that Wolfson and Gerbert were mentioning him, he argued, "does not change the fact that his acceptance of the money, and other actions, made the name-dropping effective." Second, because the foundation's gross income in 1966 was all of $115,200, the $20,000 fee was "generous in the extreme." Third, in his letter to *Life* denying any impropriety or participation in Wolfson's affairs, Fortas did not even admit that he had ever received any money from the foundation, just that he had briefly visited "Mr. Wolfson's famous horse farm." Fourth, Lambert clearly suspected that the justice had returned the money only because of Wolfson's indictment. Although the reporter admitted that *Life* had not "uncovered evidence making possible a charge that Wolfson hired Fortas to fix his case," he made the justice's association with the businessman seem anything but innocent. The article prominently displayed two sections from the American Bar Association's Canon of Judicial Ethics. One declared that "a judge's official conduct should be free from impropriety and the appearance of impropriety." The other warned against conflicts of interest that might "interfere or appear to interfere" with the fulfillment of judicial obligation.[24]

Lambert's story ignited a firestorm. In one respect, the facts proved even more damning than those he had reported. The original contract between Wolfson and Fortas, to which the reporter lacked access, stated that the financier would pay Fortas $20,000 annually for life to become a consultant and the same amount to Carol Agger, should she survive her husband. Instead of following the "cardinal rule of Washington: tell everything right away and make a clean breast of it," however, one liberal Washington insider lamented, the justice stonewalled. On

May 5, Fortas released a statement that said nothing about the lifetime contract. Instead, he insisted that he had not "accepted" a fee from the foundation, while acknowledging that it had "tendered" him one that he then returned. The justice also unequivocally denied that he had provided the financier any legal advice or services from the court. Then he maintained a watchful silence. "The high-living little judge was clearly trying to ride out the storm," *Newsweek* reported.[25]

So elliptical, incomplete, and legalistic was his statement responding to Lambert's story, however, that it just made matters worse. The *Washington Post*, usually one of Fortas's staunchest supporters, editorialized on May 6 that he had cast "a shadow over the Supreme Court." The justice *might* remove it if he put "the whole story of his dealings in this matter on the public record." If he could not, he should protect the court by resigning.[26]

Impeachment was another possibility, as was, Assistant Attorney General William Rehnquist informed Mitchell, indictment. Rehnquist subsequently said that the "arrangement with Louis Wolfson raised a serious question as to whether there might have been a violation of a criminal statute, 18 U.S.C. 205 (in substance prohibiting officers of any branch of the federal government from acting as agent or attorney in any matter to which the United States is a party)." When Robert Griffin and other congressional Republicans who had opposed Fortas in 1968 raised the specter of impeachment, the Democrats who had supported him then remained conspicuously silent. But on May 6, Nixon and Attorney General Mitchell dissuaded congressional Republicans from launching lengthy, divisive impeachment proceedings. The president kept the attention on Fortas's ethical lapses, and Mitchell implied that the justice would soon resign.[27]

The Nixon administration and Fortas's congressional antagonists increased the likelihood of that outcome by playing hardball with people and institutions important to the justice. On May 5, the day the *Life* exposé appeared, Bobby Baker's nemesis, Senator John Williams, went after Fortas's mentor, William O. Douglas. He reminded his colleagues that Douglas received $12,000 annually from the Parvin Foundation (nearly $78,000 in 2016 dollars), which was "controlled by a group of Las Vegas gamblers . . . in trouble with the Department of Justice," and he introduced a bill to penalize judges or public officials who accepted payments from tax-exempt foundations. The *Los Angeles Times* stressed "an intriguing link" between the two justices who took fees from suspicious charitable foundations when it pointed out that Carol Agger acted as the Parvin Foundation's tax attorney. On May 6, the press also disclosed that the Justice Department had "quietly" launched a grand jury investigation to reopen the question of whether Fortas's old firm, Arnold & Porter, had obstructed justice by deliberately concealing subpoenaed documents in a price-fixing case that the firm had reported as lost, which had recently turned up in Agger's office safe.

Arnold & Porter lawyers believed that the administration was sending Fortas a message that it would destroy his wife and the firm he had founded.[28]

And, the administration suggested, unless he resigned, it could ruin him too. The press reported that the Justice Department was investigating whether Fortas had violated any criminal statutes. Rumors also swirled about his private life. Those accusations the press did not disclose, probably because reporters considered them unreliable. After talking with Will Wilson's assistant at Justice, Henry Petersen, about them, Fred Graham noted that while Petersen "didn't know of the alleged morals charge(s), he said that 'Fortas and Mrs. Fortas were known to have a loose sense of morals—whatever that means.'" It was a fact that Fortas chased women. His wife had no sexual relationships outside their marriage of which any of their close friends were aware. It was also a fact that Agger tolerated her husband's philandering, since she understood she remained the most important person in his life. If that meant "Fortas and Mrs. Fortas" had "a loose sense of morals," so did plenty of other powerful Washington couples.[29]

The administration soon found more acceptable ways of smearing Fortas. Although Justice Department officials had corroborated for Lambert Fortas's receipt of a fee from the Wolfson Foundation, they still lacked hard proof he had accepted one when the *Life* article appeared. As soon as it did, the IRS subpoenaed the correspondence between Fortas and the Wolfson Family Foundation. When Mitchell and press spokesman Jack Landau arrived back in Washington from New York just after midnight the morning of May 7, Wilson and Petersen met them at the airport. They were carrying a copy of Fortas's contract with the foundation showing that Wolfson had agreed to pay $20,000 annually to Fortas for his life and to Carol Agger, should she survive him. The contract shocked Mitchell. "It can't be real!" Landau recalled the attorney general exclaiming repeatedly.[30]

Though it was, there was still no proof that Fortas had done anything illegal. As John Dean said later, the Justice Department was "not even close" to having "the goods on Fortas." Justice had no evidence that he had ever contacted a government official on Wolfson's behalf, and its lawyers knew that he had returned his first and only payment from the financier. If the administration pressed too hard, Fortas might dig in his heels. In addition to turning up the heat on his old law firm and his wife, it needed to convince someone the justice respected that he should resign.[31]

Warren's thaw toward Nixon after the dinner made him the obvious nominee. So, as John Ehrlichman later said, the administration dispatched John Mitchell to share the contract with the chief justice and to give him a chance to demonstrate his thankfulness for the president's hospitality. Particularly given his anger over Landau's earlier visit about *Alderman*, Warren probably should have refused to discuss Fortas with the attorney general. He did not.[32]

Instead, the chief justice became Mitchell's accomplice. "He can't stay," Warren said privately of Fortas afterward. The chief justice's own meeting with the attorney general helped guarantee that. The next *Newsweek* contained an article by Samuel Shaffer detailing Mitchell's May 7 "backstairs call on Chief Justice Earl Warren. The message: there was still more damaging material in the Fortas file—and it was sure to surface unless Fortas withdrew." Washington reporter Robert Shogan remembered that Shaffer's article created as much of "a sensation" as Lambert's. Mitchell encouraged the public to imagine the worst and fed the story by admitting publicly that he had seen Warren to provide him with "certain information," which he still refused to disclose.[33]

When the Nixon administration debriefed the imprisoned Wolfson, though, it received bad news. The financier had agreed to talk with Will Wilson and two FBI agents after the *Life* story appeared, and he hoped for a deal.* He provided them with a sworn affidavit on May 10 insisting that in a 1966 preindictment meeting with Fortas, the justice had dismissed the financier's violations as "technical" and indicated, the affidavit continued confusingly, that he "had or would contact Manuel Cohen of the Securities and Exchange Commission regarding this matter. Fortas indicated that he was somewhat responsible for Cohen's appointment to the Commission as Chairman [by LBJ]." As one Fortas biographer has remarked, this language proved "too vague" for Nixon administration officials, who understood that a "contact" might encompass anything from a legitimate, if ill-advised, request for an update on the proceedings to a corrupt order to shut down the prosecution. In letters to Wolfson that the financier now handed over to the Justice Department and that Mitchell promptly made available to Warren, Fortas sounded concerned about his friend's legal problems. But the correspondence did not suggest that Fortas did anything for him. Nor did the justice reach out to Cohen on Wolfson's behalf. (When Wolfson asked why after his release from prison, Fortas answered that "would have been like lighting a fuse on our own dynamite.") Wolfson also emphasized that at their last meeting before his indictment, Fortas listened sympathetically, but "made no offer of assistance nor did he indicate he would do anything." After his conviction, the financier urged the justice to ask Johnson to lobby Nixon for a presidential pardon, which he did not receive, but Fortas apparently did not do that either,

---

* Whether Wolfson got one remains unclear. The Justice Department worked hard in 1969 to avoid the impression he was benefiting from his cooperation, but it may have rewarded Wolfson by directing a resistant US attorney's office in the Southern District of New York to accept his no-contest plea in another case in 1972. Laura Kalman, *Abe Fortas: A Biography* (New Haven: Yale University Press, 1990), 363. In the odd way of Washington, Wolfson's lead defense attorney in fighting the criminal charges was William Bittman, the former Justice Department attorney who had once prosecuted Bobby Baker, who then became a DC superlawyer.

and Wolfson's pardon file in the Nixon Library reveals no indication of Johnson's involvement.[34]

Of course, Fortas and Wolfson may not have provided a faithful account of their relationship to the Justice Department and press in 1969. Fortas had lied before the Senate Judiciary Committee the previous year to hide the depth of his involvement in the Johnson White House. And just a few weeks before Wolfson talked with Wilson in May of 1969, the financier informed a skeptical *Wall Street Journal* reporter that "somebody who is as close as anybody could be" to Lyndon Johnson had assured him that a presidential pardon was his for the asking in 1968, but he had decided against doing so "because he didn't want any favors"![35]

Still, in the half century that followed Fortas's May 1969 press statement, it would become clear to most, if not all,[36] who studied the episode that Justice Fortas did nothing for Louis Wolfson beyond, perhaps, soothingly predicting orally that the government would not consider his friend's violations significant and sending him comforting letters that promised nothing. Fortas remained loyal to a fault to those he had represented. His behavior was indiscreet. But after Fortas left the court, even Attorney General Mitchell admitted that it was not criminal.[37]

Although the White House repeatedly stressed how "responsibly" it was behaving in the Fortas affair, reporters knew that the administration was playing them and suspected its officials of very dirty pool. "The statement by Attorney General Mitchell that he has taken some information of importance to Chief Justice Warren—presumably information relating to Justice Fortas—comes close to being an effort at political blackmail," the *Post* editorialized. "Although the statement does not say explicitly Mr. Mitchell knows anything more than the information already made public, that is the obvious implication, and with it comes the further implication that the Nixon Administration is prepared to use it against Justice Fortas unless the Chief Justice persuades him to resign." It was unseemly for anyone who headed "a department named Justice to feed the rumor mills by confirming the innocuous details of a story in *Newsweek* while failing to confirm or deny other details which indicate he has derogatory evidence of a serious nature against Mr. Fortas." The *New York Times* agreed that the attorney general was trafficking "in rumors and innuendo" and accused the administration of making an "ugly squeeze play" to win the justice's resignation. Meanwhile, NBC characterized Mitchell's "ominous" visit to Warren as a "deep rare intrusion into the Judicial Branch by the Executive Branch." The media called on Fortas to break his silence, since his short statement had just sparked confusion and criticism.[38]

That he refused to do. The court was taking a short recess, and Fortas had scheduled speeches in Boston, Richmond, and Memphis, which he delivered. He had received no payment beyond his travel expenses or donated his $2,000 speaker's fee (nearly $13,000 in 2016 dollars) to charitable causes "for some time," his office ostentatiously made clear. But that news backfired: The justice's agent said that Fortas had only adopted that policy recently, and the revelation that "a Supreme Court Justice, like an actor or nightclub entertainer, engages a booking agent to drum up business" revolted some. Reporters and photographers followed Fortas everywhere he went and besieged his Georgetown house.[39]

By the weekend, apparently, he was edging toward resignation—though he may have wanted to wait until term's end to announce it. "The real truth about this," he subsequently confided to Wolfson, was that the Nixon administration officials "were bound and determined to get me . . . because of my association with Johnson" and had promised Strom Thurmond a veto over Fortas's successor. "I knew that they were after me," and his arrangement with Wolfson made him vulnerable. Impeachment and/or criminal prosecution seemed possible. Fortas met with Clark Clifford at his house, who recalled that the justice had "unequivocally" decided to resign even before the start of their long conversation. "And I couldn't understand why because it didn't seem to me that the offense warranted the action." But Fortas insisted and appeared eminently rational, as well as "quite deeply" troubled by a message from the Nixon administration that if he did not resign, he would face further punishment. Whether that warning came through the press or as a more direct threat remained murky. All that was clear, Clifford said later, was that "some incident or event had persuaded him that he must resign and nothing any of us could say would change his mind."[40]

In a separate meeting at Fortas's house, William O. Douglas found that out. Adam Stolpen, a close family friend from Westport, who attended college in Washington and spent weekends with Agger and Fortas, helping them with the garden and chores and visiting with them and their friends, witnessed it. As the men stood beside the swimming pool and its bar, Stolpen remembered, Douglas pleaded with Fortas not to resign. "We" had done a firm headcount the previous night, he said, and there were not sufficient votes to ensure impeachment. "We" most likely included Douglas's long-time friend, House Judiciary Committee Chair Emanuel Celler. Everyone could see Celler was "foot-dragging on [bringing] an impeachment proceeding" against Fortas, and he would subsequently save Douglas from impeachment. The crisis would blow over, Douglas counseled. And on the one hand, perhaps that was reasonable advice. Chief Justice William Howard Taft had survived a similar scandal when the public learned that Andrew Carnegie had left a $10,000 annual annuity to him and to his wife should she outlive him (over $130,000 in 2016 dollars). On the other hand, although no one had yet officially filed articles of impeachment, the pressure for impeachment was growing in the House as the crisis continued, and it is unclear how long Celler could, or wanted to, resist it. Any impeachment attempt, as the *Wall Street Journal* said, would be "messy" and "unpredictable." Even if it ended in Fortas's favor, that would not guarantee him exemption from criminal prosecution, though, to be sure, that threat represented a bluff. (Recall that Mitchell himself later said Fortas had committed no crime.) Stolpen remembered Fortas's reply to Douglas: He himself did not matter. There was no constitutional mandate for the Supreme Court's authority; the court depended on public opinion to preserve its legitimacy. "I will not be responsible for destroying that." At that moment, Stolpen recalled, Douglas put his hand on Fortas's shoulder to comfort him, and this fastidiously controlled man began to cry.[41]

That theme of falling on his sword had run through Fortas's letter asking LBJ to withdraw his chief justice nomination the previous year, and he stressed it again in the resignation letter he submitted to Earl Warren on May 14. It included the fullest public explanation he would ever provide of his relationship with Wolfson. He explained that the financier had recruited him because of their shared interest in social welfare. The planned $20,000 lifetime annual consultant's fee, which Fortas now publicly acknowledged, was not high, he implied, since Wolfson had promised to expand the foundation's budget and its activities. Because their program had been "a long-range one," the two men had decided upon a lifetime contract with payments to Carol Agger should Fortas predecease her. Fortas had received his first and only check in 1966, and after attending a trustees' meeting in June, he had decided to terminate his association because he was busy and he had learned "that the SEC had referred Mr. Wolfson's file to the Department of Justice for consideration as to criminal prosecution." He wrote Wolfson that month cancelling the arrangement, but did not return the check until December. While the financier had sometimes sent him information about his problems, Fortas correctly observed that Wolfson had forwarded the material to "many other people" as well. "I have not interceded or taken part in any legal, administrative or judicial matter affecting Mr. Wolfson or anyone associated with him," he reiterated. Nonetheless, "the welfare and maximum effectiveness of the Court to perform its critical role in our system of government" were all-important. "Hell, I feel there wasn't any choice for a man of conscience," Fortas explained to a reporter after the court had released the news he was quitting on May 15. He had decided for himself that his resignation was right for the court and the country.[42]

Many believed that he had badly wounded both. *Los Angeles Times* Bureau Chief Robert Donovan maintained that "though the Fortas case was in certain respects the most sensational Washington has ever witnessed," it had "sickened," rather than "excited" observers. "If a Supreme Court justice latches onto a fee he should never have touched," perhaps all society was as "corrupt" as critics of the United States claimed. Citizens were "bred" to see the court as "their final bulwark against injustice," and since Warren had arrived there, "it has done more than any other institution to uphold individual rights and undo wrongs to the black, the downtrodden, the accused." Sometimes the court stirred controversy, but Americans ultimately revered it. Now, it had become a little less sacred. As "the first Supreme Court justice to resign under personal attack," Fortas had cast "a shadow of impropriety over a great institution," the *New York Times* agreed. For its part, the Nixon administration increased suspicion that it had blackmailed Fortas by denying repeatedly it had done so and by dropping talk of prosecuting him, his wife, or his old law firm now that it had secured two vacant seats at the court, Fortas's and Warren's. The House Judiciary Committee sought to write *finis* to the sorry story. A relieved Emanuel Celler had told reporters after Fortas had announced his resignation, "I feel like a woman who has been delivered of a baby." He maintained that "further action would be like feeding on a carcass." But an angry Republican on the committee publicly expressed the hope that the American Bar Association or the Judicial Conference of the United States would investigate Fortas. More condemnation quickly followed when the ABA summarily publicly declared, solely on the basis of what Fortas had said in his resignation letter to Warren, that his relationship with Wolfson violated the canons of judicial ethics.[43]

Fortas was not the only exposed liberal justice either. "One down, how many more to go?" the conservative *Chicago Tribune* asked hopefully in stressing that investments in tax shelters and relationships with foundations made at least Brennan and Douglas fair game too. Even when Douglas resigned as the Parvin Foundation's president and relinquished his $12,000 annual honorarium soon afterward, his critics continued to complain. Their disapproval grew after Parvin showed a reporter an earlier letter from Douglas discussing the foundation's response to an IRS investigation of its finances and characterizing the probe as a "manufactured" attempt "to get me off the court." Although the Parvin Foundation did valuable work in developing countries, the *New York Times* editorialized, "nothing could justify a judge in associating his name and the aura of his office with any individual or organization involved in the Las Vegas gambling community." That was mild compared to what conservatives said. "Douglas is next," Strom Thurmond vowed. One of Nixon's political espionage experts reported to John Ehrlichman that a national newspaper felt "it is on to a Fortas type exposure and is using its full weight" to examine Douglas's connections to the Parvin Foundation.[44]

From France, where he and Agger had gone to recuperate, Fortas wrote Douglas, "I should be in anguish if I thought that my own decision aggravated your problems—because I hoped that it would, whatever else it did, relieve the pressure on you," as he still believed it would. And for the present, at least, the *New York Times* considered it "doubtful" that the Justice Department would pursue the case against Douglas "if only because two such incidents might indeed damage the Court beyond repair."[45]

Earl Warren watched with dismay these developments that overshadowed the many celebrations of his tenure and departure. With Congress, which had adopted its own lame ethics code the previous year, making menacing noises about imposing one on the federal judiciary, he determined to demonstrate that it could police itself. Since the American Bar Association canons did not bind federal judges, Warren, acting in his capacity as chair of the Judicial Conference of the United States, summoned eleven judges to the court on Saturday, May 24, a week and a half after Fortas's resignation, and directed them to draft the federal judiciary's first code of ethics by early June. "The move marks the first concrete sign that Chief Justice Warren and the Federal judiciary feel an obligation to set their house in order in the wake of the recent Fortas controversy," one reporter observed.[46]

Since distinguishing "good" from "bad" moonlighting proved so difficult, the new code would bar federal judges from virtually all of it, including accepting remuneration for most teaching and lecturing, joining foundation boards, and acting as executors or trustees for estates, except in the exceptional case, and only then when the Circuit Court of Appeals determined beforehand that such an activity served "the public interest." Additionally, the code would require judges regularly to file financial disclosure statements of their investments, gifts, income, and liability with the Judicial Conference. Despite some favorable publicity for the code adopted at the June 10 meeting of the Judicial Conference, press accounts left no doubt that Warren had "rammed through" its adoption and angered some federal judges in the process. Some complained that the new restrictions represented a hasty and hysterical overreaction to the Fortas scandal and would relegate federal judges to what Judge Charles Wyzanski referred to as "a monastic magistracy."[47]

These concerns possessed some validity. "I am so sorry that the Chief Justice felt required to wind up his career by attempting to forge a chastity belt for the judiciary," John Frank, an expert on judicial ethics, wrote Hugo Black. "I doubt the necessity of the requirements and think, in any case, that they are far too strict—a burst of puritanism which will seriously interfere with the legitimate involvement of the judiciary in the life of the communities in which the judges live." Warren countered such criticism by pointing out that judges could still participate in public service and that "acquisitiveness while engaging in decision making is not a wholesome thing and can lead to great embarrassment if not illegality," as all Washington had just witnessed. Like Frank, many remained unconvinced.[48]

Even worse, the Judicial Conference, citing lack of jurisdiction, refused to apply the code to the Supreme Court at its June meeting. Warren, however, assured the conference that the justices would follow it in embracing the strictures. "I did not say this lightly, and I assure you that I had reason to believe that this would be done," he wrote one federal judge. But after a lengthy discussion, his colleagues at the court refused, as the chief justice should have anticipated. His brethren had always treated each justice as guardian of his own morality, and at least two, Black and Douglas, were known to oppose a code because it threatened judicial independence. So, as the *Washington Post* reported, the man "whose persuasive powers produced a 9-0 decision against school segregation" proved unable "to carry a Court majority for self-imposed reform," and Warren was embarrassed.[49]

By term's end, Warren could announce that Stewart, White, Marshall, and Brennan had individually agreed to follow the code, but that did not help much.* "In stark contrast," the *Los Angeles Times* acidly observed, "there is the behavior of Justice Douglas, who despite all the concern over the non-judicial activities of justices continues shamelessly to peddle his name and the prestige of his office to virtually any outlet that will give him a forum, including girlie magazines." (Douglas had recently accepted $350 for writing an article on folk singing for the racy magazine *Avant Garde*.) The Senate's Judicial Improvement Subcommittee chairman, Joseph Tydings (D-MD), stressed the "damaging anomaly." Although "much of the impropriety that gave impetus to the reforms emanated from the Supreme Court," its members had rejected the code. He cautioned that if the court did not "heal itself, Congress may feel obligated to apply its own medication." Ultimately, the judiciary abandoned Warren's reforms and punted the issue to the American Bar Association, which updated the Canon of Judicial Ethics in 1972 to encourage public reporting of outside income. By that time, it had become clear that just as Fortas's fall haunted Warren's final days as chief justice, it would also dog the court and shape its future.[50]

"The Center Seat"

The firestorm sparked by Lambert's *Life* Fortas story worried Warren Burger, and not just because he received an honorarium for his work as Mayo Foundation trustee. Though the president's behavior about Fortas was "carefully correct," Burger assured Nixon in a letter on May 8, congressional Republicans were rushing to judgment. "This week is a time for Republican leaders to 'view with dismay' and to 'be saddened' and 'disturbed' but largely silent. They should not

---

* Actually, Brennan had gone even further: he had divested himself of all investments except federal bonds; cancelled his scheduled speeches, whether or not he received a fee for them; bowed out of a scheduled teaching engagement and refused to accept new ones; and cut his ties to every organization but the Catholic Church and the court after Fortas left the court. Since he had never had much money, his decision created a hardship for him. Seth Stern and Stephen Wermiel, *Justice Brennan: Liberal Champion* (New York: Houghton Mifflin, 2010), 319–21.

'attack.'" To do so would seem unfair. It would backfire politically by suggesting that Republicans prejudged the Fortas case. Moreover, an attack would push Fortas's 1968 chief justice supporters in the Senate, who "have really nothing to say now," out of the spotlight *and* embitter them. "As a consequence when your first nomination goes to the Senate, this suppressed rage will likely assert itself and your nominee may become *their* whipping boy." As it turned out, the president's first nomination went very smoothly.[51]

It was Burger's, and it was as chief justice. On May 20, Nixon told the GOP leadership that in selecting the next leader of the court and associate justice, "he would be leaning very heavily on the Attorney General" and "got across the idea that he felt there should be some distance between the President and the men he named to the Court." Republicans should submit their recommendations of anyone but a member of the House or Senate for the chief justiceship or the Fortas vacancy to Mitchell. The Constitution's emoluments clause barred members of Congress from assuming positions for which they had voted a salary increase, and the justices had received a pay hike that session. The following day, just a week after Fortas's resignation, John Mitchell summoned Burger to the Justice Department to say that Nixon was announcing his nomination on television in what John Ehrlichman called a "prime-time spectacular" that evening.[52]

"It was highly symbolic; the Warren era was over and a Nixon Court was coming into being," Ehrlichman remembered. The president insisted on avoiding leaks and milking his selection for maximum media attention. On May 21, the White House let reporters know in the afternoon that the president would make a televised address naming the new chief justice that evening and that his nominee would attend. "This started a frantic game among them of tracking down which prospective candidates would or would not be in Washington at 7 P.M.," one journalist said. Potter Stewart was on a plane, Sophie Friendly said that her husband was on his way to his New York City home for the evening at 6:30 P.M., and William Rogers was travelling in Asia. But Mitchell cancelled a Mississippi speech. Was he staying in town because he was becoming the next chief justice or because the president had invited his cabinet members to his speech? No one knew. "The air was electric in the East Room" when Nixon entered "with the white-haired man whom a great many in the audience did not recognize." The Burgers had escaped detection by entering the White House by tunnel. Nixon secured a public relations coup and the positive press coverage he sought (figure 19). In his remarks, the nominee lauded the president for paying "tribute to all of the sitting judges of the federal and state systems in this nomination." Nixon himself alluded only implicitly to the court's travails in rating the nominee as "above all, qualified because of his unquestioned integrity throughout his private and public life."[53]

Figure 19 After nominating Warren Burger as chief justice, President Nixon looked on as Burger extolled him for "paying tribute to all of the sitting judges of the federal and state systems in this nomination." National Archives.

The following day when he met with reporters, the president proved more direct. He explained that he had made his decision in close consultation only with Mitchell, not with members of Congress or the American Bar Association. "Now, because of the Fortas matter, I determined that the appointee should not be a personal friend," the president stressed. "I determined also that if possible, I should avoid appointing somebody who would be a political friend or using the Washington vernacular, 'crony.' " And he wanted someone confirmable "without violent controversy."

He had therefore eliminated a number of individuals for the chief justiceship or the Fortas vacancy, including his close friend Charles Rhyne. Four others had taken themselves out of the running. "You all know my high regard for him," Nixon said of Herbert Brownell, whom he later identified as his top choice, originally. "You know he was the man next to Attorney General Mitchell, who was my closest adviser in selecting the Cabinet. I think he would have made a superb Chief Justice." But Brownell had warned the president that the Senate might hold up the nomination because of his actions as Eisenhower's attorney general, which included sending in federal troops to desegregate Central High in Little Rock, and Senate Judiciary Committee Chairman Eastland had delivered the same message. Tom Dewey had disqualified himself because of age. The "superbly qualified" John Mitchell had counseled the president against nominating a political intimate, Nixon continued. Justice Potter Stewart had taken the unusual step of coming to the White House and arguing that "generally speaking, because of the special role that the Chief Justice has to play as the leader of the Court, it would be very difficult to take a man from the Court and put him above the others" and that the president should choose an outsider. (In fact, Stewart had visited Nixon before the Fortas scandal erupted and what mainly motivated him to do so was the awkwardness involved in becoming chief when the Senate had already denied the position to another sitting justice.)[54]

What brought Nixon to Burger? Though he had known the judge for more than two decades, they were not chums. Moreover, the president had long believed, he volunteered to reporters, that able district and circuit court judges deserved Supreme Court appointments. Yet although some had received that reward, "more often than not Circuit Judges do not go to the Supreme Court and very, very seldom does a Judge of the Circuit Court go to Chief Justice." Burger also possessed the "leadership quality" needed by a chief justice and the right judicial philosophy. According to Nixon, his nominee advocated judicial restraint. As a "strict constructionist," Burger had written criminal law opinions that reflected "the minority view of the Supreme Court" that the president hoped would become "the majority view. But when he gets to the Supreme Court he will be his own man." Nixon hammered home that point repeatedly as he said that he had not spoken with the nominee about the job "until three minutes before we went to meet the press" and that he had never interviewed Burger about his philosophy. "He will owe his appointment to the fact that I appointed him, but he is to sit there and consider these decisions, these great questions, without any pressure from the White House." As a lawyer, the president sought a "cordial but . . . arm's length" relationship between the Supreme Court and the White House.

Obviously, and very significantly, Nixon was changing the rules of the game. While the president refused to rule out the future appointment of individuals from the legal academy or the bar "with substantial constitutional law" expertise, Nixon was reviving Eisenhower's reasoning that federal judges most deserved Supreme Court seats. "As you can tell from this appointment, naturally I would say that Appellate and District Court experience gives an individual an edge." He also made the "crony" label even more prejudicial. Yet as Dirksen had stressed during the Fortas chief justice battle, presidents had long installed the intimates Nixon put off limits on the court, often with salutary results.[55]

Whether the president accurately described the process he followed in choosing Burger is unclear. He had not yet begun to tape his deliberations, and the Nixon Library contains strangely few related documents. His remarks to the press contained at least some disinformation. Nixon had no use for Potter Stewart and his establishment credentials, for example, and it is unlikely that the president ever considered him for the job—though most of Congress, the legal academy, the reporters who covered the court, and the other justices would have acclaimed a Chief Justice Stewart. But the accuracy of the president's account does not matter. What is important for our story is that Nixon had announced a presumption in favor of judges and against cronies that henceforward would haunt the confirmation process.[56]

He had also underscored the casualness with which his administration vetted prospective nominees. Nixon apparently did decide on Burger himself, and relatively deliberately, especially when compared to the haphazard way he settled on associate justices later. But when Senate Majority Leader Mansfield voiced his certainty that the president and his advisers had reviewed the life of Nixon's nominee "with a fine-tooth comb," he overstated the case. A quick FBI investigation had occurred, and Justice Department officials had reviewed Burger's tax returns. But when Burger reasoned with John Mitchell that his doctor should give him a physical before the president made his announcement, however, the attorney general said there was no time. What other information had the Justice Department failed to nail down besides the nominee's health? Obviously, as its behavior in subsequent nominations would soon confirm, the Nixon White House and Justice Department did not yet appreciate the need for that "fine-tooth comb."[57]

In many ways Burger proved an obvious choice, given Nixon's promise in 1968 to unleash the peace forces against those of lawlessness. Earl Warren had predicted Burger's selection, as had the *Washington Post*'s Supreme Court correspondent. Some administration officials assumed, as Mitchell joked, that "Burger's the first guy to run for the job of Chief Justice—and get it."[58]

His ambitions, however, had been more modest. Mitchell had shocked him, Burger told Nixon later. "I assumed that it was Herb Brownell" and that "I was going to be second man." He remembered telling the attorney general that he was "disappointed in a way" until Mitchell explained that Brownell was too old and too close to the president. Burger had no recollection of what happened afterward until he found himself in St. John's Church across from the White House in Lafayette Square, where he had sat for an hour. Justice Department officials confirmed that the news of his selection "dazed" him. Harry Blackmun had thought that Burger had "a very fine chance" of nomination for an associate justice. Like Burger himself, though, Blackmun had never foreseen that Nixon would make his friend chief.[59]

"The Fortas affair, however, made this almost inevitable," Blackmun concluded. As Pat Buchanan, now a White House adviser, told the president, it was crucial that his "first choice not in any way be construed as 'Nixon's Fortas.'" Whatever led him to Burger, it is significant that the president justified his pick by referring to Fortas and stressing the need to avoid "cronyism." As ever, recent history played a role in the nomination process.[60]

Nixon won points for how he handled it. He had not consulted the American Bar Association, but it considered Burger "highly acceptable" anyway. "He looks, acts and talks like a Chief Justice," Senator Dirksen (and many others) observed of the nominee. Given recent events, the press raised some questions about Burger's Mayo trustee post, which the White House had skittishly tried to hide. (Burger would soon succumb to pressure to resign from the Mayo Foundation.) Yet the media largely applauded the nomination. Nixon had every reason to feel pleased with himself, and he did. When he read that the liberal *Nation* and *New Republic* mourned the end of the Warren years and complained that Burger lacked "'leadership' and 'intellectual' qualities," the president responded with a barbed quip: "Warren, of course, was an intellectual!!??" Even the slight grumbling sparked by the selection seemed halfhearted. "Conservatives were quite pleased with the nomination; liberals, by contrast, were demoralized by the Fortas affair and not disposed to attack a nominee whose only apparent vice was that he was relatively conservative," one law professor reported.[61]

Burger's confirmation hearing just two weeks later seemed straight out of a bygone era. It lasted all of one hour and fifty minutes, and it went on that long only because senators vied with each other to praise him. The Senate approved him by a seventy-four-to-three vote six days later.

While most future presidents would shun cronies when they selected justices, it turned out that Nixon himself had just pushed cronyism underground. Ironically, the leader who made presidential intimates taboo as justices endangered the independence of the court by enlisting an eager chief justice to shore up his presidency. That began to become clear when the first Watergate tapes were released in 1974. Reporters noted that Attorney General John Mitchell's successor, Richard Kleindienst, had visited the president in April of 1973. Kleindienst wanted Nixon to know that the Watergate prosecutor and his team had alerted him that John Dean, who was cooperating with them in the hope of immunity or a reduced sentence, had implicated White House aides H. R. Haldeman and John Ehrlichman in the Watergate cover-up. Kleindienst had been urging Nixon to demand the resignations of Haldeman and Ehrlichman and to appoint a special prosecutor for some time, and he now renewed his plea. "[I]ncidentally, the Chief Justice and I are very close friends," the attorney general volunteered, and

Burger suggested a distinguished Chicago attorney with a track record as an able prosecutor. Legal ethics expert John Frank noted the irony: Nixon had cited his desire to avoid cronyism as the reason for Burger's appointment. Reporters wondered what else the chief justice and members of the administration had privately discussed. They speculated that Burger's involvement would require him to recuse himself from any Watergate case before the Supreme Court or presiding over an impeachment trial.[62]

Instead, the chief justice put himself in charge of drafting the court's opinion that ultimately held that the president must hand over the tapes he tried to hold back. Nixon "reportedly used expletive-deleted language to describe Chief Justice Warren E. Burger, his once-supportive appointee and now the author of the crushing decision against him," the *Washington Post* said in 1974. It was left for Bob Woodward and Scott Armstrong to reveal, accurately, five years later in *The Brethren* that the other justices had initially considered Burger's first attempt at the tapes decision dreadful. They had hatched a successful coup to take the drafting of the opinion away from him, and he had been its author in name only.[63]

The Brethren ended its coverage of the court in 1976. It was Nina Totenberg's turn to create a stir in 1977, when she reported that the court had "secretly voted" by five to three to refuse review of the Watergate cover-up convictions of John Mitchell, H. R. Haldeman, and John Ehrlichman. Since four justices had to agree to take a case, that left Burger one vote short. She revealed that the three justices who wanted to hear the case were Nixon appointees and that Burger was delaying a public announcement of the decision in the hope of winning additional support. Legal correspondents did not usually reveal court actions before they became public. Totenberg said she had "previously received advance notice of some court opinions, but had not reported them because 'there's no profit in it except self-glorification'" and maintained that "no one actually 'leaked'" the news. However she happened on it, her information potentially compromised the court. As reporters observed, if the justices now denied review of their convictions, Mitchell, Haldeman, and Ehrlichman could make a case that publicity about the leak prejudiced their situations. If the justices took the case, court watchers would conclude that Burger had successfully persuaded a justice who had originally voted against hearing it to change his vote. (The court denied review anyway.)[64]

Then Ehrlichman published his memoir of the Nixon White House in 1982 and revealed that Nixon and Mitchell "made a constant effort to keep in touch with Burger." Ehrlichman served up the example of a White House breakfast he had attended with the president, attorney general, and chief justice in December of 1970, before Nixon began taping his conversations. The four men had privately and "openly" spoken about "the pros and cons of issues before the court," including busing and criminal procedure, he wrote. Mitchell imme-diately announced that neither he nor Nixon had any "recollection of such dis-cussions." Burger angrily knocked a camera out of the hands of a member of the CBS news team that tried to question him about the allegation. He claimed that Ehrlichman was just "trying to sell a book." At the time, it seemed as if Burger overreacted. As journalist Linda Greenhouse observed, Ehrlichman's "sketchy" account did not necessarily indicate the chief justice had breached judicial eth-ics. A discussion of "issues" did not necessarily include talk of pending cases before the court.[65]

But a decade later, in an article about the still-unreleased Nixon tapes, Seymour Hersh revealed that the archivists listening to them had told him that "Burger was more than willing to discuss any issue with the President, whether it involved politics, Watergate, or cases pending before the Supreme Court." Ehrlichman laughingly agreed. He now admitted to Hersh that his book had actually soft-pedaled the relationship between the president and chief justice.[66]

When the tapes were finally released, they bore out the archivists' observa-tions. In one 1972 conversation, Nixon and Burger discussed the court's forth-coming obscenity decision in *Miller v. California*. "I am struggling with this pornography thing," Burger said, and was "coming out hard" against it, "whether I get the support or not." (He got four other justices.) After identifying him-self as "a square," Nixon maintained that freedom of the press had "gone over-board." He also instructed the chief justice to drag his feet on busing for as long as possible. "Don't get anything in before the election, for God's sake!" The court had plenty of other "explosive issues" already, Burger reassured him. The two men also discussed the death penalty, which the chief justice reported "was still churning around in the Court," and about which Nixon volunteered he pos-sessed "mixed feelings."[67]

Burger may have proved helpful that summer when the Justice Department charged Daniel Ellsberg and Anthony Russo with theft and espionage after they leaked the Pentagon Papers to the press. Acting in his capacity as the justice re-sponsible for the Ninth Circuit, William O. Douglas issued a stay that postponed the trial. Though the solicitor general publicly called on the court to overturn it, Ehrlichman visited Burger privately to explain that Nixon would benefit from a delay until after the 1972 presidential election. The chief justice "was kind of intrigued with the political aspects of it," he reported back, and the court was soon issuing an order that it would not meet in special session to review Douglas's decision.[68]

Nixon's Watergate troubles provided more instances for contact with his chief justice. When the government indicted Mitchell, Haldeman, and Ehrlichman for their roles in covering up White House involvement in the Watergate break-in, Nixon telephoned Burger in 1973. "My heart goes out to those people who with the best of intentions were overzealous," he confided. "But as I am sure you know . . . if I could have spent a little more time being a politician last year and less time being President, I would have kicked their butts out. I didn't know what they were doing." Nixon had China and Russia to preoccupy him, the chief justice answered diplomatically, before the president jumped in to remind him that the Vietnam War had taken a toll too. Still, Nixon did not want Burger to worry: "I know you as a great jurist, probably, and as an old politician, are naturally concerned about all the hullabaloo, but it will pass, and I will survive it." But the president added that he did not "see how any of these guys can receive a fair trial." On the telephone, Burger was discreet. "It's just one of the times when the boat's rocking, and this kind of separates the men from the boys," he laughed. Later that year, when Spiro Agnew had to resign as vice president, Earl Warren reported "a rumor at the Court that Chief Justice Burger was to be the new Vice President."[69]

Chief Justice Burger never approached Fortas in importance as a presidential adviser, but it was not for lack of trying, and his relationship with Nixon was anything but arm's-length. As we will see, he peppered the president with his opinions whenever a court vacancy existed. He once telephoned the White House to say that Thurgood Marshall was "much sicker than anyone presently realizes" and to dictate a get-well message Nixon could send. As Fortas backed LBJ on Vietnam, so Burger dropped by the White House to leave a letter of support when Nixon launched the invasion of Cambodia. Like Fortas, he played the courtier: "Very properly the White House lines and all Western Union lines are blocked with loyal Americans who wish to express their support for your courageous decision." When Nixon faced a hostile White House Press Correspondents' dinner in 1971, Burger was there to soothe that his "fortitude and forbearance in the face of gross rudeness by your hosts will always have my unbounded admiration" and to remind the president that the press had also treated Washington and Lincoln savagely. The chief justice welcomed the fact that the president treated him as a political ally. "Poor, sad Abe Fortas," Burger had written Blackmun revealingly after Fortas resigned from the court. "I wonder if he really hurt the Court as much as the 5/4 & 6/3 monstrosities [of opinions] had done before l'affaire Fortas."[70]

But most of the disclosures about Burger's involvement in administration nominations, politics, and policymaking occurred decades after Nixon had left office. For the present, what mattered in 1969 was that the president had reasserted the importance of separation of powers and had apparently dramatically ended the Warren era. At a ceremony on the final day of the term that the Nixons attended, Warren administered the oath of office to his successor, and the president saluted the court and Warren as the embodiment of "fairness, integrity, dignity." According to the new White House line, Nixon might have derogated some of the court's decisions, but he defended the institution. That represented a shrewd shift in tone as the president tried to build support for a new Burger-led majority that was supposed to alter the court's direction.[71]

"Southern Discomfort," 1969–70

Richard Nixon loved to dream about whom he would put on the Supreme Court. Just six months into his presidency, he had named a new chief justice and had created a vacancy where a liberal once sat. As Fortas had realized, Nixon planned to use that vacancy to court Strom Thurmond and white Southerners angered by the Supreme Court. By capitalizing on hatred for the Warren Court in the nomination and confirmation process, the president continued to believe, he could both grow the Republican Party and unify the disparate elements within it.

It turned out, though, that he faced opposition. LBJ's nomination of Marshall and Fortas marked "the opening offensive in a persistent struggle for the Supreme Court, eased only by an occasional truce." At least Johnson made those choices when his party controlled the Senate. In 1968, the United States had entered an era of divided government and one in which a Supreme Court seat sometimes, though not always, seemed momentous. Nearly half of the twenty-three nominations to the court after 1968 occurred when one party—always the Republicans until 2016—held the presidency and the other controlled the Senate. Now, the pressure groups and the investigative journalism that would help topple Nixon's presidency loomed larger too, as senators themselves soon learned. Consequently, as during the Nixon years, the contentiousness of the process by which Supreme Court nominees were selected and confirmed grew.[1]

Nixon's Southern Strategy

By now, the court traditionally possessed a Jewish seat, just as it featured one for a Catholic and one for an African American. Because the public identified Brandeis and Frankfurter with social justice causes before they came to the court, and because Goldberg and Fortas belonged to Warren Court majorities that expanded civil rights and civil liberties, the Jewish seat also had become synonymous with liberalism. As President Nixon reminded reporters in May 1969, however, Arthur Goldberg had recently objected to "the Jewish seat." At a press conference, the former justice announced that Nixon was under no "obligation" to appoint a Jew to succeed Fortas. Goldberg condemned the idea of a "Jewish seat" on the court and claimed that the nation had reached a point "where judicial and political offices could be filled on the basis of individual merit." He insisted that he had not thought at the time of his own Supreme Court appointment "that I was occupying a Jewish seat." Did Goldberg mean it? Perhaps, but he was also mulling over a campaign to become New York's governor or senator and would have had every incentive to treat the United States as the melting pot that made race, religion, and region irrelevant to a person's success.[2]

Nixon seized upon those remarks and praised them as he spoke with reporters about his selection of Burger and the next associate justice. "I do not consider that there is a Jewish seat or a Catholic seat or a Negro Seat on the Court," the president said. He vowed to make Supreme Court appointments on the basis of "competence" and pledged that "the Court will not be used for the purpose of racial, religious, or geographical balance, at least not while I am here."[3]

Yet privately, Nixon remained fiercely opposed to Jews. "There's not going to be any Jew appointed to the Court, not because they're Jewish, [but] because there's no Jew . . . that can be right on the criminal law issue," he told Pat Buchanan. "They're all hung up on civil rights." Had he looked, Nixon might have found Jews who fit his ideological criteria, like Judge Henry Friendly, Chief Judge of the New York Court of Appeals Charles Breitel, and Third Circuit Judge Arlin Adams. But he did not.[4]

Nixon dissembled in another way. He intended to seek "geographical balance" because he saw Fortas's departure as a political opportunity. In 1968, he had attracted white suburbanites in the metropolitan South by posing as the moderately conservative elder statesman and an alternative to racist demagogues like George Wallace. Now Nixon hoped to capture the Wallace crowd and expand his party's hold over the region. Harry Dent, his adviser on Southern affairs and a former aide to Strom Thurmond, assured him that the reaction of Southern senators and newspapers to the Burger appointment was "overwhelmingly favorable," as it was to the president's vocal insistence that the Department of Health, Education, and Welfare (HEW) slow down the pace of school desegregation. "I am convinced that another such good appointment coupled with the changes now being generated at HEW should win for us a very close working relationship among most Southerners on Capitol Hill," Dent declared. Anticipating that the Senate would easily confirm his next nomination, as it had Burger, Nixon directed John Mitchell to find him a Southerner for the Fortas seat.[5]

Lewis Powell was "my first choice," Nixon claimed to Powell's biographer about the lawyer and former American Bar Association (ABA) president. The president had met Powell, a Virginia Democrat, and "knew him well by his representation as one of the preeminent legal scholars of our time." Powell's inclusion among the ranks of "preeminent legal scholars" was debatable, but without a doubt, he was a distinguished corporate lawyer. So, as Nixon recalled it, John Mitchell, the search's director, contacted the Richmond lawyer, but Powell turned the attorney general down. "It was only then that I nominated Judge Haynsworth, who was, incidentally, a very close second choice." Nixon's memory, however, was playing tricks on him. Perhaps he also engaged in wishful thinking. Although Powell suffered from some of Haynsworth's handicaps, he would face relatively easy going before the Senate after the president announced his nomination to the Court in 1971. Had the president and attorney general managed to draft Powell for the Fortas vacancy and substituted him for Haynsworth, they might have saved themselves a great deal of suffering. In reality, they only thought of Powell after the Senate turned down Haynsworth.[6]

Judge Clement Furman Haynsworth Jr. of South Carolina was a well-respected and well-off son of the old Confederacy. He looked like the kind of Southerner who wore white suits and two-tone shoes. He had graduated summa cum laude from Furman College, which his family had founded, and, like his father and grandfather, from Harvard Law. After naval service during World War II, he practiced law at South Carolina's largest law firm in Greenville, home to a hub of postwar textile mills and companies that employed him to represent them. An Eisenhower Democrat, Haynsworth had secured his seat on the Fourth Circuit in 1957 and had since become its beloved chief judge. The fifty-six-year-old seemed "shy" and "reserved," which some of his many friends attributed to his slight stutter, but never "aloof." When the administration began to focus on Haynsworth, he mourned the potential disruption in his personal life. He spent one week every month in Richmond, home of the Fourth Circuit, and the rest of his time in Greenville. There, he and his wife, "Miss Dorothy," the president of the local debutante cotillion, owned a large, handsome brick Tudor; raised camellias and roses; watched birds; and collected the art of another Carolinian, Jasper Johns (figure 20).[7]

Though he relished his life, Haynsworth recounted, "when the fire horse smells the fire, he is bound to go and if it should happen, I could not say no." The way the administration officials conducted the selection process to avoid another Fortas or Thornberry pleased him too. "Wishing to avoid every appearance that positions on the Supreme Court are given as rewards for personal friendship or political favor, they decided to turn to a review of the performance of the sitting judges," Haynsworth said. "When I met Mr. Mitchell for the first time, he informed me that he knew a great deal about me, and on our next meeting he told me that he had read a synopsis of every opinion I had ever written and a great many of the opinions he had read in full. On that basis, I survived the process of elimination of many judges whose work was reviewed and whose performance was considered," which was "very gratifying."[8]

Figure 20 Judge Haynsworth and his wife, Miss Dorothy. This photo by Alfred Eisenstaedt appeared in Marshall Frady, "Haynsworth of Greenville," *Life*, October 31, 1969.

Once again, Nixon and Mitchell had dispensed with the practice, standard under the three previous administrations, of consulting the American Bar Association before announcing a Supreme Court nomination. But Mitchell would not have needed the ABA Standing Committee on the Judiciary, which avowedly rated prospective candidates on the basis of their professional competence and integrity rather than their politics and ideology, to conclude that Haynsworth had amassed a distinguished record. After the fact, its chair, Lawrence Walsh, would testify at Haynsworth's nomination hearing that the committee unanimously deemed him "highly acceptable from the viewpoint of professional qualification" and would praise his "scholarly, well written opinions." Everyone at the court from Burger to Brennan, Harlan to Marshall, and Black to White welcomed the prospect of his nomination.[9]

Liberals off the court did not. In part that was because of the symbolism of the Haynsworth selection. South Carolinians like Strom Thurmond had been at the forefront of the battle against the Warren Court. "After fifteen long years of resisting the progress of the civil rights movement by opposing judicial nominees considered hostile to the Southern way of life," James Heath has written, "South Carolina's senators would finally, in 1969, be granted an opportunity to install one of their own on the Supreme Court" and to show off to the nation the importance of their state to the new Administration. Liberals also reacted as they did because Lewis Powell, Haynsworth's vigorous supporter, accurately described the judge's opinions as "moderately conservative." As legal ethicist John Frank, one of the judge's staunchest defenders at the time, afterward acknowledged, Haynsworth did not favor labor unions. His devoted Senate sponsor, South Carolina Democrat Fritz Hollings, who may have first suggested the judge to Nixon, characterized Haynsworth's vantage point as that of "a corporate right-to-work lawyer." As an attorney, Haynsworth had once represented the antiunion J. P. Stevens & Company and pressed the South Carolina legislature to enact the state's "right-to-work" law. And while some of the judge's opinions advanced the cause of racial equality, he was not "zealous for civil rights" either, though his tone remained refined, rather than rabid. His record on crime, Fred Graham reported, showed "no quarrel with the basic direction of the Warren Court on crime, only a tendency to go slower."[10]

As the possibility of Haynsworth's nomination was bruited about in July, the NAACP, AFL-CIO, and Leadership Conference on Civil Rights began mobilizing opposition. Founded in 1950, the Leadership Conference was an umbrella group of 125 civil rights, labor, social welfare, and religious groups. It included heavyweights such as Roy Wilkins, the executive director of the NAACP, and the NAACP's chief lobbyist, Clarence Mitchell, often called the "101st Senator" because of his influence. Its counsel was the feisty Joe Rauh, vice chair of the still-powerful Americans for Democratic Action and a Warren Court enthusiast who "wore the label 'knee-jerk liberal' as a badge of honor." The nomination's foes could also count on the support of a loose group of liberal law students, lawyers, law professors, union leaders, Americans for Democratic Action members, civil libertarians, and civil rights workers—many of them associated with the Leadership Conference, NAACP, and Marian Wright Edelman's Washington Research Project, the predecessor to the Children's Defense Fund.[11]

Though two of the judge's former clerks decried the "charges by the N.A.A.C.P. and professional liberals" in a lengthy memorandum released before Nixon announced he was nominating Haynsworth to the court, they accurately recognized that interest group allegations "automatically make headlines despite their hollow and baseless nature." The judge's antagonists insisted he opposed organized labor. They produced his dissent in one case condemning the majority's contention that racial segregation in publicly funded hospitals violated the Fourteenth Amendment's equal protection clause as "unprecedented and unwarranted." They scorned Haynsworth's insistence in an opinion that the Virginia Supreme Court should evaluate Virginia's decision to close down all public schools after the Supreme Court issued *Brown v. Board of Education* and his eight-month delay in handing it down. His detractors also condemned his sympathy for "freedom of choice" plans and other tactics that school boards adopted to delay desegregation. Like John Parker, the only Supreme Court nominee the Senate rejected between 1894 and 1968, Haynsworth maintained that the Constitution did not require integration, but simply forbade discrimination—even after the Warren Court showed impatience with the judge by reversing him.[12]

In a strange twist, Haynsworth was the protégé of Judge Parker, another Carolinian. Parker's Fourth Circuit opinions had won him the enmity of the civil rights and labor organizations that likewise decided to fight Haynsworth. Labor's opposition to Haynsworth in 1969 proved especially noteworthy. Its representatives had not testified against anyone before the Senate Judiciary Committee since Hoover nominated Parker to the court in 1930.

Nearly four decades after Parker's defeat, though, most liberals knew that Haynsworth's labor and civil rights record alone could not defeat him. Who would listen to them in the Senate? Haynsworth would appeal to many Republicans and Southern Democrats there. And the Democrats with whom liberal interest groups had relationships included people like Ted Kennedy, who had pounced on Marshall's and Fortas's opponents in 1967 and 1968 for inappropriately probing nominee ideologies. To be sure, most legislators did not fear looking like hypocrites to do what they deemed right and/or politic. Still, most in Washington agreed that the labor and civil rights issues could not win the opposition enough votes in the Senate to deny Haynsworth the appointment.[13]

But Haynsworth, who had a stock portfolio valued at more than $1 million (nearly $6.5 million in 2016 dollars), had a potential "Fortas problem" that Mitchell and the FBI, which investigated federal judges at the time of their first appointment and then administered "once-over-lightly" checks at the time of their elevation to higher courts, had inadequately vetted. Haynsworth helped launch, and owned stock in, Carolina Vend-a-Matic, a provider of vending machines that dispensed candy, coffee, and soda. In 1963, he sided with a majority of the business-friendly Fourth Circuit judges in overturning a National Labor Relations Board ruling related to Darlington Mills, a subsidiary of the notoriously antiunion Deering-Milken Company. Haynsworth and two other judges maintained that an employer could lawfully close part of a business for antiunion reasons even if the purpose was to discourage unionism in the rest of it, a decision that the Supreme Court subsequently vacated. And although Carolina Vend-a-Matic had not managed to get any vending machines into Darlington, it reaped about 3% of its annual gross margin from machines it had placed in other Deering-Milliken plants. Attorney General Robert Kennedy had publicly declared his faith in Haynsworth after the Darlington case when a lawyer for the Textile Workers Union of America relayed an anonymous allegation to the Fourth Circuit that Haynsworth had taken bribes.[14]

Nixon ignored the warning signals, all of them evident, and imprudently delayed announcing the nomination. On August 1, the *Wall Street Journal* reported that Roy Wilkins, executive director of the NAACP and chair of the Leadership Conference on Civil Rights, had protested Haynsworth to the White House, and that Clarence Mitchell had condemned him. On August 13, the AFL-CIO associate general counsel telephoned Jerris Leonard, the assistant attorney general in charge of the Civil Rights Division, at the "Western White House" in California, where Nixon was vacationing, to warn that Haynsworth's opinions were antilabor and that the judge was vulnerable on ethical grounds. That same day, Senate Minority Leader Dirksen, a Haynsworth enthusiast, leaked the prediction that Nixon would soon appoint the judge and that the Senate would approve him. On August 14, AFL-CIO President George Meany sent Nixon a telegram importuning him to pick someone else. Moreover, journalist William Eaton, who worked in the Washington Bureau of the *Chicago Daily News* and possessed ties to labor and civil rights groups, predicted that they would fight his nomination. On August 15, Haynsworth railed to a reporter against the "blatant falsehoods" alleging his conflict of interest with respect to Darlington Mills. He had not been Vend-a-Matic officer at the time of the decision, the judge added, but he refused to say whether he had owned stock in the company. As antagonism to the judge grew, the *New York Times* reported, speculation rose "that the expected nomination might be coming unglued."[15]

Nevertheless, on August 18, with Nixon still in California, his press secretary, Ron Ziegler, belatedly announced it. Ziegler also released portions of the Kennedy letter that the administration and Haynsworth insisted cleared the judge. "Since the President's intention was a badly kept secret, he had ample advance indication of how poorly the appointment would sit with champions of civil rights and others who believe the road to national unity lies in effective enforcement of constitutional guarantees of equal opportunity," the *New York Times* groused about the "disappointing" nomination of this "obscure" candidate. And indeed within three days, George Meany had thrown the resources of the AFL-CIO into fighting the nomination, Roy Wilkins was urging local chapter members to bombard their senators with mail opposing it, and labor and civil rights had combined forces through the Leadership Conference to battle it.[16]

The White House had given Haynsworth's foes plenty of time to mobilize, and the media made quick to enter the fray. Just as an investigative reporter helped bring down Fortas, so one would play a critical role in mounting the fight against Haynsworth. William Eaton characterized the nominee as "a jurist with charm and great dignity" on August 21. That day, though, a friend at the AFL-CIO telephoned Eaton and urged him to dig into the nominee's finances. Checking Securities and Exchange Commission files, the reporter discovered the news that the judge sold his stock in Carolina Vend-a-Matic for some $455,000 in 1964 (nearly $3.5 million in 2016 dollars) after ruling for Darlington Mills. Eaton, who would win a Pulitzer for his coverage of the nomination, now launched a crusade against Haynsworth and his "socialite wife." Nevertheless, Haynsworth anticipated confirmation.[17]

Then Senate Minority Leader Everett Dirksen dropped dead at the beginning of September. The hearings were postponed to enable members of Congress to go to his Illinois funeral, and Haynsworth's antagonists had more time to plan. To this point, the senators who had opposed the judge had lacked a leader. Three liberal Democratic Senate Judiciary Committee members—Birch Bayh of Indiana, Ted Kennedy of Massachusetts, and Philip Hart of Michigan— discussed strategy on the flight returning from the funeral. Hart, who had guided the fight for Fortas in 1968, did not want to take the lead, and Kennedy's reputation had recently taken a beating when he delayed reporting a fatal car accident involving a young woman to whom he was not married off Chappaquiddick Island. The three agreed that the forty-one-year-old Bayh, often labeled the "All-American Boy," would take charge of the crusade against Haynsworth.[18]

With no investigators or staff of his own to speak of, save his devoted cousin, Harry, Judge Haynsworth tried to fight back. He and Senator Hollings spent an unprecedented two days making the courtesy calls on Judiciary Committee members that until then had occurred irregularly, and the judge disclosed more about his finances than any previous nominee. And his efforts seemed to be bearing fruit. Most senators predicted a relatively easy confirmation in early September. Jacob Javits, who had become the first to declare his opposition, foresaw "a real battle" ahead. Even he, however, told reporters he expected it to end with Haynsworth's confirmation.[19]

Yet as Eaton faithfully recounted, the judge's enemies had tapped "a battery of labor lawyers" to compare companies in which the nominee owned stock with decisions in which he participated, "hoping to find a lucky match." They struck potential pay dirt when they showed he had bought a thousand shares of Brunswick Corporation valued at about $17,500 (nearly $125,000 in 2016 dollars) while a decision in its favor in which he had participated was pending. Mitchell learned of Brunswick only once the hearings finally began in mid-September, when Bayh blindsided John Frank with the news about the company as Frank defended the ethics of Haynsworth's behavior in the Darlington Mills case to the committee.[20]

"Clement F. Haynsworth Jr. went before the Senate Judiciary Committee today to establish his fitness to sit on the Supreme Court and spent most of the day explaining the affairs of an obscure vending machine company," Fred Graham wrote after the first day of hearings. Instead of presenting Haynsworth to the committee, Fritz Hollings rightly complained, he had to defend the nominee before it. That task became even more difficult when after eight long days of testimony, including two appearances by Haynsworth and one by his broker, Senate Judiciary Committee Chair James Eastland suddenly decided to end the proceeding without hearing from three constitutional experts supporting the judge, who were encouraged to submit written statements instead. That was probably a shrewd move, since it enabled Eastland to cut off some opposing witnesses, and no one seemed interested in constitutional interpretation anyway.[21]

The focus was on Haynsworth's portfolio and ethics. Though he insisted that he had done nothing wrong and that "when I went on the bench, I resigned from all such business associations I had, directorships and things of that sort," his critics could point out that the judge appeared on the books as the vice president of Carolina Vend-a-Matic until 1957, and as director until 1963. Haynsworth had also, it developed, become involved in a number of realty deals with Vend-a-Matic after he became a judge and participated in other cases involving companies that did business with Vend-a-Matic and other corporations or their subsidiaries in which he owned a small amount of stock. As for Brunswick, Haynsworth testified that his broker had alerted him to the investment opportunity after he had reached his decision in the case and he had not thought of the case at the time of the purchase. If he had, he admitted, he would not have bought it. Then there was a revelation that Haynsworth had once been "in partnership" with the notorious Bobby Baker. That development clearly horrified the White

House, though Haynsworth had not even become aware that he and Baker had invested in the same cemetery until after Nixon announced the nomination.[22]

The 1972 revision of the Canon of Judicial Ethics, a reaction to Haynsworth's travails, as well as Fortas's, directed judges to disqualify themselves in cases in which they possessed any financial interest, no matter how small. Yet Haynsworth's defenders could justify much of his specific behavior under the relatively permissive 1923 canon that still held sway. Moreover, John Frank testified, the Federal Judicial Code provided for disqualification only when judges possessed "a substantial interest" in a matter, and said that they otherwise possessed a "duty to sit." And as Frank also made clear, few expected judges to disqualify themselves when they owned stock in the supplier or subsidiary of a party to litigation. So what, then, if Haynsworth had ruled in favor of a textile company that did business with another company in which he owned stock? Assistant Attorney General Rehnquist produced a memorandum justifying the judge's ethics. Past presidents of the ABA stood by Haynsworth, and a "substantial majority" of the organization's Standing Committee on the Judiciary reaffirmed its support of him by a two-to-one majority after the airing of all his linen, with Chairman Lawrence Walsh contending that "the fact that the committee was divided" provided proof the committee had not participated in a "whitewash." Moreover, scholars largely dismissed the conflict-of-interest charges against Haynsworth as "makeweight" and "relatively insubstantial." None of that especially bothered his opponents, who simply "retreated to the safer ground" of claiming that Haynsworth was "insensitive to ethical matters" and fretting about Brunswick, which they insinuated came perilously close to insider trading and had not been the unintentional slip Haynsworth and his defenders suggested. After all, as Fortas's resignation had shown, even the 1923 canon indicated that "a judge's conduct should be free of impropriety or the impression of impropriety."[23]

Though Haynsworth was at least as well qualified to join the court as most justices in its history,* he proved an unfortunate choice for the moment. Fortas's resignation had created a moral panic about judicial ethics. "It is nothing short of astonishing that President Nixon should have nominated for the succession to

---

* After Bayh refused an invitation to debate, Hollings faced off against Senator Eagleton (D-MO) on NBC. "I think Judge Haynsworth is probably considered a moderately competent legal craftsman," Eagleton said. "But these high accolades that are being bestowed on him to make him sort of the second coming of Brandeis I find to be rather new and novel. I don't think anyone's ever held him in that high judicial esteem. But we'll put that aside." Though Haynsworth may not have been "the second coming of Brandeis," Eagleton was unfair to him. His was a respectable nomination. And as Hollings told the network, "It's the philosophy . . . that everyone opposes. But they won't say so." "Senators Eagleton and Hollings Interviewed," November 13, 1969, 7:00 A.M., Box 127, Supreme Court Judges, Haynsworth, Ethics Investigations, Hollings MSS.

Abe Fortas'[s] seat on the Supreme Court a man whose prior record as a judge raises ethical questions," the *New Republic* predictably editorialized. "Ethics are for liberals," the cartoonist Herblock joked bitterly (figure 21). AFL-CIO President George Meany came before the Senate Judiciary Committee to allege that Haynsworth did not deserve elevation because he was "opposed to labor, indifferent to civil rights and lacked ethical standards." The Leadership Conference on Civil Rights also used the hearings to attack the judge as a "laundered segregationist" whose nomination would deal "a deadly blow" to the court's "image."[24]

Meanwhile, Bayh dribbled out *tu quoque* arguments and revelations about Haynsworth's ethics to guarantee the most media attention. All the while, the senator assured the nervous nominee he was an "honest" man who appeared before the Senate Judiciary Committee at a time when Fortas's resignation required an irreproachable successor. It was "logical" to exploit the Fortas precedent Bayh's staffers assured him, for defeating Haynsworth on grounds of "his philosophy" would prove impossible, and what had been "good for the goose, . . . a great liberal jurist . . . may also be the best thing for the gander." Nixon would "certainly find someone of similar ideology" who could win confirmation if Haynsworth went down to defeat, but at least Bayh would have gained "political mileage" in the process with the civil rights groups, labor, and "the Jewish community," which was smarting from Fortas's involuntary resignation.[25]

While Pat Buchanan saw "the naming of a conservative South Carolinian to the 'Jewish seat'" as an "unmistakable affront" to many, Assistant Attorney General Rehnquist and others in the Nixon administration believed that Bayh and other liberals sought revenge for their treatment of Fortas. So did Senator Hollings, who considered Haynsworth's vilification "payback." If anything, though, the fear of seeming inconsistent after the *Washington Post* had urged Fortas's confirmation in 1968 despite the revelations about lecture fees forced its editors to declare at hearing's end in late September "reluctantly and unhappily . . . that there is no valid reason on the basis of the present record for the Senate to deny the President his choice." That did not keep Herblock, the *Post's* cartoonist, from continuing to preach against the nomination (figure 21). In one particularly devastating cartoon after Haynsworth had pledged to place his holdings in a blind trust, the cartoonist pictured "Mitchell, Nixon, Thurmond & Associates" telling the public: "None of the things my client did were wrong, and he promises to stop doing them completely" (figure 22). So, too, the *New York Times*, another Fortas supporter in 1968, backed the nomination with an obvious lack of "enthusiasm," though its editorial staff made clear its preference, which the *Post* came to share, that Haynsworth disappear.[26]

What the talk of "payback" missed was that liberals, who believed that Fortas had betrayed them by becoming involved with Wolfson, simply thought that the circumstances of his resignation had handed them a convenient weapon. As

Figure 21 A 1969 Herblock Cartoon. Copyright © The Herb Block Foundation.

John Masarro has shown, at least fifteen senators who ultimately voted against the nomination said or suggested that they did so because of the similarity to the Fortas situation. Some, like John Williams, the Republican "conscience of the Senate" from Delaware who had made Bobby Baker's life miserable and who the Nixon White House wrongly assumed controlled six votes, were doubtless sincere. So were others, such as Senate Republican Conference

"None Of The Things My Client Did Were Wrong, And He Promises To Stop Doing Them"

Figure 22 Senator Hollings maintained that Herblock's powerful cartoon cost Haynsworth's supporters five senators' votes, "exactly the number by which we fell short of confirming Haynsworth."

Chair Margaret Chase Smith, who told the president that the Brunswick news had set her to worrying about "the appearance of a double standard." And so, too, were others, such as Senator Joseph Tydings, the Maryland Democrat and one-time Haynsworth admirer who had called on Fortas to resign. Tydings now decided that Haynsworth showed insensitivity about "the cardinal rule which admonishes judges to avoid even the appearance of impropriety" and was the wrong person to "relieve the cloud over the Supreme Court created by the Fortas affair." Certainly, Haynsworth's Senate opponents included individuals in both parties otherwise predisposed to support the president. White House officials rightly suspected that for still others, however, the ethical issue supplied the "smokescreen" behind which they hid ideological opposition and/or their fear of antagonizing labor and civil rights groups.[27]

"Abe Fortas was there all the time," the AFL-CIO's legislative director recalled. According to Joe Rauh, while "Justice Fortas had a *potential* conflict of interest in his outside activities, Judge Haynsworth had an *actual* conflict of interest in a case before him at the bench." One labor leader put it more pungently for the Senate Judiciary Committee when he declared that Haynsworth made "Fortas look like an altar boy." No allegation irritated the administration so much or proved so effective. A Harris poll showed that 53% of the public had reacted negatively to the nomination, with 58% agreeing that "it looks bad to have a man with so many doubts about him taking the place of Abe Fortas."[28]

In response, William Rehnquist argued that the Fortas–Haynsworth analogy was useless. The assistant attorney general blamed the defeat of Fortas's chief justice nomination on his refusal to return to explain his lecture fees and his involvement in drafting legislation and contended that the Fortas resignation because of his tie to Wolfson was equally inapposite. In Rehnquist's telling, Democrats and Republicans had informed Fortas, "in effect," to "explain or resign"—to give an accounting of his relationship or quit, and Fortas had decided to leave the court. "The matter was not resolved by the Senate on the merits, but rather by Justice Fortas'[s] choice of resignation."[29]

Nevertheless, Fortas still stained Haynsworth. Indeed, Fortas's former partner, Paul Porter, his deputy in the chief justice battle and sounding board at the time of his resignation, wrote Haynsworth to commiserate "as a member of the bar who has directly, not vicariously, and in a closely related context, shared your ordeal." And when *Life* profiled Haynsworth, some of his supporters groused that the author had depicted the judge as "an emasculated Neanderthal spook." Yet Harry Haynsworth thanked the journalist for portraying his cousin "as a person who was completely incapable of being a wheeling-dealing Fortas like man. While I feel that your story goes too far in painting Clement as an anachronistic Southern gentleman living in another century, such an extreme view was in my opinion necessary to overcome the Fortas image painted by the Eastern Establishment press"—on which the nominee himself, like the administration, Hollings, and Senate Judiciary Committee Chair Eastland, lay most of the blame for Haynsworth's poor reception.[30]

Although the media did cover the nomination as if it were a boxing match, Dirksen's death and the opportunities it opened up for interest groups caused just as much trouble. As labor, civil rights, and religious groups got their anti-Haynsworth message out and Bayh developed their evidence into his "bill of particulars" against the judge, the Republicans fought over the next Senate leaders. When the dust settled, the new minority leader was the relatively liberal Hugh Scott of Pennsylvania, who had voted to report the Haynsworth nomination out from the Senate Judiciary Committee; the new whip, Robert Griffin of Michigan. Both represented states where labor unions and civil rights groups mattered, and according to the *New York Times*, the AFL-CIO "alone" had deployed "40 full-time lobbyists" to press senators to vote against the nomination. Despite the considerable impact of the Citizens for Decent Literature on the Fortas nomination, outside pressure groups proved more effective from the beginning this time around and even more influential.[31]

Neither Griffin nor Scott wanted to vote for the nomination. Griffin knew that if he supported it after opposing Fortas's ethics so forcefully in 1968, he would seem dangerously hypocritical, not just hypocritical. Even worse, he would look like a union antagonist in Michigan, where the United Automobile Workers' Walter Reuther was attacking Haynsworth's association "with the notorious anti-labor, anti-social textile mills of J.P. Stevens, a company that discharged 250 workers because they joined a union."[32]

Moreover, the Leadership Conference on Civil Rights was alleging that the judge would dole out rights to African Americans "with an eyedropper." African Americans in the House also attacked the nomination. "The Supreme Court of the United States is the one institution that has given us hope when everything else has been lost on the city and state level," Representative Shirley Chisholm reminded the Senate Judiciary Committee. Responsible black leaders would be rendered impotent to convince African Americans that "you don't have to riot in the Streets because the Supreme Court will uphold your rights" if Haynsworth won confirmation, she claimed. Then, at the beginning of October, Edward Brooke of Massachusetts, the first popularly elected African American in the Senate and a Republican, stood on the Senate floor publicly to ask Nixon to withdraw the nomination. Griffin and other senators surely feared looking like racists too.[33]

No surprise, then, that by early October, Griffin had joined Bayh in whipping up opposition to the nomination, despite his pledges to the administration that he would not work against it. The whip pointed to Haynsworth's ethical insensitivity and based his decision on the grounds that the Constitution trumped party loyalty. "I have said that the fact that he was a conservative was not a point against him," Griffin stressed. "I hope the next nominee will be a conservative." Unlike Griffin, who sided with six other Senate Judiciary Committee members in voting against the nomination, Scott voted with nine others to report it out on October 9. But the Pennsylvanian believed "that his vote in favor of Haynsworth could by itself defeat him in 1970." He could go no further, particularly with the Leadership Conference on Civil Rights reminding its members that Scott "needs to hear from constituents in Penna, that in view of his outstanding record in support of civil rights and social welfare causes, it would be shameful for him to support the Haynsworth nomination."[34]

With all the Republican leaders united against the nomination and some of them working hand in glove with liberal Democrats to defeat it, the administration had to rely on Republicans Roman Hruska of Nebraska and freshman Marlow Cook of Kentucky to become its shepherds. The two had little success rounding up votes in areas where unions remained strong. Ultimately just two Republicans from industrial states—Dirksen's successor, Ralph Smith in Illinois, the target of intense administration pressure, and George Murphy of California—voted for the nomination. And why should others? "A wave of anti-Haynsworth mail and telegrams was pouring into the Senators' office," John Ehrlichman recalled.[35]

"We can stimulate mail too," Ehrlichman remembered Nixon saying. "There should be letters and wires from the Farm Bureaus, Southern bar associations, the National Rifle Association and our other friends." Those "friends" included the John Birch Society. The American Medical Association was drafted too, though it later characterized its lobbying effort as a "very minor one," in which "a couple of physicians in Virginia" arranged to tell a senator, "Hey we like this guy Haynsworth." One Republican businessman in Ohio wrote a typical letter to his freshman GOP senator, William Saxbe. "We backed your recent election with generous contributions and tireless door-to-door campaigning," he said. "We will be watching you. We support Haynsworth."[36]

The AFL-CIO, NAACP, and Leadership Conference had done their job—and kept doing it—too well for such politicking to make much of a difference. "KEEP THE MAIL ON HAYNSWORTH COMING!" the secretary of the Leadership Conference exhorted member organizations during the first week of November. "Opposition to the Supreme Court nomination of Judge Clement F. Haynsworth has grown so in the Senate that if the vote were taken today his name would most likely be rejected." But the vote would not come before "mid-November, at the earliest," and now the administration was twisting arms and "stirring up mail from back home. Until a week ago, mail in most Senate offices was running overwhelmingly against confirmation," but thanks to the "White House offensive," senators were now receiving "large amounts of pro-Haynsworth letters, many of them originating in the South." So what? The judge's antagonists had carefully studied their Senate targets, none of whom wanted to lose labor and civil rights support. Saxbe, for example, ultimately voted no on Haynsworth. So would twenty-one of the thirty senators running for reelection in 1970.[37]

It did not help that although Haynsworth's fellow South Carolinian and Democrat, Fritz Hollings, was spearheading the fight, the judge hailed from

Strom Thurmond's state. The senator, who may well have won the promised veto over the seat that Fortas suspected, tried to help Haynsworth by keeping his vigorous support covert. He worked behind the scenes to mobilize Phyllis Schlafly and other conservatives in favor of the nomination. But he did testify on the nominee's behalf, and as the judge later said, there was "a great to-do that I was Strom Thurmond's boy." Nixon's congressional liaisons acknowledged that the president had "invited" a battle by naming a South Carolinian and putting his "Southern Strategy" on trial "in a forum (the Senate) where it will always given its present composition be voted down, and where the Republicans will be seriously divided." Nearly 40% of the Senate Republicans would vote against the nomination. Nixon had gambled, his team concluded, in a venue where he was lucky to win sixty votes on any controversial issue and where his administration had "poor relations" with fifteen to twenty of its forty-three Republicans.[38]

The president had also done little to ensure Haynsworth's success. His legislative team admitted that when it should have expected trouble, it was "caught napping." Nixon had been lazy too, particularly compared to LBJ. He should have announced the nomination himself, for example, and, as Hollings grumbled, made sure that people like Scott and Griffin had signed on to the judge's cause by September. Instead, the president remained in the background until after the hearings had ended and the judge's prospects had become decidedly uncertain. "If we cave in on this one, they will think that if you kick Nixon you can get somewhere," the president then told Republican senators. Who were "we" and "they"? By this time, Republicans seemed more united in their opposition to the nomination than the Democrats. Though he understood that Griffin and others disagreed, Nixon continued, he believed that if the Senate did not confirm Haynsworth, "there is no one the President can appoint" whom liberals would not undermine. Because his prestige was on the line and his attorney general under attack for inadequately investigating Haynsworth, Nixon held a press conference to accuse the judge's antagonists of "vicious character assassination" and began meeting with individual Republican senators. The president himself used "the total soft sell," one invitee said. "The other guys do the short-hair business." As Dean Kotlowski maintained, the administration's "hardball" tactics further injured Haynsworth's cause, as did Nixon's own belated lobbying of senators.[39]

The president and his team turned up the heat clownishly. "They're a bunch of amateurs," Saxbe complained to the New York Times about those running "the Administration's two lobbying centers—Harry S. Dent, Bryce N. Harlow, Kenneth E. BeLieu, Eugene S. Cowen and Clark Molenhoff at the White House and Attorney General Mitchell and William H. Rehnquist at the Justice Department." The "berserk" television appearance of Mollenhoff on behalf of the judge, for example, created a Washington joke about "the Mollenhoff cocktail—you throw it and it backfires." Even Chief Justice Burger got into the act,

Newsweek reported, "buttonholing Senators at social functions and telling them: 'If Judge Haynsworth isn't qualified to sit on the Supreme Court, then I'm not either.'" According to the magazine, his lobbying "has brought astonishment and quiet disapproval from those concerned" and had won "no visible converts." The White House publicized the information, obviously acquired improperly from the Internal Revenue Service, that six justices played the stock market. Moreover, House Minority Leader Gerald Ford revealed that his staff was studying the possibility of impeaching Justice Douglas. "If the Senate votes against a nominee for lack of sensitivity, it should apply the same standards to sitting justices," he maintained. That warning backfired too.[40]

"It will be close," William Eaton predicted on November 21 as he wrote about Haynsworth's "day of decision." It wasn't. Though Vice President Agnew was on hand to break the tie in the event of a fifty-fifty vote, the Senate defeated the nomination by fifty-five to forty-five. "Let us not get ourselves in the situation where the president's nominees shall be sent through a clearinghouse of labor and minorities," Strom Thurmond pleaded. "We need no unofficial 'second Senate.'" Interest group representatives belonging to that "second Senate" showered the judge's opponents with praise. According to the *Chicago Tribune*, "the [s]econd floor hallway of the Capitol, just outside the Senate Chamber, resembled a scene outside the locker room after the home team had won its upcoming football game," and guards had to restrain the "elated crowd" as senators left.[41]

By this time, the president had moved on. He had never cared about Haynsworth as much as LBJ did about his nominees to the court and, along with Dent, his key Southern strategist, had decided that "we may gain enormously by this incident" if the judge became "a martyr." The Haynsworth nomination might help Nixon fend off a 1972 challenge from George Wallace, and it had won him favor with South Carolina's kingmaker. "The liberal majority, with its ties to organized labor, unfortunately won out," Strom Thurmond consoled the president, but South Carolinians took comfort in the nomination of "this man we hold in such high esteem."[42]

Haynsworth took his defeat stoically. "I have been named South Carolinian of the Year, and on Friday night in New York some four hundred and fifty people turned out for a very elegant dinner and dance at which I was the honored guest, and rose twice to standing ovations," he wrote Warren Burger with evident bemusement. "In restaurants, theaters, airports, and museums in Europe and New York, and on the streets of New York, strangers recognizing me from pictures, stop me with expressions of a wish to shake my hand." At Nixon's request, he remained on the Fourth Circuit, and as "a makeup for his mistreatment," the House and Senate approved renaming the federal building in Greenville after him fifteen years later—somewhat unusually, while he was still alive. (Homer Thornberry received the same honor in Austin.) In 1969, however, the judge himself hoped that his mistreatment would serve a larger cause. "The venom that the Fortas affair has caused has now been expended and many other competing political interests have engaged in battle in the Senate to the point of apparent mutual exhaustion," Haynsworth told John Mitchell and former South Carolina governor and US Supreme Court Justice James Byrnes. "I believe that the President's next nominee, whoever he is, will be a shoo-in, and that no substantial group in the Senate will be anxious soon again to turn a reasonable appointment into a matter of great controversy."[43]

"Too Good to Be True"

Wishful thinking, especially when Nixon's next nomination proved neither "reasonable" nor "a shoo-in." Nixon's former partner Leonard Garment, the lawyer the president hoped would become "the Clark Clifford of the Republican Party," had warned Nixon that he would more easily find someone "whose record is unobjectionable on civil rights" if he looked for someone who had not written much about it. That advice may have helped lead the Administration in the direction of Lewis Powell, a Southern lawyer, instead of judge. But when he heard his name was under consideration, Powell wrote the attorney general in December of 1969 citing his age and poor eyesight as his reasons for not wanting the job, and Nixon also remained fixated on conservative Southern judges whom no one could call cronies. If Haynsworth's selection was bad for the moment, the next was just bad.[44]

Chief Justice Burger suggested Judge G. Harrold Carswell to Mitchell. Edward Gurney, a conservative who had become Florida's first Republican senator since Reconstruction, characterized Carswell as "an all-around darned good judge" and promoted him too, with the enthusiastic backing of Senator Richard Russell of Georgia, who had known the judge since birth. Attorney General Mitchell set William Rehnquist to studying the judge's opinions, and commended Carswell to Nixon after the assistant attorney general deemed him a "strict constructionist." Harry Dent, whom Nixon had directed to find a candidate "farther South and further right" after Haynsworth's defeat, championed Carswell too. And there were not many other choices, given the president's criteria. Mitchell reportedly "angrily" informed one Republican who proposed the distinguished Fifth Circuit judge, John Minor Wisdom, that Carswell's colleague was a "damned left winger" who would prove "even worse than Earl Warren."[45]

Carswell was certainly no left-winger. An alumnus of Duke, native Georgian, and son of a Democratic politician, he studied law at the University of Georgia until he joined the Navy during World War II. In 1948, he graduated from Mercer Law School in Macon, where he served in student government, rather than on law review. He returned to his small hometown and became editor of one of its two newspapers, the *Irwinton Bulletin*. At the age of twenty-eight, he unsuccessfully sought the Democratic nomination in the Georgia House of Representatives in 1948. Then Carswell changed states and parties. He married a "bubbly" Floridian described as "a petite Southern belle cheer leader type." (Had he won confirmation, the fifty-year-old Carswell would have become not just the youngest member of the court but its first Floridian.) Carswell and his wife, Virginia, built a large house in Tallahassee on ten lakefront acres that he designed and that they filled with antiques. Perhaps the influence of his father-in-law, a powerful Florida Republican, helped persuade Eisenhower administration officials to name Carswell US attorney after he had practiced law a few years, and then district judge, a position he held for eleven years. Nixon, who had only met the candidate once for a "brief handshake" years ago, had named him to the Circuit Court of Appeals a few months earlier.[46]

Hunting quail, fishing, playing bridge, partying with Tallahassee's elite, and watching Florida State University football evidently engaged Carswell more than judging. He produced some sixteen pages of published opinions annually. They proved unusually short not just in length, but also on citations, and, Fred Graham complained, "read, for the most part, like plumbers' manuals." Higher courts rarely cited and routinely reversed Carswell. Although he insisted that he was loyal to *Brown*, the judge dragged his feet in enforcing desegregation. "While there were 'worse' judges in the South when it came to civil rights issues, there simply were not *many* who were worse," concluded political scientist Bruce Kalk, who painted a damning portrait of Carswell's judicial career in the 1950s and 1960s.[47]

Perhaps Burger and others reasoned that Carswell was bulletproof. The judge had won confirmation to the Fifth Circuit despite well-publicized complaints by civil rights and labor groups that he had displayed "a strong bias against Negroes asserting civil rights claims." Criticism by one Senate Judiciary Committee Republican in 1969 that District Judge Carswell had "been repeatedly reversed and reproached by the Fifth Circuit," where the NAACP filed many of its civil rights cases, "for his rulings in cases involving desegregation of everything from reform schools to theaters" and was known by civil rights lawyers for his "prolonged temporization" had reached the Nixon administration too.[48]

Given these red flags, the White House should have scrutinized Carswell's record, but apparently no one there carefully studied the judge's background or opinions. And although Mitchell had reportedly ordered more rigorous FBI investigations of Supreme Court nominees after the Haynsworth fiasco, the bureau's check on Carswell was so "superficial," the FBI's assistant director later said, "that we never found out that he was a homosexual." Whether Carswell was gay was unclear, but he may have been bisexual, and at the time of his appointment, the *New York Times* reported that he was "viewed as being something of a swinger," whatever that meant. He was subsequently arrested for propositioning a vice squad officer in a men's room, and on another occasion, a man whom Carswell invited to his hotel room assaulted him. These incidents did not occur until the late 1970s.[49]

As the public then learned of them, it also became clear that the bureau's agents who investigated the judge in 1970 had largely just checked to see what newspapers said about him until John Pack, a gay high school teacher who had once been Carswell's neighbor, was murdered two weeks after Nixon nominated the judge to the court. A week after the killing, the sheriff's department located a watch that one of the judge's four children, Scott, had given Pack. Larry Campbell, the deputy who found it, recalled telling Robert Clark, the head of the local FBI office, about the potentially embarrassing, though "tenuous connections between Mr. Pack and the Carswell family, as well as a 'rumor around town' that Mr. Carswell had been involved in a homosexual incident some years earlier." Sources informed the *New York Times* that the news left Clark "extremely upset." Campbell subsequently said that he was not "certain" he had provided the information to Clark, though "it would have been likely we would have discussed it." What is certain is that no word of the murder ever reached the White House. Surely it would have wanted to investigate the story, if only because, as AP reported, Scott Carswell testified in the December 1970 trial of the victim's alleged killers that he had bought the watch, similar to one he wore, for his teacher after Pack admired his.[50]

When the president and Mitchell settled on Carswell, then, they knew only that civil rights groups would object to him. That suited them. Mitchell personally reviewed the judge's accomplishments. Martha Mitchell reported to guests at a Women's National Press Club event "that she had watched her husband reading background information on Carswell and that he had looked up at her, smiled broadly, and declared: 'He's just too good to be true.'"[51]

John Dean and historian David Kyvig maintained that the president made his "colossal mistake" in choosing Carswell because he trusted Mitchell and Burger and did not understand how much "the Fortas experience had changed the political culture." White House speechwriter William Safire hypothesized, however, that the president wanted to "spite" the Senate, while Joe Rauh speculated that Nixon "wanted to win with opposition from the same people who had fought him on Haynsworth." Most likely, Dean and Kyvig were right.[52]

Certainly, though, the president was fighting the last battle. He refused to send up a "trial balloon" and give Carswell's foes chance to organize this time. The press reported that the nominee's name remained "an unusually closely guarded secret." This time, too, Mitchell consulted with Griffin, Scott, and other leaders beforehand. Eager to show their loyalty after they had deserted the White House on Haynsworth, they promised support. It wasn't until the weekend before Nixon made the nomination that the press began to finger Carswell as the likely candidate. On Monday, some six weeks after Haynsworth's defeat, White House Press Secretary Ron Ziegler announced the appointment and lauded Carswell as a "strict constructionist" who satisfied Nixon's criteria, since he had "a good judicial record, an outstanding background and he is young." According to the *Chicago Tribune*, "the shadow of the Senate rejection of Nixon's last appointee . . . hung heavily" over the event. Ziegler reported that Nixon had received a complete FBI examination, which "cleared Carswell of any suspicions" and included a survey of Carswell's finances and tax returns. Roman Hruska, one of Carswell's leading Senate proponents, observed that the judge was "not a pauper, but he's far from affluent." Unlike Haynsworth, the judge was just worth about $200,000 (about $1.4 million in 2016 dollars, mostly in real estate and land) and had himself never owned any stock or bonds, though his wife had inherited some stock in her father's crate company. "It was a very thorough check," Ziegler stressed.[53]

Though it was obvious that Carswell was no Holmes and that Nixon had chosen him because of geography and because he did not own much stock, Senate approval seemed preordained. To be sure, there was grumbling. The *New York Times* editorialized that the nomination "almost suggests an intention to reduce the significance of the Court by lowering the caliber of its membership," and Fred Graham believed it would set liberals to yearning for Haynsworth. The *Wall Street Journal* acknowledged that Carswell's "outstanding qualification" was "an immunity to conflict-of-interest charges quite unusual among men of his age and standing," rather than "judicial eminence." That he was not smart enough to make much money, it implied, clinched the job for him. Predictably, the NAACP immediately condemned Carswell, while Joe Rauh maintained that the president had "again nominated an unknown, whose principal qualification for the post seemed to be his opposition to Negro rights." That might be "good Nixon-Mitchell politics in the suburbs and the South," he added, but would "only add to already dangerous racial tensions in America." Yet, as Marian Wright Edelman told Rauh, although Carswell had "a pretty tough segregationist image," that in itself "clearly isn't enough" to defeat him, and blocking the nomination was "not going to be easy going." The AFL-CIO initially refused even to oppose it because there was "no hint of a conflict of interest in Judge Carswell's financial holdings and he has not been involved in any significant labor decisions." When Carswell met with reporters briefly after Ziegler's announcement, he said, "I don't really anticipate any problems."[54]

Why should he? Senator Gurney was touting the judge's "middle of the road, moderate record on civil rights" and Carswell's unpopular decision that his own Tallahassee barber could not refuse to cut African Americans' hair to reporters. ("If Judge Carswell is confirmed, God help us, it will be the first time in history that a man ever was confirmed for writing an opinion that his racist barber ought to cut a Negro's hair," Rauh joked.) Embarrassed by their mutiny over Haynsworth, Republican senators readied themselves to play ball, as did Democrats exhausted by the previous battle. Minutes after Ziegler's announcement, Senate Minority Leader Scott, who, of course, had voted against Haynsworth, told reporters the Senate would approve the nomination "with an absolute minimum of difficulty." So, too, Robert Griffin said he was "hopeful the Senate would confirm Judge Carswell without delay," and Senate Majority Leader Mansfield reported that there was "a general feeling of good will toward the President's latest nomination." Doubtless to avoid giving the judge's opponents time for research, Senator Eastland, a Carswell supporter, announced that the Senate Judiciary Committee would begin its hearing on the nomination the following week.[55]

At 4 A.M. the day of Ziegler's announcement that Nixon had selected the judge for the court, George Thurston, a Tallahassee reporter with a penchant for green or orange socks, and his stringer, Ed Roeder, had driven 250 miles to Irwinton, a town that Carswell's Mercer Law School professor described as "the kind of place (as some of my students say) where white folks get up in the morning, walk down to the corner store, and whittle, chew tobacco, and cuss niggers." When Thurston and Roeder learned that the county courthouse housed the only extant copies of the *Irwinton Bulletin* that Carswell once edited, they went there and found the text of a speech Carswell had made in 1948 when he was running for the Georgia House. In it, he proclaimed himself as "a Southern by ancestry, birth, training, inclination, belief and practice" and contended "I yield to no man, as a fellow candidate or as a fellow citizen, in the firm, vigorous, belief in the principles of white supremacy, and I shall always be so governed." After returning to Tallahassee at 1 A.M. on January 21, Thurston telephoned Carswell, whom he knew casually, seven-and-a-half hours later, and read him the speech.[56]

The judge paused and exclaimed, "God Almighty! Did I say that? It sounds like another person." He asked the reporter to bring the documentation to the house, and when Thurston and Roeder arrived at 11 A.M., a tense Carswell invited Thurston into his bedroom for an hour-long off-the-record conversation, in which the judge must have unsuccessfully begged the reporter not to publish the story. "I've read a summary of what is attributed to me as a young candidate some twenty-two years ago," the obviously distressed Carswell then said of the speech, which he now denounced as "obnoxious and abhorrent" in a hastily arranged televised statement. "There is nothing in my private life or in my public record of some seventeen years which could possibly indicate that I harbor racist statements," he insisted. Indeed, he maintained, "I lost that election because

I was considered too liberal," which may well have been the case.* When Walter Cronkite broadcast the news story that night, though, it created a furor, particularly since the surprised and embarrassed White House had to admit that the FBI had missed the speech.[57]

More of Carswell's skeletons began coming out of the closet as other reporters, law students, and the Washington Research Project's Rick Seymour, a "mod young" Harvard Law alumnus who resembled Buffalo Bill, dug in Florida and the libraries. Within a few days of the revelations about the white supremacy speech, for example, the public had learned, thanks to Seymour's interviews with local African American civil rights leaders, that US Attorney Carswell had participated in an apparent dodge to forestall integration of a public golf course by incorporating it as a private club of which he then became a director. When two ABA Standing Judiciary Committee members questioned Carswell on January 26, the night before the Senate hearing on his nomination opened, he acknowledged having served as an incorporator and director. Nevertheless, as it had already hinted it would, the ABA committee, which had decided simply to rate court nominees as "qualified" or "unqualified" after Haynsworth, unanimously approved Carswell anyway.[58]

Other potential opponents seemed to lack the will for a brawl. On January 26, as the judge and Senator Gurney called on Senate Judiciary Committee members, George Meany did condemn the nomination as "a slap in the face to the nation's Negro citizens." The AFL-CIO, which heretofore had only opposed Supreme Court nominations because of the individual's labor record, would battle Carswell's, he now said. But some suspected that Meany, who opposed Nixon's "Philadelphia Plan" to open up more construction jobs for African Americans, was simply trying to avoid straining labor's relations with civil rights leaders to the breaking point, and it was unclear whether the AFL-CIO would go all out against the judge. "We're tired," its general counsel acknowledged privately. Joe Rauh worried that the anti-Carswell senators "didn't have their heart" in a fight either. Bayh, who was planning a 1972 presidential run, did not want to lead the opposition.[59]

So even though the Leadership Conference on Civil Rights, with the full weight of the NAACP behind it, unanimously resolved to oppose Carswell at its

---

* In a 1946 editorial, for example, Carswell had written that the gubernatorial candidate, Gene Talmadge, "has done exactly as expected, yelling 'Nigger, Nigger,' as he has for the last 20 years, and put on a show that would be a first-rate comedy were his act not a tragedy of deceit and disgrace." His 1948 white supremacy statements may well have been opportunistic. "Ol' Harrold was just playing the game," one Irwinton official told the New York Times. "Back then this county didn't hardly know what an integrationist was." Jon Nordheimer, "Carswell Reviews Copies of Papers He Edited From '46 to '48," New York Times, January 23, 1970. And see Nordheimer, "Carswell's Racist Remarks in 1948 Were for Expediency, Son of His Political Foe Says," id., January 22, 1970.

board meeting on January 28, it was waging the proverbial lonely battle. Marian Wright Edelman attributed the Leadership Conference's willingness to rush in to its short history of active opposition to Supreme Court confirmations. "One of the advantages of neophyte organizations like this," she said, "is that you don't know the political realities. So you make a fight because you think it's important, not because you think you can win." As Leadership Conference officials told their member organizations after the board meeting, "We realize there is some reluctance to take up this fight so soon after the successful campaign against the nomination of Judge Clement Haynsworth." That was an understatement. It seemed impossible to imagine that the Senate might turn down the president twice. "But the Senate must be made to recognize that confirming a man whose civil rights record is even worse than Haynsworth's is an affront to its own principles, to millions of Americans who are sickened by its seeming indifference to racism, and to the Supreme Court itself."[60]

The Judiciary Committee hearings put Carswell's views on racial justice on display. Where Carswell wanted to present himself as the antidote to the Warren Court by testifying that "the Supreme Court should not be a continuing Constitutional convention," he was forced to declare, "I am not a racist." (As LBJ would have said, the opposition made the judge deny its allegations.) "I suppose I believed" in white supremacy in 1948, he acknowledged, but he argued that "the course of 22 years of history" had changed his mind.[61]

Civil rights activists, however, saw no evidence of a true "change of heart." Though Edward Brooke was prudently remaining silent for the moment, African Americans from the House testified against the nomination. Other civil rights leaders and lawyers showcased the judge's unusually "insulting" behavior toward civil rights lawyers, whatever their race, in his courtroom. In response, the administration produced a letter from one black lawyer in the Nixon administration drafted by Rehnquist announcing that when *he* appeared before Carswell, he had always received courteous treatment. But even a Justice Department attorney who testified under subpoena acknowledged that Carswell had shown "extreme hostility" toward civil rights lawyers and had charged them with "meddling and arousing the local people." Together with the judge's decisions, which Joe Rauh eviscerated for the Judiciary Committee, his behavior, Rauh alleged, demonstrated "Judge Carswell is Judge Haynsworth with a cutting edge. He is Judge Haynsworth with a bitterness and a meanness that Judge Haynsworth never had."[62]

And while Carswell seemed more relaxed and calmer than Haynsworth, he proved even less frank. Though no one acquainted with previous hearings should have expected candor, the judge's responses still demonstrated an unusual lack of it. When the segregated golf course took center stage, the nominee initially implied that he had learned of the allegation only when he "very hurriedly" read the morning's newspaper and denied that he was one of its incorporators or directors. Carswell only changed his tune when Ted Kennedy "brandished" the articles of incorporation that the ABA representatives had shown the judge. Then Carswell insisted he had not "looked at the documents" and lamely maintained that he had sought to improve the termite-ridden clubhouse and the golf course, rather than stall integration. Even his sense of humor was challenged at the hearings once *Newsweek* reported that he had "shocked" a Georgia Bar Association audience to whom he had told "the following Negro dialect joke: 'I was out in the Far East a little while ago, and I ran into a dark-skinned fella. I asked him if he was from Indo-China, and he said, 'Naw, suh, I'se from Outdo' Gawgee.' "[63]

The judge came across not just as racist, but as a male chauvinist pig, to use a phrase becoming all the rage. He had voted to deny a rehearing in a case involving the issue of whether a corporation had legally denied employment to a mother because she had preschool-age children when it had said it would hire a similarly situated father. Carswell's was the first Supreme Court hearing at which NOW testified—not that the Senate Judiciary Committee took its president, Betty Friedan, very seriously. (The committee did, however, treat Representative Patsy Mink of Hawaii, who made the same points, respectfully, and her testimony and what she herself described as "badgering" of Senate Judiciary Committee member Hiram Fong [R-HI] helped persuade him to vote against Carswell.)[64]

Few considered Carswell intellectually impressive either, with one AFL-CIO lawyer characterizing him to the Judiciary Committee as "an undistinguished, dull graduate of the third best law school in the state of Georgia, with an undistinguished judicial record." Was this the sort of Supreme Court nominee an ostensibly meritocratic culture should produce? After damning the judge's civil rights record to the Senate Judiciary Committee, Yale Law School Dean Louis Pollak, a member of the NAACP Legal Defense Fund's board of directors, observed that Carswell possessed "more slender credentials than any other nominee for the Supreme Court put forth in this century." Pollak then gracefully withstood hostile cross-examination from Senators Thurmond and Hruska. "Suppose some would say that you are the least qualified man since 1900 to be dean of the law school at Yale University, how would you feel?" Thurmond scolded him. The dean, who was known for his modesty, decency, and sense of humor, replied, "Well I think that would be a reasonably good estimate." Meanwhile, copies of a recent article by Pollak's colleague, Charles Black, were circulating through the Senate in which that constitutional scholar assured legislators that nothing in the text, structure, or history of the Constitution stopped them from voting against a Supreme Court nominee they believed would likely prove "very bad for the country."[65]

At hearing's end, Joe Rauh begged senators not to "accept the principle that because the Senate refused to confirm someone, it thereby has to confirm somebody worse. Otherwise you will get to the point where you may never refuse to confirm anybody because there will be a threat that it will be worse the second time." Yet it appeared that the Senate would approve the nominee, in part because, one Republican senator said semifacetiously, if it did not, he had heard the administration was enrolling George Wallace's 1968 running mate, General Curtis "Bombs Away" LeMay, in law school. Art Buchwald joked that the administration was readying "Judge Caleb Robert E. Lee," who had no investments, just slaves.[66]

But it was Nixon who seemed on track for the last laugh, since even both Bayh and Pollak predicted the judge's confirmation. "If everyone in this government had to give up his job if he belonged to a restricted golf club, Washington would have mass unemployment," the president kidded at a January 30 press conference at which he admitted he had not known of Carswell's 1948 speech before George Thurston revealed it and said it would have made no difference to his decision to nominate the judge. The president predicted to reporters that the Senate would "overwhelmingly" approve Carswell. The press concurred that confirmation looked likely.[67]

It certainly did. Two-and-a-half weeks after Nixon's press conference, the Senate Judiciary Committee recommended Carswell's appointment by a vote of thirteen to four, even though by now, it had also become clear that despite the court's declaration that restrictive covenants were unconstitutional in 1948, Carswell had sold land with a covenant restricting its use to Caucasians in 1966. That information, which Nixon also shrugged off, arrived in time for inclusion in the Leadership Conference's anti-Carswell pamphlet, but not everything did. "It is a measure of the man that we have been unable to keep up with all the evidence of his unfitness for the position of Associate Justice," the Leadership Conference mentioned when it circulated "Has Judge Carswell Changed?" It then emerged that Carswell had chartered an all-white Florida State University booster club. Nevertheless, a majority of the ABA's Standing Federal Judiciary Committee reaffirmed on February 21 that the nominee was "qualified" to become a justice.[68]

The steady drip of revelations, though, gave heart to those who fought the nomination. In mid-February, the AFL-CIO escalated its attack against this "nonentity whose only appeal is to forces determined to resist progress in civil rights and human rights," and Meany now said "we are putting out just as much effort to defeat Carswell as members had done with Haynsworth." Edward Brooke became the eighteenth senator publicly to oppose Carswell on February 25 and took charge of recruiting Republican senators. That was key, for as Mary McGrory wrote in the Washington Star, "Few Republicans wanted to hear the Senate's only black member eloquently laying out the case against Carswell." And on March 8, when Bayh appeared at a Leadership Conference meeting, his attitude toward making the fight changed. Bayh "made a speech that turned. . . on" his listeners, his assistant said, "and their response turned him on." The senator would energetically lead the attack on Carswell, whom he portrayed as an undistinguished racist, even though in the middle of the nomination fight, Bayh's father-in-law murdered his second wife and killed himself. Now Nixon cheered when the media revealed that Bayh had belonged to a fraternity "formed by three ex-Confederate soldiers" and that he had flunked the bar exam three times.[69]

As the shift in rhetoric suggested, given the apparent indifference to just the judge's racial views, his antagonists had to zero in on his mediocrity as well. It turned out that Lou Pollak had made the strongest argument against the judge when he coupled Carswell's civil rights record and slender credentials. As if to compensate for its reticence with respect to Haynsworth, the *Washington Post* editorial board jumped on the anti-Carswell bandwagon in mid-February, the same day that John MacKenzie announced in its news section that the judge's opponents would focus on "a subject rarely put at issue in a contest over a Supreme Court nomination—the nominee's legal 'distinction' or lack of it." The nominee's ordinariness was something about which many could agree. "If you're only 'above average' at Mercer Law School, what does this make you," Ehrlichman and others at the White House privately scoffed about this "[b]oob."[70]

Despite the ties of loyalty to one of their own, some prominent Fifth Circuit judges obviously opposed the nomination too. No wonder: After examining his and others' decisions, "Law Students Concerned for the Court" and progressive Republicans in the Ripon Society concluded that just six of the sixty-seven Southern judges had a higher reversal rate. "[T]housands of lawyers, hundreds of [law school] professors and dozens of deans" denounced him as unfit in what Joe Califano, now a Washington superlawyer, characterized as "the revolt of the attorneys." So did over two hundred former Supreme Court clerks, who declared him mediocre, a sentiment privately shared by one of Carswell's few law professor sponsors. And on the eve of the start of the debate in the Senate, 457 lawyers, including the deans of Yale, Harvard, and the University of Pennsylvania Law School, former attorney general Ramsey Clark, and some of the nation's most distinguished law professors from all parts of the country signed a letter that FDR adviser Samuel Rosenman had circulated urging Carswell's defeat on the grounds of his racism and lack of distinction. In Tallahassee, nine of thirteen law professors at Florida State University Law School created dissension among their colleagues and consternation among the state board of regents by signing a petition opposing Carswell too.[71]

By March, the incompetence issue had become for Carswell what ethics proved for Haynsworth. The words "mediocre" and "mediocrity" would appear over and over again in the Senate floor debate, and while some of the references reflected supporters' rebuttals of the charge, the frequency was nevertheless telling. "We couldn't win if we had to make it a strictly civil rights fight," one of Carswell's opponents acknowledged later. "We had to have a cover issue." The lesson of the Fortas and Haynsworth fights, then, was that ideological differences between senators and the nominee were by themselves insufficient to defeat nominations. Opponents needed that "cover issue" to show they respected the distinction between law and politics and were not inappropriately concerned with ideology. That way, they could maintain that they respected the president's right to find someone sympathetic and only sought to make sure there was nothing else wrong with the nominee.[72]

As with Haynsworth, the administration's public responses hurt Carswell. When the *Washington Post* condemned Carswell's civil rights record, Rehnquist shot off an angry letter to the editor. He charged that the newspaper really sought "something far broader than just 'civil rights'; it is the restoration of the Warren Court's liberal majority after the departure of the Chief Justice and Justice Fortas and the inauguration of President Nixon." According to him, the *Post* must admit "all of the consequences that your position logically brings in its train: not merely further expansion of constitutional recognition of civil rights, but further expansion of the constitutional rights of criminal defendants, of pornographers, and of demonstrators." That argument, according to Rehnquist, "would make up in candor what it lacks in marketability."[73]

Some in the Senate agreed with him. Russell Long also waved the bloody shirt of the Warren Court when the debate opened on March 16, 1970. During the 1968 battle over Fortas's elevation, he remarked, "much was made of the point that he was a brilliant student. My reaction was, 'Look at those decisions on law and order . . . that have made it virtually impossible to punish criminals in this country.'" Hadn't the court suffered enough "upside down, corkscrew thinkers" who could make anything sound "logical" even as they crippled law enforcement? "Would it not appear that it might be well to take a B student or a C student who is not able to think straight, compared to one of those A students who are capable of the kind of thinking that winds up getting us a 100-percent increase in crime?" More infamously, Senator Hruska committed a fatal blunder when he publicly said of Carswell, "Even if he were mediocre, there are a lot of mediocre judges and people and lawyers. They are entitled to a little representation, aren't they, and a little chance? We can't have all Brandeises and Frankfurters and Cardozos." Did he compare Carswell to three Jews for a reason? Hruska was just having fun, an associate insisted, but people took his joke seriously, and it reflected poorly on both the nominee and the senator.[74]

Most senators reported "a light flow of Carswell mail (which seems to be running about 3 to 1 against him)" and seemed less than thrilled about the nomination. Even in the South, where a sense of regional victimization simmered and support for Carswell proved stronger, many disliked the idea of Justice

Carswell. True, Senator William Spong, a moderate Democratic lawyer from Virginia who had voted for both Thurgood Marshall and Clement Haynsworth on the grounds that "history has demonstrated" that the Senate's "examination of a nominee should be limited to his qualifications, background, experience, integrity and temperament," received death threats and plenty of angry mail when he decided "as a matter of conscience" that he could not support Carswell. "I did not ask for perfection, I only asked two things: (1) candor from a man who is to sit on the highest court in the land and (2) a reasonable competence when compared with the performance of judges either in the South or throughout the nomination," Spong rebuked one constituent. Yet many Virginians applauded Spong's stand.[75]

And where Haynsworth's hometown newspaper, after conceding that Carswell "lacks the fine judicial brilliance and sensitivity of Clement Haynsworth," editorialized that the judge was receiving "the same treatment" as Haynsworth and deserved support "simply because he is qualified," Haynsworth's booster, Senator Hollings, was less certain. "Carswell is nothing to get enthused about," Hollings wrote a friend. "I am proud of the South and when we put our foot forward, it should be our very best foot. Carswell can't even carry Haynsworth's law books." Nevertheless, the senator would "probably vote for him but I am not proud of the vote." While he did not consider Carswell a racist, "I just believe he is a mediocre lawyer and judge" and could see "no reason why I should promote him to the highest court." The best Hollings could say for Carswell, whom he ultimately did vote for, was not very good: "Of course district judges do not attract very bright young lawyers as law clerks, and perhaps on the Court the Judge will have more able assistance and grow."[76]

Despite his tepid support, the judge's chances of defeat remained less slim than his credentials. As one reporter said, "Paradoxically, while opposition to that choice was growing outside the Senate, opposition inside it seemed on the verge of collapsing." The tide had turned in the sense that the Leadership Conference on Civil Rights was no longer alone, and as Herblock made graphically clear, there was "growing public revulsion" against the judge. Yet although a Carswell impersonator dolefully sang "Nobody knows the trouble I've seen, Nobody knows but Haynsworth" in the Gridiron Club Banquet skits where Nixon and the Washington press corps mingled the Saturday night before the floor debate began, Ted Kennedy publicly proclaimed that blocking Carswell remained "a long shot." Perhaps he was trying to coax the unusually large number of uncommitted senators into declaring themselves. Bayh, however, sounded only slightly more hopeful when he said, "We have a chance of winning. Don't write us off." As the debate entered its third day, the New York Times reported, "Confident supporters of Judge Carswell did not even feel required to keep a spokesman in the all-but-empty chamber most of the day as Senator Jacob K. Javits of New York for the Republicans, and Senator Harold E. Hughes of Iowa, for the Democrats, droned through long reading of critical material." Carswell was still "likely to win," the *Washington Post* and *New York Times* predicted afterward.[77]

Like the evidence of racial insensitivity, though, the criticism of the judge and his supporters kept coming. On March 23, Arthur Goldberg intervened. Perhaps goaded by a rumor that Burger was lobbying senators for Carswell, which the chief justice had condemned as "a malicious falsehood," the former justice spoke out about the nomination. If the judge were confirmed, he would "occupy the seat of Holmes, Cardozo and Frankfurter," Goldberg told NBC. "How can it be said that Judge Carswell is qualified to sit in [it]? He is not." That morning, Anthony Lewis also marveled in the *New York Times* at the ABA Standing Federal Judiciary Committee's decision to play "a supporting role in what must be taken as a calculated effort to demean the Supreme Court" by twice bestowing its stamp of approval on Carswell.[78]

Lewis had company within the ABA power structure. Bernard Segal, then the association's president, would characterize the committee's failure to revise its vote as "without question the major mistake" in its history. "I think the President's decision to avoid picking personal friends is a very tragic one for the nation and for the Court," and represented "an over-reaction to the Fortas affair," Albert Jenner also said. "Some of Mr. Nixon's friends would make brilliant Supreme Court justices."[79]

The once-sociable Carswell had reacted to the poor publicity by withdrawing into the cocoon of his home. His admirers accused the judge's opponents of lying about his record and pointed out that he would succeed Fortas, who was no paragon. "There is a quality of obscenity about the opposition to Judge Carswell on the part of liberals who had nothing but praise for the appointments of Goldberg and Marshall and who profess horror when it is suggested that Douglas is so outrageously unfit to remain on the court that he should be impeached," the *Chicago Tribune* editorialized on March 24.[80]

It wasn't until then that the press reported the plan that the opposition had just hatched and the nomination began to seem endangered "for the first time," the *Washington Post* reported. Bayh would propose a motion to recommit the nomination to the Senate Judiciary Committee for more study. In all probability, it would die there, and the Senate would have sent a relatively polite message to the president about its constitutional responsibility to advise and consent.[81]

Predictably, Nixon turned down the fig leaf, as did a majority of the Senate Judiciary Committee. And Senator Saxbe, who was receiving lots of pressure from his Ohio constituents to buck the White House over the Supreme Court a second time, agreed to come to the administration's rescue in an effort to mend his fences. At the urging of the White House, Saxbe wrote the president to ask whether Nixon still fully supported his nominee. On April Fool's Day, the president released his affirmative reply publicly charging that the Senate's members wanted to deprive him of "the same right of choice" to "appoint" a Supreme Court justice that they had awarded every one of his predecessors. That contention ignored the Senate's overall past rejection of about one-fifth of presidential nominees to the court. It also boomeranged because when Nixon maintained that the Constitution entrusted "one person," the president, with "the power of appointment" to the court and said the Senate sought "to substitute" its "subjective judgment" for his, he derogated its authority. Was this where "strict construction" of the Constitution led? Senators wanted no part of what Scotty Reston described as Nixon's "emotional and inaccurate argument." One Republican summed up the response: "The Senate doesn't like to do very much, but it doesn't like to be told that it doesn't have the right to do very much."[82]

"This is the fight we never expected to win," the Leadership Conference said of the motion to recommit because it followed so closely on Haynsworth's defeat. "The Senate was supposedly too tired of fighting the President to fight him once again. But, incredibly we have reached a point where it is entirely possible that we *can* defeat the Carswell nomination."[83]

Not so fast. The White House used up all its political capital in defeating the motion, and Vice President Agnew cancelled his plans to throw out the first ball at the Washington Senators' game on April 6 in case he needed to break a tie. He did not. The fifty-two-to-forty-four vote against recommittal surprised few insiders, who expected Carswell's antagonists to lose.[84]

After the motion to recommit went down to defeat, though, it became clear the White House had made a fatal error as it frantically lobbied the uncommitted Republicans it had previously neglected. The senators had done what the White House wanted and now readied to vote their consciences in an up-or-down vote on Wednesday, April 8. White House officials had "shot" their "wad on recommittal," Bayh subsequently told *Time*. "They called in all their IOUs on that one. They cranked up for the wrong vote." By the *Post*'s count, and despite the fact that ten senators had not yet declared themselves, forty-eight senators opposed the nomination and forty-six favored it.[85]

On Tuesday night, Bob Dole (R-KS) told Nixon that the situation looked grim and that everything depended on Senators Marlow Cook of Kentucky and Margaret Chase Smith of Maine. If those Republicans voted for the nomination, Vice President Agnew could break the tie. Nixon had already met with Cook, a Haynsworth stalwart, for nearly an hour Monday night, but the senator refused to commit himself. The next day, Cook returned to the White House to see Nixon award twenty-one Medals of Honor to Vietnam soldiers posthumously. "Those young men showed such excellence in their short lives," he told reporters later. "When I got back to my office, I just made up my mind that I couldn't vote for Carswell for the Supreme Court and accept such lack of excellence," and he telephoned congressional liaison Bryce Harlow to tell him so.[86]

Meanwhile, Smith, who had always taken pride in not disclosing how she would vote on key issues, remained on the fence. She had seen Nixon on Tuesday and had not told him how she would vote—which did not stop the administration from spreading rumors to reporters that she had agreed to support Carswell at their meeting later. That same day, though, one of her aides told Harlow that she would side with the White House on the nomination. As Senator Cook informed Senator Brooke, Harlow immediately began spreading the news to other undecided senators. "We had to do it," an administration official rationalized. "We had good information she was going to vote 'yes,' and we thought that information might change some votes that we had to have." Brooke tracked down Smith in the Senate restaurant to let her know what was happening. Smith then approached another Republican, Richard Schweiker of Pennsylvania, in the Senate, who acknowledged he had received a call about her plans. "She had a fit of temper right there," an administration official said, and voted no soon afterward.[87]

By this time, Nixon understood that he would lose the battle. Carswell may have figured it out too. One of the two dozen friends and family members who watched the vote on twin television sets at his house said the atmosphere there represented that at "a wake."[88]

Those who packed the Senate galleries and crowded its floor, though, did not know what would happen. When the vote came, and Cook said no, they gasped loudly. When the Democratic Fulbright of Arkansas did the same, they sighed. When Winston Prouty, an administration loyalist whose Vermont constituents disliked Carswell, followed their lead, some applauded. When Smith cast her vote against the nomination, Haynes Johnson reported, "[a] cry of delight rang through the gallery." And when Agnew announced that the Senate had rejected the nomination by fifty-one to forty-five, a smaller margin of defeat than Haynsworth's, ironically, but a loss nonetheless, there was "an explosive sound of emotion," as people embraced, applauded, cheered, and congratulated the Leadership Conference's Clarence Mitchell. Once again, the Senate had rebuffed the president[89] (figure 23).

Neither the White House nor the Justice Department had acquitted itself well this time either. Indeed, while Bob Dole had carried water for Carswell, he now derided the White House lobbyists as "those idiots downtown." Others blamed the Justice Department. One Republican senator complained to a reporter about a disturbing conversation with Assistant Attorney General Rehnquist, who referred to a "Nixon mandate" to reverse the Warren Court. Others groused that the Justice Department had misled them; "Justice was overconfident; Justice failed to take the senators into its confidence; John Mitchell is inscrutable and

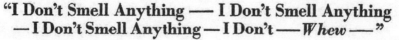

Figure 23 Despite their sense that Judge Carswell was unsavory, more senators voted to confirm him as a Supreme Court justice than voted for Judge Haynsworth. A 1970 Herblock Cartoon. Copyright © The Herb Block Foundation.

aloof, his deputy Richard Kleindienst is 'an abrasive man who wants to ram things down your throat.'" Senator Hatfield said of the attorney general, "I don't know how many times this man can come up as an embarrassment to the administration and remain a powerful figure."[90]

Martha Mitchell had previously telephoned senators' wives and staffers to threaten that she would campaign on "national television" against those who did not vote for Haynsworth. Now she contacted the Arkansas *Gazette* at 2 A.M. to urge its staff to "crucify" Senator Fulbright. She subsequently told her biographer she had done so at her husband's urging and with the president's approval. At the time, she reassured a friend that "John Mitchell says that's the time you get their attention" and defended herself by saying that "crucify" was just an "idiomatic" way of saying "Oh, I could kill you."[91]

Mrs. Mitchell had reason for frustration. "She takes his defeats as her defeats," one Justice Department staffer said, and senators and journalists who had once seen her husband as omnipotent did not point the finger at Rehnquist or Burger for Haynsworth and Carswell. They blamed Mitchell and that "great Justice Department operation" that should have known "everything about a man since the first time a diaper was put on him." The attorney general had replaced Vice President Agnew "as the radix malorum of American society," Pat Buchanan observed. "Patton's dictum—Find the Bastards and Pile On—has been adopted as the operative strategy of the liberal press." Even though the president boosted Mitchell by taking him boating on the night of Carswell's defeat, Nixon and much of his staff faulted the attorney general.[92]

But why should Mrs. Mitchell take it out on Fulbright? One-third of the Republicans had broken ranks with the administration. Some, such as Griffin and Scott, who had deserted the administration on Haynsworth and received pressure from Carswell's opponents to do so again, did not, but only because they feared doing so a second time. Although Haynsworth was the superior candidate, seven Republicans, some of them party leaders, and one Democrat who had voted against Haynsworth held their noses and backed Carswell. And clearly, lots of others who voted for Carswell had done so reluctantly too.[93]

No wonder Nixon was angry. He sought revenge for Haynsworth and Carswell by directing Representative Gerald Ford to orchestrate those impeachment proceedings against William O. Douglas. That Ford obligingly did in April 1970 one week after Carswell's defeat when he unpersuasively contended that "an impeachable offense is whatever a majority of the House of Representatives considers [it] to be at a given moment in history."[94]

And as Ford's sympathetic biographer acknowledged, he neither effectively argued that Douglas had violated federal law by practicing law on behalf of the Parvin Foundation nor claimed that the justice's ties to created a conflict of interest. Instead, Ford insisted that Douglas's "fractious behavior" signaled "the first sign of senility" and that the justice revered "hippy-Yippie style revolution," penned articles for pornographic magazines, and consorted with a gambler. It was a fool's errand, as Ford himself later admitted, that only damaged his own reputation for decency.[95]

The impeachment drive itself went nowhere. Douglas had long been fractious, and his combativeness made him, unlike Fortas, determined to fight. As a liberal icon and symbol of the Warren Court, he attracted devoted lawyers, including his prominent Columbia law classmate, former federal judge Simon Rifkind. The House Judiciary Committee chair, Emanuel Celler, had defended the Warren Court in the 1960s and befriended Douglas since the 1930s. Of course, his committee concluded that Douglas had committed no impeachable offense. When conservatives complained to Ford, they received a form letter declaring that the multitude of Democrats in Congress made it impossible "to obtain an objective committee to conduct a thorough investigation."[96]

Nixon tried to transform Carswell into another martyr. "If they vote him down, we'll send them somebody from Mississippi," he had promised Republican leaders at the peak of the fight. But after the defeat, and in "that indifferent voice he uses when he is really pissed off," he directed Pat Buchanan to draft him a statement to which the president added his own zingers. It exhorted Southerners to vote Republican in the midterm elections: "I have reluctantly concluded—with the Senate as presently constituted—I cannot successfully nominate to the Supreme Court any Federal Appellate Judge from the South who believes as I do in the strict construction of the Constitution." Carswell and Haynsworth had braved "vicious assaults on their intelligence, their honesty and their character," and their commitment to racial equality. "But when all the hypocrisy is stripped away, the real issue was their philosophy of strict construction of the Constitution, a philosophy that I share, and the fact that they had the misfortune of being born in the South," Nixon insisted. He would not impose this indignity again on a Southerner but would find another "strict constructionist with judicial experience." He understood why the Senate's "act of regional discrimination" embittered millions of Southerners, and he promised them "that the day will come when men like Judges Carswell and Haynsworth can and will sit on the High Court." Nixon then delivered the message with a dramatic display of anger in the White House Press Room, and all the networks made it their lead story on the nightly news. Harry Dent rejoiced at the inflammatory language and assured the president he had guaranteed that Haynsworth's and Carswell's rejections would become important issues in the midterm elections.[97]

While Nixon's statement rightly underscored the continuing ideological hold of liberalism and the Warren Court over many Democrats and Republicans, it remained, some of his staffers understood, a "misreading." For all its noise, the Senate still cut the president substantial slack with respect to Supreme Court nominees. Since most senators liked to think they focused on fitness, not ideology, and especially since so many of them were lawyers trained to pay lip service to the ideal of an independent Supreme Court, they needed that "cover issue." Like LBJ, who had made his mistake in nominating two liberal "cronies" so close to the 1968 presidential election, Nixon had blundered the first time in naming a Southern conservative challengeable on ethical grounds in the aftermath of the Fortas scandal. Then the president had nominated a mediocre Southern conservative. Nixon himself told Warren Burger later that while Haynsworth deserved confirmation, "I think, actually, looking back, the Carswell nomination was a mistake. He was a nice fellow, but he wasn't really up to the big league." The president had erred in permitting Mitchell and Burger to promote two vulnerable Southern conservatives, not two Southern conservatives.[98]

As Senators Bayh, Hart, Kennedy, and Tydings said in opposing the nomination, confirmable Southern "strict constructionists" did exist, though the senators did not name them. (Perhaps they feared ruining their chances by bestowing the seal of approval or worried that Nixon would turn to them.) On one level, that represented a surprising admission since Senate liberals relished forcing nominees to say that they did not understand what Nixon meant by "strict constructionist." On another, it simply reflected senatorial realism.[99]

"Raw and Bleeding"

Eighth Circuit Judge Harry Blackmun, a Harvard College and Law School alumnus, now anticipated a summons to Washington. After Nixon told the press he wanted to replace Fortas with a federal judge, Blackmun had mentally reviewed the list of Republican federal candidates of the appropriate age. Few existed, and the Chief Justice of the United States actively promoted his dear friend. To Warren Burger's delight, the *Washington Star* had already listed Blackmun as a possibility for the court in the summer of 1969, and as Haynsworth's troubles grew, a mutual friend had visited the chief justice to discuss the judge's prospects. "This bothers me somewhat although I am grateful for his interest," Blackmun wrote Burger. "Please believe me when I say that (a) I am not instigating this business, (b) I am amazed by offers of support, and (c) above all, I do not want this to be embarrassing to you in any way. I believe I need say no more. Certainly, I hope that poor guy from South Carolina holds up." As it turned out, Nixon had selected Carswell. Still, Blackmun remembered later, given the field, "it didn't surprise me that, almost immediately after the Carswell vote, I had a call from the Attorney General."[100]

The administration's desperation was evident. Blackmun recalled his surprise at the amount of time Mitchell, Rehnquist, and another Justice Department official spent interviewing him until he realized "that all three were raw and bleeding from the Haynsworth-Carswell incidents and were deeply disappointed about the Haynsworth rejection and embarrassed about the Carswell one. Some reference was made to Senator Hruska's unfortunate speech in the Senate." They did not concentrate on Blackmun's opinions, since Rehnquist had already examined them and concluded that that though sometimes "longer than necessary," they were scholarly and marked the judge as "conservative-to-moderate in both criminal law and civil rights." The biggest black mark he could find against Blackmun related to geography: "He and Chief Justice Burger both hail from Minnesota, and both practiced extensively in the Twin Cities before ascending the bench."

Instead, Mitchell and his colleagues wanted to know whether Blackmun's daughters were "hippies." Above all, though, they focused on his finances, stock ownership, and disqualification practices, since, as Rehnquist sarcastically told Mitchell, "the fact that Judge Blackmun sat in two cases involving Ford Motor Company in the early 60s, at a time when he owned 50 shares of Ford Motor Company stock, could be made a basis of an attack on his 'ethics,' or the basis for a charge that he was 'insensitive to the appearance of impropriety' in the words of the Great Statesman from Indiana," Senator Bayh. (It certainly could. Because Ford stock "generally traded in the range of $40-$50 during the 1960s," Ford Motor Company could have survived without Blackmun's investment. But the judge's Ford holdings, valued at $2000-$2500, or $12,000-$16,000 in 2016 dollars, would have seemed important to him.)[101]

The judge's answers satisfied them, and Mitchell took Blackmun to the White House. The president, who had not met with Haynsworth or Carswell before he announced their nominations, "wanted to see this animal who had been suggested to him," Blackmun believed. "Mr. Nixon was obviously irked at the Carswell events and I had the impression that he was irked at the AG [Attorney General] and the DJ [Department of Justice] staff work." How much money did Blackmun have? the president asked. "We have reached the point where we have to put paupers on the Supreme Court," Nixon tactlessly exclaimed after the judge placed his net worth, excluding his house, at about $70,000 (less than $430,000 in 2016 dollars). When Blackmun "flushed" with "annoyance," Nixon reassured him "that anyone with substantial wealth is under a disadvantage from the start," yet another lesson he had obviously drawn from the Haynsworth nomination.

The president soon took the judge's arm and guided him to a window overlooking the Rose Garden. He told Blackmun to stay "independent" from the White House and others when he came to Washington. "I should warn you, however, that the Georgetown crowd will do their best to elbow in on you" with invitations, the judge recalled Nixon saying. "I suspect that two of the Justices have fallen victim to this kind of thing. Can you resist the Washington cocktail party circuit?" Could Mrs. Blackmun? Assured that they could, Nixon told his press secretary to announce the nomination less than a week after Carswell's defeat.[102]

At least, the ABA approved. Unhappy that Senator Hruska had repeatedly used its seal of approval to defend Carswell against charges of mediocrity, the ABA had decided to seize more of a voice in the process. Instead of simply evaluating a Supreme Court nominee as "not qualified" or "qualified," it was adding a third rating for the candidate who "meets high standards" of professional competence, judicial temperament, and integrity, which it awarded Blackmun.[103]

The administration received precious little from the nomination. "I assume Judge Blackmun is highly qualified," Senator Dole told Nixon. "He is however the second Minnesotan [sic] and the second . . . man in his sixties nominated by you. I fail to see any long-term benefits in this appointment, nor any reason to select a nominee from a state whose Senators [Mondale and Humphrey, both Democrats] led the opposition in part to Haynsworth and Carswell." As another drawback, though Blackmun was not a presidential crony, he was a crony of the chief justice. After chatting up the nominee's eighty-five-year-old mother, Nina Totenberg, in her article "Judge Worries About Ties to Chief Justice: Nixon Nominee Blackmun Is Old Burger Friend," revealed that the two talked by phone about all manner of things, including opinions, weekly. "The whole tenor of the article was that I was exerting influence on the Chief Justice and that Mother was freely bragging about it," Blackmun remembered, and it so "distressed and depressed" and angered him that "I contemplated resigning from the federal bench, and, in fact, asking the President to withdraw the nomination." He fretted, too, about Burger's reaction.[104]

But when Blackmun spoke with Burger, the chief justice made no mention of Totenberg (though he did subsequently warn his friend that "female reporters" had caused "Washington 'official' wives to discuss nothing at parties except maybe favorite recipes" and that those "who depart this sound rule" often "live to rue the day"). Something else explained Burger's iciness, Blackmun's openness with the press. Hordes of reporters were pursuing the nominee with the relentlessness of "the mob at the bastille," and he had refused to categorize himself as a "strict constructionist." The judge told reporters that "I had been called both liberal and conservative and that 'I tried to call them as I see them.'" He had also admitted his personal opposition to capital punishment. Burger advised his friend "that if I felt free to give press interviews and to discuss political subjects, e.g., capital punishment, I should be prepared to discuss other political subjects when my Senate hearing came along." Just in case the message remained unclear, Nixon directed Mitchell to muzzle the judge until then.[105]

The Senate hearing on the nomination, however, proved short and anticlimactic. So what if Blackmun and Burger were lifelong intimates? Blackmun assured a sympathetic Ted Kennedy, who had every reason to agree that family relationships or friendships did not determine policy positions, "I would have no hesitation whatsoever, and he is the first person to be aware of this, in disagreeing with him, or, if I may speak for him, and this is presumptuous so to do, in his disagreeing with me." So what if Blackmun had participated in cases in which he owned stock in one of the parties? He had talked over the issue with his chief judge, who had directed him to sit anyway because his holdings were not all that substantial. Moreover, he informed the Senate Judiciary Committee that since the Haynsworth nomination, he had declined to sit in cases in which he owned stock in any of the parties. Worn-out senators unanimously approved him. Obviously, it was not just the administration that was "raw and bleeding" over the recent nominations to the court, but the Senate as well.[106]

The president tried to keep his defeats in the spotlight even as he won. He urged his staff to stress Blackmun's "strict constructionist" credentials to all and the double standard to Southern columnists. Nixon considered his new justice as "to the right of both Haynsworth and Carswell on law and order and perhaps slightly to their left, but very slightly to the left only in the field of civil rights." It was "of the highest urgency" to get the message out that Blackmun "has the same philosophy on the Constitution as Haynsworth and Carswell" lest any- one conclude "I was forced to back down by the Senate and name a liberal or even a quasi-liberal." Blackmun's judicial record resembled Haynsworth's and Carswell's, the president stressed, and he had "some of the same problems" on ethics as Haynsworth. "Incidentally," he added of Blackmun without providing further verification, "you could also point out that as far as his law school record is concerned it was not as distinguished as Haynsworth, that his grades were actually not as good as Carswell's, and having made all these points neverthe- less he got a unanimous approval by the Senate when the others had a battle in which they were the targets of vilification unprecedented in the history of the Senate."[107]

Given his political objectives, Nixon believed his lingering embrace of Haynsworth and Carswell made sense. He courted the South in 1969 and 1970 by championing them and attacking school desegregation plans that he blamed on Johnson holdovers and the other liberals he got rid of in Health, Education and Welfare. The president understood, the *Washington Star* said, that "Wallace is emerging as a greater threat to Richard Nixon than any which arises from the Democratic side."[108]

But the president never forgot other constituencies, and as Mitchell famously told civil rights activists who occupied his office in 1969 to press for Southern school desegregation, "You'd be better informed if instead of listening to what we say, you watch what we do." After the Supreme Court swatted down the Justice Department's attempt to delay school desegregation and handed down *Alexander v. Holmes*, unanimously mandating immediate desegregation that fall, Nixon became convinced that Southern school desegregation was inevitable— though he privately railed against "the Court's naïve stupidity" and its "childish" and "irresponsible" opinion. "We cannot frontally take the Court on," he told Republican leaders. "He said it would be different if we were 'present at the cre- ation,'" as Truman's secretary of state, Dean Acheson, had called the dawn of the Cold War years. "But we weren't." When Mississippi Senator John Stennis sought to embarrass the North and West by introducing an amendment that would require uniform school desegregation throughout the country, Nixon jokingly asked Mitchell at a cabinet meeting, "Which side are you on?" The attorney general answered, "In the right place; right in the middle." That was just where Nixon wanted him.[109]

By the spring of 1970, when the Carswell battle occurred, the president was emerging as desegregation's reluctant, surprisingly effective champion. "We could have demagogued it," Nixon subsequently told the media, "and we would have had massive resistance." Instead—and despite the president's frequent willingness to blame the federal courts and woo suburban whites throughout the nation by declaring his opposition to busing to achieve racial balance—Nixon put his duty to obey the law ahead of backlash politics. Less than a month after Carswell's defeat, Mitchell used Law Day to denounce "irresponsible and malicious criticism" of the Supreme Court, and to defend William O. Douglas, *Miranda v. Arizona*, and school desegregation. That summer, the administration denied tax-exempt status to segregated private schools. Southerners and conservatives reacted angrily to the president's shift leftward. One Republican told the president that his new nickname was "Mister Integrator." Strom Thurmond dedicated a Senate speech to declaring that Nixon imperiled his own chance of re-election: "I am warning the Nixon Administration—I repeat, I am warning the Nixon Administration today that the people of the South and the people of the nation will not tolerate such unreasonable policies." But thanks to a president who clearly sympathized with the South, well-placed business interests there now had the cover they needed to accept desegregation. In the words of Bruce Ackerman, "Just as his cold warrior image protected him against right-wing attacks on his rapprochement with Mao, his emphatic gestures to Dixie gained him credibility when he told the South that the time had come to accept defeat."[110]

Given his strategy, the president needed to trumpet the Haynsworth and Carswell rebuffs in 1970 to reassure those suffering from "Southern discomfort." Newspapers in the South saluted Nixon for his bravery in nominating the two men after Harry Dent spread the gospel and made heroes of Nixon, Haynsworth, and Carswell. As the midterm elections approached, Vice President Spiro Agnew and "his unabridged Webster's dictionary" traversed the Midwest and West maligning "pusillanimous pussyfooting," "the vicars of vacillation," "the nattering nabobs of negativism," and "the hopeless, hysterical hypochondriacs of history." But in Greenville, South Carolina, Haynsworth's hometown, Agnew abstained from alliteration. There, he simply promised that the president would overcome "radical liberals" and successfully name "a Southern strict constructionist" to the Supreme Court. In Raleigh, he charged the Senate with displaying "flagrant and inexcusable bias against the South" in rejecting Haynsworth and Carswell.[111]

Yet although rhetorical polarization attracted crowds, it did not pay off at the polls. The midterm elections produced some bright spots in Southern states, such as the defeat of Tennessee Senator Al Gore, a Democrat already suspect for a number of reasons besides his opposition to Haynsworth and Carswell. But they did not provide many. Carswell himself had resigned from the Fifth Circuit to seek the Republican Senate nomination, declaring "one thing for sure—everybody knows my name. I'm a household word, just like Coca-Cola" (figure 24). The idea of sending this "strict constructionist" to beard the Senate lions who had rejected him in their den tickled many, and the candidate had Nixon's surreptitious support. "The election of Carswell, of course, would be enormously effective in justifying my positions in appointing him in the first place," the president reminded an intimate whom he urged to raise money for Carswell on the sly.[112]

But Nixon did not want to interfere in a primary too obviously, Carswell lost, and Democrat Lawton Chiles won the Senate seat. (After Carswell's defeat, to the disgust of some at the White House, he became so eager "to get out of the country" that he was ready to become "Associate Justice in American Samoa.

Figure 24 Though undated, this photo of G. Harrold Carswell must have been taken after the Senate, led by Birch Bayh, defeated the former judge's Supreme Court nomination and while he was running unsuccessfully for a US Senate seat in Florida. The State Archives of Florida. Photo by Donn Dughi.

He served in Samoa during World War II and thinks this would be just great." Asked whether that appointment was "too obscure and trivial," given that Nixon had tried to put Carswell on the Supreme Court, Charles Colson wrote "*absolutely*—this is an unmitigated disaster—*Stop* it!" Carswell became a Tallahassee lawyer.)[113]

So it went. As Harry Dent told the administration, the 1970 elections just "encouraged" the Democrats. No wonder: Historians have shown how Nixon's tactics, which wrongly assumed that all white Southerners lived to destroy integration just undercut Southern Republicans. Instead, they contributed to the emergence of "new South Democrats" like Jimmy Carter of Georgia in governors' mansions and Congress, who advocated "legal compliance and color-blind progress"—as the president himself now did.[114]

Elsewhere in the country, the results disappointed the administration too. Consequently, although Nixon claimed victory in the 1970 elections in front of the cameras and privately, he also fumed behind closed doors at the prospect of a "Senate full of liberal harassers and obstructionists, some from his own party." Despite them, he remained determined to yoke the court to his goal of Republican hegemony.[115]

7

The Lost Ball Game, Or How Not to Choose Two Justices, 1971

To Warren Burger, Earl Warren, like Theodore Roosevelt, yearned to be the bride at every wedding and the corpse at every funeral. Warren was "a public man concerned almost exclusively with self" and popularity, his successor maintained. That explained why as a California official "he flagrantly violated" the constitutional rights of the accused, then somersaulted as chief justice and destroyed the Constitution in the process. Burger complained to Blackmun about the "booby traps" and "ambushes" that his "illustrious power hungry predecessor" lay for him, as well as his own isolation at the court. "It is really incredible to me how 9 men could have gotten so far from reality for so long." Like Nixon, Burger hoped Old Father Time and the Grim Reaper would cause the court's transformation.[1]

"I Will Have Named Four"

Given his loneliness, to say Burger welcomed Blackmun with open arms in 1970 after the Fortas seat had sat vacant for a record 391 days is at once trite and an understatement. "The Court is working smoothly for all the disaster of the past two years," the chief justice assured his childhood friend, and he sensed relief that "while they would not have elected me, I was not as bad as some feared!" The task was to "to get people to believe that the Court can be trusted and that it is not a political establishment," and then they would accept the results it ordered even when they did not understand its reasoning. That made it imperative "to draw away from the attitude that everything unwise or wicked is unconstitutional and that if we but search, we will find some long hidden meaning in Due Process or Equal Protection or whatnot. If this has slowed down a little—and it is far too little to suit me—it may be that the successive blows on Fortas and Thornberry followed by Haynsworth and Carswell, plus the personal tragedies within the family, took the edge off the sense of omniscience which I think this Court has exhibited in the past dozen years or more." Burger relished the idea of an intimate to whom he could voice such thoughts frankly. For his part, Blackmun shared "completely your observation that the country desperately needs reassurance about the Court" and anticipated "with more eagerness than I can express to a renewal of our old walking excursions when at least we talked things out and unloaded our gripes and frustrations."[2]

Yet Blackmun was anxious. His mother, who had known Burger as long as he had, had warned that his relationship with the chief justice—in contemporary terms, a bromance—would change. Blackmun asked two couples who knew him and Burger well for advice for that "inevitable day when Warren will be belligerently in error. Should I stand my grounds or run for the hills?" Still, Blackmun knew that he was naturally apprehensive, and these moments of doubt were, at first, few. "There will be satisfaction in working with Warren and the others," he told another mutual friend. "He is giving every indication of being a great Chief Justice." As a baseball enthusiast, Blackmun remembered joking to the other justices in 1970 that they might refer to him and Burger as the "Minnesota Twins"[3] (figure 25).

Just as Burger anticipated Blackmun's allegiance and loyalty, so did members of the court with whom Burger was proving less popular and respected

Figure 25 Justices of the Supreme Court, 1971, seated, left to right: John Harlan, Hugo Black, Warren Burger, William O. Douglas, William Brennan. Standing, left to right: Thurgood Marshall, Potter Stewart, Byron White, Harry Blackmun. Supreme Court of the United States.

than he sensed. Harlan had smilingly told Burger after one fall 1969 conference that he sounded like Felix Frankfurter. When the new chief justice thanked him for "the extravagant compliment and asked why," he was deluged with copies of Frankfurter's many memoranda ineffectually exhorting the court to change its undesirable ways. "I do not intend my efforts to be vain, and I did not leave the life of relative ease in the Court of Appeals to be frustrated," Burger vowed. That was clear, and there was suspicion of both him and Blackmun. An unsigned "Ode to the Chief Justice" in the Harlan Papers, probably written by some clerks, concluded:

> Burger is being aided and abetted
> By his yes-man, Blackmun, for whom he stood up when wedded,
> Or was it the other way around, Blackmun standing up for Berger [sic]?
> Regardless, it is plain that they still honor their old time merger:
> YOU STAND UP FOR ME AND I'LL STAND UP FOR YOU AND TOGETHER WE WILL SOW DISORDER
> TO HELL WITH THE CONSTITUTION, WE ARE FOR NIXON'S LAW AND ORDER.[4]

Law and order was indeed the chief justice's greatest concern. "It has been no secret for a dozen years that in my view the Court went to absurd lengths in criminal law," he told Blackmun. That the court had recently overturned Judge Blackmun's opinion in *Ashe v. Swenson* was symptomatic. The majority held that under the Fifth Amendment's double jeopardy clause, once a defendant had been found not guilty of robbing one individual in a burglary, the state could not try him or her again for robbing a different one in the same operation. "Even now in this term, the Court is still on its emotional binge occasionally, as in your *Ashe*," Burger told Blackmun, a case it should never have taken. "I dissented vigorously in part to make it plain that the 'new boy' was not going to be over-awed by even the most majestic nonsense." But Burger had been the only one to do so. Obviously, he expected Blackmun, whose opinion had been reversed, to join him in championing law and order and other causes in the future. "The President did not put us here alone," Burger reminded Blackmun. "It may have been one of the Good Lord's errors," but they would face the future together.[5]

God's will or not, two justices did not make a majority. So when Burger telephoned the White House in September 1971 to report that poor health was forcing Hugo Black's retirement and that John Harlan was in the hospital too, he sounded exultant. "This is it," John Ehrlichman remembered the chief justice saying, his voice heavy with "excitement and triumph." Within a week, Black had died, and Burger had informed the president that Harlan also was leaving the bench.[6]

Two giants were departing, and Nixon admired both of them. Had the president had his choice, he would have gotten rid of Douglas and Brennan instead. Still, the prospect of a "double play" delighted him. Like other presidents, he believed it easy to select justices whose votes on key issues he could predict.[7]

Here was his chance to put his stamp on the court and the GOP. During the twentieth century, only three other presidents (FDR, Taft, and Eisenhower) had enjoyed the chance to nominate four or more individuals to the Supreme Court within a three-year period, and Burger had assured the president that more justices were teetering on the edge of death or retirement. Despite Democrats' control of Congress, Nixon hoped that his Burger Court would surpass its predecessor in stature—which made his flirtations with unsuitable candidates for the court all the more surprising. Even if no further vacancies ensued, "whatever happens in the election, we will have changed the Court," Nixon informed Haldeman. "I will have named four, and Potter Stewart becomes the swing man. He's a goddamn weak reed, I must say."[8]

Stewart had provoked the president when he sided with Black, Brennan, Douglas, Marshall, and White in the "Pentagon Papers" case. There they had held that the Nixon administration's attempt to block the *New York Times* from publishing the Defense Department account of America's tortured history in Vietnam from the Franklin D. Roosevelt through Johnson years leaked by Daniel Ellsberg and Anthony Russo represented an unconstitutional prior restraint. The Pentagon Papers case sent the administration a long way down the road towards the many illegal actions for which "Watergate" would become shorthand. It inspired the president to approve the creation of the Special Investigations Unit, known as the "Plumbers" because of its determination to plug leaks that fruitlessly sought to discredit Ellsberg by burglarizing his psychiatrist's office. "Those clowns" on "the stinking Court," the president raged to J. Edgar Hoover. At least, the court's per curiam opinion had sparked dissents from Burger, Blackmun, and Harlan. Now Harlan, like Black, was leaving. Despite his conviction that Stewart had become a captive of the Georgetown cocktail circuit, Nixon had not altogether given up on him. "[I]f we can only get him on board, we'll have the Court," the president told Haldeman.[9]

Two changes in the process of selecting justices this time were intended to make it operate more smoothly. Attorney General Mitchell, who had not previously consulted with the American Bar Association before Supreme Court nominations were announced, had resolved to give the ABA's Standing Committee on the Federal Judiciary, which traditionally evaluated court nominees, a real

voice. The committee would intensively prescreen possible Supreme Court candidates before the president announced his nomination, with an eye to deciding
whether they met "high standards" of integrity, judicial temperament, and professional confidence, and were "qualified" or "not qualified." Historically, ABA
investigations had been cursory. While the Eisenhower, Kennedy, and Johnson
administrations gave the association ample time to investigate lower federal
court judges, they had expected the ABA to deliver its verdict on potential justices in twenty-four hours or less.[10]

But the days of quick-and-dirty checks had ended which carried potential risks and rewards. ABA Standing Committee on the Judiciary Chairman
Lawrence Walsh had warned Mitchell that "if the Committee's investigation
continued long enough, public disclosure was inevitable because it is impossible to question 200 lawyers and judges and law school deans about a
person under consideration for a Supreme Court vacancy and not have the
fact of the investigation leak." Committee members hoped, though, that if
the Justice Department provided them with enough time, "we could conduct a discreet investigation for a period of a few days and report on it to
you before the scope of our investigation was broadened and then became
publicly known." Another possible problem was that many of the judges, lawyers, and law school deans the ABA would poll considered themselves liberal.
Though Standing Judiciary Committee members insisted that they did not
consider politics or ideology, the views of those surveyed might color ratings.
In fact, to look back is to realize how far lawyers on the Right have come. No
Federalist Society or elite network of conservative law students, lawyers, and
judges existed in the 1970, and, Mitchell informed Nixon, "it's the people
in the larger law firms who are the cut-throat liberals." The legal profession's
powerful, after all, had supported the Warren Court and Johnson's nomination of Abe Fortas as chief justice in 1968. Still, the role of the ABA in the
process would make it less likely that the administration would "announce a
nomination and discover, too late, that the legal establishment considered it
a turkey," Fred Graham explained. Mitchell was gambling on the discretion
and professionalism of the legal profession and, perhaps, on the nature of the
ABA itself. It was no bastion of progressivism. After all, grumbled civil rights
lawyer Joe Rauh, who considered the association ultra-reactionary, when
Nixon nominated Haynsworth and Carswell, the ABA twice approved each
of them "even after the worst was known."[11]

Once again, the administration was well aware it would face the network of
liberal lawyers, law professors and students, union leaders, protesters, and civil
rights workers to which Rauh belonged. Those activists began preparing for
action as soon as Black and Harlan wrote their letters of resignation. This time,
they planned to investigate anyone they learned Nixon was seriously considering

naming, as well as actual nominees. Perhaps their existence made the administration see the importance of having the ABA on its side.[12]

As a second change in how Nixon decided on additions to the court, the White House, through John Ehrlichman, would keep watch on the Justice Department. The Justice Department and the FBI "let you down" with Haynsworth and Carswell and must now do their "homework," one adviser told the president. Based on his experience with Carswell, Egil Krogh, the head of the Plumbers and architect of the break-in at Ellsberg's psychiatrist's office, thought the White House should intervene more aggressively in choosing a justice. "We simply can't afford to play catch-up ball with a nomination again," he stressed to Ehrlichman. While the Justice Department could do the preliminary screening, he advised, the White House should secretly establish a confirmation committee to oversee the process, which it did not do, and task John Dean and Plumber David Young, a "very facile and penetrating" lawyer, with completing "something like a CIA de-briefing" of any top candidate, which was done in some instances. "My experience has shown that the FBI investigations and a casual luncheon or conversation are not sufficient to extract the kind of information we need," Krogh warned.[13]

"I Want Poff"

Though the process of vetting a nominee had changed, the objective of the White House had not. Given Black's Alabama roots, "it would be a slap to the South not to try for a Southerner," Nixon informed Mitchell. Second, the nominee "must be a conservative Southerner," with "conservative" defined as someone who was not a racist, but "against busing and against forced housing integration." (Sometimes the president also talked about finding someone strong on law and order, but not as often. Perhaps, because members of his administration privately worried that the national crime statistics from his tenure were showing few signs of improvement, he had decided to deemphasize law and order or Nixon may have thought anyone good on busing would prove right on crime.) Beyond meeting those criteria, "he can do as he pleases," and the president did not care whether he was "a socialist." Party affiliation was also immaterial. So was prior judicial experience: After all, Nixon now often pointed out, Frankfurter had none before he joined the court. Third, the nominee must be confirmable, since the president did not intend to go "halfway down the road" and find himself with "another Carswell." He must be young, too, because Nixon wanted someone who could sit on the court for twenty years.[14]

Ironically, busing in the South to achieve racial balance had become a fait accompli. The court had upheld the use of extensive school busing for schools historically segregated as a matter of law in the spring of 1971 in *Swann v. Charlotte-Mecklenburg Board of Education*. Burger wrote the opinion, and he labored mightily and not altogether successfully, to limit it. Indeed, the process of producing it became one of the instances in which his efforts to lead the court came a cropper. Though unanimous, the chief justice's opinion in *Swann* worsened his relationship with his colleagues. Court tradition required the senior associate justice in the majority to assign the opinion when the chief justice was in the minority, as Burger was when the justices first conferred. But he assigned the opinion to himself, as he would in similar circumstances for important decisions time and again. As a result, the opinion went through endless drafts as justices in the original majority insisted on changes to make it tolerable. The case, William O. Douglas said, "illustrated the wasted time and effort and the frayed relations which result when the traditional assignment procedure is not followed."[15]

The White House proved more satisfied than the justices. Nixon privately admitted that *Swann* "could have been worse." He was happy to hear Mitchell credit Burger with keeping his colleagues away from the bramble bush of de facto school segregation outside the South—and probably not dissatisfied that Martha Mitchell, a busing opponent, had angrily told the press that *Swann* showed that the Supreme Court "should be abolished." As ever, the president himself seized the opportunity at once to blame and declare himself bound by the court.[16]

Especially with George Wallace nipping at his heels, Nixon worried. As a lawyer, the president read *Brown v. Board of Education* to mean that "legally segregated education was inferior education," he explained to Ehrlichman and Haldeman. If separation of the races continued despite the removal of the legal barriers to it, "the philosophy of *Brown* would be that any segregated education, whether it was because of law or because of fact, is inferior. That is why I see the courts eventually reaching the conclusion that de facto segregation must also be legally unacceptable" even though Nixon was sure that "it is only segregated black education which is inferior and that actually segregated white education is probably superior to education in which there is too great a degree of integration of inferior black students with the white students." Given the depth and geographic breadth of the reaction against busing, the president reiterated his personal opposition to busing to achieve racial balance in August of 1971, resolved to hold it to "the minimum required by law" in the future, and revealed that his Justice Department would "disavow" the plan of the Department of Health, Education, and Welfare to use extensive busing to desegregate Austin's public schools. Housing and Urban Development Secretary George Romney's ambitious effort to reduce residential segregation by putting low-income housing in suburbs also bothered Nixon. It was not just African Americans whom whites did not want moving into their "exclusive neighborhoods," but "Italians,

Mexicans, Irish and others" too, he reasoned. "Putting a public housing project in a neighborhood of home-owners is, of course, totally wrong whether it is Black or White from an economic standpoint because it will not only reduce property values but it raises—and we have to admit—very grave questions with regard to the possibilities of increase in crime, etc." The bottom line for Nixon was that the country was "not ready at this time for either forcibly integrated housing or forcibly integrated education," and the president did not want to put anyone on the court who believed in it either.[17]

Placement of a Southern conservative on the court might pay rich political dividends, but given his bitter statement denouncing the Senate for anti-Southern bias after the Carswell defeat, why did the president think he would succeed in getting one now? Arguably, the Senate had moved a bit to the right after the midterm elections, but only very marginally. The answer soon became clear. While the Constitution's emoluments clause, which prohibited congressional members from taking a job for which they had approved a salary hike, had prevented the president from turning to a legislator in 1969, he could find his candidate in the new Congress. That was an excellent place to look, since the court had traditionally included at least one member of Congress and legislators were less likely to find fault with one of their own.[18]

The problem was the president's pick. Nixon had decided to nominate Richard Poff, a decorated World War II bomber pilot, a Virginian, and a Republican on the House Judiciary Committee. "[H]e's conservative, but he's not considered to be a racist," Nixon said, and he would become "another Blackmun," which was "basically what I'd like." Then forty-seven, Poff had served in Congress since voters in southwest Virginia elected him in 1952. He had signed both Southern manifestos, one pledging resistance to *Brown v. Board of Education* and the other vowing to resist the ineffectual 1957 Civil Rights Act. He had opposed the civil rights legislation of the 1960s, and he was tough on crime.[19]

Poff had also sponsored legislation that attacked the Warren Court by requiring Supreme Court justices to possess five years of prior judicial experience. "No one has condemned more vigorously the Supreme Court in the past decade than have I," he had boasted to one constituent. "I believe this judicial experience is absolutely necessary and reveals the temperament and philosophy of a prospective Supreme Court justice than any other method." Poff himself, though, possessed little experience practicing law and none as a judge, since he had joined Congress four years after graduation from University of Virginia Law School. Nevertheless, he really wanted to become a justice. Poff had said publicly that he would prefer a seat at the court to the presidency, and as one of his staffers admitted, "he had been running hard" for one ever since Nixon took office. "[T]he bar will never approve him," Chief of Staff H. R. Haldeman warned the president.[20]

"I want Poff," Nixon said privately and hinted publicly. Mitchell thought highly of him. "I've not been quite that impressed with him because I didn't really see him in action," the president told his attorney general. "But on the other hand, he's a young man, and he's a good lawyer, and good God, that's what we need on this Court." As Nixon exulted to Pat Buchanan, replacing Black with a "strict constructionist conservative who signed the Southern manifesto" was bound "to have a very salutary effect on our Southern friends." (Was he saying he equated "strict constructionist" with antagonism to civil rights or that he preferred a "strict constructionist" who opposed racial equality?) As an added bonus, the nomination of a Capitol insider would split Senate Democrats.[21]

Within a day of Black's resignation, the *New York Times* and *Washington Post* had identified Poff as the frontrunner. The president maintained that made a quick announcement of his selection necessary. So Mitchell spoke with ABA Standing Committee on the Judiciary Chairman Walsh. "He says he can get Haynsworth past the Bar and confirmed in a breeze," the attorney general reported. "He says he has nothing but people all over the country who come up to him" to discuss the mistreatment of one-time nominee Clement Haynsworth. But Mitchell and the president agreed, as Nixon put it, that "it's a risk we shouldn't buy. I think it looks like a petulant President . . . trying to prove to these fellows that they were wrong." Consequently, the attorney general persuaded Walsh to "go out and try to sell" Poff on the grounds that his service on the House Judiciary Committee made up for his lack of experience.[22]

Poff possessed other vulnerabilities. He would also surely face questions about why, after he joined Congress, his former law firm listed him as a partner and continued to pay him a percentage of its profits, though he did little work for it. Though some liberals like Lou Pollak and former governor "Pat" Brown of California, who had worked with Poff on the National Commission on the Reform of Federal Criminal Laws, venerated him as a lawyer and human being and welcomed the possibility of his Supreme Court nomination, others would challenge him. Anticipating his appointment, Clarence Mitchell was already denouncing him as "an affable and soft spoken individual" whose "record on civil rights matters is one of the worst in the United States Congress," while Roy Wilkins was urging Nixon not to appoint anyone who would "evoke divisive confirmation struggles." Political scientist Gary Orfield declared that he was working with some twenty students to uncover Poff's "dismal record" on civil rights. And American Federation of Labor-Congress of Industrial Organizations President George Meany, who decried Poff's "racist" past, was proclaiming that "the AFL-CIO does not believe that President Nixon's narrow election in 1968, coupled with the election of Democratic majorities in both houses of Congress in 1968 and 1970, constituted any mandate to stack the court with reactionary nonentities." Feminists, who disliked Poff's position on the Equal Rights

Amendment, were unhappy too. So was the Unitarian who lay Hugo Black to rest: Nixon complained that "the goddamn minister made a great eulogy by attacking strict constructionists" as he looked directly at the president, who had reluctantly attended, and his attorney general.[23]

But Poff had eloquently renounced his segregationist views, and he was extremely popular on Capitol Hill, even among House liberals, who joined their Republican colleagues in lobbying the president, Senate, and public on his behalf. Nixon, who welcomed the pressure, used it to push Mitchell: "Well, we have to realize John, that, you know, the House and Senate are, well, at least the House is so damn strong for this fellow, we're going to have a hell of a time if we don't appoint him." The president told Republican congressional leaders that since the court now lacked any Southerners, the administration "ought to be able to find one" and that it would prove "much more difficult for them to vote against a Southerner who's been in the House than it is against some damn judge," like Haynsworth or Carswell.[24]

Everyone agreed. Republican Whip Robert Griffin predicted that thirty-one would oppose the nomination; Senate Minority Leader Hugh Scott, thirty-six. "But either way we should have a majority," Griffin promised the president, and probably even could break a filibuster. When Haldeman warned Nixon about anti-Poff senators who would oppose confirmation, the president was unfazed. "We're going to get it," he insisted. "Scott says we can confirm him, and Scott's no tower of strength." Oddly, Nixon found that reassuring.[25]

The naysayers affected the schedule, however. The Senate minority leader had urged Nixon to name both court nominees at once. "We get a bit of maneuvering room when we get them both together," Scott explained to Nixon before leaking that advice to reporters. The senator who opposed the president on one might compensate by supporting the other and/or the other nominee might "balance" the Southerner. And indeed, though he anticipated "a hard time with our friends" in the civil rights community, the eminent Republican African American lawyer, William Coleman, was preparing to swallow Poff "and trying to work out with the Attorney General the selection of the other man, who has to be a first-rate lawyer or judge, and then see if it can be put across as a package." On Thursday, September 30, Mitchell reported to Nixon, "Because of the pressures that have been building up on Poff with the civil rights people and so forth, it became very obvious that we didn't want to get mouse-trapped by sending somebody else up with him, where we might lose Poff and get the other one in a brokerage pair[off] operation."[26]

So as it had done with Marshall, Fortas, and Thornberry, the Justice Department just forwarded Poff's name to the ABA. The Justice Department coupled it with a ten-page memorandum repeating Felix Frankfurter's oft-quoted axiom that "the correlation between prior judicial experience and fitness for the functions of the Supreme Court is zero" and arguing that Poff's experience as legislator qualified him for the court. Standing Federal Judiciary Committee members had expected the administration to submit more than one name. That might distract inquiring reporters from digging up dirt on the president's preferred choice while keeping open administration options. Given the recent conflict around Supreme Court nominees, Justice's decision seemed "crazy" to at least one ABA power broker, who told Fred Graham that the department and the White House should have "sent up several names as a smoke screen—but now if Poff draws a lot of opposition, they'll have to nominate him and have another fight or back down in public."[27]

The administration's behavior struck some inside the White House as foolish too. John Dean and David Young had spent three-and-a-half hours grilling Poff on September 25. They had submitted a lengthy memorandum covering his law firm income; health (occasional prostatitis, now cleared up; athlete's foot; and hemorrhoids); developmentally disabled uncle; drinking (nightly scotch and soda and an occasional glass of wine "but he has never been drunk in his life"); enemies (just one, a former campaign worker); extramarital affairs (one long ago); marriage (happy); and three children, one of whom was twelve and had not yet been informed he was adopted ("Poff confided that the only time he thinks about this is when he wakes up at 2 o'clock in the morning worrying about how he is going to tell him"). They had covered his reading ("the Constitution straight through two or three times a year just to get a feel on whether or not we are really carrying out what he thinks the Founding Fathers intended"); religion (committed Presbyterian, but not a "Bible quoter"); African American supporters (he thought he could find some); net worth ($200,000 to $250,000, about $1.24 million to $1.5 million in 2016 dollars); and outside income (just one honorarium on which he had paid income tax).

They had also explored his positions. If reminded that he had proposed qualifications for a Supreme Court justice he did not himself meet, Poff planned to say that both the Senate and House had rejected his suggestion. He had stayed out of the Haynsworth and Carswell fights. He considered the former an excellent, if ethically challenged, candidate for the court. To him, the latter looked qualified at first glance but was not, which was "why he was glad we were giving him a rough going over." He had "pleaded" with Ford not to launch impeachment proceedings against Douglas and had never publicly discussed Fortas. The three men had also talked about Poff's chances. He repeatedly, though never boastfully, said "he thought that he had more friends than any other man in the House except perhaps Wilbur Mills" and declared himself "absolutely convinced that if nominated he would be confirmed."

Young wrote that Poff possessed the highest morality, integrity, and patriotism. He had felt as if "I had been a priest in a confessional," but that the sinner had nothing to say. Poff had faced "the most difficult and offensive questions that a man can be asked" and answered them amiably and forthrightly.[28]

By September 30, however, Young was having second thoughts. Poff was a great man, he told Ehrlichman, but he lacked the "deeper and broader legal grounding" that the court required. If the White House restricted itself to a Southern "strict constructionist" (a term Young thought might just mean "conservative"), perhaps Poff was the best candidate. But if Nixon wanted a Southerner or "strict constructionist," people of "greater stature" existed.[29]

Others did not worry about Poff's intellect, but his prospects of surviving confirmation. It was most important to avoid another battle, and the risk of one here outweighed the advantage of the proposed nomination, Leonard Garment warned the president: Democrats with presidential hopes in 1972 and others "who wish the Administration ill can be expected to move into the contest, seeing in it an opportunity to foment a bitter controversy, to sour the political atmosphere, to open old wounds, and thereby to break the momentum of sustained Presidential achievement of recent months." What was the rush? And what was the point in presenting "these appointments as surprises"? Why not invite the input of different groups? It would save discomfort at the confirmation stage and demonstrate White House dedication to finding "the best qualified nominees at a critical point in the Court's history."[30]

That was good advice. The singular focus on Poff did reflect bad judgment by the Justice Department and White House. But the candidate had by now captivated the president. Who cared if he lacked judicial experience and had not represented clients for very long? "We all know, John, practicing law is nothing," Nixon told Mitchell on September 30. Who cared if he had signed the Southern manifesto? "He did what any damn Southerner should do," and "I'd sign the goddamn manifesto today," the president informed his attorney general. Meany and the liberals were "hypocrites." Nixon wanted to push forward, "bite the bullet and send [up] the goddamn thing. Fight it. You know, if we lose, fine." Defeat would mean that no Southerner could win appointment. But Nixon still thought the White House would win. "I don't think you're going to have more than 40 votes against him. I think it will be 35."

Mitchell hedged. Why not wait until the ABA issued its report on Poff, then take a legislative head count and decide then? But the president resisted. Get the Senate count now, he directed, because he wanted to send Poff's name up Monday and capture the week's news cycle. Would the president nominate him even if the ABA did not rate Poff qualified? the attorney general wanted to know. "Hell, yes!" Nixon answered. "I can't be giving Walsh and his people a veto in this." And while he hated to part ways with it, the ABA would look "damn small" if it said "that some God damn little lawyer out in Paducah who has practiced law for fifteen years is better qualified to be in the Supreme Court than somebody that's been on the Judiciary Committee in the House for fifteen years."[31]

But as members of the Standing Committee on the Judiciary gathered in New York at Walsh's office to evaluate the potential nominee on Saturday morning, October 2, and the Washington Research Project's Rick Seymour was driving to southwest Virginia to check Poff out, the prospective nominee shocked them. The previous evening, he had dropped a bombshell on the White House when he let John Dean know that he was considering withdrawing his name, though he had promised to sleep on it. Now he made his decision official and public. Poff cited his desire to avoid another "long and divisive confirmation battle" that could lead to a filibuster and damage his family, the court, and the country.[32]

And it was true, up to a point. His intimates promptly told reporters that while Poff had anticipated that the ABA would find him "qualified" or would express "no opposition," he had become nervous as he reviewed his own voting record. Then Senator Robert Byrd of West Virginia, a Senate Judiciary Committee member and the Democratic whip, had stopped by Poff's office Friday afternoon to warn him of a developing fight led by civil rights groups and organized labor, and, possibly, a filibuster. "I told him, 'I can't be sure what will happen, but one or two Senators were preparing to examine your background at some length,'" Byrd confirmed. He had also, however, stressed his "certainty" that Poff would ultimately win confirmation. One Poff enthusiast said that the senator's friendly and encouraging warning had devastated the congressman.[33]

Apparently, Poff also worried about what those senators would uncover. Haldeman maintained that "the real reason for his withdrawal is that as our guys were working him over on the problems he would face on confirmation, they got to the point that he has a very substantial net worth but is unable to document the sources of this money. He just doesn't have the facts. They're convinced there's nothing wrong, but that a lot could be made that would appear to be wrong." Over at the National Association for the Advancement of Colored People (NAACP), Director-Counsel Jack Greenberg heard that the ABA Standing Judiciary Committee "was prepared to vote against him by a near 2-1 vote," not because of his views on race, but because of "his role in his law firm and [with respect to] at least one former partner. Poff decided to withdraw rather than face canvassing of these relationships." Meanwhile, Poff confided to Dean that he had reached his decision principally because he and his wife had begun to fear that the adoption of his son would become public when the Senate considered his nomination. (Ironically, when the Poffs had to tell the boy about his adoptive status after he took himself out of the running because columnist Jack Anderson was about to reveal the news, the child took it well enough. Young

Tommy had "remained in a traumatic silence all day" until he got hungry, asked for dinner, and assured his parents he knew that they loved him.)[34]

Had a choice for the court ever so publicly pulled his name before the president could submit it because after two confirmation battles, he foresaw a third? Like Nixon in the Carswell and Haynsworth instances, Grover Cleveland suffered two successive defeats when he nominated William Hornblower and Wheeler Peckham to the court. But just as Nixon had prevailed with Blackmun, Cleveland had with Edward White. Poff's withdrawal, like the intense scrutiny by Dean and Young, underlined how hazardous the process of becoming a Supreme Court justice now was.

Republicans made the most of that. "It's a sad and shocking day in American history," Poff's friend, House Minority Leader Gerald Ford, said, "when leaders of the NAACP and leaders in organized labor and a few power-hungry senators can prevent an honorable, fair and qualified man from having his name submitted for the Supreme Court." In contrast, Joe Rauh saluted Poff's decision to avoid "a third nation-splitting confirmation struggle" as "an act of judicial statesmanship." However one came down, the episode underscored the messiness of the new nomination and confirmation process. Marshall's treatment by hostile Southern senators in 1967 had made its ugliness clear, and since then, the *Washington Post* observed, "the abilities and characters of Justice Fortas and Judges Haynsworth and Carswell" had been "dissected" and rejected. It was beginning to look as if the Burger and Blackmun confirmations were the anomalies.[35]

As John Dean said, Poff had gone "poof." The congressman feared that the president "would think that I had somehow run out on you," he apologetically told Nixon. "They would have made you look like the worst son of a bitch that ever came down the pike," the president consoled him, and though the administration would "probably" have prevailed, it might have taken months. "I hope you tell all the fellows that . . . we were backing you to the hilt" and that the administration had not run out on Poff, Nixon stressed. As the president began to tell the congressman that he could rest easy that the process would yield "two men on that Court . . . like Burger and Blackmun," he stopped himself. "Two individuals," he said. That was a significant correction. But before he could reveal its meaning to Poff or the public, another diversion would occur.[36]

"God, What a Guy to Have on That Court"

The White House and Justice Department were now almost back at where they began, as high-level administration officials privately acknowledged. The president's press secretary nevertheless insisted that "Congressman Poff was under consideration with a number of other people." Technically, that was correct, since Nixon, Mitchell, and White House staffers had discussed other names besides Poff's.[37]

They had agreed that if Thurgood Marshall, who Nixon thought was "God damn dumb" and whose health they liked to check, retired, they would have to appoint an African American to replace him. "That's one you've got to do," the president said. While he worried it would mean naming a progressive, he had his eye on Senator Edward Brooke, who was "basically a liberal, [as] he had to be," but "one of the few blacks [who] really talks in an intelligent way"; Equal Employment Opportunity Commission Chair William Brown, whom Ehrlichman found "very loyal"; or William Coleman. (In 1973, Nixon would expand the list to include Chicago lawyer Jewel Lafontant, whom he had named deputy solicitor general. "Why not kill two birds with one stone, get a black woman," he remarked. "When they say she isn't a towering figure, well, who the hell is a towering figure on that Court?") After speculating about whether nominating an African American would encourage Marshall to retire, the president and the attorney general had decided to wait.[38]

They had also ruled out a Jew. "When are you going to fill that Jewish seat on the Supreme Court?" Mitchell joked. "Well, how about after I die?" Nixon laughed. Nevertheless, they had briefly considered Yale Law School Professor Alexander Bickel, a Frankfurter clerk and iconoclastic Democrat who had argued the Pentagon Papers case for the *New York Times*, if his position on busing proved satisfactory. "Everybody would say well, we finally appointed a scholar," Nixon noted. Another possibility was Philadelphia District Attorney Arlen Spector, who was "strong on law enforcement." They had not mentioned Third Circuit Judge Arlin Adams, an early Nixon supporter with whom Mitchell was reportedly angry.[39]

But they had not just eliminated candidates. They had talked about the political advantage of naming a Catholic. "If he's a conservative, a Catholic conservative is better than a Protestant conservative," Nixon instructed Mitchell. That made Lawrence Walsh himself a possibility. Another ABA stalwart, former president Lewis Powell, was too old, they agreed. They had dissected the political advantage of naming a woman, discussed Judges Mildred Lillie and Sylvia Bacon, and dismissed others. They had covered Warren Burger's belief that Nixon had given him the right to name Harlan's successor. "I didn't give the Harlan seat to anybody," the president exploded, though the chief justice's suggestion of Arkansas lawyer Herschel Friday intrigued him. They had mentioned as a possibility Governor Ronald Reagan's friend, William French Smith, "a hell of a big corporation lawyer," Nixon said, whose wife the president liked. They had also spoken of Caspar Weinberger. As Nixon observed, Weinberger possessed two advantages: He was an Episcopalian with a Jewish name and he had an undeserved reputation for liberalism. Then there was Vice President Spiro Agnew.

"You'd be accused of putting him adrift in a lifeboat" and using the court as a port and give the Senate "a golden opportunity to do you in by refusing to confirm your vice president," Ehrlichman warned. They had also discussed Circuit Judge Paul Roney, and Nixon's friends, David Dyer and Charles Rhyne. Mitchell and Nixon had agreed, too, that Senator Roman Hruska "would love the part, act the part, and release the right opinions," but that he was too old. They had even mentioned J. Edgar Hoover, whom they wanted out of the FBI.[40]

It was mostly chatter and badinage, though some names would resurface. To this point, they had always focused on Poff. They had asked the ABA to concentrate on him.

Meanwhile, the Supreme Court opened its fall term with tributes to Black and Harlan on Monday, October 4, the day Nixon had hoped to nominate Poff. For the first time court watchers could recall, there were not nine chairs behind the bench at which the "grim-faced" justices sat, but seven. The court had delayed hearing all its most important cases, and some wondered whether it would remain short two members for its entire term. Once the Nixon administration had sent along the new names, the ABA would take at least a week to consider them, and Congress planned to adjourn after November. Though James Eastland remained the Democratic chair of the Senate Judiciary Committee and he could be expected to help the administration, others on it might drag the hearings out, particularly if the nominees proved controversial. Following the example of the Republicans in 1968, the Democrats might follow Robert Griffin and even argue that the winner of the 1972 presidential election should nominate the next justices.[41]

Every indication was that the president was running toward, rather than away from, another fight. After Poff withdrew, Nixon told Haldeman that he would select "a real right-winger now," whom liberals would consider "worse" and "really stick it to the opposition." When the Senate voted down Carswell, the president had spoken of nominating Senator Robert Byrd, and he now returned to the idea. The son of a West Virginia coal miner, the Democrat had worked as a butcher and grocer before he became a congressman and senator. Byrd had not gone to college. He had graduated from American University Law School, which he attended at night once he reached the Senate, but he had never practiced law and was not a member of the bar. And although Byrd, like Hugo Black, had repudiated his Klan membership, he had voted against the Civil Rights Act of 1964, the Voting Rights Act of 1965, and the nominations of Thurgood Marshall and Abe Fortas in 1967 and 1968. He had supported Haynsworth and Carswell, had opposed "activist" judges and justices, and was bombarding the White House with telegrams urging the nomination of a "strict constructionist" with no financial problems who would "uphold freedom of choice in school integration matters." What's more, since the governor of West Virginia, a Republican, would appoint Byrd's successor, his departure for the court would bring an additional Republican to the Senate.[42]

There were Southern senators with better qualifications than Byrd, such as William Spong of Virginia, a Democrat, and Howard Baker of Tennessee, a Republican. But as Haldeman said, the president considered Byrd particularly attractive "because he was a former KKK'er, he's elected by the Democrats as Whip, he's a self-made lawyer, he's more reactionary than [George] Wallace, and he's about 53." Obviously, Nixon had stopped worrying about looking "petulant." If his goal of disempowering the Warren Court required him to demean the Supreme Court as an institution, so be it.[43]

On Friday, October 8, when the president and the attorney general met, Byrd became an agenda item. Senators said he would go through Congress "like greased lightening," Nixon volunteered. "Sure, because he's part of the club," Mitchell agreed, but his selection would horrify the public and the American Bar Association would rank him "not qualified." Undaunted, the president continued his reverie. "God, what a guy to have on that Court. He wouldn't be like Potter Stewart who came down here pretty clean, nice little fellow from Ohio, and goes out to Georgetown and his wife loves the parties and the rest and then comes the big case, the *Times* case, and he goes to pieces." The senator would become "the strongest man on that Court. You couldn't budge that son of a bitch." He was "tough" about every issue Nixon cared about, including crime. It would take Byrd years to understand "the nuances" of the court's work, Mitchell predicted. "I guess it's out of the question, but I just sort of think sometimes we got to do something out of the question the way they kicked us in the ass three times now," the president said. "You get started down this road, the pressures are going to mount on you tremendously," Mitchell cautioned repeatedly. "To what, appoint more Senators?" Nixon asked. "No, to appoint Byrd."[44]

Later that day, the president traveled with Byrd to West Virginia by plane and remarked that he and the attorney general had discussed him that morning. The senator, who had already checked his chances with Eastland, assured Nixon that he could win confirmation. The president was amused to see one headline the next day: "Robert Byrd Nixon's Next Court Choice." Since the White House had not leaked it, he told Mitchell, Byrd must have.[45]

And the immediate response from Senate Democrats was surprising. Sam Ervin said that Byrd had "a very sound constitutional philosophy and would make a fine appointment." That was predictable since Ervin and Byrd were both Southerners and constitutional fundamentalists. Even George McGovern, though, the South Dakota liberal who would become the Democrats' standard-bearer against Nixon in 1972, was on board. While McGovern said he would nominate a woman himself, he maintained that Byrd's civil rights views had become more moderate, the West Virginian would make "every effort to become a great justice," and the Senate would probably confirm him. "What the hell do you think they're up to?" Nixon asked Mitchell. "They probably want to get him out of that Whip job," the attorney general speculated. "Well, I'm glad to keep the game a little open on this," the president added. "I'll bet you they're regurgitating all over the place, John," because next to Byrd, Poff was "a flaming liberal."[46]

If "they" were not regurgitating, they were nevertheless nonplussed. In 1971, as one of Byrd's staffers said, his detractors dismissed him as a "hillbilly 'Uriah Heep.'" Of course, that did not mean the Senate would not approve Byrd. By Monday, the *New York Times* was reporting "Senator Said to Be Nixon's First Choice and Easy Confirmation Is Predicted," thanks to Senate "clubbiness." As Nixon might have predicted, Byrd's prospects had topped the conversation at Democratic politician Averell Harriman's special Sunday party in Georgetown to introduce five hundred friends to his bride, Pamela. "Any U.S. senator appointed would be confirmed," Senator Scott informed the *Post*. While Abe Fortas "did laugh and started out a sentence this way: 'I don't think—guess that's enough,'" Earl Warren, Arthur Goldberg, Byron White, and Stanley Reed refused comment.[47]

The editors of the newspapers Nixon most despised did not consider Byrd's candidacy a laughing matter. "If President Nixon and Attorney General Mitchell deliberately set out to destroy the prestige and authority of the Supreme Court, they could hardly pick a more likely course than that which they now seem to be following," the *New York Times* editorialized. "Certainly not since President Truman's blatantly political appointments—such as that of Senator Minton— has the White House put forward for the Supreme Court anyone so lacking in qualifications as the junior senator from West Virginia. Even the Carswell nomination tops this one." The prospect of Byrd was "deeply distressing," the *Washington Post*'s editors agreed. "We simply do not understand what motivates the Nixon Administration to toy with the idea of taking on another divisive confirmation fight after its experiences in 1969 and 1970," they wrote plaintively on Monday.[48]

What motivated the administration was Byrd's value in embarrassing and distracting the Democrats. Left to his own devices, the president might well have nominated the senator, who genuinely appealed to him. And by the time of Byrd's death in 2010 after fifty-one years in the Senate, those on both sides of the aisle saw him as one of its giants and saluted his independence and integrity. Among other things he had voted against the nominations of Robert Bork and Clarence Thomas to the Supreme Court, attacked George W. Bush's Iraq invasion, vigorously promoted Barack Obama as a presidential candidate, and published a multivolume history of the Senate. Perhaps Nixon saw something in Byrd that became visible to others later.[49]

It seems doubtful, though. The horrified reaction of his attorney general probably prevented the president from proceeding with the idea, but he did not want the press or Senate to know that. When Spencer Rich at the *Washington Post* published a story entitled "Byrd Held Unlikely for Court: Nixon Aide Says He Is on List But 'Not on Top,' " Nixon telephoned Press Secretary Ron Ziegler. "One of our boys got off the reservation on the Byrd thing and just blew a beautiful play I am trying to make here," he complained. Ziegler was to summon Rich and insist that the administration had Byrd "under very active consideration." Reversing himself, McGovern had said on Monday that he would not vote for his colleague. All the Democratic Presidential contenders had to identify their position on the Byrd candidacy. "We're going to make them stand up and be counted." Byrd would also divert attention from the two candidates Nixon had actually chosen, a woman and a Southern man, so the opposition could not destroy them "before I get a chance to defend them."[50]

"The Woman's Seat" and an "Arkansas Harlan"

George McGovern had not been the only person who wanted to see a woman on the court. For starters, Elvera Burger, Martha Mitchell, and Betty Friedan said they did too. So did the First Lady, who volunteered that she was "talking it up" with the president but that the "best qualified" women were "too old." Reporters speculated that Pat Nixon may have referred to North Carolina Justice Susie Sharp. A "strict constructionist," Sharp was a favorite of North Carolina's senators and law professors and would become the state's first woman chief justice. Or perhaps Mrs. Nixon alluded to District Judge Sarah Hughes, who was then seventy-five, but why would her husband want to name the person LBJ had asked to swear him in as president to the court? Another possibility was Arizona Supreme Court Chief Justice Lorna Lockwood, the first woman ever to become chief justice of a state supreme court and one who could also claim Abraham Lincoln as a cousin. But she was sixty-eight, was relatively progressive, and had defended the Warren Court.[51]

In response to the talk of a woman justice, the National Women's Political Caucus, a nonpartisan group peopled mostly of liberal Democrats, had suggested ten women with the right qualifications and age. Its list included three judges—Ninth Circuit Judge Shirley Hufstedler and US District Judges Cornelia Kennedy and Constance Baker Motley. There were five academics—Soia Mentschikoff of the University of Chicago, Herma Hill Kay of Berkeley, Ellen Peters of Yale, University of Southern California Law School Dean Dorothy Nelson, and former Howard Law School Dean Patricia Harris. In the miscellaneous category were Representative Martha Griffiths, a Republican from

Michigan, and Rita Hauser, a Nixon appointee to the United Nations. Two were African American, Motley and Harris.[52]

Of these possibilities, the most "obvious" was forty-six-year-old Shirley Hufstedler, Fred Graham reported. She was a graduate of Stanford Law, where her grades placed her fifth in the class, tied with future secretary of state Warren Christopher. In addition to becoming the highest-ranked woman federal judge in the country, she had been a California superior court and appellate judge. "She is so highly regarded that during the last year she delivered both the Holmes Lecture at Harvard and the Cardozo Lecture in New York—roughly the equivalent of playing in the World Series and the Super Bowl in the same year." Jimmy Carter would make Hufstedler his secretary of education, and at her confirmation hearings, she reminisced, senator after senator would quiz her about whether she had her eyes on the Supreme Court. She was an "obvious" choice—but not for Nixon and his attorney general. Like the other candidates on the list, she had established a distinguished record, and like them, she possessed a "record of demonstrated commitment to human issues particularly civil rights and equal rights," the National Women's Political Caucus assured the president. That was not the sort of woman Nixon wanted. Everyone on the National Women's Political Caucus's list was "a left-wing red," and to top it off, an ugly "bag," he grumbled.[53]

If truth be told, he did not want a woman at all. Women were "erratic" and "emotional," Nixon volunteered to Mitchell, and did not deserve government jobs. (In another exchange, he shouted, "I don't even think women should be educated!" and in another, that they should be barred from voting.) But politically, he, his staff, and Mitchell understood, a woman at the court could help him at the polls in 1972. As Nixon said, no one would vote against him because he appointed a woman, while "one or two per cent . . . would say because he appointed a woman, I am for him," and "we got to pick up every half a percentage point we can." But a woman nominee must be "conservative." If he found such a person, he let Republican leaders know, he expected them to support her, and he anticipated confirmation. Senators "can't vote against the first woman, any more than they can vote against the first Negro. So they'll take a woman, provided she can read and write"[54] (figure 26).

The Justice Department went to work and zeroed in on fifty-six-year-old California Court of Appeals Justice Mildred Lillie, whom reporters typically described as "statuesque and vivacious" and a great cook. (One sign of changing attitudes came when the *New York Times* drew fire for extolling her "bathing beauty figure," but progress came slow: Mitchell felt compelled to assure Nixon that Lillie was no "frigid bitch."). She had a great story. Born in Iowa, she had been raised on a California farm by a single mother and had worked her way through Berkeley and its law school, where after a rough first year, she then did

JUDICIAL COOK — Justice Mildred Lillie offers buffet dinner guests homemade, rich fudge cake.
Times photo

Order in the Kitchen!
Justice Lillie Presiding

BY CECIL FLEMING
Times Staff Writer

"Food should be served with a heavy hand and a lavish heart," said Justice Mildred Lillie. "I prefer to have lots of food so no one can leave my table hungry."

These are not idle words from the statuesque and vivacious judge. She shared with us a buffet menu including two meat entrees, accompanied with a relish, salad and vegetable she feels complement each entree.

But when it comes to dessert she goes all out and has at least three—usually an assortment of cakes, her specialty.

Her busy schedule as Justice of the District Court of Appeal does not allow as much time to entertain as she desires but at least once a month she prepares a sit-down dinner for six or eight friends. At least every other month she invites about 20 for a buffet dinner in her large Wilshire district apartment.

"When you like to cook it's no burden to do the planning and preparation for friends," she said. "I do plan a meal to include some made-ahead dishes, though."

Justice Lillie confesses her love of food and plenty of it dates back to her youth, when she lived on a fruit ranch in San Joaquin Valley. Everyone was busy on the farm and, at the age of 12, it became her task to take over the family cooking.

She learned to get along with the behemoth wood stove, but still remembers the many times she had to cut the top from the cake layers that peaked in the center from too much heat at the wrong time.

"I have had my share of cooking disappointments, but everyone has," she laughed. "No one becomes much of a cook until they have had some

Please Turn to Page 26, Col. 1

Figure 26 Justice Lillie's male admirers frequently stressed that she was not just a good judge, but a good cook and baker too. Here she dispensed her signature fudge cake. Copyright ©1966 *The Los Angeles Times*. Reprinted with permission.

well enough. She applied to the Oakland District Attorney's office, only to be told by Earl Warren that he did not believe in women lawyers. As governor, however, Warren appointed her to the municipal court and later to the Los Angeles Superior Court, where she reorganized its domestic relations division. Warren's successor put her on the court of appeals in 1958, and she had been there ever since. Like many California lawyers, Nixon knew of her. "She's been a judge longer than I can remember," he said. Though Lillie was a Democrat in name, one mutual friend wrote the president, she was "as strong a Republican Conservative as I am." And on the basis of the review of her opinions by the "hard-nosed" Rehnquist, Mitchell reported to the president that she was more conservative than anyone Nixon had nominated to the court and that the California Supreme Court had reversed her frequently enough "to give her a good standing with the law and order people."[55]

To sweeten the pot, when Justice Department officials interviewed her in Washington, Lillie brought along her Italian American lawyer husband, Alfredo Falcone, whom Mitchell described as "a plodding mediocrity" with lots of debts, but "distinguished looking." That was good news at a time when Nixon's Transportation Secretary John Volpe, members of Congress, and White House strategists like Pat Buchanan were pressing Nixon to appoint an Italian American to the court. Her religion was right too. "Tell her if she isn't a Catholic to get busy, get over there, God damn it and get confirmed," the president joked to Mitchell. But she was, and an observant one, to boot.[56]

When he was not ribbing Mitchell about their proud legacy of putting the first woman on the court, Nixon radiated enchantment with their pick. "This is a chance to get a conservative in the Court and at the same time we can get a woman," he cheered. "[They] can vote against a Southerner, but they can't vote against a woman because she's conservative." Nixon also relished credit for historic firsts, and, as he said, Lillie's would become "the woman's seat."[57]

The other likely nominee, forty-nine-year old Herschel Friday, a Democrat in a leading Little Rock law firm, had been one of Burger's choices from the beginning. A graduate of Little Rock Junior College (which became the University of Arkansas at Little Rock) and University of Arkansas Law School, Friday had clerked for a US district judge for five years and taught law at the University of Arkansas before settling into private practice, where, like Mitchell, he specialized in bond law. By 1970, Friday had also defended thirteen Arkansas school districts against desegregation lawsuits, which had paid his law firm $200,000. His clients included the Little Rock School Board in the case in which the Eisenhower administration ultimately sent in federal troops after Governor Orval Faubus defied court orders to enroll African Americans at Little Rock's Central High. "I've known him, worked with him for twenty-five years, never thought of him, actually," Mitchell volunteered. "Burger keeps coming back to him."[58]

Actually, the chief justice probably preferred another Southerner he also promoted, fifty-two-year-old US District Judge Frank Johnson of Alabama. Among many other things, Johnson's decisions had ended the Montgomery Bus Boycott by desegregating buses, and helped make possible the 1965 march by civil rights activists from Selma to Montgomery. Martin Luther King maintained that the judge "gave true meaning to the word *justice*"—and at an enormous price. White supremacists bombed the house of Frank Johnson's mother. His only child committed suicide after years of ostracism. The judge himself received so many death threats that federal agents accompanied him everywhere. He had also lost many friends, including his law school buddy, George Wallace. If Nixon wanted a "strict constructionist," Johnson fit the bill. He was a law-and-order judge, and as he said, "I'm not a segregationist, but I'm not a crusader, either. I don't make the law. I don't create the facts. I interpret the law." Hugo Black had hoped Johnson would succeed him, and legal elites would have cheered the appointment. So, surprisingly, would the many Alabamians urging him on the White House who were grateful to the judge for recently dismantling school segregation in Montgomery without requiring court-ordered busing. Perhaps Nixon should have realized that both non-Southerners, who respected Johnson for the enemies he had made, and Southern whites, who recognized that the judge was not the liberal that outsiders made him, would have applauded the nomination.[59]

As a legendary figure and long-time friend and fishing companion of Burger's, a fellow Eisenhower appointee to the bench, Frank Johnson would have fit in well at the court. And while he was on his boat one day, he later recalled, he received a radio message that the chief justice needed to speak with him. When Johnson returned to shore and telephoned Washington, Burger told him that the White House would soon announce his nomination. According to Johnson, however, three Alabama Republicans in Congress derailed it by persuading Mitchell that it would ruin them.[60]

Burger believed that Friday could work too, under the right circumstances. In a letter to Mitchell that made its way into the hands of the *Washington Post's* Supreme Court reporter, the chief justice said that the Arkansan possessed "superior professional qualifications." He would prove suitable if he were coupled with a "nationally recognized" judge—which Lillie was not.[61]

Rehnquist cleared Friday on Tuesday, October 12. "It is evident from our experience in the Haynsworth and Carswell confirmation fights that a demonstrable 'red neck' hostility to civil rights on the par of a nominee, or a personal animus against any minority, could well prove fatal to chances for confirmation," he reminded the administration. But Friday's public statements had always been "in good taste," and he had developed a cordial relationship with Thurgood Marshall and other opponents. "It would seem doubtful that any evidence of personal bias, even such as the rather thin case adduced against Carswell, could be proven against Friday." His tax returns were clean; his lack of experience in public office, no detriment. "Perhaps the actual practicing lawyer is entitled to at least one prototype to represent him on the Supreme Court," and his work for the ABA constituted "a form of public service."

While his nomination would doubtless disappoint civil rights activists and labor unions, and they would "probably try to defeat" Friday, Rehnquist predicted their failure. The administration's experiences showed that opponents "cannot successfully defeat a nominee unless they are able to unfurl some banner other than their own under which they can enlist some of the more middle-of-the road members of the Senate," he stressed. In the Haynsworth case, they had used ethics; in Carswell, a combination of "mediocrity" and racism. "From what we can tell now, there is no such outside rallying point in the case of Friday." But the Arkansan's name should be sent forward as quickly as possible, he cautioned, lest the approaching 1972 election cause the "the parallel" to Fortas's chief justice nomination to become more evident.[62]

"I think Friday's going to work pretty good," Mitchell told Nixon that same day. "Is he a really successful lawyer, big in the ABA?" the president wanted to know. Yes, he was a senior partner at the largest and most successful law firm in his state and a player in the association's house of delegates and board of governors. "Is he conservative?" Nixon wondered. "No question in my mind," Mitchell answered. "I think he'll be to the right of Burger. You see he's represented all the school boards," though Mitchell did not believe that would pose a problem in his confirmation, since everyone deserved legal representation. In addition, Friday had practiced law for years with Pat Mehaffey, who was now on the Eighth Circuit and was "to the right of the Sheriff of Nottingham." Nixon wanted to make sure Friday did not have "anything like the Klan in his background." No, Mitchell said. His wife had kept a scrapbook with all his press mentions, "and Rehnquist went all the way through it, beginning to end, and it's [the record of] just a lawyer." (How much more Rehnquist had done by way of background check than review clippings Beth Friday had saved remained unclear.) And Friday did not have "any other infirmities that you had with Haynsworth." Obviously, the memories of Haynsworth and Carswell still stung over at the Justice Department. Friday appealed to Nixon too. "We forget that there's a hell of a lot of stuff before the Supreme Court that involves corporations," he reasoned. They would sell Friday as an "Arkansas Harlan."[63]

"I'd like to send these two young lawyers down to comb him over," Haldeman said. "I welcome that," Mitchell answered. Yet the president did not like the idea that the rules for selection were changing. Told that Dean and Young would ask about extramarital affairs, he wondered aloud "how in the Christ" William O. Douglas had survived confirmation. He also resisted sending them out to California to meet Lillie, though Mitchell himself liked the idea of another look at her husband. "Now look," Nixon responded, before speculating that Falcone might be a thief, "I'm not going to go for somebody like Caesar's wife" because that person would have "never done a goddamn thing." The White House needed to anticipate the opposition, Haldeman and Ehrlichman argued. In the end, the president agreed it was good to "know the worst," while stressing that the worst would not necessarily deter him. John Dean and David Young would go to Little Rock and Los Angeles.[64]

Meanwhile, the attorney general would submit a list of six possible candidates to the American Bar Association on Tuesday, October 12, with instructions to Lawrence Walsh to concentrate on Lillie and Friday and to check them out quickly. Over the attorney general's objections, the list would include Byrd. As further camouflage, it would include three judges. The first, Justice Department alumna Sylvia Bacon, a Harvard Law School graduate with a reputation for fighting crime, must have been surprised. Although she had lobbied for a seat on DC's US District Court, its circuit court of appeals, the US Court of Customs and Patent Appeals, or the US Court of Claims in 1969, Nixon had then only named her to the DC superior court. The second, Fifth Circuit Judge Paul Roney, another Harvard Law alumnus, had just taken over the seat Carswell had vacated. The third, University of Mississippi Law School graduate Charles Clark, was also a recent Nixon appointee to the Fifth Circuit, to the disgust of *Newsday*, which labeled him "the segregationists' Perry Mason" because of the many times he had defended Mississippi's status quo as an attorney. The same day that the attorney general forwarded the list to the ABA, the president announced at his news conference that Byrd was "definitely" on it, two women were "under consideration," and he would make both nominations the following week.[65]

The administration had obviously learned the value of disguising its preferred candidates from the Poff experience. But six names in one week? "I expressly warned those acting for you that such an investigation could not be conducted without all of those names becoming public within 48 hours," Walsh reminded Mitchell once the mutual finger-pointing began later. "I was told that this was an acceptable risk and requested to go ahead as rapidly as possible."[66]

It took less than twenty-four hours for the names to leak. Nina Totenberg had the list of four Southerners and two women on the Dow Jones ticker by 4:03 P.M. on Wednesday, and she and other reporters instantly figured out that Lillie and Friday were its persons of interest. Totenberg had telephoned Walsh at his summerhouse, only to be told he would not speak with her on that line. He returned her call from a pay phone. (At the time, Totenberg found him "paranoid," but after Watergate, she realized that he was not.) The reporter tried unsuccessfully to "cajole" the list from him. Was Edward Gignoux one of the names? Totenberg finally asked. That well-regarded Eisenhower appointee to the First Circuit was a fifty-five-year-old graduate of Harvard College and Law School. Along with Department of Health, Education, and Welfare Secretary Elliot Richardson and three Southerners—Frank Johnson, Fifth Circuit Judge John Minor Wisdom, and University of Texas law professor Charles Alan Wright—Gignoux appeared on just about every list that Harvard law professors made of their ideal nominees. (Mitchell, however, did not consider him a strict constructionist.) "Oh, God, I wish it were," she remembered Walsh groaning, before he refused further comment. So Totenberg began telephoning the leaders of the legal establishment whom the Standing Committee on the Judiciary was likely to contact from her booth at the Supreme Court. "Lawyers talk," she said matter-of-factly years later.[67]

Predictably, the reaction to the list was one of dismay (figure 27). Few outside their own communities had even heard of the potential nominees, only two of whom, Byrd and Friday, possessed entries in *Who's Who*. "What is the caliber of the candidates," the *New York Times* asked rhetorically about the "career politician from West Virginia, former organizer for the Ku Klux Klan, a Senator whose public record is marked by racism and reaction"; the DC judge "whose only claim to fame lies in the tough 'law and order' legislation" she wrote while at the Justice Department; the former Los Angeles "domestic relations judge"; the "Little Rock lawyer whose most notable legal work was in resisting school desegregation"; and the "two respectable if undistinguished Federal Court of Appeals judges who at least are not known to have anything against them"? The unknown and unremarkable candidates, the *Washington Post* lamented, made it clear that President Nixon insisted on treating the Supreme Court of the United States as though it were "some sort of minor commission." The *Wall Street Journal* declared that "we, and many others, feel that the President again may not be aiming high enough."[68]

The mainstream media reflected informed public opinion. Law professors and members of the bar began drafting petitions to oppose the names on the list. Rick Seymour went to Little Rock to investigate Friday's defense of school boards. Civil rights activists contended that "Nixon wants a racist Court." The National Women's Political Caucus pointedly declared that it did not support "women on the Court merely because they are women," but wanted ones who cared about human rights and deserved "the distinction they are receiving." In the Senate, some voiced regret over their votes against Haynsworth. And Bayh hinted that he would again lead the opposition if Nixon nominated anyone on the list that Ted Kennedy ranked as "one of the great insults to the Supreme Court in its history."[69]

Against this outcry stood a lonely and joyous Martha Mitchell. "Friday is my man," she told the *Washington Post* of her fellow Arkansan. She liked Lillie too. "We have just got to get a woman on the Court this time," she insisted.[70]

Prospects Being Studied for Seats on Supreme Court

Judge Sylvia Bacon   Senator Robert C. Byrd   Judge Charles Clark

The New York Times

Herschel H. Friday   Judge Mildred Loree Lillie   Judge Paul H. Roney

PRESIDENT ASKS BAR UNIT TO CHECK 6 FOR HIGH COURT

2 Women Are on the List and 4 Men From Border States or the South

MOST NOT WELL KNOWN

Potential Choices Do Not Include Leading Judicial Figures Cited Earlier

By FRED P. GRAHAM
Special to The New York Times

WASHINGTON, Oct. 13— The Nixon Administration has sent the names of six persons, including two women, to be investigated by the American Bar Association as potential nominees to the two vacant seats on the Supreme Court.

The four men on the list are all from Southern or Border states, which indicates that the vacant "Southern seat" will be filled by a man. Assuming that President Nixon follows tradition and does not name two Southerners at once, the other appointment would therefore propose the first woman Justice.

Figure 27 The media and legal profession took a dim view of Richard Nixon's reported choices for the court, Mildred Lillie and Hershel Friday, in 1971. Fred Graham, "President Asks Bar Unit to Check 6 for High Court: 2 Women Are on the List and 4 From Border States or the South; Most Not Well Known," *New York Times*, October 14, 1971.

The criticism enraged Nixon. He and Mitchell blamed the ABA for the leaks, though Totenberg "flatly" denied her source was there. "The bar broke its pick with me," the president raged to Mitchell on Thursday, and "the next time we have an appointment they aren't going to get a chance to look at it." What did its "sanctimonious" members know about judicial candidates anyway? "I mean good God, I can take a bar examination better than any of those assholes." The ABA had not embarrassed Burger and Blackmun, he added. When Mitchell tried to remind the president that he had appointed Burger and Blackmun without consulting the ABA, Nixon insisted the White House had checked them out with the bar. Not so, the attorney general responded. "Well, that was our mistake here then, I guess, . . . letting the bar have a crack at it," the president finally said. "I expect the bar to be helpful in this picture by coming out with the solid approvals of Friday and Lillie," Mitchell comforted him.[71]

Push the bar to act quickly, Nixon instructed on October 14. Tell Walsh that he and the Standing Judiciary Committee members "don't have to check too damn much for someone like Friday, who has been practicing 25 years or Lillie, who's been on the bench 25 years. Friday and Lillie ought to be checking on them rather than the other way around." In the meantime, the Administration would leak the news that it was considering other names too. Poff's name had gotten out, and they had eaten him alive. The President did not want his nominees destroyed before he had the chance to make the case for them. So, Jack Anderson and Nina Totenberg reported, a "surly" Mitchell obligingly held an off-the-record press conference complete with cocktails, only to be asked by Totenberg which expletives the president had used in discussing the ABA. (It was left for John Osborne of the *New Republic* to report that the president had said "Fuck the ABA!" and that "the operative word is one of his favorites.") Nixon's press secretary encountered an equally skeptical reaction when he said it was "incorrect to assume that there are only six people under consideration." Washington's focus, as well as that of the media, remained on Lillie and Friday.[72]

Totenberg had "impeccable" sources inside the court too, who made their own unhappiness clear. According to her, Harlan had considered sending Nixon a sharp protest from his sickbed. The seven members of the court were "extremely perturbed," with even "conservative" justices worrying that the president sought to "denigrate" it. Moreover, after reading some opinions of Lillie's, one liberal justice "promptly got drunk." Soon afterward, someone at the Supreme Court complained to the White House.[73]

Just as Mitchell had always assured Nixon that the ABA would approve Lillie and Friday, so he had promised that the chief justice would take the news of Lillie's nomination like a "good soldier," though it would prove a "very grave shock" to him. Nixon sympathized with Burger, who Mitchell reported was "dying" and telephoning him "maybe twice a day." The justices lived together as closely as astronauts "inside a space ship," the president reminded Mitchell. "You ought to soften him up a little," he instructed the attorney general on October 11, and then Nixon would tell Burger he was naming Lillie. "He's played the game with us so well that I think we should apprise him in advance," Mitchell agreed. On October 14, the attorney general reported that he had heard again from the chief justice. Burger had said that Friday was "great," but argued that "the only way to strengthen the Court" was to reserve the other vacancy for a "nationally known" judge, and reviewed "the same bunch of names." The chief justice had referred to Justice Arthur Goldberg's resignation from the court, the "completely unwarranted rejection of Judge Haynsworth and the subsequent rejection of Judge Carswell," LBJ's "seemingly hurried" effort to elevate Fortas to the chief justiceship, and Fortas's resignation in disgrace as "wounds" that had bruised the court.

Burger had also made it clear that "he's not anxious to have a woman" in his long letter to the attorney general. "No more anxious than I am," Nixon replied. "I am sure he will take it in good grace," Mitchell still insisted.[74]

That hope evaporated later that day, when Burger came to visit the attorney general with a letter resigning effective September of 1972. Of course it was a bluff, but it won him White House attention. "We've got Chief Justice problems," Mitchell informed the president and Ehrlichman on October 15. Burger said that women had not been "exposed to the judicial process long enough" and were not sufficiently "distinguished to rank a seat at the Court." The president pointed out that Lillie had served as a judge for as long as Burger. While Burger based his case on merit and qualifications, he simply did not want a woman as a colleague, Mitchell said. The chief justice had even raised the specter of the slippery slope: If the administration needed a woman justice, "you should have a Jew and a black and a Chinaman and a Burmese." Was Burger "representing others on the Court?" Nixon wondered. The attorney general inferred that "there was a rather wide discussion of the situation up there yesterday" because the chief justice had said that "Blackmun told him how great an advocate Herschel Friday was."

Nixon's immediate instinct was to accept the resignation. "They're all undistinguished," he said of the seven justices then on the Supreme Court. Tell Burger to go back and "read the editorials about him" at his appointment. "I had to defend him." Though Burger's press had been largely favorable, except at venues like the Nation and New Republic, Mitchell agreed. "I brought that subject matter up with him," the attorney general said, and the chief justice replied, 'Well, we must have been reading different editorials.'" Like most presidents, Nixon hated prima donnas, and he fumed that Burger was behaving as badly as Federal Reserve Chairman Arthur Burns. "We'd be better off having him resign now" than in an election year, he reasoned. "The Court would just fall apart," Mitchell warned. "We'll consult him, but he isn't going to name them," the president decided. "Well, we shouldn't even be consulting with him, actually," Mitchell responded, in an apparent reference to Nixon's pledge to avoid cronyism when he named Burger.

Earl Warren had ruined the court by increasing its workload, the president and the attorney general now agreed. "Warren Burger has changed that substantially, but they still consider too many cases," Mitchell said. Elderly justices compounded the problem, Nixon added, sounding like FDR trying to justify packing the court. But when the attorney general had told Burger that Black and Harlan "could not carry their load," the chief justice had responded, according to Mitchell, that "White and Potter Stewart and Brennan are so stupid that he can't assign some of the cases . . . to them because he doesn't know what they're going to write." Let him know that Lillie was "a workhorse," Nixon advised.

Since they also agreed that Burger "is really one of the best appointments we've made," they settled on a strategy by which Mitchell would inform him that "the conversation never happened and that he better go about being Chief Justice in the interest of the Court and country and stop this foolish nonsense." Tell him that just as the times had demanded an African American on the court, now they required a woman, the president directed. "It was hard for them to take a black, particularly a dumb black, and at least I have given them a bright woman." Another vacancy or two would materialize for the court. Burger had to become Lillie's "cheerleader," Ehrlichman emphasized. As Nixon and Mitchell said, the chief justice should be reminded that in Friday, he was getting half a loaf.[75]

But serious doubts were developing about that half. Not every Arkansan rejoiced at the prospect of Justice Friday, though the state's Democratic senators, John McClellan and J. William Fulbright, did. McClellan, who described Friday as "a personal acquaintance of mine for more than twenty years" and "one of the finest advocates I have ever known," proved especially enthusiastic. So were Representative Wilbur Mills, the Arkansas Trial Lawyers Association, and the Arkansas Association of Women Lawyers. In Little Rock, the *Arkansas Democrat* declared that Friday had "our support and the support of a majority of the people of Arkansas if President Nixon decides to nominate him for a seat on the Supreme Court." But the *Democrat*'s competitor, the liberal *Arkansas Gazette*, attacked the prospective nominee's suitability and accused the local bar of rallying "around Mr. Friday rather like a herd of angry bison protecting one of its own." *Gazette* editors could not think of a "better way to cultivate the segregationist South, against the blandishments of George Wallace, than to appoint the lawyer identified more than any other with the fight against school integration in Little Rock." Former governor Winthrop Rockefeller, a progressive Republican, telephoned the White House to complain that Friday was "an avid redneck segregationist whose only qualification was that he is a bond salesman friend of John Mitchell's." The president of the Arkansas AFL-CIO accused Friday's firm of "union-busting." The president of the state NAACP expressed displeasure as well. (Some liberals came to regret their objections later.)[76]

The controversial nature of the nomination, even in Arkansas, did not bother Nixon. But when Dean and Young spent October 13 and 14 in Little Rock interviewing Friday, they sounded alarm bells. After seven hours with him on Wednesday, they reported that he had no ethical problems and was "not a 'red neck,'" but "a 'lawyer' who has represented civil rights defendants." He was "clean as a hound's tooth." He was a "brilliant legal technician," and a very successful one. His Little Rock house was "substantial," and his net worth exceeded $600,000 (about $3.5 million in 2016 dollars). He belonged to an all-white

Baptist church, and he had no "association with the KKK" or any secret or racist group. Beyond "a slight case of hemorrhoids" and the loss of hearing in one ear, his health was good. He was happily married. "I've had the same girl all these years," Friday informed his interlocutors. He belonged to a luncheon club and country club that included Jewish members, but no African American ones. He liked to hunt quail and play golf. He was a registered Democrat, "but that's not the way I vote." He was not an intellectual. His extracurricular reading was restricted to *U.S. News and World Reports* and the local paper (doubtless the *Arkansas Democrat*), and Friday volunteered that he was "not the kind of person that comes home and picks up 'The Life and Times of Chief Justice Marshall.'"[77]

When they turned to civil rights and crime at the end of the day, Dean and Young began to worry. Ehrlichman reported that Dean had said, "I don't know if this man is conservative" and planned to return the next day and "hit him fresh." After hearing that, Nixon became anxious. "I can't do it if he's not conservative," the president fretted. "I wonder if we shouldn't just give out [up] on this Southern thing."[78]

Thursday morning went no better. Though Rehnquist and others at the Justice Department had spoken with Friday, they had apparently barely covered his views of the Constitution, Dean and Young reported. The potential nominee knew next to nothing about constitutional law and proved unable "to articulate his personal beliefs on many of the fundamental social issues of the times."[79]

They had reviewed issues with him, including church and state, other First Amendment questions, privacy, capital punishment, arrest, and the jury system, and found his answers largely "superficial." For all the media focus on *Miranda*, for example, Friday had no position on it. While his instincts were "conservative, rational, realistic and moderate," he showed "little evidence of a reflective and strong mind that could lead on the court or articulate a substantive conservative philosophy on fundamental issues." As Ehrlichman informed the president after another telephone call, Friday had finally told Dean, "'John, you're going to have to tell me what to say. ... I want to be with the President,'" by which he presumably meant that he intended to echo Nixon. He could coach Friday through confirmation, Dean added, but he was unsure how he would vote five years from now. "'You're going to have to tell the President for me that I cannot assure him that Herschel Friday is a conservative,'" Dean concluded, except with respect to civil rights, and there, he was uncertain how solid Friday's convictions were. Of course, Nixon also wanted to know whether Mrs. Friday was "a socialite" who would fall prey "to that goddamn Georgetown set" that could turn Friday into another Potter Stewart and leave the president resentful that "I appointed that son of a bitch," something he knew he would not feel about Lillie.[80]

But the White House had no fallback, and time was short. Given the reactions to those on the ABA list, no one else on it was a winner, and Byrd had telephoned Secretary of Treasury John Connally to say he preferred a legislator's life and did not want to be considered. (The White House kept that quiet as long as possible in the hope that the senator would "scare the liberals" into approving anyone Nixon nominated who was "not a member of the Ku Klux Klan.") When Mitchell suggested Lewis Powell again, he and the president again agreed he was too old. Why put someone on the court who would only "last four or five years" or stay there when he became senile? Moreover, Rehnquist and Senator McClellan did not share Dean's doubts about Friday, the attorney general emphasized. Given the nature of the Arkansan's law practice, the president also believed, "there is no potential for this guy to have a liberal bend." Finally, Nixon concluded, Friday was "pretty close to Burger" and had said he wanted to follow the president. They would educate him about presidential policies "for the good of the country," Nixon resolved. "I think we'd better go with Friday, John." Nobody told them that Dean had privately concluded that the Arkansan would probably "withdraw from consideration, realizing he did not have the credentials. Another session like the one we had put him through in Little Rock would do it."[81]

The four-and-a-half-hour interview with Lillie and Falcone by Dean and Young on Thursday afternoon proceeded more positively, though the staffers' written account of it damned with faint praise. Like others, Dean and Young could not resist commenting on the appearance of this large but not overweight and "rather handsome woman with excellent hearing." They had "found nothing" in the background of either her or her husband that would embarrass the administration. "We were reasonably impressed with her as an articulate woman of considerable breadth and experience from a legal as well as personal point of view." Young added that she was apparently "a most able woman" and "not an intellectual lightweight," possessed "stern and strict" views of justice, and was "confident enough to hold her own on the Court."

They had uncovered no problems in Lillie's legal education or judicial record. There was the matter of her first semester in law school, when she had received a D in one course and failed another because of her adored uncle's death, but she had made them up, and received As and Bs in every other course afterward. Obviously proud of her supervision and reorganization of the Los Angeles Domestic Relations Court, she joked, "there are God knows how many little Mildred Lillie Gonzales[s] running around California as a result of my attempts at reconciliation." She had written more than 1,160 opinions as an appellate judge, and she estimated that of her cases that the California Supreme Court then heard, it had reversed two-thirds and affirmed one-third, which she maintained was "about average" for an appellate judge. She had just sniped occasionally and indirectly at the Warren Court in her opinions by, for example, observing that precedent required her to reverse a trial court although the defendant was clearly guilty. She had never sentenced anyone to death, but seemed unworried about doing so. She knew of no newspaper editorials attacking her decisions, and she believed that lawyers in her courtroom thought she treated them fairly. "You can't be a judge and please everyone," she said, when they asked about her antagonists and advocates. She believed that the ACLU, the local Criminal Bar Association, the National Lawyers' Guild, and liberal Democrats who championed Shirley Hufstedler would oppose her, but she anticipated no problem from labor. She numbered among her supporters Governor Reagan (though he preferred William French Smith) and Los Angeles Mayor Sam Yorty, who thought "she would be an outstanding appointment because she has not gone along with the Warren criminal law decisions except as compelled to do so." Lillie also included among her referees William French Smith, the Los Angeles County sheriff, and four California Supreme Court justices.[82]

Dean and Young had found her personal life respectable too. Neither she nor Falcone had any conflicts of interest, and though some tax liens had been filed against them in the past, those issues were resolved. Falcone had once been sued for nonpayment of a bill for a defective hi-fi, but it had been settled. Asked outright if there was anything in his past that could prove embarrassing, Falcone had only mentioned the hi-fi. After a complete physical six months ago, Lillie's doctor had given her "a clean bill," and she had "no psychiatric problems." African Americans and Jews lived in her apartment house. She and Falcone were serious Catholics whom a cardinal had married. She gave speeches on Americanism, law and order, and law enforcement, but had never accepted a fee. Her reading outside work was limited to newspapers, news magazines, and recently, Mario Puzo's *The Godfather*. Her hobbies were cooking and oil painting, and she was very good at both. She did not drink much, did not gamble, and had told Dean and Young that "with an Italian husband who has a Latin temperament," she would be "crazy" to have an affair "even if I wanted to!" Though she had a different name from her husband, that was only because by the time her first husband had died, voters knew her as Mildred Lillie. She had kept "far away" from "the women's lib movement" and "personally considered it to be somewhat dangerous." That was just fine with Nixon, who was making the appointment not for the "liberals" in "women's lib" but for "decent women."[83]

If Dean and Young did not sound that enthusiastic on paper, Dean made up for it when he telephoned his impressions and also took some of the sting out of Burger's reaction to Lillie. "He says she's a goddamn jewel," Haldeman reported to the president on Friday, October 15, a "tough, able, personable, marvelous woman." Ehrlichman agreed that Dean described Lillie as "the greatest thing since sliced bread." Dean had "worked over" her husband and concluded that he was "not great" but would pose no impediment, Ehrlichman added. "He says she has all the right vibrations . . . on crime, on administration of justice, civil rights." It didn't matter that she had not issued any civil rights opinions because "we will generally find that somebody that's hard on law and order is also hard on civil rights," Nixon reasoned. He did not even flinch when his attorney general grumbled that Lillie wore "loose-fitting clothes." "Ah, she looks like most women who study law," the president reasoned. He was already planning to introduce her to the world as Mildred Falcone.[84]

Dean, however, feared that the ABA would not share his positive assessment. He liked both Lillie and the idea of a woman on the court. He remembered telling Ehrlichman, though, that her husband warranted further investigation and that the "make-no-waves" Standing Committee on the Federal Judiciary might well find Lillie "not qualified" or "at best—have no opinion" because of her sex. "But they'll never say that. She's very conservative on criminal law issues," and the committee might well base its rating on her reversal rate. Someone should review what the California Supreme Court had said about her opinions, Dean advised. While he agreed to ask the Justice Department for that evaluation, Ehrlichman seemed untroubled and did not pass along Dean's warnings to the president.[85]

He should have. Lillie herself always blamed the negative contemporary reaction of her critics on sexism, and doubtless there was some. Was she inferior to G. Harrold Carswell, who had come so close to winning a Supreme Court seat? "I had served two years on the Municipal Court, nine years on the Superior Court and 12 years on the Court of Appeal, and I had heard every kind of case imaginable," she recalled in 1980. "I think I was just as qualified as any Supreme Court justice," and "I fully believe that the fact that I was a woman was [a] very serious [problem] to them." Dean, too, thought her the victim of "shameless gender discrimination." Certainly, by the time she died in 2002, when the legal profession welcomed women, her reputation had soared.[86]

But diminishing chauvinism alone cannot explain why Lillie had become so esteemed. She had broken two records for length of service: She worked fifty-five years in the California judiciary and forty-four years as an appellate judge. In 1984, though she was a Democrat and nearly seventy, California's Republican governor, George Deukmejian, had appointed her presiding justice of her division, a position she held for eighteen years. Present and past California governors in both parties and the chief justice of the California Supreme Court lionized her when she died, and one obituary insisted that "she was staunchly backed [for a seat on the US Supreme Court] by state Supreme Court justices and the Los Angeles County Bar Association." As one of her fellow judges said, she received a send-off "worthy of a head of state" attended by "hundreds of judges and lawyers" that included the ultimate Los Angeles tribute, the shutdown of two freeways by the California Highway Patrol for her funeral cortege.

We expect reporters and their subjects to speak well of the dead. How do we explain, though, the posthumous naming of the enormous Los Angeles County Law Library after Lillie, a singular honor?[87]

Perhaps after 1971, she worked harder at judging. By 1980, Los Angeles lawyers were lining up to report that Lillie was "underrated" because she had not demonstrated "her abilities" during her early years as an appellate justice. "She's shown a remarkable tendency over the last four to six years to moderate, mellow and accept new ideas," one said.* "Her opinions today are night and day compared to the ones 10 or 15 years ago." Though they still found her "somewhat conservative," he and others agreed she had become "less predictable and dogmatic."[88]

Just as there was reason to question Friday's qualifications in 1971, though, there was then reason to question Lillie's, and many did. "A warm personality, she is not known as a judicial thinker, and even her admirers admit that she seems to go out of her way to interpret the law against criminal defendants," *Time* observed. She ran her courtroom with an iron hand, and some did not even find her warm. Over the weekend of October 16 and 17, Harvard law professor Laurence Tribe, who was coordinating a group of students who evaluated Nixon's candidates, wrote his dean, "Lillie is an abrasive, small-minded, unimaginative, embittered woman."[89]

More important, her opinions were "long, obscure, confused, and often myopically oblivious to critical issues and controlling cases." Tribe's devastating study revealed that over a four-month period in the spring and summer of 1971, the California Supreme Court had reversed four of them and had also identified serious problems with her reasoning. Despite the court's record for progressivism, it included two conservative members, and it had acted unanimously. In one case, the court intervened after Lillie had upheld the effort by the city of Los Angeles to apportion representation among city council voting districts according to the number of registered voters, rather than population. Like the city, Lillie cited as authority a 1965 Hawaii federal court decision that she neglected to mention the United States Supreme Court had subsequently challenged. When the California Supreme Court reversed, it scolded that her reliance on the

---

* Demanding in the courtroom, Lillie also remained "witty and charming"—and peppery. In 1979, she joined an opinion by her ally, Justice Robert Thompson, which included a footnote making clear what the majority thought of the allegation that they favored obscenity by the dissenter, a frequent opponent. Read together, the first letter of each of footnote two's seven sentences spelled out SCHMUCK. When the *Los Angeles Times* called attention to the note, Thompson pointed out that the German definition of "schmuck" was "jewel." Don DeBenedictis, "Justice Mildred L. Lillie," *LADJ*, September 12, 1980 ("witty"); *People v. Arno*, 90 Cal. App. 3d 505 (1979); Roger Grace, "Div. One: A Court of Appeal Division with a Tradition of Tomfoolery," *Metropolitan News-Enterprise*, January 3, 2002.

1965 decision "is not merely misplaced; it also reveals a cavalier disregard for that basic jurisprudential principle that the decision of a court of superior jurisdiction supersedes contrary holdings of inferior tribunals."[90]

Tribe could respond so quickly and effectively because he had recently spent a year clerking for California Supreme Court Justice Matthew Tobriner before he arrived at the United States Supreme Court to work for Potter Stewart. "That some (perhaps all) of the cases [written by Lillie and reversed] appear at pages of Cal. App. [California Appellate Reports] which are removed from the bound volume as soon as the California Supreme Court grants a hearing makes them so hard to locate as to create a substantial risk that they, and other opinions like them, could well be overlooked by someone without access to law clerks at the California Supreme Court," he explained at the time. He remembered that Lillie was considered "a real lightweight by the justices of California's highest court at the time I clerked there, and not just [by] the more liberal justices either. The lack of respect for Lillie wasn't ideological or, as far as I could tell, at all sexist; it simply reflected what people thought were her woeful inadequacies as a lawyer, all of them painfully evident in the weak opinions she tended to write." (That would have been news to Lillie, who, recall, had listed four of the justices as references.) After Tribe briefed reporter John MacKenzie about his research, the *Post* and *Los Angeles Times* prominently featured it on Monday morning. An FBI agent visited the Harvard professor at his office that day to demand citations to the opinions he had criticized and to inquire whether he "would say 'for the record' that she is unqualified for the Supreme Court," as he now did. The agent asked "seriously intimidating" questions about Tribe's motivation, the president of Harvard complained to the Justice Department.[91]

Many whom the FBI did not question agreed with Tribe. Nina Totenberg was new at her job and a college dropout, she remembered, but she knew enough to know that Lillie's opinions were unsound. The reporter received "a lot of help" in making the case against the judge from clerks to other California appellate judges, who thought poorly of Lillie and sent along opinions she might otherwise have missed. "How they ever thought they'd get this through is beyond me," Totenberg said of the Nixon administration. She compared the president's promotion of Lillie to George W. Bush's nomination of Harriet Miers: "It's Harriet Miersesque." Twenty UCLA Law School professors signed a petition to the White House maintaining that though the time to name a woman to the court was "long overdue . . . Justice Lillie's judicial decisions indicate that she lacks the competence to be a Supreme Court justice." The Los Angeles County Bar Association was reportedly unhappy with the idea of Lillie, too, as were other judges. One lawyer who said he spoke for Los Angeles Superior Court judges privately informed the White House that "she just does not follow and/or know the law and rather renders decisions which are completely inconsistent with case law," Dean reported. "Mrs. Lillie is a very nice person and no one has any basis to attack her other than her lack of legal judgment," where her reputation was "very bad," the attorney had said, and her husband was no great lawyer either. Roger Traynor, the celebrated former chief justice of the California Supreme Court, proved only slightly more positive when he publicly characterized Lillie as a "prodigious" and experienced worker. "I would be hard put to say she is not qualified," Traynor maintained, "but I couldn't say she is distinguished."[92]

The White House and the Justice Department, however, pressed forward. Rehnquist took the unusual step of supplying reporters with a memorandum that avoided discussion of Lillie's legal reasoning and characterized her reversal rate as "typical." His defense just supported speculation that she was a front runner, which, of course, guaranteed that reporters would continue digging. Their investigation of Los Angeles court records revealed that despite what he told Dean, Falcone had "been sued at least 22 times over the past 10 years by credit bureaus, former employees and others." Nixon considered the resultant publicity "a goddamn cheap shot." Then Rehnquist produced a memorandum justifying those lawsuits too. The assistant attorney general had not previously provided the document to the ABA Standing Committee on the Federal Judiciary, and several of its angry members questioned Rehnquist's integrity. Just as discussion of Robert Byrd qualifications, or lack of them, consumed the first weekend after Nixon's search for two justices began, so discussion of Lillie's reversal rates, Falcone's debts, Friday's defense of school boards, and other bad press filled the second.[93]

It was now Monday, October 18, and Nixon wanted to announce the nominations on Thursday. A revolt against Lillie and Friday was brewing inside the White House and on Capitol Hill, as well as at the ABA. From the president's legislative team, Charles Colson reported to Ehrlichman that he was "getting very negative sounds" on Herschel Friday and that his intelligence suggested that "we will have about the same kind of a line up we had in the Haynsworth and Carswell situations." As an additional problem, since Mitchell knew Friday, "there will be an allegation of cronyism with the Attorney General." The nomination would just give Democrats a stick with which to bludgeon the president, and they might defeat it. "As bad as I want to see an Italian on the Court (and Mrs. Lillie comes the closest to it), I think we will run into similar problems although nowhere near as severe." Colson thought the Senate would confirm her, though "not without bloodshed." Leonard Garment warned the president that whether Friday and Lillie had the qualities to succeed as Supreme Court justices was "largely guesswork" and that "there is a growing feeling" that Lillie "is not qualified." The shift from "the utopian activism of the Warren Court to the judicial realism of the Nixon Court" demanded "not lesser but larger judicial minds and talents."[94]

At his meeting with the president that Monday morning, Haldeman, too, raised doubts about both candidates. Lillie's critics were hammering away at her record. "Friday just has no distinction other than the fact that John Mitchell had known him," he said, and no one was sure he was conservative. Nixon reassured his chief of staff that "[o]rdinary" people did not worry about "whether a judge is mediocre or not." Unusually, Haldeman disagreed and said they now did "because of Carswell." To read the papers, Nixon insisted, was to think that "everybody in the country" was "just panting" for the president to name his Supreme Court nominees when a pollster would find that the subject interested just 15% of Americans. "It's not that big," Nixon maintained. "And despite all the talk about it, Carswell and Haynsworth didn't mean all that much either."[95]

Mitchell also received pushback at a White House-Justice Department staff meeting that afternoon in Ehrlichman's office to apprise him of Dean and Young's research. "I led with a bit of song and dance about our visits, entertained all questions, and I am sure—notwithstanding my efforts to the contrary—thoroughly embarrassed both Rehnquist and Mitchell with the sloppy work they had done on Herschel Friday, while more than corroborating their choice of Mildred Lillie," Dean recalled. As the meeting broke up, Dean reported that a newsman had asked him if Nixon was considering Rehnquist for the post. As Dean, who was by now promoting Rehnquist, hoped, "[t]hat got everyone's attention. When the journalist had asked Rehnquist if he might get the job, Dean related, the assistant attorney general had said that Nixon would never choose him. "'I'm not from the South, I'm not a woman, and I'm not mediocre.'" As the assembled audience chortled, Rehnquist flushed. "When the laughter stilled, he nodded his head up and down with a boyish grin. 'Yeah, I said that, but it was off the record.'"[96]

Mitchell then went in to see the president. The seed Haldeman had planted that morning now sprouted. "The Haynsworth and Carswell deal[s] sort of rubbed off on me," the president reminded his attorney general. Mitchell, however, bore unexpectedly glad tidings. Burger was singing a different song about Lillie, the Attorney General announced. The Chief Justice had been ill when he threated to resign, and he had resolved to stay in bed "and not add to our problems." (Whether Burger had really changed his tune was uncertain: Dean subsequently heard that he lobbied at least two members of the ABA Standing Committee on the Federal Judiciary committee to oppose Lillie).[97]

Yet there was bad news as well. Standing Committee on the Federal Judiciary Chairman Walsh did not think the bar would rank Lillie "qualified," though he had been unable to name any woman in her age group who was. Tribe's memorandum had dealt her a mortal blow, though the Harvard professor insisted that his work "formed but a part of a large mosaic—pieced together throughout the country—pointing toward the same general conclusion," and that "many" deserved credit for revealing her inadequacy. "Holmes and Brandeis dissented," Nixon now illogically informed Mitchell, "so they would have been reversed. Bullshit reversal rate. Goddamn them." It was not just the "mediocrity issue," Mitchell stressed. Falcone required further investigation. The committee chairman had reported that interest groups were challenging the candidates too: Walsh had just received an urgent letter from Roy Wilkins and the Leadership Conference insisting that "mediocrity on the Court is a civil rights issue. Progress has been made in the last two decades because of the preeminent stature and prestige of the Court," and endangering that stature and prestige would jeopardize the future. Walsh had informed Mitchell that he doubted the ABA would rank Friday highly, though perhaps it might award him a lukewarm "not opposed" rating. "You know these son of a bitches are all looking for somebody that's nationally known," Mitchell said. "I don't think the appointment of the first woman should be of a woman the bar says is not qualified," Nixon now informed Mitchell, and "I think they're going to rip Friday up."[98]

"A Day They're Going to Remember"

"One thing I want to do is surprise them," the president said of the ABA, his other critics, and reporters, before adding the obvious: "I want to screw them." Lewis Powell was a nationally known lawyer based in Richmond, Virginia, and past president of the American College of Trial Lawyers, American Bar Foundation, and American Bar Association. "You think Powell's the best man?" Nixon asked that Monday. "I guess," Mitchell answered skeptically. What did Burger think of him? The chief justice saw Powell as "mature" and "tough," the attorney general said. "I know that's a bit of a shock to you," Nixon now volunteered apologetically to Mitchell, but Powell was the right choice. Who cared if he was a year older than Burger? "We won't desert the South. I think Powell is perfect for that reason, and I'll just take the easy older man." Nixon decided to substitute Powell for Friday. "Virginia means a little more to us than Arkansas," he reasoned, and no one would call Powell undistinguished.

Even now, however, the president was not quite ready to give up Lillie. "Should we make a deal with Walsh if I can?" Mitchell asked. "Yes. Yes sir," Nixon enthusiastically replied. "Don't you think that really would be better? Then we can say, look, you'll get her, we'll give you Lewis Powell . . . Just say 'we just don't want the bar to say that a woman is unqualified.' "[99]

Here was a solution born of desperation. Powell had insisted in 1970 that he did not want to serve on the Supreme Court. What if he declined, and/or what if the Standing Committee on the Federal Judiciary disappointed the president about Lillie? Over the next two days, as they became increasingly frantic, the president and Mitchell tossed around several possibilities.

One was forty-five-year-old Senator Howard Baker, the Tennessee Republican who had almost defeated Hugh Scott and become Senate minority leader. "He's no crook," Nixon rationalized, and the ingrown Senate would approve him even if he were. Besides that, Scott and Griffin would throw themselves into winning Baker's confirmation "to get him the hell out of the Senate." Baker was a "good leader" and "a very persuasive political guy, and you know that court is political as hell." The president thought he would make "a damn good judge." Was the Tennessean really conservative? Mitchell wondered. Nixon thought so. In any event, the president predicted, he would side with the administration more often than Potter Stewart.[100]

Another option, the president mused, was William French Smith, "a hell of a good looking man," who had gone to Harvard Law School and chaired the University of California Board of Regents. Anyone who could ride herd on that group, Nixon reasoned, must be "a pretty good politician." No need to check up on him or submit his name to the ABA, the president said. Did Nixon know anything about Smith's clients or background? Mitchell asked. Was that information necessary? the president wanted to know. Smith was the senior partner at one of the two leading Los Angeles law firms, Gibson, Dunn & Crutcher.[101]

Another was William Mulligan, the former dean of Mitchell's alma mater, Fordham Law, a Catholic school, whom Nixon had recently put on the Second Circuit. "Every play we make to those Catholics" could help, the president and his attorney general agreed. Nixon also liked the fact that Fordham was not top tier because "this number one law school bullshit is getting me down." Though Mitchell worried that critics might call Mulligan mediocre, Nixon (naively) believed that any dean would impress the bar. He also reasoned that the deans of other Catholic law schools would rush to Mulligan's defense.[102]

The only appointment that would really pay off politically, the president and attorney general agreed, was a woman. So in the meantime, Nixon was sticking with Lillie, provisionally, and moving ahead on other fronts. But on Tuesday, while the attorney general was interviewing Baker as a possible fallback, the president telephoned with new information. A friend of his who was "a big wheel" in the Los Angeles bar had told him Lillie "would get a bad rap" from its members. That could say more about the bar than Lillie, Mitchell observed, but the signals he was receiving from the Standing Committee on the Federal Judiciary remained discouraging. "The bar may take us off the hook on the damn thing," Nixon now said hopefully. He had definitely turned against her. If Lillie received a "not qualified" rating from the Standing Committee, the White House and Justice Department could leak it, and women would blame the ABA, not the administration. "The bar has . . . big broad shoulders," the president rationalized. "[L]et them take the wrath of women."[103]

The following day, the ABA made its evaluations official. The Standing Committee on the Federal Judiciary split six-six on Friday, with half its members reporting him "not qualified" and the other half declaring itself not opposed to his nomination. "Why do you think they pissed on Friday?" Nixon wondered. "Civil rights," Mitchell answered. "Well, they'll do the same on Powell then, won't they?" Nixon asked. He too had a history of involvement with Southern school boards seeking to slow desegregation. "Nobody's going to have a chance," Mitchell laughed. The administration would use this sorry episode as an excuse to terminate its practice of asking the committee to prescreen potential nominees. "Boy, did Mitchell get burned," the president told Press Secretary Ron Ziegler. "This whole thing with the ABA is his idea, not mine."[104]

The vote against Lillie proved even more damning, with eleven members deeming her "not qualified." Leak that, Nixon directed: "She's the best qualified woman, but she's not qualified for the Supreme Court. Jesus, that's great."[105]

As the president hoped, the news of the ratings hit the press on Thursday, October 21, the day he planned to announce his nominations. When the ABA accused the Justice Department of releasing the information, Mitchell maintained that neither his department nor the White House had done so. Nixon enjoyed the machinations. He directed Ziegler to say that given the president's own background as a lawyer schooled in attorney–client privilege, the ABA's lack of respect for confidentiality had dismayed him. He also wanted Ziegler to take advantage of a *New York Times* report that morning that he was set to nominate Herschel Friday that day and that Lillie's candidacy "might be faltering." "Be sure to keep them haring off in the wrong direction," the president directed. "We'll give them a day that they're going to remember."[106]

On Tuesday, October 19, Mitchell had sounded out Powell and Baker—a combination that Nixon labeled "Southern strategy with a vengeance." Powell remained unenthusiastic. In fact, by his account, he twice told Mitchell no that day and recommended that the administration proceed with Herschel Friday. He and his wife did not want to move to Washington. He preferred his life as a lawyer to that of a judge. Civil rights activists would criticize his tenure as chair of the Richmond School Board and the Virginia State Board of Education, his condemnation of Martin Luther King's embrace of civil disobedience, and his membership in an all-white country club. Liberals would assail his client roster of huge corporations and his investments. He owned $1.5 million in stock holdings (nearly $9 million in 2016 dollars), and he had seen what happened to Clement Haynsworth. He had already turned the job down on grounds of age the previous year, and he was older now. When his name bubbled up again after

Harlan and Black retired, Powell had written his children, "I feel strongly . . . that a younger man should be put on the bench at this time when we have had a long period of ultra liberal control on the Court" so that the president could restore a "reasonable balance" to it. Moreover, Powell had a serious, deteriorating eye condition, and he had to check with his doctor.[107]

Powell thought he had turned down the nomination, but Mitchell had heard a maybe—or so he reported to the president. "Powell will do it if he possibly can," he informed Nixon. But he had to speak with his doctor about his eyes. Obviously sensing Powell's responsiveness to the call of duty, Mitchell had told him how much his appointment would benefit the country. "I think if you called him up and asked him, he would do it if he was blind," Mitchell informed Nixon. By now, the president had embraced the Powell prospect. "It would give us a terribly prestigious appointment," he enthused. "[T]wo years of Powell is worth twenty of anyone else, and that's the damn truth."[108]

Baker, Mitchell reported to Nixon, had been "knocked . . . off his feet with surprise," and he did not want to join the court either. Baker had pointed out that a justice's $60,000 salary would be cut in half by taxes, to which Mitchell had replied that he could supplement his salary by writing articles and giving talks, à la Justice Douglas. (Nixon added that they could "arrange" some additional money.) The senator then disappeared for the rest of the day and, though he had promised to telephone Mitchell by 5 P.M., was unreachable all evening. But the attorney general seemed more worried about Powell than Baker. What if they got the latter, but not the former? he asked Nixon.[109]

One option, Mitchell now added early Tuesday evening, was "this Bill Rehnquist over here that everybody is so high on." (Like Dean, White House aide Richard Moore was promoting him.) The forty-seven-year-old was an "arch-conservative" and a "tough guy," he had excelled at Stanford Law, and Lawrence Walsh had even asked why the administration did not nominate someone like Rehnquist. It was a change in tune for Mitchell. "It'd be a great appointment," the attorney general had originally told the president after Nixon mentioned that Senator Barry Goldwater had recommended Rehnquist, a fellow Arizonan, early in October, "but what the hell do you get out of that, politically?" (Perhaps Rehnquist might help out the administration and his chances by having a sex change, the president joked.) It was Nixon who waxed lukewarm now about how the man he variously referred to as "Renchburg" or "Rensler," and complained "dressed like a clown" and looked "Jewish" could help him. "How the hell could you just put a guy who's an assistant attorney general on the Court?" Nixon asked. Smith and Mulligan interested him more.[110]

That Tuesday night, the president thought he might have nailed down Powell. Unlike LBJ, Nixon did not enjoy lobbying people to accept jobs, but he made an exception in this case. "Warren Burger is extremely anxious to have a top-flight appointment at this time, and what happens in the next five years is terribly important," the president telephoned Powell to say. While Nixon stressed what Powell could do for the court, he also made it clear how much the criticism of his candidates had damaged the administration. "[W]ell, let's put it quite bluntly, nobody could claim that you were a mediocrity," Nixon laughed. Would Powell accept the appointment? "I think the answer is affirmative Mr. President," Powell responded. "I am a fairly patriotic guy." But he refused to commit until he spoke with his wife and law partners, and he also warned that Haynsworth's opponents would be gunning for him. "There will be plenty of black leaders who will think that I was not active enough in adding integration in Virginia." Powell added, "I'm sure that the Attorney General's office is familiar with what I have written."[111]

Mitchell was not. There had apparently been no FBI checks or personal data questionnaires. At the very least, before making the announcement, the administration should have examined Powell's finances, public statements, and writings for matters that might spark controversy. No one did, more than superficially. Though Mitchell had at least looked at Powell's speech challenging Martin Luther King and knew by Tuesday night that he supported wiretapping, the attorney general could still not tell the president which law school Powell had attended. (The answer was Washington and Lee, where Powell was first in his class, with a year of postgraduate study at Harvard Law to appease his status-conscious father.) Nixon was so desperate to meet his self-imposed deadline that the administration concentrated exclusively on persuading Powell, whom the president still considered "so old" and who would become the fourth most elderly Supreme Court nominee ever, to take the job instead of investigating his suitability for it. The president reported that the potential nominee had mentioned that, whatever he decided, he appreciated the telephone call. "[T]hat worries me when he says that." Powell always told him that too, the attorney general replied. The Virginian had not closed the door, they agreed, but Nixon did not know "how far" he had left it open.[112]

On Wednesday afternoon, Nixon learned that Powell had accepted. "I wasn't expecting that," he remarked. That night, however, the Powells reconsidered. They did not want to leave Richmond or Jo Powell's elderly mother with whom they lived. The prospective nominee tried to withdraw Thursday morning before Nixon's announcement later that day. "The Attorney General received that news with obvious shock and displeasure and said that the matter had already passed the point of no return," Powell remembered. "He said the President had relied on my acceptance the previous afternoon; that he was committed to make the scheduled broadcast; and it would not be possible to find a replacement for me in the course of a single day." The Virginian reluctantly decided to allow the White House to proceed with his nomination.[113]

Actually, by that point, the president had a potential substitute. On Thursday morning, Howard Baker finally told Mitchell he would take the job, though he seemed only marginally more enthusiastic about doing so than Powell. "I don't think it's going to disturb him too much" if Nixon went in another direction, Mitchell observed. And after rejecting Rehnquist Tuesday afternoon, Nixon became belatedly interested in him when he learned that Rehnquist had served as a law clerk to Robert Jackson. Nixon admired Frankfurter's partner in advocating judicial restraint and regretted that Jackson never became chief justice. Only one Supreme Court clerk, Byron White, had ever before become a justice, and Nixon's aide, Richard Moore, told the president that appointing Rehnquist to the court "would be an impressive thing." And there was his record at Stanford. "Stanford's an elite law school, right?" the president asked, only to be assured that it was the Harvard of the West Coast. Consequently, Nixon could have chosen Baker and Rehnquist had Powell bowed out—though he and his Justice Department had still done little in the way of vetting either.[114]

Baker's star, however, was falling and Rehnquist's rising. How had the senator done in law school? Nixon now asked the attorney general. Once again, Mitchell could not answer, though by now, he could tell the president that Rehnquist had ranked first at Stanford. If Baker "had an outstanding record, so that I can say that he and Powell both had outstanding records, that's one thing," Nixon added. "But if it's a jackass record," he would choose Rehnquist and send Baker word he could join the Supreme Court if he wished when the next vacancy occurred. Powell and Baker would give him "two Southerners, which is not good," while Powell and Rehnquist would give him one "man who's unknown, but with a hell of a record." By conversation's end, the president had resolved to opt for the record, though Rehnquist's WASP background disappointed Nixon because he still wanted a Catholic. "Tell him to change his religion," the president kidded Mitchell, and get him "baptized and castrated" or "circumcise[d] "—"No, that's the Jews," Nixon remembered of circumcision, just in time.[115]

By now, though, the president had become anxious about the very leaks in the White House and Justice Department that had recently served his interest. He resolved to discuss the candidates only with Mitchell and Richard Moore. Not even Haldeman would know their identities. Nixon would write the speech himself. "Are you going to ignore the Bar?" Mitchell wanted to know. "I'm not even going to mention the Bar," Nixon responded. When Ron Ziegler told the press just before noon that the president had reached a decision and would address the nation that evening, the press secretary pointedly observed that the Constitution gave the Senate the duty to consent to the nomination, not the ABA.[116]

What about the also-rans Nixon had hung out to dry? After Lillie had been dragged through the mud and the president had announced his nominees, Mayor Yorty blasted the administration's "shoddy" treatment of her, and the president of the Los Angeles County Bar Association belatedly held a news conference to declare, "The bar wishes the public to know it has the utmost confidence in the integrity, dedication and conscientiousness of Mildred L. Lillie." Even Friday's most implacable local foe, the *Arkansas Gazette,* decried the "abominable" way Nixon had handled the nominations. Friday himself had been informed that the White House would telephone him an hour before the announcement. As friends met at his house in anticipation of a celebration and reporters gathered near his front lawn, the telephone rang. It was not Nixon, but Mitchell, who characterized it as "the hardest telephone call" he would ever make and blamed the ABA rating. "What happened?" the lawyer's friends shouted as he put down the receiver. "It didn't turn out the way we thought," his wife remembered him saying nearly a quarter century later. "He had on his face his little smile that I knew meant he was very hurt." A class act, Friday expressed the hope he had not "brought any discredit to the state." He also spoke out on behalf of the organization to which he had devoted so much energy for the last two decades and defended the ABA's role in selecting justices, though he admitted that its verdict in his particular case had left him "shattered."[117]

Soon after Mitchell's call, Nixon announced he had selected Powell and Rehnquist. "Presidents come and go, but the Supreme Court, through its decisions, goes on forever," and "by far the most important appointments" they made were to the court. Consequently, two criteria had guided him. The first was excellence, the need to people the court with "the very best lawyers in the Nation."[118]

The second was "judicial philosophy." What did that mean? He had not won the Presidency "by being loved," Nixon informed Moore. "I'm not going to miss this opportunity to say that these two guys are conservative." Sensing that "strict constructionist" had outlived its usefulness, Nixon replaced that label with "constitutionalist." It was the justice's duty, he emphasized, "to interpret the Constitution and not to place himself above the Constitution or outside the Constitution," or "twist or bend the Constitution in order to perpetuate his personal political and social views." Honest justices would differ about constitutional interpretation, he added, as did Justices Harlan and Black, the "Constitutionalists" he was now replacing. Avoiding the swamp of busing, Nixon limited himself to law and order in explicating his views. "As a judicial conservative, I believe that some court decisions have gone too far in the past in weakening the peace forces as against the criminal forces in our society," the president continued. "I believe we can strengthen the hand of the peace forces without compromising our precious principle that the rights of individuals must always be protected."[119]

Then, finally, the names. He was giving the court a Southerner, a Westerner, and two individuals who had graduated first in their class from law school—one, a former clerk to Justice Robert Jackson, "one of the most outstanding members of the Supreme Court in the past half-century," and "the President's lawyer's lawyer"; the other, a lion of the bar who reminded the president of another Virginian, Chief Justice John Marshall. Nixon closed with the admonition that "it is our duty as citizens to respect the institution of the Supreme Court of the United States." As soon as the president concluded his fourteen-minute speech, Mitchell informed the ABA that the administration would no longer submit potential nominees before the president sent them to the Senate.[120]

The next day, Nixon addressed a "disappointed, but resigned" audience of several thousand, who belonged to the National Federation of Republican Women. He felt "somewhat lonely," he volunteered, because he was the only man on the dais. "I must say that's a better break than a woman gets when she goes before the American Bar Association," he quipped—before suggesting that when the association's "jury of 12 decides on the qualifications of individuals that the President of the United States, through the Attorney General, submits to them for consideration, the jury should have at least one woman on it." He knew that many in the audience, including the First Lady, wanted to see a woman on the court, he continued. After all, the women in attendance mobbed Martha Mitchell, who made her disappointment at the failure to select both Lillie and Friday obvious. ("Your wife gives the impression that you let her down," the attorney general, who introduced himself as "Mr. Martha Mitchell," was told by a guest. "She may have given you that impression, but she gave me hell!" he affirmed.) Nixon stressed to the National Federation of Republican Women that "we have made a beginning. There will be a woman on the Supreme Court," he promised. Mitchell repeated that message too.[121]

For the present, the president and his attorney general signaled, it should be enough that Nixon had launched serious discussion of that prospect, revealed the sexism of the Establishment bar, divided the Democrats with his Byrd decoy, and named two conservatives who led their class. (As ever, Nixon disdained hierarchy at the same time it held him in its thrall. He privately told Chief Justice Burger that he had been third in his class at Duke and that class rank meant "nothing.") Nixon instructed Mitchell to get the word out "to all Southerners that Rehnquist is a reactionary bastard, which I hope to Christ he is." But what most tickled the president was his success in leading the media down the garden path. As when he announced he was going to China, he had astonished reporters.[122]

And though some might say that Nixon and Mitchell had been searching for Southern bigots or incompetents, the nominations made the harrowing selection process worthwhile for Burger. "I think all of these distasteful things will fade away," the chief justice told Nixon's personal secretary. "I think all of us listen too much to the *Washington Post*—in Iowa and across the country they get it straight from the President. These two nominations are just tops." Powell had said that he could no longer work over fifty hours a week, Nixon cheerily confided to the chief justice, but he would have clerks. "He doesn't have to read the fine print. What you need him for is conferences." Obviously, the president did not know much about how the Supreme Court went about its business, and the appreciative chief justice did not bother trying to educate him.[123]

Others shared Burger's thankfulness. Pat Buchanan chortled that liberal commentators like Eric Sevareid and Dan Rather who had talked of a crisis if Nixon named Lillie and Friday were "swallowing their spit" after the president's announcement. They now predicted confirmation, though Rather did marvel at how the president "managed to cause so much controversy, so much division, so many hard feelings, so much potential political damage to himself and . . . to the Nation's institutions." (Nixon's answer: "[T]he President did not cause the controversy, the press did!") An internal White House memorandum summarizing press and editorial reaction found consensus that the choices represented "both a surprise and an improvement upon those expected to get the nod," and that the "approving" reaction reflected "relief." But there was no media agreement, the memorandum made clear, on whether the six names submitted to the bar had represented "a smokescreen" or whether the president really had intended to choose Lillie and Friday, though an "increasing number" correctly believed he did and credited the ABA and Senate opposition for his turnaround. "In several cases, usually from those generally critical of the Admin, the pre-choice handling of the nomination is sharply rapped as a 'curious charade,'" the memorandum reported—or, as the New Republic put it, "slapstick, banana peel and all, directed by Keystone Kop Mitchell."[124]

The hard part was over now. When the opposing party controls the Senate, the administration generally struggles more in winning the confirmation of justices than in choosing them. In this case, however, Nixon experienced more difficulty as he careened from candidate to candidate in the selection phase. That was why the administration ultimately had to settle for one individual Nixon had always dismissed as too elderly, Powell, and another, Rehnquist, whom the president considered obscure.

In contrast, winning the confirmations of Rehnquist and Powell proved relatively easy. The liberal network had spent its energy on fighting Haynsworth, Carswell, Poff, and the six individuals on the ABA's list. Ironically, Rehnquist looked more conservative than Haynsworth or Carswell. But as one activist pointed out, "it takes time to dig out the facts and to collect and excerpt a nominee's public statements, to pass them around and explain them to potential allies in the fight," and liberals did not have any. Grateful to be spared Lillie and Friday, senators were now anticipating the Christmas recess. Moreover, as LBJ had believed in 1968, and Hugh Scott told Nixon in 1971, sometimes a president more easily sells two Supreme Court nominees together than just one. The two can complement and compensate for each other. Senate Judiciary Committee Chair Eastland made sure Powell and Rehnquist did in this case by scheduling their confirmation hearings together. In the words of Deputy Attorney General Richard Kleindienst, Eastland held "the confirmation of the popular Powell hostage to the confirmation of Rehnquist."[125]

The American Bar Association Standing Committee on the Federal Judiciary had resolved to press ahead with its evaluations of Rehnquist and Powell for the Senate with or without administration encouragement. It did not view them as equally desirable. Committee members unanimously bestowed on Powell their highest rating. In contrast, while no one doubted Rehnquist's intelligence, some apparently questioned his devotion to civil rights and civil liberties. Nine members declared him "one of the best persons available for appointment to the Supreme Court," but three would say only that he was "qualified."[126]

Rehnquist was indeed potentially vulnerable, though in the rush, there was little time to expose that. The Washington Research Project dispatched Rick Seymour to explore how the nominee had behaved in the brass-knuckles atmosphere of Phoenix politics, where Republicans in the early 1960s were frequently accused of preventing minorities from voting. There was talk that since he had become involved in Arizona politics through the 1964 Goldwater–Johnson race, Rehnquist himself had engaged in voter intimidation of African Americans and Latinos. According to civil rights activists in Phoenix, he had also fought a public accommodations law in 1964, a move to integrate its schools in 1967, and the open housing legislation of 1968. Feminists also mistrusted Rehnquist, though once again, no one much cared.[127]

Then there was his record as assistant attorney general. Rehnquist had ineptly investigated Haynsworth, Carswell, Friday, and Lillie when Nixon wanted to nominate them to the Court. It seems unlikely he acted out of a desire to sabotage the president or attorney general, both of whose photographs Rehnquist subsequently hung in his Court chambers. Perhaps Rehnquist, another Warren Court antagonist, shared the President's goal of disempowering the justices on it by any means necessary or other issues prevented him from paying his full attention to vetting the prospective nominees, a task he may have considered beneath him. Or maybe graduation at the top of his class had not qualified him to do the equivalent of document discovery. Rehnquist was also suspected—by John Dean, at least—of involvement in the administration's attempts to remove two liberals, Fortas and Douglas, from the bench. He had publicly decried the Warren Court and demanded the repeal of the exclusionary rule. He had denounced the "barbarians of the new left" who practiced civil disobedience, defended the administration's mass arrest of thousands of demonstrators against the Vietnam War in 1971, warned federal employees who criticized the war that they might lose their jobs, and claimed that the president could constitutionally send troops into battle without consulting Congress. He had told one Senate committee that the federal government had the unlimited right to collect data on anyone it wished and championed wiretapping. Moreover, he had drafted a possible constitutional amendment to ban "forced busing to achieve racial balance" in public schools, though reporters and the public would not learn that until 1972.[128]

The Leadership Conference on Civil Rights and NAACP would oppose him. So would the ACLU, which had never before fought a candidate for public office—a step it would not take again until President Reagan nominated Robert Bork as a justice in 1987. But one did not need to belong to the liberal network to predict that Rehnquist would encounter rough sledding before the Senate Judiciary Committee. Reporters assumed that Rehnquist, himself a long-time advocate of forceful questioning of Supreme Court nominees, would receive "the third degree" as he sought to explain his controversial views.[129]

Compared to Rehnquist, confirming Powell looked like a snap. That was why Eastland made the Senate take up both nominations jointly and scheduled Powell's appearance before the Senate Judiciary Committee first. "If a separate hearing had been held for each nominee," Deputy Attorney General Richard Kleindienst remembered, "Powell's would have been concluded in one day; Rehnquist's perhaps never," particularly with the specter of the 1972 election looming.[130]

Yet as Powell realized, he was not unassailable. He and his partner talked with Clement Haynsworth, who counseled him to avoid the media. Haynsworth also confided that "the mistake he made was in not preparing himself to testify in the same way that you would prepare for a major trial," and cautioned that even the Justice Department had not indicated "the type of examination that he could expect from members of the Judiciary Committee." Consequently, Powell drafted lawyers in his firm as his "staff" to get him ready for confirmation and anticipate every senator's question. He did not count on an easy time in front of the Judiciary Committee for all the reasons he had given Nixon and Mitchell when he argued against his own appointment. Additionally, liberals knew, Powell had publicly disparaged some of the Warren Court's criminal procedure decisions. He had also denounced the "outcry against wiretapping" as "a tempest in a teapot" and declared that "the radical left" had created a myth of government repression, and "law-abiding citizens have nothing to fear." Civil rights activists, civil libertarians, labor, feminists, and liberals all viewed him skeptically—though less critically than Rehnquist, and some in the civil rights community actively supported Powell. But what if activists uncovered the summer 1971 confidential memorandum that the Virginian had written for the chamber of commerce claiming that "Communists, new leftists and other revolutionaries" had mounted a "broad, shotgun attack on the system" and setting out a road map by which businessmen could "conduct guerilla warfare" against the propagandists? Jack Anderson, who publicized the memo after it was leaked to him in 1972, thought it might have raised questions about Powell's evenhandedness toward business.[131]

Powell's biographer shrewdly observed that the Virginian needed Rehnquist. Rehnquist's youth made up for his age—though Powell's sixty-four years also made him seem less threatening. As James Eastland said, "all those liberals" supported the Richmond lawyer because he was "old" and they thought he would die soon. Even more important, Rehnquist's evident conservatism distracted liberals from focusing too closely on Powell's record. Rehnquist shielded Powell, but the administration still sent out FBI officials to question Laurence Tribe, Rick Seymour, Marian Wright Edelman, and others about whether they planned to fight both nominees.[132]

The presentation of the nominees as two halves of the same walnut to the Senate Judiciary Committee served the administration well. Powell had a relatively easy time of it. For his part, Rehnquist denied he had intimidated Arizona voters, and Seymour, whose research revealed that the nominee had tried to stop his fellow Republicans from doing so, considered the charge unfounded. Rehnquist also claimed that his votes had changed since he opposed the open accommodations law. Further, he fenced ably with senators who asked him whether he would roll back "the march of progress" made by the Warren Court. The nominee volunteered that since *Brown v. Board of Education* had been "unanimous" and "repeatedly reaffirmed," there could "be no question but what that it is the law of the land." Meanwhile, the attorney general cited attorney–client privilege in defense of his refusal to testify to Rehnquist's work at the Justice Department.[133]

A small roadblock materialized after Rehnquist had testified when the NAACP released two affidavits from African Americans attesting to the nominee's intimidation of black Phoenix voters in 1964. Nina Totenberg also produced "two highly respected members of the Negro community in Phoenix," a minister and his wife, who told her, and swore in affidavits submitted to the Senate Judiciary Committee, that if the man harassing African American voters in 1964 had not been Rehnquist, "then 'he was his twin brother.'" These allegations, along with the discovery by Seymour and a graduate student that Rehnquist was on the mailing list of Arizonans for America, a right-wing group that included many John Birchers, helped to justify Rehnquist's opponents' demand to postpone reporting the nomination out of committee for a week. Yet the appearance of a name on a mailing list was thin gruel, and Rehnquist submitted written answers to the Judiciary Committee denying membership in either Arizonans for America or the John Birch Society and insisting that he had not engaged in voter harassment. As Totenberg said, both the Senate Judiciary Committee and the media paid "relatively little attention" to the matter. (The accusation of voter intimidation acquired more weight at the time of Rehnquist's chief justiceship nomination in 1986. At that time, the former US attorney of Phoenix, a Democratic appointee of JFK's, reluctantly testified before the Senate that the nominee had intimidated Latino and African American voters in south Phoenix.)[134]

As expected, the Senate Judiciary Committee unanimously endorsed Powell and a majority supported Rehnquist. Predictably, Birch Bayh, Philip Hart, Ted Kennedy, and another liberal Democrat opposed the latter's nomination on the grounds that he was "'outside the mainstream of American thought' on civil rights." But no one expected the hostile senators to prevail on the Senate floor. Consequently, one Administration official brightly predicted to the President on December 4, "It now appears that the 'Conservative Twins' will join the 'Minnesota Twins' on the Supreme Court before the end of the month."[135]

On Monday, December 6, the day before the Senate was to vote on Powell, though, Washington began buzzing with a new story about Rehnquist. Someone had alerted *Newsweek*'s Robert Shogan to a memorandum in Justice Jackson's Library of Congress Papers that Rehnquist had written when he was Jackson's clerk as the court considered *Brown*. It defended the "separate but equal" doctrine the court lay down in *Plessy v. Ferguson* that *Brown* famously overruled. The memo maintained that Thurgood Marshall and others seeking school desegregation were asking "the Court to read its own sociological views into the Constitution" and urging on it "a view palpably at variance with precedent and probably legislative history." The conclusion startled many, given the sacred role *Brown* had assumed in constitutional discourse and American history: "I realize that it is an unpopular and unhumanitarian [sic] position, for which I have been excoriated by 'liberal' colleagyes [sic], but I think Plessy v. Ferguson was right and should be reaffirmed."[136]

Confronted, Rehnquist insisted in a letter to Eastland that the Judiciary Committee chair read aloud to the Senate on Wednesday, December 8, that "I wish to state unequivocally that I fully support the legal reasoning and the rightness from the standpoint of fundamental fairness of the *Brown* decision." The "I" in the memorandum, he maintained, referred to his boss. Rehnquist was expressing Jackson's "tentative views" before he had abandoned them to join his brethren, and he had drafted the memo at the justice's direction. Jackson's longtime secretary, Elsie Douglas, immediately branded the nominee a liar.[137]

What if the memo had surfaced before Rehnquist testified under oath to the Senate Judiciary Committee? What if he had not attributed it to Jackson? And what if he had not pledged allegiance to *Brown*? Would the *Newsweek* revelations have sunk his nomination? Probably not. To be sure, the Rehnquist confirmation did confirm the special place *Brown* had come to occupy in constitutional culture. As Brad Snyder has written, ironically, Rehnquist canonized *Brown*.[138]

Nevertheless, reporters understood that Bayh, the leader of a quixotic filibuster against Rehnquist backed by the Leadership Conference, was waging "a losing battle." Journalists observed that even the nominee's antagonists agreed they had not persuaded the public or the Senate "that Mr. Rehnquist was dangerously insensitive to individual freedoms and civil rights." For his part, Bayh insisted that "under normal circumstances, if it were not the tail end of a session, if all of us were not so preoccupied with our own responsibilities, and if all of us were not so anxious to return to our constituents and families, . . . the Senate would be up in arms" over the *Newsweek* revelations.[139]

The Senate clearly wasn't. In fact, as soon as the article appeared on Monday, and even before Eastland read Rehnquist's letter in the chamber, William Proxmire of Wisconsin, a maverick Democrat who had voted against Haynsworth and Carswell, surprised the Senate. He signaled that he would vote for the confirmation of Rehnquist, who had been born and raised in Milwaukee. The White House still counted "70 for, 23 opposed, 5 undeclared and 2 absent." On Wednesday, the count was 69 for, 18 against, 10 undecided, and 3 absent. That senators wanted to leave town and that Majority Leader Mansfield had promised to hold the vote on the nominee before letting them do so was helping. So were Rehnquist's credentials. Laurence Tribe, for one example, wrote the *Boston Globe* to deny he was building the kind of case against the nomination that he had helped to develop against Lillie. "Though I personally believe he should not be confirmed, I am undertaking no systematic effort to press that view on others since I believe that, despite my ideological differences with Mr. Rehnquist, his appointment by the President at least reflects a standard of intellectual excellence and legal distinction that shows respect for the Supreme Court as an institution." As Joe Rauh put it, law professors did not mobilize against the nominee because "they think that a reactionary A student is better than a reactionary C student."[140]

Rehnquist's critics were speaking to an empty chamber anyway. Beyond unveiling the nominee's letter to Eastland, his supporters did not even dignify the charges against Rehnquist with responses. Most senators did not want to go to the mat with the president over another court pick. Charles Colson was not just flattering Nixon when he said that nominee's survival was "more a reflection on you than Rehnquist."[141]

The Senate still approved of Powell more. He won confirmation by eighty-nine to one. When the president contacted Powell, the Virginian embodied modesty. "I'm very much aware that I'm the beneficiary of some opposition to Rehnquist," he said.[142]

Rehnquist's vote proved narrower, sixty-eight to twenty-six. Chief Justice Hughes had received exactly the same vote, Nixon assured Rehnquist in a congratulatory telephone call on December 10. "Just be as mean and rough as they said you were." ABC News announced that "[a] long era of liberalism on the Court may have come to an end"[143] (figure 28).

That Nixon recognized the flaws in the process that led him to celebrate two afterthoughts soon became evident. He anticipated three additional vacancies. "There is Douglas—Powell will be over 70—at least one [justice—Marshall?] has serious physical disabilities," he reported to his speechwriters. "Let me tell you about . . . future appointments," he directed Burger when they got together in the summer of 1972. Without "consulting any of your other colleagues," the chief justice should ready himself for vacancies. "I don't want to have a situation develop where we have an opening, and we don't have three or four good names." Nixon himself "wouldn't have thought of Rehnquist," he confided, but he wanted more justices like him. Forget about the Jewish seat. "If it comes down to the question of just picking a Jew because he's a Jew, I'm not going to do it," particularly since Nixon already employed plenty of them. "I am not going to go for this business, except on the color—the black thing. You have to have a black for a black." Burger sympathized. "Getting a really outstanding Negro is harder than getting the outstanding Jew," he remarked. Burger should take a look at William Brown at the Equal Employment Opportunity Commission, the

Figure 28 Powell and Rehnquist receiving their commissions to the US Supreme Court from President Nixon, December 22, 1971. Nixon Library.

president instructed. The chief justice should remember William French Smith for vacancies other than Marshall's and also that "I want to move away from the Ivy League." Burger volunteered that his opinion of White had improved. If his plane went down, "Byron White would be the guy unless you brought in somebody from the outside."[144]

Of course, Burger did not die, and no more vacancies materialized. After 1971, the membership of the "Nixon Court" remained static. As Fred Graham wrote privately, that meant anyone interested in "the theme of the turnabout caused by the new Nixon appointees" must focus on "Warren Burger's pompous conniving; Harry Blackmun's timidity; Lewis Powell's aristocratic manipulations; [and] William Rehnquist's Teutonic conservatism."[145]

Still, in the second half of the twentieth century, only Eisenhower named more Supreme Court justices. For Nixon, that was insufficient. "The main point that I am afraid that you and your colleagues have not considered is that in our elation over finally having the 'Nixon Court' we are now stuck with whatever decisions the new Supreme Court majority hands down," the president scolded top advisers after the Powell and Rehnquist appointments. Like senators and representatives, "Supreme Court Justices are softened up by the media they read, the communities they live in, the parties they attend, and the very air they breathe on the Potomac. It is bound to happen to one or more of our new majority on the Court and then we will have lost the ball game."

Regardless of whether the president correctly diagnosed the reasons for change, he did identify a problem. Within four years, a "softened" Blackmun had declared his independence from Warren Burger. Powell also proved more "centrist" than conservative. A year after his arrival, he handed down an opinion as circuit justice rejecting the attempt by the Augusta, Georgia, school system to delay busing its students in compliance with *Swann*. Nixon publicly attacked the "Powell decision" and used it to justify obviously antibusing legislation of dubious constitutionality that he was vainly proposing as the presidential election loomed.[146]

But what did Nixon think the ball game was? The scattershot and incoherent way he dealt with the Supreme Court reflected both administration ineptitude and his lack of interest in most issues on the court's docket. As Kevin McMahon and Stephen Engel have stressed, despite his acrid rhetoric, the president remained most invested in the court for strategic political reasons. Beyond that, he cared about it very little, if at all. So, while it was ironic that the court that Nixon helped create led to his own resignation by forcing him to turn over the Watergate tapes in a unanimous opinion, it was not so startling that it also upheld busing as a means of achieving racial balance in schools outside the South, respected some rights of criminal defendants, and constitutionalized the right to abortion (which the president worried fostered "permissiveness" but thought was necessary to get rid of mixed race babies and those conceived as the result of rape).[147]

Like many, but not all, historical topics, the Burger Court seems more important as it recedes in time. Constitutional experts in the 1980s portrayed it as the "counter-revolution that wasn't" because they believed that the Burger Court did not roll back Warren-era jurisprudence. Equally distinguished scholars today emphasize its erosion of the equality that undergirded Warren Court opinions. They show that the Burger Court chomped, rather than nibbled, on its predecessor's desegregation and criminal procedure decisions. By protecting corporate speech in political campaigns, Burger and his colleagues also lay the foundation for the Roberts Court's transformation of the electoral process in the next century.[148]

Yet it was the opportunity to exploit the court for political reasons that apparently most engaged Nixon. It appealed to him at least as much as the chance to create a new body that confirmed or undercut the legacy of its predecessor—depending on which scholars have described the Burger Court, when they have written, and where they have looked. The president attacked the Warren Court as part of his drive to make the GOP the majority party, and he used seats on the Burger Court to cultivate constituencies and to compensate for disappointments he inflicted on conservatives. Even so, as Rehnquist's letter affirming *Brown* showed, the Warren Court did not go away, and neither did the sixties.

Epilogue

Surely no one who has read this far would say that Johnson and Nixon provided a model for how presidents should choose Supreme Court justices. True, given LBJ's interests, Abe Fortas represented an excellent choice in 1965. Still, most probably agree that contemporary justices should be less involved with the presidents who select them than Fortas remained with LBJ. A justice who can't break the habit of advising a president risks damaging the court by disclosing its secrets and possesses less time for its pressing business. Thurgood Marshall represented an inspired selection for 1967. But if Johnson wanted to reward Fortas in 1968 by making him chief justice, the president should have coupled his nomination with someone other than Homer Thornberry. And if LBJ hoped to maintain the ideological direction of the Warren Court, he might more prudently have nominated another chief justice altogether. Nixon did not score enough political points by naming Clement Haynsworth and Harrold Carswell in 1969 and 1970 to compensate for the damage those two nominations did to his administration. In 1971, he just floundered until he happened upon Lewis Powell and William Rehnquist.

Thankfully, future Supreme Court nominee hunts occurred less haphazardly—though as one attorney general said, the element of "Russian roulette" remained, as searches uncovered numerous "qualified" prospects, and administration lists and rankings of prospects changed. Nixon did not really care whether his nominees were qualified. Both the Nixon and Johnson administrations investigated potential nominees carelessly: Just as Nixon should have been aware of Carswell's 1948 speech, LBJ should have known about Fortas's lecture fees. The contemporary nomination process in our information age looks very different, thanks to more carefully vetted selections.[1]

So why is the story set out here significant? Some scholars condemn the modern process of Supreme Court confirmation as a circus. As Elena Kagan famously did while still a law professor, they criticize the vague and vapid responses it elicits from nominees and "the selling of Supreme Court nominees" like toothpaste to pressure groups, the public, and others. Perhaps our story shows that those who *celebrate* the contemporary process as one of democracy's triumphs are correct. Carswell might well have become a justice but for interest group mobilization. Maybe this book demonstrates that as messy as the modern process of Supreme Court nomination and confirmation became in the sixties, the system—at least as it existed through the Kagan confirmation in 2010—"worked" and we should rejoice, rather than regret, that it routinely came to involve not just the president and Senate, but interest groups, the media, and the public.[2]

Unlike lawyers, though, historians hate the argument that just because matters were one way in the past, they should stay that way in the present. As Herbert Gutman said, the "value of historical understanding is that it transforms historical givens into historical contingencies." When we see how Johnson and Nixon's decisions reflected their contemporary concerns, we may come to realize that the patterns they helped establish need not bind us at a different moment. The past may never be dead or even past, but why should it become authoritative? Consequently, I would not say this story provides a justification for how things should be. It may, however, help explain how and sometimes even why they became the way they are—though any historian will stress the difficulty of decoding causation. As Senator Richard Durbin (D-IL) remarked in 2001, "Congressmen, Senators and Presidents come and go. Supreme Court Justices hang around forever. The hand of Richard Nixon, who has been gone from this city in an official role, is still on the Supreme Court 25 years later." So is that of Lyndon Johnson. In my view, the story mattered for the court. It helped shape the way the Warren Court is remembered. It may have influenced the nomination process, and it definitely affected the confirmation process.[3]

1 First Street, SE

The fallout from the confirmation battles of the sixties changed the court as an institution by altering its membership, atmosphere, leadership, and, perhaps, doctrinal output. Many inside the Supreme Court Building at 1 First Street had revered Earl Warren, a former governor who guided the court with ease. Warren's colleagues, a generation of law clerks turned law professors, and other scholars all but canonized him as the court's one true "Super Chief" after he left it.[4]

Even many of the young now claimed Warren as one of their own. As he stepped down from the court's helm in 1969, the *Harvard Law Review* editors dedicated the issue to "Chief Justice Earl Warren who with courage and passion led a reform of the law." When Warren spoke at the University of California, San Diego, in 1970 as antiwar sentiment engulfed the campuses, a student in renaissance dress suddenly materialized with a trumpet. "For 35 seconds the notes of the cavalry charge echoed across the dark concrete," the *San Diego Union* reported. Then the musician and his co-conspirators began unfurling a banner. "A hush fell over the throng, most of whom expected the worst in student graffiti, perhaps 'F—k the Chief Justice,'" one professor in the audience recalled. But to the university administrators' relief, the banner said, " 'Right on, Big Earl!' The crowd roared its approval." Warren beamed, then attacked those who believed that social justice was divisible from law and order.[5]

Warren Earl Burger wasn't there that day, but as at San Diego and in the law reviews, Earl Warren often upstaged him. In one instance in 1972, for example, Chief Justice Burger, who had appointed a blue-ribbon panel to study the problems of the federal judiciary, had but to seem supportive of its idea of a national court of appeals meant to improve the quality of the Supreme Court's opinions by reducing their quantity. In addition to resolving some conflicts between the circuits, the judges on the proposed "mini-Court" would screen all certiorari petitions to decide which cases the Supreme Court should consider. Instantly, Warren summoned into existence an army of his former law clerks to denounce this "junior supreme court." Like the court-curbing proposals of the 1950s and 1960s, Warren charged, a national court of appeals entailed "a scuttling of the Supreme Court." And so, despite frequent complaints about overwork from Burger and the newer Nixon appointees, the proposal and others like it went nowhere.[6]

Even without comparing him to Warren, many would still have objected to the new chief justice. From the beginning, complaints abounded about Burger's high-handed administration of the federal judiciary, his inappropriate lobbying for it, and the way he ran the justices' meetings. "All talking at once," Harry Blackmun recorded of the "Conference" in 1980. "Such a kindergarten!" According to some, Burger also hogged the big opinions and, as in *Swann*, even changed his vote when he was in the minority to maintain control over assigning them. As these and other allegations filtered out to the media, the chief justice became obsessed with leaks. Though he once formed the Ad Hoc Committee on Court Secrecy to plug them, the disclosures about the court's most sensitive opinions and its justices only became more sensational.[7]

Many of the most damaging stories involved Burger, who loathed most reporters and received terrible press. "I have been warned that the media will grasp any stick or stone to beat the Court—and me personally as the 'lightning rod' until we bow to their demands," the chief justice confided to Justice Powell in 1979. One article in *Time* that November, "Inside the High Court: After a Decade It Is Burger's in Name Only," was written with the cooperation of Justices Byron White, William Rehnquist, and Lewis Powell, who took the unusual step of speaking with the reporters together in the vain hope of producing a good story. "Byron, Bill and I did agree that it might be helpful, by conversation, to let the other Justices know that the three of us interviewed the reporters together, and that we actually spoke well of the Chief Justice as well as of the Court as an institution," Powell recorded of their futile effort at damage control. They could only take comfort in their "combined judgment . . . that in light of the forthcoming Woodward/Armstrong book, the Chief's concern about the *Time* article will subside into memory quite quickly."[8]

Some solace. When published a month later, Bob Woodward and Scott Armstrong's *The Brethren: Inside the Supreme Court* did eclipse everything. But it also painted Burger as a paranoid, pompous dissembler who could not guide his colleagues, abused his power, and saw law as the basest form of politics. Despite the court's historic emphasis on protecting the secrecy of its deliberations, the book was written with the help of five justices and a multitude of clerks. *The Brethren* was a blockbuster, and as Justice Powell lamented, it made two points: "(1) the Chief Justice is an arrogant dunce, and (2) the Court is so torn by dissension and discord that it cannot perform effectively its constitutional duty. Each of these messages is totally false."[9]

Were they? Of course, in the aftermath of the book's publication, the justices circled the wagons around Burger and insisted all was well. But whether or not the chief justice actually was an "arrogant dunce," the Blackmun, Brennan, Douglas, and Powell Papers, and, to a lesser extent, the Stewart and Rehnquist Papers, read together and in conjunction with contemporary press accounts, suggested that a number of justices—even, perhaps especially, Burger's boy-hood friend, Harry Blackmun—considered him one a good part of the time. So did their clerks, many in the media, and Warren, who labeled his successor a "horse's ass." Despite Justice Powell's herculean efforts to create harmony, the Burger Court was a less happy place than the Warren Court.[10]

When Burger resigned as chief justice before the 1986 midterm elections while the Republicans still held the Senate (and, perhaps, to take advantage of that), one pundit accounted for the kind assessments of his tenure by explaining that everyone wanted to see him go. "Liberals have disliked him ever since he was appointed by Richard Nixon to preside over a retreat from Warrenesque activism," while conservatives believed he had "botched" the task. "Quick, somebody, throw him a retirement party before he changes his mind." One internal Reagan administration memorandum promoting Rehnquist as the next chief justice portrayed him as everything Burger was not. He could direct what has been "a generally rudderless Court. . . . No one can question the depth of his scholarship or intellect, the clarity of his philosophical vision or his ability to build a consensus to implant that vision in the Court's decisions. Moreover, he enjoys a warm collegial relationship with, and is genuinely respected by, all of his fellow justices, even those with whom he often disagrees." Is it any wonder that when Rehnquist became the next chief justice, he modeled himself as the anti-Burger?[11]

If the changes wrought by the 1967–71 battles over its membership left an imprint on the court as an institution, did they also make a difference to the doctrine it produced?

What if Fortas had hidden his relationship with LBJ in 1968 more adeptly, avoided "Flaming Creatures," and just said no to the lecture fees, or if LBJ had named Goldberg, Brennan, or someone else chief justice? The possibilities are intriguing. By the late 1960s, for example, some thought that the Warren Court was on the verge of singling out wealth as a suspect classification. Perhaps a Fortas, Goldberg, or Brennan court might have subjected laws that sustained economic, as well as gender and racial, inequality to strict scrutiny. Perhaps it would have required regional busing to achieve racial balance in the schools, announced indigent women's right to government-funded abortions, and forced Americans to focus more on how class, like race and gender, divides us. Who knows?[12]

Memories

We do know that the sixties confirmation battles helped shape the way the Warren Court was remembered. Some do hold "misty water-colored" recollections of Earl Warren and his stewardship. Indeed, many liberal law professors and their students under "the spell of the Warren Court" transformed it into "judicial Camelot." Nevertheless, memories of "the way we were" because of Warren Court opinions suffered. Beginning with *Brown v. Board of Education,* many in the legal community portrayed the Warren Court as a "countermajoritarian" force whose accomplishments or atrocities, depending on the speaker's point of view, occurred in defiance of popular will. Even contemporary celebrations of Warren and his court often reinforced the theme that it soldiered on alone. In full, that *Harvard Law Review* editors' 1969 dedication to Warren read, "to Chief Justice Earl Warren who with courage and compassion led a reform of the law while the other branches of government delayed."[13]

Yet Warren and his court often followed public opinion during the 1950s, and the chief justice, LBJ, and congressional liberals saw each other as partners when the Warren Court moved into full throttle in the 1960s. As academic lawyers and political scientists have recently stressed, in reality, the Warren Court was actually majoritarian. Its members, one said, "removed the blocks to majority rule that were lurking within the system" and "knew what was majority sentiment and what wasn't." And though the Warren Court did become a lightning rod during the 1960s, many more Americans at the time accepted it than we recall. Liberals retained the power of voice in the Senate and elsewhere until after Watergate. Remember the support for Marshall in 1967 and for Fortas initially in 1968. Even if his baggage doomed Fortas, it seems possible that LBJ could have won the confirmation of another liberal in 1968. The withdrawal of Fortas's nomination was a sign that liberalism was on the ropes, but not that it was down and out. The defeats of Haynsworth and Carswell made clear it retained some vitality.[14]

The reverence for Warren was clear when he died on July 9, 1974, twelve days before the court handed down the opinion compelling Nixon's surrender of the Watergate tapes, and reportedly after exclaiming "Thank God!" three times when Justice Brennan informed him what it would say. Chief Justice Burger arranged for his predecessor's flag-draped coffin to lie in state in the Supreme Court's main hall, the first time any justice had received that honor. The chief justice, eight associate justices, and former justices Fortas, Goldberg, and Clark lined the building's fifty-three marble steps as the pallbearers carried the coffin into the court (figure 29). During the next day and a half, while Warren's clerks stood watch, some nine thousand people paid their respects.[15]

No commemoration, of course, offers reason to urge a return to the Warren Court. Like the confirmation struggles that accompanied the Warren Court and followed Warren's departure, though, this one helps remind us that it is ahistorical to call the Warren Court in its heyday countermajoritarian. In the context

Figure 29 Earl Warren's funeral, July 12, 1974. Supreme Court of the United States.

of the sixties, the court's liberalism, like that of LBJ's Great Society, was hardly radical—which was why many radicals then detested liberalism. Even now, many Warren Court opinions remain largely intact.

Yet today, even liberals run away from the Warren Court because they accept the cartoonish image promoted by its opponents with relatively little success during the confirmation struggles of the sixties. Democrats try to respect and reject the Warren Court by relegating it to history. Think of the approving announcement by the *New Republic*'s legal correspondent that in nominating Judges Ruth Bader Ginsburg and Stephen Breyer to the court, the Democrats had "weaned themselves from Warrenism at last." President Clinton had escaped "the ideological excesses" of the Warren Court and ended "the age of judicial heroics." Recall what happened when candidate Obama called for justices who showed empathy: Prominent conservative Kenneth Starr wondered if that was code for Warren Court types. Not so, said Obama, who maintained before and after his election that judicial "activists" of the sixties "ignored the will of Congress" and "democratic processes."[16]

Thus, even as confirmation hearings feature nominees, beginning with Rehnquist in 1971, ritualistically swearing fealty to *Brown*, they underline the bipartisan acceptance of the caricature of the Warren Court its opponents advanced in the earlier confirmation battles. The Warren Court, Mark Tushnet reminds us, has molded the contemporary Republican Party, just as Republicans have shaped the Warren Court into an invaluable whipping boy. "Ever since 1968, when Richard Nixon ran on a platform attacking Chief Justice Earl Warren, the Republican Party's position on the Supreme Court has helped to unite its otherwise anomalous coalition of anti-abortion activists, law-and-order forces, gun-rights advocates and anti-regulatory business interests—not to mention many whites who still, deep down, blame the federal courts for the leveling effects of civil rights," John Witt observed recently. That's powerful glue. No wonder Clinton and Obama proceeded so cautiously in making nominations to the court.[17]

Nomination

In 2015, the Supreme Court was composed of three women and six men, three Jews and six Catholics. For the first time in its history, it included no Protestants. Four justices had grown up in New York City. All had attended Harvard or Yale Law School. One was African American. All except Justice Kagan had prior judicial experience, and all except Kagan were not presidential friends before their nomination. During the sixties, politicians, academics, lawyers, presidential intimates, and judges became justices. How did presidents come to select members of the court from this much narrower group?

The sixties struggles likely influenced the nomination process in a number of ways. The events described in this book may have affected the arrival of women at the court and helped end the tradition of geographical representation. They helped cause the disappearance of the "Jewish seat" for more than twenty years. They also confirmed the symbolic importance of a place at the Supreme Court table for women and minorities and contributed to the institutionalization of the "black" seat. The contests of the sixties heightened expectations that nominees should possess prior judicial experience. Finally, they made presidential friends untouchable for decades.

It may seem a stretch to attribute the arrival of women justices to Mildred Lillie. Of course, the women's movement had something to do with their nominations too. Yet while Lillie was not the first woman considered for an appointment, she was, thanks to perceptions of the growing political power of women, the first examined so seriously. As Nixon hinted to Republican clubwomen in 1971, his interest in her ensured that every president after him would face pressure to name the first woman to the court. After submitting an all-male list of Supreme Court candidates to the American Bar Association (ABA) in 1975 that leaked, the Ford administration received so many complaints that President Ford's special assistant on women admonished him about the political fallout. Attorney General Edward Levi obediently sent forward a revised list to the ABA that included two women—neither of whom received serious consideration. When Jimmy Carter nominated Ninth Circuit Judge Shirley Hufstedler as his first secretary of education four years later, an enthusiastic *Washington Post* alluded to her "perennial mention as the female most likely to be the first of her kind named an associate justice of the Supreme Court (a prospect that is still live)."[18]

No vacancy on the court materialized during Carter's Presidency, but Ronald Reagan capitalized on the demand for a woman justice in his 1980 race against Carter. Realizing that his opposition to the Equal Rights Amendment distressed some women voters, Reagan proclaimed it "time for a woman to sit among our highest jurists." The Republican promised "that one of the first vacancies in my administration will be filled by the most qualified woman I can possibly find, one who meets the high standards I will demand for all court appointments."[19]

Though President Reagan knew and liked Lillie, and his California friends recommended her when Justice Potter Stewart retired, he settled on Arizona judge Sandra Day O'Connor instead. Reagan did not face what John Mitchell called "Chief Justice problems," since by now, Burger acknowledged the political force of the women's movement and had come to see a woman justice as inevitable. Indeed the chief justice cultivated O'Connor before her nomination and promoted her to the administration. From the perspective of the president, who may have found her, O'Connor was a nearly ideal nominee. She had done almost as well at Stanford Law as her friend and classmate, William Rehnquist, and, one feminist wrote with grudging admiration, was "as much of a conservative as you can find in a qualified woman, and as much of a feminist as you can find in a conservative." Yet religious and social conservatives rightly suspected that O'Connor would not prove a secure vote against abortion. They launched what New Right leader Paul Weyrich described as a campaign of "intense opposition" to her nomination even as they understood that the momentum to put a woman on the court had become so great that "we were unlikely to get a single vote." Sure enough, the Senate approved O'Connor by ninety-nine to zero.[20]

That she hailed from Arizona, while Stewart came from Ohio, was unimportant. The tradition of geographical representation on the court had been on the wane since the Civil War. But ironically, it was Nixon who, having vainly tried to keep it alive in 1969 and 1970 by nominating a Southerner, sounded its death knell when he consecutively appointed two Saint Paul natives. Once the court housed Minnesota Twins in Burger and Blackmun, it was not a big step to a court with justices from every New York borough but Staten Island.

Meanwhile, thanks in part to Nixon's anti-Semitism, the "Jewish seat" vanished for two decades just as the "black seat" became sacred. The Jewish seat did briefly seem on its way to revival when Ronald Reagan nominated Judge Douglas Ginsburg to the court in 1987 after the Senate shot down the nomination of Ginsburg's DC Circuit colleague, Robert Bork. The White House considered Douglas Ginsburg's Judaism a plus. Ethnic solidarity, administration officials correctly predicted, might lead Jewish liberals, who had worked against Bork, a Christian, because they believed he opposed abortion and gender and racial equality, to treat a Jewish conservative more kindly.[21]

But after Reagan withdrew Ginsburg's nomination, the Jewish seat became a historical curiosity. During this period, "I considered myself the Jewish justice," the Catholic Justice Scalia remarked to a friend. "The New York-raised judge was shocked that he had to teach his colleagues how to pronounce 'yeshiva' (Chief Justice Rehnquist . . . called it 'ye-shy-va') and, Scalia added proudly, . . . 'I even told them what a yeshiva is.'"[22]

That only got the court so far. When Bush I became president, articles appeared in the *New York Times* and *Jerusalem Report* pointing out that no Jew had served on the court for twenty years and asking what had happened to the Jewish seat. Ninth Circuit Judge Stephen Reinhardt, a Jewish liberal, first raised the question. Reinhardt recognized that as American Jews' politics had become more diverse, "the nomination of a Jew no longer automatically means that humanitarian concerns or causes will be advanced." Yet the beauty of a Supreme Court seat was that it required a presidential nomination and a Senate confirmation but not, for better or worse, election. "It is wrong that the only branch of government in which Jews have been able to reach the top has now been closed to them at that level for an entire generation," he insisted. Reinhardt blamed the absence of a Jewish justice in part on Nixon, but he also faulted Jews themselves, who had maintained "a conspiracy of silence." His Ninth Circuit colleague, Alex Kozinski, a prominent conservative, agreed that the lack of Jews on the court "has been an issue among Jews for 20 years, but most aren't willing to speak out on it." When New York Times reporter David Margolick set out to determine whether the victims deserved any part of the blame, he found that despite Jews' presence at the highest levels of the legal profession, for many of them, "even touching the topic is taboo." Was it because they feared seeming "chauvinistic or parochial"? Margolick wondered.[23]

Perhaps, and it may also have reflected the fact that some Jews had turned against affirmative action. How could they then support "a quota" on the court? "Most Jewish organizations, and I think most Jews in general, don't think there's a need for a Jewish seat," and considered the Jewish seat "passé," one prominent spokesman told the Jerusalem Report. "You can't oppose the quota system in daily life and then demand one for the Supreme Court."[24]

The subject reemerged when Clinton became president. Should American Jews agitate for the revival of the Jewish seat? At a time when ethnics/minorities/women were lobbying for a Supreme Court nomination, some suggested that Clinton could please Jewish voters by nominating a Jewish justice.[25]

DC Circuit Judge Ruth Bader Ginsburg's ethnicity/religion did play a role in her appointment, but not a large one. Clinton had spoken of his interest in reviving the Jewish seat, but he had other Jews on his list of prospects, which included non-Jews as well. The president found his way to Ginsburg haphazardly. At first, he delighted liberals by saying he wanted to name someone with "a big heart." He courted New York Governor Mario Cuomo and Secretary of Interior Bruce Babbitt, but Cuomo dithered, and environmentalists told the president that they needed Babbitt where he was. Then Clinton interviewed Ginsburg and loved her story—which, beginning with LBJ and Marshall, had become a more important element of the selection equation. In announcing her nomination, the president observed that Ginsburg "argued and won many of the women's rights cases before the Supreme Court in the 1970's" and that many who admired her "say she is to the women's movement what former Supreme Court Justice Thurgood Marshall was to the movement for the rights of African-Americans." That accolade, he rightly judged, was the highest "an American lawyer" could receive. But it also surely helped that Ginsburg had a reputation as a moderate. She had angered the Left by defending the Pentagon's right to dismiss gays, and she had annoyed feminists by labeling Roe v. Wade divisive. Ginsburg was appointable, that is, because she was not overtly ideological. So was First Circuit Judge Stephen Breyer, another Jew and a one-time Goldberg clerk, who was considered even more of a centrist. Beset by the Whitewater probe and allegations of ethical impropriety in 1994, Clinton selected Breyer to replace Harry Blackmun.[26]

These nominations disappointed some who saw a historic passion for social justice undergirding the Jewish seat. "Particularly for organizations that have fought these battles, there is a sense of frustration, of lost opportunity," the president of one liberal interest group told the *New York Times*. "Breyer may be phenomenally talented, but he's not Blackmun and Ruth Ginsburg is not necessarily Thurgood Marshall. There's almost an irony here that the Court is becoming more conservative, losing the liberal powerhouses and getting moderates in exchange."[27]

What are we to make of such assessments? Not much. Definitions of "greatness" in justices are time bound. The generation of law professors who hailed Holmes gave way to the one that worshipped Warren. So, too, views of the justices often evolve, just as the justices themselves sometimes do. Blackmun, once dismissed as Burger's clone, had been transformed into a "liberal powerhouse"! And Ginsburg became a liberal icon.[28]

Did the Ginsburg and Breyer nominations mean that religion, or at least Judaism, had become irrelevant to presidential calculations in Supreme Court nominations? In a 2002 address at the law school named after Brandeis, Justice Ginsburg said so. Maintaining that she was so secure that she proudly displayed a mezuzah on the doorpost to her Supreme Court chambers, she nevertheless contended that "no one regarded Ginsburg and Breyer as filling a Jewish seat. Both of us take pride and draw strength from our heritage, but our religion was simply not relevant to President Clinton's appointments." Instead, theirs were, quite simply, American success stories. "What is the difference between a New York City garment district bookkeeper and a Supreme Court justice?" she asked rhetorically. "One generation—the difference between the opportunities open to my mother, a bookkeeper, and those open to me."[29]

Just as Nixon's anti-Semitism drove the Jewish seat into retirement for more than two decades, so Jewish ambivalence about claiming a "Jewish seat" probably helped keep it there for so long. One reason for the lapsing of the "Jewish seat" and the survival of LBJ's "black" seat lay in interest group mobilization or, really, lack of concerted Jewish mobilization. After the Parker nomination battle in 1930, interest groups came to prominence in modern judicial politics when the Citizens for Decent Literature charged Fortas with peddling porn and liberals dug for skeletons in the closets of Haynsworth and Carswell. In contrast to Jews, and just as women clambered for one of their own as a justice, African Americans signaled more enthusiasm for the "black seat."

Small surprise, then, that Nixon planned to replace Marshall with an African American. Presidents carefully cultivated African Americans to nominate in the event that Thurgood Marshall retired, as the Carter administration apparently made clear it wanted him to do. President Carter, for one example, was reportedly ready to nominate Solicitor General Wade McCree to replace Marshall. Bush I named Clarence Thomas.[30]

Interest group mobilization proved crucial in winning Justice Thomas's confirmation. The opposition of civil rights groups and feminists had helped doom Robert Bork. As some had foreseen during the Thurgood Marshall nomination fight, African Americans had become a significant voting bloc in the South, and senators fretted about alienating them by backing Bork. In the case of the Thomas nomination, Southerners and their constituents would again prove significant. But this time, the White House had put up a conservative African American born in a Georgia shack and opposed to affirmative action and packaged him as a Horatio Alger hero. Civil rights activists might remain quiet to help him, and some African Americans might champion Thomas because they liked his message. If that happened, the administration could break up the old anti-Bork coalition. Consequently, two white Republican Southerners let the White House know "that we needed to split the blacks on this issue, because if they all lined up against Thomas," they and others would have a hard time voting to confirm. The Bush administration's subsequent success in promoting its nominee as "the living embodiment of the President's empowerment agenda" and exploiting "the popular support for Judge Thomas outside the beltway," despite "strong liberal interest group opposition inside the beltway" and Anita Hill's attention-grabbing allegations that the nominee had sexually harassed her, made some in the White House hopeful that "the confirmation of Judge Clarence Thomas to the U.S. Supreme Court constitutes a major turning point in American life." Perhaps those liberal interest groups had "become increasingly divorced from their rank and file" and were even "on the run."[31]

In another good omen for that Administration and its successors, Republican senators had stood by their President. Seventeen Republicans had voted against Haynsworth; thirteen against Carswell; and six against Bork. Just two Republicans stood with the forty-six Democrats who voted against Thomas, while eleven Democrats joined forty-one Republicans to confirm him. As the ideological gulf between Democrats and Republicans hardened in the years following the Thomas nomination, "[p]arty loyalty toward the nominees of your party's presidential nominations for the Court" would harden into "a matter of political faith."[32]

Significantly, Justice Thomas arrived at the US Supreme Court after having served on the DC Circuit for a year and a half. The emphasis on prior judicial experience dated back to Eisenhower and also reflected the troubled battles of the sixties. When ill health finally forced William O. Douglas off the court while the Democrats still controlled Congress in 1975, Chief Justice Burger cited the past as reason to intervene in the selection process. "A nominee with substantial judicial experience would have several marked advantages; the adjustment to the work of the Court would be expedited because of familiarity with the enormous amount of 'new law' in recent decades; insulation from controversy and partisanship by reason of judicial service is also likely an advantage (as it was to Justice Blackmun and me)," he wrote President Ford. "For my part, I am compelled to be candid in saying that we have had all we can sustain of functioning with a 'crippled court' since 1969. The delays in 1969-1970 hurt the Court and the country."[33]

The president ignored the chief justice's offer to help with the selection process and instead instructed Attorney General Edward Levi to "look for the best" and not to consider "politics." Levi's work transformed the process that LBJ and Nixon had treated as their private domain. He developed the systematic evaluations of candidates in relationship to each other that future administrations would adopt. After study, Levi placed three prospects at the top of his list: Seventh Circuit Judge John Paul Stevens, Brigham Young University President Dallin Oaks, and Yale Law School Professor Robert Bork. Once the administration had consulted with the ABA Standing Committee on the Federal Judiciary, as all presidents but Nixon and Bush II dutifully did, the three top candidates of the White House were all circuit court judges. They were Seventh Circuit Judge John Paul Stevens, fifty-five; Third Circuit Judge Arlin Adams, fifty-four; and Seventh Circuit Judge Philip Tone, fifty-two. Ford chose Stevens.[34]

Here was the hardening of Eisenhower and Nixon's norms. Nixon himself had told reporters that a judicial career gave a prospective nominee the "edge" when he nominated Warren Burger. Then he saw how the criterion boxed him in as he searched for replacements for Black and Harlan. Yet it turned out that appellate judges indeed possessed the "edge." Here, too, was evidence that the thirteen bills introduced in Congress requiring Supreme Court justices to possess prior judicial experience between 1965 and 1967 by Warren Court foes like Richard Poff had borne fruit. Though none became law, the expectation of prior judicial experience solidified during the 1970s. Federally elected officeholders disappeared from the court (figure 30).[35]

Significantly, despite William Rehnquist's warning that a court made up only of judges risked resembling "the judiciary in civil law countries," which did "not command the respect and enjoy the significance of ours," prior judicial experience became a prerequisite for every justice over the next three and a half decades, beginning in 1975. Possibly one reason for what we might call "the judicial turn" is that as the United States moved politically right after the mid-seventies, the experience with the Warren Court helped convince some conservatives

Figure 30 The contemporary Supreme Court lacks its historic breadth. Elena Kagan was the first nominee since Powell and Rehnquist to lack prior judicial experience. Ben Sargent, copyright 2010 Austin American Statesman. Reprinted with permission of UNIVERSAL UCLICK. All rights reserved.

that those named to the court with deep roots in politics, like former governor Earl Warren, Senator Hugo Black, Securities and Exchange Commission Chair William O. Douglas, and LBJ intimate Abe Fortas, viewed law as politics—even though Justice Brennan, who was responsible for much of the Warren Court's work, came to the court from the judiciary. "Perceptions of the Warren Court's activism fueled a debate about the judiciary; critics wanted the Court to stop legislating from the bench," one law professor hypothesized. "Picking candidates with judicial (as opposed to political) experience may be seen as a way of pursuing this end." Or, as another put it, "The technocrats we've acquired . . . are somewhat a reaction to what the Warren Court did, and to the feeling that if we can just pick very safe people," new justices would not share its activist tendencies.[36]

Scholars also stressed presidents' desire for "predictability." Presidents viewed how a judge voted on lower courts as a reliable indicator of how a justice would decide cases. As one Justice Department official involved in Reagan's

1986 selections of Chief Justice Rehnquist and Justice Scalia wrote of the ideal nominee, "*we* must know what he thinks now, and *he* must have thought about issues enough that he will be unlikely to change his mind. For either, several years of federal judicial experience (since so many issues critical to us are dealt with little if at all by state courts), some time in academia, or a considerable body of written work introduced elsewhere is desirable." But at most, Reagan and his key partners thought in terms of "and," not "or." In his contemporary account of how the president decided on nominees, the White House counsel stressed that Reagan, Attorney General Meese, and he "were all of the view that sitting judges . . . who had clearly articulated philosophy were the most likely to remain steadfast in their views." While academic and/or government experience provided a plus, that is, judicial experience was the key.[37]

Some also explained presidents' preference for judges by pointing to their need to select a candidate with a strong resume who could win confirmation to the Supreme Court. Since federal judges who became justices had already survived the confirmation process at least once, they were supposedly not just predictable, but confirmable too. Thus, Pat Buchanan told Reagan's chief of staff that the president's "best bet for confirmation is a sitting jurist—who has already run the ga[u]ntlet of the Judiciary committee and the full Senate," even though their earlier confirmations did not help Clement Haynsworth, G. Harrold Carswell, Robert Bork, or Douglas Ginsburg.[38]

Sometimes, prior judicial experience does prove a good indicator of how a judge will vote in key cases and his or her confirmability. Sometimes, it doesn't. Careful empirical research has demonstrated the inaccuracy of presidential assumptions about both confirmability and predictability. While Supreme Court nominees Thurgood Marshall and Ruth Bader Ginsburg enjoyed relatively painless experiences before the Senate, compared to winning their nominations to the court of appeals, federal judges have not routinely enjoyed smooth Supreme Court confirmations. They have also proved no more likely to respect precedent or set aside their own policy preferences as justices than the "politicians" who preceded them on the court. In fact, they have followed the questionably judicious pattern of disproportionately ruling "in favor of their home [circuit] court." It has also become clear that conservative nominees can prove at least as "activist" as liberal ones.[39]

And the court may lose something when it draws so many of its members from the judiciary. Exhibit A, Linda Greenhouse reminds us, is *Clinton v. Jones*. There the justices reached the outlandish conclusion that requiring a sitting president to defend himself against claims of sexual harassment would not harm him. Moreover, when members of the court are drawn from a professional elite, credentials become crucial, which helps explain why all of the justices went to Harvard or Yale, and most did exceptionally well there. In the past, justices trod a wider path: It wasn't until sixty years ago, when Stanley Reed retired and Charles Whittaker joined the court, that all the justices even had attended law school. Doubtless it is useful for doctrinal analysis to people the court with a number of top graduates from elite schools—particularly if future presidents acknowledge that Harvard and Yale are not the only two in existence (figure 31). It is valuable, too, to draw some of the justices from "the judicial monastery," though perhaps one might hope for more justices with experience as trial, as well as appellate, judges. But a bench composed only of such individuals lacks its historic breadth. When Clinton had his opportunity to reshape the court, his adviser, Walter Dellinger, reminded him and others involved in the selection process of that. "I said when Thurgood Marshall retired that the court had lost its only—. . . and people expected me to say 'black justice.' But what I said was 'national figure,'" he remembered.[40]

It may also prove useful to take Supreme Court justices from the helms of other branches of government. The last justice with experience as a member of Congress was Hugo Black. Yet, as one of Poff's promoters reminded Nixon in 1971, "Since the founding of the Court, over thirty Justices have had previous service in Congress." More tellingly, "there has never been a year when the Court was without a former member of either the Congress or Continental Congress."

Figure 31 The contemporary Supreme Court also lacks its historic intellectual diversity. Nick Anderson editorial cartoon used with permission of Nick Anderson, the Writers Group, and the Cartoonist Group. All rights reserved.

Congress has its own problems, to be sure, but it might prove useful to add the perspective of legislators to the court. A number of commentators have noted the contemporary court's scorn for Congress and politicians, which legislators who become justices might help mute. They might even convince skeptics on the court of the value of legislative history.[41]

And why should William Howard Taft be the only former chief executive on the court in American history, particularly since his record there proved inspirational in some ways? As chief justice, Taft helped secure congressional enactment of the Judiciary Act of 1925, which vastly increased the discretionary nature of the court's docket; managed the federal courts and organized them as the third branch of government; obtained the funding for the Supreme Court building; and had the imagination to select Cass Gilbert to design it. Like former legislators, former presidents often do possess an unusual store of knowledge about law and politics, skills at compromise and conciliation, and useful contacts. Why shouldn't a president who could persuade former president Barack Obama to become a justice nominate him?[42]

Over the same period that the expectation of judicial experience bloomed, that of placing presidential intimates like Fortas on the court withered. Drawing on his experience in the Nixon White House, Pat Buchanan warned Reagan's chief of staff, "Any friend of the President's who can be painted as a 'crony' will be torn to pieces." When filling his first court vacancy, Clinton passed over his Arkansas friend, the distinguished Eighth Circuit judge, Richard Arnold, for the Supreme Court and awarded the position to Ruth Bader Ginsburg. While Arnold's status as a WASP male counted against him, his biographer reported, "speculation arose—and was confirmed by a member of Clinton's staff—that White House wariness toward Arnold's appointment to the Supreme Court had more to do with the fact that he was from Arkansas and a friend of the Clintons." When the president received a second court vacancy, he again considered Arnold. This time, Arnold's Eighth Circuit colleagues voiced their fear that he would not receive the nod to succeed Harry Blackmun *because* he was Clinton's friend and from Arkansas. They fretted needlessly, since Arnold's health did more to explain why he did not get the job, but significantly, they worried.[43]

Then, when Bush II nominated White House Counsel Harriet Miers in 2005, some complained that she lacked judicial experience ("If Approved, a First-Time Judge, Yes, but Hardly the First in Court's History," one *New York Times* headline felt compelled to remind readers), while others cried cronyism. Invoking history, David Greenberg told the Fortas story in *Slate*. He concluded: "The practice of naming presidential pals began to wane decades ago, and, as John Roberts might say, the wisdom of avoiding cronyism is now a settled matter."[44]

This "wisdom" is mystifying for several reasons. Lyndon Johnson was not the last president to practice cronyism with respect to the court. Although Nixon justified his choice of Chief Justice Burger by citing the need to maintain distance from the judiciary, Burger belonged to his political circle and shared political information about the court privately with him, just as Fortas did with LBJ. Admittedly, Burger's relationship to Nixon is no argument for cronyism. Still, given the value of transparency, surely it is preferable for a justice to be an overt crony like Fortas than a relatively covert one like Burger. More important, we deal out too many excellent prospects when we eliminate presidential intimates, be they exceptionally smart people, like Fortas, or reliable and trusted individuals of high character, like Homer Thornberry. Yes, some cronies who became justices were mediocrities, but not all of them. Recall, for example, John Marshall, David Davis, the first Harlan, Louis Brandeis, Harlan Fiske Stone, Felix Frankfurter, William O. Douglas, Hugo Black, and Robert Jackson. Presidential cronies have populated the court since Washington appointed Jay. Presidents and those who help them select justices could benefit from the reminder that Supreme Court justices need not be federal judges with whom they have no connection.

That mold has already been chipped. It may be noteworthy that in nominating Elena Kagan, Obama selected someone without judicial experience whom he explicitly called a "friend." (In addition to having taught law with Obama at Chicago, Kagan had served as the president's solicitor general and had many political and social contacts with administration insiders.) Yet, as a former Harvard Law School dean and solicitor general, Justice Kagan occupied a special place in the pantheon. Moreover, but for the Senate, which blocked Clinton's attempt to nominate her to the great feeder of the DC Circuit, Kagan would have arrived at the court from the bench. Perhaps her selection launched a new era in the nomination process; more likely, it did not.[45]

Confirmation

Whether or not the Kagan nomination proves a game changer, the 1967–71 contests over the court's membership, taken in their entirety and proximity to one another, heralded the birth of the contemporary confirmation process. Sarah Binder and Forrest Maltzman usefully divide commentators into two groups. Do they believe in the Ecclesiastes "nothing-new-under-the-sun theory of judicial selection," which treats "ideological conflict over the makeup of the bench" as an "ever-present force in shaping the selection of federal judges and justices"? Or do they subscribe to the "big bang theory" that identifies "a breaking point in national politics, after which prevailing norms of deference and restraint in judicial selection have fallen apart" and posits "a sea change in appointment politics, evidenced by the lengthening of the confirmation process and the rise in confirmation failure"? In the latter case, commentators often point to the Bork battle and contend that it rang in the modern era of partisan confirmation politics. In the words of Senator Orrin Hatch, "Democrats captured the Senate in 1986 . . . and conspired with leftist legal gurus that dramatically politicized the process."[46]

The Bork battle was indeed politicized. And liberals and conservatives grasped at whatever precedents helped them to justify contesting and championing Bork. Senate Judiciary Committee Chair Joe Biden argued that historically, and as late as the Fortas and Carswell fights, the Senate focused on ideology. Only recently, Biden maintained, had the Senate restricted its review to the more "narrow standard" of character and professional competence. His fellow liberals seized on the ideological argument that Southerners like Strom Thurmond had made against Thurgood Marshall twenty years earlier and maintained that Bork's confirmation would change the "balance" of the court. For its part, the Reagan administration wrongly claimed, "In the 1960s, when Justices Goldberg, Fortas and Marshall were being placed on the Supreme Court—resulting in a body that consisted of (at best) two judicial conservatives—the 'balance' theory was never raised." And Thurmond and others who had inveighed against Marshall in 1967 and Fortas in 1968 on grounds of ideology now insisted that the Senate only justifiably rejected a nominee because of ability and character. Naturally the Reaganites framed the Fortas story so as to make the case that LBJ's nominee had not become chief justice because of his character flaws, not ideology.[47]

We expect politicians to ransack the past and flip-flop on their positions. Of course, as the *New York Times* noted, "Both Sides in Bork Debate Seek the Blessing of History." And someone might legitimately tell the story of the 1968 chief justice fight in a way that made ideology all-important and Fortas the first to be "Borked" or focused on LBJ's insistence on coupling Fortas and Thornberry and on Fortas's extrajudicial activities and lecture fees.[48]

Yet the claim that Bork was the first to be "Borked" doesn't seem altogether right. That's not to say it's implausible. We know that Reagan did think of pairing Rehnquist's chief justice nomination with either that of Scalia or Bork in 1986. His administration considered Scalia and Bork the leading exponents of judicial restraint and admired Scalia's commitment to separation of powers and Bork's to original intent. The White House counsel observed that Reagan "seemed intrigued by Judge Scalia, who was young enough to serve on the Court for an extended period of time, and [would] be the first Italian-American appointee to the Supreme Court." Presumably for reasons of youth and/or ethnicity, Scalia, fifty, got the nod over Bork, fifty-nine, and the Senate unanimously confirmed him in 1986. (If Powell shielded Rehnquist in 1971, Rehnquist provided cover for Scalia fifteen years later.) Thus, Bork's ordeal the next year "must" signal a shift.[49]

Bork himself characterized earlier confirmation struggles as "essentially" but not "overtly" political. He specifically mentioned only Haynsworth's. That makes sense: Why would a conservative meritocrat like Bork want to become the bedfellow of Abe Fortas or Harrold Carswell? "In my case," Bork continued, "after the most minute scrutiny of my personal life and professional record, all that was available to the opposition was ideological attack, and so politics came fully into the open. I had criticized the Warren court, and this was the revenge of the Warren Court."[50]

Well, maybe, though if so, Bork's experience provides further testimony to the lasting scars of the sixties. But it may also be that Bork could have won confirmation in 1986 before the Republicans lost the Senate. In fact, one 1986 administration memorandum promoting him pointed out that Bork had been "considered the frontrunner for the next seat on the Supreme Court since the beginning of the first Reagan Administration," that "even liberals respect Bork's intellectual force," and that he might experience easier going than other candidates before the Senate Judiciary Committee "because he is 'much older and less radical' than some of the alternatives" and "is thought to be about as liberal a nominee as the Democrats believe they will get from President Reagan." Perhaps divided government does not explain the contentiousness of recent confirmation battles. Still, it is worth remembering that like Haynsworth and Carswell, and unlike Scalia and Rehnquist in 1986, Bork faced a Democratically controlled Senate in 1987.[51]

The 1987 Bork fight *was* significant. Bork himself contended that the opposition defeated a nominee solely because of ideology, without a "cover." But as A. E. Dick Howard has countered, the Bork battle did not so much "change" as intensify "everything."[52]

Indeed, in a number of ways beyond the allegation that Bork would alter the "balance" of the court, the confirmation politics of 1987 recalled the old battles. As with Haynsworth, Bork's opponents had plenty of lead time. That was the reason Ted Kennedy had his speech condemning "Robert Bork's America" ready for delivery within an hour after Reagan announced the nomination. As with Haynsworth and Carswell, the media and interest groups undermined the nominee. They plunked down a plethora of "well-publicized 50-page 'reports' finding that Judge Bork's records or views are particularly antagonistic" to their point of view and alleging that Bork was not the moderate defender of judicial restraint the president wanted to sell him as, "but rather a result oriented right wing activist," the White House counsel complained. "I don't think anybody imagined the kind of campaign you'd have," Reagan's communications director said. Consequently, as with Haynsworth and Carswell, the White House was caught off guard at a time when it had already alienated conservative groups by portraying Bork as a centrist, a tactic that seemed particularly hypocritical after a "senior White House aide" was quoted in *Newsweek* calling Bork a "right-wing zealot." And like the Nixon White House, the Reagan administration sometimes behaved as if all grass-roots sentiment was equal as it circulated memoranda enumerating the groups that backed Bork's nomination. Too often, the administration did not acknowledge that the American Latvian Association or National Association of Wholesale-Distributors would not devote the vigor to promoting the nomination that the Leadership Conference, People for the American Way, and feminist groups gave to fighting it.[53]

The Reagan White House marketed Bork as poorly as the Nixon administration had sold Haynsworth and Carswell. By contrast, liberals who in many cases had cut their teeth on earlier confirmation fights successfully updated their old playbooks, and the Senate rejected Bork by fifty-eight to forty-two. The White House now learned, one veteran said, "that it is entirely unrealistic to expect that a nominee's ideology—or more precisely the contents of his judicial philosophy—can escape scrutiny by the Senate." Administration officials shouldn't have needed the Bork battle to teach them that.[54]

Bork's defeat did not still the echoes from the past. As after the failure of the Haynsworth nomination, the president vowed to nominate an ideological clone, then sent up the name of someone vulnerable. The "cover issue" became important again as Judge Douglas Ginsburg had to withdraw his nomination amid a welter of conflict-of-interest charges, allegations about his truthfulness, and, above all, disclosures by National Public Radio's Nina Totenberg that he had smoked marijuana. "We never stop learning lessons do we?" a White House postmortem concluded. "The brief Ginsburg battle gave us a glimpse of what the post-Bork era will bring us. Everything is fair game to a voracious media. Fed by behind-the-scenes leakers, innuendo specialists and people who appear willing to lie to the FBI but spill their guts to NPR, the media have taken to dining out on Supreme Court nominees." Once again, the study of recent history might have taught the White House something. The media had helped shape confirmation controversies since the sixties.[55]

Now Reagan sent up the name of Ninth Circuit Judge Anthony Kennedy. And it may have been here, in the wake of the Ginsburg embarrassment, that the modern vetting process emerged in all its glory. Kennedy faced more than ten hours of FBI interviews and a three-hour session with the attorney general and White House counsel in which he was asked, among other things, whether he liked "kinky sex," how many women he had slept with in college, and whether he had ever contracted a sexually transmitted disease, shoplifted as a child, and shown cruelty to animals. As Harry Blackmun had done before him, Kennedy then sailed through an exhausted Senate. He proved almost as much of a changeling on the court as Blackmun did when he won confirmation after the Haynsworth and Carswell fights.[56]

So the Bork battle doesn't mark the beginning of the contemporary confirmation process, which is the child of the sixties. And that process has not always
been contentious, now or then. Justices Kennedy, Scalia, Blackmun, Powell,
Stevens, O'Connor, and Ruth Bader Ginsburg won confirmation by a unanimous, or nearly unanimous, vote. Though each confirmation follows its own
script and the process has changed over the past half century, it has often sparked
the concerns that reverberated during 1967–71. Contemporary commentators
frequently condemn the "kabuki confirmations," or carefully choreographed
and highly stylized performances in which nominees pretend to answer senators' queries—as most of them have been doing since the Warren era. They show
frustration about White House "packaging" of the nominee. They chart the intense media scrutiny that can turn hearings into spectacle. They marvel at interest group mobilization. And they understand that nominees and justices can
become more vulnerable because of a "cover issue" than ideology.[57]

Ghosts of the Sixties

The sixties have cast a long shadow over the confirmation process too, particularly since the last justice to win approval in 2010, Justice Kagan, clerked for
Justice Marshall (figure 32). Though the *Wall Street Journal* reported that she had
accused the Warren Court of "overreaching" in her Oxford thesis, Republicans
mentioned Marshall repeatedly on day one of her hearing. Would she, like
Marshall, use law to help the disadvantaged? a Republican asked on day two.
Like other nominees since 2000, this one placed great emphasis on her own neu-
trality and objectivity, and she responded, "you'll get Justice Kagan, you won't
get Justice Marshall, and that's an important thing." That didn't answer his question, the senator observed. A *Washington Post* op-ed semifacetiously entitled
"Kagan May Get Confirmed, but Thurgood Marshall Can Forget It" put it this
way: "Did Republicans think it would help their cause to criticize the first African
American on the Supreme Court, a revered figure who has been celebrated with
an airport, a postage stamp and a Broadway show?" Yes, Republicans did. Yet
with a Democratic president and Democratic Senate, Kagan received confirmation, but by the relatively slim vote of sixty-three to thirty-seven. Clearly, the
nomination and confirmation process had become even more partisan in the
twenty-first century.[58]

The next vacancy, a surprise, underlined that. Control of the Senate had
changed hands in the midterm elections after Kagan's confirmation. When
Justice Scalia died, President Obama now faced Republicans in the Senate led by
Majority Leader Mitch McConnell. During the sixties, McConnell had worked
as a legislative assistant to Senator Marlow Cook (R-KY), a sometime thorn in

Figure 32 The beginning of Senate confirmation hearings for Supreme Court nominee Elena Kagan, 2010. The contemporary nomination and confirmation process was born between 1967 and 1971. Alex Wong/Staff Editorial #: 102501070. Collection: Getty Images News.

Nixon's side. Though Cook worked hard for Haynsworth's confirmation, he had provided a pivotal vote against Carswell.

McConnell had defended Cook's votes and presidential power in a 1970 article, "Haynsworth and Carswell: A New Senate Standard of Excellence." Tellingly, McConnell chose a quotation from the French poet and essayist Paul Valéry as his epigraph: "All politicians have read history; but one might say they read it only in order to learn from it how to repeat the same calamities all over again." Because twentieth-century senators had decided to judge Supreme Court nominees on the basis of "qualifications and not politics or ideology," they had often "sought to hide their political objections beneath a veil of charges about fitness, ethics and other professional qualifications," McConnell explained. Instead, he argued, senators really should judge nominees only on the basis of whether they possessed competence, distinction, temperament, ethical probity, and a clean life off the bench free of "prior criminal conviction" or "debilitating personal problems such as alcoholism or drug abuse." By those standards, he maintained, Haynsworth deserved confirmation, while Carswell did not. "The Senate should discount the philosophy of the nominee" unless he were "a Communist or a member of the Nazi party," McConnell concluded. "In our politically centrist society, it is highly unlikely that any Executive would nominate a man of such extreme views of the right or the left as to be disturbing to the Senate," and "the true measure of a statesman may well be the ability to rise above partisan political considerations to objectively pass upon another aspiring human being." So, too, thirty-five years later, during the Bush II years, Senator McConnell continued to defend executive authority when he proclaimed that "the President, and the President alone, nominates judges" and accused "my friends on the other side of the aisle" of altering "the Senate's 'advise and consent' responsibilities to 'advise and obstruct'" for the first time since ratification of the Constitution.[59]

In 2016, however, McConnell and his Republican colleagues assumed the role of Senator Robert Griffin in the Fortas fight. Scalia's body was barely cold before McConnell declared that the next president should choose the next justice. "The fact of the matter is that it's been standard practice over the last nearly 80 years that Supreme Court nominees are not nominated and confirmed during a presidential election year," Senate Judiciary Committee Chair Charles Grassley (R-IA) insisted. Though Grassley was wrong, Republicans on the Senate Judiciary Committee vowed not to hold a confirmation hearing. They pointed to a June 1992 speech by Obama's vice president, Joe Biden, during another period of divided government. As Senate Judiciary chair, Biden had then argued that if a Supreme Court vacancy materialized (it didn't), Bush I should "not name a nominee until after the November election is completed." If the president did, the Judiciary Committee "should seriously consider not scheduling confirmation hearings on the nomination until after the campaign season is over."[60]

President Obama responded to Republicans by insisting on his responsibility to nominate and calling on the Senate to "do your job." As the Nixon White House might have done, Obama's floated a trial balloon. Its trial balloon, however, was designed to appeal to the opposition party and was the popular Hispanic Republican governor of Nevada, Brian Sandoval. McConnell and company proved unimpressed, and the governor pulled a Poff and removed himself from consideration.[61]

By this point in the process, even the possibilities of a Republican filibuster and constitutional crisis seemed tame. "Senate Republicans Lose Their Minds on a Supreme Court Seat," the New York Times editorialized two weeks after Scalia's death. All that seemed certain was that any debate that occurred would feature "lofty empty rhetoric and reliance on questionable precedent by all sides" and that "both Republicans and Democrats and their followers will make use of the still-controversial Senate reaction to a Supreme Court nomination in 1968 by President Lyndon Johnson." No matter what Republicans, Democrats, and their followers said about those questionable precedents, that still-controversial reaction, and that still-controversial nomination, it seemed clear that they would accuse each other of hypocrisy as well.[62]

Obama's eventual nomination of Merrick Garland did nothing to resolve the situation. As Clinton had done in selecting Ginsburg and Breyer, the president had chosen an outstanding candidate cut near the center. Sometimes, McConnell justified his refusal to hold hearings on grounds of principle and maintained that the next president should name the next justice. At others, he pointed out that the National Rifle Association and National Federation of Business opposed Garland as someone who would move the court "dramatically to the left." And Republicans didn't just fail to schedule hearings. Many refused even to meet the nominee. When they gathered to choose Donald Trump as their nominee in Cleveland that summer, Republicans seemed certain they were on the correct course. Trump, who had promised to nominate conservative prolife justices who would respect the Second Amendment, tweeted that "if the Dems win the Presidency, the new JUSTICES appointed will destroy us all!" and gave a Nixonian acceptance speech that dwelled on the need for law and order. "Scalia's ghost" loomed large over the convention, the *Charlotte Observer* announced in an article whose "highlights" observed that "Republicans are reminding delegates in Cleveland about the Supreme Court every chance they get," "The next president could reshape the court for a generation," and "The issue could be enough to get some voters off the couch." The Democrats resorted to equally histrionic rhetoric.[63]

Then in September, and unusually for a presidential candidate, Trump released the names of twenty-one potential court nominees that he had assembled with the help of the Heritage Foundation and Federalist Society. All on his list were individuals in the mold of Justice Scalia, who "will protect our liberty with the highest regard for the Constitution," he stressed, "and I will choose only from it in picking future Justices of the United States Supreme Court." Notably, almost all his possible choices were federal appeals judges and state supreme court justices, though Trump did make an exception for one senator, Utah's Mike Lee. Fewer than a quarter had gone to law school at Harvard or Yale. "If the list has a main theme, it is that there are plenty of good judges who went to law school at places like Notre Dame, Marquette, the University of Georgia and the University of Miami," one columnist wrote.[64]

When Trump won the presidency in November and the Republicans maintained control of the Senate, Garland presumably stopped preparing for his confirmation hearing. Clearly, one analyst observed, "Senate Republicans' strategy of not even considering Garland, of letting the American people decide who gets to fill Scalia's seat worked." And if Senate Republicans ended the filibuster for Supreme Court nominees, as the Democrats had done for lower court federal judges in 2013, and if all Republicans approved of the Presidential picks, they would just require a bare majority in the Senate to prevail in ratifying President Trump's selections.[65]

Might the United States be headed for a future in which a president could only successfully nominate a justice when his or her party controlled the Senate? That would politicize the nomination and confirmation process, and ultimately the Supreme Court, more than ever. In the era of divided government that began in 1968 and has continued with intermittent interruptions afterwards, could that also leave the court without personnel for such extended periods that it might ultimately "just disappear"? Historians are poor prognosticators. Time will provide the answer.[66]

ACKNOWLEDGMENTS

Though other authors and those mentioned find them irresistible, acknowledgments are often boring. There are too few synonyms for the verb *to thank*. Nevertheless, it is a pleasure to declare my appreciation, to use a particularly clunky one, for the many people who helped me write this book.

I am grateful to the LBJ Library for releasing the Johnson tapes early and to the Miller Center for providing access to them online and, in some instances, for transcribing conversations for me. I am indebted to Stanley Kutler, who introduced me to John Dean, and to John Dean for his great generosity in sharing his Nixon transcripts. Luke Nichter at nixontapes.com kindly provided me with tapes in the best possible listening format and some transcripts too. Then there are the archivists across the country who welcomed me to their collections and/or swiftly responded to my requests for items. I am very, very grateful to them and for the kind and efficient individuals who helped me track down illustrations. Thankfully, too, a number of people extended themselves to answer my sometimes frantic queries for information and materials, including John Jacob, Bruce Kalk, Dorissa Martinez, Jenny Mandel, Tony Mastres, Steve Petteway, Rick Seymour, Ross Tomlin, Nina Totenberg, and Laurence Tribe.

I benefited from opportunities to present my research at the American Society for Legal History annual meeting, Boston University, Cambridge, NYU, Oxford, UCLA, UCSB, and the University of Pennsylvania.

While I was at work on this project, I lost, in chronological order, four beloved cheerleaders and critics—my father, my mother-in-law, my dissertation adviser, and my mother. I so miss them all, and I am so grateful to have had them for so long. I have been especially thankful for those who stepped into the editorial breach. Hope Firestone enabled me to finish the book. Judy Shanks channeled her "inner Newton" and attacked my prose in every chapter. Barry Friedman, Sarah Barringer Gordon, Ariela Gross, John Henry Schlegel, and Larry Zacharias tackled portions of the project. For taking on the entire manuscript and providing invaluable criticism and other assistance, I will always be indebted to Richard Bernstein, Dan Ernst, John Jeffries, Pnina Lahav, Sanford Levinson, William E. Nelson, Scot Powe, Brad Snyder, Adam Stolpen, and Mark Tushnet. For research assistance, I thank Ron Krock, Jaclyn Reinhart, Sydney Soderberg, and Paul Warden.

At Oxford University Press, Dave McBride proved the editor of my dreams and Katie Weaver provided invaluable assistance. And I thank my very able production and copy editors, Mary Jo Rhodes and Danielle Michaely; proofreader Timothy DeWerff; and indexer John Grennan.

I am much obliged, too, to friends from A to Z, who, in addition to those mentioned earlier, gave me all kinds of vital aid and/or support at one time or another: Christine Adams; Pat Bagley; Pamela Blum; Mort and Penn Borden; Cyndi Brokaw; Elliot and Mary Brownlee; Guido Calabresi; Jane DeHart; Lupe Diaz; Mercedes Eichholz; Bill Felstiner; Carolyn Agger Fortas; Ethel and Lucy Garr; Jesus Gil; Dan Gordon; Jamie, Mira, and Talia Gracer; Tom Green; Denis Grunfeld; A. J. Hinojosa; Risa Katzen; Barbara Kern; Elliott Lee; Charles Li; Alice and Tremper Longman; Eva Madoyan-Ktoyan; Daniel and David Marshall; Harriet and Serena Mayeri; Kate Metropolis; Melissa Murray; Aiko Noda; Tom Pejic; Daniel and Jeff Richman; Irma Rico; Bladey Kalman Runge and Chris Runge; Todd Ryan; Kate Saltzman-Li; Connie, John, and Ward Schweizer; Eran Shalev; Gary Silk; Dennis Ventry; Vicky Woeste; Candace Waid; the Westlake girls of 1971; and Rosemarie Zagarri.

Most of all, I thank W. Randall Garr.

NOTES

Abbreviations for Sources Consulted

MANUSCRIPT COLLECTIONS

Bayh MSS
Birch Bayh Papers, Modern Political Papers Collection, Indiana University, Bloomington, IN

Black MSS
Hugo LaFayette Black Papers, Manuscript Division, Library of Congress, Washington, D.C.

Blackmun MSS
Harry A. Blackmun Papers, Manuscript Division, Library of Congress

Brennan MSS
William J. Brennan Papers, Manuscript Division, Library of Congress

Brennan TH MSS
William J. Brennan Term Histories, Manuscript Division, Library of Congress

Brownell MSS and Brownell Add'l.
Herbert Brownell Jr. Papers and Additional Papers, Eisenhower Library, Abilene, KS

Celler MSS
Emanuel Celler Papers, Manuscript Division, Library of Congress

Charns MSS
Alexander Charns Papers, Southern Historical Collection, Louis Round Wilson Special Collections Library, University of North Carolina, Chapel Hill, Chapel Hill, NC

Cheney MSS
Richard Cheney Papers, Ford Library, Ann Arbor, MI

Clifford MSS
Clark M. Clifford Papers, Manuscript Division, Library of Congress

Contested Materials MSS
White House Special Files, Contested Materials Collection, Nixon Library, Yorba Linda, CA

Dent MSS
Harry Dent Papers, Nixon Library

Eaton MSS
William J. Eaton Papers, Howard Gotlieb Archival Research Center, Boston University

Ervin MSS
Sam J. Ervin Papers, Southern Historical Collection, Louis Round Wilson Special Collections Library, University of North Carolina

Fortas-Thornberry MSS
Special File Pertaining to Abe Fortas and Homer Thornberry, LBJ Library, Austin, TX

Frank MSS
John Paul Frank Papers, Manuscript Division, Library of Congress

Fortas MSS
Abe Fortas Papers, Manuscripts and Archives, Yale University Library, New Haven, CT

Goldberg MSS
Arthur J. Goldberg Papers, Manuscript Division, Library of Congress

Gossett MSS
William T. Gossett Papers, Bentley Historical Library, University of Michigan, Ann Arbor, MI

Graham MSS
Fred P. Graham Papers, Manuscript Division, Library of Congress

Griffin MSS
Robert P. Griffin Papers, Clarke Historical Library, Central Michigan University, Mount Pleasant, MI

Harlan MSS
John Marshall Harlan Papers, Seeley G. Mudd Manuscript Library, Princeton University, Princeton, NJ

Hart MSS
Philip A. Hart Papers, Bentley Historical Library, University of Michigan

Hartmann MSS
Robert Hartmann Papers, Ford Library

Haynsworth MSS
Clement F. Haynsworth Jr. Papers, Special Collections and Archives, Furman University, Greenville, SC

Hollings MSS
Ernest F. "Fritz" Hollings Papers, South Carolina Political Collections, Hollings Special Collections Library, University of South Carolina, Columbia, SC

Katzenbach MSS
Nicholas deB. Katzenbach Papers, JFK Library, Boston, MA

Kilpatrick MSS
James J. Kilpatrick Papers, Albert and Shirley Small Special Collections Library, University of Virginia, Charlottesville, VA

Leadership Conference MSS
Leadership Conference on Civil Rights Papers, Manuscript Division, Library of Congress

B. Marshall MSS
Burke Marshall Papers, JFK Library

T. Marshall MSS
Thurgood Marshall Papers, Manuscript Division, Library of Congress

McClellan MSS
John L. McClellan Papers, Archives and Special Collections, Ouachita Baptist College, Arkadelphia, AR

Mink MSS
Patsy T. Mink Papers, Manuscript Division, Library of Congress

Morris MSS
Robert P. Morris Papers, Special Collections, Louisiana State University, Baton Rouge, LA

NAACP MSS
NAACP Papers, Manuscript Division, Library of Congress

Parker MSS
John Johnston Parker Papers, Southern Historical Collection, Louis Round Wilson Special Collections Library, University of North Carolina

Poff MSS
Richard Harding Poff Papers, Albert and Shirley Small Special Collections Library, University of Virginia

Pollak MSS
Louis H. Pollak Papers, Manuscripts and Archives, Yale University Library

Porter MSS
Paul Porter Papers, LBJ Library

Powell MSS
Lewis F. Powell Jr. Papers, Powell Archives, Washington & Lee University, Lexington, VA

Rauh MSS
Joseph L. Rauh Papers, Manuscript Division, Library of Congress

RFK AG MSS
Robert F. Kennedy Attorney General Papers, JFK Library

RFK Senate MSS
Robert F. Kennedy Senate Papers

Rogers MSS
William P. Rogers Papers, Eisenhower Library

Rosenthal MSS
Jacob "Jack" Rosenthal Papers, JFK Library

Russell MSS
Richard B. Russell Jr. Papers, Special Collections, Richard B. Russell Library for Political Research and Studies, University of Georgia, Athens, GA

Safire MSS
William Safire Papers, Manuscript Division, Library of Congress

Schlesinger MSS
Arthur Schlesinger, Jr. Papers, Archives and Manuscripts, New York Public Library

Scott MSS
Hugh Scott Papers, Albert and Shirley Small Special Collections Library, University of Virginia

Smith MSS
Margaret Chase Smith Papers, Margaret Chase Smith Library, Skowhegan, ME

Soberloff MSS
Simon Ernest Soberloff Papers, Manuscript Division, Library of Congress

Sorensen Papers
Theodore Sorensen Papers, JFK Library

Spong MSS
William Belser Spong Papers, Albert and Shirley Small Special Collections Library, University of Virginia

Stewart MSS
Potter Stewart Papers, Manuscripts and Archives, Yale University

Talmadge MSS
Herman E. Talmadge Papers, Special Collections, Richard B. Russell Library for Political Research and Studies, University of Georgia

Thurmond MSS
Strom Thurmond Papers, Special Collections, Strom Thurmond Institute of Government and Public Affairs, Clemson University, Clemson, SC

Thurston MSS
George Lee Thurston III Family Papers, Clarke Historical Library, Central Michigan University

Walters MSS
Johnnie M. Walters Papers, South Carolina Political Collections, Hollings Special Collections Library, University of South Carolina

Warren MSS
Earl Warren Papers, Manuscript Division, Library of Congress

White MSS
Theodore H. White Papers, JFK Library

White House Special Files, Special Member Office Files, Nixon Library
Colson MSS	Charles W. Colson
Dean MSS	John W. Dean III
Ehrlichman MSS	John D. Ehrlichman
Harlow MSS	Bryce N. Harlow
Krogh MSS	Egil Krogh
Young MSS	David R. Young Jr.

Whitman MSS
Ann C. Whitman Papers, Administration Series, Eisenhower Library

OTHER ABBREVIATIONS
DDEL	Dwight D. Eisenhower Library, Abilene, KS
JFKL	John F. Kennedy Library, Boston, MA
LBJL	Lyndon B. Johnson Library, Austin, TX

RMNL	Richard M. Nixon Library, Yorba Linda, CA
GRFL	Gerald Ford Library, Ann Arbor, MI
RWRL	Ronald Reagan Library, Simi Valley, CA
GHWBL	George H. W. Bush Library, College Station, TX
WJCL	William J. Clinton Library, Little Rock, AR
NARS	National Archives
NPR	National Public Radio
POF	President's Office Files
PPF	President's Personal Files
WHCF	White House Central Files

ABBREVIATIONS RELATED TO TAPES CITED

MC	Presidential Recordings Program, Miller Center
EOB	Executive Office Building
OVAL	Oval Office
NT	Nixontapes.org, http://nixontapes.org/
Transcripts	Transcripts of Conversations and Meetings Collection, LBJ Library
WHT	White House Telephone

ORAL HISTORIES ABBREVIATIONS

COHP	Oral History Project, Columbia University
GRFOH	Oral History, Ford Library
LBJOH	Oral History, LBJ Library
OHLC	Oral History, Library of Congress

NEWSPAPERS, PERIODICALS, AND OTHER PUBLICATIONS CITED

ABFJ	*American Bar Foundation Journal*
AC	*Augusta-Courier*
AD	*Arkansas Democrat*
AG	*Arkansas Gazette*
AHR	*American Historical Review*
AJ	*Alabama Journal*
AJLH	*American Journal of Legal History*
AmSp	*American Speech*
AvG	*Avant Garde*
AzSLJ	*Arizona State Law Journal*
BCLR	*Boston College Law Review*
BG	*Boston Globe*
BLJ	*Blackletter Law Journal*
BrLJ	*Brandeis Law Journal*
BuffLR	*Buffalo Law Review*

CA	*Commercial Appeal*
CaLH	*California Legal History*
CaLR	*California Law Review*
CarLR	*Cardozo Law Review*
CDD	*Chicago Daily Defender*
CDN	*Chicago Daily News*
CJR	*Columbia Journalism Review*
CKLR	*Chicago-Kent Law Review*
CLR	*Columbia Law Review*
CO	*Charlotte Observer*
ConComm	*Constitutional Commentary*
CorLR	*Cornell Law Review*
CPD	*Cleveland Plain Dealer*
CR	*Congressional Record*
CSM	*Christian Science Monitor*
CT	*Chicago Tribune*
Daed	*Daedalus*
DFP	*Detroit Free Press*
DK	*Daily Kos*
DLJ	*Duke Law Journal*
DMR	*Des Moines Register*
Dr	*Drake Law Journal*
Esq	*Esquire*
FHQ	*Florida Historical Quarterly*
FLR	*Fordham Law Review*
Fort	*Fortune*
GaSJLH	*Georgia Journal of Southern Legal History*
Gaz	*The Gazette*
GB	*Green Bag*
GN	*Greenville News*
HaCLQ	*Hastings Constitutional Law Quarterly*
Ham	*Hamline Law Review*
HE	*Human Events*
Hi	*The Hill*
HLPR	*Harvard Law and Policy Review*
HLR	*Harvard Law Review*
HLRec	*Harvard Law Record*
HofLR	*Hofstra Law Review*
InN	*Indianapolis News*
JAH	*Journal of American History*
JBSBull	*John Birch Society Bulletin*

JerP	*Jerusalem Post*
JerR	*Jerusalem Report*
JHS	*Journal of the History of Sexuality*
JPL	*Journal of Public Law*
JSCH	*Journal of Supreme Court History*
KyLJ	*Kentucky Law Journal*
LADJ	*Los Angeles Daily Journal*
LAT	*Los Angeles Times*
LDS	*Lewiston Daily-Sun*
LHR	*Law and History Review*
Li	*Life*
LSI	*Law and Social Inquiry*
MA	*Montgomery Advertiser*
MetNe	*Metropolitan News Enterprise*
MinnLR	*Minnesota Law Review*
MLR	*Michigan Law Review*
MSLR	*Michigan State Law Review*
Na	*Nation*
NCLR	*North Carolina Law Review*
NEWS	*Newsweek*
NEWSD	*Newsday*
NewT	*New Times*
NO	*National Observer*
NR	*National Review*
NT	*Nashville Tennesseean*
NwULR	*Northwestern University Law Review*
NY	*New Yorker*
NYDN	*New York Daily News*
NYLSLR	*New York Law School Law Review*
NYMag	*New York Magazine*
NYP	*New York Post*
NYT	*New York Times*
NYT Mag	*New York Times Magazine*
NYULR	*New York University Law Review*
OB	*Ohio Bar*
OHSLJ	*Ohio State Law Journal*
OP	*Oakland Post*
PAMagH&B	*Pennsylvania Magazine of History and Biography*
PI	*Philadelphia Inquirer*
POL	*Politico*

POQ	*Public Opinion Quarterly*
PSCHA	*Proceedings of the South Carolina Historical Association*
PSQ	*Presidential Studies Quarterly*
RAH	*Reviews in American History*
RLR	*Rutgers Law Review*
SBCS	*San Bernardino County Sun*
SCarLR	*South Carolina Law Review*
SCH	*Supreme Court History*
SCHSY	*Supreme Court Historical Society Yearbook*
SCR	*Supreme Court Review*
SDU	*San Diego Union*
SFE	*San Francisco Examiner*
SHT	*Sarasota Herald-Tribune*
Sla	*Slate*
SLPD	*Saint Louis Post Dispatch*
SLR	*Stanford Law Review*
StP	*Saint Petersburg Times*
Ti	*Time*
TNR	*The New Republic*
TPM	*Talking Points Memo*
TxLR	*Texas Law Review*
UCDLR	*University of California, Davis Law Review*
UCLR	*University of Chicago Law Review*
UPLR	*University of Pennsylvania Law Review*
URLR	*University of Richmond Law Review*
USA	*USA Today*
USN	*US News and World Report*
VA	*Victoria Advocate*
VaLR	*Virginia Law Review*
VF	*Vanity Fair*
W&LLR	*Washington & Lee Law Review*
W&MBRJ	*William & Mary Bill of Rights Journal*
WCR	*Western Criminology Review*
WDN	*Washington Daily News*
WMLR	*William Mitchell Law Review*
WoLJ	*Women Lawyers Journal*
WP	*Washington Post*
WS	*Washington Star*
WSJ	*Wall Street Journal*
YLJ	*Yale Law Journal*

CONGRESSIONAL HEARINGS AND REPORTS

Roy Mersky and J. Myron Jacobstein, Compilers. *Supreme Court of the U.S. Hearings and Reports on Successful and Unsuccessful Nominations of Supreme Court Justices by the Senate Judiciary Committee.*

Nomination of Felix Frankfurter
Hearings Before a Subcommittee of the Committee on the Judiciary, U.S. Senate, Seventy-Sixth Congress, First Session, on the Nomination of Felix Frankfurter to Be an Associate Justice of the Supreme Court, January 11 and 12, 1939, Volume 4

Nomination of Frank Murphy
Copy of the Original Handwritten Minutes of the U.S. Senate Committee on the Judiciary on the Nomination of Frank Murphy to Be an Associate Justice of the Supreme Court, 1939, Volume 4

Nomination of Earl Warren
Copy of the Original Transcript of Hearings Held by the U.S. Senate Committee on the Judiciary on the Nomination of Earl Warren to Be Chief Justice of the Supreme Court, 1954, Volume 5

Nomination of John Harlan
Hearings Before the Committee on the Judiciary, U.S. Senate, Eighty-Fourth Congress, First Session, on Nomination of John Marshall Harlan, of New York, to Be Associate Justice of the Supreme Court of the United States, February 24 and 25, 1955, Volume 6

Nomination of William Brennan
Hearings Before the Committee on the Judiciary, U.S. Senate, Eighty-Fifth Congress, First Session, on Nomination of William Joseph Brennan, Junior, of New Jersey, to Be Associate Justice of the Supreme Court of the United States, February 26 and 27, 1957, Volume 6

Nomination of Potter Stewart
Report to Accompany the Nomination of Potter Stewart, Eighty-Sixth Congress, First Session, Executive Report, No. 2, April 29, 1959, Volume 6

Nomination of Charles Whittaker
Hearing Before the Committee on the Judiciary, U.S. Senate, Eighty-Fifth Congress, First Session, on Nomination of Charles E. Whittaker, of Missouri to Be Associate Justice of the Supreme Court of the United States, March 18, 1957, Volume 6

Nomination of Byron White
Hearing Before the Committee on the Judiciary, U.S. Senate, Eighty-Seventh Congress, Second Session, on Nomination of Byron R. White, of Colorado, to Be Associate Justice of the Supreme Court of the United States, April 11, 1962, Volume 6

Nomination of Arthur Goldberg
Hearings Before the Committee on the Judiciary, U.S. Senate, Eighty-Seventh Congress, Second Session, on Nomination of Arthur J. Goldberg, of Illinois, to Be Associate Justice of the Supreme Court of the United States, September 11 and 13, 1962, Volume 6

Nomination of Abe Fortas
Hearing Before the Committee on the Judiciary, U.S. Senate, Eighty-Ninth Congress, First Session, on Nomination of Abe Fortas, of Tennessee, to Be an Associate Justice of the Supreme Court of the United States, August 5, 1965, Volume 7

Nomination of Thurgood Marshall
Hearings Before the Committee on the Judiciary, U.S. Senate, Ninetieth Congress, First Session, on Nomination of Thurgood Marshall, of New York, to Be an Associate Justice of the Supreme Court of the United States, July 13, 14, 18, 19, and 24, 1967, Volume 7

Nominations of Abe Fortas and Homer Thornberry, Part 1
Hearings Before the Committee on the Judiciary, U.S. Senate, Ninetieth Congress, Second Session, on Nomination of Abe Fortas, of Tennessee, to Be Chief Justice of the United States and Nomination of Homer Thornberry, of Texas, to Be Associate Justice of the Supreme Court of the United States, July 11, 12, 16, 17, 18, 19, 20, 22, and 23, 1968, Volume 9

Nominations of Abe Fortas and Homer Thornberry, Part 2
Hearings Before the Committee on the Judiciary, United States Senate, Ninetieth Congress, Second Session, on Nomination of Abe Fortas, of Tennessee, to Be Chief Justice of the United States and Nomination of Homer Thornberry, of Texas, to Be Associate Justice of the Supreme Court of the United States, Part 2, September 13 and 16, 1968, Volume 9A

Report to Accompany the Nomination of Abe Fortas
Report Together With Individual Views to Accompany the Nomination of Abe Fortas, Ninetieth Congress, Second Session, Executive Rept. No. 8, September 20, 1968, Volume 9A

Nomination of Warren Burger
Hearing Before the Committee on the Judiciary, U.S. Senate, Ninety-First Congress, First Session, on Nomination of Warren E. Burger, of Virginia, to Be Chief Justice of the United States, June 3, 1969, Volume 7

Nomination of Clement Haynsworth
Hearings Before the Committee on the Judiciary, U.S. Senate, Ninety-First Congress, First Session, on Nomination of Clement F. Haynsworth Jr., of South Carolina, to Be Associate Justice of the Supreme Court of the United States, September 16, 17, 18, 19, 23, 24, 25, and 26, 1969, Volume 10

Report to Accompany the Nomination of Clement Haynsworth
Report Together With Individual Views, Nomination of Clement F. Haynsworth Jr., Executive Rept. No. 91-12, Ninety-First Congress, First Session, November 12, 1969, Volume 10

Nomination of George Harrold Carswell
Hearings Before the Committee on the Judiciary, U.S. Senate, Ninety-First Congress, Second Session, on Nomination of George Harrold Carswell, of Florida, to Be Associate Justice of the Supreme Court of the United States, January 27, 28, and 29 and February 2 and 3, 1970, Volume 11

Report to Accompany the Nomination of George Harrold Carswell
Report Together With Individual Views to Accompany the Nomination of George Harrold Carswell, Ninety-First Congress, Second Session, Executive Rept. 91-14, February 27, 1970, Volume 11

Nominations of William Rehnquist and Lewis Powell
Hearings Before the Committee on the Judiciary, U.S. Senate, Ninety-Second Congress, First Session, on Nominations of William H. Rehnquist, of Arizona, and Lewis F. Powell Jr., of Virginia, to Be Associate Justices of the Supreme Court of the United States, November 3, 4, 8, 9, and 10, 1971, Volume 8

Report to Accompany the Nomination of Lewis Powell
Report Together With Individual Views to Accompany the Nomination of Lewis F. Powell Jr., Ninety-Second Congress, First Session, Executive Rept. No. 92-17, November 23, 1971, Volume 8

Report to Accompany the Nomination of William Rehnquist
Report Together With Individual Views to Accompany the Nomination of William H. Rehnquist, Ninety-Second Congress, First Session, Executive Rept. No. 92-16, November 23, 1971, Volume 8

Nomination of Justice William Rehnquist
Hearings Before the Committee on the Judiciary, U.S. Senate, Ninety-Ninth Congress, Second Session, July 29, 30, and 31 and August 1, 1986, Volume 12A

Hearings on the Judicial Nomination and Confirmation Process
Hearings on the Judicial Nomination and Confirmation Process Before the Senate Committee, 107th Congress, 1st Session, June 26 and September 4, 2001

Preface

1. Katherine Schulten, "Scalia's Death Offers Best Chance in a Generation to Reshape Supreme Court," *NYT*, February 22, 2016; Remarks on the Death of Supreme Court Justice Antonin Scalia in Rancho Mirage, California, http://www.presidency.ucsb.edu/ws/index.php?pid=111571&st=scalia&st1=death; Burgess Everett and Glenn Thrush, "McConnell Throws Down the Gauntlet: No Scalia Replacement Under Obama," *POL*, February 13, 2016.
2. Remarks on the Nomination of Merrick B. Garland to Be a United States Supreme Court Associate Justice, March 16, 2016, http://www.presidency.ucsb.edu/ws/index.php?pid=115077&st=merrick+garland&st1=; Tom Clark, Sanford Gordon, and Michael Giles, "How Liberal Is Merrick Garland?," *WP*, March 17, 2016.
3. For those who see the Bork battle as the turning point, see, for example, Ethan Bronner, *Battle for Justice: How the Bork Nomination Shook America* (New York: W. W. Norton, 1989); and epilogue, infra. I argue that "the sixties" only ended in 1975 in Laura Kalman, *Right Star Rising: A New Politics, 1974-1980* (New York: W. W. Norton, 2010).
4. Laura Kalman, "The Constitution, the Supreme Court, and the New Deal," 110 *AHR* 1052 (2005); Jeff Shesol, *Supreme Power: Franklin D. Roosevelt vs. the Supreme Court* (New York: W. W. Norton, 2010); Philip Cooper, *Battles on the Bench: Conflict Inside the Supreme Court* (Lawrence: University Press of Kansas, 1995), 94 (quoting Chief Justice Stone on the "difficulty in herding my collection of fleas").
5. Lucas Powe, *The Warren Court and American Politics* (Cambridge, MA: Belknap, 2000), 494.
6. William Faulkner, *Requiem for a Nun* 73 (New York: Vintage, 2011); Fred Graham, "Conversation with Potter Stewart," n.d., Box 11, Graham MSS; Graham, "Conversation with Bill Rehnquist," March 23, 1973, id.
7. Editor's Note, *Taking Charge: The Johnson White House Tapes, 1963-1964*, ed. Michael Beschloss (New York: Simon & Schuster, 1997), 547 (quoting Mildred Stegall memorandum, January 29, 1973).
8. Id., 550–51; Laura Kalman, *Abe Fortas: A Biography* (New Haven: Yale University Press, 1990).
9. David Shreve, "Preface," *Lyndon B. Johnson: The Presidential Recordings: Lyndon B. Johnson, The Kennedy Assassination and the Transfer of Power, November 1963-January 1964 I*, ed. Max Holland (New York: W. W. Norton, 2005), xxxvii (lightning); Bruce Schulman, "Taping History," 85 *JAH* 571, 578 (1998); Kelley Shannon, "Friends, Family Remember Lady Bird," *WP*, July 14, 2007 (quoting LBJ Foundation Chair Tom Johnson).

Chapter 1

1. Lyndon Johnson, *The Vantage Point: Perspectives of the Presidency 1963-1969* (London: Weidenfeld and Nicolson, 1971), 12, 21. The most illuminating accounts of the first days of Johnson's presidency are provided in *Taking Charge: The Johnson White House Tapes, 1963-64*, ed. Michael Beschloss (New York: Simon and Schuster, 1997), and Robert Caro, *The Years of Lyndon Johnson: The Passage of Power* (New York: Alfred Knopf, 2012), 319–605.

2. Earl Warren, *The Memoirs of Chief Justice Earl Warren* (Lanham: Madison, 2001), 352–54.

3. Between Bill Moyers and Eugene Rostow, November 24, 1963, 3:00 P.M., K6311.02, PNO2, Max Holland, ed., *The Presidential Recordings: Lyndon B. Johnson: The Kennedy Assassination and the Transfer of Power I, November 22–30, 1963* (New York: W. W. Norton, 2005), 129–31.

4. Johnson, *The Vantage Point*, 25–26; To Joseph Alsop, November 25, 1964, 10:40 A.M., K6311.02, PNO 17-18, *The Kennedy Assassination and the Transfer of Power I*, 148, 152–55; Walter Jenkins, Memorandum: Various Considerations Today, November 25, 1963, WHCF Ex FG1, LBJL (reporting what Fortas said he told proponents).

5. Laura Kalman, *Abe Fortas: A Biography* (New Haven: Yale University Press, 1990), 217 ("communist plot," quoting Fortas); Caro, *The Passage of Power*, 440–42.

6. Johnson, *The Vantage Point*, 26.

7. To Abe Fortas, November 29, 1963, 1:15 P.M., K6311.04, PNO 12, *The Kennedy Assassination and the Transfer of Power I*, 258, 259, 262.

8. To Abe Fortas, November 29, 1963, 262; Warren, *The Memoirs of Chief Justice Earl Warren*, 356; Nicholas Katzenbach, *Some of It Was Fun: Working with RFK and LBJ* (New York: W. W. Norton, 2008), 135.

9. To Richard Russell, November 29, 1963, 8:55 P.M., K6311.06, PNO 14–16, *The Kennedy Assassination and the Transfer of Power I*, 356, 367; Richard Russell to Halcyon Bell, September 1, 1961, Series I, Subseries C, Box 18, Folder 19, Russell MSS ("indignation and contempt"); Russell to Homer Bone, March 10, 1961, id. ("Warren and his leftist").

10. To Richard Russell, November 29, 1963, 356–57, 364–65 (emphasis in the original); To Charles Halleck, November 29, 1963, 6:30 P.M., K6311.05, PNO 22, *The Kennedy Assassination and the Transfer of Power I*, 324, 326; To James Eastland, November 29, 1963, 7:03 P.M., K6311.06, PNO 3, id., 338, 339.

11. Willard Edwards, "Clash Hinted Over Warren Probe Role," *CT*, December 3, 1963.

12. Susan Douglas, *Where the Girls Are: Growing Up Female with the Mass Media* (New York: Times Books, 1995), 113.

13. John Kennedy, Inaugural Address, January 20, 1961, http://www.presidency.ucsb.edu/ws/?pid=8032.

14. Joseph Califano, *The Triumph & Tragedy of Lyndon Johnson: The White House Years* (New York: Simon and Schuster, 1991), 174, 100, 175; Merle Miller, *Lyndon: An Oral Biography* (New York: G.P. Putnam's Sons, 1980), 298 (quoting George Reedy).

15. To Walter Reuther, January 14, 1965, 10:40 A.M., WH6501.03, PNO 1, MC#6729, ("Kennedy cult," "cornpone"); To Walter Reuther, May 14, 1965, 4:19 P.M., WH6505.12, PNO 6, #8326, id. ("My Mexicans").

16. Calvin Trillin, "Reflections: Back on the Bus: Remembering the Freedom Riders," *NY*, July 25, 2011.

17. David Farber, *The Age of Great Dreams: America in the 1960s* (New York: Hill and Wang, 1994), 105; LBJ Library Staff, "Religion and President Johnson," http://www.lbjlib.utexas.edu/johnson/archives.hom/faqs/Religion/religion_hm.asp; Sylvia Ellis, *Freedom's Pragmatist: Lyndon Johnson and Civil Rights* (Gainesville: University of Florida Press, 2013), 129.

18. Richard Goodwin, *Remembering America: A Voice From the Sixties* (Boston: Little Brown, 1988), 256-58. See Lucas Powe, *The Warren Court and American Politics* (Cambridge, MA: Harvard University Press, 2000).

19. Califano, *The Triumph & Tragedy of Lyndon Johnson*, 54–55 (repeating a story about a senator that Humphrey had told him and adding: "Whether the story is exaggerated or not, the conviction with which Humphrey told it reflected his awe at Johnson's vote-getting determination."); From Richard Russell, March 6, 1965, 12:05 P.M., WH6503.03, PNO 1-2, #7026-27, *Reaching for Glory: Lyndon Johnson's Secret White House Tapes, 1964-1965*, ed. Michael Beschloss (New York: Simon and Schuster, 2001), 210; Rowland Evans and Robert Novak, *Lyndon B. Johnson: The Exercise of Power* (New York: Signet, 1968), 115; Julian Zelizer, *The Fierce Urgency of Now: Lyndon Johnson, Congress, and the Battle for the Great Society* (New York: Penguin, 2015). See especially id., 6–7, where Zelizer addressed liberals' regret that President Obama did not prove another LBJ.); Arthur

Schlesinger, Jr. , *Journals 1952–2000*, ed. Andrew Schlesinger and Stephen Schlesinger (New York: Penguin, 2007), 236–7.

20. Arthur Schlesinger Jr. to Robert Kennedy, December 15, 1963, Personal Correspondence File, Box 11, Schlesinger, Arthur, RFK Senate MSS.

21. Drew Pearson, "Fortas Resisted Arm Twists by LBJ," *BG*, February 4, 1965, 15; Califano, *The Triumph & Tragedy of Lyndon Johnson*, 208 ("two").

22. Jeff Shesol, *Mutual Contempt: Lyndon Johnson, Robert Kennedy, and the Feud That Defined a Decade* (New York: W. W. Norton, 1997); Robert Dallek, *Lone Star Rising: Lyndon Johnson and His Times, 1908–1960* (New York: Oxford University Press, 1991), 572, 578–81; Philip Graham, Notes on the 1960 Democratic Convention, July 19, 1960, Personal Correspondence File, Box 11, Schlesinger, Arthur, RFK Senate MSS; LBJ-Sorensen Telephone Conversation, June 3, 193, Subject Files, Box 30, Civil Rights Legislation, RFK Senate MSS ("humiliated"); Alexander Bickel, "Robert F. Kennedy: The Case Against Him for Attorney General," *TNR*, January 9, 1961, 15, 18 ("The sum of it all is that Mr. Kennedy appears to find congenial the role of prosecutor, judge and jury, all consolidated in his one efficient person").

23. Katzenbach, *Some of It Was Fun*, 134.

24. Id., 149–50. Robert Kennedy to James Wechsler, February 4, 1964, Box 241, 29-L, RFK AG MSS ("the President"); Schlesinger, *Journal*, 253, 215, 229, 213 ("President Kennedy," "intimate," "new," "Lyndon Johnson as he [RFK] calls him," "obviously"); (Schlesinger maintained in December 1963 "that what Bobby would like most of all is to be Secretary of State, presumably with Sarge [Shriver, RFK's brother-in-law] as Vice President." Id., 217); "Robert Kennedy Backed as '64 Vice President," *NYT*, December 24, 1963; "Robert Kennedy Rejects Bid for Vice-Presidency," id., January 29, 1964; Tom Wicker, "Kennedy Gains in Primary: New Hampshire Vote Drive May Embarrass Johnson," id., March 16, 1964; "Robert Kennedy Seen Undecided: Is Said Not to Have Made Up Mind on Vice Presidency," id., April 26, 1964; "Kennedy Hints Hope for Vice Presidency," June 30, 1964, id.; John Galbraith to Lyndon Johnson, July 21, 1964, Box 238, 29-G, RFK AG MSS ("tactless").

25. McGeorge Bundy to Robert Kennedy, n.d., Box 242, Bundy, RFK Senate MSS (National Security Adviser Bundy was one of those RFK obviously suspected of drawing too close to LBJ.); John Galbraith to Robert Kennedy, August 25, 1965, Senate Personal File, Box 4, Galbraith, id.; Robert Kennedy to John Galbraith, September 15, 1965, id. (insider accounts). RFK took pains to avoid open warfare. Several days after the assassination, his deputy press secretary, Jack Rosenthal, confided to a reporter that "the one thing that bothered me [about the new president] was what seemed like LBJ's shit-kick kind of style." The next day, a piece about the mistrusting Kennedy men reported that LBJ's "wheeler-dealer" style offended a high Justice Department official. When Kennedy asked Rosenthal to trace down the source of the quotation with the reporter, Rosenthal learned what had happened. "He didn't want to report back empty-handed so he gave in my reaction unattributed," and the person writing the story "assumed that any reaction had to be from a high Justice Department official. And, unable to use the term 'shit-kick,' translated it into what he regarded as a publishable synonym. I sat frozen for a moment. How could I ever explain that to the stricken RFK? But there was no choice. I went back in . . . and said, hard as it was to believe, I was the source. 'Thank god!' RFK exclaimed. Huh? It turned out that Bill Orrick, Assistant Attorney General for the Civil Division had been at a dinner party the night before and made scathing, wheeler-dealer comments about LBJ. If he, a truly high-ranking official close to RFK had been the source, LBJ would have taken it as a serious sign. But nothing coming from a second-tier flak would be so regarded." Jack Rosenthal, Jody Matthewson story, Box 5, Personal Notes, Undated, Rosenthal MSS.

26. Enid Nemy, "Mrs. Fortas: Law Is Her Life, Too," *NYT*, July 25, 1968 ("at least"); Max Frankel, *The Times of My Life and My Life with The Times* (New York: Random House, 1999), 291.

27. To Katharine Graham, December 2, 1963, 11:10 A.M., K6312.01, PNO 19, *The Presidential Recordings: Lyndon B. Johnson: The Kennedy Assassination and the Transfer of Power II, December, 1963*, ed. Robert Johnson and David Shreve (New York: W. W. Norton, 2005), 38, 39, 41, 42, 45–46; Ted Sorensen to John Gardner, December 24, 1963, Chronological File, Box 83, Sorensen MSS ("greatest man"); Ted Sorensen, *Counselor: A Life at the Edge of History* (New York: Harper, 2008), 382.

28. Bobby Baker with Larry King, *Wheeling and Dealing: Confessions of a Capitol Hill Operator* (New York: W. W. Norton, 1978), 22, 154, 176–77.

29. Rowland Evans and Robert Novak, *Lyndon B. Johnson: The Exercise of Power* (New York: Bantam, 1966), 351; Caro, *The Passage of Power*, 276–318.

30. Caro, *The Passage of Power*, 276–80, 308-09 (reporters, "protégé"); David Shreve, "Preface," *Lyndon B. Johnson: The Presidential Recordings: The Kennedy Assassination and the Transfer of Power I* (Estes), lxiv–lxv; "The 'TFX' Case," *NYT*, February 26, 1963 (reporting that "TFX" had "been dubbed by capital wags the 'LBJ' because of the Vice President's presumed influence in the award of the contract"); Kalman, *Abe Fortas*, 222 (Fortas's formulation).

31. Chalmers Roberts, "Abe Fortas Withdraws as Lawyer for Baker," *WP*, December 3, 1963.

32. Caro, *The Passage of Power*, 318 ("I think"); Baker, *Wheeling and Dealing*, 193–97; and see, for example, "Insurance Man Quizzed in Bobby Baker Case: Closed-Door Probe is Preview to Senate Hearing Tuesday on Alleged Kickback," *LAT*, November 28, 1965; E.W. Kenworthy, "FBI Discredits Payoff Charges by Baker Witness: Reynolds Told Senate Panel of $100,000 Given During TFX Plane Negotiations," *NYT*, March 3, 1965; William Moore, "Assail Smear of Reynolds as Retaliation: Warning from High-Up, Williams Says," *CT*, March 5, 1965; Lawrence Stern, "Ruin, Disgrace and Exile Seen as Reynolds' Fate," *WP*, May 14, 1965; "Farewell to Bobby Baker," *WP*, July 3, 1965.

33. Cabell Phillips, "Senators to Push Inquiry on Baker: Rules Panel to Investigate Business Affairs of Former Secretary to the Majority," *NYT*, October 24, 1963; Robert Johnson, *All the Way with LBJ: The 1964 Presidential Election* (New York: Cambridge University Press, 2009), 216 ("flouted"); Califano, *The Triumph & Tragedy of Lyndon Johnson*, 116 ("skirt[ed]," Hay-Adams).

34. From Clark Clifford, December 4, 1963, 6:25 P.M., K6312.03, PNO 23, *The Presidential Recordings: Lyndon B. Johnson: The Kennedy Assassination and the Transfer of Power II, December 1963*, ed. Robert Johnson and David Shreve (New York: W. W. Norton, 2005), 147, 148; Lyndon Johnson to Robert Kennedy, January 2, 1964, Confidential File, Box 238, 29-J, RFK AG MSS. "I honor you for the decision you have made to stay on the job," Clifford wrote RFK. "I have some understanding of how difficult it has been for you, but it is so important to so many people that you continue on" and "the right and decent and honorable course for you." Clifford to Kennedy, January 13, 1964, Box 237 29-C, id.

35. To Walker Stone, January 6, 1964, 3:48 P.M., WH6401.06, PNO 4, #1196, *The Kennedy Assassination and the Transfer of Power III, January 1964*, ed. Kent Germany and Robert Johnson (New York: W. W. Norton, 2005), 175, 179; To Martin Luther King, January 15, 1965, 12:06 P.M., WH6501.04, PNO 1-2, #6736-37; *Reaching for Glory*, 159, 163.

36. From Whitney Young, January 6, 1964, 3:55 P.M., WH6401.06, PNO 5, #1197, *The Kennedy Assassination and the Transfer of Power III*, 181, 182–83; To Roy Wilkins, January 6, 1964, 5:12 P.M., WH6401.06, PNO 8, #1200, id., 190, 192, 194.

37. To Robert Kennedy, May 28, 1964, 11:45 A.M., WH6405.11, PNO 9-10, #3539-3540, *The Presidential Recordings: Lyndon B. Johnson: Toward the Great Society VI, April 14, 1964-May 31, 1964*, ed. Guian McKee (New York: W. W. Norton, 2005), 914, 924; To Robert Kennedy, July 21, 1964, 8:00 P.M., WH6407.11, PNO 3, #4288, *Taking Charge*, 464, 465; To John Connally, July 23, 1964, 5:31 P.M., WH6407.13, PNO 2, #4320-23, id., 466, 468 ("this fellow"); Shesol, *Mutual Contempt*, 165–66; FBI Report, September 18, 1964 (riot situations), Box 1, File: Civil Rights General, 1962–1965, Rosenthal MSS.

38. To Clark Clifford, July 29, 1964, 2:17 P.M., WH6407.18, PNO 4, #4392, *Taking Charge*, 478, 479, 480.

39. Johnson, *All the Way with LBJ*, 151–52 (reporters); To Hubert Humphrey, March 6, 1965, 11:25 A.M., WH6503.02, PNO 8-9, #7024-25, *Reaching for Glory*, 206; Randall Woods, *LBJ: Architect of American Ambition* (Free Press: 2006), 532 ("hydrophobia").

40. Cabell Phillips, "Rusk Post Desired: Friends Report Robert Kennedy Wants to Be Secretary of State," *NYT*, August 1, 1964, "Kennedy Voices a Wry Regret: Sorry That He 'Took So Many Over the Side With Me,'" id., August 7, 1964; "The Kennedy Blitzkrieg," id., August 22, 1964; R. W. Apple Jr., "How Kennedy Did It: 27 Days of Hard Politicking," id., August 26, 1964.

41. "Germans Shot Down, Imprisoned Katzenbach," *WP*, September 4, 1964.

42. Susannah Clark, "A Day in the Sun: Table Talk with Nicholas Katzenbach '39," *Exe Bull* 8 (Winter 2009) (Wallace); Benjamin Welles, "Cool-Nerved Statesman: Nicholas deBelleville Katzenbach," *NYT*, October 19, 1968.

43. From Abe Fortas, October 14, 1964, 3:56 P.M., WH6410.08, PNO 6-7, #5876-77, *Reaching for Glory*, 54, 59; To Abe Fortas and Clark Clifford, October 14, 1964, 8:02 P.M., WH6410.09, PNO 3, #5880, id., 61; To Abe Fortas and Clark Clifford, October 14, 1964, 8:32 P.M., WH6410.09, PNO 4, #5881, id., 64; Johnson, *All the Way with LBJ*, 252–58 (political operative, IRS, safe; Johnson suggests that in giving Fortas the order to clear the safe, LBJ engaged in obstruction of justice.)

44. To John Connally, October 14, 1964, 8:45 P.M., WH6401.09, PNO 4, #5882, *Taking Charge*, 66, 68 ("What's"); Remarks at the Civic Center Arena in Pittsburgh, October 27, 1964, http://www.presidency.ucsb.edu/ws/index.php?pid=26674&st=&st1=, ("Bobby Baker, Walter Jenkins, and Billie Sol Estes"); To Nicholas Katzenbach, October 15, 1964, 7:26 A.M., WH6410.11, PNO 1, #5891, id., 81, 82, 83 (remaining quotations).

45. Laura Kalman, *Right Star Rising: A New Politics* (New York: W. W. Norton, 2010), 24–25 (Goldwater's 1964 campaign); Anthony Lewis, "Goldwater Stand on Court Decried: Prominent Lawyers Assail 'Broadside Attacks,'" *NYT*, October 12, 1964; Lady Bird Johnson, Tape Recorded Diary, January 13, 1965, *Reaching for Glory*, 158, 159 (New York: Simon and Schuster, 2001).

46. "LBJ Vote Credited for Bob Kennedy's Defeat of Keating," *WP*, November 4, 1964; To Bill Moyers and McGeorge Bundy, November 4, 1964, 9:56 A.M., WH6411.03, PNO 5, #6158, *Reaching for Glory*, 111, 114 (Kennedy's lack of gratitude); From Edwin Weisl Sr., November 4, 1964, 12:46 P.M., WH6411.04, PN0 10, #6174, id., 119, 120, 122 ("is going," media, running ahead of RFK).

47. "The Johnson Landslide," *NYT*, November 4, 1964; Zelizer, *The Fierce Urgency of Now*, 8–9, 164.

48. Jack Rosenthal to John Mashek, November 28, 1964, Box 2, Rosenthal MSS; Rowland Evans and Robert Novak, "Katzenbach: A Cliff-Hanger with Good Grip," *BG*, November 20, 1964, 11.

49. To Abe Fortas, November 4, 1964, 1:00 P.M., WH6411.05, PNO 1, #6175, *Reaching for Glory*, 123, 124–25; To Abe Fortas, November 11, 1964, id., 10:30 P.M., WH6411.18, PNO1-2, #6335-36, id., 139, 140 ("vastly" "knight," "Senator Williams").

50. To J. Edgar Hoover, November 17, 1964, 1:37 P.M., WH 6411.22, PNO 11-12, #6385-86, MC. Two other intimates had potential. One, Edwin Weisl Sr., Wall Street lawyer, philanthropist, and movie mogul, had provided political and investment advice to LBJ and his wife since the late 1930s. "I told him that I felt I was too old," recalled Weisl, then nearly sixty-seven. Edwin Weisl, Interview by Joe Frantz, May 13, 1969, LBJOH, 34. LBJ settled for awarding Weisl responsibility for all New York federal appointments, rather than giving it to the state's new senior Democrat, Robert Kennedy. Beschloss, *Reaching for Glory*, 366 (patronage). Another possibility, Donald Cook, had chaired the Securities and Exchange Commission and currently presided over the nation's largest privately owned power company. Cook's brother, however, had been a member of the Communist Party. Worse, Cook himself had once queried an SEC commissioner on behalf of Bobby Baker and the Mortgage Guaranty Insurance Company of Milwaukee, colloquially known as MGIC or MAGIC, in which Baker had invested for himself and members of Congress. "Don't do it," Senate Minority Leader Everett Dirksen of Illinois advised LBJ when the president asked about an appointment for Cook. "If he's got the MAGIC touch on him, you're going to catch hell as sure as shootin'. . . . We can defend him, and I'm sure, get him confirmed, but . . . you know damn well someone will say . . . 'That son of a bitch was in MAGIC up to his ears.' And you can't live it down, no matter how long he serves." To Everett Dirksen, March 16, 1965, 12:55 P.M., WH6503.07, PNO 4, #7070, *Reaching for Glory*, 228, 22; and see To J. Edgar Hoover, November 17, 1964, 1:37 P.M., WH6411.22, PNO 11, #6835, MC (interest in Cook, American Electric Power Company president, for Justice Department); From Cartha "Deke" DeLoach, November 20, 1964, 4:23 P.M., WH6411.25, PNO 12, #6431, id. (interest in Cook for Justice Department or Treasury, brother); LBJ did subsequently offer the treasury secretary position to Cook, which he declined. Frank Porter, "Fowler New Treasury Secretary," *WP*, March 19, 1965.

51. Katzenbach, *Some of It Was Fun*, 156–58.

52. To Richard Russell, January 22, 1965, 11:15 A.M., WH6501.04, PNO 6-7, #6741-42, *Reaching for Glory*, 166, 167; To James Eastland, January 22, 1965, 11:40 A.M., WH6501.05, PNO 1, #6743, id., 167, 168.

53. Kalman, *Abe Fortas*, 231–32. If this conversation occurred on the telephone, Johnson did not tape it.

54. Clark Clifford with Richard Holbrooke, *Counsel to the President: A Memoir* (New York: Random House, 1991), 439–40.

55. From Nicholas Katzenbach, January 15, 1965, 1:38 P.M., WH6501.04, PNO 4, #6739, *Reaching for Glory*, 163, 164.

56. Katzenbach, *Some of It Was Fun*, 158; Lady Bird Johnson, January 27, 1965, Tape-Recorded Diary, *Reaching for Glory*, 169.

57. Katzenbach, *Some of It Was Fun*, 163; To Nicholas Katzenbach, March 10, 1965, 9:00 A.M., WH6503.04, PNO 9, #7047, *Reaching for Glory*, 224.

58. Special Message to Congress: The American Promise, March 15, 1965, http://www.presidency.ucsb.edu/ws/index.php?pid=26805&st=selma&st1=; Katzenbach, *Some of It Was Fun*, 167–68.

59. Katzenbach, *Some of it Was Fun*, 173; *Breedlove v. Suttles*, 302 U.S. 277 (1937).

60. Katzenbach, *Some of It Was Fun*, 173; Gary May, *Bending Toward Justice: The Voting Rights Act and the Transformation of Democracy* (2013), 152–59; To Nicholas Katzenbach, January 14, 1965, 10:40 A.M., WH6501.03, PNO 1, #6729, MC; To Nicholas Katzenbach, April 7, 1965, 9:17 A.M., WH6504.02, PNO 10-11, #7323–24, *Reaching for Glory*, 269–71; Byron Hulsey, *Everett Dirksen and His Presidents: How a Senate Giant Shaped American Politics* (Lawrence: University Press of Kansas, 2000), 187–97, 199–202, 210–13.

61. Bruce Ackerman provides a full account of this story in *We the People 3: The Civil Rights Revolution* (2013), 83–116. The quotations are from id., 108, 103, 108, 114. See Harper v. Va. Bd. Of Elections, 383 U.S. 663 (1966); William Eskridge and John Ferejohn, *The Republic of Statutes: The New American Constitution* (New Haven: Yale University Press, 2010), 26. What "superstatutes," such as the Sherman Antitrust Act of 1890, the Social Security Act of 1935, and the Voting Rights Act of 1965, "have in common is that each (1) embodied a new principle or policy displacing common law baselines, responsive to important social or economic challenges facing the country; (2) was drafted and enacted after a process of publicized institutional deliberation responsive to the voices and needs of We the People; and (3) stuck in the public culture, after a period of implementation and formal confirmation by Congress after further public discussion."

62. To Clarence Mitchell, May 4, 1965, 8:45 P.M., WH6505.05, PNO 1, #7580, MC; From Birch Bayh, May 7, 1965, 4:45 P.M., WH6505.06, PNO 9-10, #7603-04, *Reaching for Glory*, 313, 314.

63. To Walter Reuther, May 14, 1965; From Birch Bayh, May 7, 1965, *Reaching for Glory*, 314, n.4 ("insult and blasphemy").

64. Nathan Miller, *FDR: An Intimate History* (Garden City: Doubleday, 1983), 327 (quoting Harry Hopkins); Barry Cushman, "The Hughes Court and Constitutional Consultation," 23 *JSCH* 79 (1998, #1).

65. Katzenbach, *Some of It Was Fun*, 161, 204; Alexander Wohl, *Father, Son, and the Constitution: How Justice Tom Clark and Attorney General Ramsey Clark Shaped American Democracy* (Lawrence: University Press of Kansas, 2013), 249–50 ("here's"). Especially since "[t]he closest LBJ came to seeking a political favor" from Katzenbach was his request that the attorney general name young Weisl, however (Katzenbach, *Some of It Was Fun*, 204), Weisl and Vinson's failure to thank the president rankled LBJ. "Reckon they don't know who appointed them?" Johnson asked Katzenbach, who replied that he reckoned they were just "young fellas." They ought to know better then, the president groused. "Nobody's ever been appointed that hasn't come kissed me with a letter or telegram. It's a matter of humaneness. You acknowledge your Christmas presents, don't you?" To Nicholas Katzenbach, March 30, 1965, 10:03 A.M., WH6503.15, PNO 5, #7185, MC.

66. To Nicholas Katzenbach, August 6, 1965, 6:10 P.M., WH6508.02, PNO 5, #8514, MC ("Think"). Johnson made the comment about Mrs. Katzenbach's boyfriends during a

discussion with his attorney general about the Justice Department's comptroller general). LBJ badgered Katzenbach about appointments during the debate over the Voting Rights Bill: "I gave in and just agreed to get raped by your crowd in Wisconsin, so I'm going to put in your man—Governor Whatever-His-Name-Is, this ex-politician," former Wisconsin Governor John Reynolds, as a federal judge. "I don't want you and Ramsey ever talking to me about standards anymore." When Katzenbach replied, wryly but respectfully, "Mr. President, they have very high standards [in Wisconsin]," LBJ answered, "The hell they have!" Laughing, he added that he could supply Katzenbach and Clark with plenty of one-time congressmen and governors for judgeships. The president yielded this time, though he did so reluctantly. To Nicholas Katzenbach, April 7, 1965, 9:17 A.M., WH6504.02, PNO 10-11, #7323-24, *Reaching for Glory*, 269. LBJ conflated judicial appointments at all levels into one and made it his. As he said, "In fifty years, I don't want to have a lot of ex mayors and ex governors on my Supreme Court." To Walter Reuther, January 14, 1965, 10:04 A.M., WH6501.03, PNO 1, #6729, MC ("my Supreme Court").

67. To Nicholas Katzenbach, April 7, 1965. Compare, for example, LBJ's very negative comments about Turner in From Ramsey Clark, WH6611.06, PNO3, November 23, 1966, 6:54 P.M., #11053.

68. To Nicholas Katzenbach, April 7, 1965.

69. From Abe Fortas, June 28, 1965, 3:00 P.M., WH6506.08, PNO 9, #8204, MC.

70. Id.; Katzenbach, *Some of It Was Fun*, 177; From Ramsey Clark, January 25, 1967, 8:22 P.M., WH6701.09, PNO 2, #11408, MC ("burr-head"). "For quite a while I had felt the need for some clear-cut determination of my status," Cox wrote Chief Justice Warren. "Last month I told the President of my feeling, submitting a resignation in order to return home to New England but saying that if he wished, I would be proud and happy to continue as his Solicitor General." Archibald Cox to Earl Warren, July 14, 1965, Box 362, General, Warren MSS.

71. Juan Williams, *Thurgood Marshall: American Revolutionary* (New York: Three Rivers, 1998), xiv ("He"); Carl Rowan, *Dream Makers, Dream Breakers: The World of Justice Thurgood Marshall* (Boston: Little, Brown 1993), 218, 451.

72. To Martin Luther King, January 15, 1965, 160.

73. Wendell Pritchett, *Robert Clifton Weaver and the American City: The Life and Times of an Urban Reformer* (Chicago: University of Chicago Press, 2008), 265; From Roy Wilkins, November 4, 1965, 10:50 A.M., WH6511.01, PNO 5, #9105, MC ("martyr"). Wilkins did not sound that enthusiastic about Weaver in To Roy Wilkins, October 30, 1965, 4:03 P.M., WH6510.03, PNO 11, #9048, id.

74. To Martin Luther King, January 15, 1965, 160 ("charge"); To Roy Wilkins, January 16, 1964, 1:20 P.M., WH6401.15, PNO 3-4, #1383-84, *The Kennedy Assassination and the Transfer of Power III*, 554 ("tell," "real"); To John McClellan, January 16, 1964, 4:20 P.M., WH6401.15, PNO 6, #1386, id., 561, 564 ("peter"); From Jack Valenti, January 23, 1964, WH6401.20, PNO 5, #1504, id., 763, 764 (meetings and telephone calls); To Carl Rowan, February 20, 1964, 11:10 A.M., WH66402.19, PNO 9, #2137, *The Presidential Recordings: Lyndon B. Johnson: Toward the Great Society IV, February 1, 1964-March 8, 1964*, ed. Robert Johnson and Kent Germany (New York: W. W. Norton, 2007), 637 (cars); To Kermit Gordon, February 20, 1964, 11:20 A.M., WH6402.19, PNO15-17, #2143-45, id., 640 (cars); To Nicholas Katzenbach, July 9, 1965, 2:00 P.M., WH6507.03, PNO 1, #8326, MC ("another").

75. Charles Zelden. *Thurgood Marshall: Race, Rights and the Struggle for a More Perfect Union* 126–27 (New York: Routledge, 2013); Mark Tushnet, *Making Civil Rights Law: Thurgood Marshall and the Supreme Court, 1936-1961* 4 (New York: Oxford University Press, 1994) ("irony").

76. To Thurgood Marshall, July 7, 1965, 1:30 P.M., WH6507.01, PNO 7, #8307, *Reaching for Glory*, 385, 386; Thurgood Marshall, Interview I by T.H. Baker, July 10, 1969, LBJOH, 8-9.

Chapter 2

1. To Walter Reuther, August 5, 1964, 2:54 P.M., WH6408.07, PNO 6, #4727, MC ("the King"); and LBJ also alluded to the impact of the defeat of court packing on FDR's agenda. in calls to Robert Jones, August 5, 1964, 2:45 P.M., WH6408.07, PNO 4, #4725, id.; To Olin Teague,

August 5, 1964, 2:56 P.M., WH6408.07, PNO 7, #4728, id.; To George Mahon, August 5, 1964, 3:05 P.M., WH6408.07, PNO 11, #4732, id.; To John Flynt, August 5, 1964, 3:10 P.M., WH6408.07, PNO 12, #4733, id.

2. Garrison Nelson with Maggie Steakley and James Montague, *Pathways to the US Supreme Court: From the Arena to the Monastery* (New York: Palgrave Macmillan, 2013), 71.

3. Laura Kalman, *The Strange Career of Legal Liberalism* (New Haven: Yale University Press, 1996), 19–20. ("superlegislature"); Alexander Bickel and Harry Wellington, "Legislative Purpose and the Judicial Process: The Lincoln Mills Case," 71 *HLR* 1, 2–3 (1957) ("sweeping"); Morton Horwitz, "The Warren Court and the Pursuit of Justice," 50 *W&LLR* 5, 11 (1993) ("common"); Jim Newton, *Justice for All: Earl Warren and the Nation He Made* (New York: Riverhead, 2006), 347 ("dumb").

4. Fred Graham, undated profile of Hugo Black (c. 1968) ("robes"), Box 3, Hugo Black, Graham MSS; Hugh Grant to Hugo Black, May 18, 1954, Box 31, Hugh Grant, Black MSS ("betrayed"). John Frank to Yousuf Karsh, November 14, 1963 ("senior"), Frank MSS.

5. Richard Hasen, "Celebrity Justice: Supreme Court Edition," 19 *GB* 2d 157, 160 (2016) ("He was perhaps the first real Celebrity Justice."); Christopher Schmidt, "Beyond the Opinion: Supreme Court Justices and Extrajudicial Speech," 88 *CKLR* 487, 496 (2013) ("Some justices are more interested in talking about themselves than others. On the one end of the spectrum, we have Justice William O. Douglas, easily the most prolific author ever to sit on the High Court. Early in his career on the Court, Douglas desperately wanted to be President, and some of his writing and many of his speeches in the 1940s and early 1950s had the feel of campaign advocacy.... Once he gave up on his political aspirations, Douglas turned his attentions to other pursuits: three divorces and subsequent alimony payments left him chronically short of money, which drove him to write more books, several of them autobiographical. Furthermore, Douglas had a remarkable story to tell about his life—some of which apparently was true.") But see Jonathan Turley, "Justice Scalia Is a Political Star—And That's Bad for the Supreme Court," *WP*, January 21, 2011 (making the case that Justice Scalia was the court's "first real celebrity justice").

6. Mapp v. Ohio, 367 U.S. 643 (1961); Engel v. Vitale, 370 U.S. 421 (1962); School District of Abington Tp. v. Schempp, 374 U.S. 203 (1963).

7. Anders Walker, "'To Corral and Control the Ghetto': Stop, Frisk, and the Geography of Freedom," 48 *URLR* 1223, 1224, 1237–38 (2014); and see Walker, "The New Jim Crow? Recovering the Progressive Origins of Mass Incarceration," 41 *HCLQ* 845, 860 (2014); Corinna Lain, "God, Civic Virtue, and the American Way: Reconstructing Engel," 67 *SLR* 479, 534, 513 (2015); Sarah Barringer Gordon, *The Spirit of the Law: Religious Voices and the Constitution in Modern America* (2010), 88, 155; Mary Dudziak, *Cold War Civil Rights: Race and the Image of American Democracy* (2000); John MacKenzie, "'All Deliberate Speed' Was Unwise Policy, [Justice Hugo] Black Feels: Sheds Some New Light," *WP*, December 4, 1968; Alan Freeman, "Legitimizing Racial Discrimination Through Antidiscrimination Law: A Critical Review of Supreme Court Doctrine," 62 *MinnLR* 1049 (1978); William Eskridge and John Ferejohn, *A Republic of Statutes: The New American Constitution* (2010), 42 ("neither"); and see Erwin Chemerinsky, *The Case Against the Supreme Court* (New York: Penguin, 2014), 155; Justin Driver, "The Constitutional Conservatism of the Warren Court," 100 *CaLR* 1011 (2012); Kalman, *The Strange Career of Legal Liberalism*, 52–53, 82–86.

8. The Senate Judiciary Committee File on Clark is full of complaints. (See, for example, William Jevis to Senator Pat McCarran, August 7, 1949, Senate Judiciary Committee Nominations, NARS: "In view of the latter's record, his constant anti-labor bias, his Klan-like disregard for the Negro people's rights, and his strong tendency to overlook the Bill of Rights and fundamental American constitutional liberties, makes him an inadequate choice for that honorable job."); *CR*, August 18, 1949, S11720 (Remarks of Senator Johnson); Dwight Eisenhower to H.L. Hunt, September 24, 1953, WHCF OF 100-A, Box 321, Supreme Court, DDEL ("formerly").

9. Herbert Brownell to Ed Cray, December 16, 1993, Brownell Addl. MSS, Box 2, CR (1), Eisenhower Library; Brownell interview with Ed Cray, September 6, 1991, CR (3), id.; The President's News Conference, September 30, 1953, http://www.presidency.ucsb.edu/ws/index.php?pid=9709.

10. Herbert Brownell with John Burke, *Advising Ike: The Memoirs of Attorney General Herbert Brownell* (Lawrence: University Press of Kansas, 1993), 180–81 ("such experience"); Diary, February 5, 1957, Whitman MSS, Brownell, 1957 (1).

11. Plessy v. Ferguson, 163 U.S. 537, 559 (1896); Constance Baker Motley, "Thurgood Marshall," 68 *NYULR* 205, 210, 211 (1993) (quotation of dissent); David Yalof, *Pursuit of Justices: Presidential Politics and the Selection of Supreme Court Nominees* (Chicago: University of Chicago Press, 1999), 54; Learned Hand to Dwight Eisenhower, October 22, 1954, Box 539, Learned Hand, Harlan MSS; Ethel McCall to Potter Stewart, February 15, 1972, Box 586, Folder 137, Stewart MSS (eyesight).

12. Yalof, *Pursuit of Justices*, 57–61 ("show"); Brownell, *Advising Ike*, 179–80; Joel Grossman, *Lawyers and Judges: The ABA and the Politics of Judicial Selection* (New York: Wiley, 1965), 72; Philip Yeager and John Stark, "The Supreme Court in Transition," *NYT*, March 10, 1957; Dwight Eisenhower to M. Hartley Dodge, October 4, 1956, WHCF OF 100-A, Box 321, Supreme Court (2), DDEL ("warm").

13. Bernard Schwartz, *Super Chief: Earl Warren and His Supreme Court—A Judicial Biography* (New York: New York University Press, 1983), 326 and see, for example, id., 216, 224, 260 on Whittaker's wavering and alignment; Brownell, *Advising Ike*, 180–81; Yalof, *Pursuit of Justices*, 61–63 ("verifiably").

14. Dwight Eisenhower to William Rogers, September 17, 1958, Box 4, President Eisenhower, Rogers MSS.

15. Fred Graham, Interview of Justice Potter Stewart, February 17, 1979, Series IV, Box 624, Folder 33, Stewart MSS.

16. Seth Stern and Stephen Wermiel, *Justice Brennan: Liberal Champion* (New York: Houghton Mifflin, 2010), 138–39; Eisenhower to William Rogers, May 12, 1958, Box 4, President Eisenhower Correspondence, Rogers MSS. Rogers replied: "Those who criticize the Supreme Court on the ground that it is 'legislating' usually mean that, in their view, the Justices are playing too expansive a role; that they are injecting too much personal philosophy into their decisions; and that they are determining what they think the law ought to be, instead of giving effect to the way statutes enacted by Congress in the way Congress intended. Sometimes the complaint that judges are 'legislating' is a careless charge made primarily because the critic does not find particular court decisions to his liking. In other instances, the criticism, though made sincerely and without bias, stems from a grossly over-simplified notion of 'law,' " since, Rogers observed, many of the most crucial phrases such as "commerce," "due process," and "equal protection" were open to many different interpretations. While Congress had the authority to limit the court's jurisdiction, Rogers himself opposed jurisdiction stripping, even though he believed that "too often the Supreme Court decides cases based on what it thinks the law should be rather than what Congress intended," the court's opinions were "much too long and often confusing even to an experienced lawyer," and he disliked the court's recent practice of changing "its decisions on the same set of facts, especially within short periods of time." Rogers to Eisenhower, May 27, 1958, id. For the justices' views on Eisenhower and his lack of support for them, see Schwartz, *Super Chief*, 173–75. For the argument that Eisenhower deserves greater credit for his leadership on civil rights, see David Nichols, *A Matter of Justice: Eisenhower and the Beginning of the Civil Rights Revolution* (New York: Simon and Schuster, 2007).

17. L. Arthur Minnich, Memorandum for the President, October 13, 1953, WHCF OF 100-A, Box 321, Supreme Court (1), DDEL.

18. Counsel, Analysis of Charges Against Honorable Earl Warren, Nominee for Chief Justices of the United States, February 11, 1954, Sen 83B-A3, Box 51, Senate Judiciary Committee Nominations, NARS.

19. Drew Pearson, "Langer Fight on Warren Has Revenge Basis," *SBCS*, February 24, 1954; Hearing of the Senate Judiciary Committee, Executive Session, Nomination of Earl Warren, February 20, 1954, Senate Judiciary Committee Nominations, Box 51, NARS.

20. Jim Newton, *Justice for All: Earl Warren and the Nation He Made* (New York: Riverhead, 2006), 282–91; Hearing of the Senate Judiciary Committee, Nomination of Earl Warren, February 20, 1954; Nelson, *Pathways to the US Supreme Court*, 131: "From 1789 to 1965, 69 of the 99 successful nominations (69.7 percent) were confirmed by a voice vote and six voted

nominations were confirmed with votes of less than half of the eligible senators who could vote on their nominations."

21. Denis Rutkus, "Supreme Court Appointment Process: Roles of the President, Judiciary Committee and the Senate," February 19, 2010, 23–24; Denis Rutkus, Elizabeth Rybicki, Betsy Palmer, Todd Tatelman, Richard Beth, Michael Koempel, and Judy Schneider, eds., *Supreme Court Nominations: Presidential Nomination, the Judiciary Committee, Proper Scope of Questioning of Nominees, Senate Consideration, Cloture, and the Use of the Filibuster* (Alexandria: Capitol Net, 2010); Dion Farganis and Justin Wedeking, *Supreme Court Confirmation Hearings in the U.S. Senate: Reconsidering the Charade* (Ann Arbor: University of Michigan Press, 2014), 2.

22. J. H. von Sprecken to Harley M. Kilgore, January 11, 1955, Sen 84B-A3, Box 19, Senate Judiciary Committee Nominations, NARS ("scalawag"); Brad Snyder, "How the Conservatives Canonized *Brown v. Board of Education*," 52 *RLR* 383, 400–403 (2000); Stern and Wermiel, *Justice Brennan*, 113–119; Lucas Powe, *The Warren Court and American Politics* (Cambridge, Belknap, 2000), 102-03; Nomination of Charles Whittaker, 5–34.

23. Powe, *The Warren Court and American Politics*, 98 ("democratic"); Jencks v. U.S., 353 U.S. 657 (1957); Yates v. U.S., 354 U.S. 298 (1957); Watkins v. U.S., 354 U.S. 178 (1957); Sweezy v. New Hampshire, 354 U.S. 234 (1957); Schware v. Board of Bar Examiners, 353 U.S. 232 (1957); Konigsberg v. State Bar of California, 353 U.S. 252 (1957); "The Supreme Court: The Temple Builder," *Ti*, July 1, 1957 ("Not"); "The Law: After the Swerve," id., July 8, 1957 ("swerve"); Newton, *Justice for All*, 366–67; Robert Caro, *The Years of Lyndon Johnson: Master of the Senate* (New York: Vintage, 2002), 1030–33.

24. "High Court Critics Subject Stewart to Barbed Queries," *WP*, April 10, 1959; "Badgering Judges," id., April 11, 1959; "A History of Supreme Court Nominations," July 12, 2009, NPR, http://www.npr.org/templates/story/story.php?storyId=106528133 (turning point); Senate Judiciary Committee Papers re Nominations, Stewart, 86B-A3, Box 35, Hearing held before Committee on the Judiciary, Nomination of Potter Stewart to Be Associate Justice of the Supreme Court of the United States, April 9, 1959, NARS.

25. Report to Accompany Nomination of Potter Stewart, Minority Views, 5, 10. Though Eastland and Johnston signed the report, another member of the committee, John McClellan, also cast a negative vote. Warren Durfee, "Senate Unit Approves Stewart in Court Job," *WP*, April 21, 1959.

26. *CR*, 86th Congr., 1st Sess., May 5, 1959, S6693–6711.

27. Sheldon Goldman, *Picking Federal Judges: Lower Court Selection from Roosevelt through Reagan* (New Haven: Yale University Press, 1997), 81; Judge Simon E. Sobeloff, 1894-1973, https://www.law.umaryland.edu/marshall/specialcollections/sobeloff/fourthcircuit.html.

28. Henry Abraham, *Justices, Presidents, and Senators: A History of U.S. Supreme Court Appointments from Washington to Bush II*, 5th ed. (Lanham: Rowman & Littlefield, 2008), 137, 141–43, 153–54, 157–58.

29. Roger Newman, *Hugo Black: A Biography* (New York: Pantheon, 1994), 239–42; Lori Ringhand, "Aliens on the Bench: Lessons in Identity, Race and Politics From the First 'Modern' Supreme Court Confirmation Hearing to Today," 2010 *MichSLR* 795, 835 (2010); Nomination of Felix Frankfurter, 107–28; Nomination of Frank Murphy; William Wiecek, *The Oliver Wendell Holmes Devise History of the Supreme Court of the United States XII: The Birth of the Modern Constitution: The United States Supreme Court, 1941-1953* (New York: Cambridge University Press, 2006), 438. "There are millions of Americans, among whom I am one, who regretted the hasty action of the Senate in confirming Justice Black without investigating this aspect of his life, which, at the time his confirmation was pending in the Senate, had been extensively referred to," one Boston Democratic member of Congress indignantly told the Senate Judiciary Committee chair. John McCormack to Henry Ashurst, September 13, 1937, Senate Judiciary Committee Nominations, Sen 75B-A4, Hugo Black, NARS.

30. John Maltese, *The Selling of Supreme Court Nominees* 36-44, 50-69 (Baltimore: Johns Hopkins, 1995); John Frank, "Are the Justices Quasi-Legislators Now?" 81 *NwULR* 921 (1990) ("the beginning of *ideological* controversy—as distinguished from purely

political controversy—begins in 1881 with Justice Matthews." Id. Emphasis in the original); Kenneth Goings, *The NAACP Comes of Age: The Defeat of Judge John J. Parker* (Bloomington: Indiana University Press, 1990); John Parker to H. H. Williams, May 26, 1930, Box 8, Folder 130, Parker MSS.

31. Joseph Crespino, *Strom Thurmond's America* 105-108 (New York: Hill and Wang, 2012), 105, 108 ("war"); James Heath, *To Face Down Dixie: South Carolina's War on the Supreme Court, 1954-1970* (DPhil, University of Warwick, 2015), 100–16; Peter Fish, "Spite Nominations to the United States Supreme Court: Herbert C. Hoover, Owen J. Roberts, and the Politics of Presidential Vengeance in Retrospect," 77 *Ky. L. J.* 549, 561, 567–68 (1988-89). Grossman, *Lawyers and Judges*, 168 ("given").

32. Newton, *Justice for All,* 382–83, 405–6; Arthur Goldberg OHLC, Set I: Sixth Interview with Goldberg (by Daniel P. Moynihan), Reel 3, LCOH, Series II: Box 89, Folder 7, 1, Goldberg MSS; Edwin Guthman and Jeffrey Shulman, *Robert Kennedy in His Own Words: The Unpublished Recollections of the Kennedy Years* (New York: Bantam, 1989), 66, 115 (quotations). Warren's assessment may have been unduly harsh. See Note, " 'Just One More Vote for Frankfurter': Rethinking the Jurisprudence of Judge William H. Hastie," 117 *HLR* 1639 (2004).

33. Yalof, *Pursuit of Justices,* 77–80 (Freund); Dennis Hutchinson, *The Man Who Once Was Whizzer White: A Portrait of Justice Byron R. White* (New York: Free Press, 1998), 173–78, 312–322, 457 ("ideal," "non-ideological"); *CR,* April 11, 1962, S6331 (Remarks of Senator Russell); Nomination of Byron White, 11–14. Louis Brandeis had served as secretary or clerk to Chief Justice Horace Gray of the Massachusetts Supreme Judicial Court, a pioneer in developing "the modern clerkship," before Gray's appointment to the United States Supreme Court. Brad Snyder, "The Judicial Genealogy (and Mythology) of John Roberts: Clerkships from Gray to Brandeis to Friendly to Roberts," 71 *OHSLJ* 1149, 1155 (2010).

34. Arthur Schlesinger Jr., *Robert Kennedy and His Times* (Boston: Houghton Mifflin, 1978), 378–79 (quotations); Powe, *The Warren Court and American Politics,* 205 (stroke); Baker v. Carr, 369 U.S. 162 (1962); Colegrove v. Green, 328 U.S. 549, 556 (1946) ("political thicket").

35. See David Stebenne, *Arthur J. Goldberg: New Deal Liberal* (New York: Oxford University Press, 1996), 1–6, 309–10.

36. Goldberg LCOH; Lewis Wood, "Truman Watches Burton Take Oath: New Supreme Court Justice Ascends Bench," *NYT,* October 2, 1945; Elisabeth Bumiller, "Lengthy Practices Prepare Court Nominee for His Senate Hearing," id., September 1, 2005.

37. "Areas of Inquiry by the Senate Judiciary Committee," nd., Series II, Box 44, Folder 2, Goldberg MSS.

38. Nomination of Arthur Goldberg, 22, 24; "Wirtz Sworn In for Labor; Goldberg Confirmed as Justice," *NYT,* September 26, 1962; Barry Goldwater to the President, August 30, 1962, WHCF EX FG 535/A, Box 194, JFKL; the letters protesting the nomination are in Sen 87B-A3, Box 38, Senate Judiciary Committee Nominations, NARS.

39. Yalof, *Pursuit of Justices,* 70.

40. Conversation with George Harrison, August 20, 1962, 11:33 A.M., Dictabelt 33.4, Cassette K, *The Presidential Recordings: John F. Kennedy: The Great Crises I July 30-August 1962,* ed. Timothy Naftali (New York: W. W. Norton, 2001), 656 ("I don't); Tom Wicker, "Washington: Mr. Johnson's Surprise Choice," *NYT,* July 21, 1965.

41. Powe, *The Warren Court and American Politics,* 209 (fifth vote); Undated Statement, Series I, Box 165, Folder 3, Goldberg MSS. Dorothy Goldberg made use of this statement for her memoir, *A Private View of a Public Life* (New York: Charterhouse, 1975), 171–74; NAACP v. Button, 371 U.S. 415 (1963); Gideon v. Wainwright, 372 U.S. 335 (1963); Wong Sun v. United States, 371 U.S. 471 (1963); Ker v. California, 374 U.S. 23 (1963); Fay v. Noia, 372 U.S. 391 (1963); Gray v. Sanders, 372 U.S. 368, 381 (1963).

42. "High Court Found Imperiled by Foes: Brennan Discerns Danger in Uninformed Criticism," *NYT,* August 30, 1963; The President's News Conference, June 27, 1962, http://www.presidency.ucsb.edu/ws/index.php?pid=8735; Christopher Hickman, *The Most Dangerous Branch: The Supreme Court and Its Critics in the Warren Court Era* (PhD dissertation, George Washington University, 2010), 173–76 (religious groups); Lain, "God, Civic Virtue, and the

American Way," 538; Barry Friedman, *The Will of the People: How Public Opinion Has Influenced the Supreme Court and Shaped the Meaning of the Constitution* (New York: Farrar, Straus and Giroux, 2009), 269, 273; Barry Friedman, "The Birth of an Academic Obsession: The History of the Countermajoritarian Difficulty, Part, Part V," 112 *YLJ* 153, 210 (2002). See Sara Mayeux, "What Gideon Did," 116 *CLR* 15, 52–67 (2016), for the argument that Gideon had a much greater impact.

43. Frank Shanahan, "Proposed Constitutional Amendments: They Will Strengthen Federal-State Relations," 49 *ABAJ* 631 (July 1963); Charles Black, "Proposed Constitutional Amendments: They Would Return Us to the Confederacy," id., 637; Earl Warren to Arthur Freund, June 10, 1963, Box 660, Constitutional Amendment 1963, Warren MSS ("astounded"); Warren to Paul Ringler, May 13, 1963, id. ("shameful"); Information Service, American Bar Association, "Proposals for Amending the Constitution Approved by the General Assembly of the States: A Summary of State Legislative Action," id. (May 1964); Newton, *Justice for All*, 426. Warren wrote Freund: "I am well aware that you have been conducting practically a one-man crusade against these proposals to amend the Constitution, and I want you to know that I am most appreciative." Warren to Arthur Freund, May 2, 1963, Box 660, Constitutional Amendment 1963, Warren MSS. Arthur Freund and Paul Freund were cousins.

44. Charles Mohr, "Goldwater Sees Presidency Peril," *NYT*, September 12, 1964; Robert Thompson, "School Prayers Given Support by Goldwater," *LAT*, October 11, 1964; Charles Mohr, "Goldwater Says He'd Curb Court: Also Stresses States' Rights in Swing Through South," *NYT*, September 16, 1964.

45. Frank Porter, "Prominent Lawyers Rebuke Goldwater: Many Bar Leaders," *WP*, October 12, 1964 ("catch," "ultimate"); Anthony Lewis, "Goldwater Stand on Court Decried: Prominent Lawyers Assail 'Broadside Attacks,'" *NYT*, October 12, 1964; Richard Toth, "Lawyers Hit Goldwater in High Court Attacks," *LAT*, October 12, 1964; "Goldwater Scored for Court Attacks," *NYT*, September 3, 1964 ("violent"); Drew Pearson, "Goldwater Court Plan Claimed," *LAT*, August 4, 1964; Michael Flamm, *In the Heat of Summer: The New York Riots of 1964 and the War on Crime* (Philadelphia: University of Pennsylvania Press, 2016), 20-22. But see Walter Murphy and Joseph Tanenhaus, "Public Opinion and Supreme Court: The Goldwater Campaign," 32 (1) *POQ* 31, 347 (1968) (hypothesizing that many conservatives "connected the work of the Court with the liberalism of the last thirty odd years in great part because of Goldwater's campaign" and that the Republican may have made much of the animus toward the court previously relegated to the Far Right "morally and intellectually respectable").

46. Fred Rodell, "The 'Warren Court' Stands Its Ground," *NYT Mag*, September 27, 1964; Reynolds v. Sims, 377 U.S. 533, 624–25 (1964).

47. Griffin v. County School Board of Prince Edward County, 377 U.S. 218 (1964); Griffin v. Maryland, 378 U.S. 130 (1964); v. Florida, 378 U.S. 153 (1964); Barr v. City of Columbia, 378 U.S. 146 (1964); Bell v. Maryland, 378 U.S. 226 (1964); Bouie v. City of Columbia, 378 U.S. 347 (1964); Hamm v. City of Rock Hill, 379 U.S. 306 (1964); McLaughlin v. Florida, 379 U.S. 184 (1964); New York Times v. Sullivan, 376 U.S. 254 (1964); Jacobellis v. Ohio, 378 U.S. 184 (1964), Quantity of Books v. Kansas, 378 U.S. 205 (1964); Aptheker v. Secretary of State, 378 U.S. 500 (1964); Malloy v. Hogan, 378 U.S. 1 (1964); Massiah v. U.S., 377 U.S. 201 (1964).

48. Newman, *Hugo Black*, 540–48 ("nigras"); Bell v. Maryland, 378 U.S. 343; Schwartz, *Super Chief*, at 630 (1983) ("buried"); Christopher Schmidt, "Divided by Law: The Sit-ins and the Role of the Courts in the Civil Rights Movement," 33 *LHR* 93, 118-29 (2015); Christopher Schmidt, "The Sit-Ins and the State Action Doctrine," 18 *W&MBRJ* 767, 800 (2010) ("opinions"). Black is buried in Arlington.

49. Rodell, "The 'Warren Court' Stands Its Ground."

50. Jim Cannon to Messrs. Elliott, Lansner, Bernstein, Bradlee, Iselin, Roberts, Miss Sain, "Talk With President Johnson on July 14, 1965," Box 32, Interview with Lyndon Johnson, White MSS.

51. Alexander Wohl, *Father, Son, and the Constitution: How Justice Tom Clark and Attorney General Ramsey Clark Shaped American Democracy* (2013), 288 ("passive").

52. Robert Dallek, *Flawed Giant: Lyndon Johnson and His Times: 1961-1973* (New York: Oxford University Press, 1998), 233.

53. From Tom Clark, October 5, 1965, 7:31 P.M., WH 6510.01, PNO 21, #9021, MC; Hugo Black to Lyndon Johnson, December 3, 1963, Box 35, Black MSS; William O. Douglas, *The Court Years 1939-1975: The Autobiography of William O. Douglas* (New York: Random House, 1980), 85; Dorothy Goldberg to Robert Goldberg, December 27, 1963, Series I: 1962-66, Miscellaneous, Goldberg MSS; Newton, *Justice for All*, 478.

54. Sanford Levinson, Book Review, 75 *VaLR* 1429, 1439 (1989), quoting G. Edward White, *The Oliver Wendell Holmes Devise History of the Supreme Court of the United States: The Marshall Court and Cultural Change, 1815-1835*, vols. 3–4 (New York: Macmillan, 1988), 198; http://www.americanbar.org/content/dam/aba/migrated/cpr/pic/1924_canons.authcheckdam.pdf.

55. To Arthur Goldberg, April 9, 1964, 12:28 P.M. WH6404.06, PNO 2, #2944, *The Presidential Recordings: Lyndon B. Johnson: Toward the Great Society V, February 1, 1964-May 31, 1964*, ed. David Shreve and Robert Johnson (New York: W. W. Norton, 2007), 866; Newton, *And Justice for All*, 390–91 (consultation).

56. Ethan Greenberg, *Dred Scott and the Dangers of a Political Court* (Lanham: Lexington, 2009), 68–79; "Vinson Excelled in Federal Posts," *NYT*, September 9, 1953; Jim Mann, "Court Rejected Chief Justice's View in '52 Steel Dispute: Book Says Vinson Advise Truman to Seize Mills," *LAT*, August 24, 1982; James St. Clair and Linda Gugin, *Chief Justice Fred M. Vinson of Kentucky: A Political Biography* (Lexington: University Press of Kentucky, 2002), 216–17; "With All Deliberate Impropriety," *NYT*, March 24, 1987; Philip Elman, Interviewed by Norman Silber, "The Solicitor General's Office, Justice Frankfurter, and Civil Rights Litigation, 1946-1960: An Oral History," 100 *HLR* 817 (1987).

57. From Nicholas Katzenbach, May 14, 1965, 7:25 P.M., WH6505.12, PNO 14, #7679, *Reaching for Glory: Lyndon Johnson' Secret White House Tapes, 1964-1965*, ed. Michael Beschloss (New York: Simon and Schuster, 2001), 323–24.

58. Barbara Perry, *A "Representative" Supreme Court? The Impact of Race, Religion, and Gender on Appointments* (New York: Greenwood, 1991). See, for example, From Abe Fortas, September 22, 1966, WH6609.11, PNO 3, #10821, MC (in which Johnson, who had decided to appoint Thurgood Marshall to the court, worried that he would be "overdoing" things by making another African American, William Coleman, solicitor general), and To James Eastland, June 23, 1968, 9:09 A.M., WH6806.03, PNO 4, #13135, id. (in which Johnson referred to the inadvisability of bringing Goldberg back to court if Fortas became chief).

59. To McGeorge Bundy, November 6, 1964, 3:45 P.M., WH6411.11, PNO 9, #6275, MC; To Nicholas Katzenbach, November 11, 1964, 7:38 P.M., WH6411.16, PNO 3, #6326, id. (judicial ambition); Carroll Kilpatrick, "LBJ Gives Celebrezze Court Seat," *WP*, July 28, 1965 ("There have been rumors off and on for months that Celebrezze wanted to leave the Cabinet for a judgeship.")

60. Betty Beale, *Power at Play: A Memoir of Parties, Politicians and the Presidents in My Bedroom* (Washington, DC: Regnery Gateway 1993), 58, 133 ("marvelous," cat bill); Jack Smith, "Lemmeowt! It Seems That a Cat, Too, Is Entitled to Lives, Liberty and the Purrsuit of Happiness," *LAT*, November 4, 1990; Arthur Schlesinger, Jr. *A Thousand Days: John F. Kennedy in the White House* (Boston: Houghton Mifflin, 1965), 138-39.

61. "Arthur Schlesinger, Jr., *Journals 1952-2000*, ed. Andrew Schlesinger and Stephen Schlesinger (New York: Penguin, 2000), 211. (As Schlesinger said of Stevenson, with whom he had worked closely for many years, "[h]e had many moments of petulance, querulousness, indecision." Id., 239); Jeff Broadwater, *Adlai Stevenson and American Politics: The Odyssey of a Cold War Liberal* (New York: Twayne, 1994), 193–94, 199; "Senate or U.N.?," *NYT*, May 2, 1964; "Another Senator Kennedy?," id., May 16, 1964; Lady Bird Johnson, Tape-recorded Diary, July 23, 1965, *Reaching for Glory*, 405-06.

62. From McGeorge Bundy, June 24, 1965, 10:00 A.M., WH6506.07, PNO 2, #8186 *Reaching for Glory*, 369, 370 ("peace").

63. George Ball, *The Past Has Another Pattern: Memoirs* (New York: W. W. Norton, 1982), 382; To Dean Rusk, July 15, 1965, 9:12 A.M., WH6507.03, PNO10-11, #8335-356, *Reaching for Glory*, 391, 392; To Richard Russell, July 19, 1965, 6:09 P.M., Citation No. 8352, WH6507.04, PNO 13, #8352, MC (second thoughts).
64. John Kenneth Galbraith, *A Life in Our Times: Memoirs* (New York: Ballantine, 1981), 455–56; Daily Diary, July 16, 1965, LBJL; Lyndon Johnson, *The Vantage Point: Perspectives of the Presidency, 1963-1969* (London: Weidenfeld and Nicolson, 1971), 543–44.
65. Daily Diary, July 16, 1965, LBJL; Galbraith, *A Life in Our Times*, 456–57; Johnson, *The Vantage Point*, 543; "Goldberg Says LBJ Lied in His Book," *WP*, October 27, 1971; see Arthur Goldberg, Interview by Ted Gittlinger, March 23, 1983, LBJOH, 1, 18. But compare. Neil Sheehan, "Goldberg Disputes Johnson Memoirs on U.N. Post," *NYT*, October 27, 1971 (when Sheehan contacted Galbraith, Galbraith had confirmed that Goldberg "certainly gave me" the impression of, at least, initial boredom). Johnson's own account of the timing of the Goldberg appointment is muddled. There, he said he first mentioned the possibility of the Department of Health, Education, and Welfare or the UN to Goldberg on the plane to Stevenson's burial on July 19, 1965. Johnson, *The Vantage Point*, 543–44. That seems too late. On the other hand, Dorothy Goldberg's memory that Johnson first telephoned Goldberg about the appointment on July 16, 1965, probably placed the conversation too early. Goldberg, *A Private View of a Public Life* 193. The President's Daily Diary of July 16, 1965, includes no call to Goldberg.
66. Daily Diary, July 17, 1965, LBJL; Goldberg LBJOH, 2; Daniel Moynihan, Letter to the Editor, "Did Arthur Goldberg Want U.N. Post," *NYT*, November 1, 1971; and see Daniel Patrick Moynihan, Letter to the Editor, "Supreme Sacrifice," id., November 24, 1996.
67. Cartha DeLoach to Clyde Tolson, July 19, 1965, Part 3 of 3, http://vault.fbi.gov/abe-fortas/Abe%20Fortas%20Part%2003%20of%2003/view; Landon Storrs, *The Second Red Scare and the Unmaking of the New Deal Left* (Princeton: Princeton University Press, 2013). The eleven Senators were Senator Cannon (D-UT), Eugene McCarthy (D-MN), Paul Douglas (D-IL), Robert Kennedy (D-NY), Edward Kennedy (D-MA), Thomas Kuchel (R-CA), Everett Dirksen (R-IL), Roman Hruska (R-NE), Bourke Hickenlooper (R-IA), Norris Cotton (R-NH), and George Murphy (R-CA).
68. To Richard Russell, July 19, 1965; From Arthur Goldberg, July 19, 1965, 8:28 P.M., WH6507.05, PNO 3, #8355, MC.
69. From Arthur Goldberg, July 19, 1965; Califano, *The Triumph and Tragedy of Lyndon Johnson*, 39; Goldberg LBJOH, 1 ("enmeshed," "egotistical"); Kathleen Teltsch, "Search on at U.N. for Vietnam Pact," *NYT*, August 5, 1965; Dallek, *Flawed Giant*, 234; "Search on at U.N. for Vietnam Pact," *NYT*, August 5, 1965; Stebenne, *Arthur J. Goldberg*, 348 ("picked," "logical," "mind"); From Arthur Goldberg, July 19, 1965, 9:00 P.M., WH6507.05, PNO 7, #8359, *Reaching for Glory*, 399 ("proud," "I").
70. From Arthur Goldberg, July 19, 1965, 8:28 P.M. WH6507.05, PNO 7, #8359, MC (letter, "We'll"); Laura Kalman, *Abe Fortas: A Biography* (New Haven: Yale University Press, 1990), 241–44 ("delighted," "touched"). Johnson reproduced Fortas's letter in *The Vantage Point*, 544-45.
71. Goldberg, *A Private View of a Public Life*, 196 ("stone age"); Dorothy Goldberg to Robert Goldberg, December 27, 1963, I: Miscellaneous, 1962-66, Goldberg MSS ("nothing"), Dorothy Goldberg to Darlings, April 24, 1972, Part II: Box 1, Folder 1, Goldberg MSS ("increasingly." "I think some of this [feeling that he should have stayed on the court] has crept into the book," she continued about her memoir, *A Private View of a Public Life*.); Remarks Upon Announcing the Nomination of Arthur J. Goldberg as U.S. Representative to the United Nations, July 20, 1965, http://www.presidency.ucsb.edu/ws/?pid=27097; Raymond Daniell, "Some at U.N. Are Critical; Arabs Decline to Comment," *NYT*, July 21, 1965; Lloyd Garrison, "U.S. Holds Talks to Avert Arab Attacks on Goldberg," id., July 22, 1965. Joseph Alsop, "Matter of Fact," *WP*, August 2, 1965. Fred Graham, "Senate Confirms Goldberg Unanimously for the U.N. Post," *NYT*, July 24, 1965; "The Goldberg Appointment," id., July 21, 1965. Warren's reaction to the news of Goldberg's appointment was typical of that at the court. "The Chief Justice was surprised and shocked," his great friend, Fairmont Hotel owner and philanthropist Ben Swig, wrote Goldberg. "He told me he felt as though he were losing his right arm with your leaving the Supreme Court. I have never heard anyone speak in such

glowing terms as the Chief Justice did of you." Benjamin Swig to Arthur Goldberg, July 21, 1965, Series I, Box 36, Folder 7, Goldberg MSS. "As our 1965 term approaches, I am more keenly aware of the fact that I will no longer be able to feel your presence on the Court with all that has meant to me—the warmth of your friendship and my confidence in your views of the law," Warren wrote by hand to Goldberg on October 1, 1965, id. "It leaves a great void for me as we launch into another year of decision making. In the three years you were with us you made a great impact on the jurisprudence of the Court, and I had hoped so much that you would be here not only as long as I will be, but for a long time thereafter. I understand, however, what caused you to accept your new and great responsibility and I honor you for it. . . . I know it was a great wrench for you to tear up your roots here and embark on such a hazardous adventure, but one never goes wrong in following his conscience." See also William O. Douglas to Arthur Goldberg, July 20, 1965, id.; John Harlan to Arthur Goldberg, July 21, 1965, id.; and the letter from the court acknowledging his resignation, October 4, 1965, id.

72. To John Galbraith, July 20, 1965, 12:06 P.M., WH6507.05, PNO 10, #8362, MC.

73. To Abe Fortas, July 21, 1965, 4:31 P.M., WH6507.06, PNO 6, #8370, *Reaching for Glory*, 401, 402.

74. To Ramsey Clark, July 23, 1965, 4:25 P.M., WH6507.07, PNO5-6, #8381-82, MC.

75. Kalman, *Abe Fortas*, 184, 241 ("used," "lucky"); Nicholas Katzenbach, Memorandum for the President, Re: Supreme Court Vacancy, July 22, 1965, WHCF EX FG 535/A, Box 360, LBJL.

76. Kalman, *Abe Fortas*, 244; To Abe Fortas, July 28, 1965, 11:48 A.M., WH6507.09, PNO 2, #8406, MC.

77. Califano, *The Triumph and Tragedy of Lyndon Johnson*, 48–50; Johnson, *The Vantage Point*, 545.

78. Kalman, *Abe Fortas*, 243-45 (Douglas, "jurisprudential"); From Arthur Goldberg, WH6507.09 PNO 8, July 28, 1965, 7:20 P.M., #8412, MC ("whole"); Hugo Black to Earl Warren, August 3, 1965, Box 347, Hugo Black, Warren MSS. Lee Epstein, Richard Posner, and William Landes also consider Fortas the equivalent of a federal employee at the time of his appointment in *The Behavior of Federal Judges: A Theoretical and Empirical Study of Rational Choice* (Cambridge: Harvard University Press,2013), 118.

79. Interview with Adam Stolpen, January 2014; William O. Douglas to Hugo Black, August 1, 1965, Box 60, Douglas, Black MSS; Excerpts From Editorial Comments on the Appointment of Honorable Abe Fortas as Associate Justice of the United States, Nomination of Abe Fortas, 3–6; From Michael Mansfield, July 30, 1965, 10:00 A.M., WH6507.09, PNO 11, #8415, *Reaching for Glory,* 417.

80. From Nicholas Katzenbach, July 28, 1965, 9:20 P.M., WH6507.09, PNO 9, #8413, MC; Senate Judiciary Committee 38/A-A3, Fortas Nomination Files, No. 105, NARS; "Fortas the Fixer," *HE*, August 7, 1965.

81. Nomination of Abe Fortas, 8–21, 23–33; Mary McGrory, "Hearing on Fortas Confirmation Casts Shadows of Bad Old Days," *LAT*, August 10, 1965.

82. Griswold v. Connecticut, 381 U.S. 479 (1965); Nomination of Abe Fortas, 1965, 42, 50, 57; Ervin's specific reference was to "Josh Billings' mule that don't kick to no rule whatsoever," a point of departure he also used in discussing the Warren Court's disrespect for precedent with the press: "I am inclined to think that the precedent to which some Members of the Supreme Court are most faithful is the precedent set by Josh Billings' mule, which didn't kick according to no rule." Quoted in Karl Campbell, *Senator Sam Ervin: Last of the Founding Fathers* (Chapel Hill: University of North Carolina Press, 2007), 192.

83. To Joseph Kennedy, September 24, 1965, 1:05 P.M., WH6509.07, PNO 8, #8902; John MacKenzie, "Panel Likely to Approve Morrissey," *WP*, October 3, 1965; "Morrissey Drops Federal Court Bid," *NYT*, November 6, 1965.

84. To Richard Russell, July 19, 1965; To Nicholas Katzenbach, August 6, 1965, 6:10 P.M., WH6508.02, PNO 5, #8514, MC; "Senate Committee Supports Marshall's Appointment," *NYT*, July 30, 1965.

85. To Nicholas Katzenbach, August 9, 1965, 3:31 P.M., WH6508.03, PNO 9, #8526, MC ("better relations"); *CR*, August 11, 1965, S20055 (Remarks of Senator Thurmond); "Senate Confirms Fortas for High Court: Gardner and Marshall Also Approved in Voice

Vote," *NYT*, August 12, 1965. The three senators who spoke against the nomination were Republicans: John Williams of Delaware, Strom Thurmond of South Carolina and Carl Curtis of Nebraska.

86. Califano, *The Triumph and Tragedy of Lyndon Johnson*, 59.

87. From John McCone, August 18, 1965, 12:10 P.M., WH6508.05, PNO 9, #8550, MC ("powder," "absolutely"); From Martin Luther King, August 20, 1965, 5:10 P.M., WH6508.07, PNO 12, #8578, id.; David Carter, *The Music Has Gone Out of the Movement: Civil Rights and the Johnson Administration, 1965-1968* (Chapel Hill: University of North Carolina Press, 2009), 61 (target); Michael Flamm, *Law and Order: Street Crime, and the Crisis of Liberalism in the 1960s* (New York: Columbia University Press, 2005), 46-49; Michael Flamm, *In the Heat of the Summer: The New York Riots and the War on Crime* (Philadelphia: University of Pennsylvania Press, 2016), 188, 254; Statement by President Upon Announcing a Program of Assistance to Los Angeles, August 26, 1965, http://www.presidency.ucsb.edu/ws/?pid=27189; Califano, *The Triumph and Tragedy of Lyndon Johnson*, 59–62.

88. Harry McPherson, Memorandum for the President, September 12, 1966, 7:00 P.M., Box 15, File: Harry McPherson, Katzenbach MSS; and see Harry McPherson, *A Political Education* (Boston: Little Brown, 1972), 355–58.

89. Carter, *The Music Has Gone Out of the Movement*, 90–92 Remarks to the Delegates to the White House Conference "To Fulfill These Rights." June 1, 1966, http://www.presidency.ucsb.edu/ws/?pid=27624; McPherson, *A Political Education*, 349; Address of Solicitor General Thurgood Marshall, June 1, 1966, Series II, Box 62, White House Speeches, B. Marshall MSS.

90. "Corinna Lain, "Countermajoritarian Hero or Zero: Rethinking the Warren Court's Role in the Criminal Procedure Revolution," 152 *UPLR* 1361, 1413-16 (2004); "Support for Police Seen at Low Point," *NYT*, February 4, 1966 ("red-necked"); "Crime: Meaningless Statistics?," *Ti*, August 19, 1966 (quoting Columbia sociologist Sophia Robinson); Fred Graham, *The Self-Inflicted Wound* (New York: Macmillan, 1970), 67–85 (academic reaction and statistics); Ramsey Clark, *Crime in America: Observations on Its Nature, Causes, Prevention and Control* (New York: Simon and Schuster, 1970), 11, 44–45, 321; Dennis Loo and Ruth-Ellen Grimes, "Polls, Politics, and Crime: The 'Law and Order' Issue of the 1960s," 5 *WCR* 50, 55-57 (2004); David Timothy Ballantine, "Managing the Backlash: Senator Ernest F. 'Fritz' Hollings and the Marshall and Fortas Supreme Court Nominations," *PSCHA* 2013 19, 20 (euphemism); "The Cities: The Crucible," *Ti*, January 26, 1968 ("crime in the streets," "omnibus"); "Crime & the Great Society," id., March 24, 1967 ("disgrace," "foundation"); "Violence in America," id., July 28, 1967 ("Negro riots," "greatest," "violence").

91. Carter, *The Music Has Gone Out of the Moment*, 108–9; Peniel Joseph, *Stokely: A Life* (New York: BasicCivitas, 2014), 114–15, 173, 103, 125; "Carmichael Says the War Is for Johnson, Not Him," *NYT*, November 1, 1966 ("Johnson's war," "If Lyndon").

92. Carter, *The Music Has Gone Out of the Movement*, 109, 117 ("father"); The President's News Conference at the LBJ Ranch, July 5, 1966, http://www.presidency.ucsb.edu/ws/index.php?pid=27705.

93. Carter, *The Music Has Gone Out of the Movement*, 112; From Abe Fortas, September 22, 1966, 8:30 A.M., WH6609.11, PNO 4, #10822 (blaming Carmichael); Joseph, *Stokely*, 146–47.

94. Harper v. Virginia State Board of Elections, 383 U.S. 663 (1963); South Carolina v. Katzenbach, 383 U.S. 301 (1966); Katzenbach v. Morgan, 384 U.S. 641 (1966); Brown v. Louisiana, 383 U.S. 131, 142 (1966); John MacKenzie, "Justice Black Blisters 5-to-4 Ruling: Louisiana Sit-In Conviction Reversed," *WP*, February 24, 1966; William O. Douglas to Abe Fortas, n.d., Brown v. Louisiana, Fortas MSS.

95. Case History, October Term, 1965, Series II, Box 6, Folder 8, xiv, Brennan TH MSS; Hugo Black to Elizabeth Wenger, December 9, 1969, Box 73, Requests for Personal Opinions 1960-71, Black MSS ("Never"); John Frank, Memorandum for the Files, July 5, 1968, Box 1,

Folder 11, Frank MSS ("zealot," "like"); Kalman, *Abe Fortas*, 250–54, 321 (Fortas's causes). See, for example, Abe Fortas to Hugo Black, February 27, 1966, Box 60, Abe Fortas, Black MSS: "How wonderful-how satisfying it has been for me to see the gradual, and now fairly complete, acceptance not only of many of your stoutly held positions, but also of your quality as a lawyer and judicial statesman! . . . I hope you don't mind my saying that I'm so proud of you!"

96. Miranda v. Arizona, 384 U.S. 436, 501 (1966); July 27, 1966, Lewis Powell to James Vorenberg, July 6, 1966, Box 22, Justice—National Crime Commission, Katzenbach MSS.

97. Lain, "Countermajoritarian Hero or Zero?," 1421, 1418; and see Yale Kamisar, "The Warren Court and Criminal Justice," in *The Warren Court: A Retrospective*, ed. Bernard Schwartz (New York: Oxford University Press, 1996), 116, 120–21, 29 (Though Miranda was initially criticized for going "too far, . . . to a considerable extent the Warren Court was criticized for what its critics had anticipated it would do [but what, it turned out, the Court did not really do." Id., 121); Flamm, *Law and Order*, 58 ("dodged," "deliberately").

98. Fred Graham, "The Law: Marshall and the Activists," *NYT*, September 3, 1967; Lain, "Countermajoritarian Hero or Zero?," 1421–24; Graham, *The Self-Inflicted Wound*, 9. (Graham himself stressed in the book that there was not necessarily any causal relationship between Warren Court decisions and the increasing crime rate while maintaining that the court's actions may have "contributed substantially to the deterioration in public order that took place" id., 4, 285–86. As he said, though, "there is a logic to the charge that the concentration of liberal decisions from the Warren Court during the 1960s did contribute to the deteriorating crime situation, and the charge is still made, even if it can never be proved." Id., 286)

99. To Abe Fortas, October 3, 1966, 8:16 A.M., WH6610.2, PNO 1, #10912, MC; The President's News Conference, November 6, 1966, http://www.presidency.ucsb.edu/ws/index.php?pid=27994&st=johnson&st1=; Michael Nelson, *Resilient America: Electing Nixon in 1968, Channeling Dissent, and Dividing Government* (Lawrence: University Press of Kansas, 2014), 60 (in the Senate, "the GOP's three-seat gain was grounded in victories by liberal and moderate candidates: Mark Hatfield in Oregon, Charles Percy in Illinois, Edward Brooke in Massachusetts, and Howard Baker in Tennessee.")

100. Adderly v. Florida, 385 U.S. 39, 54, 55 (1966); Fred Graham, "A Supreme Court Split: Clash of Black and Douglas Suggests Shift of Bench to Conservative Tone," *NYT*, December 14, 1966.

101. Walker v. Birmingham, 388 U.S. 307, 321, 349 (1967); Shuttlesworth v. Birmingham, 394 U.S. 147 (1969); Powe, *The Warren Court and American Politics*, 278–80.

102. Case History, October Term 1966, xxxii, Series II, Box 6, Brennan TH MSS ("magnificent," "blistering"). See, for example, "Dr. King Loses Plea; Faces 5 Days in Jail," *NYT*, June 13, 1967; Joseph Kraft, "Whither the Supreme Court?," *LAT*, June 16, 1967.

103. From Abe Fortas, August 16, 1965, 9:53 A.M., WH6508.05, PNO 1, #8542, MC ("talk"); To Abe Fortas, August 30, 1965, 3:44 P.M., WH6508.13, PNO 10, #8676, id. ("stories"); Dan Morgan, "Foes' Brickbats Only Spurred His Will to Fight, Says Bress," *WP*, October 22, 1965; Robert Asher, "Senate Confirms Bress as Prosecutor by 49-14," id., October 23, 1965.

104. From Abe Fortas, January 4, 1966, 7:05 P.M., WH6601.02 PNO 5, #9240, MC; From Nicholas Katzenbach, January 4, 1966, 7:24 P.M., WH6601.02, PNO 7, #9422, id.; From Ramsey Clark, January 25, 1967, 8:22 P.M., WH6701.09, PNO 2, #11408, id. ("conscientious," complaining about Myer Feldman).

105. Drew Pearson and Jack Anderson, "The Bobby Baker Trial: The Most Important Issue Involved Is the Use of Wiretapping," *WP*, January 8, 1967 ("sensational"); Richard Harwood, "Baker Says He Went to LBJ First for Aid," id., January 21, 1967; Bobby Baker with Larry King, *Wheeling and Dealing: Confessions of a Capitol Hill Operator* (New York: W. W. Norton, 1978), 212–18; From Ramsey Clark, January 29, 1967, 10:45 A.M., WH6701.09, PNO 8, #11414, MC ("Aw," "all of us"); To Abe Fortas, January 4, 1966, 7:40 P.M., WH6601.02, PNO 8, #9423, id. ("destroyed," "murdered"); From Abe Fortas, January 10, 1966, 8:40 P.M., WH6601.06, PNO 11, #9477, id. ("commitment," "bad").

106. From Abe Fortas, January 10, 1966 (Justice leaks); To Ramsey Clark, November 23, 1966, 6:56 P.M., WH6601.06, PNO 3 (antitrust); To Abe Fortas, January 11, 1967, 3:45 P.M., WH6701.03, PNO 3, #11333, id. ("gut"). To get a sense of the stories that concerned LBJ, see, for example, Miriam Ottenberg, "Baker Conflict of Interest Charge by Jury Is Blocked by Law Loophole," *WS*, January 9, 1966.

107. Schlesinger, *Journals*, at 260; David Broder, "Kennedy's Vietnam Plea Spurs Popularity on Democratic Left," *NYT*, February 21, 1966; To Nicholas Katzenbach, March 17, 1966, 10:02 P.M., WH6603.08, PNO 1-2, #9895-96, MC; To Nicholas Katzenbach, April 29, 1966, 12:59 P.M., WH6604.05, PNO 2, #10060, id. For a prescient analysis of Kennedy's evolution with respect to the Vietnam War, see Joseph Palermo, *The Politics of Race and War: Robert F. Kennedy and the Democratic Party* (PhD dissertation, Cornell University, 1998).

108. To Abe Fortas, December 22, 1966, 3:41 P.M., WH6612.08, PNO 9, #11189, MC; To Nicholas Katzenbach, March 29, 1965, 6:24 P.M., WH6503.14, PNO 12-13, #7179-80, *Reaching for Glory*, 251, 252-53.

109. John MacKenzie, "Ginzburg, Black Lose on Appeals: Hearings Refused in Tax Evasion, Obscenity Cases," *WP*, May 3, 1966; MacKenzie, "Use of 'Bug' Is Admitted by Justice," id., May 25, 1966; MacKenzie, "Black Asks Dismissal of Tax Case," id., May 28, 1966 ("tainted"); Richard Harwood, "U.S. Releases Text of 'Bugs' on Baker," id., November 16, 1966; Athan Theoharis, ed., *From the Secret Files of J. Edgar Hoover* (Chicago: Ivan R. Dee, 1991), 152-53. See Alexander Charns, *Cloak and Gavel: FBI Wiretaps, Bugs, Informers, and the Supreme Court* (Urbana: University of Illinois Press, 1992), 39-42. LBJ complained that while the media identified Black as his onetime neighbor, "I wouldn't know him if I met him on the street." To Ramsey Clark, July 13, 1966, 11:39 P.M., WH6701.01, PNO 7, #10407.

110. Charns, *Cloak and Gavel* (Urbana: University of Illinois Press, 1992), 56; To Ramsey Clark, July 13, 1966, 11:39 P.M., WH 6607.01, PNO 8, #10408, MC.

111. Wohl, *Father, Son, and Constitution*, 315-17; Jeff Shesol, *Mutual Contempt: Lyndon Johnson, Robert Kennedy, and the Feud that Defined a Decade* (New York: W. W. Norton, 1997), 349-53; Morton Mintz, "Kennedy Hints FBI Wiretapping," *WP*, June 27, 1966; To John McCormack, January 11, 1967, 7:12 P.M., WH6701.03, PNO 10, #11342, MC; Cartha DeLoach to Clyde Tolson, June 15, 1966, *From the Secret Files of J. Edgar Hoover*, 166 ("finger").

112. Nicholas Katzenbach, *Some of It Was Fun: Working With RFK and LBJ* (New York: W. W. Norton, 2008), 187; Charns, *Cloak and Gavel*, 59 ("greatest crisis"), and see 60-62; Cartha DeLoach to Clyde Tolson, June 6, 1966, *From the Secret Files of J. Edgar Hoover*, 163-64 ("fronting"). "I cannot refrain from observing that there has been a constant feeding to the press by individuals in the Department of snide and caustic criticisms of the FBI following the death of President Kennedy," Hoover complained in July 1965. J. Edgar Hoover, Memorandum for the Attorney General, July 21, 1965, Box 3, Memoranda 1965, Rosenthal MSS.

113. Cartha DeLoach, *Hoover's FBI: The Inside Story by Hoover's Trusted Lieutenant* (Washington, DC: Regnery, 1997), 393, 54-55; Jeremy Roebuck and Allison Stelle, "Villanova Professor's Quest Reveals LBJ Vendetta Against George Hamilton," *PI*, September 1, 2014; Samahon v. Federal Bureau of Investigation, 40 F. Supp. 3d 498 (2014); Stern and Wermiel, *Justice Brennan*, 267; Michael Tigar, *Fighting Injustice* (Chicago: American Bar Association, 2002), 52-59 (Deprived of his clerkship, Tigar went to work for Edward Bennett Williams and helped him defend Bobby Baker. Id., 71-74, 202); Cartha DeLoach to Clyde Tolson, June 14, 1966, *From the Secret Files of J. Edgar Hoover*, 268-72.

114. DeLoach to Tolson, June 14, 1966; J. Edgar Hoover, Memorandum for Personal Files, June 14, 1966, Charns MSS ("trying," "patsy").

115. DeLoach to Tolson, June 14, 1966; and see DeLoach to Tolson, June 21, 1966 and June 23, 1976, *From the Secret Files of J. Edgar Hoover*, 273-75. LBJ aide Marvin Watson, told DeLoach that LBJ "did not want to be seen as undermining" Katzenbach. Charns, *Cloak and Gavel*, 61. Charns discusses the resolution of the Hoffa at 80-84.

116. Robert Kennedy to Nicholas Katzenbach, July 13, 1966, Box 5, Personal Correspondence, RFK Senate MSS.

117. To Ramsey Clark, July 13, 1966, 11:39 P.M., WH6607.01, PNO 7, #10407, MC; Richard Harwood, "Hoover Bugged Black's Suite, High Court Told," *WP*, July 14, 1966; "Bugging, American Style," July 15, 1966, id. The relevant language in the supplemental memorandum said, "records of oral and written communications within the Department of Justice reflect concern by Attorneys General and the Director of the Federal Bureau of Investigation that the use of listening devices by agents of the government should be confined to a strictly limited category of situations. Under Departmental practice in effect for a period of years prior to 1963, and continuing into 1965, the Director of the Federal Bureau of Investigation was given authority to approve the installation of devices such as that in question for intelligence (and not evidentiary) purposes when required in the interest of internal security or national safety, including organized crime, kidnappings and matters wherein human life might be at stake. Acting on the basis of the aforementioned Departmental authorization, the Director approved installation of the device involved in the instant case." Supplemental Memorandum for the United States, Box 8, Wiretapping Memoranda 1966-67, Rosenthal MSS. See "Statement by a Spokesman," July 13, 1966, id., and Jack Rosenthal, Memorandum for the File, July 13, 1966, id., for discussion of Justice Department interpretations of the memorandum for the press.

118. Jean White, "Hoover, Kennedy Step Up Bugging Row," *WP*, December 12, 1966 ("all but"); George Lardner, "RFK Extended Use of 'Bug,' Hoover Asserts," id., December 11, 1966 ("not only"); "J. Edgar: Oh, Yes You Did; Bobby: Oh, No I Didn't," *NYDN*, December 12, 1966.

119. Cartha DeLoach to Clyde Tolson, September 12, 1966, *From the Secret Files of J. Edgar Hoover*, 267–268 (quotations); Charns, *Cloak and Gown*, 64–68, 72–73.

120. William O. Douglas, Draft separate opinion, n.d., Box 1397, Douglas MSS (Douglas substituted "studied effort" for "powerful and studied effort" in a subsequent draft and deleted the sentence beginning "And in light of the power and influence of the group behind the present effort." Id.); William O. Douglas, *The Court Years 1939–1975: The Autobiography of William O. Douglas* (New York: Random House, 1980), 256–57; Charns, *Cloak and Gown*, 67–68 (reprinting Fortas note).

121. Charns, *Cloak and Gown*, 73–77; Black v. United States, 385 U.S. 26 (1966); Berger v. New York, 388 U.S. 41 (1967); Katz v. United States, 389 U.S. 347, 358 n.23 (1967); Graham, *The Self-Inflicted Wound*, 22–24 ("rights"); Louis Kohlmeier, "Bugging, Crime and the Court Flip-Flop," *WSJ*, January 12, 1968; Lain, "Countermajoritarian Hero or Zero?," 1436 ("pro-law enforcement"); Orrin Kerr, "The Fourth Amendment and New Technologies: Constitutional Myths and the Case for Caution," *MLR*, 801, 824 (2004) (arguing that Katz was far less revolutionary than subsequent generations of scholars have suggested). Justice Black, who had little use for the Fourth Amendment and was now telling his clerks that the court was "coddling criminals," issued the lone dissent, which, his biographer observed, revealed his obliviousness "to the dangers of uncontrolled wiretapping." Newman, *Hugo Black*, 558–59.

122. Katzenbach, *Some of It Was Fun*, 187.

123. From Joseph Califano, December 21, 1966, 8:45 A.M., WH6612.07, PNO 1, #11174, MC (Justice and RFK staff); From Abe Fortas, December 17, 1966, 10:45 A.M., WH 6612.04, PNO 2-3, #11149-11150; Shesol, *Mutual Contempt*, 309–27.

124. Juanita Roberts to Abe Fortas, August 29, 1966, WH6608.13, PNO 16, #10653, MC (time not noted); From Abe Fortas, December 17, 1966 ("opened"); William Manchester, *The Death of a President*, 324–28 (New York: Harper & Row, 1967); Manchester, "Flight from Dallas," *Look*, February 21, 1967. The identity of the person to whom Hughes gave the book remained unclear for the time being, and it was not until 1979 that the Johnson Library acknowledged possession of the book. "Mystery Still Lingers Over Kennedy's Bible: Judge Hughes Says She Handed Book to First Person She Saw After Giving Oath," *LAT*, February 8, 1967; November 22, 1963: Tragedy and Transition, More About the Missal used on Air Force One for the Oath of Office on 11/22/63," http://transition.lbjlibrary.org/missal. But leaks at least ensured that the public learned that it was an unopened missal, not a precious family Bible. See Andrew Glass, "Catholic Church Not Bible, Used by Johnson for Oath at

Dallas," *WP*, February 24, 1967 ("The missal was still wrapped in cellophane and resting in a cardboard box.")

125. From Abe Fortas, December 17, 1966, 10:45 A.M., WH6612.04, PNO 2, #11149, MC ("spies"); From Eunice Shriver, December 18, 1966, 6:55 P.M., WH6612.04, PNO 8, #11155, id.

126. From Abe Fortas, December 7, 1966, 10:45 A.M., WH6612.04, PNO 3, #11150, id.; Abe Fortas to Sarah Hughes, August 29, 1966, 1:30 P.M., WH6608.15M PNO7 #10666, id.; To Abe Fortas, August 29, 1966, 9:30 A.M., WH 6608.15, PNO 4, #10657, id. ("first battle") See Sam Kashner, "A Clash of Camelots," *VF*, August 31, 2009 and Shesol, *Mutual Contempt*, at 353-63 for accounts of the Kennedys' evolving relationship with Manchester and their lawsuit.

127. Louis Harris, "The Harris Survey: Book Dispute Lowers the Kennedys' Image," *LAT*, January 31, 1967; "Polls Say Dispute Hurt Mrs. Kennedy," *NYT*, February 1, 1967; Katzenbach, *Some of It Was Fun*, 211.

Chapter 3

1. Fred Graham, "The Law: Marshall on the Stand," *NYT*, July 30, 1967.
2. To J. Edgar Hoover, June 29, 1966, 10:24 A.M., WH6606.07, PNO 12-13, #10285-86, MC; "President Honors Ball on Retirement," *NYT*, October 7, 1966; From Abe Fortas, September 22, 1966, 8:30 A.M., WH6609.11, PNO 4, #10822, MC (eggs); To Nicholas Katzenbach, September 20, 1966, 8:35 P.M., WH6609.10, PNO 7, #10814, id.
3. Clark Clifford with Richard Holbrooke, *Counsel to the President: A Memoir* (New York: Random House, 1991), 440. "He was just as wrong as he could be," LBJ said of Clifford. "And I thought a fellow that could make a wrong decision on that might make other wrong ones. So it didn't bother me much. But I just thought it was unbelievable. Here's a man [Secretary of State Dean Rusk] that I think in due time will have to move out on account of his health, on account of his money, and on account of the political situation, and on account of a lot of things. But to run for cover now would be bad. And then for another man to insist on getting a contract, getting it sealed, and getting it notarized, that you would throw the guy out in not over six months. You just can't do that. God Almighty." To Abe Fortas, October 3, 1966, 8:16 A.M., WH6610.02, PNO 1, #10912, MC.; Arthur Schlesinger, Jr., Journals, July 28, 1966, Schlesinger MSS (reporting that Clifford might become the next Secretary of State. "He has been mentioned for some time as a possible successor to George Ball as Undersecretary. Last spring he told David Ginsburg that he would not take this job unless he were assured rather speedy promotion to the Secretaryship.")
4. Nicholas Katzenbach, *Some of It Was Fun: Working with RFK and LBJ* (New York: W. W. Norton, 2008), 211–12.
5. Tom Lambert, "Key Post Moves Startle Capital: Katzenbach Moving into State Department," *LAT*, September 22, 1966; To Nicholas Katzenbach, September 22, 1966, 8:05 P.M., WH6609.11, PNO 9, #10827, MC.
6. To Abe Fortas, September 24, 1966, 12:48 P.M., WH6609.12, PNO 1, #10832, MC; John MacKenzie, "Clark Long a Contender for Attorney General," *WP*, September 23, 1966.
7. Remarks at the Swearing In of Ramsey Clark as Attorney General, March 10, 1967, http://www.presidency.ucsb.edu/ws/index.php?pid=28123 (LBJ remembered Ramsey Clark in "knee pants"); From Ramsey Clark, January 25, 1967, 8:22 P.M., WH6701.09, PNO 2, #11408; Mimi Clark Gronlund, *Supreme Court Justice Tom C. Clark: A Life of Service* (Austin: University of Texas Press, 2010), 224 (quoting LBJ as telling Ramsey Clark, "Don't expect to be attorney general. . . . I can't appoint a Texan.").
8. Katzenbach, *Some of It Was Fun*, 212–13; Alexander Wohl, *Father, Son, and the Constitution: How Justice Tom Clark and Attorney General Ramsey Clark Shaped American Democracy* (Lawrence: University Press of Kansas, 2013), 309 ("Technically it was not true that Tom Clark would have to resign if Ramsey was appointed attorney general; he could recuse himself on any number of cases, and Ramsey would not actually have to sign the Justice Department's

briefs submitted to the Court. . . . But Johnson clearly was focused on making a change on the Court."); To Everett Dirksen, September 21, 1966, 11:41 A.M., WH6609.10, PNO 10, #10817, MC; From Everett Dirksen, September 22, 1966, 5:00 P.M., WH6609.11, PNO 7, #10825, id. ("don't"). See Lee Epstein and Jeffrey Segal, *Advice and Consent: The Politics of Judicial Appointments* (New York: Oxford University Press, 2005), 79 (discussing "the throw Momma from the bench" strategy, Republicans espoused to force the Ninth Circuit's Betty Fletcher to take senior status, so President Clinton could appoint her son to the Ninth Circuit).

9. From Abe Fortas, September 22,1966, 8:30 A.M., WH6609.11, PNO 3-4, #10821-22, MC.

10. From Abe Fortas, September 22, 1966; Seth Stern and Stephen Wermiel, *Justice Brennan: Liberal Champion* (Boston: Houghton Mifflin, 2010), 288–89, 295 ("drift," "acutely."). " 'Hugo changed, the man changed, right in front of us,' noted Justice Brennan. 'It was so evident. We talked about it much, the Chief and Bill Douglas probably more than anyone else. Bill especially was really hurt. We lost our fifth vote,' Brennan continued, his voice rising. 'Those of us who cared for him certainly felt sad. We were afraid it would hurt him in history and in academia.' In early 1966 Earl Warren observed: 'Black has hardened and gotten old. It's a different Black now.'" Roger Newman, *Hugo Black: A Biography* (New York: Pantheon, 1994), 570.

11. From Abe Fortas, September 22, 1966.

12. Id.; From Abe Fortas, October 6, 1966, 6:02 P.M., WH6610.03, PNO 7, #10929, MC (steer).

13. From Abe Fortas, September 22, 1966; From Ramsey Clark, November 24, 1966, 6:45 P.M., WH6611.06, PNO 1–3, #11051–11053, MC; Daily Diary, November 23, 1966, LBJL ("belt destroyed on President's instruction"); Joseph Califano, *The Triumph & Tragedy of Lyndon Johnson: The White House Years* (New York: Simon & Schuster, 1991), 159–63; From Ramsey Clark, March 28, 2967, 4:00 P.M., WH6703.04, PNO 6, #11654, MC ("Damn," "Talk"); Baltimore & Ohio R.R. Co. v. U.S., 386 U.S. 372, 459, 463 (1967); "High Court Blocks Pennsy-Central Merger Till Small Lines' Fate Is Set," *WSJ*, March 28, 1967; Penn-Central Merger Cases, 389 U.S. 486 (1968).

14. From Abe Fortas, September 22, 1966.

15. To Nicholas Katzenbach, September 24, 1966, 12:57 P.M., WH6609.12, PNO 2, #10833.

16. To Nicholas Katzenbach, September 28, 1966, 5:16 P.M., WH6609.13, PNO 2, #10848, MC.

17. To Abe Fortas, October 3, 1966; From Abe Fortas, October 6, 1966 ("exactly"); Fred Graham, "Justice Retiring," *NYT*, March 1, 1967. Johnson continued to go out of his way to send the Clarks the message that Tom Clark's retirement was mandatory. Could Clark become attorney general if his father served on the court? he asked Ramsey in January of 1967. Ramsey replied that he did not think that there was a conflict. He thought his father was "at the height of his judicial power, and I'm a little concerned, too, because I think he, more than any other member of the Court, stands for a lot of things that the American public is pretty strong for now, tough law enforcement and things . . . where I really don't agree with him." But the question of a conflict of interest was for others to decide. "My judgment, is, if you . . . became Attorney General, he'd have to leave the Court" because "every taxi driver in the country" and every member of the court would say "the old man couldn't judge . . . fairly" cases that "his own boy's" submitting, LBJ stressed. "When you do that, you, I think, lose the best friend we got on the Court. I mean, the best philosophically speaking . . . I think he believes about what I believe. I think you're too damn radical . . . liberal. I think you got a little of that dash of the University of Chicago in you." How had LBJ gotten the idea that the University of Chicago Law School, one of the country's more conservative elite law schools, was the bastion of either liberals or radicals? And why did he continue to harp on the necessity of Clark's retirement after he had received Tom Clark's promise that he would do so? Did LBJ think that Clark might renege on the promise? That seems unlikely. More probably, LBJ was letting Ramsey know how much trouble he was taking to make him attorney general. From Ramsey Clark, January 25, 1967, 8:22 P.M., WH6701.09, PNO 2, #11408, MC.

18. To Abe Fortas, October 3, 1966.

19. To Ramsey Clark, October 3, 1966, 5:57 P.M., WH6610.02, PNO 7, #10918, MC; To Abe Fortas, October 3, 1966; Clifford, *Counsel to the President*, 444–45.

20. From Ramsey Clark, January 25, 1967.

21. Id.; Louis Martin. Interview I by David McComb, May 14, 1969, LBJOH, 17; Charles Zelden, *Thurgood Marshall: Race, Rights, and the Struggle for a More Perfect Union* (New York: Routledge, 2013), 138; Mark Tushnet, *Making Constitutional Law: Thurgood Marshall and the Supreme Court* (New York: Oxford University Press, 1997), 21–22; Katzenbach, *Some of It Was Fun*, 189 ("midafternoon"); Juan Williams, *Thurgood Marshall: American Revolutionary* (New York: Three Rivers Press, 1998), 330 (rumors, "first black"); Abe Fortas to William O. Douglas, March 21, 1967, Box 782, Abe Fortas, Douglas MSS; Louis Kohlmmeier, "Ramsey Clark Appointed Attorney General: His Father, Justice Tom Clark Will Retire," *WSJ*, March 1, 1967. Every justice on the Court attended Ramsey Clark's swearing-in ceremony. Earl Warren, Memorandum to the Brethren, March 9, 1967, Box 58, Clark, Tom, Black MSS.

22. Fortas to Douglas, March 21, 1967; Kohlmeier, "Ramsey Clark Appointed Attorney General;" David Yalof, *Pursuit of Justice: Presidential Politics and the Selection of Supreme Court Nominees* (Chicago: University of Chicago Press, 1998), 89–90.

23. Williams, *Thurgood Marshall*, 177–78, 330, (aides); Robert Dallek, *Flawed Giant, Lyndon Johnson and His Times 1961–1973* (New York: Oxford University Press, 1998), 440 ("suspense").

24. Michael Parrish, *Felix Frankfurter and His Times: The Reform Years* (New York: The Free Press, 1982), 275; Arthur Schlesinger, Jr., *The Coming of the New Deal* (Boston: Houghton Mifflin, 1958), 531; The Reminiscences of Thurgood Marshall, 1992, COHP, 106; Williams, *Thurgood Marshall*, 9.

25. Loving v. Virginia, 388 U.S. 1 (1967); Dorothy Roberts, "Loving v. Virginia as a Civil Rights Decision," 59 *NYLSLR* 175, 176 (2014–15); Daily Diary, February 10, 1968, LBJL; Daily Diary, July 14, 1968, id. ("a negro"). LBJ apparently first saw the film on February 10, 1968. Daily Diary, February 10, 1968, id.

26. From Ramsey Clark, June 13, 1967, 7:59 A.M., WH6706.01, PNO 5, #11905, MC.

27. From Ramsey Clark, January 25, 1967; From Ramsey Clark, June 13, 1967; John Mackenzie, "LBJ Names Marshall to Court," *WP*, June 14, 1966; Thurgood Marshall to Clinton Riggs, March 4, 1966, U.S. Solicitor General File, October Term 1965, Westover v. U.S., Folder 1, T. Marshall MSS.

28. Remarks at Reception for the Presidential Scholars, June 13, 1967, http://www.presidency. ucsb.edu/ws/?pid=28301; The Reminiscences of Thurgood Marshall, 106–8, 162–63; Jim Newton, *Justice for All: Earl Warren and the Nation He Made* (New York: Riverhead, 2006), 480; Martin, LBJOH, 17–18; Daily Diary, June 13, 1967, LBJL.

29. The Reminiscences of Thurgood Marshall, 108, 110; Daily Diary, June 13, 1967; Martin, LBJOH, 17–18.

30. The Reminiscences of Thurgood Marshall, 108–9; Daily Diary, June 13, 1967 (which records the call to Mrs. Marshall "at some point during this A.M." and has the president taking the receiver and telling "her the good news himself"); Carl Rowan, *Dream Makers, Dream Breakers: The World of Justice Thurgood Marshall* (Boston: Little, Brown, 1993), 297.

31. Thurgood Marshall Nominated to Supreme Court, http://www.youtube.com/ watch?v=ri0NwkwkkoE; Remarks to the Press Announcing the Nomination of Thurgood Marshall as Associate Justice of the Supreme Court, June 13, 1967, http://www.presidency. ucsb.edu/ws/?pid=28298.

32. The President's News Conference, June 13, 1967, http://www.presidency.ucsb.edu/ws/ index.php?pid=28299.

33. Remarks at a Reception for the Presidential Scholars, June 13, 1967, http://www.presidency. ucsb.edu/ws/index.php?pid=28301&st=thurgood+marshall&st1.

34. LBJ, Memorandum for Marvin Watson, July 25, 1967, WHCF FX FG 535/A, Box 360, LBJL ("every leading"); John Macy, Memorandum for the President, July 24, 1967, id. ("colloquial-isms"); Big Mouth, "Lauds LBJ for Naming Thurgood," *CDD*, July 1–July 7, 1967, id.; "The Supreme Court: Negro Justice," *Ti*, June 23, 1967 (McKissick).

35. "Marshall to the Court . . . ," *NYT*, June 14, 1967.

36. Howard Ball, *A Defiant Life: Thurgood Marshall and the Persistence of Racism in America* (New York: Crown, 1998), 194; "Thurgood Marshall," *TNR*, June 24, 1967; "T.R.B. From Washington," id.

37. Capital Briefs: "LBJ 'Packs' the Court," *HE*, June 24, 1967, 4; James Kilpatrick, "Term's End," *NR*, July 25, 1967; "Mr. Justice Marshall," *WSJ*, June 15, 1967; "The Supreme Court: Negro Justice" ("If Thurgood Marshall's qualifications for the Supreme Court were unimpeachable, his selection was also politically astute—an act of official beatification that brought cheers from virtually every segment of the civil rights spectrum and should earn the Administration points among disenchanted Negro voters in next year's election."); "At Long Last," *WP*, June 14, 1967. See also "Good Man for Supreme Court," *CPD*, June 14, 1967; "A Big First," *SFE*, June 14, 1967; "A Choice Appointment," *NT*, June 14, 1967; "Marshall to the Supreme Court," *PI*, June 14, 1967; "The Marshall Appointment," *SLPD*, June 14, 1967; "Eminently Qualified," *DMR*, June 15, 1967; "Another Marshall on the Supreme Court," *CSM*, June 16, 1967; "Mr. Marshall's Nomination Is Both Fitting and Just," *DFP*, June 15, 1967; "Mr. Justice Marshall," *News*, June 26, 1967.

38. "The Cities," *Ti*, August 11, 1967; Joseph Califano, *Inside: A Public and Private Life* (New York: Public Affairs, 2004), 169.

39. Andrew Glass, "75 Invade Capitol Hill for Rat Bill," *WP*, August 8, 1967; John Herbers, "Bill to Curb Riots Approved by House Committee," *NYT*, July 12, 1967 (reporting warnings of possible unconstitutionality by House Judiciary Committee Chair Emanuel Celler); Herbert Mitgang, "The Ground Rules—If Any—of Protest," id., July 17, 1967; Harry McPherson, Memorandum for the President, July 26, 1967, LBJ Handwriting File, June 1967 (3), LBJL; Malcolm McLaughlin, *Urban Rebellion in America: The Long, Hot Summer of 1967* (New York: Palgrave Macmillan, 2014), xi, 166–67.

40. Daniel Lucks, *Selma to Saigon: The Civil Rights Movement and the Vietnam War* (Lawrence: University Press of Kansas, 2014), 252 ("Public"); Annual Message to Congress on the State of the Union, January 10, 1967, http://www.presidency.ucsb.edu/ws/?pid=28338; "No Staying Power?," *TNR*, January 21, 1967; McLaughlin, *Urban Rebellion in America*, 141–50.

41. "The Other 97%," *Ti*, August 11, 1967 ("You've Got"); Whitney Young to the President, June 14, 1967, WHCF EX FG 535/A, Box 360, LBJL.; Bernard Roschco, "Survey: What the Black Press Said Last Summer," 6 *CJR* 6 (Fall 1967).

42. Wil Haygood, *Showdown: Thurgood Marshall and the Supreme Court Nomination That Changed America* (New York: Knopf, 2015), 6, 133–37; Zelden, *Thurgood Marshall* (New York: Routledge, 2013), 127; Alan Burch to James Eastland, September 26, 1961, Sen 87B-A3, Senate Judiciary Nominations, Thurgood Marshall, Box 42, NARS. The committee stopped delegating Supreme Court nominations to subcommittees for study after Warren's appointment as chief justice in 1954.

43. Richard Revesz, "Thurgood Marshall's Struggle," 68 *NYULR* 237, 239–47 (1993); John Carroll, Philip Hart, Thomas Dodd, Edward Long to James Eastland, Senate Judiciary Committee Nominations, August 23, 1962, Box 42, NARS ("The delays have been intolerable. The hearings have been extended far longer than necessary. The full Committee on the Judiciary has a responsibility to insure that the Senate shall have a chance to pass on this nomination."); Alfred Kelly, "Clio and the Court: An Illicit Love Affair," 1965 *SCR* 119 (1965); Gilbert Ware, *William Hastie: Grace Under Pressure* (New York: Oxford University Press, 1984), 227-247.

44. Robert Van Keuren to Thurgood Marshall, November 9, 1967, Box 32, Folder 5, T. Marshall MSS; Marshall to Van Keuren, November 22, 1967, id.

45. Williams, *Thurgood Marshall*, 316; John Herbers, "Coleman Backed by Katzenbach: Nominee for Appeals Bench a Moderate on Race Issue, Attorney General Says," *NYT*, July 13, 1965; John MacKenzie, "Segregation Dead; Says Coleman; Unit Votes Job Approval," *WP*, July 14, 1965 As opposed to Williams, who suggested that LBJ threatened to withdraw his support from Coleman if Marshall did not win appointment as solicitor general, MacKenzie seemed to imply that the Marshall appointment might have been calculated to take the sting out of Johnson's decision to name Coleman to the bench.); "Naming Marshall, Or Any Negro to Supreme Court Is a Dirty Shame," *AC*, June 26, 1967, Box 490, Folder 15, McClellan MSS; The Hardshaws to John McClellan, June 14, 1967, id. ("Please").

46. Brad Snyder, "How the Conservatives Canonized *Brown v. Board of Education*," 52 *RLR* 383, 411–12 (2000); Paul Collins and Lori Ringhand, *Supreme Court Confirmation Hearings and Constitutional Change* (2013), 167.

47. "Out of a Cocoon," *Ti*, September 27, 1976 ("black brothers"); Steven Lawson, *Black Ballots: Voting Rights in the South, 1944–1969* (1976), 331; David Timothy Ballantyne, "Managing the Backlash: Senator Ernest F. 'Fritz' Hollings and the Marshall and Fortas Supreme Court Nominations," *PSCHA* 2013 19, 21–22.

48. Linda Greene, "The Confirmation of Thurgood Marshall to the United States Supreme Court," *BLJ* 27, 50 (1989); Roy Reed, "Marshall Named for High Court, Its First Negro," *NYT*, June 14, 1967 ("silence"); Herman Talmadge to Jesse Kite Sr., April 23, 1968, Series VII.A., Box 341, Riots, Talmadge MSS ("small bloc") and L. M. Todd, August 3, 1967, August 3, 1967, id. ("Judges on the Supreme Court," "majority"); "Johnson Calls Nominee 'Best Qualified,' and Rights Leaders Are Jubilant—Southerners Silent on Confirmation," *NYT*, June 14, 1968.

49. Chris Asch, *The Senator and the Sharecropper: The Freedom Struggles of James O. Eastland and Fannie Lou Hamer* (New York: New Press, 2008), 113–17, 270; Sherry Laymon, *Fearless: John L. McClellan: United States Senator* (Mustang: Tate, 2011), 168, 189, 250–52; Karl Campbell, *Senator Sam Ervin: Last of the Founding Fathers* (Chapel Hill: University of North Carolina Press, 2007), 109–10; Geoffrey Kabaservice, *Rule and Ruin: The Downfall of Moderation and the Destruction of the Republican Party, From Eisenhower to the Tea Party* (New York: Oxford University Press, 2012), 143 ("great"); Joseph Crespino. *Strom Thurmond's America* (New York: Hill and Wang, 2012), 165–67, 6, 103, 121.

50. Thurgood Marshall, Court of Appeals Decisions, n.d., Box 354, Folder 13963, Ervin MSS and Box 40, Folder 38, McClellan MSS (The second sentence was added by hand to Ervin's copy.).

51. Strom Thurmond to J. C. Phillips, July 18, 1967, Subject Correspondence: 1967, Nominations 3, Strom Thurmond MSS; Michael Flamm, *In the Heat of the Summer: The New York Riots of 1964 and the War on Crime* (Philadelphia: University of Pennsylvania Press, 2016), 70.

52. Strom Thurmond to Lyndon Johnson, March 2, 1967, Supreme Court Nominations 3, Thurmond MSS; Greene, "The Confirmation of Thurgood Marshall to the Supreme Court," 30 ("decidedly"); Thurmond to Mr. and Mrs. Ed. Hall, June 15, 1967, Supreme Court, Nominations 3, Thurmond MSS; Thurmond to Jno. Murray, July 4, 1967, id. ("original intent").

53. Nomination of Arthur Goldberg, 44; Kenneth Kmiec, "The Origin and Current Meanings of Judicial Activism," 92 *CaLR* 1441, 1445–49 (2004); Sam Ervin to Pat Thomas, September 7, 1967, Ervin MSS.

54. Denis Rutkus, "Supreme Court Appointment Process: Roles of the President, Judiciary Committee, and Senate," in *Supreme Court Nominations: Presidential Nomination, the Judiciary Committee, Proper Scope of Questioning of Nominees, Senate Consideration, Cloture, and the Use of the Filibuster*, ed. Denis Rutkus, Elizabeth Rybicki, Betsy Palmer, Todd Tatelman, Richard Beth, Michael Koempel, and Judy Schneider (Alexandria: Capitol Net, 2010), 1, 49 (roll call); Richard Beth and Betsy Palmer, *Supreme Court Nominations: Senate Floor Procedure and Practice, 1789-2009* (Washington, DC: BiblioGov, 2009), 20, 40–41 (hearing length). See Paul Collins and Lori Ringhand, "The Institutionalization of Supreme Court Confirmation Hearings," 41 *LSI*, 126 (2016).

55. John McClellan to Thomas Gallaher, August 12, 1967, Box 410, Folder 38, McClellan MSS ("one," "my belief"); McClellan to Ulys. Lovell, July 24, 1967, id. ("more conservative"); Nomination of Thurgood Marshall, 3–4, 6.

56. Nomination of Thurgood Marshall, 3–7, 12, 9, 10, 13; Fred Graham, "Senate Confirmation of Marshall Delayed by McClellan Questions; High Court Nominee Ruffled—Backing Expected When Hearings Resume Today," *NYT*, July 14, 1967.

57. Graham, "Senate Confirmation of Marshall Delayed" ("vote"); John MacKenzie, "Marshall Grilled by Senate Critics but Signs Point to Easy Sailing for Court Post," *WP*, July 14, 1967.

58. Ronald Ostrow, "Marshall Target of South's Frustration," *LAT*, July 18, 1967 (Hastie); Nomination of Thurgood Marshall, at 149-50, 158.

59. Nomination of Thurgood Marshall, 55, 64; Fred Graham, "Marshall Balks at Ervin Queries: Refused to Comment about Court's Confession Rule," *NYT*, July 15, 1967.

60. Nomination of Thurgood Marshall, 120, 98–99; Stovall v. Denno, 355 F. 2d 731 (1966); 388 U.S. 293 (1967); Fred Graham, "Marshall Asked About His Rulings: Southerners Critical of Past Record of Court Nominee," *NYT*, July 19, 1967.

61. Nomination of Thurgood Marshall, 161.

62. Id., 163–79; Crespino, *Strom Thurmond's America*, 215. See especially Kennedy's sarcastic questions to Thurmond at 163, which the record shows provoked laughter in the hearing room and led Eastland to call for order and Kennedy's request that Thurmond answer his own questions for the record at *CR*, S12543, S12547, August 30, 1967.

63. Nomination of Thurgood Marshall, 179–81.

64. Id., 176; Herbert Aptheker, *A Documentary History of the Negro People in the United States* (Secaucus, NJ: Citadel, 1951).

65. Nomination of Thurgood Marshall, 181–84.

66. James Furman to Strom Thurmond, August 16, 1967, Subject Correspondence/Nominations 3, 1967, Thurmond MSS; "The Judiciary: Kite Flying & Other Games," *Ti*, July 28, 1967; "White Rednecks," *NYT*, July 21, 1967; "Inquisition," *WP*, July 23, 1967. "Yes, I can answer the question[s] I posed to Mr. Marshall since I did extensive research for these hearings," Thurmond wrote another skeptic. "Although I would not expect the average person, the average lawyer, or many judges to be capable of answering these questions, I would expect answers from a lawyer who has devoted his entire practice to Constitutional questions concerning the 13th and 14th amendments. I feel that Mr. Marshall has displayed a lack of sufficient comprehension in his own area of expertise." Thurmond to Mrs. Arthur Ward, July 26, 1967, Subject Correspondence/Nominations 3, 1967, Thurmond MSS.

67. Nomination of Thurgood Marshall, 189–90, 196–197.

68. The Reminiscences of Thurgood Marshall, 157–58 *CR*, August 30, 1967, S24649 (Remarks of Senator Thurmond); Everett Dirksen, Interview II by Joe Frantz, March 21, 1969, LBJOH, 10.

69. Report Accompanying Nomination of Thurgood Marshall, Minority Views of Mr. Ervin, 16, 5, 9, 17. Smathers of Florida voted against recommending the nomination to the Senate but did not sign the minority report.

70. Report Accompanying Nomination of Thurgood Marshall, 2–3.

71. Greene, "The Confirmation of Thurgood Marshall," 48–49; *CR*, August 30, 1967, S24657 (Remarks of Senator Mansfield).

72. The Reminiscences of Thurgood Marshall, 155–56 (Asked by an interviewer in the 1990s if he shared LBJ's assessment, "Marshall merely shrugs and says, 'How do I know?'" "Looking Back," in *Supreme Justice: Speeches and Writings Thurgood Marshall*, ed. J. Clay Smith [Philadelphia: University of Pennsylvania Press, 2003], 303, 306); Neil McFeeley, *Appointment of Judges: The Johnson Presidency* (Austin: University of Texas Press, 1987), 113. Haygood suggested that at one point after the hearing began, LBJ had become so concerned about his nominee's prospects that he had hatched a backup plan to nominate the distinguished African American Republican lawyer William Coleman in the event of Marshall's defeat. Haygood, *Showdown*, 110–17. But in his autobiography, Coleman puts his White House conversation about a possible nomination in "early 1967," before Johnson nominated Marshall, and LBJ's Daily Diary, which may not be wholly accurate, does not place Coleman at the White House between May 12 and December 7 of 1967. William Coleman with Donald Bliss, *Counsel for the Situation: Shaping the Law to Realize America's Promise* (Washington, DC: Brookings, 2010), 177–78. The six southerners who voted for Marshall were J. William Fulbright (D-AR), William Spong (D-VA), Albert Gore (D-TN), Ralph Yarborough (D-TX), John Tower (R-TX), and Howard Baker (R-TN). The five who absented themselves were Harry Byrd (D-VA), B. Everett Jordan (D-NC), John McClellan (D-AR), Richard Russell (D-GA), and George Smathers (D-FL).

73. *CR*, August 30, 1967, S24640, S24654 (Remarks of Senator Javits and Hart).

74. Graham, "The Law: Marshall and the Activists"; John MacKenzie, "Supreme Court Was Main Target in Marshall Quiz," *WP*, September 4, 1967; Ronald Ostrow, "Takes Rap for Court: Marshall Target of South's Frustration," *LAT*, July 18, 1967.

75. Charles Mohr, "The Zest is Gone, But Johnson's Ego Survives Setbacks," *NYT*, August 4, 1968; Tom Wicker, "In the Nation," id., September 14, 1967.

76. Max Frankel, "Why the Gap Between L.B.J. and the Nation," *NYT Mag*, January 7, 1968.

77. Allen Matusow, *The Unraveling of America: A History of Liberalism in the 1960s* (New York: Harper and Row, 1984), 314, 32 ("sleeping," "corporate"); James Miller, *Democracy Is in the Streets: From Port Huron to the Siege of Chicago* (New York: Simon and Schuster, 1987), 223. Arthur Schlesinger thought that whereas "the leftists of the early sixties" viewed JFK as within "their orbit of discourse," they saw LBJ as "a creature from outer space." Arthur Schlesinger, Jr., *Journals 1952-2000* (New York: Penguin, 2007).

78. "Leaders Divided on Aims of March," *WP*, October 20, 1967; Joseph Loftus, "Guards Repulse War Protesters at the Pentagon," *NYT*, October 22, 1967 (Spock); Daily Diary, October 22, 1967, LBJL; George Wilson, "Chronology of Pentagon Siege: A Day for Peace Saw Futile Charges, Bloody Heads, Mass Arrests," *WP*, October 23, 1967. The Defense Department put the number in front of the Pentagon at twenty thousand. Robert McNamara with Brian VanDeMark, *In Retrospect: The Tragedy and Lessons of Vietnam* (New York: Times Books, 1995), 304. The *Wall Street Journal* estimated it at thirty thousand to thirty-five thousand; Frederick Taylor, "Antiwar Demonstrators March on Pentagon; 2,500 Troops, Marshals Contain the Crowd," *WSJ*, October 23, 1967.

79. Walter Pincus, "McCarthy a 1-Man Show: Senator is Challenging Johnson Without a Staff," *WP*, December 3, 1967; McNamara, *In Retrospect*, 311; Max Frankel, "M'Namara Takes World Bank Post: War Shift Denied," *NYT*, November 30, 1967; Richard Harwood, "McNamara Accepts Job as Head of World Bank: Will Leave Pentagon in Early '68," *WP*, November 30, 1967.

80. Arthur Schlesinger, Jr., Journals, July 28, 1966, Schlesinger MSS; Drew Middleton, "Goldberg's Future: Diplomat Must Soon Decide Whether to Resign or Stay in His U.N. Post," *NYT*, December 6, 1967; Drew Pearson, "Goldberg: Next to Leave?," *LAT*, December 5, 1967; Chalmers Roberts, "Goldberg's Departure Is Denied," *WP*, December 7, 1967; The Presidents News Conference, December 4, 1967, http://www.presidency.ucsb.edu/ws/index.php?pid=28581; "President: A Slap at the 'Kennedy Kids,'" *LAT*, December 10, 1967.

81. "Marvin Watson Entered the President's Office at 2:35 P.M., Wednesday, December 6, 1967, for Meeting Between President and Ambassador Arthur Goldberg," Transcripts, LBJL; From Joseph Califano, April 27, 1968, 11:14 A.M., WH6804.03, PNO 2, #12939; "Chill Lingers in Goldberg's U.N. Farewell: A Three-Year Dream Down the Brain," *CT*, April 29, 1968; Louis Fleming, "Goldberg Resigns: U.N. Envoy Makes Frosty Exit," *LAT*, April 26, 1968.

82. Clifford, *Counsel to the President*, 465-67, 473, 476; Joseph Palermo, *The Politics of Race and War: Robert F. Kennedy and the Democratic Party, 1965-1968* (PhD, Cornell University, 1998), 235–57. See, for example, *Mark Lawrence, The Vietnam War: A Concise International History* (New York: Oxford University Press, 2008), 122–23. For a contemporary satire of the military's assurances of "light at the end of the tunnel," see Art Buchwald, "'We Have Enemy on the Run,' Says Gen. Custer at Big Horn," *WP*, February 6, 1968.

83. Gene Roberts, "Wallace Derides War Protesters: Cry of 'Pseudo Intellectuals' Wins Him Applause," *NYT*, October 29, 1967 ("scum," "bearded"); Homer Bigart, "Wallace Considers Entering Primary in New Hampshire," id., April 1, 1967 ("chicken"); Ben Franklin, "Wallace in Race; Will 'Run to Win,'" id., February 9, 1968; James Strong, "Executives Cheer Talk by Wallace: Hits Actions of High Court," *CT*, February 17, 1968 ("If").

84. Michael Nelson, *Resilient America: Electing Nixon in 1968, Channeling Dissent and Dividing Government* (Lawrence: University Press of Kansas, 2014), 119, 122 ("victorious"); David Broder, "Nixon Warns About 'Crisis of the Spirit,'" *WP*, February 4, 1968 (remaining quotations).

85. "McCarthy's Total Vote 230 Shy of Johnson's," *LAT*, March 16, 1968; "Poll Finds Vote for McCarthy Was Anti-Johnson Not Antiwar," *NYT*, March 18, 1968; David Broder, "Senator Enters Presidency Race," *WP*, March 17, 1968; "Cambridge Group of Academicians to Help Kennedy," *NYT*, March 25, 1968. "'Why not come out for McCarthy?'" Arthur Schlesinger Jr. asked Robert Kennedy just before he announced his decision to run. "'Every McCarthy delegate will be a potential Kennedy delegate. He can't possibly win, so you will be the certain inheritor of his support.' He looked at me stonily and said, 'I can't do that. It would be too humiliating. Kennedys don't act that way.'" Arthur Schlesinger Jr., *Robert Kennedy and His Times* (Boston: Houghton Mifflin, 1978), 856.

86. Clifford, *Counsel for the President*, 511–30; Palermo, *The Politics of Race and War*, 347–54.

87. The President's Address to the Nation Announcing Steps to Limit the War in Vietnam and Reporting His Decision Not to Seek Reelection, March 31, 1968, http://www.presidency.ucsb.edu/ws/index.php?pid=28772&st=i+shall+not+seek&st1=vietnam; Califano, *The Triumph and Tragedy of Lyndon Johnson*, 271–72; Horace Busby, *The Thirty-First of March: An Intimate Portrait of Lyndon Johnson's Final Days in Office* (New York: Farrar, Straus and Giroux, 2005), 229, 230 (quotations).

88. Busby, *The Thirty-First of March*, 235; Peniel Joseph, *Stokely: A Life* (New York: BasicCivitas, 2014), 254–59; Jean White, "McKissick Refused to Meet LBJ," *WP*, April 11, 1968 ("It was just the old team—the people who don't represent anybody," said Floyd McKissick's second-in-command at CORE, Roy Innis.); James Yuenger, "LBJ Pleads for Racial Peace," *CT*, April 6, 1968; Califano, *The Triumph & Tragedy of Lyndon Johnson*, 279 ("Goddamn!"); Ben Gilbert and the staff of the *Washington Post, Ten Blocks From the White House: Anatomy of the Washington Riots: An Anatomy of the Washington Riots of 1968* (London: Pall Mall, 1968), 79.

89. Carl Solberg, *Hubert Humphrey: A Biography* (New York: W. W. Norton, 1984), 332–33; Ben Franklin, " 'City' of the Poor Begun in Capital: Abernathy Vows to 'Plague Pharaohs of Nation' for Help Against Poverty," *NYT*, May 14, 1968; Jack Nelson, "Poor People's Drive in Trouble," *LAT*, June 10, 1968 ("last dream"); David Jewell and Paul Valentine, "The Troubles of Resurrection City," *WP*, June 21, 1968.

90. "Marchers Besiege Court: Panes Broken, 3 Arrested in Hill Protest," *WP*, May 30, 1968; "Fishing-Rights Case," id., June 3, 1968; Earl Caldwell, "High Court Building Stormed in Demonstration by the Poor," *NYT*, May 30, 1968; Puyallup Tribe v. Department of Game, 391 U.S. 392 (1968); John Davis, Memorandum to the Chief Justice, May 31, 1968, Box 359, Sundry Memos to the Court, Warren MSS.

91. Fred Graham, "Fortas Condemns Columbia Protest," *NYT*, May 24, 1968 ("totally," "White Uncle Toms"); Abe Fortas, *Concerning Dissent and Civil Disobedience* (New York: A Signet Special Broadside published by the New American Library), 52–55; Herbert Mitgang, "Broadsides, 1968," *NYT*, June 9, 1968.

92. Elliot Fremont-Smith, "Books of the Times: Freedom and Procedure," *NYT*, May 27, 1968 ("signal"); Tom Farer Book Review, 69 *CLR* 320, 320–21, 333, 324, 326, 329 (1969) (Farer then taught at Columbia Law School); Howard Zinn, *Disobedience and Democracy: Nine Fallacies on Law and Order* (New York: Vintage, 1968), 7; Laura Kalman, *Abe Fortas: A Biography* (New Haven: Yale University Press, 1990), 283–84; Martin Duberman, *Howard Zinn: A Life on the Left* (New York: New Press, 2012), 140–46. The *Times* and other newspapers serialized Fortas's broadside. See, for example, Abe Fortas, "Justice Fortas Defines the Limits of Civil Disobedience," *NYT Mag*, May 12, 1968.

93. U.S. v. O'Brien, 391 U.S. 367, 389 (1968); "Decision Shocks O'Brien," *NYT*, May 28, 1968; Irene Johnson, Catherine Allsup, Mary Suzuki Little to Earl Warren, June 9, 1968, Box 660, Court Subject File, Demonstrations, Warren MSS (stating intention to burn draft cards "in solidarity with draft resisters" and asking for appointment with Warren); Claudia Levy, "Women Burn Draft Cards at Court: G-Man Plays Role of Newsman," *WP*, June 18, 1968.

94. Green v. County School Board of New Kent County, 391 U.S. 430, 438 (1968); Ward Just, "Nixon, RFK Aim at Crime, Urban Rioting," *WP*, May 31, 1968; Ward Just, "Wallace Cheered, HHH and Nixon Applauded," id., August 1, 1968 ("insane"); "Wallace Sees Nixon Role in School Ruling," *LAT*, September 15, 1968 ("agreed," "destruction"); "Mr. Nixon on Integration," *NYT*, September 6, 1968.

95. Nelson, *Resilient America*, 120 ("Never in American political history had a presidential nominee raised crime as a significant issue. Four years earlier, Goldwater had refused campaign aides' advice to do so."); "63% in Gallup Poll Think Courts Are Too Lenient on Criminals," *NYT*, March 3, 1968; John Averill, "Court-Haters Have Their Day," *LAT*, May 15, 1968 ("one of"); "Court Decisions Ripped by Nixon," *CT*, May 31, 1968.

96. Miranda v. Arizona, 384 U.S. 436 (1966); U.S. v. Wade, 388 U.S. 218 (1967); Mallory v. U.S., 354 U.S. 449 (1957); Robert Semple, "Nixon Decries 'Lawless Society' and Urges Limited Wiretapping," *NYT*, May 9, 1968; Fred Graham, "Congress Tackles the Court," id., May 22, 1968; Graham, "Senate Upholds Supreme Court on Review Issue," id., May 21, 1968; "Senate Decision on the Courts," *LAT*, May 22, 1968.

97. Christopher Hickman, *The Most Dangerous Branch: The Supreme Court and Its Critics in the Warren Era* (PhD dissertation, George Washington University, 2010), 401 ("fascist"); "Nixon Links Court to Rise in Crime," *NYT*, May 31, 1968 ("green"); Nixon Campaign Statements, 1968, The Supreme Court, n.d., WHCF EX FG 51, Folder 6, LBJL.

98. Terry v. Ohio, 392 U.S. 1 (1968); Earl Warren to Samuel Pryor, June 20, 1967, Warren MSS; Lucas Powe, *The Warren Court and American Politics* (Cambridge: Belknap: 2000), 406–7.

99. William Stuntz, *The Collapse of American Criminal Justice* (Cambridge: Belknap, 2011), 218, 236 ("dramatically," "elaborate"); Stuntz, "The Political Constitution of Criminal Justice," 119 *HLR*, 781, 817 (2006) ("Trials are the system's Potemkin village, a piece of pretty scenery for display on Court TV while real cases, and lives, are disposed of more casually off-camera."); Stuntz, "Unequal Justice," 121 *HLR*, 1969, 2006-07 (2008) (Warren Court decisions "allowed politicians to attack black crime indirectly by condemning the white judges who protected black criminals, not the criminals themselves," which enabled conservatives "to appeal to more than racist whites," put street crime on the national agenda "for the first time in history," and since "politicians couldn't change the constitutional rulings that prompted so much controversy, . . . their criticisms were unburdened by the need to exercise governing responsibility."); George Fisher, *Plea Bargaining's Triumph: A History of Plea Bargaining in America* (Palo Alto: Stanford University Press, 2003), 202–4; Naomi Murakawa, *The First Civil Right: How Liberals Built Prison America* (New York: Oxford University Press, 2014); Sara Mayeux, "What Gideon Did," 116 *CLR* 16, 69, 78–82, 87 (2016); Anders Walker, " 'To Corral and Control the Ghetto': Stop, Frisk, and the Geography of Freedom," 48 *URLR*, 1223, 1224, 1242-45 (2014); Sibron v. New York, 392 U.S. 40 (1968); L. Michael Seidman, "Akhil Amar and the (Premature?) Demise of Criminal Procedure Liberalism," 107 *YLJ*, 2281, 2282 (1998) ("bandwagon").

100. Francis Gregory and Raymond Fisher, Opinions of William J. Brennan, October Term, 1967, Notes, II, Box 6, Folder 10, Brennan TH MSS, xxxvii; Terry v. Ohio, 392 U.S. 39 (1968); Fred Graham, "Yes for 'The Frisk,' " *NYT*, June 16, 1968 ("Since the Court has been under heavy fire in Congress for allegedly being too generous in extending defendants' rights, the Court was widely suspected of political backpedaling.")

101. Ed Cray, *Chief Justice: A Biography of Earl Warren* (New York: Simon and Schuster, 1997), 494; Kenneth Reich, "Ex-Sen. Kuchel Dies; Last of State's GOP Progressives," *LAT*, November 23, 1994 ("I"); Willard Edwards, "Capitol Views: Kuchel Confident of Appointment to Federal Court," *CT*, June 29, 1968 (Edwards was the first journalist to link Warren's resignation to Kuchel's loss); Nelson, *Resilient America*, 199 ("Nixon had accumulated many enemies during his twenty-two years in public life, but none who despised him longer and in greater detail than Warren.").

Chapter 4

1. Jim Jones, Memorandum for the Record, June 13, 1968, EX FG535, Box 360, LBJL; Michael Flamm, *Law and Order: Street Crime, Civil Unrest, and the Crisis of Liberalism in the 1960s* (New York: Columbia University Press, 2005), 140; Joseph Califano, *The Triumph and Tragedy of Lyndon Johnson: The White House Years* (New York: Simon & Schuster, 1991), 305, 307.

2. Donald Stephenson, *Campaigns & the Court: The U.S. Supreme Court in Presidential Elections* (New York: Columbia University Press, 1999), 183–84.

3. Laura Kalman, *Abe Fortas: A Biography* (New Haven: Yale University Press, 1990), 311–13 (intimacy); Bernard Schwartz, *Super Chief: Earl Warren and His Supreme Court—A Judicial Biography* (New York: New York University Press, 1983), 720.

4. Ed Cray, *Chief Justice: A Biography of Earl Warren* (New York: Simon and Schuster, 1997, 497 ("good"); Warren Christopher, Memorandum, Power of the President to Nominate and of the Senate to Confirm Mr. Justice Fortas to Be Chief Justices of the United States and Judge Thornberry to Be Associate Justices of the Supreme Court, July 11, 1968, http://www.justice.gov/sites/default/files/olc/opinions/1979/04/31/op-olc-v003-p0152.pdf; Earl Warren, Interview by Joe Frantz, September 21, 1971, LBJOH, 21 ("good"); To James 4 Eastland, June 23, 1968, 9:09 A.M., WH6806.03, PNO 3-5 #13134-36, MC ("I think

Warren would prefer Goldberg [to Vance or Clifford]. As a matter of fact, he told me he would. I just don't believe I could have Fortas as Chief Justice and bring Goldberg back."); Robert Young, "LBJ Selects Fortas to Be Chief Justice," *CT*, June 27, 1968 (letters); Earl Warren to John Massaro, December 10, 1973, Box 667, Chief Justice Retirement, Warren MSS. "As you know, I wanted you to be Chief Justice and so urged," Fortas subsequently wrote Goldberg. "Perhaps this uproar would not have occurred—but perhaps you're reasonably satisfied that you had no occasion to find out!" Abe Fortas to Arthur Goldberg, July 26, 1968, I: 43, Folder 7, Goldberg MSS. I have found no evidence that he recommended Goldberg as chief justice, but Fortas did sometimes drop Goldberg's name when the conversation with LBJ turned to the appointment of justices.

5. Malvina Stephenson, Radio Broadcast, June 23, 1968, Box 418, Chapter 1, Griffin MSS ("While"); Stephenson, Radio Broadcast, June 22, 1968, id. ("He is definitely"); Robert Griffin, "The Senate Stands Taller: The Fortas Case" (Griffin's unpublished memoir of the Fortas fight, hereafter "The Fortas Case"), Box 284, Griffin MSS; Philip Warden, "Tells Warren Resigned to Outflank Ev: Reporter Overhears Dirksen Reference," *CT*, July 1, 1968; "Washington Wire," *WSJ*, June 14, 1968.

6. Marjorie Hunter, "Leading Fortas Foe: Robert Paul Griffin," *NYT*, September 28, 1968 ("Casual," "years," "nearly"); "The Fortas Case"; Questionnaire for Candidates for Senator of Michigan, n.d., Box 291, Griffin Biographical, Box 291, Griffin MSS (describing Romney as the contemporary man he admired most). How many of the court's decisions Griffin agreed with was unclear, but he had opposed the jurisdiction-stripping provision of the Safe Streets Act.

7. Griffin, "The Fortas Case"; American Law Division to Robert Griffin, June 26, 1968, Supreme Court Justices Appointed During the Last Year of a President's Term in Office, Box 285, Various Materials, Griffin MSS (John Marshall [Adams], John Catron [Jackson], Peter Daniel [Van Buren], Samuel Nelson [Tyler], William Woods [Hayes], Melville Fuller [Cleveland], George Shiras [Harrison], Howell Jackson [Harrison]) (compare Nominations of Abe Fortas and Homer Thornberry, Exhibit 7, Supreme Court Nominations Made During the Last Year of a President's Last Term in Office [that the Senate did not confirm], Part 1, 400); Charles Fairman to Warren Christopher, June 30, 1968, Box 2, Fortas-Thornberry MSS.

8. Their letter is reprinted in Nominations of Abe Fortas and Homer Thornberry, Part 1, 3–6. See, for example, Geoff Earle, "Senators Spar Over 'Thurmond Rule,'" *Hi*, July 21, 2004; Andrew Rosenthal, "The 'Thurmond Rule,'" *LAT*, July 12, 2012.

9. To Abe Fortas, June 21, 1968, 3:51 P.M., WH6806.02, PNO 8-11, #13127-13130, MC; Fred Graham, "Warren, 75, Set to Stay on Job, but Backs Age Limit on Service," *NYT*, March 19, 1966; Interview with Adam Stolpen, January 2014; Notes From Fortas re His Prospective Appointment as CJ, June 17, 1968, Box 1782, Douglas MSS: "1. All requests will be honored. Girls will be permitted in chambers at any hours. I assume that's why Brother Douglas wants clean towels. 2. Toilet paper will be unnecessary. There will be no more diarrhea—of words or otherwise. 3. There will be free booze every Friday, in lieu of Conference. 4. Every son of a bitch anybody doesn't like will be fired. The foregoing I pledge on my word as a Candidate for Vice President."

10. Geoffrey Stone, "Understanding Supreme Court Confirmations," 2011 *SCR* 381, 414, n. 56 (2011); William O. Douglas, Box 956, Autobiography Drafts, Douglas MSS.

11. To Abe Fortas, June 21, 1968; Horace Busby, *The Thirty-First of March: An Intimate Portrait of Lyndon Johnson's Final Days in Office* (New York: Farrar, Straus and Giroux, 2005), 86 (compliment). He worried about people who did not seem to have a "philosophy," by which he meant political ideology, LBJ told Fortas. "I think a lot of people worry that I'm the same way, but I really rather think that I'm for the people. And if I can find where it is, I think that's where I go. I don't know. Sometimes I get lost down the road," the president laughed, "and get in the wrong pasture, but I'm searching." To Abe Fortas, June 21, 1968.

12. To Abe Fortas, June 21, 1968; Clark Clifford with Richard Holbrooke, *Counsel to the President: A Memoir* (New York: Random House, 1991), 488–89.

13. To Abe Fortas, June 21, 1968; To James Eastland, June 23, 1968 (Vance's background); James Yuenger, "Cyrus Vance: The New-Breed Troubleshooter," *CT*, June 2, 1968. Clifford wrote about the impact of Vance's turnaround on LBJ in Clifford, *Counsel to the President*, 514, 518.

14. To Abe Fortas, June 21, 1968; Lyndon Johnson, *The Vantage Point: Perspectives on the Presidency* 325-26 (London: Weidenfeld and Nicolson, 1971); Joseph Thorndike, "Historical Perspective: Sacrifice and Surcharge," http://www.taxhistory.org/thp/readings.nsf/cf7c-9c870b600b9585256df80075b9dd/6b24abb33fe1996c852570d200756a5d?OpenDocument; Robert Hershey, "Henry Fowler Is Dead at 91; Former Treasury Secretary," *NYT*, January 5, 2000. Others shared LBJ's impression. "Among friends, over a bourbon and water, Fowler has a fine talent for Southern-style anecdote and humor—which fails to show up in his ponderous, legalistic speeches, often with portentous titles like 'A Program for a New Step Forward in Realizing the American Dream,'" noted one admiring profile. Hobart Rowen, "Fowler Leaving Mark at Treasury," *WP*, November 14, 1968. Fowler received his LLB from Yale in 1932 and his SJD in 1933, the same year Fortas received his LLB. Recently, Fowler had persuaded LBJ to support a 10% tax on individual and corporate income taxes as an inflation-fighting and revenue-raising measure.

15. To Abe Fortas, June 21, 1968.

16. Robert Thomas, "Homer Thornberry, Appeals Judge, Dies at 86," *NYT*, December 13, 1995 ("eminently"); Homer Ross Tomlin, *Homer Thornberry: Congressman, Judge, and Advocate for Equal Rights* (Fort Worth: TCU Press, 2016), 15, 19, 24, 37–38.

17. Tomlin, *Homer Thornberry*, 31, 52, 96–98; Daily Diary, June 21, 1968, LBJL. Mrs. Thornberry had flown back to Washington from the LBJ ranch with the Johnsons on June 18. Daily Diary, June 18, 1968, id.

18. Tomlin, *Homer Thornberry*, 118–24; Thomas, "Homer Thornberry, Appeals Judge."

19. Tomlin, *Homer Thornberry*, 129 ("qualified," "better," "ambition"); Remarks at the Swearing In of Homer Thornberry as Judge, U.S. Court of Appeals, Fifth Circuit, July 3, 1965, http://www.presidency.ucsb.edu/ws/?pid=27065americanpresidency.org; Homer Thornberry, Interview by Joe Frantz, December 21, 1970, LBJOH, 36 ("proud," "which"); U.S. v. State of Texas, 252 F. Supp. 234 (1966); U.S. v. Jefferson County Board of Education, 372 F. 2d 836 (1966); Wade McCree to Philip Hart, July 1, 1968, Box 174, Fortas, Hart MSS. See the memorial tributes to Thornberry by Congressman J. J. Pickle, Fifth Circuit Judge Thomas Reavely, and District Judge Sam Sparks in 79 *TxLR* 943–50 (1996).

20. To Everett Dirksen, June 22, 1968, 8:02 A.M., WH6806.03, PNO 1, #13132, MC; Byron Hulsey, *Everett Dirksen and His Presidents: How a Senate Giant Shaped American Politics* (Lawrence: University Press of Kansas, 2000), 207, 229–31, 248–50.

21. To Everett Dirksen, June 22, 1968; George Tagge, "Ev Tells How LBJ Picked Fortas," *CT*, October 22, 1968.

22. Kalman, *Abe Fortas*, 327 ("really"); Clifford, *Counsel to the President*, 555–56 (Clifford recounted the conversation just after it occurred to an associate, who made notes of it. Id., 686, n. 3); Griffin, "The Fortas Case."

23. Larry Temple, Interview by Joe Frantz, June 26, 1970, 7; Warren Christopher, Memorandum for Larry Temple, The Fortas and Thornberry Nominations, December 20, 1968, Box 3, Fortas-Thornberry MSS (names discussed with Clark).

24. James Reston, "Washington: The Next Chief Justice," *NYT*, June 23, 1968.

25. Lyndon Johnson, *The Vantage Point: Perspectives of the Presidency 1963-1969* (London: Weidenfeld and Nicolson, 1970), 547 (Eastland as source of intelligence on Republicans); To James Eastland, June 23, 1968; James Eastland, Interview by Joe Frantz, February 19, 1971, LBJOH, 12;. For Johnson's irritation over Carmichael, see Alexander Wohl, *Father, Son, and the Constitution: How Justice Tom Clark and Attorney General Ramsey Clark Shaped American Democracy* (Lawrence: University Press of Kansas, 2013), 338–41; Lonnie Brown, "A Tale of Prosecutorial Indiscretion: Ramsey Clark and the Selective Non-Prosecution of Stokely Carmichael," 62 *SCarLR* 1, 18–23 (2010). Clark maintained that there was not enough evidence for an indictment, which would be politically ill-advised anyway.

26. To James Eastland, June 23, 1968; for Eastland's irritation about Marshall, see Hugh Jones, *The Defeat of the Nomination of Abe Fortas as Chief Justice of the United States: A Case Study in Judicial Politics* (PhD, Johns Hopkins University, 1979), 52–53.

27. Griffin, "The Fortas Case"; Daily Diary, June 22, 1968, LBJL; To Mike Mansfield, June 23, 1968, 8:43 A.M., WH6806.03, PNO 2, #13133 ("Drew told Art he had called on the President to ask him to appoint Arthur and that the President had said Of course Art had all the qualities but he didn't think the country would accept two Jews on the bench.") The day after Goldberg resigned from the UN, William Brennan wrote him and Dorothy Goldberg, "I don't have to tell you how hard it's been for us not to have you here as colleagues—& how hard it was even to accept your leaving us. Nothing is closer to hearts & hopes than that you return to us, & I have not accepted the possibility that you may not." William Brennan to Arthur and Dorothy Goldberg, n.d., I: Box 42, Folder 4, Goldberg MSS.

28. The President's News Conference at the National Press Club, January 17, 1969, http://www.presidency.ucsb.edu/ws/index.php?pid=29355; Robert Kaiser, "Resurrection City Falls—With a Song," *WP*, June 25, 1968; Remarks at the Swearing In of George Ball as UN Ambassador, Arthur Goldberg, June 25, 1968, http://www.presidency.ucsb.edu/ws/?pid=28955; James Bill, *George Ball: Behind the Scenes in Foreign Policy* (New Haven: Yale University Press, 1997), 76–78; Dorothy Goldberg Journal, June 27, 1968.

29. Christopher, The Fortas and Thornberry Nominations; Daily Diary, June 24, 1968; Drew Pearson and Jack Anderson, "Fortas Support Is Keyed to SACB," *WP*, July 11, 1968; To Everett Dirksen, July 11, 1968, 8:26 A.M., WH6807.01, PNO 5, #13205, MC.

30. Daily Diary, June 24, 1968, LBJL; From Edwin Weisl Sr., June 25, 1968, 1:05 P.M., #13138 (no recording), Transcripts, id.

31. Temple, LBJOH, August 7, 1970, Tape 6, 8; To Everett Dirksen, June 27, 1968, 3:57 P.M., WH6806.04 PNO6, #13146-13147, MC ("dumbbell," "I don't think").

32. Johnson, *The Vantage Point*, (New York: Holt, Rinehart and Winston, 1970), 545; To Everett Dirksen, June 26, 1968 ("only"); To Mike Mansfield, June 26, 1968, 9:44 A.M., WH6806.04, PNO 5, #13145, MC.

33. Daily Diary, June 25, 1968, LBJL; Christopher, The Fortas and Thornberry Nominations.

34. Christopher, The Fortas and Thornberry Nominations (Eastland bulletin); Mike Manatos, Memoranda for the President, June 25, 1968, 3:00 P.M. and 4:15 P.M., Box 1, Fortas-Thornberry MSS.

35. To Everett Dirksen, June 25, 1968, 4:53 P.M., WH6806.03, PNO8, #13140. As the *New York Times* was also to editorialize, the nation's courts "would be decimated" if nominees were excluded because they were friends of the president. "Justice for Mr. Fortas," *NYT*, September 27, 1968.

36. To Ralph Yarborough, June 25, 1968, 5:35 P.M., WH6806.04, PNO 1, #13141: To Abe Fortas, June 21, 1968; To Leon Jaworski, June 25, 1968, 5:56 P.M., WH6806.04, PNO 3, #13143, MC.

37. Johnson, *The Vantage Point*, 545; Daily Diary, June 25, 1968, LBJL; Thornberry, LBJOH,

38. Early in June, Russell had provided his view of the situation to his fellow Georgian, Judge Griffin Bell: "The President discussed this appointment [Lawrence's] with [ABA Standing Committee on the Federal Judiciary Chairman] Albert Jenner in person and Jenner told him that he could not understand the attitude of the Attorney General. Some of the group who are familiar with the FBI tell me there has never been a better report made on any prospective District Judge. The President is in a particular position, but I believe that he will eventually over-ride the Attorney General if he [Clark] does not change his mind. At the President's direction, he [Clark] came up to explain the matter to me and I was amazed and outraged to find that he apparently based his opposition to Alex on the statement of some anonymous person whose entire statement was impeached from one end to the other and on the views of a preacher named Hooten. In addition, [W. W.] Law, the thoroughly discredited head of the [Savannah] NAACP, opposed him and apparently some of the other NAACP chapters did so on his request. All three of the Negro members of the Bar in Savannah strongly endorsed Alex." Richard Russell to Griffin Bell, June 7, 1968, Series VII, Box 17, Southern District Judgeship, Alexander Lawrence, Folder 1, Russell MSS. Who discredited Law, apparently an extremely effective civil rights leader, Russell did not indicate. http://www.georgiaencyclopedia.org/articles/history-archaeology/w-w-law-1923-2002.

38. From Ramsey Clark, June 26, 1968, 9:18 A.M., WH 6806.04, PNO4, #13144; Don Oberdorfer, *Senator Mansfield, The Extraordinary Life of a Great American Statesman and Diplomat* (Washington, DC: Smithsonian, 2003), 337–42; Marjorie Hunter, "Senate Coalition May Block Action on Warren's Post," *NYT*, June 23, 1968 ("thoughts").

39. To Mike Mansfield, June 26, 1968.

40. Mike Manatos, Memorandum for the President, June 26, 1968, Wednesday, 9:30, Box 1, Fortas-Thornberry MSS; Daily Diary, June 26, 1968, LBJL; Johnson, *The Vantage Point*, 547; James Eastland, LBJOH, February 19, 1971, 13.

41. The President's News Conference, June 26, 1968, http://www.presidency.ucsb.edu/ws/index.php?pid=28959.

42. But see Jones, *The Defeat of the Nomination of Abe Fortas as Chief Justice of the United States: A Case Study in Judicial Politics*, 8–9: "The most significant factor in Fortas' defeat was time," and Johnson could not have won the confirmation of anyone other than a US senator in the last months of 1968. He also quoted a Washingtonian who described time as the "life-blood of the anti-Fortas forces." Id., 140.

43. Mike Manatos, Memorandum for the President, June 26, 1968, Box 1, Fortas-Thornberry MSS; John Mackenzie, "Warren to Stay If Senate Delays Action on Fortas: 'Continuing' Nature of Court Cited," *WP*, July 6, 1968; To Ramsey Clark, July 1, 1968, 4:26 P.M., WH6807.01, PNO 1, #13201, MC ("believe"); Eastland, LBJOH, 14; Fairman to Christopher, June 30, 1968 (describing vacancy question as insubstantial); Legislative Reference Service, Library of Congress, July 9, 1968, "The Vacancy Issue Raised by the Impending Retirement of Chief Justice Warren and Its Effect on the Power of the Senate to Advise and Consent to His Successor's Nomination," July 9, 1968, Box 125, Folder 1968 January-July Judicial Background (3), Scott MSS (concluding "(1) that the Chief Justice has not submitted his unequivocal resignation or retirement from the Court, and consequently, that his office is not now vacant, but (2) that notwithstanding the absence of a vacancy, the Senate is not precluded from carrying out its constitutionally conferred function at this time."); John Harmon, Memorandum Opinion for the Attorney General, April 12, 1979, Presidential Appointees—Resignation Subject to the Appointment and Qualification of a Successor, 3 Op. Off. Legal Counsel 152 (1979); Charles Cooper, Nominations for Prospective Vacancies on the Supreme Court," July 9, 1986, 10 Op. Off. Legal Counsel 108, 111 (1986) ("In our view, the President's constitutional power to nominate Justices for anticipated vacancies is limited only by his term of office."); Califano, *The Triumph and Tragedy of Lyndon Johnson*, at 308 (Dirksen).

44. Griffin, "The Fortas Case"; Press Conference, June 27, 1968, Box 292, Courts, Warren Resignation, Griffin MSS. In addition to Griffin and Murphy, the original signatories were Gordon Allott (Colorado), Howard Baker Jr. (Tennessee), Wallace Bennett (Utah), Frank Carlson (Kansas), Norris Cotton (New Hampshire), Carl Curtins (Nebraska), Paul Fannin (Arizona), Hiram Fong (Hawaii), Clifford Hansen (Wyoming), Len Jordan (Idaho), Jack Miller (Iowa), Thruston Morton (Kentucky), Karl Mundt (South Dakota), Strom Thurmond (South Carolina), John Williams (Delaware), and Milton Young (North Dakota). Within two days, John Tower of Texas had added his name to the list.

45. Bob Fleming, Memorandum for the President, June 26, 1968, Box 1, Fortas-Thornberry MSS (network reaction); Robert Semple, "Nixon Repudiates Any Wallace Tie," *NYT*, June 27, 1968 (reporting that as Nixon flew from New York to Lansing on June 26, he told newsmen that "because of the Court's 'transcendent importance' a 'new President with a fresh mandate' should be allowed to choose this own Chief Justice" and that when he arrived in Michigan and learned Johnson had nominated Fortas, he responded: "I felt that it would have been wise for the President to have delayed the appointment of the new Chief Justice until the new President had been elected. It would have been wise for him to ask Chief Justice Warren to serve during the fall term."); Don Irwin, "Fortas Naming Timed Wrong," *LAT*, June 27, 1968 (reporting Nixon had termed Fortas's approval "quite likely"); "The Political Court," *WSJ*, June 27, 1968; Griffin, "The Fortas Case" (press reaction, Marge Griffin).

46. To Ramsey Clark, July 1, 1968.; From Abe Fortas, June 28, 1968, 8:53 A.M., WH6806.04, PNO 7-8, #13148-49, MC; Thomas Foley, "Nixon Gets Discreet Aid of Smathers: Retiring Senator's Office to be Near White House," *LAT*, December 18, 1968; Barefoot Sanders, Memorandum for the President, June 28, 1968, Box 1, Fortas-Thornberry MSS (headcount).

47. Califano, *The Triumph and Tragedy of Lyndon Johnson*, 309; ("assumed") Joseph Califano, Memorandum for the President, June 29, 1968, Box 1, Fortas-Thornberry MSS (Porter's draft); Robert Albright, "Smathers Lauds LBJ on Court Selections," *WP*, July 2, 1968; Mike Manatos, Memorandum, July 2, 1968, Box 2, Fortas-Thornberry MSS ("we," "Griffin effort"); Chronology: Events Relating to Supreme Court Nominations, September 25, 1965, Box 418, Griffin MSS (Taken From Daily Newspapers and Wire Service Accounts); Chapter 9, id. ("definitely").

48. Richard Russell to Lyndon Johnson, July 1, 1968, Office Files of Larry Temple, Box 1, LBJL; Robert Griffin, Interview by Michael Gillette, March 2, 1979, LBJOH, 9. Griffin recalled a telephone conversation with Russell as he arrived in Michigan for the Fourth of July recess; Russell's legislative assistant remembered that the critical conversation occurred in Russell's Washington office. Compare Griffin, LBJOH, 9, and Powell Moore, Interview by Michael Gillette, January 23, 1976, LBJOH, January 23, 1976, 21. Griffin made no mention of any communication with Russell in his memoir, which was incomplete, and simply referred to "indications, in informal ways, that opposition to the nominations, particularly that of Justice Fortas, was beginning to crystallize on the Democratic side." Griffin, "The Fortas Case."

49. Robert Griffin, Notes, n.d., Box 285, Abe Fortas, Griffin MSS. These notes were apparently made in August.

50. Joe Frantz, Richard B. Russell Lecture, April 3, 1979, Series AVA, Subseries 79–1, Russell MSS ("foot," "there," emissaries); Mike Manatos, Memorandum for the President, July 9, 1968, Box 2, Fortas-Thornberry MSS.

51. Richard Russell, Memorandum, July 13, 1968, Series XVIII, Exhibit B, Box 2, Folder 2, Alexander Lawrence nomination, Russell MSS; "Alexander A. Lawrence, A U.S. Judge in Georgia," *NYT*, August 22, 1979.

52. Warren Christopher to Wayne Morse, July 27, 1968, Box 2, Fortas-Thornberry MSS (nominations of Lewis Morgan to Fifth Circuit; Lawrence to Georgia, Southern District; Orma Smith to Mississippi, Northern District; Hugh Bownes to New Hampshire).

53. Douglas Martin, "James J. Ling, Who Built Conglomerates, Dies at 81," *NYT*, December 26, 2004 ("collected"); Joseph Califano, Memorandum for the President, June 29, 1968, 7:30 P.M., Box 1, Fortas-Thornberry MSS (Henry Ford, Austin); Jim Gaither to Joseph Califano, July 2, 1968, Box 4, id. (Eastern Airlines); "Senator Cites Pressure on Court," *WP*, July 4, 1968 (Senator Allott's complaints that "the Administration is trying to pressure big corporations into helping it win Senate approval of President Johnson's Supreme Court Nominations"); News from the AFL-CIO, June 28, 1968, Box 174, Fortas, Hart MSS; Telegram, Walter Reuther to Philip Hart, n.d., id.; Statement by the AFL-CIO Executive Council on Confirmation of Justice Fortas, September 16, 1968, Jim Gaither to Joseph Califano, July 1, 1968, Box 2, Fortas-Thornberry MSS ("business and the free enterprise").

54. Bruce Murphy, *Fortas: The Rise and Ruin of a Supreme Court Justice* (New York: Morrow, 1988), 299 ("After"); Matt Kohl, Recorded Message, July 11, 1968, WH6807.01, PNO 6, #13206, MC; Griffin, "The Fortas Case" ("Jewish," "handle"); Hyman Bookbinder to Philip Hart, September 25, 1968, Box 174, Fortas, Hart MSS ("first"); For Immediate Release, Statement by American Jewish Committee, September 18, 1968 ("exploiting"); Harry McPherson, Memorandum for the President, July 11, 1968, Box 5, Fortas-Thornberry MSS ("there"); Peter Lisagor, "B'nai Brith Mobilizes Against Fortas Foes," *NYP*, July 3, 1968; Memorandum of message left by Eugene Wyman, June 28, 1968, Box 1, Fortas-Thornberry MSS. The anti-Semitism issue did not even possess much traction in New York, where Javits's Democratic antagonist in the Senate race, Paul O'Dwyer, unsuccessfully tried to siphon off the Jewish vote by accusing him of insufficient sensitivity to the role of anti-Semitism in explaining the Senate's opposition to Fortas. Sidney Zion, "Says Paul O'Dwyer: 'The Times Seem to Have Caught Up With Me': Paul O'Dwyer of County Mayo Is Going for the Jewish Vote," *NYT*, August 11, 1968; "Javits Wins," id., November 11, 1968.

55. To Ramsey Clark, July 1, 1968, WH6807.01, PNO 1, 4:26 P.M., #13201, MC ("like," "sober"); From Cartha "Deke" DeLoach, July 1, 1968, 5:02 P.M., WH6807.01, PNO 2, #13202, id.

56. Nominations of Abe Fortas and Homer Thornberry, Part 1, 312, 365–94, 1110–13, 1115–23; Fred Graham, "Senate Panel Bids Officials Explain Pro-Fortas Memo," *NYT*, July 23, 1968; Robert Johnson, "LBJ and the Fortas Nomination," 41 *JSCH* 103, 109 (#1, 2016).

57. "Hart, 'Conscience of Senate,' Dies of Cancer at 64," *LAT*, December 27, 1976; Philip Hart to Berrien Eaton, September 4, 1968, Box 174, Hart MSS.

58. John Goldsmith, *Colleagues: Richard B. Russell and His Apprentice Lyndon B. Johnson* (Macon, GA: Mercer University Press, 1998), 162; "Subsiding Tempest," *WP*, July 4, 1968.

59. Califano, *The Triumph and Tragedy of Lyndon Johnson*, 308; Kalman, *Abe Fortas*, 335.

60. Thomas Keck, "Party Politics or Judicial Independence? The Regime Politics Literature Hits the Law Schools," 32 *LSI* 511 (2007); Barry Friedman, *The Will of the People: How Public Opinion Has Influenced the Supreme Court and Shaped the Meaning of the Constitution* (New York: Farrar, Straus and Giroux, 2009), 277; Corrina Lain, "Countermajoritarian Hero or Zero? Rethinking the Warren Court's Role in the Criminal Procedure Revolution," 152 *UPLR* 1361 (2004). But see Richard Pildes, "Is the Supreme Court a 'Majoritarian' Institution?," 2010 *SCR* 103 (2010).

61. Johnson, "LBJ and the Fortas Nomination," 111 (break); Nominations of Abe Fortas and Homer Thornberry, Part 1, 49, 52–54.

62. Nominations of Abe Fortas and Homer Thornberry, Part 1, 103–6.

63. Califano, *The Triumph and Tragedy of Lyndon Johnson*, 313, 315; Murphy, *Fortas*, 234–68; Kalman, *Abe Fortas*, 221–40, 293–312.

64. Nominations of Abe Fortas and Homer Thornberry, Part 1, 104–5, 169, 107, 166; Jones, *The Defeat of the Nomination of Abe Fortas*, 100 ("Most of what is known about the Johnson-Fortas relationship between 1965-68 became known after 1969."). "Abe—architect of our Vietnam policy—sat in the five cases raising the question of the constitutionality of the war—absent a declaration of war," William O. Douglas told Fred Rodell. "I could not tell . . . whether he was being hammered on that or not." Quoted in Kalman, *Abe Fortas*, 311. Douglas evidently wrote Brennan to ask whether any senator had raised the issue, for Brennan replied, "I really don't know whether any concern was expressed about Abe's sitting in 'Viet Nam' type cases. My impression is that the concern went to his relationship with the President without regard to particular matters." William Brennan to William O. Douglas, August 5, 1968, Box 1780, Brennan, Douglas MSS. See Fred Graham, "Fortas Is Grilled on His Non-Judicial Role," *NYT*, July 21, 1968: "During the past Court term, Fortas voted with the Johnson Administration's position and upheld the legality of the law that made draft-card burning a crime. He also remained silent when two justices insisted that the Court should consider young men's claim that the Vietnam war draft is unconstitutional. No one would argue that his decisions were biased, but it must have seemed strange to the young men who lost those decisions to learn last week that Fortas had taken part in conferences concerning Vietnam war strategy." In the floor debate on the Fortas nomination, Griffin did cite Fortas's failure to recuse himself in the draft-card burning case and two cases raising the issue of the constitutional permissibility of the draft in the absence of a former declaration of war as evidence that the executive matters in which the justice had participated had already come before the court. Griffin, "The Fortas Case"; U.S. v. O'Brien, 391 U.S. 367; Holmes v. U.S., 391 U.S. 936 (1968); Hart v. U.S., 391 U.S. 956 (1968).

65. Nominations of Abe Fortas and Homer Thornberry, Part 1, 105, 109–14, 167–68; Griffin, "The Fortas Case." Where he had once declined to focus on the justice's extrajudicial activities, for example, the senator now leapt on the chance to "have a little fun" at Fortas's expense by demonstrating that the justice had not made full disclosure of them the following day. Griffin, "The Fortas Case."

66. Amalgamated Food Employees Union v. Logan Valley Plaza, 391 U.S. 308 (1968); Nominations of Abe Fortas and Homer Thornberry, Part 1, 126–61, 170-71, 337; Part II, 1355, 1304; Griffin, "The Fortas Case" (eighteen minutes).

67. Nominations of Abe Fortas and Homer Thornberry, Part 1, 336–37; Philip Warden, "Delay Action on Fortas as Chief Justice," *CT*, September 5, 1968 ("general philosophy"); Griffin, "The Fortas Case"; Meg Greenfield, "In 1968, Read 'Crime' for 'Communism': Law and Order Issue Stirs Memories of Fifties," *LAT*, August 25, 1968; Abe Fortas to Philip Hart, July 20, 1968, Box 174, Fortas, Hart MSS. For some years, Hugh Scott lived at 3260 N

Street, two blocks down from Fortas, and the two were on a first-name basis. Scott wrote one constituent: "The hearings before the Senate Judiciary Committee, on which I serve, have not produced evidence which caused me to question the qualifications of Justice Fortas or the right of the President to appoint him, in spite of press reports to the contrary. I do not agree with all of the opinions of Justice Fortas or other members of the Court. I have opposed, and even helped reverse by legislative action, some recent Supreme Court tendencies. I strongly supported Title II of the Crime Control and Safe Streets Act which permits voluntary statements made by defendants to be admitted into evidence, thus off-setting the effects of the Supreme Court decisions in the Miranda and Mallory cases. I do not, however, believe that differences of opinion, even strong differences in some areas, should prejudice my consideration of the nominee's legal qualifications." Hugh Scott to C. Harrison Mann, October 2, 1968, Box 125, Folder 1968 July-October, Scott, MSS.

68. Nominations of Abe Fortas and Homer Thornberry, Part 1, 182, 185.

69. James Clayton, "The Mallory Story: From Death Cell to Freedom," *WP*, June 30, 1957; "Mallory Sought in D.C. Beating," id., January 5, 1958; "Freed Here on Legal Technicality: Andrew Mallory Indicted for Rape of Young Philadelphia Housewife," id., April 23, 1960; Paul Valentine, "Mallory, of Famed Decision, Slain by Philadelphia Police," id., July 12, 1972; Nominations of Abe Fortas and Homer Thornberry, Part 1, 182, 185, 191; Jones, *The Defeat of the Nomination of Abe Fortas*, 189 (possibility of premeditation).

70. Nominations of Abe Fortas and Homer Thornberry, Part 1, 191–92; John McKenzie, "Fortas Berated for Two Hours," *WP*, July 19, 1968.

71. Nominations of Abe Fortas and Homer Thornberry, Part 1, 219; "The Senate: Fortas at the Bar," *Ti*, July 26, 1968.

72. John MacKenzie, "4 Noted Attorneys Endorse Fortas," *WP*, August 3, 1968 ("vicious"); MacKenzie, "Bar Unit Blasts Senate Critics of Court in Fortas Quiz," id., August 8, 1968; Fred Graham, "Law Dean Assails Critics of Fortas: Yale Official Warns Bar of Assault on Constitution," *NYT*, August 7, 1968; "Head of Bar Assails Griffin for Battle Against Fortas," id., August 13, 1968; Murphy, *Fortas*, 447 (White House).

73. Mark Silverstein, *Judicious Choices: The Politics of Supreme Court Confirmations* (New York: W. W. Norton, 2007), 26-27 ("scapegoat," "effective"); John James Lucier to Strom Thurmond, July 19, 1968, Box 45, Fortas Speech/Statement Drafts/Folder 1, Legislative Assistant Series, Thurmond MSS.

74. Nominations of Abe Fortas and Homer Thornberry, Part 1, 277, 251; Fred Graham, "Thornberry Bars Senate Questions on Past Decisions: Appearing Before Senate Judiciary Panel He Takes the Same Position as Fortas Did," *NYT*, 1968; Griffin, "The Fortas Case."

75. Jones, *The Defeat of the Nomination of Abe Fortas*, 201, 274, n. 148, 256–58, 281–82.

76. Ken Fanucchi, "Porn Fighter Grapples With Evil: Attorney Clancy, Battling on Many Fronts, Sees Smut as Poisonous to Family," *LAT*, August 6, 1978 ("reported"); Nomination of Abe Fortas, at 302 ("girlie"); Whitney Strub, "Perversion for Profit: Citizens for Decent Literature and the Arousal of an Antiporn Public in the 1960s," 15 *JHS* 258, 302 (2006) ("humorless").

77. Nominations of Abe Fortas and Homer Thornberry, Part 1, 294; Schackman v. California, 388 U.S. 454 (1967).

78. Joseph O'Meara, "Obscenity Issue and Fortas," *WP*, September 11, 1968; Charles Rembar, "Fortas Record Reviewed," *NYT*, September 22, 1968; Murphy, *Fortas*, 460; Nominations of Abe Fortas and Homer Thornberry, Part 1, 306–9; L. A. Powe, "The Obscenity Bargain: Ralph Ginzburg for Fanny Hill," 35 *JSCH* 166, 167 (#2, 2010).

79. "Stamping Out Smut Means Stopping Abe Fortas," Box 125, Judicial Background 1968-69, n.d. (5), Scott MSS; "Profiles: All Pockets Open," *NY*, January 6, 1973; Daniel Schreiber, *Susan Sontag: A Biography* (Chicago: Northwestern, 2014). "So what if Susan Sontag thinks this film is worthwhile (meaning, it gives her a chance to say something new in her column), or that some professor somewhere gives his class a cheap thrill by showing it a dirty film," Fortas's clerk, Dan Levitt, wrote in his memo on Jacobs. "There are other crit-ics who would classify this film as pornographic trash, and thousands of professors who wouldn't use this film on a bet." Fortas wrote next to the first sentence "I will stick with them." Jacobs v. People of New York, No. 600, O.T. 1966, Box 27, Fortas MSS; Jacobs v. New York, 388 U.S. 431 (1967).

80. Larry Meyer to Cecil Holland, Obscenity Issue—Fortas Hearings, December 20, 1968, Box 418, Pornography Becomes an Issue, Griffin MSS; Griffin, "The Fortas Case" ("Thanks").

81. John Corry, "Washington Report: Strom's Dirty Movies," *Harper's*, December 1968 ("Mostly"); "The Congress: The Fortas Film Festival," *Ti*, September 20, 1968; Brian Frye, "The Dialectic of Obscenity," 35 *HamLR* 212 , 264 (2012) To George Smathers, July 25, 1968, 11:30 P.M., WH6807.02, PNO 8, July 25, 1968, #13218, MC. 11:30 P.M.

82. To George Smathers, July 28, 1968; Meyer to Holland, December 20, 1968; Nominations of Abe Fortas and Homer Thornberry, Part 1, 347, 360; "Thurmond Brandishes Nude Pictures, Wants More Testimony From Fortas," *AG*, Box 528, Folder 12, McClellan MSS.

83. To George Smathers, July 28, 1968; Mike Manatos, Memorandum for the President, July 25, 1968, Box 7, Fortas-Thornberry MSS.

84. Morton Mintz, "Griffin Says 40 Ready to Block Vote on Fortas," *WP*, July 31, 1968 ("crude"); Jim Wood, Memorandum to Senator McClellan, Jacobs v. New York, September 9, 1968, Box 508, Folder 60, McClellan MSS; and see Wood to McClellan, September 9, 1968, id. In 1967, over Douglas, Fortas, and Brennan's dissent, most justices held in "one of the Court's first major gay rights cases" that an Immigration and Nationality Act provision barring aliens "afflicted with psychopathic personality" from the United States constitutionally excluded homosexuals. Marc Stein, *Sexual Injustice: Supreme Court Decisions From Griswold to Roe* (Chapel Hill: University of North Carolina Press, 2010), ix, 11–12, 61–92; Boutillier v. the Immigration and Naturalization Service, 387 U.S. 118 (1967); Joe Patrice, "LBJ, FBI, and SCOTUS All Spying on George Hamilton Because . . . Gay Stuff," September 2, 2014, http://abovethelaw.com/tag/tuan-samahon/; Samahon v. Federal Bureau of Investigation et. al., Case No. 2:12-CV 04839, Pennsylvania, Eastern District Court, August 22, 2012. But see David Sklansky, "One Train May Hide Another: *Katz*, Stonewall, and the Secret Subtext of Criminal Procedure," 41 *UCDLR* 875 (2007) (suggesting that the court's interest in protecting gays might lie at the core of its creation of modern criminal procedure).

85. Frye, "The Fortas Film Festival," 266; James Kilpatrick, "Fortas: His Confirmation Could Turn on Film Decision Alone," *LAT*, August 13, 1968; Strom Thurmond Reports to the People: "Fortas on Filth," August 5, 1968, Volume XIV, No. 28, Box 508, Folder 60, McClellan MSS.

86. "Court Poll Leans to Conservatives: Gallup Finds Public Is 5-3 Against Nominee," *NYT*, April 19, 1970 (reporting on polls taken asking this question in June 1968, June 1969, and April 1970); Lou Harris, "Poll: Fortas Gets 'Yea,' Court Gets 'Nay,'" *StP*, August 12, 1968; Jones, *The Defeat of the Nomination of Abe Fortas*, 286, 383–84 (press support for nomination); Philip Hart to Robert Howlett, August 6, 1968, Box 174, Thornberry, Hart MSS ("solid"); Philip Hart to Eugene Bogan, August 9, 1968, Box 174, Fortas, id. ("superbly"); John MacKenzie, "4 Noted Attorneys Endorse Fortas," *WP*, August 3, 1968 ("lunatic"); "Independent Judiciary," *NYT*, August 14, 1968 ("small"); see, for example, Louis Pollak to John Lindsay, August 23, 1968, Box 44, Abe Fortas, Pollak MSS ("grave"); "Head of Bar Assails Griffin for Battle Against Fortas," *NYT*, August 13, 1968; Alexander Bickel to Anthony Lewis, October 22, 1968, Abe Fortas, Box 44, Pollak MSS (responding to Lewis's comment that "Mr. Justice Fortas deserves more of the blame than you attribute to him, and I think some worthy liberal should admit as much." Anthony Lewis to Alexander Bickel, October 17, 1968, id. Bickel replied to Lewis that he did not want to blame Fortas publicly because of "the enemies he has made"—presumably among racist demagogues and rabid anticommunists.); Kalman, *Abe Fortas*, 350 (reporting that Paul Porter had asked iconic liberal Joe Rauh if liberals remained silent on the Fortas nomination because they so mistrusted LBJ and were so alienated by the Vietnam War, only to have Rauh accuse him of being "paranoid" and insist, "I have never seen an issue on which liberals are more united than they are on Abe Fortas.") When Philip Hart complained that his mail was running against Fortas's confirmation, one surprised Democrat wrote him that "all liberal Democrats assume you know we are in favor of confirmation, so you can easily imagine who has been writing to you." Barbara Miatech to Philip Hart, September 6, 1968, Box 174, Fortas, Hart MSS. Yet although liberals did unite behind Fortas, they did not leave the kind of extensive paper trail in their usual places, the Rauh or Leadership Conference on Civil Rights Papers, that they put

down in opposing some of Nixon's nominees to the court). See John MacKenzie, "Liberals Torn Over Fortas," *WP*, September 22, 1968.

87. George Reedy, Memorandum for the President, July 30, 1968, 9:30 A.M., Box 7, Fortas-Thornberry MSS; Johnson, *The Vantage Point*, 547.

88. Philip Hart to Geoffrey Gilbert, August 1, 1968, Box 174, Fortas, Hart MSS; Califano, *The Triumph and Tragedy of Lyndon Johnson*, 315; From Everett Dirksen, August 27, 1968, 11:15 A.M., WH6808.03, PNO 1, #13323, MC; Barefoot Sanders, Memorandum for the President, July 30, 1968, Box 2, Fortas-Thornberry MSS; Jones, *The Defeat of the Nomination of Abe Fortas*, 203 (LBJ's refusal to give up).

89. George Gallup, "High Court Gets a Low Rating," *WP*, July 10, 1968; "Fortas Says He Was Outraged by Critics," *LAT*, July 25, 1968; Fred Graham, "Fortas, in Rejoinder to Thurmond, Warns Against Some 'Professed Friends of Law and Order,' " *NYT*, August 4, 1968; Paul Porter to James R. Jones, August 7, 1968, Box 5, Porter MSS.

90. Abe Fortas to Earl Warren, July 25, 1968, Box 97, Folder 1983, Fortas MSS.

91. Abe Fortas to John Harlan, July 24, 1968, id.; Fortas to William O. Douglas, July 26, 1968, id.; Fortas to William O. Douglas, July 26, 1968, Box 1782, Abe Fortas, Douglas MSS.

92. Fortas to Douglas, July 26, 1968; "Independent Judiciary," *New York Times*, August 14, 1968; Kalman, *Abe Fortas*, 345; Irving Spiegel, "Javits Asks Nixon for Aid on Fortas," *NYT*, August 18, 1968 Jacob Javits to Louis Pollak, September 20, 1968, Box 44, Abe Fortas, Pollak MSS ("I spoke to Mr. Nixon during the week of August 22, urging him to repudiate the threatened filibuster and was most pleased by his recent statement along these lines."); Abe Fortas to William O. Douglas, August 7, 1968, Box 1782, Douglas MSS ("I," "If").

93. John Ehrlichman, *Witness to Power: The Nixon Years* (New York: Simon and Schuster, 1982), 113; Patrick Buchanan, *The Greatest Comeback: How Richard Nixon Rose From Defeat to Create a New Majority* (New York: Crown, 2014), 276–78; Peter Holmes to Senator, August 23, 1968, Meeting on Fortas-Thornberry Nominations With Senate Backers, Box 285, Strategy Meeting, Griffin MSS (communications between Republicans and Nixon over issue); George Lardner Jr. and Michael Dobbs, "New Tapes Reveal Depth of Nixon's Anti-Semitism," *WP*, October 6, 1999.

94. Robert Albright and Chalmers Roberts, "Thurmond: The GOP's Kingmaker," *WP*, August 11, 1968; Bruce Kalk, *The Origins of the Southern Strategy: Two-Party Competition in South Carolina, 1950-1972* (Lanham: Lexington Books, 2001), 82; Joseph Crespino, *Strom Thurmond's America* (New York: Hill and Wang, 2012), 219 (describing Thurmond as "indefatigable in holding the South for Nixon"); Max Frankel, "Humphrey Terms Nixon 'a Wiggler' on Crucial Issues," *NYT*, September 12, 1968; Marquis Childs, "Nixon Role Urged in the Fortas Case," id., September 13, 1968; Max Frankel, "Humphrey Scores 'the Same Nixon,' " *NYT*, September 14, 1968; Don Oberdorfer, "Filibuster Opposed by Nixon," *WP*, September 14, 1968; Marjorie Hunter, "Griffin Rebukes Nixon for Stand Opposing a Filibuster on Fortas," *NYT*, September 15, 1968; Robert Shogan, *A Question of Judgment: The Fortas Case and the Struggle for the Supreme Court* (Indianapolis: Bobbs-Merrill, 1972), 180; Philip Warden, "G.O.P. Plank Slaps at Fortas Nomination," *CT*, August 3, 1968; Address Accepting the Presidential Nomination at the Republican National Convention, August 8, 1968, http://www.presidency.ucsb.edu/ws/?pid=25968.

95. The Walker Report to the National Commission on the Causes and Prevention of Violence, *Rights in Conflict: The Violent Confrontation of Demonstrators and Police in the Parks and Streets of Chicago During the Week of the Democratic National Convention* (New York: Bantam, 1968), 5; From Ramsey Clark, August 29, 1968, 11:29 A.M., WH6808.04, PNO 5, #13334; Robert Hughes, "A Step by Step Chronicle of Confrontation, Chaos," *CT*, August 20, 1978 (Cronkite); Jack Gould, "TV: Covering the Chaos in Chicago," *NYT*, August 31, 1968; David Farber, *Chicago '68* (Chicago: University of Chicago Press, 1998), 206 (public reaction); "LBJ Panel to Probe Chicago," *WP*, September 5, 1968; To Frank Stanton, August 29, 1968, 7:12 P.M., WH6808.05, PNO 3, #13342, Transcripts, LBJL (predictably, LBJ told the president of CBS that he blamed the coverage on Robert Kennedy's crowd); David Janson, "Daley's TV Film Shows Convention Week Clashes: Daley Gives Film Version of Clashes," *NYT*, September 16, 1968; "Fear of Poor Reception Linked to Decision by Johnson to Skip Convention Visit," id., September 1, 1968.

96. Marjorie Hunter, "Returning Democrats Are In for Trouble," *NYT*, September 1, 1968.

97. Philip Warden, "Delay Action on Fortas as Chief Justice: Committee Fails to Get Quorum," *CT*, September 5, 1968; Marjorie Hunter, "Johnson Told Hope of a Fortas Victory Is Fading in Senate," *NYT*, September 6, 1968; Remarks of Senator Philip Hart, National Press Club, September 4, 1968, Box 174, Fortas, Hart MSS; The President's News Conference, September 6, 1968, http://www.presidency.ucsb.edu/ws/index.php?pid=29101 (Mansfield, Dirksen); Philip Warden, "LBJ Plans to Fight for Fortas," *CT*, September 6, 1968; Philip Dodd, "Tries to Force Committee to Act on Fortas," id., September 10, 1968.

98. To Ramsey Clark, September 12, 1968, 5:16 P.M, WH6809.02, PNO 5, #13413, MC; Morton Mintz, "Dirksen, GOP Master of the U-Turn Follows a Familiar Route on Fortas," *WP*, October 1, 1968.

99. Robert Griffin, "Advice and Consent: The Fortas -Thornberry Issue," National Press Club, Box 508, Folder 60, McClellan MSS; DeVier Pierson, Memorandum for the President, September 11, 1968, Box 7, Fortas-Thornberry MSS ("swearing"); Nominations of Abe Fortas and Homer Thornberry, Part 2, 1361–64; Kalman, *Abe Fortas*, 353–54.

100. Meyer to Holland, December 20, 1968 (suitcases, "enticing"); Robert Griffin, Memorandum to the Chairman and Members of the Committee on the Judiciary, September 9, 1968, Box 508, McClellan MSS.

101. Christopher, The Fortas and Thornberry Nominations (LBJ and Clark); Marjorie Hunter, "Fortas Refuses to Appear Again in Senate Inquiry," *NYT*, September 14, 1968.

102. Larry Meyer to Cecil Holland, American University Seminar Fund, November 1, 968, Box 418, Chapter 11, Griffin MSS; Griffin, "The Fortas Case."

103. "The DC Lecture Biz: Party Conversation Getting Dull? Rent Senator for the Evening," *WP*, October 17, 1971; Nominations of Abe Fortas and Homer Thornberry, Part 2, 1285–1304; Kalman, *Abe Fortas*, 322, 326–27, 351–53. Porter had received contributions from Maurice Lazarus of Federated Department Store, Troy Post of Great America Corporation, Paul Smith of Philip Morris, and investment bankers Gustave Levy and John Loeb. Lazarus, Post, and Smith had been his clients, and Post's son was appealing the conviction. See Paul Porter to Gustave Levy, February 2, 1968, and to Maurice Lazarus, February 9, 1968, Paul Porter Papers, Box 5, Johnson Library (restlessness); Paul Porter to Troy Post, February 7, 1968, to Gustave Levy, February 9, 1968 (informed Fortas of their contributions).

104. Jones, *The Defeat of the Nomination of Abe Fortas*, 242–43, 266, n.63; Griffin, "The Fortas Case" ("This"); Ronald Ostrow and Robert Jackson, "Even Supporters Question Fortas' Accepting Fee," *LAT*, September 21, 1968; Nominations of Abe Fortas and Homer Thornberry, Part 2, 1298, 1351 ("somewhere," "fee").

105. Richard Russell to Lyndon Johnson, September 26, 1968, Box 3, Fortas-Thornberry MSS; Meyer to Holland, November 1, 1968 ("Senators Spong, Pearson, Aiken, Prouty, Dirksen, Hruska, Cooper, Boggs, and Dodd"); Griffin, "The Fortas Case" ("above"); James Yuenger, "Drop Fortas, LBJ Urged," *CT*, September 15, 1968 ("serious"); "The Real Threat to Law and Order," *WP*, September 22, 1968; "Justice for Mr. Fortas," *NYT*, September 27, 1968.

106. Ramsey Clark, Interview by Harri Baker, June 3, 1969, LBJOH, 11–13; J. J. Maloney, "Did J. Edgar Hoover Blackmail Justice Abe Fortas?," *Crime*, October 9, 2009, http://www.crime-magazine.com/did-j-edgar-hoover-blackmail-justice-abe-fortas; Marc Stein, "Did the FBI Try to Blackmail Supreme Court Justice Abe Fortas?," July 18, 2005, http://historynews-network.org/article/13170.

107. Benjamin Welles, "Clark Declares Foes of Fortas Play Politics and Oppose Rights," *NYT*, September 14, 1968; Califano, *The Triumph and Tragedy of Lyndon Johnson*, 316–17.

108. Mike Manatos, Memorandum for the President, September 16, 1968, Box 3, Fortas-Thornberry MSS.

109. Report to Accompany the Nomination of Abe Fortas, 11, 12, 39, 41, 18, 21.

110. Ronald Ostrow, "Dirksen Won't Support Fortas Cloture, May Not Vote for Him," *LAT*, September 28, 1968 ("arms," "obstinate"); "The Real Threat to Law and Order," *WP*, September 22, 1968 ("so long," "great"); Robert Albright, "GOP to Lead a Filibuster Against Fortas," id., September 20, 1968.

111. Willard Edwards, "Seek End of Fortas Fight: Expect Senate to Say There Is No Vacancy," *CT*, September 24, 1968; Ronald Ostrow, "Mansfield Forces Action Today on Fortas

Nomination," *LAT*, September 25, 1968; Johnson, *LBJ and the Fortas Nomination*, 16 ("The Majority Leader opened debate with a speech that one correspondent noted 'left some doubt at just how totally Mansfield himself viewed the brilliance of Johnson's selection of Fortas.'"); Robert Albright, "Senate Acts to Open Debate on Fortas Today," *WP*, September 25, 1968; Griffin, "The Fortas Case"; Fred Graham, "Critics of Fortas Begin Filibuster, Citing 'Propriety,'" *NYT*, September 26, 1968; Robert Albright, "Fortas Debate Opens With a Filibuster: Fee Held Unfortunate," *WP*, September 26, 1968; Eastland LBJOH, 14.

112. Philip Dodd, "Fortas Dealt New Blow: Dirksen to Vote 'No' on Bid to Curb Debate," *CT*, September 28, 1968 ("things," Witherspoon); Witherspoon v. Illinois, 391 U.S. 510; Hulsey, *Everett Dirksen and His Presidents*, 267; "Leader Says Bar May Reconsider Stand on Fortas," *LAT*, September 28, 1968 ("facts"); "Sen. Griffin Wins Once Lonely Battle to Block Court Change," *CT*, October 3, 1968 ("psychological"); Fred Graham, "Fortas Receives Critical Setback as Dirksen Shifts," *NYT*, September 28, 1968 ("hell"; ABA President Gossett "was quoted by some news sources in Detroit as saying that he would ask the committee to review its endorsement. Reached by telephone tonight, he stated that this was not so and, to his knowledge, the bar association's investigation was closed.").

113. "Fortas Dealt New Blow" ("ghost"); Fortas to William O. Douglas, September 26, 1968, Box 1782, Fortas, Abe, Douglas MSS; Christopher, *The Fortas and Thornberry Nomination*.

114. Fred Graham, "Warren Looks to Future, Hoping to Speed Justice," *NYT*, September 30, 1968; Carl Solberg, *Hubert Humphrey: A Biography* (New York: W. W. Norton, 1984), 380–86.

115. From Everett Dirksen, October 1, 1968, 10:31 A.M., WH6810.01, PNO 1, #13501, MC; and see From John McCormack, October 1, 1968, 10:45 A.M., WH6801.01, PNO 3, #13503, id.

116. From Ramsey Clark, October 1, 1968, 11:05 A.M., WH 6810.01, PNO 4-5, #13504-05, MC.

117. Fred Graham, "Fortas Jewels Stolen as Senate Debated Nomination," *NYT*, October 13, 1968; "Bare $22,160 Jewel Theft from Fortas," *CT*, October 13, 1968; Griffin, "The Fortas Case" (quotations); Fred Graham, "The Votes Are Not There for Fortas," *NYT*, September 29, 1968. Jones suggests that Griffin was "used" by Thurmond and Southern Democrats. Jones, *The Defeat of the Nomination of Abe Fortas*, 10.

118. To Clark Clifford, October 1, 1968, 5:40 P.M., WH6810.01, PNO 8, #13508, MC. Lou Pollak had suggested that the Senate majority leader raise the possibility of paralyzing the Senate to White House aide Joe Califano: "If I were the President I would tell Senator Mansfield that I wanted the filibusterers to be put to the test of carrying their filibuster on to the very end of the session. That is to say, I would not let the Senate go on to other business (let alone withdraw the nominations) if a couple of cloture votes fail. The American people are entitled to see 'a little band of willful men' actually hold up (and not merely threaten to hold up) the entire legislative process—and in the bargain, defy the majority of their colleagues who would vote to confirm, if given the opportunity." Pollak to Califano, September 7, 1968, Box 44, Abe Fortas, Pollak MSS. Mansfield did not run these old-fashioned kinds of filibusters.

119. To Clark Clifford, October 1, 1968.

120. To Abe Fortas, October 1, 1968, 6:06 P.M., WH6810.01, PNO9, #13509, MC.

121. "Fortas Letter and Statement by Johnson," *NYT*, October 3, 1968; John MacKenzie, "Johnson Withdraws Fortas Nomination," *WP*, October 3, 1968; Kalman, *Abe Fortas*, 300.

122. Fred Graham, "Fortas Abandons Nomination Fight; Name Withdrawn," *NYT*, October 3, 1963 (reporting that Capitol Hill was "swept with rumors of possible nominees," including Tom Kuchel, Philip Hart, Arthur Goldberg, Clark Clifford, Henry Fowler, and Cyrus Vance); From Barefoot Sanders, October 11, 1968, 3:54 P.M., WH6810.03, PNO 14, #13536, MC; To Mike Manatos, October 11, 1968, 3:55 P.M., WH 6810.03, PNO 15, #13537, id.; Bryce Harlow, Memorandum for Richard Nixon, November 24, 1968, Nixon Presidential Returned Materials MSS, Box 7, Folder 2 ("I find that Strom Thurmond did try to get, but did not get, a firm agreement with LBJ that no additional Supreme Court Justice nominations would be sent to the Senate."); Robert Young, "LBJ Won't Pick New Chief Justice Now; Warren Remains," *CT*, October 11, 1969; Elsie Carper, "Sanders, Bress Judgeships Blocked," *WP*,

October 10, 1968; To Mike Mansfield, October 16, 1968, 9:34 A.M., WH6810.04, PNO 5, #13546, MC; Marjorie Hunter, "Congress Defers Plan to Adjourn," *NYT*, October 12, 1968; Robert Young, "LBJ Weighing Senate Call on Atom Pact," *CT*, November 28, 1968. LBJ did resubmit the names of Sanders and four other potential judicial nominees in January 1969 after he thought Nixon had approved them. The new president, however, withdrew all of the nominations and resubmitted only one of them. Ironically, it was that of District Judge Matthew Byrne, who presided over the Pentagon Papers trial discussed in chapter 7 and who lambasted the administration for its misconduct. Neil McFeeley, *Appointment of Judges: The Johnson Presidency* (Austin: University of Texas Press, 1987), 128–32; Martin Arnold, "Pentagon Papers Charges Are Dismissed; Judge Byrnes Frees Ellsberg and Russo, Assails 'Improper Government Conduct,'" *NYT*, May 11, 1973.

123. Kalman, *Abe Fortas*, 356; Daily Diary, October 10, 1968, 1:01 P.M-2:02 P.M., LBJL; To Mike Mansfield, October 6, 1968, 9:34 A.M., WH6810.04, PNO5, #13546, MC; McFeeley, *Appointment of Judges: The Johnson Presidency*, 118–20.

124. To Abe Fortas, October 17, 1968, 9:19 A.M., WH6810.05, PNO 8, #13357, MC.

125. To Ramsey Clark, October 14, 1968, 11:51 P.M., WH6810.03, PNO 19, #13541, MC; Rowland Evans and Robert Novak, "Inside Report: LBJ, Ike and the GOP," *WP*, August 5, 1965.

126. From Earl Warren, December 5, 1968, 11:15 P.M., WH6812.01, PNO 4, #13804, MC; John MacKenzie, "Nixon and Justice Warren: Rivalry to Reconciliation," *WP*, July 11, 1974; Don Irwin, "Nixon Asks Warren to Remain Till Court Term Ends in June," *LAT*, December 5, 1968.

127. From Earl Warren, December 5, 1968; Drew Pearson, "The Washington Merry-Go-Round: Nixon Call to Warren Undercut LBJ," *WP*, December 7, 1968; "Charge Nixon Foiled Lyndon on High Court," *CT*, December 11, 1968; Fred Graham, "Dirksen Tests G.O.P. Sentiment if Johnson Nominates Goldberg," *NYT*, December 13, 1968.

128. Barefoot Sanders, Memorandum for the President, December 9, 1968, WHCF EX FG 535, Box 359, LBJL; "Thurmond Reports a Johnson Retreat," *NYT*, December 10, 1968 (stating that a news conference, Thurmond had said that LBJ "had toyed with the idea of calling a special session of Congress to nominate Arthur J. Goldberg as Chief Justice but abandoned it when it looked as thought it would run into trouble."); McFeeley, *Appointment of Judges*, 117–20; David Kyvig, *The Age of Impeachment: American Constitutional Culture Since 1960* (Lawrence: University Press of Kansas), 76 ("lie").

129. Johnson, *The Vantage Point*, 546.

130. Allen Otten, "Politics and People: Court Stakes," *WSJ*, March 18, 1970. In the judgment of *Wall Street Journal* reporter Louis Kohlmeier, it was Johnson's insistence on coupling Fortas with another crony that doomed Fortas, and had he handled the nominations correctly, LBJ "probably could have won confirmation even of Abe Fortas to be the next Chief Justice." Louis Kohlmeier, *God Save This Honorable Court: The Supreme Court Crisis* (New York: Scribner's, 1972), 89. According to Philip Hart's biographer, LBJ sent out serious feelers to Hart about whether he wanted the Chief Justiceship, James Eastland even promised the senator that he would not fight the nomination, and Hart "probably could have been confirmed" had he chosen to seek the chief justiceship. "I sent back word—thanks, but no thanks," Hart recalled, and "there never was a formal offer. I said I was comfortable in the Senate." Michael O'Brien, *Philip Hart: Conscience of the Senate* (East Lansing: Michigan State University Press, 1995), 121–23. John Masarro develops the argument that ideology lay behind voting patterns, though he also blames Fortas's defeat on Johnson's timing and management of the nomination in *Supremely Political: The Role of Ideology and Presidential Management of Unsuccessful Supreme Court Nominations* (Albany: State University of New York Press, 1990), 1–77.

131. Fred Graham, "The Stakes Are Large in the Fortas Dispute," *NYT*, September 22, 1968; "Sen. Griffin Wins Once Lonely Battle to Block Court Change"; Phyllis Schlafly, "What the Vote on Abe Fortas Means," December 1, 1968, Insight on the News, Box 528, McClellan MSS; Buchanan, *The Greatest Comeback*, 278; Whitney Strub, *Perversion for Profit: The Politics of Pornography and the Rise of the New Right* (New York: Columbia University Press, 2010) 7, 120; Kalman, *Abe Fortas*, 356, 357 (Fortas, Lady Bid Johnson); Philip Hart to

Lois Brodsky, November 11, 1968, Box 174, Fortas, Hart MSS; Ronald Ostrow, "Scholars See Trouble Ahead for High Court," *LAT*, October 3, 1968 (Bickel).

Chapter 5

1. Robert Mason, *Richard Nixon and the Quest for a New Majority* (Chapel Hill: University of North Carolina Press, 2004); Donald Stephenson, *Campaigns and the Court: The U.S. Supreme Court in Presidential Elections* (New York: Columbia University Press, 1999), 184.
2. Tom Wicker, *One of Us: Richard Nixon and the American Dream* (New York: Random House, 1991), 9. If he had to practice law for the remainder of his life, Nixon confided to one associate after he became a Wall Street lawyer, "I would be mentally dead in two years and physically dead in four." Patrick Buchanan, *The Greatest Comeback: How Richard Nixon Rose From Defeat to Create the New Majority* (New York: Crown Forum, 2014), 35.
3. James Rosen, *The Strong Man: John Mitchell and the Secrets of Watergate* (New York: Doubleday, 2008), 50, 490, 71 ("dour" [quoting William Safire], "lawyer's lawyer"); Saul Friedman, "Richard Kleindienst: The 'Mr. Tough' of Justice Department," *CT*, February 24, 1972; John Carmody, "Jerry Leonard—a Team Man in Justice's Civil Rights: Potomac Profile," *WP*, March 8, 1970; John Dean, T*he Rehnquist Choice: The Untold Story of the Nixon Appointment that Redefined the Supreme Court* (New York: Free Press, 2001), 16.
4. Douglas Hallett, "A low-level memoir of the Nixon White House," *NYT*, October 20, 1974; J.Y. Smith, "H.R. Haldeman Dies," *WP*, November 13, 1993 ("President's"); Robert Semple, "White House 'Fireman:' John Daniel Ehrlichman," *NYT*, November 10, 1969; Alissa Rubin, "Nixon Loyalist Ehrlichman Is Dead at 73," *LAT*, February 16, 1999; John Dean, *Blind Ambition: The End of the Story* (Palm Springs: Polimedia, 2009).
5. Laura Kalman, *Right Star Rising: A New Politics, 1974-1980* (New York: W. W. Norton, 2010), 7.
6. James Patterson, *Grand Expectations: The United States 1945-1974* (New York: Oxford University Press) 720–22. Compare, for example, Bruce Schulman, *The Seventies : The Great Shift in American Culture, Society and Politics* (New York: Free Press, 2001), 25, 27, which after conceding the case that can be made for Nixon as "the last interventionist liberal," argues that he should be seen as "the first of the conservatives" with Joan Hoff, *Nixon Reconsidered* (New York: Basic, 1994), 49, which stresses that in domestic policy, he "exceed[ed] the accomplishments of the New Deal and Great Society. "For a fascinating discussion of historians' transformation of Nixon into a liberal, see David Greenberg, *Nixon's Shadow: The History of an Image* (New York: W.W. Norton, 2003), 304-37.
7. Alderman v. U.S., 394 U.S. 165 (1969) (Alderman involved behavior before the Safe Streets Act expanded the right of government to eavesdrop in criminal cases and those affecting national security); Fred Graham, "High Court Faces Plea on Wiretaps," *NYT*, March 13, 1969.
8. Earl Warren, *The Memoirs of Chief Justice Earl Warren* (Lanham: Madison, 2001), 337–41; Bernard Schwartz, *Super Chief: Earl Warren and His Supreme Court* (New York: New York University Press, 1983), 750–52; Seth Stern and Stephen Wermiel, *Justice Brennan: Liberal Champion* (New York: Houghton Mifflin, 2010), 311–13; William Brennan to Earl Warren, March 18, 1969, enclosing his March 17 memorandum describing the incident, Box 348, Brennan, Warren MSS; Douglas Martin, "Jack C. Landau, Who Fought For Rights of News Reporters, Is Dead at 74," *NYT*, August 20, 2008. Warren said in his memoirs that Landau was very tense, and when I worked briefly as his intern in the 1970s, I found him excitable.
9. Fred Graham, "High Court Hints Easing of Disclosure of Bugging," *NYT*, March 25, 1969 (Senate); Giordano v. United States, 394 U.S. 310 (1969).
10. Warren, *The Memoirs of Chief Justice Earl Warren*, 341; John Crewdson, "Secret Bid to Court Is Laid to Mitchell," *NYT*, May 17, 1973 (reporting Landau's incredulity at Mitchell's denial); Linda Mathews, "Ex-Aide Says Mitchell Sent Him to See Justices in 1969 Wiretap Case," *LAT*, May 17, 1973 (disbarment); John MacKenzie, "Mitchell Aide Tells of Call on Justices," *WP*, May 16, 1973.
11. William O. Douglas, *The Court Years, 1939-1975: The Autobiography of William O. Douglas* (New York: Random House, 1980), 259, 139; Ex Parte Quirin, 317 U.S. 1 (1942).

12. Dinner Honoring Chief Justice Earl Warren, WHCF EX FG 51, Box 1, Folder 1, RMNL; Earl Warren to Richard Nixon, April 25, 1969, id.; "Nixons Fete Warren at White House," *NYT*, April 24, 1969 (menu); "Guests at the White House," *WP*, April 24, 1969.

13. "Nixons Fete Warren at White House" (Rogers, Agnew, Dewey); Julius Duscha, "Chief Justice Burger Asks: If It Doesn't Make Good Sense, How Can It Make Good Law?," *NYT Mag*, October 5, 1969 ("turned"); Warren Burger to Herbert Brownell, January 12, 1969, Box 107, Brownell MSS (discussing "imperative" need for Nixon to appoint MacKinnon and another former prosecutor whom Nixon also nominated to the DC circuit, Roger Robb); Burger to Brownell, December 11, 1968, id., urging MacKinnon; Richard Nixon to the Attorney General, Box 65, Folder 227-OA 3052, Krogh MSS (relaying Burger's plea for "two strong men" on the DC Circuit Court of Appeals).

14. Warren Burger to Herbert Brownell, Friday (c. October 1968), Box 107, Brownell MSS. See, for example, Fred Graham, "Court Scored by Top Judge Here: A Jurist Nixon May Name Urges Curbs on Liberal Trend," *NYT*, November 10, 1968, (referring to Friendly as someone "who has been mentioned as a possible Nixon appointee to the Supreme Court"); John O'Melveny to Earl Adams, January 6, 1969, WHCF Ex FG 51, Box 1, Folder 1, RMNL (quoting letter from Friendly to Henry Dreyfuss asking if Adams could do anything to help him: "Anyway it seems to me the best thing Nixon could do on that [the chief justiceship] is to promote Mr. Justice Stewart, who has solid Republican support from Ohio; such faint hopes as I have are directed rather to the vacancy this would create.")

15. Joel Grossman, *Lawyers and Judges: The ABA and the Politics of Judicial Selection* (New York: John Wiley, 1965), 143.

16. Duscha, "If It Doesn't Make Good Sense" ("There"); Richard Nixon to Harold Stassen, June 25, 1969, WHCF EX FG 51/A, Box 3, Folder 5, RMNL (occasion of first meeting); "Harold E. Stassen, Who Sought G.O.P. Nomination for President 9 Times, Dies at 93," *NYT*, March 5, 2001.

17. Duscha, "It Doesn't Make Good Sense" ("liberal"); Warren Burger to Harry Blackmun, n.d., c. May 1963, Box 50, Folder 10, Blackmun MSS; Burger to Blackmun, Labor Day 1967, Box 50, Folder 15, id. ("if," "guys"); Burger to Blackmun, n.d., c. 1961, Box 50, Folder 8, id. ("Bastards," "horrible"); Burger to Blackmun, May 21, 1970, Box 51, Folder 3 ("absurd"); Harry Blackmun to E. Barrett Prettyman, April 10, 1964, Box 50, Folder 12, id. ("scrapper," "many"); Herbert Brownell, Memorandum to General Eisenhower, September 16, 1965, Box 107, Brownell MSS ("As"). "No, indeed, I am not mad," Burger wrote after Blackmun had rejected yet another proposed trip in the early 1960s. "It surely will look funny as Hell when we finally get to that tour with sturdy nurses pushing our wheel chairs and we two fiddle with our hearing aids. I can just hear it: 'What did you say? Girls, what girls, I don't see any girls.'" Warren Burger to Harry Blackmun, May 31, c. 1962, Box 50, Folder 11, Blackmun MSS.

18. Daily Diary, February 4, 1969, RMNL; Richard Nixon, Memorandum for the Attorney General, February 13, 1969, Box 54, Folder 277, Krogh MSS ("ablest"); Richard Kleindienst, Memorandum for John Ehrlichman, February 18, 1969, id. ("fruitful"); Warren Burger to Richard Nixon, March 2, 1969, Box 294, Haldeman Personnel Material, RMNL.

19. Warren Burger to Harry Blackmun, n.d. (c. March 31, 1969), Box 51, Folder 1, Blackmun MSS; Burger to Blackmun, September 17, 1969, Box 51, Folder 2, id.

20. "Nixons Fete Warren at White House."

21. "William Lambert; Pulitzer-Winning Journalist," *LAT*, February 10, 1998 ("father"); Don Oberdorfer, "The Gathering of the Storm That Burst Upon Abe Fortas," *WP*, May 16, 1969; Alan Weinberger, "What's In a Name?—The Tale of Louis Wolfson's Affirmed," 39 *HofLR* 645, 676–78 (2011); U.S. v. Wolfson, 394 U.S. 946 (1969). At the time of the chief justice battle, Robert Griffin had also heard the rumor of Fortas's connection to Wolfson, and his staff had vainly tried to interest the FBI in investigating it. When the FBI's Cartha DeLoach, however, told a Griffin staffer that the FBI could not proceed without the approval of Attorney General Ramsey Clark, the senator's representative replied that Griffin would not pursue the matter because he was sure that Ramsey Clark, who "fully endorsed Fortas," would never approve an investigation that could "discredit him." Laura Kalman, *Abe Fortas: A Biography* (New Haven: Yale University Press, 1990), 360.

22. Bruce Murphy, *Fortas: The Rise and Ruin of a Supreme Court Justice* (New York: Morrow, 1998), 555 (confirmation); Will Wilson, *A Fool for a Client: Richard Nixon's Free Fall Toward Impeachment* (Austin: Eakin, 2000), 18–19. Wilson maintained that he had done nothing wrong in confirming the story. He also said the meeting with Lambert at which he did so occurred after he had met with Wolfson's attorney and been informed of the Fortas–Wolfson relationship and after he had taken Wolfson's statement, which seems unlikely, since other accounts indicate that his confirmation preceded Wolfson's statement. Id., 17. Cf., for example, Murphy, *Fortas*, 556: "The department had yet to see the actual documents about which Lambert was reporting, and had not yet spoken to Wolfson himself. The Nixon official knew, though, that confirming the story anyway would ensure its publication." Wolfson's statement was dated May 10.

23. Time v. Hill, 385 U.S. 374 (1967); OVAL 733-010, June 14, 1972, 2:54 P.M., Nixon, Burger, Sanchez, Bull, Unknown Participant, NT; Kalman, *Abe Fortas*, 363 ("off").

24. Kalman, *Abe Fortas*, 322–25; John Frank, *Clement Haynsworth, the Senate, and the Supreme Court* (Charlottesville: University Press of Virginia, 1991), 13 (see infra for a discussion of Taft). 25. Kalman, *Abe Fortas*, 365;

25. "The Furor Over Fortas," *News*, May 19, 1969. While Hugo Black, whom Fortas consulted during the crisis, refused to say much about their conversations to his friend and former clerk, John Frank, "he was outspoken that Fortas's major tactical error was his statement immediately upon the publication of the *Life* article. Black felt that the only tactical thing to do was to bring out every last bit of the worst of the matter—whatever could be most criticized—voluntarily. This is about what he did in 1937 in the Klan matter. The want of full disclosure at the time of the first statement made the Fortas situation impossible." John Frank, "Visit of May 20, 1969, with Justice Black," n.d., Box 1, Folder 11, 1967–71, Frank MSS. Fortas later agreed he had erred in not fully explaining his relationship with Wolfson quickly. Benjamin Bradlee, "Fortas: 'Wasn't Any Choice for a Man of Conscience,'" *WP*, May 16, 1969.

26. "A Shadow Over the Supreme Court," *WP*, May 6, 1969.

27. William Rehnquist, Memorandum to John Ehrlichman, October 10, 1969, Buchanan Briefing Book, Backup, Box 13, Haynsworth, RMNL ("arrangement"); Robert Jackson, "Congressmen Call on Fortas to Quit," *LAT*, May 6, 1969; John MacKenzie, "Fortas Is Silent as Criticism on Hill Continues," *WP*, May 8, 1969; Robert Shogan, *A Question of Judgment: The Fortas Case and the Struggle for the Supreme Court* (New York: Bobbs-Merrill, 1972), 242–44; Leadership Meeting, May 6, 1969, Box 6, Scott MSS.

28. Jackson, "Congressmen Call on Fortas to Quit"; Ronald Ostrow and Robert Jackson, "Fees Paid to Fortas, Douglas Connected to 1968 Stock Case," *LAT*, May 9, 1969 ("intriguing"); Fred Graham, "Fortas's Old Firm Faces U.S. Inquiry," *NYT*, May 7, 1969 ("quietly"); "Finding of Missing Data in Fortas Safe Probed," *WS*, May 7, 1969; Kalman, *Abe Fortas*, 366–67.

29. "Justice Department Reported Studying Fortas-Wolfson Tie," *NYT*, May 9, 1969; Kalman, *Abe Fortas*, 375; Fred Graham, conversation with Bill Lambert, August 29, 1969, Box 6, Graham MSS; interview with Henry Petersen, December 24, 1969, id.

30. Kalman, *Abe Fortas*, 367.

31. Dean, *The Rehnquist Choice: The Untold Story of the Nixon Appointment That Redefined the Supreme Court*, 9.

32. John Ehrlichman, *Witness to Power: The Nixon Years* (New York: Simon and Schuster, 1982), 116.

33. Schwartz, *Super Chief*, 762 ("can't"); Kalman, *Abe Fortas*, 368-69; "Justice Abe Fortas on the Spot," *News*, May 19, 1969, 29 (Copies were available on the weekend of May 10.); Shogan, *A Question of Judgment*, 252–53.

34. Murphy, *Fortas*, 552–54, 568; Kalman, *Abe Fortas*, 361; Bob Woodward, "Fortas Tie to Wolfson Is Detailed," *WP*, January 23, 1977 ("lighting"); Wolfson Pardon File, Egil Krogh Chron File, Box 1, Memos, April 1969, RMNL. Wolfson's plans to make the correspondence public after he left prison in 1970 upset Fortas, who flew to Florida and talked him out of talked him out of it by warning that the "crooked" and "dirty" would interpret them to mean that Fortas's foundation post "was nothing but a cover-up and that what was really happening was that I was taking a gratuity from you in terms of the statute and

supplementing my salary" and was also practicing law illegally. Unfortunately for Fortas, Wolfson secretly taped the meaning, and the *Post*'s Bob Woodward got hold of the transcript in 1977 and released its highlights. "Things are quiet now and I have reached a point where I think I can resume my life," Fortas told Wolfson. The former justice worried that the public would think he had written Wolfson handwritten letters "because he wanted to hide something." While he understandably hoped the letters would remain "buttoned up," they did not add up to a hard case against him. Woodward, "Fortas Tie to Wolfson Is Detailed."

35. Stanley Penn, "Wolfson's World: Industrialist, Facing a Year in Jail Friday, Turns Cold Shoulder Toward Wall Street," *WSJ*, April 22, 1969.

36. The skeptic is a significant one, the legendary New York District Attorney Robert Morgenthau. Before his retirement in 2009, Morgenthau told a reporter that in investigating Wolfson, he had proceeded "against the wishes of Wolfson's friends in the Kennedy and Johnson administrations" and that he was convinced that LBJ had replaced Nicholas Katzenbach as attorney general in 1966 because "he refused to block Mr. Morgenthau's indictment and subsequent conviction of Wolfson." James Freeman, "The Weekend Interview with Robert Morgenthau: The World's District Attorney," *WSJ*, December 26, 2009; and see Terry Carter, "The Boss," 96 *ABAJ* 35, 39 (June 2010). But there is no reference to Wolfson on any of Johnson's tape-recorded conversations, which appear to cover that moment in the history of his administration intensively, and the relatively small file of letters and memoranda from or about Wolfson in the LBJ Library seems "relatively harmless." Murphy, *Fortas*, 552. Of course, it is impossible to prove a negative, and Johnson could have pressured Katzenbach on Wolfson's behalf, as Morgenthau believed. Still, given his suspicions about Katzenbach's loyalty and how many other sensitive subjects the president was discussing with Katzenbach on tape at the time, it seems likely that he would have done so in a recorded conversation. The tapes and documentary evidence suggest that it is more likely that LBJ got rid of the attorney general because of his frustration over Katzenbach's role in the Bobby Baker and Fred Black cases and his relationship with Robert Kennedy than because Katzenbach did not shut down Wolfson's indictment.

37. Weinberger, "What's in a Name," 672–73; Shogan, *A Question of Judgment*, 263.

38. Kalman, *Abe Fortas*, 370; "The Plot Thickens in the Fortas Affair," *WP*, May 13, 1969; "Slander by Indirection," *NYT*, May 14, 1969; "Fortas," POF, Annotated News Summary, Box 30, Folder 5, RMNL; Max Frankel, "Washington's Dinner Guests Are Served War, Want, and Fortas," *WP*, May 12, 1969; *CR*, May 16, 1969, S 12795 (Remarks of Senator Gore): "A cloud needs to be lifted from the Department of Justice, too. For this Capitol is rife with rumors of the practice of intimidation—even blackmail."

39. Kalman, *Abe Fortas*, 370-71; "At Speech Tonight: Fortas Curbs the Press," *WS*, May 8, 1969 ("The justice's office said the booking agent had been under instruction 'for some time.' But the agent said the instructions had been passed down in the past few days."); John Barnes to William Spong, May 9, 1969, Box 64, Judiciary Supreme Court Fortas 1969, Spong MSS ("actor"). The *Washington Post*'s society reporter noted that journalists and photographers kept the Fortases' R Street mansion "under almost constant 24-hour surveillance." Maxine Cheshire, "VIP: Fortases Cancel Annual Party," *WP*, May 20, 1969.

40. John MacKenzie, "Fortas Bars Speech Amid Talk He'll Quit," *WP*, May 14, 1969; Woodward, "Fortas Tie to Wolfson is Detailed" ("real," "I"); Kalman, *Abe Fortas*, 373-75 ("quite"); Clark Clifford to John Frank, February 3, 1987, Box 24, Folder 20, Clifford MSS ("[s]ome incident"); Clark Clifford with Richard Holbrooke, *Counsel to the President: A Memoir* (New York: Random House, 1991), 558-59. The *Chicago Tribune* reported on Tuesday, May 13, that Fortas had "been given until Wednesday to resign from the Supreme Court or the justice department will release information that administration officials believe will lead to his impeachment. . . The department has sent word to Fortas that he already has 'been extended unusual courtesy' because of the nature of the court and the respect that must be maintained in it. However, he was informed this courtesy is not open-ended and unless he resigns the information will be released." Philip Warden, "Hear Fortas Told: Quit: Ultimatum Attributed to Justice Department," *CT*, May 13, 1969. The *Chicago Tribune* had never been a fan of

Fortas's or the Warren Court's, and its reporters may have had better sources at Nixon's Justice Department than their colleagues at other newspapers.

41. Interviews with Adam Stolpen, January 2014 and January 2016; Email, Adam Stolpen to Laura Kalman, January 6, 2016; Warren Unna, "Congress Greets Fortas Resignation With Relief," *WP*, May 16, 1969 ("foot-dragging"); Frank, *Clement Haynsworth*, at 13 (Taft); "Fortas Case Nearing Close," *WSJ*, May 16, 1969. Stolpen believes the exchange he witnessed occurred over the weekend; the *Post*, in its most complete account of the events leading up to the resignation, put Douglas at Fortas's house Monday night, May 12. *Newsweek* reporter Robert Shogan, who wrote a book about the resignation, had Douglas at Fortas's house on Tuesday night, May 13; and Douglas himself recalled that he "sat up with him [Fortas] two nights" urging him not to resign with some success the first night and none the second, an account Fortas later told a biographer was an "an absolute fabrication." Compare Oberdorfer, "The Gathering of the Storm That Burst Upon Abe Fortas"; Shogan, *A Question of Judgment*, 259; Douglas, *The Court Years*, 358; Murphy, *Fortas*, 571. The reports of sightings of Douglas and others are surely incomplete. The media kept watch at the main entrance to the house on R Street, but there was also a garage entrance to the property off an alley on the south side of the property, which was not visible, through which the couple's friends sometimes entered and which Carol Agger used to elude the press. Kalman, *Abe Fortas*, at 371.

The chain of events leading up to Fortas's actual decision to submit his letter of resignation on the late afternoon of May 14 is not entirely clear, either. On Tuesday, May 13, Fortas met with the other justices to discuss his situation. He spoke of quitting then. Kalman, *Abe Fortas*, 373. When he also abruptly cancelled a speech to the Judicial Conference of the First Circuit scheduled that evening, rumors began circulating that his resignation would come soon. MacKenzie, "Fortas Bars Speech Amid Talk He'll Quit." Shogan said that Fortas summoned his secretary, Gloria Dalton, to begin work on his resignation statement that night. Shogan, *A Question of Justice*, 259. Perhaps Fortas had reached his final decision, although he might simply have wanted to have the letter ready in case he concluded that he needed it.

According to John Dean, who was then still working at Justice, the principals there were getting edgy by the following day. "I was called to the attorney general's office on the morning of May 14, 1969," Dean remembered. "Will Wilson was with John Mitchell; they were discussing the Fortas case, and the weakness of building a criminal case against Fortas. Mitchell told me that if they could not convince Fortas to resign, the Justice Department might formally submit a report to the House of Representative[s] calling for his impeachment." The Attorney General directed Dean "to prepare myself to talk with congressional leaders to determine if there might be bipartisan support for such an undertaking," though Mitchell remained "hopeful that 'his talk with Chief Justice Warren would do the trick.' I was only to familiarize myself with the impeachment process. I left the meeting with the impression there was more interest in scaring the bejesus out of Fortas than successfully prosecuting him." Dean, *The Rehnquist Choice*, 293, n. 34.

That same morning, House Judiciary Committee member Clark MacGregor (R-MN), a Congressional point person on the Fortas matter for the administration, submitted a letter to Celler formally requesting that the Judiciary Committee "initiate a preliminary informal investigation" beginning "at 10:00 A.M. on Tuesday, May 20th and that you as Chairman of the Committee invite Mr. Justice Fortas and Attorney General John N. Mitchell to appear at that time before the full membership of the Committee." Remarks of Representative MacGregor, *CR*, May 14, 1969, H12470. Apparently, Mitchell had already assured MacGregor that he would cooperate, and he did tell newsmen on the evening of May 14 that he "would be delighted to testify." Fred Graham, "Hearing Urged in House," *NYT*, May 15, 1969. The attorney general may even have pressed MacGregor to publicize his letter to raise the heat on Fortas. When Celler got it, he went to the House floor. "Mr. Speaker, obviously I have been much concerned with matters involving Associate Justice Abe Fortas," he said, and he mentioned MacGregor's demand. The ranking Judiciary Committee Republican, William McCulloch of Ohio, and he were "conferring," Celler assured his colleagues, "and shall propose such steps as are appropriate at the proper time. I ask the Members of the House to have patience. Patience is bitter, but sometimes it bears rich fruit." McCulloch then seconded Celler's request. Remarks of Representatives Celler and McCulloch, CR, May 14, 1969, H12452; Aldo Beckman, "Secret Data Made Fortas Break at End: Quit After Move for House Quiz," CT, May 18, 1969.

By the *Tribune* account, Fortas remained optimistic at this point that Celler would prevent a hearing from taking place—"so confident that he permitted his staff, anxious to try to dissuade [sic] public opinion, to release to the press a survey showing that 80 per cent of the mail he had received was favorable to him." Later that day, however, Mitchell met with Celler and McCulloch and showed them his dossier of Fortas-Wolfson materials. Celler now jumped ship. He decided a hearing must occur and that impeachment was the likely outcome. By mid-afternoon, the justice, who "was set out to ride out the storm and resign at the end of the current term," had learned of Celler's change of heart, and had learned that a House investigation, "the one thing that Fortas was determined to avoid. . .was inevitable." Beckman, "Secret Data Made Fortas Break at End." Mitchell refused to answer questions from newsmen on the evening of May 14 about whether he had met with Celler and McCulloch earlier that day (Graham, "Hearing Urged in House"), but it subsequently became clear that he indeed had seen them the afternoon of May 14 (Umma, "Congress Greets Fortas Resignation With Relief"), and he or someone close to him may have given the story to the *Tribune* later.

The *Tribune* story was likely intended to make the case that Fortas was behaving stubbornly and to justify the pressure on him as essential to securing his resignation. It seems more likely to me, as it was to Clifford and Stolpen, that he had definitely decided to resign earlier, particularly since Carol Agger was urging her husband to quit. Kalman, *Abe Fortas*, 372. A proud person, Fortas would have wanted to leave with his head high, and he could have authorized the release of the news about his mail to show he still possessed substantial support.

The White House learned that Fortas was definitely resigning when Warren telephoned at 4:20 on May 14. Nixon heard at 4:45 that Fortas's letter, which arrived by messenger around 5:30, was coming. But because the President had scheduled an address about Vietnam that evening and did not want to distract attention from it, the White House decided to announce it at noon the following day. Oberdorfer, "The Gathering of the Storm that Burst Upon Abe Fortas;" Dean, *The Rehnquist Choice*, 10–11. On the evening of May 14, the *Chicago Tribune* reported, a friend of Nixon's who had once been in Congress, Patrick Hillings, told friends in Congress he spoke with at a party that Fortas was resigning. Philip Warden and Aldo Beckman, "Fortas Agrees to Quit, Nixon Aid [sic] Says," CT, May 15, 1969; Beckman, "Secret Data Made Fortas Break at End."

42. Fred Graham, "Fortas Quits the Supreme Court; Defends Dealings with Wolfson," NYT, May 16, 1969; "Fortas'[s] Letter to Warren on His Ties to Wolfson Foundation," WP, May 16, 1969; Bradlee, "Fortas: 'Wasn't Any Choice for a Man of Conscience:'" "How Fortas Looks at It," NYT, May 16, 1969. Wolfson had also, for example, asked Senator Richard Russell for help with the Justice Department during LBJ's Presidency. Richard Russell to Louis Wolfson, November 18, 1967, Series I, Subseries C, Box 14A, Folder 4, Judiciary, Russell MSS. Among others, Wolfson enlisted Senator Russell Long to make the case for a pardon with Nixon. John Ehrlichman to Russell Long, May 12, 1969, Egil Krogh Chron File, Box 1, Memos, May 1969, RMNL. While the White House and Warren had agreed the former would release news of Fortas's resignation at noon, the court ultimately released it and did so early. "The fact is that Justice Fortas became over-wrought on reading of the release of Wolfson's statement [acknowledging the lifetime contract] in the morning paper, and himself called the Court's press relations man to have him release the news of his resignation," Warren explained to Nixon. "I am sure he would not have been moved to do this under normal conditions. It was really a matter of little importance, but in his troubled state of mind it assumed abnormal importance." Earl Warren to Richard Nixon, May 16, 1969, Box 353, Fortas, Warren MSS. See Ronald Ostrow and Robert Jackson, "$20,000-a-Year Lifetime Offer to Fortas Told: Prison Statement to FBI by Wolfson Says Jurist Agreed to Take Retainer," LAT, May 15, 1969; John MacKenzie, "Wolfson Airs Fee to Fortas: $20,000 Set As Annual Fee, He Tells FBI," WP, May 15, 1969.

43. Robert Donovan, "The Sounds of Silence: A Saddened Capital Ponders Question of Corrupt Society," LAT, May 16, 1969; Sidney Zion, "The Court Crisis: Shadow of Impropriety Over a Great Institution," NYTMag, May 18, 1969; Robert Jackson, "Senators Demand Full Fortas Story: But Doubts Arise as to Vigor of Justice Department Investigation," LAT, May

17, 1969; "The Fortas Case Cannot Be Closed," *WP*, May 18, 1969; Christopher Lydon, "Wolfson File Inactive," *NYT*, July 21, 1969; John MacKenzie, "Fortas Breached Ethics, ABA Says," *WP*, May 21, 1969. "I passed the ball yesterday to Mr. Celler, and he elected to drop it today," MacGregor told reporters the day after news of Fortas's resignation had become public, and Celler had told reporters that "[a]s far as the Judiciary Committee is concerned, it is a closed chapter." "Congress, Showing Relief, Drops Fortas Inquiry Plan," *NYT*, May 16, 1969 (quoting Celler and MacGregor). The chairman of the Sitting Committee on Professional Ethics, Walter Armstrong, did not participate in drafting the informal opinion. The remaining seven members agreed that Fortas's behavior violated the canons. They divided, however, over the value of making the report public, with five of them making the case for release, and two arguing against. Benton Gates to William Gossett, May 18, 1969, Gossett MSS; "American Bar Committee Says Fortas Violated Judicial Ethics Canons, May 20, 1969, id.

44. "One Down, How Many More to Go?," *CT*, May 17, 1969 (and see "Douglas Must Go," id., May 22, 1969; "Fortas Fallout," *HE*, May 24, 1969); "A Salutary Reform," *NYT*, May 24, 1969 ("nothing"); Barnard Collier, "Douglas Says Tax Inquiry Aims to Get Him off Court," id., May 26, 1969; Ronald Ostrow and Robert Jackson, "Douglas Letter to Parvin Sharpens Court Controversy," *LAT*, May 27, 1969; George Lardner, "Celler Raps Douglas on Letter to Parvin," *WP*, May 28, 1969; Strom Thurmond Reports to the People: "Douglas Is Next," Press Release 15, no. 19, Thurmond MSS; Thurmond to Claude Ragsale, May 28, 1969, Correspondence, 1969, Box 28, Nominations 3, id.; Jack Caulfield to John Ehrlichman, "Newspapers Investigate Possible Justice Douglas Impropriety," June 4, 1969, Box 39, Folder 510, Supreme Court (2), Ehrlichman MSS.

45. Abe Fortas to William O. Douglas, May 28, 1969, Box 1782, Abe Fortas, Douglas MSS; Zion, "The Court Crisis."

46. Fred Graham, "Warren Seeking a Code of Ethics," *NYT*, May 23, 1969 ("move"); Robert Jackson, "Judges Meet to Frame First Code of Ethics for U.S. Bench," *LAT*, May 25, 1969.

47. John MacKenzie, "Warren Is Seeking Strict Code," *WP*, May 30, 1969; "The Honor of the Court," *NYT*, June 15, 1969; "Warren on Modernizing the Courts," *WP*, June 5, 1969; Fred Graham, "Warren Is Accused of Pushing Through New Judges' Code," *NYT*, June 13, 1969 ("rammed"); Charles Wyzanski to Earl Warren, May 19, 1969, Box 719, Ethics, Warren MSS; and see Judge Robert Ainsworth, "Judicial Ethics—A Crisis of Confidence," *OB*, September 14, 1969, Box 720, Ethics: General Correspondence, id.

48. John Frank to Elizabeth and Hugo Black, July 15, 1969, Box 462, John Frank, Black MSS; Earl Warren to Robert Ainsworth, October 1, 1969, Box 719, Ethics, Warren MSS; and see, for example, Henry Friendly to Judge Lumbard, n.d., Box 529, Ethics, Harlan MSS (complaining that the resolution forced federal judges "to go through the humiliating task of begging permission to receive compensation for teaching, for giving established lectures, for writing books"; that it failed to provide judges with "elementary due process"; and that it was "exceedingly ill-considered").

49. Warren to Ainsworth, October 1, 1969 ("I," embarrassment); John Mackenzie, "Warren Fails to Get Ethics Code Now," *WP*, June 18, 1969 ("persuasive").

50. "Ethics and the Supreme Court," *LAT*, June 19, 1969; William O. Douglas, "Appeal of Folk Singing: A Landmark Opinion," *AG*, March 7, 1969; "Tydings Assails Supreme Court for Inaction on Code of Ethics," *WP*, June 19, 1969.

51. Warren Burger to Richard Nixon, May 8, 1969, WHCF EX FG 51, Box 1, Folder 1, RMNL (emphasis in the original).

52. POF, Pat Buchanan, Memorandum to the President, May 21, 1969, One Observer's Notes of Legislative Leadership Meeting, May 20, 1969, May 21, 1969, Box 78, RMNL; Ehrlichman, *Witness to Power*, 117.

53. Ehrlichman, *Witness to Power*, 117; Robert Donovan, "Nixon Nominates His Chief Justice," *LAT*, May 22, 1969; H. R. Haldeman, *The Haldeman Diaries: Inside the Nixon White House* (New York: G. P. Putnam's Sons, 1994), 60–61; Remarks Announcing the Nomination of Judge Warren Earl Burger to Be Chief Justice of the United States, May 21, 1969, http://www.presidency.ucsb.edu/ws/?pid=2063.

54. Conversation with Newsmen on the Nomination of the Chief Justice, May 22, 1969, http://www.presidency.ucsb.edu/ws/index.php?pid=2065&st=nixon&st1=burger id.; John MacKenzie, "Fortas's Presence on High Court Deterred Stewart From Top Job," *WP*, May 28, 1969. Nixon explained in his memoir, "As the search continued, I developed five criteria for the selection process. The next Chief Justice must have a top-flight legal mind; he must be young enough to serve at least ten years; he should, if possible, have experience both as a practicing lawyer and as an appeals court judge; he must generally share my view that the Court should interpret the Constitution rather than amend it by judicial fiat; and he must have a special quality of leadership that would enable him to resolve differences among his colleagues, so that, as often as possible, the Court would speak decisively on major cases with one voice or at least with a strong voice for the majority opinion." Richard Nixon, *RN: The Memoirs of Richard Nixon* (New York: Grossett & Dunlap, 1978), 419. Nixon mentioned Eastland's warning to Burger in OVAL 733-010, June 14, 1972, NT, Burger.

55. Conversation with Newsmen on the Nomination of the Chief Justice, May 22, 1969.

56. See chapter 7; MacKenzie, "Fortas's Presence on High Court Deterred Stewart From Top Job": "Many close observers of the Court considered Stewart to have been, in addition to the Justice most eligible for promotion, the one least likely to stir the human jealousies of his colleagues."

57. Ehrlichman, *Witness to Power*, 113; Conversation with Newsmen on the Nomination of the Chief Justice, May 22, 1969 (FBI); Richard Kleindienst, *Justice: The Memoirs of Attorney General Richard Kleindienst* (Ottawa: Jameson, 1985), 112–13 (tax returns); Duscha, "Chief Justice Burger Asks: 'If It Doesn't Make Good Sense, How Can It Make Good Law?'" (health); OVAL 733-010, June 14, 1972 (health); Donovan, "Nixon Nominates His Chief Justice" (Mansfield).

58. Bob Woodward and Scott Armstrong, *The Brethren: Inside the Supreme Court* (New York: Simon and Schuster, 1979), 11 (Warren); John MacKenzie, "Burger, a 'Law and Order' Judge, Seen in Running for High Court," *WP*, April 29, 1969; Dean, *The Rehnquist Choice*, 14 ("run").

59. OVAL 733-10, June 14, 1972; Harry Blackmun to George Register, May 28, 1969, Box 90, Folder 6, Blackmun MSS; Kleindienst, *Justice*, 114 ("dazed").

60. Blackmun to Register, May 28, 1969; Pat Buchanan, Memorandum to the President, May 6, 1959, WHCF, Box 1, Folder 1, EX FG 51.

61. John MacKenzie, "Burger Got $6000 From Foundation," *WP*, May 23, 1969 John MacKenzie, *The Appearance of Justice* (New York: Charles Scribner's Sons, 1974), 162; Nomination of Warren E. Burger, 1 (ABA rating); Bryce Harlow, Memorandum for the President: Appointment of Chief Justice, May 22, 1969, WHCF EX FG 51, Box 1, Folder 9, RMNL; Herbert Klein, Memorandum for the President, May 27, 1969, WHCF EX FG 51/A, Box 3, Folder 4, id. ("We have found no editorial wholly critical of the nomination."); Alexander Butterfield to John Ehrlichman, June 2, 1969, Box 65, Folder 277-0A 3032, Krogh MSS ("of course"); Earl Maltz, *The Chief Justiceship of Warren Burger* (Columbia: University of South Carolina Press, 2000), 10 ("Conservatives").

62. Meeting: The President and Kleindienst, EOB, April 15, 1973, 11:12 P.M., *The Presidential Transcripts* (New York: Dell, 1974), 376, 386, 392, 400 ("Incidentally," Burger's support for Chicago lawyer Barnabas Sears); John MacKenzie, "Crossing the Judicial Line," *WP*, June 13, 1974; Linda Mathews, "Transcripts Indicate Kleindienst Got Burger's Advice in Scandal," *LAT*, May 3, 1974 (John Frank).

63. Lou Cannon, "The Last 17 Days of the Nixon Reign," *WP*, September 29, 1974 ("reportedly"); Bob Woodward and Scott Armstrong, "The Tapes Case: A Revolt Against Burger," *WP*, December 7, 1979; Woodward and Armstrong, *The Brethren*, 309–47. On the basis of his reading of the documents from the period, Justice Powell's authorized biographer, John Jeffries, deemed the account of the Nixon Tapes case in *The Brethren* "a surprisingly complete and accurate account of the evolution of the Court's opinion" that represented "a triumph of investigative reporting." John Jeffries, *Justice Lewis F. Powell, Jr.: A Biography* (New York: Fordham, 2001), 392.

64. T. R. Reid, "Leak Places High Court in Dilemma," *WP*, April 27, 1977 (quotations); "High Court Reported to Oppose a Review of Nixon Aides' Case," *NYT*, April 22, 1977; William Safire, "Equal Justice Under Leak," *NYT*, April 28, 1977; Morton Mintz, "Court Bars

Review on Watergate," *WP*, May 24, 1977. See also Stephen Wermiel, "High Court Holds Very Low Opinion of Its Recent Leak: Book Next Month Could Lead to Even Tighter Secrecy: Disclosures Involve Burger," *WSJ*, November 26, 1979. The *New York Post* speculated that the source was Justice Stewart, who was "said to be a close friend of Totenberg's," with a leering innuendo that Totenberg accurately characterized as "sexist." Stewart's secretary denied he was the source. "Leak Places High Court in Dilemma." As Totenberg said, when she wrote Stewart to apologize for embarrassing him: "You and I know perfectly well that this sort of speculation would never have occurred if a man had broken this story." Nina Totenberg to Potter Stewart, April 28, 1977, Box 598, Folder 322, Stewart MSS.

65. Ehrlichman, *Witness to Power*, 133; Phil Gailey, "Mitchell Challenges Ehrlichman Account," *NYT*, December 11, 1981; "CBS Says Burger Knocked Camera From Man's Hands," *WP*, December 17, 1981; "Burger Says Ehrlichman Selling Book," id., December 18, 1981; Linda Greenhouse, "The Issues All Justices Confront out of Court," *NYT*, December 11, 1981.

66. Seymour Hersh, "Nixon's Last Cover-Up: The Tapes He Wants the Archives to Suppress," *NY*, December 14, 1992, 76, 81. Nixon stalled on releasing his papers too. Stanley Kutler, "What Is Nixon Still Hiding? Sixteen Years After Watergate, He Still Won't Release His Papers," *WP*, January 10, 1988.

67. WHT 035-051, January 2, 1973, 8:30 A.M., Nixon, Burger, NT.

68. Dean, *The Nixon Defense*, 129–30, 136.

69. WHT 046-138, May 22, 1973, 9:27 A.M., Nixon, Burger, NT; Earl Warren to Benjamin Swig, Box 119, Box 119, Chief Justice Personal, Warren MSS; and see James Reston, "A New Problem for President," *NYT*, October 11, 1973 (reporting Burger as a possibility).

70. Dwight, Message for the President, May 22, 1970, WHCF EX FG 51, Box 1, Folder 3, RMNL; Warren Burger to Richard Nixon, April 30, 1970, PPF, Box 6, Burger, RMNL; Richard Reeves, *President Nixon: Alone in the White House* (New York: Simon and Schuster, 2001), 321; PPF, Warren Burger to Richard Nixon, May 10, 1971, Box 6, Burger, RMNL; Warren Burger to Harry Blackmun, September 17, 1969, Box 51, Folder 2, Blackmun MSS.

71. "Burger is Sworn as Chief Justice; Warren Praised," *NYT*, June 24, 1969; Remarks at the Swearing In of Warren E. Burger as Chief Justice of the United States, June 23, 1969, http://www.presidency.ucsb.edu/ws/?pid=2017. See, for example, Address to the Nation Announcing Intention to Nominate Lewis F. Powell, Jr., and William H. Rehnquist to be Associate Justices of the Supreme Court of the United States, October 21, 1971, http://www.presidency.ucsb.edu/ws/index.php?pid=3196&st=powell&st1=rehnquist: "We have had many historic, and even sometimes violent, debates throughout our history about the role of the Supreme Court in our Government. But let us never forget that respect for the Court, as the final interpreter of the law, is indispensable if America is to remain a free society."

Chapter 6

1. John Ehrlichman, *Witness to Power: The Nixon Years* (New York: Simon and Schuster, 1982), 115; Donald Stephenson, *Campaigns and the Court: The U.S. Supreme Court in Presidential Elections* (New York: Columbia University Press, 1999), 183–84 ("opening"); Garrison Nelson with Maggie Steakley and James Montague, *Pathways to the US Supreme Court: From the Arena to the Monastery* (New York: Palgrave Macmillan, 2013), 117.

2. Barbara Perry, *A "Representative" Supreme Court? The Impact of Race, Religion, and Gender on Appointments* (New York: Greenwood, 1991), 78; "Mansfield Vows Close Study of Future Court Nominees; 'Jewish Seat' Opposed by Goldberg," *WP*, David Stebenne, *Arthur J. Goldberg: New Deal Liberal* (New York: Oxford University Press, 1996), 375–76. Dorothy Goldberg felt differently. "The Fortas case is just too hurting and painful to think and talk about—hurting to the court, hurting to the ethical distances that high office necessarily impose, hurting to the Jewish community that must be like Caesar's wife all the time: purer the pure," she wrote her children. "Dad may say that the seat is not a Jewish seat, that he thought we had outgrown such a provincialism, that a justice has to be chosen for merit and not his religious affiliation—but there is too much picking and probing and trying to find others similarly vulnerable as Fortas for anyone to believe that there is not also an anti-Jewish exultance

in the atmosphere." Dorothy Goldberg to Darlings, May 21, 1969, Part II, Box 1, Folder 1, Goldberg MSS.

3. Conversation with Newsmen on the Nomination of the Chief Justice, May 22, 1969, http://www.presidency.g.ucsb.edu/ws/?pid=2065. Nevertheless, William Safire urged Nixon to avoid the subject of the "Jewish seat" altogether. "If the President is not going to appoint a Jew, nothing he says beforehand is going to placate that community. People like Arthur Goldberg may say publicly that this should not be a consideration, but deep down few Jews believe this. If the President is going to appoint a Jew, he should not say beforehand that no ethnic considerations apply, because he will seem to be trying to lay the groundwork for not appointing one, and then seem to be changing his mind under pressure." Safire to H. R. Haldeman, Presentation of Supreme Court Appointments, May 20, 1969, WHCF EX FG 51A, Box 3, Folder 4, RMNL.

4. John Dean, *The Rehnquist Choice: The Untold Story of the Nixon Appointment That Redefined the Supreme Court* (New York: Free Press, 2001), 147–48.

5. Id., 15–16; Harry Dent, Memorandum for the President, May 26, 1969, WHCF EX FG 51/A, Box 3, Folder 4, RMNL; Matt Lassiter, *The Silent Majority: Suburban Politics in the Sunbelt South* (Princeton, NJ: Princeton University Press, 2006), 232–39.

6. Richard Nixon to John Jeffries, March 15, 1990, Carton 319, Retirement Subject Files: Biography, Powell MSS.

7. B. J. Phillips, "'A Gentle Man': Clement Furman Haynsworth," *WP*, September 7, 1969; Ernest Hollings with Kirk Victor, *Making Government Work* (Columbia: University of South Carolina Press, 2008), 14 (Johns). "We have an extremely pleasant life in Greenville," Haynsworth wrote an acquaintance. "We live in the house we always dreamed of. We would not swap it for anything, and we dread the thought of being uprooted." Clement Haynsworth to Charles Alan Wright, August 22, 1969, Haynsworth MSS.

8. Clement Haynsworth to Brainerd Chapman, August 4, 1969, Haynsworth MSS ("fire"); Clement Haynsworth to Elizabeth Hirsch, August 5, 1969, id. ("Wishing," "When").

9. Nomination of Clement Haynsworth, 138-40; Clement Haynsworth to Warren Burger, September 20, 1969, Haynsworth MSS; William Brennan to Judge and Mrs. Haynsworth, id., August 10, 1969; Byron White to Haynsworth, id., September 10, 1969; Black to John Frank, September 8, 1969, id.; John Harlan to Clement Haynsworth, August 19, 1969, Box 549, Haynsworth, Harlan MSS; Thurgood Marshall to S. Sidney Ulmer, November 7, 1983, Box 34, Folder 2, T. Marshall MSS ("I consider Judge Haynsworth as one of the greatest of Federal judges and for that reason I have great respect for him"); John Frank, *Clement Haynsworth, the Senate and the Supreme Court* (Charlottesville: University Press of Virginia, 1991), 28.

10. James Heath, *To Face Down Dixie: South Carolina's War on the Supreme Court* (DPhil, University of Warwick, 2015), 254; Lewis Powell to William Spong, November 4, 1969, Box 288, Folder 10, Powell MSS; "Possible High Court Choice Hit," *WP*, August 7, 1969; Frank, *Clement Haynsworth*, 20, 21 ("zealous"); Hollings, *Making Government Work*, 143, 145; Bruce Kalk, *The Origins of the Southern Strategy: Two-Party Competition in South Carolina, 1950-1972* (Lanham: Lexington Books, 2001), 102 (legislature); Richard Harwood, "Haynsworth's Defeat: 'Contemporary Man'?," *WP*, November 23, 1969 (J. P. Stevens); William Eaton, "Why Haynsworth Lost: AFL-CIO Opposition Lit Fuse," *CDN*, November 22/23, 1969, reprinted in *The Pulitzer Prize Archive: National Reporting, 1941-1986*, ed. Heinz-Dietrich Fisher II: 200 (Munich: KG Saur, 1988); Fred Graham, "Nixon and His Motives: Politics and Attitude on Crime Viewed as Possible Reasons for Court Choice," *NYT*, August 19, 1969. Haynsworth had also written an imaginative habeas decision that the Warren Court emphatically affirmed. Rowe v. Peyton, 383 F. 2d 70, 715 (1967); Peyton v. Rowe, 391 U.S. 54, 57-58 (1968).

11. John MacKenzie, "Nixon May Delay Court Appointment Until August," *WP*, July 20, 1969 (Haynsworth a "leading contender"); Michael Parrish, *Citizen Rauh: An American Liberal's Life in Law and Politics* (Ann Arbor: University of Michigan Press, 2011), 4, 226–29; Eaton, "Why Haynsworth Lost"; E. W. Kenworthy, "The Haynsworth Issue: A Study in Pressure Politics," *NYT*, November 21, 1969; "Civil Libertarians Hit Haynsworth Selection," *WP*, August 19, 1969. Not all groups in the Leadership Conference on Civil Rights joined in the

opposition. The Anti-Defamation League and ACLU abstained "because we do not wish to prevent the Leadership Conference from taking a position on this matter." Sol Rabkin to Arnold Aronson, September 3, 1969, Part 1, Box 105, Folder 5, Leadership Conference MSS. See, for example, "Memorandum of Leadership Conference on Civil Rights Concerning Judge Haynsworth," September 9, 1969, Part 1, Box 105, Folder 5, id.

12. Daniel Grove and Louis Natali, to Dear Sir, August 16, 1969, Box 6, Folder 5, Eaton MSS; Simkins v. Moses H. Cone Memorial Hospital, 323 F. 2d 959, 971 (1963); Dillard v. School Board of City of Charlottesville, 308 F. 2d 920, 927 (1962); Griffin v. Board of Supervisors of Prince Edward County, 332 F. 2d 332 (1963); Griffin v. County School Board of Prince Edward County, 377 U.S. 218, 234 (1964); Bowman v. County School Board of Charles County, Virginia, 382 F. 2d 326 (1967); "Judges: The Haynsworth Record," *Ti*, October 17, 1969 (delay); Kalk, *The Origins of the Southern Strategy*, 102-3. Parker's gloss on Brown came to be known as the "Parker Principle." Kenneth Goings, *The NAACP Comes of Age: The Defeat of Judge John J. Parker* (Bloomington: Indiana University Press, 1990), 85–87.

13. "Although labor and civil rights forces, and some senators remained convinced throughout that Haynsworth's judicial philosophy was the key issue, it was commonly understood in the Senate that there would have been no threat to the nomination if ethics had not been made central. That was the legacy of the Fortas resignation, as most senators saw it." Lyle Denniston, "Haynsworth Vote: The Anatomy of a Nominee's Defeat," *WS*, November 23, 1969.

14. Lamar Alexander to Bryce Harlow, n.d., Box 10, Haynsworth, Harlow MSS, RMNL (lack of vetting); William Eaton, "Nixon to Tighten Judicial Screening of U.S. Judicial Appointments," *CDN*, October 6, 1969 ("once-over"); Darlington Manufacturing Company v. National Labor Relations Board, 325 F. 2d 682 (1963); Textile Workers Union of America v. Darlington Manufacturing Co., 380 U.S. 263 (1965); Frank, *Clement Haynsworth*, 22; William Eaton, "Haynsworth's Dual Role in Case Is Cited," *CDN*, August 16, 1969; Eaton, "Haynsworth Attacked by AFL-CIO Attorney," id., August 30, 1969; Nomination of Clement Haynsworth, 106–7, 13–15; John MacKenzie, "Kennedy Disputes Testimony RFK 'Cleared' Haynsworth," *WP*, September 18, 1969; Eaton, "Why Haynsworth Lost." "There is a widespread impression that Haynsworth was nominated after sloppy staff work, that had Attorney General Mitchell checked more carefully into the judge's business dealings he would never have been picked," a reporter observed in 1970. "But Mitchell now flatly denies this. 'There was an F.B.I. check, and there were no surprises, except for the intensity of the opposition.'" The FBI check was not apparently that thorough and there were other surprises. John Steele, "Haynsworth v. The U.S. Senate," *Fort*, March 1970.

15. "Washington Wire," *WSJ*, August 1, 1969; Eaton, "Why Haynsworth Lost" (Dirksen); Richard Harwood, "Haynsworth's Defeat," *WP*, November 23, 1969 (Leonard); James Wooten, "Carolinian Seen in Line for the Court," *NYT*, August 13, 1969; E. W. Kenworthy, "The Haynsworth Issue," (Meany); "A.J.C. Opposes Judge," *NYT*, August 16, 1969; William Eaton, "Haynsworth Rapped by Rights Groups," *CDN*, August 14, 1969; "Haynsworth Says U.S. Inquiry Cleared Him of Union Charges," *NYT*, August 16, 1969.

16. Neil Sheehan, "C.F. Haynsworth Named by Nixon for High Court," *NYT*, August 19, 1969; Frank, *Clement Haynsworth*, 22, 26–27; "Mr. Justice Haynsworth," *NYT*, August 19, 1969 (quotations); Warren Weaver, "Rights and Labor Leaders Oppose Nomination," id., August 19, 1969; "Labor to Oppose Senate Confirmation of Judge Haynsworth," *NYT*, August 21, 1969; Roy Wilkins to Members of the Board of Directors, August 21, 1969, Part IX, Box 16, Folder 1, NAACP MSS; G. A. Gallenthin, "The Effect of Interest Groups on the Confirmation of Clement F. Haynsworth of South Carolina, To Be Associate Justice of the Supreme Court of the United States," December 25, 1970, Part IX, Box 16, Folder 3, id.

17. John Hohenberg, ed., *The Pulitzer Prize Story II: Award-Winning News Stories, Columns, Editorials, Cartoons and News Pictures, 1959-1980* (New York: Columbia University Press), 318 ("charm"); William Eaton, "Why Haynsworth Lost"; Eaton, "Haynsworth's Stock Holdings Put at Million," *WP*, September 16, 1969 ("socialite"); Eaton, "How Profits of Haynsworth's Firm Soared," *CDN*, August 26, 1969; Gallenthin, "The Effect of Interest Groups on the Confirmation of Clement Haynsworth" (citing author's contemporary interview with Eaton about the friend and Eaton's remark that "these were published in order

to stir public opinion and require Haynsworth to expose his finances before the upcoming Senate Judiciary Committee"); Clement Haynsworth to Circuit Judges, August 21, 1969, Box 13, Clement Haynsworth, Sobeloff MSS: "With all of the flurry news of my appointment has occasioned, I do not know whether I can look forward to the pleasure of being with you on the Fourth Circuit in the future. If I am confirmed, I would leave the Fourth Circuit with the greatest regret, for I have been extremely happy in my associations. I would much prefer to work and debate with you fellows than with the Supreme Court Justices, and the Supreme Court would be really enticing to me only if I could take all of you with me. . . . If Judge [Harrison] Winter is shortly to succeed me as Chief Judge, it seems to me that he would benefit by assuming the routine duties of that office now when I am available for discussion with him when he would like it, and it would be a great relief to me."

18. John MacKenzie, "Haynsworth Hearings Delayed for a Week," WP, September 9, 1969; William Eaton, "Haynsworth Battle: Judge's Foes Lack Leader," CDN, August 20, 1969; Eaton, "Why Haynsworth Lost"; Richard Lyons, "Man in the News: Indiana's Long-Winning Liberal," NYT, July 26, 1980("All-American"). "I could see the gathering storm and then Senator Dirksen died and we had to move fast," Hollings wrote a Haynsworth supporter. "The Administration sat back as if they knew how to handle the situation and we never got back in the ball park."Ernest Hollings to Robert Small, November 28, 1969, Box 127, Haynsworth General Pro (3), Hollings MSS.

19. William Eaton, "Haynsworth Pays Visit to Senate," CDN, September 5, 1969 (quoting a "Senate insider" as saying of the visits, "It may not be traditional—but it's smart"); Fred Graham, "Haynsworth Confirmation Faces Little Opposition in the Senate," NYT, September 4, 1969 (Javits). Haynsworth described Harry Haynsworth as "my staff" in a June 26, 1971, conversation with John Frank, Haynsworth MSS.

20. Eaton, "Why Haynsworth Lost" ("battery," "lucky"); Ronald Ostrow, "Haynsworth Stock Purchase During Firm's Case Disclosed," LAT, September 21, 1969; Nomination of Clement Haynsworth, 128; Frank, Clement Haynsworth, 43. Though Nixon press secretary Ron Ziegler "seemed to imply that the Administration may have known in advance of Bayh's questioning that Haynsworth acquired the Brunswick shares before his court ruling was announced, . . . a Justice Department source said this was definitely not the case. 'We spent a frantic Thursday night,' this source said, referring to efforts to collect information about Haynsworth's ownership of Brunswick." Ronald Ostrow, "Haynsworth Recalled to Testify in Stock Purchase Controversy," LAT, September 23, 1969.

21. Nomination of Clement Haynsworth, 37, 590–625 (the three supporting witnesses were Charles Wright of the University of Texas Law School, G. W. Foster of the University of Wisconsin, and William Van Alstyne of Duke); Frank, Clement Haynsworth, 52–53; Fred Graham, "Haynsworth Talks of Vending Business Before Senate Unit," NYT, September 17, 1969. For the testimony of Haynsworth's broker, Arthur McCall, see Nomination of Clement Haynsworth, 263–70.

22. Graham, "Haynsworth Bought Stock After Ruling for Company," NYT, September 21, 1969; Graham, "No Impropriety, Haynsworth Says," NYT, September 24, 1969; James Wieghart, "Haynsworth Linked to Realty Deals," CDN, September 30, 1969; William Eaton, "New Double-Sale Real Estate Deal by Haynsworth Bared," CDN, November 10, 1969; Warren Weaver, "The Case Against Judge Haynsworth: Three Ethical Questions," NYT, October 21, 1969; Christopher Lydon, "White House Denies Any Haynsworth-Baker Link," id., October 5, 1969; Memorandum for the File: Reports and Rumors About Relationship Between Haynsworth and Robert G. (Bobby) Baker, October 4, 1969, Box 39, Supreme Court (2), Ehrlichman MSS.

23. Frank, Clement Haynsworth, 40-45 ("makeweight". As Frank conceded, "Brunswick, while involving an insubstantial amount, was at least arguably more open to criticism" than Vend-a-Matic. Id., 93); John Maltese, The Selling of Supreme Court Nominees (Baltimore: Johns Hopkins, 1995), 73 ("relatively"); John MacKenzie, "Senate Backers of Haynsworth's Reply to Charges," WP, September 11, 1969 (citing release of news about Rehnquist memorandum by Haynsworth's backer, Senator Hruska, as "the latest in a series of extraordinary moves by Judiciary Committee members"); Fred Graham, "Bar Unit Endorses Haynsworth Again,

but Vote Is Divided," *NYT*, October 13, 1979; Kalk, *The Origins of the Southern Strategy*, 106 ("retreated," "insensitive"); Nomination of Clement Haynsworth, 81, 470–71.

24. "Haynsworth Nomination," *TNR*, October 4, 1969, 7; Herblock, "Ethics Are for Liberals," October 3, 1969; *Herblock: The Life and Work of the Great Political Cartoonist with a DVD Containing Over 18,000 of His Major Cartoons*, ed. Haynes Johnson and Harry Katz (New York: Herblock Foundation and Library of Congress in association with W. W. Norton, 2009); Nomination of Clement Haynsworth, 163, 465, 423.

25. Nomination of Clement Haynsworth, 81; Tom Connaughton and Bob Keefe, "Judge Haynsworth's Conflicts of Interest," n.d., Judiciary Committee Nominations, Supreme Court Haynsworth Working File 1969, Bayh MSS.

26. Pat Buchanan, "The Forgotten Americans," July 1969, WHCF, EX FG 51, Box 1, Folder 1, RMNL; Jeffries, *Justice Lewis F. Powell, Jr,* 225 (Rehnquist); John MacKenzie, "Haynsworth Proposes Custody of Holdings," *WP*, October 7, 1969; "None of the Things My Client Did Were Wrong," October 8, 1969; Johnson and Katz, *Herblock*; Herb Block, "Herblock's History—Political Cartoons From the Crash to the Millennium," http://www.loc.gov/exhibits/herblocks-history/cartoon.html; Hollings, *Making Government Work*, 148–49 ("payback," "five votes"); "The Confirmation of Judge Haynsworth," *WP*, September 29, 1969; Clarence Mitchell and Joseph Rauh, Letters to the Editor: "The Case Against Judge Haynsworth," *WP*, October 5, 1969 ("Ultimately the position of the *Washington Post* seems to rest on it having urged the confirmation of Justice Fortas a year ago, and hence feels embarrassed to oppose Judge Haynsworth."). "A Way Out of the Haynsworth Affair," *WP*, October 9, 1969; "The Senate and the Judge," *NYT*, September 27, 1969; ". . . And Again, Judge Haynsworth," id., October 6, 1969.

27. John Masaro, *Supremely Political: The Role of Ideology and Presidential Management in Unsuccessful Supreme Court Nominations* (Albany: State University of New York Press, 1990), 80–81, 87; Warren Weaver, "Two Senators Split on Haynsworth: Williams of Delaware Says He Is Against Nominee, Aiken to Vote for Him," *NYT*, November 20, 1969; Bryce Harlow, Memorandum for the President, October 20, 1969, WHCF, Name File, Clement Haynsworth (4), RMNL ("On the Republican side the key vote is Williams. If he votes 'aye' he will influence Aiken [VT], Boggs [DEL], Cooper [KY], Dole [KS], Jordan [IDA] and Prouty [VT]." Ultimately, Aiken, Boggs, Dole, and Jordan all voted yes, and Cooper and Jordan voted no); Carol Hoffecker, *Honest John Williams: U.S. Senator from Delaware* (Newark: University of Delaware, 2000), 9, 222–23; Margaret Chase Smith to Richard Nixon, September 30, 1969, WHCF EX FG 51/A, Box 3, Folder 7, RMNL; John Ehrlichman for the President, October 13, 1969, id. (Brunswick); Statement of Senator Joseph D. Tydings, October 9, 1969, Box 127, Supreme Court Nominations, Clement Haynsworth (2), Hollings MSS; Clark Mohlenhoff to Clement Haynsworth, November 28, 1969, Haynsworth MSS ("smokescreen").

28. Steele, "Haynsworth v. The U.S. Senate" ("Abe"); Joe Rauh to Dear Senator, Box 35, Folder 5, Rauh MSS; Nomination of Clement Haynsworth, 354 ("altar boy"); Louis Harris, "Haynsworth Opposed by 53% in Poll," *WP*, November 17, 1969. Spencer Rich, "Fortas Impact Is Hurting Haynsworth," *WP*, November 16, 1969.

29. William Rehnquist, Memorandum for John Ehrlichman, October 10, 1969, Box 39, Supreme Court, Ehrlichman MSS; "Haynsworth's Past and Fortas's Not Alike, White House Asserts," *NYT*, October 12, 1969.

30. Paul Porter to Clement Haynsworth, November 25, 1969, Haynsworth MSS; Marshall Frady, "Haynsworth of Greenville," *Li*, October 31, 1969; John Frank to Haynsworth, November 12, 1969, Haynsworth MSS ("spook"); Ernest Hollings to Leon Wolfstone, October 16, 1969, Box 127, Supreme Court Judges, Clement Haynsworth Pro (1), Hollings MSS; Warren Weaver, "Eastland Assails 'Liberal Press' as Haynsworth Debate Opens," *NYT*, November 14, 1969; Harry Haynsworth to Marshall Frady, November 7, 1969, Haynsworth MSS. Haynsworth himself wrote Frady that while "many Greenvillians are in a state of apoplexy and consternation," others thought it "not as bad as it might have been, while still others are pleased that it makes me appear a very different kind of man than Mr. Justice Fortas." Clement Haynsworth to Frady, November 7, 1969, id. He said the media was "substantially" to blame for his defeat in a December 3, 1987 interview with Robert Morris,

Series II, Morris MSS. See Kalk, *The Origins of the Southern Strategy*, 108, for Administration feeling about the press. Herbert Klein to Ben Bradlee, October 27, 1969, WHCF, Name File, Clement Haynsworth (1), RMNL (accusing *Post* of burying endorsement of Haynsworth by sixteen former American Bar Association residents and trumpeting poll by American Trial Lawyers Association that opposed him); Assistant Attorney General Johnnie Walters to C. Stanley Blair, December 9, 1969, Box 1, Nominations and Appointments, 1969-1987, Walters MSS (complaining about the *Post's* November 20, 1969 "five-column article with a five-column headline reading 'Montgomery [Maryland] Teachers Oppose Haynsworth.'").

31. Jules Witcover, "Hugh Scott—Pussycat on a Hot Tin Roof," *WP*, February 24, 1975; Kenworthy, "The Haynsworth Issue" ("alone" "40"); "Haynsworth Case: Senator Birch Bayh's Bill of Particulars and Senator Ernest F. Hollings' Detailed Answer," November 18, 1969, Box 128, Supreme Court Haynsworth Statements, Hollings MSS.

32. Spencer Rich, "Judge Vote Could Hurt Senators," *WP*, November 9, 1969; Reuther's remarks, made at the September 19, 1969, meeting of the United Automobile Workers' Foundry Wage and Hour Council Meeting in Cleveland, are noted in Box 6, Folder 4, Eaton MSS.

33. Nomination of Clement Haynsworth, 424, 479; Fred Graham, "Negroes in House Oppose Haynsworth," *NYT*, September 26, 1969; Graham, "Brooke Bids Nixon Drop Haynsworth," id., October 2, 1969. Some in the NAACP thought Brooke had waited too long. Kivie Kaplan to Edward Brooke, October 7, 1969, Part IX, Box 16, Folder 5, NAACP MSS.

34. Richard Nixon, Memorandum for Bryce Harlow, October 21, 1969, WHCF EX FG 51/A, October 21, 1969, Box 3, Folder 8, RMNL ("I have noted that Griffin apparently is lobbying quietly against Haynsworth behind the scenes. I think you should have a frank talk with him along these lines, that we understand his own position, but that as the Whip attempting to work directly against the President will be very hard for most people to justify or understand"); Bryce Harlow, Memorandum for the Staff Secretary, October 23, 1969, id. ("I discussed the attached with Senator Griffin. He will not work against the Haynsworth nomination, he says."); E.W. Kenworthy, "All But One of Eleven Senators Regarded as Undecided Vote Against Haynsworth: Williams and Griffin Held Most Persuasive," *NYT*, November 22, 1969 ("I," "I"); Rowland Evans, "Griffin Bowed to Groups Back Home in Opposing Haynsworth," *LAT*, October 13, 1969; John MacKenzie, "Haynsworth Approved by Senate Unit," *WP*, October 10, 1969; Bryce Harlow Memorandum for the President: 5:00 P.M. Haynsworth Meeting with GOP Senators, October 29, 1969, WHCF, Name File, Clement Haynsworth (3), RMNL ("his vote"); Marvin Kaplan to Washington Representatives and Heads of National Organizations, October 4, 1969, Part 1, Box 5, Leadership Conference MSS ("needs"); Dean Kotlowski, "Unhappily Yoked? Hugh Scott and Richard Nixon," 125 *PaMagH&B*, 233, 245-47 (July 2001).

35. Bryce Harlow, Memorandum for the President, October 28, 1969, WHCF EX FG 51/A, Box 3, Folder 8, RMNL (referring to Hruska and Cook as "your principal lieutenants in the Senate struggle"); Bryce Harlow, Memorandum for the President, October 30, 1969, WHCF, Name File Clement Haynsworth (3), RMNL (Smith committed to voting for Haynsworth if White House needed his vote); Ehrlichman, *Witness to Power*, 120.

36. Ehrlichman, *Witness to Power*, 120; "A.M.A. Confirms and Justifies Lobbying for Haynsworth in '69," *NYT*, July 4, 1975; Haynes Johnson, "Haynsworth Case: Politics of Pressure," *WP*, November 20, 1969 (Saxbe). According to the John Birch Society, "from all we can learn, confirmation of the appointment is anything but certain at the present time. We hereby emphatically request and urge, therefore, that our members not only pour a huge flood of telegrams and letters into Washington at once, in favor of such confirmation, but that you get all of the friends you can, who are not members of the Society to do the same." The John Birch Society wanted the letters and telegrams sent to Nixon, the two senators from each author's state, and Senators Griffin, Mathias, Eastland, Smith, Dole, Pearson, Williams, Boggs, Dodd, Jackson, Fulbright, Gore, Ellender, McGee, Packwood, and Miller. "There are many very different reasons why various Senators have been placed on this list. But we believe that using the list is the best way to get the most effectiveness out of your barrage of messages. And we do mean a barrage, to which we hope *every member* of the Society will be responsible from five to ten such messages altogether." *JBS Bull*, November 1969. Packwood reported getting

thirty pro-Haynsworth letters a day. Kenworthy, "All But One of Eleven Senators Regarded as Undecided Vote."

37. Arnold Aronson to Participating Organizations, November 5, 1969, Box 35, Folder 5, Rauh MSS; Jerry, Memorandum for Ron Ziegler, October 6, 1969, Haynsworth Mail Survey, WHCF, Name File, Clement Haynsworth (4), RMNL (reporting that pro-Haynsworth mail had dramatically increased, thanks to administration show of support for him); Warren Weaver, "Haynsworth Lost Aspirants' Vote: Only 9 of 30 Running in '70 Backed Nixon's Choice," *NYT*, November 23, 1969.

38. John Frank, Notes on June 26, 1971, Conversation, Haynsworth MSS ("boy"); Alexander to Harlow, n.d.; Phyllis Schlafly to Strom Thurmond, October 31, 1969, Box 29, Confirmation 1969, Thurmond MSS, and the other materials and letters in id., Boxes 28–29; Harry Dent, *The Prodigal South Returns to Power* (New York: John Wiley, 1978), 208. See also John MacKenzie, "Nixon May Delay Court Appointment Until August," *WP*, July 20, 1969 (Thurmond's "curious" public promotion of Judge Donald Russell as support for Haynsworth gathered strength. As MacKenzie said, Thurmond's behavior "could make a Haynsworth nomination more palatable to Northern liberals," and it "puzzled and somewhat amused" politicians and others, "since Thurmond must have known his endorsement was a kiss of death for Russell, former South Carolina Governor and short-term U.S. Senator."); Hollings, *Making Government Work*, 144 (the White House must have told Thurmond to "lie low"); Leon Panetta and Peter Gall, *Bring Us Together: The Nixon Team and the Civil Rights Retreat* (Philadelphia: J. B. Lippincott, 1971), 333 ("There was even one published story that Thurmond only pretended to back another judge just so it wouldn't appear that he was dictating the Haynsworth choice. It was the sort of story we were inclined to believe by this time"). That story was apparently by Aldo Beckman, "Thurmond Baffles Foe in Naming of Justice," *CT*, August 19, 1969.

39. Alexander to Harlow, n.d.; Ernest Hollings to R. K. Wise, December 9, 1969, Box 127, Clement Haynsworth (4) (Pro), Hollings MSS; Hollings to F. A. Ramsaur, October 6, 1969, Box 127, Supreme Court Judges, Clement Haynsworth Pro (1), id. ("The going is rough because the President appointed the fellow in August, and two months later six Republicans called for his withdrawal. The National Chairman of the Republican Party also talks of his withdrawal, and the whip, Bob Griffin, is actively trying to turn some commitments I have so he won't have to vote . . . Things really got out of hand the middle of the last week . . . You can fairly well hold the line if the Republicans hold their side of it. Up until Sunday we had only four Democrats asking the President to withdraw the nomination. Now, like the sheep dog that has tasted blood, everybody is hollering."); Hollings to W. C. Boyd, March 24, 1970, Box 127, Supreme Court Judges G. Harrold Carswell 1970 (2), id. ("It was the Republicans wo defeated Haynsworth. Daily we had their leader, Scott of Pennsylvania, and the Republican Whip, Griffin of Michigan, shouting for the President to withdraw the appointment.") The administration took an equally dim view of Hollings. Harry Dent wrote John Mitchl, "Senator Hollings has been helping on the Haynsworth matter, but he has also been chopping up the President on this subject. He is contending the Administration has fallen down on the job, and even when the President made his strong public statement the other day, Hollings threw cold water on his comments, indicating the President has to control his own party and he can't do this just by making headlines. I just want you to know that he is playing this thing for Hollings for all it is worth." Harry Dent, Memorandum for the Attorney General, October 23, 1969, Box 6, Haynsworth (2), Dent MSS, RMNL); Nixon, "Remarks at an Informal Meeting With Members of the White House Press Corps on Judge Haynsworth's Nomination to the Supreme Court," October 20, 1969, http://www.presidency.ucsb.edu/ws/index.php?pid=2 271&st=vicious+character+assassination&st1=; Robert Young, "Nixon Assails Haynsworth Foes as Character Assassins," *CT*, October 20, 1969; Pat Buchanan, Memorandum for the President, October 21, 1969, "One Observer's Notes of Legislative Leadership Meeting, Tuesday, October 14, 1969," WHCF, EX FG 51/a Box 3, Folder 7, RMNL ("cave in," "no one"); Haynes Johnson, "Haynsworth Case: Politics of Pressure," *WP*, November 20, 1969 ("soft sell," "short-hair"); Dean Kotlowski, "Trial by Error: Nixon, the Senate, and the Haynsworth Nomination," 26 *PSQ* 71, 80 (Winter, 1996).

40. Kenworthy, "The Haynsworth Issue: A Study in Pressure Politics," *NYT*, November 21, 1969 (Saxbe, "two"); Steele, "Haynsworth v. the U.S. Senate (1969)" ("beserk," "Mollenhoff cocktail"); Ernest Hollings to Clark Mollenhoff, November 12, 1969, Box 127, Supreme Court Judges, Haynsworth Pro (4), Hollings MSS ("you came on too strong for these Senators in doubt. They had become touchy and your strong positive position for Judge Haynsworth immediately triggered them into a defensive position"); "Newsweek Says Burger Seeks Haynsworth Votes," *NYT*, November 10, 1969; Spencer Rich, "Ford Eyes Ousting Douglas: Move is Linked to Senate Vote on Haynsworth," *WP*, November 8, 1969. The information about stock ownership is from Leadership Meeting Notes, October 14, 1969, Box 6, Leadership Meeting Notes July-December, Scott MSS ("Six present justices own securities."); Fred Graham's interview with Potter Stewart, Box 624, Folder 33, Stewart MSS. "Graham: At one point, the White House announced the fact that while Haynsworth owned stocks, so did six or seven members of the current Court. Stewart: Well, I remember that, seeing it on television news one evening. And I thought to myself, how could they know that? And the only way they could possibly know that, it occurred to me, was by look-ing at the income tax returns of the Justices," which both Graham and Stewart agreed was inappropriate and possibly illegal. Id. John Frank later asked Haynsworth about the truth to rumors that "the administration, discovering that it was running into opposition in its own party, and feeling that it had made its Southern gesture and that was all that was required of it, figured it would buy peace by not making a militant effort" and had not used "the major political power of the sort that an administration really uses when it really wants to go some-place." Haynsworth, however, thought the administration had worked hard for him. Frank, Notes on June 26, 1971, conversation. Perhaps this was in part because when Nixon met with Haynsworth after the defeat of the nomination the president told him "that never in history had a President put the efforts of the White House staff so earnestly behind a nom-inee for the Court." John Ehrlichman, Meeting Between the President of the United States and Judge Haynsworth, December 4, 1969, Box 39, Supreme Court (1), Ehrlichman MSS. Obviously, Nixon did not take LBJ's promotion of Fortas's promotion of Fortas as Chief Justice into account. In all likelihood, the administration worked harder than the rumors suggested, but not as hard as Haynsworth believed.

41. William Eaton, "Haynsworth Faces Day of Decisions," *CDN*, November 21, 1969; *CR*, November 21, 1969, S35380 (Remarks of Senator Thurmond); Philip Warden, "Haynsworth Denied Post: Senate Bars Nixon Court Choice," *CT*, November 22, 1969 (Agnew); Aldo Beckman, "Haynsworth Opponents Greeted by Elated Crowd in Capitol Hall," *CT*, November 22, 1969.

42. Richard Nixon, PPF Memorandum for Bob Haldeman, November 24, 1969, Memoranda From the President, Box 1, Folder 12, RMNL ("martyr"); Harry Dent, Memorandum for the President, November 17, 1969, Box 5, Folder 40, Contested Materials MSS ("If Haynsworth is confirmed this will further help the [political] situation [in the South] because of the President's good work on the nomination. However, even if we fail, and the President comes back with another Southerner, this could bring bigger political dividends down that way."); Robert Donovan, "Is the Price Too High? Nixon Took Bold Gamble on Haynsworth, War Disunity," *LAT*, November 22, 1969; Strom Thurmond to Richard Nixon, November 24, 1969, Judiciary Committee Records, Box 271, Thurmond MSS. But see "Please Gentlemen, Knock It Off," *GN*, November 24, 1969, Box 127, Supreme Court Judges, Clement Haynsworth Con (5), Hollings MSS (asking that Thurmond and Hollings stop blaming each other's party for the defeat and reporting that "our people are hurt, deeply resentful, angry over slurs hurled at the nominee and the entire state during the acrimonious national debate preceding the Senate's action").

43. Clement Haynsworth to Warren Burger, February 16, 1970, Haynsworth MSS; Clement Haynsworth to John Mitchell, November 26, 1969, id.; Haynsworth to James Byrnes, November 26, 1969, id; Hollings, *Making Government Work*, 149 ("makeup"); "Senate Views on Haynsworth Changed," *WP*, March 15, 1977; Karlyn Barker, "Haynsworth: Reputation Rebuilt 10 Years Afterward," id., April 9, 1979; Renaming Ceremony, May 3, 1983, Clement F. Haynsworth Jr. Federal Building, Box 3, Clement Haynsworth, Walters MSS.

44. Leonard Garment, *Crazy Rhythm: My Journey From Brooklyn, Jazz and Wall Street to Nixon's White House, Watergate, and Beyond* . . . (Cambridge, MA: Da Capo, 2001), 146 (Clifford); Leonard Garment, Memorandum for the President, January 9, 1970, Box 39, Supreme Court (1), Ehrlichman MSS; Lewis Powell to John Mitchell, December 12, 1969, Box 288, Folder 5, Powell MSS; Jeffries, *Justice Lewis F. Powell, Jr*, 1–2, 227.

45. Dean, *The Rehnquist Choice*, 19 (Burger); Robert Semple, "Southerner Named to Supreme Court," *NYT*, January 20, 1970 (Gurney); Aldo Beckman, "Carswell Court Nominee," *CT*, January 20, 1970 ("all"); "Carswell Supports Legal Precedents: Favored by Russell," *WP*, January 20, 1970; Bruce Kalk, "The Carswell Affair: The Politics of a Supreme Court Nomination in the Nixon Administration," 42 *AJLH*, 261, 267-68 (1998) (Dent); Dent, *The Prodigal South*, 210; Bill Lawrence, "Judging the Judge," *WP*, April 25, 1971 ("angrily").

46. Fred Graham, "Carswell May Make Some People Long for Haynsworth," *NYT*, January 25, 1970 (law review); Martin Waldron, "Supreme Court Choice: George Harrold Carswell," id., January 20, 1970 ("bubbly," "cheerleader"); B.J. Phillips, "'Eisenhower Philosophy': Carswell," *WP*, January 27, 1970; Kenneth Reich, "Whites, Blacks: Judge Carswell—as Viewed in His Home Town," *LAT*, January 23, 1970; Robert Semple, "Southerner Named to Supreme Court," *NYT*, Jan 20, 1970 ("brief").

47. Phillips, "'Eisenhower Philosophy'"; "Court Nominee Likes Bridge and Football," *CT*, January 20, 1970; Graham, "Carswell May Make Some People Long for Haynsworth"; Kalk, "The Carswell Affair," 274 ("While"); and see, for example, the discussion of Carswell's decisions by Joe Rauh in Nomination of George Harrold Carswell, 278–307.

48. John MacKenzie, "Rights Groups Hit Bench Nominee," *WP*, June 12, 1969; Richard Harris, *Decision* (New York: Ballantine, 1972), 29–30 (quoting Republican Senator Charles "Mac" Mathias of Maryland). The *Washington Post* also subsequently reported that it had come into possession of a letter from Burger to Mitchell deeming Carswell "well qualified for promotion" from the US District Court to the Fifth Circuit. "Could this have been part of what led Mitchell to believe that Carswell was Supreme Court caliber a year later?" John MacKenzie, "Crossing the Judicial Line," *WP*, June 13, 1974.

49. Eaton, "Nixon to Tighten Screening of U.S. Judicial Appointees," October 6, 1969; Waldron, "Supreme Court Choice" (something"); Dean, *The Rehnquist Choice*, 19–21 ("superficial," "gay"); "Ex-Judge Carswell Arrested in Florida," *CT*, June 27, 1976; "Judge Carswell Beaten by Youth in Hotel Room," *LAT*, September 11, 1979; "G. Harrold Carswell, 72, Dies; Rejected for Supreme Court," *WP*, August 1, 1992.

50. John Crewdson, "F.B.I. Began Inquiry of Carswell in '70: Agents Apparently Failed to Tell Nixon About Family Ties to a Teacher Later Slain," *NYT*, September 19, 1976 (quotations); "Prober's Memory Hazy on Linking Carswell, Pack," *SHT*, September 23, 1976 (AP story about Carswell testimony); "Defendant Denies Part in Murder of Teacher," *SPT*, December 2, 1976 (UPI story about the trial).

51. Harris, *Decision*, 24-25; "The Seventh Crisis of Richard Nixon," *Ti*, April 20, 1970 ("watched"); Winzola McLendon, *Martha: The Life of Martha Mitchell* (New York: Ballantine, 1979), 119.

52. Dean, *The Rehnquist Choice*, 19 ("colossal"); David Kyvig, *The Age of Impeachment: American Constitutional Culture Since 1960* (Lawrence: University Press of Kansas, 2008), 91 ("Fortas"); William Safire, *Before the Fall: An Inside View of the Pre-Watergate White House* (New York: Doubleday, 1975), 267; Harris, *Decision*, 25 (Rauh). Charles Colson maintained that the White House did not study Carswell's decisions at all until after the nomination's announcement. Maltese, *The Selling of Supreme Court Nominees*, 14.

53. "Not Too Rich Nor Rightist: Nixon Names Southern U.S. Judge to Top Court: GOP Heads Pleased," *WSJ*, January 20, 1970 (weekend, Hruska); Fred Graham, "Nixon Preparing to Announce Nominee to Supreme Court; Tight Secrecy Maintained," *NYT*, January 16, 1970 ("trial balloon," "unusually"); Semple, "Southerner Named to Supreme Court" ("strict," "good"); Aldo Beckman, "Carswell Court Nominee," *CT*, January 20, 1970 ("shadow," "thorough"). Indeed, Carswell's antagonists would not find much in the way of conflicts of interest, though they looked hard, and there may have been some potential ammunition in Carswell's relationship with a conservative local millionaire from whose lawsuit, it was alleged, the judge had failed to disqualify himself and his dismissal of a lawsuit against a bank from which

Carswell borrowed money and of which his father-in-law was a director. Kenneth Reich, "Inquiry into Carswell Activities Widening; Critics Study Dismissal of $15,000 Suit Against Bank," *LAT*, February 15, 1970. Journalists did find that Carswell was "a man who has rarely had spare cash available to invest, and who has gone increasingly into debt over the years as he has traveled in high social circles on a Government salary." Fred Graham, "Carswell's Opponents Find a Steadily Growing Debt but No Conflicting Investments," *NYT*, February 9, 1970.

54. Jules Witcover, "Political Message? Carswell Choice Will Help GOP in South," *LAT*, January 20, 1970; "From Obscure to Unknown," *NYT*, January 21, 1970; Graham, "Carswell May Make Some People Long for Haynsworth"; "Judicial Qualifications," *WSJ*, January 22, 1970; "The Symbols of a Nomination," *WP*, January 21, 1970; Ted Lacey, "NAACP in War on New Nixon High Court Choice," *CDD*, January 21, 1970; Robert Semple, "Southerner Named to Supreme Court," *NYT*, January 20, 1970 (Rauh); Marian Wright Edelman to Joseph Rauh, January 21, 1970, Box 24, Folder 2, Rauh MSS; Harry Bernstein, "AFL-CIO Won't Fight Nixon's Court Choice," *LAT*, January 22, 1970; Robert Donovan, "OK of Florida Judge Expected for High Court," id., January 20, 1970 ("I").

55. Aldo Beckman, "Carswell Court Nominee," *CT*, January 20, 1970 (Gurney); Pinkney v. Meloy, 241 F. Supp. 943 (1965); Nomination of George Harrold Carswell, 305 ("If"); "Not Too Rich nor Rightist" (Eastland, Scott); "Expect Quick O.K. in Senate for Carswell," *CT*, January 21, 1970 (Griffin, Mansfield).

56. This information is taken from Morris Abram's unpublished piece on Thurston on which Thurston commented in the George Thurston MSS, and George Thurston to John Cummings, December 10, 1974, id. (hereafter Abram piece).

57. Abram piece; "Excerpts from Carswell Talk," *NYT*, January 22, 1970 (quotations); "Carswell Disavows '48 Speech Backing White Supremacy," id., January 22, 1970; Fred Graham, "Carswell Speech Missed in Check: White House Held Unaware of Nominee's 1948 Talk," *NYT*, January 23, 1970. "I fail to see why I should feel ashamed of the report on Judge Carswell's 1948 speech," George Thurston subsequently wrote a critic. "Rather, I would feel deeply ashamed for the rest of my life if having discovered the speech which he reported in his own newspaper, with his own typographical emphasis on the white supremacy passage, I had failed to report the speech. I did not write the speech for him. I didn't make the speech for him. I didn't publish the speech for him. . . . I took great care to call attention to the age and circumstances of the speech in my story, and to provide Judge Carswell with an opportunity (which, fortunately he used) to rebut the words at the same time as I reported them." Thurston to Alice Brown, April 10, 1970, Thurston MSS.

58. Fred Graham, "Carswell: Defeat From the Jaws of Victory," *NYT*, April 12, 1970 ("mod," "Buffalo Bill"); "Rick Called," January 20, 1970, Box 24, Folder 2, Rauh MSS; Richard Seymour to Marian Wright Edelman, January 26, 1970, id.; Abram Piece (rumors); Email, Richard Seymour to Laura Kalman, October 16, 2015; "Twenty Questions for Judge Carswell," n.d., Part 1, Box 108, Folder 6, Leadership Conference MSS; Spencer Rich, "Memo Cited as Proof Carswell Was Evasive," *WP*, April 3, 1970; Robert Maynard and Bruce Gilpin, "Rights Issue: Carswell Among Founders of Segregated Golf Club," *WP*, January 27, 1970; Fred Graham, "Meany Will Fight Carswell Choice," *NYT*, January 27, 1970 (Seymour's role); Spencer Rich, "Memo Cited as Proof Carswell Was Evasive: Signed by 2 ABA Members," *WP*, April 3, 1970; Linda Greenhouse, "Bar Panel Is Said to Back Carswell," *NYT*, January 26, 1970; Aldo Beckman, "American Bar Gives Approval to Carswell for High Court," *CT*, January 27, 1970.

59. Fred Graham, "Meany Will Fight Carswell Choice"; "Contempt of Court," id., January 28, 1970 ("Skeptics may conclude that the primary motivation for the Meany move is a desire to defuse the anger felt by many civil rights organizations over the exclusionist policies toward Negroes practiced by many construction unions. The A.F.L.-.C.I.O. head is himself the target of much of this anger for his leadership in the fight to block the Administration's 'Philadelphia Plan' for faster admission of blacks to skilled building jobs."); Alfred Baker Lewis to Clarence Mitchell, January 28, 1970, Part IX, Box 14, Folder 8, NAACP MSS ("I see George Meany has taken a stand against Carswell because he is unfair to Negroes. No doubt he is trying to be friendly to us to take the heat off our objection to the exclusion of the skilled unions in the building trades and some others. But anything that will strengthen the cooperation between

us & organized labor, no matter how tenuous, is good. They did give us some real help in defeating Haynsworth."); Richard Harwood, "The Fight to Reject Judge Carswell," *WP*, April 12, 1970 ("tired"); Willard Edwards, "Capitol Views: Drama Pervades Carswell Quiz," *CT*, January 29, 1970 (Rauh); Marvella Bayh with Mary Lynn Kotz, *Marvella: A Personal Journey* (New York: Harcourt Brace Jovanovich, 1979), 199–200.

60. William Greider, "Finding the Skeletons in Nominees' Closets," *WP*, October 22, 1971 (Edelman); Arnold Aronson to Participating Organizations, January 30, 1970, "Judge G. Harrold Carswell," Part II, Box 59, Folder 5, Leadership Conference MSS.

61. Ronald Ostrow, "Carswell Declares 'I'm Not a Racist,'" *LAT*, January 28, 1970; Nomination of George Harrold Carswell, 20, 10, 23–24, 21–22, 320.

62. Fred Graham, "Senators Are Told Carswell Was 'Insulting' to Negro Lawyers," *NYT*, February 3, 1970; John MacKenzie, "Carswell Defends Conduct: Judge Denies Discourtesy to Rights Lawyer," *WP*, February 6, 1970; Fred Graham, "Senator and Black Lawyer in Dispute on Praise for Carswell," *NYT*, March 31, 1970; Richard Lyons, "Negro Official Denies Pressure for Carswell," *WP*, February 3, 1970 ("extreme," "meddling"); Nomination of George Harrold Carswell, 305.

63. Ostrow, "Carswell Declares 'I'm Not a Racist,'" (comparison of demeanors); Nomination of George Harrold Carswell, 11, 31–32, 36–37, 68–70, 270, 323–24; Fred Graham, "Carswell Denies He Tried to Balk Club's Integration," *NYT*, January 28, 1970 ("brandished"); Fred Graham, "Carswell Denies Being Hostile to Rights Lawyers; Committee's Vote Put Off," *NYT*, February 6, 1970 ("shocked," "Negro dialect").

64. Jane Mansbridge and Katherine Flaster, "Male Chauvinist, Feminist, Sexist, and Sexual Harassment: Different Trajectories in Feminist Linguistic Innovation," 80 *AmSp* 256, 261 (Fall 2005); William Eaton, "Judge Hit on New Front: Carswell Male Supremacist, Rep. Patsy Mink Charges," *CDN*, January 29, 1970; Patsy Mink to Richard Harris, Box 388, Folder 7, Mink MSS ("badgering"); Phillips v. Martin Marietta Corporation, 416 F. 2d. 1257 (1969); Nomination of G. Harrold Carswell, at 81–84, 88–91. After Friedan testified, Bayh said, "I sat here with a great deal of interest not only listening to the words but sensing some of the reaction in the hearing. At the risk of being critical or stepping on toes, I think the fact of some of the reaction here is evidence of a certain amount of male smugness that some of us have." Id., 98.

65. Nomination of George Harrold Carswell, 218, 242, 252–53; Charles Black, "A Note on Senatorial Consideration of Supreme Court Nominees," 79 *YLJ*, 657, 664 (1970); On Pollak's character, see Laura Kalman, *Yale Law School and the Sixties: Revolt and Reverberations* (Chapel Hill: University of North Carolina Press, 2005).

66. Nomination of George Harrold Carswell, 305; Warren Weaver, "Carswell's Foes Are Stalling for Time," *NYT*, March 22, 1970 (reporting remarks of Senator Mark Hatfield to reporters about LeMay); Art Buchwald, "Son of Old South Waits in the Wings," *WP*, February 5, 1970.

67. The President's News Conference of January 30, 1970, http://www.presidency.ucsb.edu/ws/?pid=2558 For predictions of confirmation, see, for example, Joseph Alsop, "Liberals Played into Hands of President on Two Judges," *WP*, February 2, 1970; Frank Mankiewicz and Tom Braden, "Carswell Probably Will Be Confirmed Despite Antipathy to Negro Rights," id., February 3, 1970; "The Supreme Court: Approaching the Bench," *Ti*, February 9, 1970 (predicting confirmation)

68. Ronald Ostrow, "Senate Panel Resumes Carswell Study Today: Swift Committee Approval and Eventual Confirmation Expected but Battles Looms," *LAT*, February 16, 1970; "Carswell Tract Was Restricted: Florida Land Sold in 1966 Had 'Caucasian' Clause," *NYT*, February 13, 1970; "Senate Unit, 13–4, Backs Carswell," id., February 17, 1970 (the four opposed were Hart, Kennedy, Bayh, and Tydings); Aldo Beckman, "President Shrugs Off Carswell Land Deal," *CT*, February 14, 1970; Leadership Conference on Civil Rights to Dear Senator, March 16, 1970, Part 1, Box 108, Folder 6, Leadership Conference MSS; "Has Judge Carswell Changed?," n.d., Box 24, Folder 2, Rauh MSS; Fred Graham, "Carswell Chartered White Club to Aid Florida State U. in 1953," *NYT*, February 21, 1970; Graham, "Bar Group Reaffirms Carswell as Qualified," *LAT*, February 22, 1970 (Walsh said "all nine members present voted to support this second endorsement of President Nixon's selection for the vacant court seat. Three committee members were absent.").

69. Frank Porter, "AFL-CIO Hits Carswell as 'Insult,'" *WP*, February 17, 1970; Robert Smith, "Brooke Opposes Carswell; Criticizes Stand on Human Rights," *NYT*, February 26, 1970;

Edward Brooke, *Bridging the Divide* (New Brunswick: Rutgers University Press, 2007), 196-97 (quoting McGrory); Richard Harwood, "The Fight to Reject Judge Carswell: Rights Group Waged Lonely Struggle, Then Bayh 'Turned On' One Night," *WP*, April 12, 1970; "Bayh Father-In-Law Kills 2d Wife, Self," *CT*, April 2, 1970; Television Report, March 26, 1970, POF, Annotated News Summary, Box 31, Folder 6, RMNL (March 24); "Mediocrity?," *InN*, March 25, 1970, Box 31, Folder 7, id.

70. John MacKenzie, "Carswell Will Be Challenged on Legal Credentials," id., February 16, 1970; The Qualifications of Judge Carswell (III), id. February 16, 1970; Masarro, *Supremely Political*, at 116 "[b]oob"); Herbert Klein, *Making It Perfectly Clear: An Inside Account of Nixon's Love-Hate Relationship with the Media* (New York: Doubleday, 1980), 339. (After recounting how UCLA demonstrators had pelted him with marshmallows over the Carswell nomination, Nixon media adviser Herb Klein reflected that while he would "defend Haynsworth again, . . . Carswell was a bad choice.") "I think it quite clear that your testimony marked the turning of the tide on Carswell," one friend wrote Lou Pollak. "Prior to that everyone was focusing on the race issue, and it was you who made the first loud clear statement that important as this issue was, even more important was the fact that he is simply not qualified." Louis Hector to Louis Pollak, April 8, 1970 Box 41, File: Carswell (1), Pollak Papers.

71. Jack Bass, *Unlikely Heroes* (Tuscaloosa: University of Alabama Press, 1990), 319–23; "Judge Carswell and His Colleagues," *WP*, March 19, 1970; John MacKenzie, "Carswell's Record as Judge Scored by Ripon Society," id., March 6, 1970; Joseph Kraft, "Size of Vote Against Carswell Shows Rising Taste for Quality," id., April 7, 1970; "Judge Carswell: The Method and the Merits," id., April 6, 1970; Joseph Kraft, "Size of Vote Against Carswell Shows Rising Taste for Quality," id., April 7, 1970 ("Thousands"); "Judge Carswell: An Addendum," id., April 4, 1970; "Over 200 Supreme Court Law Clerks Urge Senate Rejection of Carswell," Senate Judiciary Committee, Nominations: Supreme Court, Carswell 1970, Bayh MSS; Charles Alan Wright to Ernest Hollings, January 30, 1970, Box 127, Supreme Court Judges G. Harrold Carswell 1970 (1), Hollings MSS ("[T]here is nothing in his record to suggest that he is more than an ordinary competent lower court judge. His opinions are rather plodding and he applies precedents in what seems a mechanical fashion." For Wright's public defense of Carswell, see his March 18, 1970, letter to Roman Hruska, reprinted in the *CR*, March 26, 1970, S9615–16.); "457 Lawyers Urge Defeat of Carswell," *WP*, March 13, 1970; Joseph Califano, *Inside: A Public and Private Life* (New York: Public Affairs, 2004), 196; "Carswell Opposed at Florida U. Rally," *WP*, April 4, 1970 ("It was disclosed this week that [Regents Chairman D. Burke] Kibler, a law partner of Sen. Spessard Holland [D-FL] had written Joshua Morse, dean of the Florida State law school, complaining about the nine law faculty members who signed a letter opposing Carswell. The letter, dated, March 19, stated, 'I am sure you realize, Josh, how imprudent action such as this makes the task of those of us trying to get adequate funding for the University even more difficult.' "); "Florida Prof Hits Attack on Carswell," *CT*, March 21, 1970 (quoting a senior faculty member as characterizing the petition as an "unwarranted personal attack" on Carswell).

72. Richard Harwood, "The Fight to Reject Judge Carswell," *WP*, April 12, 1970. See David Greenberg, "The New Politics of Supreme Court Appointments," *Daed* 5, 8 (Summer 2005).

73. William Rehnquist, Letter to the Editor, *WP*, February 14, 1970.

74. Henry Abraham, *Justices, Presidents, and Senators: A History of the U.S Supreme Court Appointments from Washington to Bush* II 12 (New York: Rowman & Littlefield, 2008, 5th ed.) (quoting Long and Carswell); Warren Weaver, "Carswell Attacked and Defended as Senate Opens Debate on Nominee," *NYT*, March 17, 1970; "A Conversation with Wally Johnson, Rehnquist's Lawyer," http://nixonfoundation.org/news-details.php?id=78.

75. "Battle Over Carswell: The 'Silent Ones' Will Now Decide," *NYT*, March 15, 1970 ("light") William Spong to Laverhne Saint, December 28, 1971, Box 65, Judiciary Rehnquist, Spong MSS ("History," "examination"); "Spong Got Threats for Court Stand," *WP*, December 15, 1970; William Spong to William Irwin, April 10, 1970, Box 63, Judiciary Supreme Court Carswell, Spong MSS ("matter"); Spong to C. B. Settle, January 7, 1971, id. ("It was not an easy thing for me to oppose Carswell and the opposition resulted in some very unpleasant times for members of my family."); Spong to B. J. Weafer, April 14, 1970, id. ("perfection"), and see, for example, Richard Fredland to Spong, February 4, 1970, Box 62, id. ("At a time

when confidence in the governmental system we have [is] so much in need of bolstering, it would seem that President Nixon could find from among some 500-plus Federal judges and a multitude of state judges someone of less offensive background than Judge Carswell for the Supreme Court. Please vote against this poor choice.").

76. "Hollings Should Support Carswell," *GN*, March 28, 1970, Box 127, Supreme Court Judges G. Harrold Carswell (1), Hollings MSS; Ernest Hollings to Fulton Creech, March 24, 1970, id., Folder 2; Ernest Hollings to Professors Webster Myers, Douglas Wickham, William McAninch, E. D. Wedlock, April 6, 1970, id., Folder 3 ("Of course").

77. Harris, *Decision*, at 123 ("Paradoxically"); Katz and Johnson, *Herblock*, "I Don't Smell Anything—I Don't Smell Anything—I Don't Smell Anything-I Don't—Whew—," March 11, 1970; Kenneth Reilly, *Nixon's Piano: Presidents and Racial Politics From Washington to Clinton* (New York: Free Press, 1995), 6; "Kennedy Pessimistic on Carswell Defeat," *WP*, March 12, 1970; "Battle Over Carswell: The 'Silent Ones' Will Now Decide," *NYT*, March 15, 1970 (Bayh); Warren Weaver, "Carswell Debate Is Losing Impetus: Judge's Backers Confident He Will Be Confirmed," *NYT*, March 18, 1970, 124; Spencer Rich, "Carswell Margin Narrows: Carswell Still Likely to Win Despite Rising Opposition," *WP*, March 20, 1970.

78. "Burger Denies Report He Lobbied for Carswell," *WP*, March 27, 1970 (and see Burger to Harry Blackmun, April 27, 1970, denouncing the "false reports about [his] 'lobbying' for Haynsworth and Carswell," http://digitalcommons.law.scu.edu/cgi/viewcontent.cgi?article=1067&context=historical); "Goldberg Asserts Carswell Is Not Fit for Supreme Court," *NYT*, March 23, 1970; Anthony Lewis, "The American Bar: A Failure of Responsibility," id., March 23, 1970.

79. Bass, *Unlikely Heroes*, 319 (Segal); Tom Herman, "The Bar on How to Pick a Justice," *WSJ*, April 6, 1970 (Jenner).

80. Kenneth Reich, "Carswell Reported Astonished by Senate Response to Charges," *LAT*, March 29, 1970; Kenneth Reich, "Carswell's Friends Start to Fight Back," id., March 29, 1970; "Carswell Critics Accused of Lying," *WP*, March 30, 1970; "The Seat Warmed by Goldberg and Fortas, *CT*, March 24, 1970.

81. Spencer Rich, "Nomination Appears in Danger," *WP*, March 26, 1970; Richard Harris, *Decision*, 137–42.

82. Exchange of Letters with Senator William B. Saxbe on the Nomination of Judge G. Harrold Carswell to the Supreme Court, April 1, 1970, http://www.presidency.ucsb.edu/ws/?pid=2931; James Eastland, John McClellan, Sam Ervin, Charles McC. Mathias, Roman Hruska, Robert Griffin, Hugh Scott, Hiram Fong, Marlow Cook, n.d., Box 68, Folder 1969, Nomination of G. Harrold Carswell (2), Scott MSS ("The undersigned, being a majority of the members of the Senate Judiciary Committee, believe that no useful purpose would be served by further hearings on the matter of Judge Carswell and, therefore, urge our colleagues of the Senate to vote against the motion to recommit on Monday, April 6."); Harris, *Decision*, 170 ("like," quoting Senator Bob Packwood); James Reston, "Washington: President Nixon's Gamble," *NYT*, April 3, 1970; Fred Graham, "Bayh Says Nixon Errs on His Role," id., April 3, 1970.

83. Arnold Aronson to Participating Organizations, Re: The Carswell Nomination, March 30, 1970, Part I, Box 108, Folder 9, Leadership Conference MSS.

84. William Timmons, Memorandum for the President, Judge Carswell Report, April 3, 1970, WHCF, G. Harrold Carswell, Name File (1); Warren Weaver, "Carswell Opponents Draft a Plan to Block Vote," *NYT*, March 24, 1970; Fred Graham, "Nixon Sees Peril to His Authority in Carswell Fight," id., April 2, 1970 (Agnew).

85. "The Seventh Crisis of Richard Nixon" (quotations); Spencer Rich, "Carswell Decision Is Today: Mrs. Smith, Sen. Cook Hold Key to Result," *WP*, April 8, 1970.

86. "The Seventh Crisis of Richard Nixon." (Dole); Rich, "Carswell Decision Is Today"; Daily Diary, April 6, 1970, RMNL; Aldo Beckman, "The Carswell Vote: Rebuff to Pressure: Indignation an Element in Defections," *CT*, April 10, 1970 (Cook).

87. Beckman, "The Carswell Vote" (quotations); Brooke, *Bridging the Divide*, 197–98; Willard Edwards, "Capitol Views: Mrs. Smith Dotes on Vote Secrecy," *CT*, April 21, 1970; Telegram, Margaret Chase Smith to Kermit Lansner, Editor, *News*, April 16, 1970, Smith Statement: G. Harrold Carswell, Smith MSS (blaming rumor on President's staff or a

Newsweek reporter, not Nixon himself and asking the magazine to publish her telegram). Pat Buchanan claimed that after Carswell's defeat, Smith was "selling her anti-Supreme Court and anti-ABM votes to the young openly" and that he was "getting readings from Maine that our best chance up there may involve doing a deal to get Mrs. Smith not to run again." Buchanan, Memorandum for Bill Timmons, October 18, 1971, Box 1, Folder 9, Contested Materials MSS. Smith ran in 1972, however, and Democrat Bill Hathaway defeated her.

88. Kenneth Reich, "Judge Relieved that 'It's Over,'" *LAT*, April 9, 1970.

89. Haynes Johnson, "In Senate: A Gasp . . . Then Cheers," *WP*, April 9, 1970. Prouty reported to the White House that his mail was "running 25-1 against" Carswell (Telephone Calls, Congressional, April 1, 1970, WHCF EX FG 51A (2), RMNL. "Daddy wouldn't let on, but it hurt us all," Carswell's son, Scott, said later. "Terribly . . . This going after him for being a bigot, a racist," which his children found "preposterous." Paul Hendrickson, "Rejected: "Rejected: The Private Pain of Wearing the Public Stamp," *WP*, March 10, 1989. Where one hundred senators had weighed in on Haynsworth, just ninety-six did on Carswell. Senators Bennett (R-UT) and Mundt (R-SD), both of whom had voted for Haynsworth, were absent for the Carswell vote.

90. Harris, *Decision*, 107 ("idiots"); Haynes Johnson, "2d Mitchell 'Mess' Hit by Senators: Carswell Fight Leaving Resentment in Party," *WP*, April 5, 1970.

91. Nan Robertson, "Martha Mitchell: Capital's Most Talked-About Talkative Woman," *NYT*, May 1, 1970 ("national"); "Mrs. Mitchell Asks Paper to Crucify Fulbright for Vote," *WP*, April 10, 1970; McLendon, *Martha* (New York: Ballantine, 1979), 116–23 ("John"); Myra McPherson, "Martha Mitchell Wants to Stay and Fight," *WP*, May 1924, 1970 ("idiomatic," "Oh"); Jerol Garison , Interview with John Woodruff, October 31, 2000, http://pryorcenter.uark.edu/projects/Arkansas Gazette/WOODRUFF-John/transcripts/JWoodruff.pdf; The Bayh camp was aware of reports that Senator Fulbright [D-AR] had told constituents "that since he had opposed Fortas he would have to be consistent and oppose Haynsworth; otherwise he might be accused of being anti-Semitic." J. Bill Becker to Al Barkan, National Director, COPE AFL-CIO, October 16, 1969, Bayh Senate Judiciary Committee Nominees: Haynsworth, Letters, Bayh MSS.

92. Marlene Cimons, "Outspoken Southern Belle: Mrs. Mitchell Breaks Mold of Cabinet Wife," *LAT*, January 4, 1970 ("defeats"); Robert Semple, "Who Likes Mitchell? Someone Named Nixon," *NYT*, April 19, 1970; Johnson, "2d Mitchell 'Mess' Hit by Senators" ("operation," "diaper"); James Rosen, *The Strong Man: John Mitchell and the Secrets of Watergate* (New York: Doubleday, 2008), 116–17; POF, Pat Buchannan, Memorandum for the President, December 15, 1969, to January 10, 1970, Annotated News Summaries, Box 31, Folder 4, RMNL.

93. Chronology, n.d., Judiciary Committee, Nominations: Supreme Court—Carswell, Staff File: Richard Harris 1970, Bayh MSS; Memorandum for the President, April 6, 1970, WHCF EX FG 51A, Box 4, Folder 2, RMNL, singling out Scott and Griffin for supporting the nominations. Unbeknownst to the White House, apparently, Griffin had almost withdrawn his backing. Harris, *Decision*, 187. The seven Republicans who voted against Haynsworth and for Carswell were John Sherman Cooper (KY), Robert Griffin (MICH), Len Jordan (ID), Jack Miller (IA), William Saxbe (OH), Hugh Scott (PA), and John Williams (DEL). The one Democrat was Alan Bible (NE). Scott subsequently characterized "his vote for Carswell as his 'worst mistake.' " Kotlowski, "Unhappily Yoked," 247.

94. Ehrlichman, *Witness to Power*, 122, 130–31; William Timmons, Memorandum for the President, April 13, 1970, WHCF EX FG 51, Box 1, Folder 3, RMNL; Remarks by Rep. Gerald R. Ford, Republican Leader, prepared for delivery on the floor of the US House of Representatives, April 15, 1970, http://www.fordlibrarymuseum.gov/library/speeches/700415.pdf.

95. Remarks by Rep. Gerald R. Ford, April 15, 1970; James Cannon, *Time and Chance: Gerald Ford's Appointment with History* 100-01 (New York: Harper Collins, 1994), 80–81; Kyvig, *The Age of Impeachment*, 93–106.

96. William O. Douglas, *The Court Years 1939-1975: The Autobiography of William O. Douglas* 364(New York: Random House, 1980); William O. Douglas to Emanuel Celler, March 24, 1967, Box 315, Celler, Douglas MSS (apologizing for missing a celebration for Celler because he had not received the invitation. "I wanted you to know that if we had known about it we would have been the first to arrive and the last to leave."); Celler to Douglas, November 14, 1975, id. ("I like to remember that our friendship goes back to your SEC days and I glory in that relationship. You have always been an inspiration to me during my years in Congress."); Statement of Chairman Emanuel Celler on the Final Report of the Special Subcommittee on H.Res. 920, Investigation of William O. Douglas, Box 338, Justice William O. Douglas, Celler MSS; Gerald Ford to Dear xxxxxxxxxx, form letter, Ford Congressional, R15, Hartmann MSS

97. Patrick Buchanan, POF, Memorandum for the President: Notes From Legislative Leadership Meeting, March 3, 1970, Box 80, RMNL ("If"); William Safire, *Before the Fall: An Inside View of the Pre-Watergate White House,* 268 ("indifferent," Nixon's additions) and see Ehrlichman, *Witness to Power,* 127–28; Richard Nixon, Statement About Nominations to the Supreme Court, April 9, 1970, http://www.presidency.ucsb.edu/ws/?pid=2456; Harry Dent, Memorandum for the President: Southern Actions Based on the President's Carswell Statement, April 21, 1970, WHCF Ex FG 51A, Box 4, File 5, RMNL; Dent, *The Prodigal South,* 212. "Contrived though his show of anger may have been, it left those of us who witnessed the performance in person frozen in our chairs for seconds after he whirled from the microphones and, with Attorney General Mitchell behind him, vanished from view. The President's spoken remarks were derived from an even stronger and, in its language, more impassioned written statement that we were handed after he had returned to the Oval Office." John Osborne, "The Nixon Watch: Rage at the White House," *TNR,* May 2, 1970; and see Safire Diary, April 27, 1970, Box 35, Folder 11, John Mitchell, Safire MSS; Television Report, April 10, 1970, Box 74, Folder 5: Carswell, Safire Papers.

98. Dean, *The Rehnquist Choice,* 23 ("misreading"); WHT 733-10, June 14, 1972, 2:54 P.M., Nixon, Burger, NT. Though the number of lawyers in Congress had declined since the mid-19th century, almost 60% of its members in the 1960s were lawyers. Nick Robinson, "The Declining Dominance of Lawyers in U.S. Federal Politics," Robinson, Nick, The Declining Dominance of Lawyers in U.S. Federal Politics (November 1, 2015). HLS Center on the Legal Profession Research Paper No. 2015-10. Available at SSRN: http://ssrn.com/abstract=2684731 or http://dx.doi.org/10.2139/ssrn.2684731

99. Report together with Individual Views to accompany the nomination of George Harrold Carswell, 91st Congress, 2d Sess., Executive Report 91-14, February 27, 1970, Individual Views of Messrs. Bayh, Hart, Kennedy, and Tidings, 13, Senate Judiciary Committee Report. Nixon's list of 150-odd possible nominees for the court has not survived. Dean, *The Rehnquist Choice,* 13, 294, n.42. On the Fourth Circuit, Fifth and Eighth Circuits, most of the conservative judges of the right age—people like, say, Herbert Boreman and Pat Mehaffy—were generally too old and/or too conservative to win confirmation. Consequently, Nixon probably was right to look to district judges once the Senate rejected Haynsworth if he insisted on a Southern judge. He was wrong, however, to choose Carswell.

100. James Simon, Interview with Justice Blackmun, May 7, 1991, Box 108, Folder 2, Blackmun MSS; Linda Greenhouse, *Becoming Justice Blackmun: Harry Blackmun's Supreme Court Journey* (New York: Times Books, 2005), 45 (Burger's delight); Harry Blackmun to Warren Burger, November 13, 1969, Box 51, Folder 2, Blackmun MSS.

101. Harry Blackmun, Undated and Untitled Memorandum on Appointment, Box 1548, Folder 10, Blackmun MSS; William Rehnquist, Memorandum to the Attorney General Re: Judicial Selection, Box 1549, FOIA Nomination Materials, Blackmun Papers. (While this memorandum is dated July 10, 1969, it cannot have been written then, since it refers to the Haynsworth and Carswell battles.); Brent Fisse and John Braithwaite, *The Impact of Publicity on Corporate Offenders* 49 (Albany: SUNY Press, 1984) ("generally").

102. Blackmun, Undated and Untitled Memorandum on Appointment; Spencer Rich, "Hill Gets Data on Blackmun: Blackmun's Net Worth Is $125,000, Justice Dept. Tells Senate," *WP*, April 16, 1970.

103. John MacKenzie, "Dissatisfied ABA Aides Seek New Role on Court Nominees," *WP*, April 4, 1970; Fred Graham, "Blackmun to Get Broad A.B.A. Study: Panel Adds Third Category of Evaluation—Change Is Linked to Criticism," *NYT*, April 19, 1970; Fred Graham, "Bar's Top Rating Given Blackmun: Panel Unanimously Declares the Supreme Court Choice Meets 'High Standards,'" id., April 29, 1970; Graham, "Early A.B.A. Vote on Court Is Asked: Mitchell Is Urged to Consult on Prospective Nominees," id., May 18, 1970.

104. Bob Dole, Memorandum for the President, April 14, 1970, Box 1549, Folder 8, Blackmun MSS; Nina Totenberg, "Judge Worries About Ties to Chief Justice: Nixon Nominee Blackmun Is Old Burger Friend; President Is Reassuring," *NO*, April 20,1970; Blackmun, Undated and Untitled Memorandum on Appointment.

105. Blackmun, Undated and Untitled Memorandum on Appointment; Warren Burger to Harry Blackmun, April 27, 1970,http://digitalcommons.law.scu.edu/cgi/viewcontent.cgi?articl e=1067&context=historical; PPF, Memoranda from the President, Memorandum for the Attorney General, April 22, 1970, Box 2, Folder 4, RMNL. "When I was first nominated for this Bench, I was severely criticized by the Chief Justice for submitting to a press conference at Rochester," Blackmun recorded later. "Actually, it was the best thing I could have done, for it cleared the atmosphere, got the press off my back, and I believe helped tremendously in the unanimous confirmation vote both in the Senate Judiciary Committee and in the full Senate." Memorandum, December 4, 1982, Cable News Network Broadcast, Box 1441, Folder 3, Blackmun MSS.

106. Nomination of Harry Blackmun, 40; Frank, *Clement Haynsworth*, 119-21.

107. PPF, Memorandum for Bob Haldeman, April 13, 1970, Memoranda from the President, Box 2, Folder 4, RMNL ("to the right," "highest," "same," "forced"); PPF, RN Tape May 13, 1970, Memoranda From the President, Box 2, Folder 5, id. ("Incidentally," "some").

108. Matt Lassiter, *The Silent Majority: Suburban Politics in the Sunbelt South* (Princeton: Princeton University Press, 2006), 232–39; Panetta, *Bring Us Together*, at 350-71; Gareth Davies, *See Government Grow: Education Politics from Johnson to Reagan* 129 (Lawrence: University Press of Kansas, 2007) (*Star*).

109. Claudia Levy, "30 'Occupy' Attorney General's Office," *WP*, July 2, 1969; Alexander v. Holmes County Board of Education, 396 U.S. 19 (1969); Dean Kotlowski, *Nixon's Civil Rights: Politics, Principle and Policy* (Cambridge: Harvard University Press, 2001), 30–31; POF, Annotated News Summary, January 13, 1969, Box 31, Folder 4, RMNL; POF, Pat Buchanan, Memorandum for the President, February 17, 1970, Meeting Series, Box 8/80, id. ("childish," "irresponsible," "We"); POF, Jim Keogh, Memorandum for the President's File, Cabinet Meeting, February 18, 1970, Box 80, Meeting Series, id. "When Holmes v. Alexander came out the 'liberal' press began the rewards-and-punishment ploy," Warren Burger recalled for Harry Blackmun. "Suddenly I was a 'true liberal,' I had cast off my sponsor, 'cut the umbilical cord,' a la Holmes and TR. This was supposed to give me a taste of what the *Post, Newsweek* and the *Times* could do for me and my 'image' if I would 'play ball.' It was nauseous. But I had seen some good men 'hooked' by this cynical technique and more important I never have and never will play to the Law Review galleries, the *Post* or anyone else. Neither have you. You did not have the *Post* to contend with but I survived 14 years of the worst it could hit me with. Unbelievably they courted me at one stage, pointing out how they would like to credit an 'enlightened moderate'—always, of course, if he minded his Ps and Qs—and cooperated a bit with 'David' [Bazelon]." Burger to Harry Blackmun, April 27, 1970,

110. Statement About Desegregation of Elementary and Secondary Schools, March 24, 1970, http://www.presidency.ucsb.edu/ws/?pid=2923; Remarks to Eastern Media Executives Attending a Briefing on Domestic Policy in Rochester, New York, June 18, 1971, http:// www.presidency.ucsb.edu/ws/index.php?pid=3049&st=eastern+media+executives &stl= ("demagogued"); Lassiter, *The Silent Majority*, 245; Kotlowski, *Nixon's Civil Rights*, 23–38; Davies, *See Government Grow*, 129-34; Fred Graham, "Mitchell Warns of Danger in Attacks on High Court," *NYT*, May 2, 1970; POF, Harry Dent, Report on Meetings of Southerners and Other Conservatives with the President, August 6, 1970, Memoranda

for the President, Box 81, RMNL ("Mister"); "Thurmond Warns of Nixon Defeat in '72 Over Desegregation," *LAT*, July 18, 1970; Bruce Ackerman, *We the People 3: The Civil Rights Revolution* (Cambridge: Belknap, 2014), 250.

111. Warren Weaver, "Haynsworth: It Was Not a Total Loss for Nixon," *NYT*, November 23, 1969; Kevin Phillips, "Nixon's Southern Discomfort," *HE*, July 31, 1971; Wiley Wasden to Richard Nixon, April 13, 1970, WHCF EX FG51A, Box 4, Folder 5, RMNL (enclosing favorable press from Southern papers); Dent, *The Prodigal South*, 212; "Traveler Agnew Volubly Verbalizes Viewpoints," *NYT*, September 20, 1970 ("unabridged"); James Naughton, "Agnew Pledges the South a Seat on the Supreme Court," *NYT*, October 27, 1970 (Greenville); William Chapman, "South to Get Court Seat, Agnew Says," *WP*, October 27, 1970 (Raleigh).

112. "Politics: A New Household Word," *Ti*, May 4, 1970; PPF, Richard Nixon, Memorandum for Bebe Rebozo, April 21, 1970, Memoranda From the President, Box 2, Folder 9, RMNL; Haldeman, *The Haldeman Diaries*, 152 ("real vindication").

113. George Bell, Memorandum for Charles Colson, May 7, 1971, WHCF, Name File, G. Harrold Carswell (3).

114. Dent, *The Prodigal South*, 178; Lassiter, *The Silent Majority*, 249, 271–75; Randy Sanders, *Mighty Peculiar Elections: The New South Gubernatorial Campaigns of 1970 and the Changing Politics of Race* (Baton Rouge: LSU Press, 2002); Jason Sokol, *There Goes My Everything: White Southerners in the Age of Civil Rights, 1945-1975* (New York: Knopf, 2006).

115. Press Commentary on the Election Results, November 8, 1970, Box 73, Folder 11, Campaign 1970, Safire MSS; Richard Nixon, Memorandum for H. R. Haldeman, November 22, 1970, Box 49, Folder 54, Contested Materials MSS ("The wisdom of our trying to get across our version of the campaign results is shown by the fact that over half of the staff memoranda understandably reflect the current mood among the columnists in Washington—that we had 'lost' in 1970—the gain of two in the Senate, the minimal loss of 9 in the House, obviously failed to get through to most of the people who listened to the media, including members of our staff, except for the political sophisticates like [strategists Murray] Chotiner and [Harry] Dent. This means, again, emphasis needs to be given to what I have mentioned on several occasions previously—the need for staff members who work and live in Washington, and who are constantly exposed to the Washington press corps and the Washington chit chat, to get a balanced point of view. Otherwise, they are going to reflect the downbeat attitude of most of Washington to everything that we are doing."); Rick Perlstein, *Nixonland: The Rise of a President and the Fracturing of America* (New York: Scribner, 2008), 535 ("Senate.").

Chapter 7

1. http://www.theodore-roosevelt.com/alice.html; Warren Burger to Harry Blackmun, September 21, 1969, Box 51, Folder 2, Blackmun MSS; Burger to Blackmun, September 17, 1969, id. ("incredible").

2. Warren Burger to Harry Blackmun, May 21, 1970, Box 51, Folder 3, Blackmun MSS ("get people"); Burger to Blackmun, June 5, 1970, Box 90, Folder 6; Blackmun to Burger, May 26, 1970, Box 51, Folder 3, Blackmun Papers.

3. Harry Blackmun, "A Tribute to Warren E. Burger," 22 *WMLR* 15, 16 (1996); Linda Greenhouse, *Becoming Justice Blackmun: Harry Blackmun's Supreme Court Journey* (New York: Times Books, 2005), 51; Blackmun to Alice and Bob Damkroger, June 2, 1970, Box 1358, Folder 1, id.; Blackmun to Myrtle and John Briggs, May 14, 1970, Box 1576, Folder 11, id.; (Blackmun put a, similar question to Judge Edward Devitt, May 22, 1970, id. He was obviously well aware Burger could be bossy.); Blackmun to Joseph Ryan, June 2, 1970, Box 1359, Folder 9, Blackmun MSS ("satisfaction"); Unsigned undated document, Box 1442, Folder 1, Blackmun MSS ("Twins"). Blackmun's mother struck an optimistic tone about the future of her son's relationship with Burger in a letter to the Chief Justice: "There is no doubt in my mind that both of you have been led by a Higher Power to continue your work together at this crucial stage in the history of the Court and I am sure each of you will be given the courage to meet the challenges that will come and try to discover in those challenges what is best for our country." Theo Blackmun to Warren Burger, n.d. (c. May, 1970), Box 1360, Folder 5, Blackmun Papers.

4. Warren Burger to Lewis Powell and William Rehnquist, March 14, 1972, Box 326, Folder 2, Powell MSS; "An Ode to the Chief Justice," n.d., Box 490, Burger, Harlan MSS.

5. Warren Burger to Harry Blackmun, May 21, 1970, Box 51, Folder 3, Blackmun MSS; Ashe v. Swenson, 397 U.S. 436 (1970); Burger to Blackmun, June 30, 1971, Box 1403, Folder 5, Blackmun MSS ("The President," "It").

6. John Ehrlichman, *Witness to Power: The Nixon Years* (New York: Simon and Schuster, 1982), 133.

7. OVAL 576–11, September 20, 1971, 11:47 A.M., Haldeman, NT.

8. OVAL 576-5, September 18, 1971, 10:05 A.M., Haldeman, NT.

9. WHT 6–84, July 1, 1971, 6:00 P.M., Hoover, NT; New York Times v. United States, 403 U.S. 713 (1971); Oval 576–5 ("[I]f").

10. "ABA Unit Asks Voice in High Court Selection," *LAT*, May 18, 1970; John MacKenzie, "ABA to Aid in Picking Justices," *WP*, July 28, 1970.

11. "Attorney General Mitchell Terminates Association's Advance Screening of Supreme Court Nominees," 57 *ABAJ* 1175, 1176 (December 1971); EOB 291–11, October 18, 1971, 3:47 P.M., Ehrlichman and Mitchell, NT ("cut-throat"). See Steven Teles, *The Rise of the Conservative Legal Movement: The Battle for Control of the Law* (Princeton: Princeton University Press, 2008).

12. Egil Krogh to David Young, Supreme Court Nomination, n.d., Box 17, Poff/Supreme Court, Young MSS ("You can bet that the army of students, the ACLU, the ADA, and the Universities are putting to work . . . will focus on every possible weakness in background."); William Greider, "Finding the Skeletons in Nominees' Closets," *WP*, October 22, 1971.

13. Fred Graham, "How to Pick a Justice or Two," *NYT*, October 3, 1971 (Ehrlichman); OVAL No. 577–3, September 20, 1971, 12:45 P.M., Burns, NT (The adviser was Arthur Burns.). Egil Krogh, Memorandum for John Ehrlichman, September 24, 1971, Box 17, Friday/Lillie/ Supreme Court, Young MSS.

14. Oval 576–6, September 18, 1971, 10:40 A.M., Mitchell, NT (quotations); WHT 10–2, September 24, 1971, 1:52 P.M., Colson, id. (Frankfurter). See John Ehrlichman, Memorandum for H.R. Haldeman, November 6, 1971, Box 5, Folder 59, Contested Materials MSS ("The nationwide crime statistics for the last three years have not been very good. On the other hand, Washington, D.C.'s record has been excellent, given all the problems of this place. In truth, the difference is that we have poured an unbelievable amount of money into law enforcement in the District and it is governed by a dictatorship rather than an elected Mayor and City Council. We've been able to do a lot of things in the management of the city government that the electorate would never have stood for if they had had any say in it. And it's gotten results. I'm not sure how this issue can be handled in the coming campaign . . . "[A]ll in all it is not a good national record and we're going to be on the defensive in this area and we'd better start laying some plans right now for meeting the political onslaught. There is no sign that the statistics are going to get any better in the coming year.")

15. Swann v. Charlotte-Mecklenburg School District, 402 U.S. 1 (1971); Earl Maltz, *The Chief Justiceship of Warren Burger, 1969-1986* (Columbia: University of South Carolina Press, 2000), 12 ("[H]is efforts to assert intellectual leadership over the Court often degenerated into fiascoes."); Bernard Schwartz, *Swann's Way: The School Busing Case & The Supreme Court* (New York: Oxford University Press, 1986), 111, 86–88 (Douglas).

16. Kevin McMahon, *Nixon's Court: His Challenge to Judicial Liberalism and Its Political Consequences* (Chicago: University of Chicago Press, 2011), 104–5 ("worse," Mitchell); "Abolish High Court—Martha Mitchell," *CT*, April 22, 1971. "There is resentment against the decision," Harry Dent informed the president with relief once Swann was handed down, "but it seems to fall on the Court." Dent, Memorandum for the President, April 21, 1971, WHCF Ex FG 51, Box 1, Folder 6, RMNL.

17. PPF, Nixon, Memorandum for John Ehrlichman, January 28, 1971, Memoranda From the President, Box 3, Folder 12, RMNL; Dean Kotlowski, *Nixon's Civil Rights: Politics, Principle and Policy* 54-62 (Cambridge: Harvard University Press, 2002 (frustration with Romney and desire to avoid firing him); Dov Grohsgal, *Southern Strategies: The Politics of Southern Desegregation and the Nixon White House* (PhD dissertation, Princeton University, 2013), 203–9.

18. John Dean, *The Rehnquist Choice: The Untold Story of the Nixon Appointment That Redefined the Supreme Court* (New York: Free Press, 2001), 34.
19. OVAL 576–6, September 18, 1971; Ben Franklin, "Poff Factors: Civil Rights and Privacy," *NYT*, October 3, 1971.
20. Dean, *The Rehnquist Choice*, 90; Richard Poff to Bessie Hawes, June 28, 1967, Box 448, Supreme Court, 1967, Misc., Poff MSS; Franklin, "Poff Factors: Civil Right and Privacy," *NYT*, October 3, 1971 (quoting Poff as having said in 1970, "I would rather be on the United States Supreme Court than be President" and alluding to his "low key but persistent personal campaign for a seat on the Supreme Court—'he has been running hard since 1969,' a Poff aide conceded this week"); OVAL 575–2, September 17, 1971, 1:17 P.M., Haldeman, NT.
21. OVAL 575–2, September 17, 1971, 1:17 P.M., Haldeman, NT ("want"); WHT 9–101, September 20, 1971, 7:40 P.M., Mitchell, id. ("impressed," "But," Mitchell's view); WHT 9–112, September 22, 1971, 11:14 A.M., Buchanan, id.
22. OVAL 576–6, September 18, 1971 (need for speed); WHT 9–101, September 20, 1976; WHT 9–101, September 20, 1976, Mitchell, NT (quotations); Robert Semple, "Justice Black, 85, Quits High Court, Citing His Health," *NYT*, September 18, 1971; Carroll Kilpatrick, "Hugo Black Quits Supreme Court, Cites Bad Health," *WP*, September 18, 1971.
23. OVAL 581–4, September 30, 1971, 10:07 A.M., Mitchell (law firm), NT; Paul Edwards, "Why Did Poff Shun Chance at Court?" *WP*, October 12, 1971 (law firm); Clarence Mitchell to Quentin Burdick, September 27, 1971, Box 39, Folder 4, Rauh MSS; Leadership Conference, Press Release, September 27, 1971 (Wilkins), Rauh MSS; "ADA Rejects Poff Candidacy to Supreme Court Nomination," Press Release, Box 39, Folder 4, id.; John MacKenzie, "Court Fitness of Poff Is Attacked: Foes Dig Into Records," *WP*, September 27, 1971; "Meany Indicates Labor Might Oppose Poff," *CT*, September 30, 1971 ("racist"); "Meany Warns Against Court Reactionaries," *LAT*, September 27, 1971 (("narrow"); "Acts to Avoid Long Battle in Senate on Confirmation," *NYT*, October 3, 1971 (feminists); OVAL 580–13, September 29, 1971, 11:55 A.M., Haldeman and Kissinger, NT ("minister"); Jack Greenberg to Louis Pollak, September 28, 1971, Box 57, Supreme Court Vacancies, 1971-72, Pollak MSS: "Joe Rauh (to whom I read your letter) is nevertheless determined to do battle and says that Clarence Mitchell feels very, very strongly that Poff should be opposed as vigorously as possible." Pollak, then in England, had tried to defend Poff to his NAACP colleagues on the grounds "that he has a first-rate legal mind and is otherwise a good person" and "that we do not have the right to insist that only people who would decide cases the way we would like them decided have the right to sit on the Court." William Coleman to Louis Pollak, October 1, 1971, id. (summarizing and agreeing with Pollak's position). For Brown's recommendations of Poff for a Supreme Court seat, see Edmund G. Brown to Nixon, April 9, 1970, WHCF, Name File, Richard Poff (4), RMNL, Edmund G. Brown to Nixon, September 30, 1971, Folder 3, id.
24. Thomas Foley, "Nixon Urged to Name Poff to Supreme Court: Celler and McCulloch of Judiciary Panel Say Virginian Would Make Good Justice," *LAT*, September 23, 1971; see, for example, petition from eighty-three signatories in Congress to Richard Nixon, September 21, 1971, WHCF, Name File, Richard Poff 1971-72 (10) and Gerald Ford to Richard Nixon, September 22, 1971, id., (6) ("There is no more honorable, decent Member of the Congress than Dick Poff."); WHT 9–101, September 20, 1971 ("Well"); OVAL 579–10, September 28, 1971, 4:23 P.M., Hugh Scott, Robert Griffin, Gerald Ford, Leslie Arends, Clark MacGregor, Ron Ziegler, George Shultz, and John Ehrlichman, NT; OVAL 580–13, September 29, 1971.
25. OVAL 579-10, September 28, 1971 ("But"); OVAL 580–13, September 29, 1971.
26. OVAL 579-10, September 28, 1971 ("We"); OVAL 581-4, September 30, 1971, 10:07 A.M., Mitchell, NT; Fred Graham, "A.B.A. Panel to Meet Tomorrow on Poff," *NYT*, October 1, 1971 (reporting divisions within Administration over whether Poff's name should be sent alone or as part of "balanced 'ticket,' with Scott "said to favor the ticket approach"); William Coleman to Louis Pollak, October 1, 1971, Box 57, Supreme Court Vacancies, Pollak Papers.
27. Richard Kleindienst to Lawrence Walsh, September 23, 1971, WHCF EX FG 51, Box 1, Folder 6, RMNL (quoting Frankfurter, "Law and the Mirror of Justices," 105 *UPLR* 781, 795 [1957]; OVAL 581-4, September 30, 1971); Graham, "How to Pick a Justice or Two," October 3, 1971.

28. John Dean and David Young, Memorandum for John Mitchell and John Ehrlichman, September 27, 1971, Meeting with Representative Richard Poff, September 25, 1971, 2:30-6:30 P.M., Box 75, Supreme Court Appointments (1), Dean MSS.

29. David Young, Memorandum for John Ehrlichman, September 30, 1971, Box 17, Supreme Court Nominations, Young MSS.

30. Leonard Garment, Memorandum for the President, September 30, 1971, WHCF EX FG 51, Box 1 (6), RMNL.

31. OVAL 581-4, September 30, 1971.

32. Greider, "Finding the Skeletons in Nominees' Closets" (Seymour); Dean, *The Rehnquist Choice*, at 117-20; John MacKenzie, "Poff Rules Out High Court Post, Cites Opposition: Move Adds to Confusion on Vacancies," *WP*, October 3, 1971.

33. Ben Franklin, "Senator Warned Poff of a Floor Battle," *NYT*, October 6, 1971 (quotations); Franklin, "Poff Is Reported to Have Feared a Senate Filibuster," id., October 5, 1961.

34. H. R. Haldeman Diaries, October 2, 1971, RMNL; Jack Greenberg to Louis Pollak, October 15, 1971, Box 57, Supreme Court Vacancies, 1971-1972, Pollak MSS; Dean, *The Rehnquist Choice*, 93, 121; Jack Anderson, "The Washington Merry Go-Round: Poff put Family Above Dream Career," *WP*, November 2, 1971. "Of course many are saying that the prospective opposition of the NAACP and the liberal forces caused Poff to withdraw," William Coleman wrote Lou Pollak. "I am pretty sure this was not the case, but on the other hand I guess the liberal forces do better by having people think they have that power." William Coleman to Louis Pollak, October 11, 1971, Box 57, Supreme Court Vacancies, 1971–72, Pollak MSS.

35. MacKenzie, "Poff Rules Out High Court Post" (Ford and Rauh); "Mr. Poff Steps Aside," *WP*, October 6, 1971.

36. Dean, *The Rehnquist Choice*, 101; WHT 585–15, October 5, 1971, 5:29 P.M., Poff, NT. Poff would later become a justice on the Virginia Supreme Court. Paul Vitello, "Richard H. Poff, Who Withdrew Court Bid, Dies," *NYT*, July 2, 2011.

37. See, for example, "How Poff Rejected Life Goal," *CT*, October 6, 1971: "Ronald L. Ziegler, Nixon's press secretary, has declared that it was not correct that the President was 'starting from scratch' in seeking a replacement for Poff. But high administration officials here said flatly that the White House had counted so heavily on Poff's successful ascension to the court that no alternate nominees came immediately to mind when the young, popular Virginia conservative abruptly and publicly declined on Saturday."

38. Oval 576-11, September 20, 1971, 11:47 A.M., Haldeman (health); OVAL 865–14, February 28, 1973, 9:12 A.M.; John Dean, *The Nixon Defense: What He Knew and When He Knew It* (New York: Viking, 2014), 244 (health, "dumb," Lafontant); OVAL 576–6, September 18, 1971 ("That's," Brooke, Brown, Coleman).

39. OVAL 576–6, September 18, 1971, 10:40 A.M., Mitchell, NT (Bickel); WHT 9–101, September 20, 1971 (Jewish seat); OVAL 575–2, 1116, September 17, 1971, 1:17 P.M., Haldeman, NT (Spector). "I do understand that Judge Arlin M. Adams is on the list of ten," William Coleman reported to Pollak. "He is Jewish, and, I guess, his appointment is a possibility as he was a very early supporter of Mr. Nixon even when the political leaders in Pennsylvania were supporting Governor Rockefeller. Friday night at a dinner party, however, Arlin said he felt his chances were killed because of the Sister Jogues Egan opinion [in which Adams set aside the contempt conviction of a nun Coleman represented, who refused to tell a grand jury what she knew about the plan of Philip Berrigan and other antiwar activists to kidnap Henry Kissinger and to engage in other actions protesting the Vietnam War. Adams's majority opinion instructed the district court to hold a hearing to decide whether the questions asked of Egan grew out of information obtained by federal agents in an illegal wiretap on her order's telephones. Donald Jamison, "Court Upholds Nun in Berrigan Inquiry," *NYT*, May 29, 1971]. In fact, he remarked that Mitchell had seen him in London, given him hell for writing it and given him even more hell that it caused a 47-page opinion which has resulted in upsetting all of the Government's grand jury investigations involving political or other so-called radical movements. I think Arlin is as good as you could expect Nixon to appoint." William Coleman to Louis Pollak, October 11, 1971, Box 57, Supreme Court Vacancies 1971-72, Pollak MSS.

40. WHT 9–101, September 20, 1971, ("Catholic conservative"); OVAL 575–7, September 17, 1971 ("hell," Agnew, Hoover); OVAL 576–5, September 18, 1971 (Mrs. Smith); WHT 9–101, September 20, 1971, 7:40 P.M., Mitchell, NT (Walsh); OVAL 581–4, September 30, 1971 (Powell, Lillie, Bacon); OVAL 576–6, September 18, 1971 (remainder).

41. Fred Graham, "Burger Hails Black and Harlan as Supreme Court Opens With Two Vacancies," *NYT*, October 5, 1971; Ronald Ostrow, "Supreme Court Pays Tribute to 2 Justices," *LAT*, October 5, 1971 ("grim"); John MacKenzie, "High Court Puts Off All Major Cases," *WP*, September 25, 1971.

42. H. R. Haldeman, *The Haldeman Diaries: Inside the Nixon White House* (New York: G. P. Putnam's Sons, 1994), 147; Robert Byrd to Richard Nixon, January 12, 1970, WHCF EX FG 51, Box 1, Folder 3, RMNL ("I plan to send this same telegram to the President every day this week"); Byrd to Kenneth BeLieu, January 12, 1970, id.

43. Haldeman, *The Haldeman Diaries* 361. Though Spong's opposition to Carswell would have made him a nonstarter, Nixon later considered Baker, as will be seen later in this chapter.

44. OVAL 587–3, October 8, 1971, 10:04 A.M., Mitchell and Ehrlichman, NT.

45. Daily Diary, October 8, 1971, RMNL; "Robert Byrd: Nixon's Next Court Choice," *WDN*, October 9, 1971;" WHT 11-26, October 11, 1971, 8:57 A.M., Mitchell, NT. See also, for example, "Call Byrd High Court Choice," *CT*, October 10, 1971; John Herbers, "Robert Byrd Considered for Supreme Court Seat," *NYT*, October 10, 1971; "Call Byrd High Court Choice," *CT*, October 10, 1971.

46. WHT 11–26, October 11, 1971; Thomas Foley, "Byrd Called Unlikely High Court Nominee," *LAT*, October 11, 1971 (McGovern); George Lardner, "Byrd Reported on Nixon List for Court Seat," id., October 10, 1971.

47. David Corbin, *The Last Great Senator: Robert C. Byrd's Encounters with Eleven United States Presidents* (Dulles: Potomac, 2012), 290 ("hillbilly"); Robert Sherrill, "The Embodiment of Poor White Power," *NYT*, February 28, 1971; Ben Franklin, "Evidence Grows That Byrd Will Get High Court Seat," *NYT*, October 11, 1971; Dorothy McCardle, "A Georgetown Party for 500 Closest Friends," *WP*, October 11, 1971.

48. "How to Undermine the Court," *NYT*, October 12, 1971; "The President, the Court and Senator Byrd," *WP*, October 11, 1971.

49. Adam Clymer, "Robert C. Byrd, 1917-2010: A Pillar of the Senate, A Champion of His State," *NYT*, June 29, 2010; Corbin, *The Last Great Senator*, 215–16, 221, 225–28, 271–78, 285.

50. Spencer Rich, "Byrd Held Unlikely for Court," *WP*, October 12, 1971; WHT 11–49, October 12, 1971, 8:40 A.M., Ziegler, NT; OVAL 590–2 ("One," "We're"), October 13, 1971, 11:06 A.M., Haldeman, id. ("chance").

51. "Woman on the Court," *WP*, September 30, 1971 (Elvera Burger); Dorothy McCardle, "Friendly Venom Over the Court," id., October 23, 1971 (Martha Mitchell); "Woman on Court Urged by Feminist," id., October 5, 1971 (Friedan); Fred Graham, "Nixon Problem: Woman Justice?," *NYT*, September 24, 1971 ("talking"); "Pat Believes Age Is a Factor in Putting Woman on the Court," *CT*, September 25, 1971; Lynn Lilliston and Marlene Cimons, "Women Front-runners for High Court," *LAT*, September 30, 1971 (speculation); Anna Hayes, *Without Precedent: The Life of Susie Marshall Sharp* (Chapel Hill, University of North Carolina Press, 2008); Sonja David, *Lady Law: The Story of Arizona Supreme Court Justice Lorna Lockwood* (Chandler: Brighton, 2012); Lorna Lockwood, "An Independent Judiciary," 51 *WoLJ* 117, 119 (1965).

52. Carroll Kilpatrick, "Nixon Widens Criteria for Court Nominee," *WP*, September 21, 1971; Ken Clawson, "Nixon May Nominate Woman: Mitchell Tells of 'Serious' Consideration," id., September 24, 1971; "Caucus Offers 10 Women for Supreme Court," *LAT*, September 28, 1971. An earlier version had included some especially unlikely names, such as those of Carol Agger and Pauli Murray. See Isabelle Shelton, "The Women Who Qualify for the Court," *WS*, September 21, 1971, Box 389, Folder 4, Mink MSS: "The list the caucus is drawing up for submission to the White House, currently includes Judge Hufstedler, Rep. Griffiths, Patricia Harris, the District's Judge Bernita Shelton Matthews and tax lawyer Caroline Ager [*sic*] (Mrs. Abe Fortas, wife of a former justice), Judge Cornelia Blanche Kennedy of the U.S. District Court of Michigan, District lawyer Marguerite Rawalt, Brandeis University professor

Pauli Murray, and Mrs. Rita Hauser, a Nixon appointee to the United Nations' Commission on Human Rights."

53. Graham, "Nixon Problem: Woman Justice?,"; Lee Edmon, Shirley Hufstedler OH, January 13, 2007, 58, 94; http://www.americanbar.org/content/dam/aba/directories/women_trailblazers/hufstedler_interview_3.authcheckdam.pdf; OVAL 580-13, September 29, 1971, 11:55 A.M., Haldeman, and Kissinger ("left-wing"); OVAL 579-10, September 28, 1971 ("bag"). Mitchell would tell Nixon that Hufstedler is "a left-winger and her husband is a leading left-handed Democrat." EOB 291-11, October 18, 1971, 10:04 A.M.

54. OVAL 581–4, September 30, 1971 ("one or," "we got," "erratic," "emotional"); OVAL 587–3, October 8, 1971 ("educated"); OVAL 589-2, October 12, 1971, 5:28 P.M., Ehrlichman, NT (vote); OVAL 579-10, September 28, 1971 ("can't vote against").

55. WHT 11–40, October 11, 1971, 8:57 A.M., Mitchell, NT ("frigid," "standing"); OVAL 581–4, September 30, 1971 ("longer"); Cecil Fleming, "Order in the Kitchen! Justice Lillie Presiding," *LAT*, April 7, 1966; "Potential High Court Nominees," *NYT*, October 14, 1971; Barbara Martin, "Sketch of Judge Lillie," id., October 23, 1971; "Oral History of Justice Mildred Lillie, California Court of Appeals," 5 *CaLH* 65 (2010) (by Mary Blackstone); Blanche Seaver to Richard Nixon, September 24, 1971, WHCF, Name File, Mildred Lillie (3), RMNL; OVAL 587–3, October 8, 1971 ("hard-nosed"). Mitchell's list of eligible women included DC Superior Court Judge Sylvia Bacon, Assemblywoman Constance Cook (R-NY), Martha Griffiths, Representative Margaret Heckler (R-MA), Shirley Hufstedler, Cornelia Kennedy, Jewel Lafontant, Mildred Lillie, Soia Mentschikoff, Constance Baker Motley, Dorothy Nelson, Ellen Peters, and Susie Sharp. It was not a very good list from Nixon's perspective, because it included liberals. "Only two Democrats on the list (Sharp and Lillie) were deemed true 'conservatives.' And of the five Republicans listed, only Cornelia Kennedy possessed even minimal judicial experience." It was reduced to four—Heckler, Kennedy, Lillie, and Peters, and Mitchell indicated that he supported Lillie. David Yalof, *Pursuit of Justices, Presidential Politics and the Selection of Supreme Court Nominees* (Chicago: University of Chicago Press, 1999), 118–19, 120–21.

56. WHT 11–40, October 11, 1971 (Volpe, husband); John Dean, "Musing on a Belated Visit With California Justice Mildred Lillie," https://verdict.justia.com/2015/01/09/musing-belated-visit-california-justice-mildred-lillie (Lillie later laughingly recalled "the lanky and pleasant young man at the Justice Department who had carried her bags [who] was now Chief Justice of the United States," William Rehnquist.); WHT 11–35, October 11, 1971, 12:37 P.M, Mitchell, NT ("confirmed"); Mario Biaggi and other members of Congress to Richard Nixon, October 14, 1971, WHCF EX FG 51, Box 1, Folder 6, RMNL; Patrick Buchanan, "Memorandum for the President," September 29, 1971, id.

57. WHT 11–33, October 11, 1971, 12:31 P.M., Mitchell, NT (teasing); OVAL 589–1, October 12, 1971, 4:20 P.M., Mitchell, and Ehrlichman, id. ("chance," "vote"); OVAL 581–4, September 30, 1971 ("woman's").

58. "Amounts Received by Friday's Firm in School Suits," *AD*, October 14, 1971; OVAL 576–6, September 18, 1971.

59. Jack Bass, "Frank M. Johnson Jr.," http://www.encyclopediaofalabama.org/article/h-1253 (King); John MacKenzie, "Crossing the Judicial Line," *WP*, June 13, 1974 (Burger's promotion of Johnson to Mitchell); "Judges: Interpreter in the Front Line," *Ti*, May 12, 1967 ("I'm"); Roger Newman, *Hugo Black: A Biography* (New York: Pantheon, 1994), 622 (Black's hope). Because Burger's papers are sealed until 2026 and the portion of Frank Johnson's papers involving his possible 1971 appointment to the Supreme Court is also closed, there is little contemporary archival information about his possible nomination, save in the Nixon Library, where there are many endorsements of him from Alabamians, including the mayor of Montgomery, the entire Montgomery police department, the *Alabama Journal*, and the *Montgomery Advertiser*. Earl James to Richard Nixon, September 24, 1971, WHCF, Name File, Frank Johnson (6); Edward Wright to Richard Nixon, September 23, 1971, RMNL; "Johnson in for Black," *AJ*, September 21, 1971, September 21, 1971, id., (1); "Why Not Judge Johnson?," *MA*, September 28, 1971, id. ("Although Judge Johnson may not appreciate it, coming from such a hair shirt as *The Advertiser*, he would be a good choice. And now even the lawyers of this area appear to agree by overwhelming margins, as do many blacks. Strange

bedfellows, Judge, but there it is."). Though Johnson had his Alabama detractors, he also had powerful support. As an unsigned memo in John Dean's papers said, "Johnson is best known nationally for his rulings in civil rights cases. . . . But Judge Johnson's civil rights decisions are best viewed in the context of his total performance as a judge and in light of his overall commitment to reason, moderation, and the supremacy of law. . . . In the past 12 months, the prevailing local attitude toward Judge Johnson has changed markedly, perhaps in recognition of the fact that he helped bring the state's school systems through a turbulent and trying period relatively intact. . . . Judge Johnson is a 'law and order' judge in the best sense of the term. . . . The U.S. Attorney's office, in fact, currently has a 98% conviction rate in his court. But if Johnson is tough in criminal cases, he is also fair." The memo concluded by touting Johnson as "a Southerner who would be confirmed virtually without opposition, and who would provide the Supreme Court with the capacity for work it so desperately needs and with the intellectual leadership it no longer seems to have. The appointment of Judge Johnson would tend to unite the country, rather than divide it again; and it would be a recognition, not of the darkness from which the South is striving to emerge, but of all that is worth preserving in the South, and in the American tradition." Judge Frank M. Johnson Jr., n.d., Box 76, Supreme Court Vacancies (2), Dean MSS. In contrast, William Coleman was unimpressed. "There is a push for Frank Johnson," he reported to Lou Pollak. "One of his supporters called me, and when he was finished I was left somewhat disgusted. Judge Johnson's supporters are saying that he ought to be appointed because he is a strict constructionist and 1) he has never decided a civil rights case where he has gone one inch beyond the existing Supreme Court decisions; (2) that he has never ordered busing in any school desegregation cases; (3) that he is a very strict judge in criminal matters; (4) that he is the only judge that has ever issued an injunction against Martin Luther King. In other words, men have to do terrible things to achieve their ambitions, particularly when the leadership of the country is of such low moral character." William Coleman to Louis Pollak, October 11, 1971, Box 57, Supreme Court Vacancies, 1971-72, Pollak MSS.

60. Jack Bass, *Taming the Storm: The Life and Times of Judge Frank M. Johnson, Jr. and the South's Fight for Civil Rights* (New York: Doubleday, 1993), 78, 275–76 (Johnson did not explain why it would have ruined the GOP).

61. MacKenzie, "Crossing the Judicial Line" (Burger's urging of Friday to Mitchell).

62. William Rehnquist, Memorandum for the Attorney General, Possible Bases for Opposition to Senate Confirmation of Herschel Friday, October 12, 1971, Box 75, Supreme Court Nominees (1), Dean MSS.

63. OVAL 587–3, October 8, 1971 ("work," "Is he," "Arkansas Harlan"); OVAL 589–1, October 12, 1971.

64. OVAL 589–1, October 12, 1971.

65. Id., Milton Young to Harry Flemming, May 15, 1969, WHCF, Name File, Sylvia Bacon (2), RMNL; "Setback for Justice," *Newsd*, October 27, 1969, WHCF, Name File, Charles Clark (2), id. (complaining about Clark's appointment to the Fifth Circuit); The President's News Conference, October 12, 1971, http://www.presidency.ucsb.edu/ws/index.php?pid=3186.

66. "Attorney General Mitchell Terminates Association's Advance Screening of Supreme Court Nominations," 1177.

67. Conversation with Nina Totenberg, July 14, 2015; OVAL 596–3, October 19, 1971, 10:14 A.M., Mitchell, NT (Gignoux); Paul Weiner, "Law School Professors Ponder," *HLRec*, October 15, 1971.

68. Fred Graham, "President Asks Bar Unit to Check 6 for High Court," *NYT*, October 14, 1971 (*Who's Who*); "Camera Obscura," id., October 15, 1971; "Mr. Nixon and the Court: Doing It the Hard Way," *WP*, October 14, 1971; "The Supreme Court Puzzle," *WSJ*, October 18, 1971.

69. Greider, "Finding the Skeletons in Nominees' Closet" (petitions and Seymour); "Nixon Wants a Racist Court," *CDD*, October 18, 1971; William Raspberry, "Bigots for High Court," *WP*, October 13, 1971; "Six in Court Race Not Checked Yet," *NYT*, October 17, 1971 (feminists); Warren Weaver, "Some Regret Votes Against Haynsworth," id., October 18, 1971; Ronald Ostrow, "Bayh Indicates He'd Fight Confirmation of 6 on Court List," *LAT*, October 16, 1971 (Kennedy).

70. Dorothy McCardle, "Martha's Man Is Friday," *WP*, October 5, 1971.

71. WHT 11–86, October 14, 1971, 9 A.M., Mitchell, NT; "Attorney General Mitchell Terminates Association's Advance Screening of Supreme Court Nominees," 1176.

72. WHT 11-86, October 14, 1971; John Osborne, "Chosen Two," *TNR*, November 6, 1971, 12; PPF, Richard Nixon, Memorandum to Bob Haldeman and Ron Ziegler, April 14, 1972, Memoranda From the President, Box 3, Folder 18, RMNL (describing Osborne and *Time*'s Hugh Sidey as dishonest and "totally against us"); Ronald Ostrow, "High Court List May Number 15," *LAT*, October 15, 1971; Fred Graham, "Nixon Court List May Be Enlarged: Husband of Woman Judge in Numerous Debt Suits," *NYT*, October 15, 1971; Ken Clawson and John MacKenzie, "ABA List for Court Not Final," *WP*, October 15, 1971; Jack Anderson, "The Washington Merry-Go-Round: Nixon Bent on Law-and-Order Court," id., October 21, 1971 (expletive); Nina Totenberg, "Intrigue and Agony: How Nixon Picked Two Men for the Court," *NO*, November 6, 1971 ("surly").

73. Conversation with Nina Totenberg, July 14, 2015 ("impeccable"); Totenberg, "Intrigue and Agony."

74. OVAL 581–4, September 30, 1971 ("soldier," "space"); OVAL 587-3, October 8, 1971 ("dying," "twice"); WHT 11–26, October 11, 1971 ("soften," "game"); OVAL 593–11, October 15, 1971 ("great," "only," "nationally," "same"), MacKenzie, "Crossing the Judicial Line" (quoting from the letter, which the *Post* had acquired); WHT 11-86, October 14, 1971 ("not anxious," "No," "grace"). Burger, who employed one woman law clerk during the 1970s, routinely segregated clerks from their spouses at his annual black-tie dinner for them at the Supreme Court until 1985. "It was the unvarying practice that clerks and spouses gathered together at the Court for cocktails, but separated for the dinner, when Mrs. Burger would gather the spouses and lead them off to dine at another venue." Joseph Zengerle, "Changing of the Chiefs," 9 *GB* 2d 175, 175 (2006). Of course, he was not the only justice who had trouble adjusting to women at the court, and there were questions about the treatment of African Americans as well. See, for example, Seth Stern and Stephen Wermiel, *Justice Brennan: Liberal Champion* (Boston: Houghton Mifflin, 2010), 473–80; Nina Totenberg, "The Last Plantation," *NewT*, July 26, 1974.

75. OVAL 593–11, October 15, 1971.

76. "Friday Leads Court List, Source Says," *AG*, October 15, 1971 (Fulbright, McClellan, Mills); John McClellan to John Smith, October 18, 1971, Box 571, Folder 28, McClellan MSS ("Herschel Friday has my total and unequivocal support for appointment to the Supreme Court of the United States"); Telephone Memorandum, November 2, 1971, From Mr. Long to Buddy Whiteaker, Re: Herschel Friday, Box 575, Folder 3, McClellan MSS (suggesting that Fulbright's support might be less enthusiastic than McClellan's); John McClellan to Everett Jordan, n.d., id. ("personal," "one"); Statement, n.d., id. (statement that McClellan would have given had Friday gotten the nod); "Lawyers Endorse Friday," *AD*, October 17, 1971 (trial lawyers); "Women Lawyers Support Friday; Labor Does Not," id., October 19, 1971; "Our Man Friday," id., October 15, 1971 ("support"); "Mr. Nixon's List for the High Court," *AG*, October 15, 1971 ("better"); "From the People: The Gazette and Herschel Friday," id., October 19, 1971; "The Central Issue in the Friday Matter," id., October 19, 1971 ("bison"); John Whitaker, Memorandum for John Ehrlichman, October 14, 1971, Box 17, Friday/Lillie/Supreme Court, Young MSS ("avid"); Fred Graham, "Friday Among Six Nixon Considering for Supreme Court," *NYT*, October 14, 1971 (Rockefeller's preference for a Republican); John Bennett, "Nixon's Court List Irks Arkansas GOP," *CA*, October 15, 1971; "Unionists Oppose Choice of Friday," *NYT*, October 21, 1971; "Judge Merit, Not Clients, ACLU Says," *AG*, October 16, 1971; "AFL-CIO Chief Attacks High Court Candidate," *CA*, October 20, 1971; Roy Reed, "Arkansas Liberals Divided Over Potential Supreme Court Nominee's Role in Integration Resistance," *NYT*, October 18, 1971 (NAACP); David Margolick, "At the Bar," id., April 1, 1994. (" 'I grew to know him better,' " Mr. [Philip] Kaplan [a Little Rock attorney who had opposed him in 1970] said. " 'I learned he was a very gracious, wonderful man, a person who was very giving of his time and his resources, a leader of a profession I love, a man who set an example for kindness and gentility in an age where they're not always at a premium.' . . . Mr. Friday's death, at 72, brought condolences from President Clinton and was front-page news in *The Arkansas Democrat-Gazette*. The newspaper was filled for days afterward with large—in some cases,

full-page—paid tributes that noted not only that he had built Arkansas's largest law firm and headed the state bar association but also that he was perhaps the state's leading citizen.").

77. John Dean and David Young, Memorandum for Attorney General John Mitchell and John Ehrlichman, "Interview with Herschel Friday," October 13, 1971, 12:00-7:15 P.M., October 14, 1971, 9:45-11:30 A.M., Box 17, Friday/Lillie/Supreme Court, Young MSS; Dean, *The Rehnquist Choice*, 159–60.

78. OVAL 592–6, October 14, 1971, Unknown time (between 9:36 A.M., and 11:08 A.M., Haldeman, Ehrlichman and Ziegler, NT.

79. Dean and Young, Interview with Herschel Friday ("He also stated that this was the most detailed discussion of this kind he had had with anyone in connection with his nomination").

80. Id.; EOB 289–15, October 14, 1971; Dean, *The Rehnquist Choice*, 160–61, 171.

81. EOB 289–15, October 14, 1971, ("last," "potential," "good," "think," discussing Byrd's withdrawal); Elsie Carper, "Byrd Says He Pulled His Name Off List," *WP*, October 27, 1971; OVAL 593–6, October 15, 1971, 9:10 A.M., Peterson, NT ("member"); Dean, *The Rehnquist Choice*, 174 ("withdraw"). John Ehrlichman's notes on his meetings with Nixon indicated that Friday and Lillie were getting the nod. Ehrlichman, Notes of a Meeting With President, October 12, 1971, Box 6, III (1), Ehrlichman MSS; Notes of Meeting With President, October 15, 1971, id.

82. John Dean and David Young, Memorandum for Attorney General John Mitchell and John Ehrlichman, October 15, 1971, Interview with Justice Mildred Lillie, October 14, 1971, 3:30–8:00 P.M., Box 17, Friday/Lillie/Supreme Court, Young MSS; Sam Yorty recommendation, January 28, 1969, WHCF, Name File, Mildred Lillie (3); and see Sam Yorty to Richard Nixon, September 20, 1971; Mildred Lillie to John Dean, October 19, 1971, Box 75 (4), Dean MSS (Attorney General Evelle Younger; LA County Peter Pitchess and four Supreme Court justices—Chief Justice Donald Wright, Justice Louis Burke, Justice Stanley Mosk, and Justice Marshall McComb); OVAL 581–4, September 30, 1971; WHT Tape 13–8, October 26, 1971, 11:13 A.M., Reagan, NT ("My heart was with Smith," Reagan told Nixon.).

83. Dean and Young, Interview with Justice Mildred Lillie, October 14, 1971; OVAL 594–2, October 18, 1971. Dean and Young commented on her painting in the report. For her cooking, see, for example, Cecil Fleming, "Order in the Kitchen! Justice Lillie Presiding," *LAT*, April 7, 1966; Earl Johnson, "Introduction: Oral History of Justice Mildred Lillie," 5 *CaLH* 65, 68 (2010).

84. OVAL 593–7, October 15, 1971, Haldeman ("jewel," "tough"); OVAL 593–11, October 15, 1971, 10:38 A.M., Mitchell and Ehrlichman ("loose," "Ah").

85. Dean, *The Rehnquist Choice*, 176–77.

86. Don DeBenedictis, "Justice Mildred L. Lillie," *LADJ*, September 12, 1980; John Dean, "Musing on a Belated Visit With California Justice Mildred Lillie," https://verdict.justia.com/2015/01/09/musing-belated-visit-california-justice-mildred-lillie. In a lengthy memoir recorded in the twilight of her career, Lillie spoke circumspectly about the sexism that women attorneys faced and did not even mention the Supreme Court incident. Lillie, "Oral History of Justice Mildred L. Lillie," 5 *CaLH* 71, 131 (2010).

87. "Presiding Justice Mildred Lillie Dies; Served 55 Years on Bench," *MetNE*, October 29, 2002 (Governors Gray Davis and George Deukmejian, Chief Justice Ronald George); Johnson, "Introduction: Oral History of Justice Mildred Lillie," 65, 69–70 (funeral); M. Roger Grace, "Perspectives: Deservedly, Justice Lillie Will Be Honored," *MetNE*, November 3, 2003.

88. DeBenedictis, "Justice Mildred L. Lillie."

89. "The Nation: Nixon's Not So Supreme Court," *Ti*, October 25, 1971; Paul Weiner, "Law School Professors Ponder," *HLRec*, October 15, 1971 (group of students); Laurence Tribe, Memorandum to Dean Sacks, Judge Mildred Lillie, October 17, 1971 (I am grateful to Laurence Tribe for providing me with a copy of this memorandum).

90. Calderon v. City of Los Angeles, 4 Cal. 3d 251, 257 (1971); Holt v. Richardson, 238 F. Supp. 468 (1965); Burns v. Richardson, 384 U.S. 73 (1966). Burns may have been somewhat more ambiguous than the California Supreme Court suggested. See Sanford Levinson, "One Person, One Vote: A Mantra in Need of Meaning," 80 *NCLR* 1269, 1282–84 (2002). The two conservatives on the California Supreme Court were Justices Marshall McComb and Louis Burke.

91. Email, Laurence Tribe to Laura Kalman, July 14, 2015; "FBI on Campus," *HLRec*, November 19, 1971; John MacKenzie, "Researcher Cites Judge Lillie's Sharp Reversals: High Court Candidate's Record Hit," *WP*, October 18, 1971; John MacKenzie, "Researcher Cites State Supreme Court Reversals of Justice Lillie," *LAT*, October 18, 1971; Laurence Tribe, Memorandum to Dean Sacks, October 28, 1971 ("say 'for the record' ") (memorandum given to me by Laurence Tribe); Robert Jackson, "Harvard's Bok Raps FBI Reaction to Lillie Study," *LAT*, December 25, 1971 ("seriously"); "U.S. Aide Defends Nominee Inquiry: Denies the F.B.I. Intimidated a Harvard Law Professor," *NYT*, December 26, 1971.

92. Conversation with Nina Totenberg, July 14, 2015; UCLA Law Petition, October 19, 1971, WHCF, Name File, Mildred Lillie (1), RMNL; Rowland Evans and Robert Novak, "Where Was Mitchell?," *WP*, October 25, 1971 (Los Angeles County Bar Association); Joan Sweeney, "County Bar Official Defends Justice Lillie," *LAT*, October 23, 1971; John Dean, Memorandum for John Ehrlichman, October 20, 1971, Box 75, Folder 2, Dean MSS (reporting telephone call of Paul Iverson); MacKenzie, "Researcher Cites Judge Lillie's Sharp Reversals" (Traynor).

93. "Administration Firmly Defends Justice Lillie's Judicial Record," *LAT*, October 20, 1971; Graham, "Six in Court Race Not Checked Yet: Husband of Woman Judge in Numerous Debt Suits"; Fred Graham, "FBI Is Checking 2 on Court List: Investigates Background of Friday and Judge Lillie," *NYT*, October 19, 1971; OVAL 594–2, October 18, 1971; Nina Totenberg, "Intrigue and Agony" (Rehnquist memorandum, ABA reactions).

94. Charles Colson, Memorandum for John Ehrlichman, Supreme Court Nominations, October 18, 1971, Box 110, Supreme Court, Colson MSS; Leonard Garment, Memorandum for the President, Supreme Court Appointments, October 18, 1971, Box 193, Supreme Court Nominations, Haldeman MSS; Leonard Garment, Memorandum for the President, Supreme Court, October 20, 1971, WHCF EX FG 51 (6) ("guesswork," "feeling," "qualified"); and see Herbert Klein, Memorandum for the Attorney General, October 19, 1971, Box 17, Friday/Lillie/Supreme Court, Young MSS, in which the White House communications director recorded his surprise at what happened after he addressed "a group which appeared to be conservative and which applauded my mention of Vice President Agnew and laughed vigorously at a one-liner in which I said, 'we finally discovered a new way to get a name slandered: say he is a Southerner and suggest him for the Supreme Court.' " Four people had privately criticized the list of six to him. "I find, in a number of circles of those who support us, skepticism regarding what they know about the records of the six names sent to the ABA."

95. OVAL 594–2, October 18, 1971; EOB 291–11, October 18, 1971.

96. Dean, *The Rehnquist Choice*, 190–91.

97. EOB 291–11, October 18, 1971; Dean, "Musings on a Belated Visit with Mildred Lillie."

98. EOB 291–11, October 18, 1971; Laurence Tribe to the Editor, *BG*, November 4, 1971 (letter given me by Laurence Tribe), responding to "Tribe Builds Case Against Rehnquist," id., November 4, 1971 (claiming that Tribe's "research on Judge Mildred L. Lillie led the ABA to declare her unqualified for the nomination"); Roy Wilkins to Lawrence Walsh, October 19, 1971, Part I, Box 130, Folder 6, Leadership Conference MSS.

99. EOB 291–11, October 18, 1971.

100. Id.; WHT 11–138, October 19, 1971, Mitchell, NT ("good," "persuasive," no crook"); OVAL 596–3, October 19, 1971 (Scott and Griffin, "damn," Potter Stewart).

101. EOB 291–11, October 18, 1971.

102. Id. (mediocre); WHT 11–143, October 19, 1971, 5:38 P.M., Mitchell, NT ("play"); WHT 11–138, October 19, 1971, 3 P.M., Mitchell, NT ("bullshit," Catholic deans).

103. OVAL 596-3, October 19, 1971 (woman); WHT 11-31, October 19, 1971, 12:54 P.M., Mitchell; WHT 11–157, October 20, 1971, 9:19 A.M. ("The bar," "[L]et").

104. WHT 12–25, October 20, 1971, 6:17 P.M., NT, Mitchell ("Why," "Civil," "Well"); "Attorney General Mitchell Terminates Association's Advance Screening of Supreme Court Nominees"; OVAL 596–3, October 19, 1971; EOB 281–70, October 21, 1971, 10:07 A.M., Haldeman and Ziegler, NT ("Boy," "This").

105. WHT 12–15, October 20, 1971; WHT 12–25, October 20, 1971 ("She's).

106. John MacKenzie, "ABA Says 2 Unfit for Court," *WP*, October 21, 1971; Spencer Rich, "Hill Sets Nominee Reviews: ABA Dispute Continues on Court 'Leaks,' " *WP*, October 23, 1971; Ronald Ostrow, "Justice Department Accused of Leak on Bar Rating of Pair for Court: ABA Committee Says Administration Disclosed Adverse Appraisals of Mildred Lillie and Friday; Mitchell Denies It," *LAT*, November 2, 1971; Fred Graham, "Nixon Is Expected to Pick Arkansan for Seat on Court," *NYT*, October 21, 1971; EOB 281–70, October 21, 1971 ("haring," "remember").

107. OVAL 596–3, October 19, 1971 ("Southern strategy"); Lewis Powell to Herschel Friday, October 25, 1971, Box 289, Folder 13, Powell MSS (Friday recommendation); Jeffries, *Justice Lewis F. Powell, Jr.* 2, 237 (reasons, stock); John McKenzie, "Stocks Seen Problem for Powell," *WP*, October 31, 1971; Lewis Powell to Jody, Penny, Molly, and Lewis, September 23, 1971, Box 288, Folder 7, Powell MSS.

108. WHT, 11–133, October 19, 1971, 1:26 P.M., Mitchell, NT ("prestigious," "blind"); WHT 11–138, October 19, 1971 ("[T]wo years").

109. OVAL 596-3 ("Powell"); WHT 11–133, October 18, 1971 ("knocked off"); WHT 11–143, 5:38 P.M.; WHT 11–155, October 19, 1971, 8:19 P.M., Mitchell, NT ("I can't find him," Mitchell told Nixon); WHT 11–157, October 20, 1971, 9:19 A.M., Mitchell, id. ("arrange"); OVAL 596-3.

110. WHT 11–143, October 19, 1971 ("this," "arch," "tough," Walsh, sex change); WHT 10–65, October 6, 1971, 8:25 A.M., Goldwater, id. (Goldwater, "Rensler"); Dean, *The Rehnquist Choice*, 86, 129–30 ("Renchburg," "clown," Dean and Moore); OVAL 587–3, October 8, 1971 ("great").

111. WHT 11–153, October 19, 1971, 7:49 P.M., Powell, NT.

112. WHT 11–155, October 19, 1971, 8:19, Mitchell, id.; WHT Tape 12–9, 4:13 P.M., Mitchell, id. ("so old"); Joel Grossman and Stephen Wasby, "The Senate and Supreme Court Nominations: Some Reflections," 1972 *DLJ* 557, 575 (1972) (fourth oldest); WHT 12–15, October 20, 1971, 5:33 P.M., Mitchell (law school, wiretapping, King); Jeffries, *Justice Lewis F. Powell, Jr.*, 39 (class rank and postgraduate study at Harvard).

113. EOB 282–26, October 20, 1971, 4:23 P.M., Moore, NT ("expecting"); Lewis Powell to Eppa Hunton, April 21, 1975, Box 1, Folder 17, Powell MSS; Jeffries, *Justice Lewis F. Powell, Jr.*, 7-9.

114. WHT 12–28, October 21, 1971, 9:33 A.M., Mitchell, NT ("don't"); EOB Tape 282–26, October 20, 1971.

115. WHT 12–28, October 21, 1971; WHT12-13, October 20, 1971, 4:44 P.M., Mitchell, NT ("Tell," "baptized"). To nit-pick, while Rehnquist had been editor-in-chief of the *Stanford Law Review* and had the highest grades of anyone in his class, Stanford did not officially rank its students at the time.

116. WHT 12–30, October 21, 1971, 9:45 A.M., Mitchell ("ignore," "mention"); EOB 281–34, October 21, 1971, 1:17 P.M., Moore; Carroll Kilpatrick, "Nixon Names Powell, Rehnquist," *WP*, October 22, 1971 (Ziegler).

117. "Yorty Assails Nixon Action," *LAT*, October 22, 1971; "County Bar Official Defends Justice Lillie," id., October 23, 1971; "Nixon's Nominations to the Supreme Court," *AG*, October 23, 1971 ("abominable"); Margolick, "At the Bar" hardest," "What," "It," "He"); "Nixon's Actions Concerning Friday Pondered," *CA*, November 7, 1971 (blame); "Friday Learned at 5:30 Decision 'No,' Sources Say," *AD*, October 22, 1971 ("discredit"); John Scudder, "Friday Defends ABA," *AD*, October 28, 1971 ("shattered").

118. Address to the Nation Announcing Intention to Nominate Lewis F. Powell, Jr., and William H. Rehnquist to Be Associate Justices of the Supreme Court of the United States, October 21, 1971, http://www.presidency.ucsb.edu/ws/index.php?pid=3196&st=powell&st1=rehnquist.

119. Id.; EOB 281–34, October 21, 1971.

120. Address to the Nation, October 21, 1971; Kilpatrick, "Nixon Names Powell, Rehnquist" (Mitchell).

121. Dorothy McCardle, "GOP Women: Resigned," *WP*, October 22, 1971; "Mrs. Mitchell Hits Rejection of Nominee," *LAT*, October 24, 1971; Remarks at the National Federation of Republican Women, October 22, 1971, http://www.presidency.ucsb.edu/ws/index.php?pi

d=3197&st=national+federation+of+republican+women&st1=; " Woman Next, President Vows," *LAT*, October 22, 1971; McCardle, "Friendly Venom," October 23, 1971 ("Your,", "She").

122. WHT 12-68, October 21, 1971, 9:03 P.M., Burger , NT("nothing"); WHT 12-62, October 21, 1971, 8:40 P.M., Mitchell, id. ("reactionary," "I"); WHT12-119, 3:29 P.M., October 25, 1971 Buchanan, id.

123. Chief Justice Burger to Rose Mary Woods, October 21, 1971, PPF, President's Speech File, Box 69, Nominations to Supreme Court, October 21, 1971, RMNL ("distasteful," "think"); WHT 12–68, October 21, 1971.

124. WHT 12-119, October 25, 1971, 3:29 P.M., Buchanan; POF, John Huntsman, Memorandum for Charles Colson, October 23, 1971, Box 35, Annotated News Summaries, October 21-30, 1971 (1), RMNL; Special Report on the Nominations to the Supreme Court, October 24, 1971, Box 17, Supreme Court Nominations, Young MSS; "Court Appointments," *TNR*, November 6, 1971. But see Joseph Alsop, "Nixon's 'Aunt Sallies,'" *WP*, December 15, 1971 (Liberals played into Nixon's hands by opposing Lillie and Friday, which enabled the President to make "the quick switch he had always planned.").

125. Spencer Rich, "Hill Reaction Is Favorable to Nominees," *WP*, October 22, 1971; Leon Friedman, "Rehnquist: He Was a Very Elusive Target," *NYT*, December 12, 1971 ("takes"); Richard Kleindienst, *Justice: The Memoirs of Attorney General Richard Kleindienst* (Ottawa: Jameson, 1985), 123.

126. Nominations of William Rehnquist and Lewis Powell, 1, 2–5.

127. Spencer Rich, "Rehnquist Civil Liberties Stance Eyed: Rehnquist Critics Design Game Plan for His Defeat," *WP*, October 26, 1971 (Seymour); Fred Graham, "Rehnquist's Statements Indicate He Would Be an Activist Pressing Conservative Views," *NYT*, November 3, 1971; Richard West, "Rehnquist Backed by Liberals in Hometown: Opposition to Supreme Court Nominee in Phoenix Spearheaded by NAACP Leaders," *LAT*, October 30, 1971; Fred Graham, "Rehnquist Role in Election Confirmed," *NYT*, November 3, 1971; Nominations of William Rehnquist and Lewis Powell, Jr., 421–32. When Reagan nominated Rehnquist as Chief Justice in 1986, it would also be revealed that the deed to Rehnquist's Phoenix house in the 1960s contained a restrictive covenant barring its sale or lease "to any person not of the white or Caucasian race" and that the deed to his Vermont vacation home had one prohibiting its lease or sale to Jews. Glen Elsasser, "Charges of Bias Dogging Rehnquist," *CT*, August 1, 1986; Ronald Ostrow and Robert Jackson, "Second Rehnquist Deed Heats Up Senate Hearing," *LAT*, August 1, 1986.

128. Dean, *The Rehnquist Choice*, 262-63; Jenkins, *The Partisan*, 77, 82-87; "Rehnquist Civil Liberties Stance Eyed," October 26, 1971; Graham, "Rehnquist's Statements Indicate He Would Be An Activist," *NYT*, November 3, 1971; West, "Rehnquist Backed by Liberals in Hometown"; James Clarity, "Senators Assail Campus Violence; Inquiries Urged: Justice Department Chiefs Also Critical," *NYT*, May 2, 1969 ("barbarians"); Mary Perry, "Cold, Hard Examination Shows Up Conservatism of Rehnquist and Powell," *OP*, November 11, 1971; David Andelman, "Rehnquist Urged a Busing Ban in 1970 Memos to White House," *NYT*, March 17, 1972.

129. "Rehnquist Court Bid Blasted by A.C.L.U.," *CT*, December 6, 1971; Ronald Ostrow, "ACLU Takes Rare Stand, Opposes Bork," *LAT*, September 1, 1987; William Rehnquist, "The Making of a Supreme Court Justice," *HLRec*, October 8, 1959; Glen Elsasser, "Rehnquist Will Undergo Third Degree," *CT*, October 31, 1971.

130. Kleindienst, *Justice*, 123.

131. Clifford Kuhn and George Butler, "'An Opportunity to be Heard': An Oral Interview with Lewis F. Powell, Jr.," 1 *Ga.J.SLH* 413, 427 (1991) ("mistake," "type"); Eppa Hunton, Memorandum to File, Nomination of Lewis F. Powell, Jr. For Associate Justice of the Supreme Court of the United States, July 30, 1975, Box 294, Folder 8a, Powell MSS (media); Lewis Powell, "Civil Liberties Repression: Fact or Fiction?—Law-Abiding Citizens Have Nothing to Fear," reprinted in Nominations of William Rehnquist and Lewis Powell, 213–216 ("outcry," "tempest," "radical," "law-abiding"); Jeffries, *Justice*

Lewis F. Powell, Jr., 232–36 (antagonists and supporters); Lewis Powell, Memorandum for Eugene Syndor, "Attack on American Free Enterprise System," August 23, 1971, http://law2.wlu.edu/deptimages/Powell%20Archives/PowellMemorandumTypescript.pdf; Jack Anderson, "The Washington Merry Go Round: FBI Missed Blueprint by Powell," *WP*, September 29, 1972. http://law2.wlu.edu/deptimages/Powell%20Archives/PowellMemorandumTypescript.pdf.

132. Jeffries, *Justice Lewis F. Powell Jr.,* 10, 229 (see, for example, Nominations of William Rehnquist and Lewis Powell, 344–45, 420); John MacKenzie, "FBI Queries Possible Opponents of 2 Supreme Court Nominees," *WP*, October 29, 1971.

133. Email, Richard Seymour to Laura Kalman, July 30, 2015; Nomination of Justice William Rehnquist, 984–1078.

134. Fred Graham, "2 Negroes From Phoenix, Arizona, Say Rehnquist Harassed Blacks at Polls in 1964," *NYT*, November 16, 1971; Nina Totenberg, "Recollection of Rehnquist—Or a 'Twin': Was It He at Bethune Precinct?," *NO*, December 4, 1971; Clarence Mitchell and Joe Rauh to James Eastland, November 22, 1971, Box 39, Folder 12, Rauh MSS (justification for delay); Curt Mathews, "Data Link Rehnquist with Right-Wing Group," *SLPD*, November 17, 1971; "Rehnquist Called an Ex-Bircher," *NYP*, November 9, 1971; Robert Ravitch, "Last-Ditch Rights Effort Expected Today for New Quiz on Rehnquist," *LAT*, November 18, 1971; Charles Baker to Inner Circle, November 19, 1971, Box 40, Folder 2, Rauh MSS (crediting Seymour with delay); "Link Rehnquist, Right Wing Unit," *CT*, November 18, 1971 (crediting graduate student with delay); Glen Elsasser, "Rehnquist Deadline is Delayed," id., November 19, 1971; Fred Graham, "Rehnquist Denies Arizona Charges: Tells Four Senators He Didn't Challenge Voters There," *NYT*, November 21, 1971; Nina Totenberg, "The Confirmation Process and the Public: To Know or Not to Know," 101 *HLR* 1213, 1215 (1988) ("relatively"); Nomination of Justice William Rehnquist, 144–52, 984–1134; Stuart Taylor, "4 Rebut Testimony by Rehnquist on Challenging of Voters in 60's," *NYT*, August 2, 1986. Seymour himself continued to believe that Rehnquist had not engaged in voter intimidation. Email, Richard Seymour to Laura Kalman, November 10, 2015: "I believe my 1971 sources were correct and everything else is a mixture of confusion, desire, and an echo chamber."

135. Fred Graham, "Senate Panel Ends Its Questioning of Powell With No Apparent Opposition to His Court Nomination," *NYT*, November 9, 1971; Ronald Ostrow, "Four Senate Liberals Charting Strategy to Block Rehnquist," *LAT*, November 11, 1971 (the fourth liberal Democrat was Senator John Tunney of California); John MacKenzie, "Judiciary Unit Delays Vote on Both Nominees," *WP*, November 12, 1971; Thomas Ronan, "Senator Kennedy Hints Opposition to Rehnquist," *NYT*, November 17, 1971; "High Court Vote Faces Filibuster,"*WP*, November 18, 1971; "Rehnquist, Powell Win Endorsements of Judiciary Panel," *LAT*, November 23, 1971; John MacKenzie, "Minority Report Hits Rehnquist," *WP*, December 1, 1971 ("outside"); Clark MacGregor, Memorandum for the President, December 4, 1971, WHCF EX FG 51/A, Box 4, Folder 12, RMNL.

136. "Memo From Rehnquist," *News*, December 13, 1971; William Rehnquist, "A Random Thought on the Segregation Cases," http://www.gpo.gov/fdsys/pkg/GPO-CHRG-REHNQUIST/pdf/GPO-CHRG-REHNQUIST-4-16-6.pdf.

137. Fred Graham, "Rehnquist '52 Schools Memo Reported," *NYT*, December 6, 1971; Graham, "Rehnquist Says '52 Memo Outlined Jackson's Views," id., December 9, 1971 ("wish," "tentative"); "Text of Rehnquist Letter to Senator Eastland, and Memo of 1952 on Rights Cases," id., December 9, 1971; Fred Graham, "2 Oppose Rehnquist," id., December 10, 1971 (Douglas); John MacKenzie, "Controversy Deepens Over Rehnquist Memo," *WP*, December 10, 1971; Brad Snyder, "How the Conservatives Canonized Brown v. Board of Education," 52 *RLR* 383, 442–46, 451–57 (2009) (discussing the case against Rehnquist for lying and the scholars who have made it, though as Snyder says at id. 455, Mark Tushnet suggests Rehnquist's testimony was "at least partially truthful"); Brad Snyder and John Barrett, "Rehnquist's Missing Letter: A Former Law Clerk's 1955 Thoughts on Justice Jackson and Brown," 53 *BCLR*, 631, 634, n. 10 (2012).

138. Brad Snyder, "How the Conservatives Canonized Brown v. Board of Education," 431–46.

139. Glen Elsasser, "Senate Gets Cloture Plea on Rehnquist," *CT*, December 9, 1971 ("losing"); "Rehnquist's Backers Say Critics Have Begun a Senate Filibuster," *NYT*, December 8, 1971 ("insensitive"); Clarence Mitchell, "Telegram to 35 Senators," December 9, 1971, Part I, Box 130, Folder 6, Leadership Conference MSS; *CR*, December 7, 1971, S45201 (Remarks of Senator Bayh).

140. Graham, "Rehnquist Says '52 Memo Outlined Jackson's Views" (Proxmire); POF, News Summary, December 7, 1971, Annotated News Summary, Box 37, RMNL (all networks had noted "Proxmire's surprise support"); William Timmons, Memorandum for the President, Bill Rehnquist's Nomination, December 6, 1971, WHCF Executive FG 51/A, id.; Eugene Cowen and Tom Korologos, Memorandum for the President, Rehnquist Vote Update, December 8, 1971, EX FG 51/A, id.; Willard Edwards, "How Rehnquist Filibuster Failed," *CT*, December 14, 1971; "Tribe Builds Case Against Rehnquist," *BG*, November 4, 1971; Tribe to the Editor, November 4, 1971; Friedman, "Rehnquist: He Was A Very Elusive Target" (Rauh).

141. Graham, "Rehnquist's Backers Say Critics Have Begun a Filibuster," *NYT*, December 8, 1971 (empty); WHT 16–97, December 10, 1971, 8:16 P.M., Colson.

142. WHT 16–27, December 6, 1971, 6:44 P.M., Powell, NT.

143. WHT 16–86, December 10, 1971, 5:18 P.M., Rehnquist, id.; POF, News Summary, December 11, 1971, Annotated News Summaries, Box 37, RMNL.

144. OVAL 733–10, June 14, 1972, 2:54 P.M., Burger, NT; POF, Ray Price, Memorandum for the President's File, Meeting With Price Staff, July 24, 1972, Memoranda for the President, Box 89, RMNL.

145. Fred Graham to Sterling Lord, October 8, 1974, Box 28, God Save This Honorable Court, Graham MSS.

146. PPF, Richard Nixon, Memorandum From the President for John Ehrlichman, January 28, 1972, Memoranda From the President, Box 3, Folder 12, RMNL; and see Edward Morgan, POF, Memorandum for the President's File, March 6, 1972, Memoranda for the President, Box 8 (similar complaint); Greenhouse, *Becoming Justice Blackmun*, 122–25; Drummond v. Acree, 409 U.S. 1228 (1972); Labor Day Message, September 3, 1972, http://www.presidency.ucsb.edu/ws/?pid=3557; Kevin McMahon, *Nixon's Court: His Challenge to Judicial Liberalism and Its Political Consequences* (Chicago: University of Chicago Press, 2011), 108–9, 232.

147. McMahon, *Nixon's Court*, 69–82; Stephen Engel, *American Politicians Confront the Court: Opposition Politics and Changing Responses to Judicial Power* (Cambridge: Cambridge University Press, 2011), 304–21. See, for example, U.S. v. Nixon, 418 U.S. 683 (1974); Keyes v. School District, No. 1, 413 U.S. 189 (1973); Argersinger v. Hamlin, 407 U.S. 25 (1972) (broadening right to counsel); U.S. v. U.S. District Court, 407 U.S. 297 (1972) (requiring warrant before electronic surveillance in domestic security cases); Roe v. Wade, 410 U.S. 113 (1973); "Nixon: Abort Interracial Babies," *TNR*, June 22, 2009.

148. Compare, for example, Vincent Blasi, ed., *The Burger Court: The Counter-Revolution That Wasn't* (New Haven: Yale University Press, 1983), with Linda Greenhouse and Michael Graetz, *The Burger Court and the Rise of the Judicial Right* (New York: Simon and Schuster, 2016); Earl Maltz, *The Coming of the Nixon Court: The 1972 Term and the Transformation of Constitutional Law* (Lawrence: University Press of Kansas, 2016). See, for example, Milliken v. Bradley, 418 U.S. 717 (1974) (striking down regional busing against equal protection challenge); Daindridge v. Williams, 397 U.S. 471 (1970) (denying fundamental right to welfare); San Antonio Independent School District v. Rodriguez, 411 U.S. 1 (1973) (upholding state system of public school financing through property taxes against claims that it violated federal equal protection guarantees); and the cases constricting defendant protections in lineup identifications, and search-and-seizure and right-to-counsel situations (e.g., Kirby v. Illinois, 406 U.S. 682 [1972]; U.S. v. Ash, 413 U.S. 300 [1973]; Schneckloth v. Bustamonte, 412 U.S. 218 [1973]; Scott v. Illinois, 440 U.S. 367 [1975]); and campaign financing, Buckley v. Valeo, 424 U.S. 1 [1976]; Citizens United v. Federal Election Commission, 558 U.S. 310 [2010]).

Epilogue

1. Edward Levi, Interviewed by Victor Kramer, 1989, 95-NLF-031, Box 1, Composite Oral History Accessions, GRFOH.

2. Michael Comiskey provides a valuable overview of the debate in *Seeking Justices: The Judging of Supreme Court Nominees* (Lawrence: University Press of Kansas, 2004). For laments about the current process, see, for example, *Judicial Roulette: Report of the Twentieth Century Fund Task Report on Judicial Selection* (New York: Priority Press, 1988); Stephen Carter, *The Confirmation Mess: Cleaning Up the Federal Appointments Process* (New York: Basic, 1994); Elena Kagan, "Confirmation Messes Old and New," 62 *UCLR* (1995); John Maltese, *The Selling of Supreme Court Nominees* (Baltimore: Johns Hopkins Press, 1995); Christopher Eisgruber, *The Next Justice: Repairing the Supreme Court Appointments Process* (Princeton: Princeton University Press, 2007). For an engaging defense of the contemporary process, see Paul Collins and Lori Ringhand, *Supreme Court Confirmation Hearings and Constitutional Change* (Cambridge: Cambridge University Press, 2013).

3. Henry Abelove, Betsy Blackmar, Peter Dimock, and Jonathan Schneer, eds., *Visions of History*, Interview, Herbert Gutman (New York: Pantheon, 1983), 187, 203; Hearings on the Judicial Nomination and Confirmation Process, September 4, 2001, 87.

4. See, for example, Laura Kalman, *The Strange Career of Legal Liberalism* (New Haven: Yale University Press, 1996) (Warren worship); Bernard Schwartz, *Super Chief: Earl Warren and His Supreme Court: A Biography* (New York: New York University Press, 1983), 771 ("Brennan, more than any of the Justices, missed Warren. He used to refer to him as the 'Super Chief'—a title that was soon adopted by those in the Court who were growing increasingly nostalgic about the Warren years."). Pressed to compare Warren and Burger as chief justices, in an interview before his death to be published posthumously, Potter Stewart extolled the former and kept quiet about the latter. "I will say this: That Chief Justice Warren had instinctive qualities of leadership, which meant that he had great tact and sensitivity to the other person's feelings and point of view. He had been, after all, an extremely successful . . . politician, . . . and a very, very popular one. And he did have those instinctive qualities of sensitivity to a very marked degree." Fred Graham, Interview of Justice Potter Stewart, February 17, 1979, Box 624, Folder 33, Stewart MSS.

5. The dedication appears above Archibald Cox, "Chief Justice Earl Warren," 83 *HLR* 1 (1969); Michael Parrish, "Earl Warren and the American Judicial Tradition," 1982 *ABFJ* 1179 (1982); Peter Brown, "Earl Warren Fears U.S. Racial Chaos: Calls for Change of Attitude in UCSD Address," *SDU*, October 17, 1970, Box 830, Folder 3, Warren MSS. See Provost John Stewart to Warren, October 22, 1970, id.: "I am sure that you are enough in touch with young people (as you proved so well last Friday afternoon) to understand that the words of the banner that came fluttering down from the residence hall behind us were a very affectionate compliment. 'Right on, Big Earl' is the kind of friendly and humorous approval that one doesn't hear or see too often on campuses these days."

6. Fred Graham, "Burger Panel Will Propose a National Court of Appeals to Screen Cases," *NYT*, November 8, 1972; Warren Burger to John Ehrlichman, December 22, 1972, WHCF, EX FG 51, Folder 8, RMNL ("I have no definite conclusions about the recommendations as yet, but I recall the history of the creation of the Circuit Court of Appeals in the late 1880s when a great many people said the sky was falling then. History has shown that the creation of the Circuit Courts did not constitute a wall between the people and the Supreme Court."); Paul Freund, "Why We Need a National Court of Appeals," 59 *ABAJ*, 247 (March 1973); Eugene Gressman, "The National Court of Appeals: A Dissent," id., 253; Lewis Powell, "An Overworked Supreme Court," Box 327, Folder 6, Supreme Court, Correspondence With Fellow Justices, Powell MSS; William O. Douglas to Lewis Powell, July 7, 1972, id. ("One's perspective changes over the years. But I really think that in terms of the present rate of activity inside the Court the job of an Associate Justice does not add up to more than about four days a week."); Earl Warren, Memorandum to My Law Clerks, November 8, 1972, Box 733, National Court of Appeals (1), Warren MSS; Earl Warren to Peter Ehrenhaft, November 8, 1972, id. ("scuttling") (The former chief justice rebuked Ehrenhaft, his one former clerk who broke ranks and dared publicly

to promote the national court of appeals. Id.,); Linda Mathews, "Earl Warren Denounces Proposal to Set Up 'Junior Supreme Court,'" *LAT*, May 3, 1972; Warren Weaver, "Burger Supports Proposal for a New National Court of Appeals," *NYT*, June 4, 1975; John MacKenzie, "New Court Plan Backed by Five Justices," *WP*, June 13, 1975; Stephen Wermiel, "Bar Group Opposes Plan to Establish New Appeals Court," *WSJ*, February 12, 1986.

7. See, for example, "Cracker Barrel Justice," *WP*, August 12, 1970; "The Chief Justice as Administrator-in-Chief," id., February 16, 1971; John MacKenzie, "Chief Justice Denies Lobbying Charge," id., October 14, 1972; "Burger's Lobbying Tactics: 'Shouting and Yelling,'" *CT*, October 17, 1978; Linda Greenhouse, "Lobbying by Burger Provokes Criticism," *NYT*, November 19, 1978; Harry Blackmun, Notes, February 27, 1980, and March 19, 1980, Box 116, Folder 2, Blackmun MSS; Evan Thomas, "Inside the High Court: After a decade it is Burger's in Name Only," *Ti*, November 5, 1979 (opinions and reporting that "Burger regularly dismisses such assertions as fables"); Nina Totenberg and Fred Barbash, "Burger Loved the Law But Not the Hassle," *WP*, June 22, 1986 ("But nothing so annoyed the other justices as the way Burger handled the chief's traditional function of assigning opinions. Normally, the chief decides which justice will write what opinion, but only if he is in the majority. Other justices say that on many occasions Burger voted with the majority, assigned the opinion to the person he thought would write the narrowest decision, and then switched to the dissenting side at the end. Some justices called it the 'Burger-bait-and-switch.' Then too, some justices charge that Burger often 'passed' instead of voting, in order to hold onto the assignment function. It is hard to understand how a person of his political acumen could so consistently alienate colleagues." Totenberg was one of Burger's least favorite reporters.); "Abortion on Demand," *Ti*, January 29, 1973; Warren Burger to Potter Stewart and William Rehnquist, March 15, 1973, Box 1571, Folder: October Term 1972 Court Memoranda, Douglas MSS (Ad Hoc Committee on "Court Security"); William Rehnquist and Potter Stewart, Memorandum to the Conference, June 18, 1973, id. (reporting on leaks involving when an opinion would be handed down and/or how it would be decided, and sometimes how the justices' deliberations changed about the issue over time with respect to the abortion cases, Flood v. Kuhn, 407 U.S. 258 [1972], and others); William Safire, "Equal Justice Under Leak," *NYT*, April 28, 1977 (leaks about Watergate-related cases); Josh Marshall, "Plugging a Leak: Justice Burger Plays Detective," *Ti*, May 7, 1979; "Rites of Spring," *Esq*, May 22, 1979 ("The increasingly heavy-handed, supercilious Chief Justice Warren Burger is now so disliked by so many clerks—and in many cases by the justices they work for—that there's a kind of sadistic pleasure derived from giving Burger's number one enemy, the press, a tidbit or two.").

8. Warren Burger to Lewis Powell, July 20, 1979, Box 326, Folder 17, Powell MSS ("warned"); Thomas, "Inside the High Court"; Lewis Powell, Memorandum, Time Magazine Article on the Court, November 26, 1979, Box 327, Folder 15, Powell MSS.

9. Bob Woodward and Scott Armstrong, *The Brethren: Inside the Supreme Court* (New York: Simon and Schuster, 1979), Lewis Powell to George Gibson, December 11, 1979, Box 351, Folder 25 Powell MSS ("arrogant dunce"); Powell to Powell Clerks, January 16, 1980, id.; David Margolick, "On the Trail of the High Court Sleuths," *NLJ*, February 19, 1979; David Garrow, "The Supreme Court and the Brethren," 18 *ConComm* 303 (2001); Stephen McAllister, "Justice White and the Brethren," 15 *GB* 2d 159 (2012). Garrow reminds us that clerks had been leakers for decades. David Garrow, "'The Lowest Form of Animal Life?' Supreme Court Clerks and Supreme Court History," 84 *CorLR* 855 (1999). So had justices. Richard Davis, *Justices and Journalists: The U.S. Supreme Court and the Media* (New York: Cambridge University Press, 2011), 77–79, 130–41. Still, the leaking with respect to *The Brethren* was extraordinary. As Clyde Spillenger has also shown, scholars such as Alexander Bickel and Alpheus T. Mason had taken readers "inside" the Supreme Court long before Woodward and Armstrong. See Clyde Spillenger, "Reading the Judicial Canon: Alexander Bickel and the Book of Brandeis," 79 *JAH* 125 (1992); Spillenger, "Lifting the Veil: The Judicial Biographies of Alpheus T. Mason," 21 *RAH* 723 (1993). But biographers did not receive as much attention as Woodward and Armstrong.

10. "Writer Quotes Warren: Burger a 'Horse's Ass,'" *LAT*, March 19, 1975. Powell's attempts to keep the peace are chronicled in his correspondence with his fellow justices and the chief justice, Boxes 326 and 327, Powell MSS.

11. TRB, "Empty Robe," *TNR*, July 14, 1986; "William Rehnquist," n.d., Peter Wallison, OA 14287, Box 3, Supreme Court, Rehnquist/Scalia Notebook I Candidates (1), RWRL; Linda Greenhouse, "How Not to Be Chief Justice: The Apprenticeship of William H. Rehnquist," 154 *UPLR*, 1365, 1367 (2006).

12. See Robert Kagan, "What If Abe Fortas Had Been More Discreet?," in *What If? Explorations in Social-Science Fiction*, ed. Nelson Polsby (Lexington: Lewis, 1982), 153, 179 (Kagan speculated that "America probably would not be very different today in any obvious, tangible way" but that a Fortas court's opinions "would have had a different tone than those of the Burger Court, a tone that invited rather than cautioned against the 'discovery' of new rights in the Constitution, that put greater stress on the value of equality, and that voiced the necessity for judicial activism to protect the less powerful rather than deference to economic constraints or majority sentiment."); Frank Michelman, "Foreword: On Protecting the Poor Through the Fourteenth Amendment," 83 *HLR* 7 (1969).

13. Alan and Marilyn Bergman, "The Way We Were," http://www.alanandmarilynbergman.com/lyrics_pages/twww.htm; Kalman, *The Strange Career of Legal Liberalism*, 4, 27–52; Russell Caplan, "The Paradoxes of Judicial Review in a Constitutional Democracy," 30 *BuffLR* 451, 456 (1981) ("Camelot").

14. Linda Greenhouse, "The Separation of Justice and State," *NYT*, July 1, 2001 (quoting Lucas "Scot" Powe, "removed," "knew"); Lucas Powe, *The Warren Court and American Politics* (Cambridge: Belknap, 2000); and see Barry Friedman, *The Will of the People: How Public Opinion Has Influenced the Supreme Court and Shaped the Meaning of the Constitution* (New York: Farrar, Straus and Giroux, 2009), 237–38; Corrina Lain, "Countermajoritarian Hero or Zero? Rethinking the Warren Court's Role in the Criminal Procedure Revolution," 152 *UPLR* 1361 (2004); Robert Dahl, "Decision-Making in a Democracy: The Supreme Court as a National Policy Maker," 6 *JPL* 279 (1957); Justin Driver, "The Constitutional Conservatism of the Warren Court," 100 *CaLR* 1101 (2012); Laura Kalman, *Right Star Rising: A New Politics* (New York: W. W. Norton, 2010). The Reagan White House even cited the certainty that Rehnquist's Brown memo to Jackson would resurface as one argument against nominating him as chief justice. After a redacted paragraph, Wallison wrote, "On top of all the other considerations raised above, the confirmation process will undoubtedly cause Rehnquist's old memorandum to his former boss, Justice Jackson to reemerge. In that memorandum, Rehnquist had argued against the principles adopted in Brown v. Board of Education. An allegation of racial prejudice is absolutely one of the last things the President's judicial nominees need at this time." Universal support for Brown, the Warren Court's most well-known decision, had become a given. William Rehnquist," n.d., Supreme Court, Rehnquist/Scalia Notebook II Candidates (3), OA 14287, RWRL.

15. Schwartz, *Super Chief*, 772 ("Thank God!"); Ed Cray, *Chief Justice: A Biography of Earl Warren* (New York: Simon and Schuster, 1997), 528; Jim Newton, *Justice for All: Earl Warren and the Nation He Made* (New York: Riverhead, 2006), 515; "Warren's Body to Lie in Repose," *WP*, July 11, 1974; "Public, Court Pay Respects to Warren," *LAT*, July 12, 1974; Lesley Oelsner, "Earl Warren Is Buried in Army Rites at Arlington," *NYT*, July 13, 1974.

Moreover, the members of the 1962–69 Warren Court majority are still lionized in popular culture and public memory. Who besides Justices Oliver Wendell Holmes, Ruth Bader Ginsburg, and Antonin Scalia have been the subjects of celebratory plays and films? William O. Douglas, Thurgood Marshall, and Abe Fortas. The Federal Judicial Center is housed in the Thurgood Marshall Building. In the 1980s, federal courthouses were named for Warren Court legal liberals even as the Reagan administration advocated the rollback of Warren-era jurisprudence.

On the one hand, so what? That the Kansas City federal courthouse is named after Justice Charles Whittaker suggests it's not hard to get a courthouse. But on the other, Warren, Brennan, Black, and Marshall are among the very few members of the court to have been honored with postage stamps. Baltimore Washington Airport is now Thurgood Marshall Airport. One of University of California, San Diego's six colleges bears the Marshall name. "A Short History of Thurgood Marshall College," http://provost.ucsd.edu/marshall/40th/history/short-history.html. Another, Warren, houses the Black, Brennan, Douglas, Goldberg, Frankfurter, Harlan, and Stewart apartment complexes and residence halls and Earl's Place, a coffee shop and mini-mart. Fortas's career and one of the Warren era's most celebrated decisions provided the plot for the 1980 movie of "Gideon's Trumpet," with Jose Ferrer playing Fortas. A 1990 Douglas Scott play, "Mountain," starring Len Carriou, focused on Douglas. Twenty years later, Thurgood Marshall became the subject of a one-person "bioplay" written by George Stevens Jr. and an HBO film, "Thurgood," with Laurence Fishburne portraying Marshall.

16. Jeffrey Rosen, "Even Stephen," *TNR*, June 5, 1994; Mark Silverstein, *Judicious Choices: The New Politics of Supreme Court Confirmations* (New York: W. W. Norton, 2d. ed. 2007), 80; "What the President Should Look for in a Judicial Nominee," American Bar Association, August 8, 2008, https://www.c-span.org/video/?280373-2/presidential-candidates-judicial-selection (comments of Kenneth Starr); John Rollett, "Forum: Reversed on Appeal: The Uncertain Future of President Obama's 'Empathy Standard,' " /http://yalelawjournal.org/the-yale-law-journal-pocket-part/supreme-court/reversed-on-appeal:-the-uncertain-future-of-president-obama's-%22empathy-standard%22; Barack Obama, *The Audacity of Hope: Thoughts on Reclaiming the American Dream* (New York: Three Rivers, 2006), 82; Remarks to the White House Press Pool and an Exchange With Reporters, April 28, 2010, http://www.presidency.ucsb.edu/ws/index.php?pid=87815&st=supreme+court&st1= ("ignored," "democratic"); Charlie Savage and Sheryl Stolberg, "Obama Says Liberal Courts May Have Overreached," *NYT*, April 30, 2010.

17. Mark Tushnet, *The Constitution of the United States of America: A Contextual Analysis* (Oxford: Hart, 2009), 228; Emily Bazelon and John Witt, "Senate Republicans and the Supreme Court: Where Is This Headed Exactly?," *NYT Mag*, February 24, 2016.

18. Beverly Cook, "The First Woman Candidate for the Supreme Court—Florence E. Allen," 1981 *SCHSY* 19 (1981); Hannah Brenner and Renee Knake, "Shortlisted," October 10, 2016, https://papers.ssrn.com/sol3/papers.cfm?abstract_id=2850599; Patricia Lindh, Memorandum for the President, November 17, 1975, WHCF FG 51, Box 137, November 17, 1975, Supreme Court of the United States, GRFL; David Yalof, *Pursuit of Justices: Presidential Politics and the Selection of Supreme Court Nominees* (Chicago: University of Chicago Press, 1999), 129–30; "The Hufstedler Nomination," *WP*, October 31, 1979; Marlene Cimons, "Hufstedler Leaves With No Regrets," id., November 17, 1980.

19. Larry Stammer and Eleanor Randolph, "Reagan Vows to Appoint Women to Supreme Court," *LAT*, October 15, 1980.

20. Ellen Goodman, "He's Done It Again," *WP*, July 14, 1981 ("as much"); Paul Weyrich to William Armstrong, September 28, 1987, David McIntosh, OA 16531, Box 1, Bork (2), id. ("intense," "vote"). See the letters from influential Angelenos recommending Lillie for the court; Mildred Lillie to Ronald and Nancy and Ronald Reagan, n.d, id. (thanking them for including her and her husband as guests at a state dinner in 1982); Edwin Meese to Preston Hotchkis, July 9, 1981, id. (thanking him for "your letter recommending Mildred Lillie" and adding: "She would make a fine choice for a high judicial appointment. We will keep her credentials in mind should a similar vacancy come up."); Michael Ulhmann to Edwin Meese, July 6, 1981, OA 2408, Box 7, Appointment: Supreme Court (1), RWRL (warning that people in right-to-life movement were saying that "the nomination of Judge O'Connor would trigger a nasty political protest against the President" and might provoke "a potentially disastrous political firefight"). For Burger's role, see Joan Biskupic, *Sandra Day O'Connor: How the First Woman on the Supreme Court Became Its Most Influential Justice* (New York: Harper Collins, 2009) 72–73; Linda Hirshman, *Sisters in Law: How Sandra Day O'Connor and Ruth Bader Ginsburg Went to the Supreme Court and Changed the World* (New York: Harper Collins, 2015), 128–31. As Hirshman also says, "Many men have claim to the role of godfather to the future Justice O'Connor," including Burger, Arizona senator Barry Goldwater, and Justice Rehnquist. "But in all of this historical inquiry almost no one focuses on the obvious Godfather—Reagan himself. Before he died, Attorney General William French Smith, who was undoubtedly at the center of any Supreme Court nomination process, told an aide that in 1980 Reagan had given him a short list with O'Connor's name written on it in Reagan's own hand." Id., 131. Neither Smith's internal administration history of O'Connor's nomination nor his memoir indicates where he got her name. William French Smith, "History of the Nomination of Justice Sandra Day O'Connor," September 1981, FG 051, Box 2, 29000-327999, RWRL; William French

Smith, *Law and Justice in the Reagan Administration: Memoirs of an Attorney General* (Stanford: Hoover, 1991), 63–70.

21. The "pro" column for Ginsburg included the following items: "Very bright," "very conservative," "age: 41," "conservatives' first choice," "Jewish." Judge Douglas H. Ginsburg, Duberstein Files, n.d., Series 1, Box 3, Nomination of Douglas Ginsburg, RWRL. A White House memorandum reported that "the initial reaction to the nomination in the Jewish community was very much a wait and see attitude," which represented an improvement, from the administration perspective, over its reaction to Bork. Rebecca Range, Memorandum for Tom Griscom, Weekly Report on Public Efforts to Support Judge Ginsburg, November 6, 1987, FG 051/14/546240-546519, RWRL.

22. Nathan Lewin, "The Supreme Court's Jewish Gentile: My Memories of Justice Scalia," February 15, 2016, http://www.jta.org/2016/02/15/news-opinion/obituaries/the-supreme-courts-jewish-gentile-my-memories-of-justice-scalia.

23. David Margolick, "At the Bar: Jews on the Supreme Court: Were They Different and Why Are There None Now?," *NYT*, December 22, 1989; Stephen Reinhardt, "Jewishness and Judging: A Judge's Thoughts on *Two Jewish Justices*," 10 *CarLR* 2345, 2356–57 (1989) ("nomination," "wrong").

24. Eric Fettman, "Splitting Chairs," *JerR*, October 25, 1990 (quoting spokesman Richard Cohen); Tom Tugend, "Conspiracy of Silence," *JerP*, August 27, 1991. For the arguments in favor of election, see Richard Davis, *Electing Justice: Fixing the Supreme Court Nomination Process* (New York: Oxford University Press, 2005), 170–78.

25. Jonathan Broder, "Jewish Justice," *JerR*, June 17, 1993; and see Andrea Stone, "Groups Call 'Jewish Seat' a Myth," *USA*, June 15, 1993.

26. William J. Clinton, Exchange with Reporters in Atlanta, March 19, 1993, http://www.presidency.ucsb.edu/ws/?pid=46357 ("big heart"); Background Briefing by Senior Administration Officials, June 14, 1993, http://www.ibiblio.org/pub/archives/whitehouse-papers/1993/Jun/Background-Briefing-on-Judge-Ginsburg-Selection ("With many factors that were listed, that was a factor. But it was not a very important factor. It was something that if you find the right person and that person happened to be Jewish, then you could say you fill the Jewish seat. But really, it was not a driving factor. There were a number of people on the list that were Jewish, many more that were not Jewish."); Remarks Announcing the Nomination of Ruth Bader Ginsburg to Be Supreme Court Justice, June 14, 1993, http://www.presidency.ucsb.edu/ws/?pid=46684%20; Martin Walker, "Clinton Plays It Safe With Supreme Court Nomination," *Gaz*, June 15, 1993; Ruth Marcus, "Judge Ruth Ginsburg Named to High Court; Clinton's Unexpected Choice Is Women's Rights Pioneer," *WP*, June 15, 1993; Neil Lewis, "High Court Nominee Faces Easy Road Through Senate," *NYT*, July 20, 1993 ("In his first nomination to the Supreme Court, President Clinton has signaled that he was not embarking on an ideological counterrevolution, hoping to balance the Republican appointees with a clearly liberal jurist.").

27. Linda Greenhouse, "The Nation; Judged in the Shadow of the Ghosts of the Past," *NYT*, May 22, 1994 (quoting Arthur Kropp, president of People for the American Way).

28. Linda Przybsyzewski, "The Dilemma of Judicial Biography or Who Cares Who Is the Great Appellate Judge? Gerald Gunther on Learned Hand," 21 *LSI* 135, 138 (1996); Nina Totenberg, "Notorious RBG: The Supreme Court Justice Turned Cultural Icon," October 26, 2015, http://www.npr.org/sections/itsallpolitics/2015/10/26/450547606/notorious-rbg-the-supreme-court-justice-turned-cultural-icon. "Whether we are judging beauty contests, dog shows, concert pianists, politicians or judges, we always will approach decisions with a body of built-in prejudices. As Bert Parks once remarked of the Miss America judges, there are titty men and leg men. So will it ever be with deans and professors rating the high court." James Kilpatrick to John Masarro, December 29, 1980, Box 34, Supreme Court, Kilpatrick MSS. Ginsburg, who co-founded the ACLU's Women's Rights Project and then became the ACLU's General Counsel, has herself suggested that because of the increasingly partisan nature of confirmation proceedings, she could not reach the Supreme Court now because "my ACLU connection would probably disqualify me." Garrison Nelson with Maggie Steakley and James Montague, *Pathways to the US Supreme Court: From the Arena to the Monastery* (New York: Palgrave, 2013), 236. Perhaps. Still, at the time that Clinton nominated her, she was perceived as a moderate.

29. Ruth Bader Ginsburg, "From Benjamin to Brandeis to Breyer: Is There a Jewish Seat?," 41 *BrLJ* 229, 234–35 (2002). Ginsburg continued to celebrate the historical significance of Judaism for the American experience. Indeed, she appeared repeatedly—dressed in judicial robes!—in the 2009 documentary "Yoo-Hoo, Mrs. Goldberg," about Gertrude Berg, the star of a popular radio and television show from 1929 to 1956. As Molly Goldberg on the show, Berg regularly leaned out the window of the Bronx apartment she shared with her lower middle-class Jewish family to shout "Yoo hoo" to her neighbors across the air shaft and exchange gossip in heavily accented English. Like the show, the documentary celebrated the big-hearted *yiddeshemama* (though Ginsburg carefully stressed that *her* mother never leaned out a window and shouted "Yoo hoo" at anyone), http://www.mollygoldbergfilm.org/about.php.

    It remained unclear, however, how much Jews were affecting life at the court. In 1995, the court was scheduled to hear oral argument on Yom Kippur. According to news reports, when Ginsburg and Breyer protested, Chief Justice Rehnquist said that they could listen to a tape recording of the oral arguments later. But that would not have allowed either of them to question the attorneys. It was just when Rehnquist was scheduled for surgery on Yom Kippur too that court was postponed. Timothy Phelps, "U.S. Court Conflict Focuses on Yom Kippur," *Gaz*, October 16, 1995. At this time, Rehnquist was still holding Christmas parties at the court, despite clerks' protests. Tony Mauro, "Roberts Adheres to Precedent on High Court Revelry," December 16, 2005 http://www.freerepublic.com/focus/f-news/1542168/posts. Only in 2003 did the court adjust its calendar to take into consideration the High Holidays. Charles Lane, "High Court Yields to High Holy Days," *WP*, September 1, 2003.

30. Juan Williams, *Thurgood Marshall: American Revolutionary* (New York: Three Rivers, 1998), 362, 372–73.

31. Jane Mayer and Jill Abramson, *Strange Justice: The Selling of Clarence Thomas* (New York: Houghton Mifflin, 1994), 173–82; Ed Carnes, Memorandum for Mark Paoletta, "Conversation with Ollie Delchamps about Judge Clarence Thomas and Delchamps['s] Conversations With Senators Heflin and Shelby," Clarence Thomas Alphabetical Subject Files, Box 5, OA ID 45504-602, Heflin-Belchamps Conversation, GHWBL; Charles Kolb to Boyden [Gray], "Domestic Policy After the Thomas Confirmation," December 5, 1991, Case No. 29230ICU, FG0511, 292301CU, id.

32. Nelson, *Pathways to the US Supreme Court*, at 151–53.

33. Warren Burger to Gerald Ford, November 10, 1975, Box 11, Supreme Court Nomination: Letters to the President, November 10-27, 1975, Cheney MSS.

34. Edward Levi, GRFOH ("look"); Yalof, *Pursuit of Justices*, 16, 126-30; Bill Barnhart and Gene Schlickman, *John Paul Stevens: An Independent Life* (De Kalb: Northern Illinois, 2010), 184–92. Burger learned from Ford's rebuff, and when he visited Reagan to tell him of his retirement, he carried with him a list of the six chief justice candidates he recommended. (For Burger's visit to Reagan, see Peter Wallison, Memorandum for the File, August 29, 1986, Peter Wallison, Supreme Court, Rehnquist Scalia General Selection Scenario, OA 14287 (1) [indicating that Burger had recommended Justices Rehnquist and White, DC Circuit Judges Bork and Scalia, Ninth Circuit Judge Clifford Wallace, and International Court of Trade Judge Edward Re]. The administration, however, did its own search and concentrated on Justices O'Connor and Rehnquist, Judges Bork and Scalia, Ninth Circuit Judges Anthony Kennedy and Clifford Wallace, Fifth Circuit Judge Patrick Higginbotham, and Second Circuit Judge Ralph Winter. After discussion of the issue with Reagan and Attorney General Meese, officials zeroed in on Rehnquist, Bork, and Scalia. Id.) Somewhat unusually, Burger also testified before the Senate Judiciary Committee on behalf of Judge Robert Bork. "'If Bork Is Not in Mainstream, Neither Am I,' Burger Testifies," *LAT*, September 23, 1986; Mary Clark, "My Brethren's (Gate) Keeper? Testimony by U.S. Judges at Others' Supreme Court Confirmation Hearings: Its Implications for Judicial Independence and Judicial Ethics," 40 *AzSLJ* 1181 (2008).

35. Henry Abraham, *Justices, Presidents, and Senators* (Lanham: MD: Rowman and Littlefield, 5th ed., 2007), 46.

36. Lee Epstein, Jack Knight and Andrew Martin, "The Norm of Prior Judicial Experiences and Its Consequences for Career Diversity on the U.S. Supreme Court," 91 *CaLR.* 903 (2003) (quoting Rehnquist at 908 and establishing that there is a norm of prior judicial

experience at 909-18); Yalof, *Pursuit of Justices*, at 170-71; Kevin O'D. Driscoll, "The Origins of a Judicial Icon: Justice Brennan's Warren Court Years," 54 *SLR* 1005 (2002); A. E. Dick Howard, "The Changing Face of the Supreme Court," 101 *VaLR* 231, 256 (2015) ("Perceptions," "Picking"); Linda Greenhouse, "The Separation of Church and State," *NYT*, July 1, 2001 (quoting Powe on "technocrats"). Though David Souter had but half a year on the First Circuit, he had logged twelve as a judge and justice in New Hampshire's courts. From John Stevens to Samuel Alito, only Justice O'Connor did not possess experience in the federal courts, and she had served six-and-a-half years as an Arizona judge. Coincidentally, perhaps even partially as a result, the court grayed further. Whereas the average justice from 1788 to 1970 retired or died at age sixty-eight-and-a-half and remained at the court for nearly fifteen years, the average justice from 1970 to 2005 retired or died at age seventy-nine-and-a-half and served there for twenty-six years. See Steven Calabresi and James Lindgren, "Term Limits for the Supreme Court," in *Reforming the Court: Term Limits for Supreme Court Justices*, ed. Roger Cramton and Paul Carrington (Durham: Carolina Academic Press, 2006), 15, 56–57; Judith Resnik, "Democratic Responses to the Breadth of Power of the Chief Justice," id., 181, 184 ("[B]eing a federal judge may correlate with longevity and even be good for one's health.").

37. "If Approved, a First-Time Judge, Yes, but Hardly the First in Court's History," *NYT*, October 4, 2005 ("predictability"); Roger Clegg, "The Ideal Candidate," n.d., Peter Wallison, Supreme Court Rehnquist Scalia, General Selection Scenario (1), OA 14287, RWRL (emphasis in the original); Peter Wallison, Memorandum for the File, August 29, 1986.

38. Pat Buchanan, Memorandum for the Chief of Staff, July 10, 1985, 2 FG051, 275543, RWRL.

39. Lee Epstein, Andrew Martin, Kevin Quinn, and Jeffrey Segal, "Circuit Effects: How the Norm of Federal Judicial Experience Biases the Supreme Court," 157 *UPLR* 833, 834, 868-77 (2009); Thomas Keck, *The Most Activist Supreme Court in History: The Road to Modern Judicial Conservatism* (Chicago: University of Chicago Press, 2004).

40. Greenhouse, "The Separation of Justice and State" (quoting Dellinger); Nelson *Pathways to the US Supreme Court*, 48-49, 229; Howard, "The Changing Face of the Supreme Court," 251–52; David O'Brien made the point about Whittaker in his interview with Lewis Powell, February 16, 1987, Retirement, Subject Files, Record Carton 322, Powell MSS. "I think I'm one of the few people who serve on the Court in this century who came directly from the Bar," Powell reflected. "I speak in a prejudiced fashion I suppose, I think the Court would be a bit stronger if there were more lawyers here who practiced law longer. . . . I can never prove that and that shows a bias that I have but I do think the necessity of the rough and tumble of law practice and seeing the effect of cases on clients and the experience I had over the years as a lawyer that has been helpful to me." But Powell also wished he had judicial experience. "[I]deally I think it would have been fine if I'd had say 20 years of law practice and 5 years sitting on the bench before coming up here." Id. Richard Posner has stressed the importance of increasing the number of justices who possess experience as trial judges. David Lat, "Judge Richard Posner on SCOTUS: 'The Supreme Court Is Awful,'" October 24, 2016 http://abovethelaw.com/2016/10/judge-richard-posner-on-scotus-the-supreme-court-is-awful/ ; "Judge Richard Posner Corrects the Record Regarding His Supreme Court Comments, October 28, 2016, http://abovethelaw.com/2016/10/judge-richard-posner-corrects-the-record-regarding-his-supreme-court-comments/.

41. John Marsh to Richard Nixon, September 23, 1971, WHCF, Name File, Richard Poff (2), RMNL; Statement by Sanford Levinson, Senate Committee Hearings on the Judicial Nomination Process: Hearing Before the Senate Committee on the Judiciary Subcommittee on Administration Oversight and the Courts on Should Ideology Matter? Judicial Nominations 2001, June 26, 2001, 50 *DrLR* 515, 520 (2002); Statement by Mark Tushnet, id., 561, 566 ("someone sensitive to the realities of the national legislative process would not dismiss legislative history as a guide to interpreting statutes"); Jeff Shesol, "The Court's Contempt for Congress," *NY*, December 4, 2013. While experience as a Congressional staffer or within the Executive Branch is surely valuable to a justice, it is not quite the same as service as a member of Congress or President. Garrison Nelson compares the Congressional staffers/Executive Branch underlings to "the picadors who ride on horseback and poke at the bull"

and members of Congress and presidents to "the matadors who must confront the enraged bull on foot, armed only with cape and sword." Nelson, *Pathways to the US Supreme Court*, 53.

42. Lewis Gould, *Chief Executive to Chief Justice: Taft Betwixt the White House and Supreme Court* (Lawrence: University Press of Kansas, 2014); Robert Post, "The Supreme Court Opinion as Institutional Practice: Dissent, Legal Scholarship and Decisionmaking in the Taft Court," 85 *MinnLR* 1267, 1267–73 (2001); Robert Post, "Judicial Management and Judicial Disinterest: The Achievements and Perils of Chief Justice William Howard Taft," 1 *SCH* 50 (1998); Abby Phillip and Anne Gearan, "Could Obama Be the Next Supreme Court Justice? Hillary Clinton Is Intrigued," *WP*, January 26, 2016; "White House: Obama Doesn't Want to Be a Supreme Court Justice," January 28, 2016, http://talkingpointsmemo.com/livewire/white-house-obama-supreme-court. Given contemporary partisanship, surely no president would look to predecessors from another party. Although a justice need not possess a law degree, politicians and the public expect one, which means that only a Democratic president could pull off appointing a former chief executive. The last two Republican presidents to possess law degrees since Taft are dead, and in any event, Richard Nixon, who resigned from the Supreme Court and California bars to dodge disbarment, something he did not avoid in New York, would not be credible even if he were among the living. So, too, Bill Clinton, who resigned from the Supreme Court bar and was suspended from the Arkansas bar, is not viable.

43. Patrick Buchanan, Memorandum for the Chief of Staff, July 10, 1985; Polly Price, *Judge Richard S. Arnold: A Legacy of Justice on the Federal Bench* (Amherst, MA: Prometheus, 2009), 329–30, 333–41; Theodore McMillan, Floyd Gibson, Donald Lay, Gerald Heaney, Myron Bright, Donald Ross, J. Smith Henley, John Gibson, George Fagg, Pasco Bowman, Roger Wollman, Frank Magill, C. Arlen Beam, James Loken, David Hansen, Morris Arnold to Lloyd Cutler and Bruce Lindsey, April 29, 1994, WHORM Alpha File, Richard Arnold, FG 051, Box 1, OA62672 OA ID 21853, WJCL.

44. Gary Fields, "Miers'[s] Lack of Judicial Experience Requires Questioning, Specter Says," *WSJ*, October 10, 2005; David Rosenbaum, "If Approved, a First-Time Judge, Yes, but Hardly the First in Court's History," *NYT*, October 4, 2005; Randy Barnett, "Cronyism," *WSJ*, October 4, 2005; David Greenberg, "Supreme Court Cronyism: Bush Restarts a Long and Troubled Tradition," *Sla*, October 5, 2005.

45. Remarks on the Nomination of Solicitor General Elena Kagan to Be a Supreme Court Associate Justice, May 10, 2010, http://www.presidency.ucsb.edu/ws/index.php?pid=87859&st=elena+kagan&st1=americanpresidency.org.

46. Sarah Binder and Forrest Maltzman, *Advice and Dissent: The Struggle to Shape the Federal Judiciary* (Washington, DC: Brookings, 2009), 7; Ethan Bronner, *Battle for Justice: How the Bork Nomination Shook America* (New York: W. W. Norton, 1989), 124–25, 297; Statement by Orrin Hatch, Hearings on the Judicial Nomination and Confirmation Process," September 4, 2001, 144, 145.

47. *CR*, July 23, 1987, S20908-20915 (Remarks of Senator Biden); "Washington Talk: A Side-Bar Battle," *NYT*, September 4, 1987 (Thurmond); Joe Rodota, Memorandum for Thomas Griscom: Ideology and Supreme Court Nominations, July 2, 1987, FG051, 516586, RWRL; "Abe Fortas," July 2, 1987, id.; "'Balance' on the Supreme Court," n.d., James Baker, Series I, Judge Bork, Nomination of (2), id.; Materials on Judge Robert Bork, FG 051, 492978 (1) ("There is no historical or constitutional basis for making the Supreme Court as it existed in June 1987 the ideal standard to which all future Courts must be held."). Biden himself had changed his message. In 1986, after the Democrats won control of the Senate, Senate Judiciary Committee Member Joe Biden, its incoming chair, suggested the irrelevance of nominee ideology. "Say the Administration sends us Bork and, after our investigation, he looks a lot like another Scalia," he told one newspaper. "I'd have to vote for him and if the [special interest] groups tear me apart, that's the medicine I'll have to take. I'm not Teddy Kennedy." Howard Kurtz, "Choosing His Battles, Working by Consensus," *WP*, December 9, 1986. By the time the Reagan Administration nominated Bork in 1987, however, Biden, was singing a different tune, perhaps in part because he was now running for the presidency himself.

48. Laura Mansnerus, "Bork Sides in Bork Debate Seek the Blessings of History," *NYT*, September 13, 1987.

49. Peter Wallison, Memorandum for the File, August 29, 1986. The Justice Department also suggested that "as the first Italian-American nominated to the Court, he would have the support of a non-ideological constituency whose exertions in his behalf might sway fence-setting Democrats in an election years." Peter Wallison, "Antonin Scalia," Supreme Court, Rehnquist/ Scalia Notebook 1, Candidates (3), OA 14287, RWRL.

50. Robert Bork, *The Tempting of America: The Political Seduction of Law* (New York: Simon and Schuster, 1990), 348–349.

51. Peter Wallison, "Robert H. Bork," n.d., Supreme Court Rehnquist/Scalia, Notebook II, Candidates (1), OA 14287, Box 3, RWRL; Kevin McMahon, "Presidents, Political Regimes, and Contentious Supreme Court Nominations: A Historical Institutional Model," 32 *LSI* 919, 925 (2007).

52. Howard, "The Changing Face of the Supreme Court," 301.

53. Bronner, *Battle for Justice*, 98–99 (Kennedy's speech). One Bush administration policy paper that pointed out that Reagan had spoken with Democratic leaders who warned that Bork would prompt a fight drily continued: "The consultation did not diffuse the controversy surrounding the nomination, but did get Bork opponents a full week to make their case in the press with no opponents." C. Boyden Gray, Counsel to the President, Memorandum for the President, February 18, 1992, "The History of Presidential Consultations With the Senate on Supreme Court Nominations," n.d., FG 051, Box 357, GHWBL; Arthur Culvahouse, Memorandum for Howard Baker, Kenneth Duberstein, William Ball, Thomas Griscom, September 8, 1987, FG051, 5 506706, RWRL ("well-publicized," "senior," "very," "zealot"). "The past two weeks have evinced a continuing criticism of the White House's characterization of Judge Bork as a mainstream jurist. Senator Biden, the ACLU and other Bork opponents describe our characterizations of Bork as a 'mainstream' jurist as intellectually dishonest. Some of Judge Bork's right wing supporters think that it is an extremely poor strategy destined to ensure Judge Bork's defeat. The mainstream jurist *is* our strategy; there is no time for another strategy; and it is true that Judge Bork is a mainstream jurist." Emphasis in the original); Morton Blackwell to Ronald Reagan, September 30, 1987, Bork Subject File: Peter Keisler, Memos (10), RWRL (complaining that "the White House strategy has been to encourage conservative groups to work the grassroots for Bork while itself presenting Bork as another Earl Warren, only smarter"); Ronald Reagan to Morton Blackwell, October 21, 1987, id. ("Morton, I think there was a distortion of our position as to his philosophy. We never portrayed him as an Earl Warren type, nor did we ever use the word 'moderate.' It's possible some might have used that term in repudiating the charge that he was some kind of radical, but not any of us here in the Administration, to my knowledge."); Stephen Wermiel, Gerald Seib, Jeffrey Birnbaum, "Losing Battle: How Reagan's Forces Botched the Campaign for Approval of Bork," *WSJ*, October 7, 1987 (quoting Communications Director Tom Griscom, "I don't think"). On the American Latvian Association and National Association of Wholesaler-Distributors, see Culvahouse to Baker, Duberstein, Ball, and Griscom, September 8, 1987; Rebecca Range, Update on Pro-Bork Activity, n.d., Series I, Subject Files, OA 15172, Box 1, Bork (5), RWRL; Dan Danner, Memorandum for Rebecca Range, Business Support/Activity for Bork, September 22, 1987, id.; Tom Gibson, Memorandum for the Chief of Staff, Office of Public Affairs Activities in Support of Judge Bork, October 15, 1981, David McIntosh, OA 16531, Box 3, Bork White House Pro Bork Activities—Baker Memo (2), id.

54. Dinesh D'Souza, Memorandum for Gary Bauer, Life After Bork, October 14, 1987 ("ideology"), David McIntosh, OA 16531, Box 3, Bork WHO Postmortem (1), RWRL; Dinesh D'Souza, Recommended Strategy for Judge Ginsburg's Nomination, November 4, 1987, David McIntosh, OA 16531, Box 3, Ginsburg (2), id.: "Lessons from the failed strategy to get Judge Bork confirmed: First, it is entirely unrealistic to expect that a nominee's judicial philosophy will escape detailed scrutiny by the Senate. Second, the argument that President Reagan has an inalienable right to his own man on the court carries little or no weight; just as the President has the Constitutional mandate to appoint, the Senate has a complementary right to reject. Third, the audience for the hearing is not just the Senate but also the American public, and a nominee who cannot convince the people watching him on TV is in a weakened position. Fourth, we no longer have any grounds for believing that the swing votes needed to confirm Judge Ginsburg are automatically predisposed in his favor: liberal Republicans feel

no obligation to vote with the President, and Southern Democrats cannot be counted on to vote as soul mates. Fifth, the side that seizes the initiative and the agenda enjoys a tremendous advantage. In Bork's case we fought entirely on turf defined and delineated by Bork's critics. Our arguments to the effect that Bork didn't hate women and blacks and actually voted in their favor lots of times carried no weight and, in fact, inspired derision. Sixth, this [is] an extremely high stakes contest for both sides. The left can no more be expected to let this one slide through than they could be to acquiesce in the Bork case. We appeared surprised at their vehemence the last time. We should be prepared now."

55. "All Things Considered: Ginsburg Exclusive," *NPR*, 1987 (Reagan maintained that Ginsburg had been framed by "some people who knew him while he was teaching at Harvard" who considered him too conservative and who leaked his "infrequent" usage of marijuana before he became a judge to destroy his candidacy. Ronald Reagan to Alan Brown, November 20, 1987, FG 051, 529937, Handwriting File, RWRL); Dan to Pat, November 10, 1987, Memorandum: Death of a Thousand Cuts, Trial by Media, and the Next Nominee, David McIntosh, OA 16531, Box 3, Ginsburg (2), RWRL ("We," "brief"); Ronald Reagan to George Murphy, October 29, 1987, FG051, 526881, Handwriting File, RWRL: "By the time you get this I will have announced another nominee for the Supreme Court. I promise you he'll be as conservative as Judge Bork. There is no way I'd go for a touch of liberalism to win over the lynch mob. We'll see if they have the nerve to repeat their scandalous performance. I don't think they will. Of course, in the meantime, we have to face up to the loss of a nominee who was, in my opinion, the most outstanding candidate in 50 years."

56. Josh Lederman, "White House Lawyers Are Scouring a Life's Worth of Information About President Obama's Potential Picks for the Supreme Court from the Mundane to the Intensely Personal," *USN*, February 16, 2016.

57. Richard Brust, "No More Kabuki Confirmations," 95 *ABAJ* 39 (October 2009); Jeff Shesol, "Should Justices Keep Their Opinions to Themselves?," *NYT*, June 29, 2011; Eric Segall, "A Liberal's Lament on Kagan and Health Care: Should Elena Kagan Recuse Herself in the ACA Case?," *Sla*, December 8, 2011.

58. Nathan Koppel, "Kagan Criticized the Warren Court in Thesis," *WSJ*, May 19, 2010; Mark Walsh, "Supreme Court Nominations: 'You'll Get Justice Kagan, You Won't Get Justice Marshall,'" http://www.abajournal.com/news/article/sessions_to_kagan_i_would_have_to_classify_you_as_a_legal_progressive/, June 29, 2010; Dana Milbank, "Kagan May Get Confirmed, but Thurgood Marshall Can Forget It," *WP*, June 29, 2010; Geoffrey Stone, "Understanding Supreme Court Confirmations," 2010 *SCR* 381, 456 (2011).

59. A. Mitchell McConnell Jr., "Haynsworth and Carswell: A New Senate Standard of Excellence," 59 *KyLJ* 7, 13, 32, 33, 34 (1970); "Sen. Mitch McConnell in 2005: 'The President, and the President Alone, Nominates Judges," *DK*, February 13, 2016.

60. Burgess Everett and Glenn Thrush, "McConnell Throws Down the Gauntlet: No Scalia Replacement Under Obama," *Pol*, February 13, 2016, http://www.politico.com/story/2016/02/mitch-mcconnell-antonin-scalia-supreme-court-nomination-219248; "Grassley Statement on Justice Scalia," February 13, 2016, http://www.grassley.senate.gov/news/news-releases/grassley-statement-justice-scalia; Chuck Grassley, "Supreme Court Vacancies in Presidential Election Years: 'The Biden Rules,'" February 22, 2016, http://www.grassley.senate.gov/news/news-releases/supreme-court-vacancies-presidential-election-years-%E2%80%9C-biden-rules%E2%80%9D; David Herszenhorn and Julie Davis, "Joe Biden Speech From 1992 Gives G.O.P. Fodder in Court Fight," *NYT*, February 22, 2016; Paul Finkelman, "A History of Supreme Court Nominations in Election Years," http://blog.oup.com/2016/02/supreme-court-nominations-election/; Amber Phillips, "Why Joe Biden's 1992 Supreme Court Comments Aren't a Silver Bullet for Republicans," *WP*, February 23, 2016. See generally Robin Kar and Jazon Mazzone, "The Garland Affair: What History and the Constitution Really Say About President Obama's Powers to Appoint a Replacement for Justice Scalia," 91 *NYULR* 53 (2016).

61. Lindsey Ellefson, "Obama Fights Back at GOP Refusing to Vote on SCOTUS Nominee: #Do Your Job," February 23, 2016, http://www.mediaite.com/online/obama-fights-back-at-gop-refusing-to-vote-on-scotus-nominee-doyourjob/; Barack Obama, "A Responsibility I Take Seriously," February 24, 2016; http://www.scotusblog.com/2016/02/

a-responsibility-i-take-seriously/; Chris Cilizza, "The Fix: Is Floating Brian Samdoval's Name for SCOTUS Just an Elaborate Troll of Senate Republicans?," *WP*, February 24, 2016; Julliet Elperin, "Sandoval Bows Out of Supreme Court Consideration," id., February 25, 2016; Dahlia Lithwick, "The Case for Nominating Elizabeth Warren to the Supreme Court," *Sla*, February 26, 2016, *Sla*, February 26, 2016, (characterizing trial balloon as brilliant).

62. Jeff Shesol, "How to Recognize a Constitutional Crisis," *NY*, February 19, 2016; "Senate Republicans Lose Their Minds on a Supreme Court Seat," *NYT*, February 24, 2016; Rick Hasen, "An Adult Conversation About the Fight to Fill Justice Scalia's SCOTUS Seat," February 26, 2016, *TPM* Café: Opinion, http://talkingpointsmemo.com/cafe/debate-scotus-nomination-obama ("lofty"); Lyle Denniston, "Judiciary Panel Chair: Wait on Court Until After Election," February 13, 2016, http://www.scotusblog.com/2016/02/judiciary-panel-chair-wait-on-court-until-after-election/ ("both").

63. Amita Kelly, "McConnell: Blocking Supreme Court Nomination About a Principle, Not a Person," *NPR*, March 16, 2016, http://www.npr.org/2016/03/16/470664561/mcconnell-blocking-supreme-court-nomination-about-a-principle-not-a-person ("principle"); Steve Benen, "On Supreme Court, Republicans Can't Keep Their Story Straight," March 21, 2016 http://www.msnbc.com/rachel-maddow-show/supreme-court-republicans-cant-keep-their-story-straight; Eric Bradner, "McConnell: No Lame Duck Confirmation," http://www.cnn.com/2016/03/20/politics/mitch-mcconnell-supreme-court-donald-trump/, March 20, 2016 (National Rifle Association and National Federation of Business); Mitch McConnell and Chuck Grassley, "McConnell and Grassley: Democrats Shouldn't Rob Voters of Chance to Replace Scalia," *WP*, February 18, 2016; Taylor Batten, "Scalia's Ghost Hovers Over RNC," *CO*, July 21, 2016, http://www.charlotteobserver.com/opinion/opn-columns-blogs/taylor-batten/article91108692.html (highlights and Trump tweet); Elizabeth Chan, "President Donald Trump Would Transform the Supreme Court—and Upend Our Most Fundamental Rights: The Fate of the Supreme Court Hinges on the Next Election," September 14, 2016, https://www.hillaryclinton.com/feed/republican-president-could-nominate-many-four-supreme-court-justices-should-terrify-you/.

64. "Donald J. Trump Finalizes List of Potential Supreme Court Justice Picks," September 23, 2016, https://www.donaldjtrump.com/press-releases/donald-j.-trump-adds-to-list-of-potential-supreme-court-justice-picks; Adam Liptak, "Trump's Supreme Court List: Ivy League? Out. The Heartland? In," *NYT*, November 14, 2016 ("If").

65. Adam Liptak, "What the Trump Presidency Means for the Supreme Court," *NYT*, November 9, 2016 (quoting the Cato Institute's Ilya Shpairo); Burgess Everett, "GOP Could Nuke Filibuster for Supreme Court Nominees," *POL*, November 18, 2016, http://www.politico.com/story/2016/11/gop-supreme-court-filibuster-nuclear-option-231582.

66. Bazelon and Witt, "Senate Republicans and the Supreme Court;" Jonathan Chait, "Will the Supreme Court Just Disappear?," *NYT Mag*, February 21, 2016.

INDEX